THE GLADSTONE–GRANVILLE

Edited by Agatha R

With a supplementary introduction ... Matthew

Agatha Ramm's two volumes containing the correspondence between Gladstone and his Foreign Secretary, Lord Granville, conducted at the height of British colonial power during the years 1868–1876, were published originally in 1952. These volumes are now available in a single volume, and provide the mass of government papers with 'the enlivening touch', drawing skilfully, as Dr Ramm did, on papers in the British Museum, and the files held in the Public Record Office. The correspondence contained in the volumes is between two men who wrote to each other privately, but about matters which were, as Matthew states, 'the very stuff of official diplomatic exchange'. *The Gladstone–Granville Correspondence* was therefore a private commentary on colonial and foreign policy. It is not, however, limited to explaining the details of British foreign policy, but also includes letters exchanged in the long period of opposition during Disraeli's government, 1874–1880. Dr Ramm's interest in a wide range of political and non-political matters, such as details of political life, how the secretarial office worked, how Gladstone and Granville related to the rest of the Cabinet and how to handle the Queen, is also apparent. This *Reprint* will therefore be of great interest to scholars of British history.

THE GLADSTONE–GRANVILLE CORRESPONDENCE

Camden Classic Reprints is a select series of classic editions which are reissued on behalf of the Royal Historical Society by Cambridge University Press. The series serves to bring to light editions of private papers or diaries of particular historical significance which have been unavailable for some time. Each volume contains a new introduction by a recognised expert in the field which contains fresh insights informed by recent historical scholarship, and which places each text in an appropriate historical context.

The first titles in the series are:

1 *Kingsford's Stonor Letters and Papers 1290–1483* edited by CHRISTINE CARPENTER
2 *Thomas Wright's Political Songs of England* edited by PETER COSS
3 *Richard Symonds's Diary of the Marches of the Royal Army* edited by C. E. LONG with a supplementary introduction by Ian Roy
4 *Encomium Emmae Reginae* edited by ALISTAIR CAMPBELL with a supplementary introduction by Simon Keynes
5 *The Gladstone–Granville Correspondence* edited by AGATHA RAMM with a supplementary introduction by H. C. G. Matthew

THE GLADSTONE–GRANVILLE CORRESPONDENCE

Edited by

AGATHA RAMM

with a supplementary introduction by

H. C. G. MATTHEW

CAMDEN CLASSIC REPRINTS 5

FOR THE ROYAL HISTORICAL SOCIETY
University College London, Gower Street, London WC1E 6BT

PUBLISHED BY THE PRESS SYNDICATE OF THE UNIVERSITY OF CAMBRIDGE
The Pitt Building, Trumpington Street, Cambridge CB2 1RP, United Kingdom

CAMBRIDGE UNIVERSITY PRESS
The Edinburgh Building, Cambridge, CB2 2RU, United Kingdom http://www.cup.cam.ac.uk
40 West 20th Street, New York, NY 10011–4211, USA http://www.cup.org
10 Stamford Road, Oakleigh, Melbourne 3166, Australia

First published by the Royal Historical Society in the Camden Third Series as volumes LXXXI and LXXXII in 1952
Reprinted with a supplementary introduction by Cambridge University Press 1998

First published 1998

Printed in the United Kingdom at the University Press, Cambridge

Typeset in MT Old Style 10/11 pt [CE]

A catalogue record for this book is available from the British Library

Library of Congress cataloguing in publication data applied for

ISBN 0 521 64208 6 hardback
ISBN 0 521 64559 x paperback

INTRODUCTION

H. C. G. MATTHEW

The publication of Agatha Ramm's edition of the Gladstone–Granville correspondence was a notable event in the historiography of Gladstone and consequently of the nineteenth century in general. The two volumes in the Camden series which are the subject of this introduction and reprint were published in 1952 (Camden third series LXXXI and LXXXII). They covered 1868–1876. The next two volumes, covering 1876–1886, were published by the Clarendon Press, Oxford, in 1962. Scholarly editing of nineteenth-century historical documents was not then in vogue. Scholarly editing was something practised mainly by medievalists; even eighteenth-century scholarly editions (other than literary editions) were unusual. In the 1920s and 1930s, the nineteenth century was still seen as almost contemporary history. The three- or four-decker biography was the usual means of publishing political correspondence. There were editions of letters, but these were presented as volumes that sold to the general reader. Consequently, scholarly apparatus, if there was any, was kept to a minimum, and a good deal of political and certainly of diplomatic detail was simply excluded. A trail was being blazed by Arthur Aspinall, whose *Letters of King George IV* began to be published in 1938 and whose *Three Early Nineteenth Century Diaries* were also published in 1952.

Gladstone was something of an exception to this. Morley's biography had, in the tradition of the 'three-decker', included a great deal of valuable and original material (F. W. Hirst, who was Morley's research assistant for the *Life*, describes their procedures in *In the Golden Days* (1947) and their shortcomings are analysed by M. R. D. Foot in 'Morley's Gladstone: a reappraisal', *Bulletin of the John Ryland's Library* (1969)). In his lifetime Gladstone had been generous in making material available to historians and biographers – Purcell's notorious biography of Cardinal Manning and C. S. Parker's *Papers of Sir Robert Peel*, for example, drew on the Gladstone Papers, with the aged politician personally sorting through them to find the relevant letters. Parker's *Peel*, especially, showed the dangers of too rapid transcription. Almost from his death in 1898, Gladstone had been unusually and effectively served by those working in his vast collection of papers, initially kept in the Octagon at Hawarden Castle, somewhat to their cost, for while the stone structure was an excellent barrier to fire, it was much less so to damp. In 1910 D.C. Lathbury, son of Thomas Lathbury (1798–1865), the historian of the non-jurors, published Gladstone's *Correspondence on Church and Religion* in two volumes, an excellent selection, accurately transcribed and competently if lightly edited. Its purpose was to correct what was seen as Morley's neglect and misunderstanding of Gladstone's religion. Published at a time of very different political priorities, the volumes did not sell, and the Gladstone family, whose members had encouraged Lathbury in his enterprise, were embarrassed and discouraged. However, Philip Guedalla very successfully bridged the gap between the needs of the general reader and the requirements of the scholar with his *Gladstone and Palmerston* (1928). Guedalla came at his subject *via* his biography of Palmerston (1926), and he conceived his edition as the first volume of *The Palmerston Papers*, which is in fact the leading title on the title page, though the book is always known by its subtitle, no more of the series being published.

Guedalla was next asked by the Gladstone family to edit the letters written between Queen Victoria and the Prime Minister she most disliked. The result was *The Queen and Mr. Gladstone*, 2 volumes (1933). There was a polemical background to this undertaking. The Gladstone family were annoyed, and Herbert Gladstone was infuriated, by G. E. Buckle's editing of the second series of *The Letters of Queen Victoria*, published in three volumes (1926–1928), covering 1862–1885. Herbert Gladstone retaliated with *After Thirty Years* (1928), in which he tried to answer Buckle point by point and document by document. This approach was not very effective. Guided by the cooler nerve of Henry Neville Gladstone, the family then decided that the best way to nail Buckle (and the Queen) was to publish as extensively as was then viable the complete correspondence between the Queen and Gladstone, and Guedalla was commissioned to do this. This was an effective method. It followed the thinking of the Cabinet in 1885–1886, when it had supported the publication of the journal of Charles George Gordon on the condition that nothing be left out, for complete publication would show how erratic and even mad Gordon had been. Because Gladstone had kept copies of all his letters to the Queen, as well as the originals of all her letters to him, it was possible for Guedalla to do his transcribing and editing at Hawarden and not under the scrutiny of those in charge of the Royal Archives. Indeed the whole edition was prepared independently of Windsor. The proofs were sent to George V who was alarmed to discover just how immoderate his grandmother's language had on occasion been; though Clive Wigram, his secretary, he argued that 'one feels that, as it were, she needs a little "protection from herself"' (Wigram to Guedalla, 30 August 1933, cited in H. C. G. Matthew, *Gladstone 1809–1898* (1997)). Guedalla and the Gladstones withstood this pressure, which even included requests to exclude letters already printed by Buckle! The publication in fact achieved the result for which the Gladstone family had sought, and it sold very well – probably the best-selling set of Victorian political correspondence. Other inter-war editions included *The Gladstone Papers* (1930) – a few extracts to give the flavour of the papers transferred to the British Museum at that time – and A. Tilney Bassett's *Gladstone to his Wife* (1936), quite accurately transcribed but very much in the tradition of *belles-lettres* editing.

The Second World War pushed back the Victorians into the realm of the clearly historical. What had been an area for battle-by-edition became a subject more suited to scholarly historians. This as reinforced in the case of Gladstone by the marked decline of the Literal Party in the 1940s, though it would be wrong to suggest that Gladstone has ever lost his capacity for topicality. Agatha Ramm's prefaces of both sets of two volumes of Gladstone–Granville letters thank Dame Lillian Penson 'for the guidance under which the project of publishing this correspondence first took shape ...' Lillian Penson was appointed in 1918 as an editor of the peace handbooks prepared for the Paris peace conference; she subsequently assisted G. P. Gooch and H. W. Temperley in editing *British Documents on the Origins of the War 1898–1914*, which were published between 1926 and 1938, her assistance being acknowledged on the title pages of volumes VIII, IX and X, to the last of which she added a 'Note on the Arrangement of Documents, &c.' In her note, Penson remarked that in addition to the official collections in the Foreign Office, there were many private collections in the Foreign Office, and that a number of private papers had become available, including those of Sir Edward Grey, Sir Arthur Nicolson, and Lord Lansdowne, which had been used together with the official correspondence. Partly under Penson's influence, a series which in its early volumes had been rather strictly confined to official documents and correspondence became more inclusive and contained material of the sort traditionally written by politicians as a parallel commentary to the official exchange of opinion.

Dr Ramm's edition took this tradition much further, for her publication was of the correspondence between two men who wrote to each other only privately, but on subjects which were the very stuff of official diplomatic exchange. In the period her four volumes cover, Gladstone was three times First Lord of the Treasury (1868–1874, 1880–1885, 1886) and Granville was twice Colonial Secretary (1868–1870, 1886) and twice Foreign Secretary (1870–1874, 1880–1885). A Colonial and Foreign Secretary was, of course, in frequent official correspondence with his Governors or with his Ambassadors and Ministers (often also paralleling this with his own private exchanges with them). The Prime Minister as a matter of course saw all the important official exchanges, and Granville sometimes showed him some of the private comment. Gladstone as Prime Minister rarely wrote directly to Ambassadors and Ministers (though he did on occasion) and his views usually reached them *via* his Foreign Secretary. He wrote rather more often to Colonial Governors if need arose. The Gladstone–Granville correspondence was thus a private commentary on colonial and foreign policy, conducted at the height of British power and responsibility. From the point of view of view of academic writing in the diplomatic school, such a publication was a notable departure. As Dr Ramm observed, 'In short, the correspondence gives to the mass of government papers, which the historian normally uses, the enlivening touch ...' (preface to Vol. I, p. xviii). But this was to be no mere Guedalla-style edition, with a *belle lettriste* tone. Dr Ramm edited the Gladstone–Granville correspondence, private as it was, with full scholarly rigour. Her edition showed an exceptional mastery of the Gladstone Papers in the British Museum, all the more remarkable since Tilney Bassett's excellent catalogue of the Gladstone Papers in the Museum was not published until after the publication of the first two of Dr Ramm's volumes. It also brought into play the splendid resources of the files in the Public Record Office, where she acknowledges the help of H. N. Blakiston, whose *The Roman Question. Extracts from the despatches of Odo Russell from Rome, 1858–1870* was published in the same year as Dr Ramm's second pair of volumes. The public Record Office was in those days in Chancery Lane, close to the British Museum, and it was possible in each institution to order volumes in large numbers for rapid searching, and, by a twenty-minute walk, to connect the work in each. Dr Ramm's footnotes are almost a scholarly conversation conducted in their archives; the reader is drawn into the complexity of the questions under discussion in the correspondence, which is often allusive and, as it was mostly written as *addenda* to daily meetings, presupposes intimate knowledge of the people and issues with which it deals.

Dr Ramm's editing is by no means confined to explaining the details and personalities of foreign policy. The correspondence deals also with the long period of opposition during Disraeli's government of 1874–1880. Here the edition was much more than giving 'the enlivening touch' to official documents, for this was the first scholarly editing of letters on a vital and controversial period of liberal opposition. Whether in or out of government, Gladstone and Granville were always active on a wide range of political and non-political matters. Dr Ramm showed a very early interest in questions which have become of more interest to historians recently, such as the details of political life, how the secretarial office worked, how her two correspondents related to the rest of the Cabinet, and how to handle the Queen.

The result of the publication of these two volumes was not merely to set new standards – that Dr Ramm certainly did for nineteenth-century British political editing – but to set standards which continue to challenge any historian working in the same field. For Dr Ramm's footnotes not only supply the necessary and expected information. They take the reader a step further, a reference more than he or she anticipates; yet they are brief and uncluttered. The *Gladstone–Granville Correspondence* is a remarkable compilation, whose editing organically associates the reader with the two correspondents, one an aimiable whig and a rather underrated foreign secretary, the other a man of whom Agatha Ramm later wrote: 'His life ... spanned nearly the whole of the nineteenth century with all its social, intellectual and political changes. He had some part, often a decisive one, in all of them ... his life was unusual, not because he was a noble or even pleasant character, but because he was extraordinarily able, active and courageous' (Agatha Ramm, *William Ewart Gladstone* (1989), p. 1).

INTRODUCTION TO THE 1952 EDITION

I

THE Gladstone papers in the British Museum and the smaller collection of Granville papers in the Record Office are the two most important private collections at present available to the student of late Victorian England. They originated in that borderland of government business which escaped the formality and impersonality of the administrative machine. These private papers are part of the documentation of government but have neither the finality nor remoteness of the official letter or memorandum. Indeed, they are important precisely because they take the historian behind the documents which formally shaped events to the documents which record, however fragmentarily, the genesis of action and policy, and mirror the day-to-day practice of the art of getting things done.

At the date, about 1868, when these collections become politically most important, the machinery of government, and the civil service especially, was just entering upon one of its phases of phenomenal expansion and reorganization and was rapidly building up departmental independence and self-consciousness. The private letter was the minister's defence for his personal control against the encroachments of the office. It sheltered, also, from parliament as well as the office, tentative early steps in his shaping of legislation or policy. It was often the means to speed and smoothness. The size of Gladstone's collection of papers was not merely the outcome of the activity of an exceptional personality. It was partly due, after 1868 at least, to the character of the office he held. This accumulation of private letters to document a public career arose because the business of the prime minister, reflecting the historical process which had created his office, still largely bore the stamp of personal and private negotiation. It was carried on, more than that of any other minister, outside formal departmental methods. The prime minister's private office and not the Treasury housed his business. Although the assistant private secretaries to the prime minister were sometimes taken from the establishment of the Treasury, one in 1882 eventually becoming principal secretary, the private office was a distinct and recognizable institution well before the term became current.

The Gladstone papers, for the years after 1868, originated then in the mass of documents which gradually assembled in the private secretaries' rooms at number 10 Downing Street, and were taken, as each ministry ended, for storing to Hawarden. The Granville papers began to take shape in the private secretary's room at the Colonial Office. Thence, when Granville changed his place, in June 1870, they were taken under Meade's control to the new Foreign Office, where the latter continued to act as private secretary until May 1871. There they were left, through the Conservative interlude, until the second Liberal administration and Granville's return to the Foreign Office. The greater part were bound in the Foreign Office. Thus the disorderliness of Granville's correspondence, which Lord Acton deplored, fearing it might cause the loss of letters from Gladstone, was in fact curbed. The Granville papers were deposited in the Record Office in three lots: one direct from the Foreign Office,[1] the second from the Dowager Countess Granville in 1937, and the third an additional deposit made in 1938.[2] The politically important part for the first two Liberal administrations is mainly to be found in the series of bound volumes.[3] Letters which were accidentally or deliberately withheld from the secretaries, including a few from Gladstone, and all letters for the period when the Liberals were out of office became separated from the rest and were not bound.[4] The politically important part of the Gladstone papers has, with the exception of certain classes, been bound by the British Museum where they are now deposited.[5]

The form in which the two collections now exist has been influenced by the activities of Gladstone's and Granville's private secretaries. Gladstone's economical and strictly disciplined methods of doing business imposed a routine on secretarial practice. This was maintained with remarkable consistency and continuity.[6] The work was shared at first between a principal and an assistant secretary with some additional help.[7] During the second administration there were two assistant secretaries and additional help was still necessary. The duties of these men included, first, the copying of all the out-going letters. Few letters written by Gladstone, even the briefest notes, escaped copy, or at least record. Thus when the Granville papers contain letters from Gladstone of which there is no copy in the Gladstone collection there is always an explanation. Some were written at Granville's house when Gladstone had called and found him away from home and were left behind as substitute for talk; some resembled minutes and immediately went on in the circulation boxes, with the dispatches on which they commented; some were written on the backs of letters from Granville which were then returned to him; some were written in the Commons; a few were notes passed across during a cabinet meeting. Gladstone while in office kept a letter-book into which all the letters he wrote in his public capacity, except those to the Queen and others especially confidential, were normally copied by one of the private secretaries, or, if trivial, at least noted. Gladstone's letter-books [8] constitute then a very important class in his collection of papers. The letters in them follow each other chronologically day by day. Thus on the rare occasions when Gladstone failed to date or incompletely dated a letter, the date can often be exactly supplied from the letter-book. The confidential letters,

[1] F.O. 362/1–5 and 97/621, being some of the private correspondence with British representatives in America, Austria and France, 1870–74, and Morocco, 1880–85.

[2] Both G.D. 29. [3] G.D. 29/32–212.

[4] The boxes of these papers are G.D. 29/18–31; they contain also papers belonging to the years before 1868.

[5] Add. MSS. 44086–835; see A. T. Bassett, *Descriptive Catalogue*, Add. MS. 44835B.

[6] Cf. the accounts for the first and second administrations respectively of Lord Kilbracken, *Reminiscences* (1931), pp. 87–90, and G. Leveson Gower, *Years of Content, 1858–86* (1940), pp. 162–5. See also E. W. Hamilton, *Mr. Gladstone* (1898), pp. 79–83.

[7] Between 1872 and 1874 when the principal secretary, F. C. Cavendish, was a member of parliament, there were two assistants who did the real work, W. B. Gurdon, who had assisted Algernon West, Cavendish's predecessor, and A. Godley. When Gladstone became chancellor of the exchequer in 1873 E. W. Hamilton joined his private staff.

[8] Add. MSS. 44536–48 for 1868–85.

kept out of the letter-books, were also copied, but the copies of these were filed with the letters received from the correspondent concerned.

The letters coming in to Gladstone all passed through the secretaries' hands before they reached him. They were classified and most of them docketed with a précis of the contents and a suggested answer. Those from colleagues in the cabinet and some other recognizable classes, however, went on unopened to him. These then were not docketed with the rest. Sometimes they were rather meagrely docketed by Gladstone himself with the name of the writer and the date. If not, they were more fully docketed by one of the private secretaries with the correspondent's name, the date, and a note of the subject, when they reached him after being answered. Lord Granville's letters to Gladstone were often imperfectly dated, misdated or not dated. There are not always copies among Granville's own papers to supply these deficiencies of dating and the docketing is only a guide. The substance of the letter shows clearly sometimes that Gladstone's date on the docket was, as one would expect, the date when he received the letter and not necessarily the date when Granville wrote it. In the documents below the date has frequently been supplied. This has perforce been taken from the docket, except when internal evidence has established another date with some certainty, and may not always, therefore, be exact. On the whole, then, secretarial practice left little or no mark on the bulk of the politically important in-coming correspondence, except in so far as it was handed over to the secretaries for filing and safe keeping.

Granville's secretarial routine was fashioned by Foreign Office practice. R. H. Meade, who created it, was trained in the Foreign Office. Granville had already employed him in 1864–66 at the Privy Council Office and in 1868 imported him into the Colonial Office. He conformed to older habits of patronage, for succeeding colonial secretaries took their private secretaries from the office establishment. Meade, who returned to the Colonial Office in 1871, was succeeded by T. F. Wetherell (1871–76), Arthur Nicolson (1872–74), and T. H. Sanderson (1880–85), who preserved his practice. Henry Hervey of the Foreign Office, as Granville's précis writer during both his terms there, shared the care of his correspondence.

Lord Granville, we are told, 'opened all his letters himself, and found by experience that most of them, if left alone, would answer themselves'.[1] But when he did reply it was the duty of the secretaries to copy the answer and to file the copy with the in-coming letters from that correspondent. Many of Lord Granville's letters, however, escaped them. Thus many of those published below are preserved only in the original in the Gladstone papers. The docketing of in-coming correspondence with the name of the writer, the date of the letter and a précis of its contents was done by the private secretaries with the fullness and regularity of Foreign Office practice. This good docketing laid the foundation for the systematic arrangement of the papers. Many of the letters, however, which Lord Granville received suffered from his casual way with papers and were not passed on punctually to the secretaries. Then, if a letter was imperfectly dated the latter sometimes found difficulty in placing it. The docket in that case expressly recorded the date when the secretary received it and so provides an approximate guide. On the very few

[1] Lord Kilbracken, *Reminiscences* (1931), p. 102.

occasions (e.g. no. 71) where this difficulty has arisen with a letter written by Gladstone of which no copy exists, the subject matter has established the exact date. While in the Gladstone papers the evidence of the private secretaries' work is most noticeable in the full copying of the out-going correspondence, in the Granville papers it is chiefly apparent in the good docketing of the in-coming correspondence and in the ultimate arrangement of the whole collection which probably represents their system of filing.

The significance of the private secretaries' activities to a modern editor of the Gladstone-Granville correspondence in these two collections may now be summarized. They have, in the first place, created two texts normally with rare and slight verbal differences, of the majority of the letters exchanged. The version printed below is, wherever possible, the version actually received by the correspondent. In a few cases (e.g. nos. 279 and 378) this was apparently a copy and not the holograph. The copy has been printed when it is the only version that has been traced. In the second place, the private secretaries' docketing has helped to some extent to solve difficulties of dating, and to facilitate the chronological arrangement according to the date of writing. When more than one letter was written on the same day, it has been possible sometimes to decide which was the earlier by the writer's numbering, by the substance, or by telegrams marked with the time of sending, if, as sometimes happened, a telegram and letter went off simultaneously. The rule of bringing a letter as near as possible, having regard to its date, to the one it answers has sometimes settled a doubtful order. When Gladstone and Granville each wrote simultaneously to the other, each opening a new subject, Gladstone's letter has been put first. The secretaries' docketing has sometimes also explained the subject of a letter or cleared up an obscure allusion. In the third place, both collections, and especially the Granville, reflect in their arrangement the way the papers were filed and kept. There is a separate sequence of sixteen volumes [1] in the Gladstone collection of correspondence with Granville, longer than any other single sequence, except that with the Queen, and a similar sequence of thirteen volumes [2] of Gladstone correspondence in the Granville papers which represents a contemporary classification.

II

The Gladstone-Granville correspondence must be read in its context. The run of volumes containing the correspondence forms, in both collections, part of a central block of papers made up of single volumes or runs of volumes, one volume or sequence of volumes for each of Gladstone's and Granville's principal correspondents. The most valuable of these sequences, again in both collections, is probably that containing correspondence with the Queen. In the Gladstone papers, this forms at present a separate section that is not generally available. An extensive selection from it was published by Philip Guedalla in *The Queen and Mr. Gladstone.* In the Granville papers, fourteen volumes [3] contain the Queen's letters, either in her own hand or written on her behalf by Charles Grey or Henry Ponsonby, and some copies of Granville's replies. Here the practical working of a relationship which was of supreme importance to the smooth running of the Liberal government

[1] Add. MSS. 44165–80. [2] G.D. 29/57–62, G.D. 29/123–9. [3] G.D. 29/32–45.

is illustrated. Lord Granville held the confidence of the Queen during the first administration. The correspondence bears witness to the part this enabled him to play in the general easing of the relations between the crown and the government, as well as to the Queen's share in the making of foreign policy and the character of the interest she took in it. In 1876 Lord Granville with other peers opposed the Royal Titles Bill in the Lords and lost the Queen's favour. The correspondence in the second administration reflects the change wrought by this 'quarrel' and by the piquancy and subtlety of Disraelian practice during the intervening period.

Next in interest are the volumes of correspondence with colleagues in the administration, both inside and outside the cabinet. They consist mostly of in-coming letters but with some copies of the out-going. This class of correspondence—classified 'special' in the index of the Gladstone papers—includes some exchanges with correspondents outside the official range, as for example Gladstone's correspondence with Cardinal Manning or Granville's with F. Harrison Hill of the *Daily News* or with Earl Russell.

Passing beyond the central class of papers: much of the correspondence with men in public life, but mostly outside the cabinet, falls, in the Granville papers, into a sequence of volumes that runs alphabetically through a number of writers (e.g. G.D. 29/75 R–S contains correspondence with Earl Spencer as well as with Rogers and the Speaker), and ends with a volume of copies of Granville's letters to the same correspondents (G.D. 29/77). In Gladstone's papers most of the important letters come in one or other of the sequences of volumes of 'special' correspondences, but there are letters of some importance from writers on the fringe of the administrative and political world or in other walks of life. These are preserved in a general series,[1] at present 'folio-ed', but not bound. Here the letters are kept in order of date of writing and not alphabetically. Occasionally letters which would normally be expected in one or other of the 'special' sequences have found their way here, including one from Lord Granville.

Both collections contain a third and highly interesting class of document: those thrown out directly by the mechanism of cabinet government. In the Granville papers the quantity is small,[2] though of sufficient interest to whet the appetite for more. They are mostly notes in which individual members of the cabinet recorded their opinion on documents circulated by Granville with a request for a statement of views: a method of doing the work of a cabinet meeting when there was insufficient occasion for oral discussion. In the Gladstone papers the quantity is very much larger [3] and the character rather different. In kind these papers are of two sorts: first, an almost overwhelming mass of argumentation in memoranda from Gladstone's hand, which served the dual purpose of clearing his own mind and giving a point of departure for cabinet discussion. Most, but not all, were circulated either to the cabinet as a whole or to those heads of department closely concerned. Expressions of opinion on these memoranda or on other memoranda circulated in the cabinet

[1] Add. MSS. 44416–91 for 1868 to July 1885.

[2] 6 volumes: G.D 29/68–70, G.D. 29/143–5.

[3] Add MSS. 44756–69 for Gladstone's political and other memoranda 1868–85; Add. MSS. 44637–46 for notes on the cabinets for 1868–85.

are scattered through the Gladstone papers in the sequences of ' special ' correspondence. The second sort of cabinet paper, which the historian may well regard as the prize of the whole collection, is a series of tabulated notes by the prime minister of subjects discussed in each cabinet meeting and of the decisions taken. Each note begins on a separate sheet headed by the date, place and time of the cabinet (sometimes on the back of a summons to a cabinet meeting). Occasionally, in Gladstone's absence, the note is by Lord Granville. These notes on cabinet meetings are not to be confused with the regular prime minister's letter to the sovereign after the cabinet or with the cabinet minute of the eighteenth and earlier nineteenth century. They would seem, however, to point forward to the modern cabinet procedure with its agenda and minutes. These notes seem to combine the character of agenda and acta. It seems reasonable to conjecture that the numbered headings for discussion were often jotted down preparatory to the cabinet and the brief note of the decision taken, which is sometimes clearly squeezed between two lines already written, added afterwards. Some, however, are written throughout in the past tense (e.g. 1. Lord Granville opened discussion on . . .) and would seem to be solely acta. All are very short and rarely give any indication of the course of discussion, though sometimes they record the way opinion divided. Occasionally they note absences. They show a good deal of regularity in the cabinet practice during the period. A normal weekly cabinet was held during session on a Saturday. It was not unusual for one or other of the ministers—most often Lord Granville during the first administration—to go down to dine and sleep at Windsor or Osborne afterwards. Occasionally the ' ordinary ' meeting was on a Friday. In between were meetings summoned at longer or shorter notice according to the urgency of business. Out of session, cabinets were held on a programme generally mapped out in advance by the prime minister and beginning usually about the middle of October, if there were no autumn session, and supposing ministers had not been recalled for exceptional business (as on 30 September 1870). This short series of out-of-session cabinets normally outlined the legislative programme for the coming session.

In addition to the block of central correspondence, the ' general ' correspondence and the cabinet papers, there is in the Granville collection another relevant class of document : that is the whole body of papers arising from Lord Granville's position as foreign secretary.[1] It is well known that the private letters exchanged between the nineteenth-century foreign secretaries and the British representatives abroad acquired a regularity and continuity that gave a special character to this correspondence however much individual practice varied. Lord Granville's letters to the ambassadors were irregular on the whole and infrequent, though they often show him at his most characteristic : easy, brief and pointed. The private correspondence with Thornton in 1870–71 is of particular importance, since the first tentative reopening of negotiations on the Alabama claims was not recorded in the dispatches. The private correspondence with foreign representatives resident in London, which

[1] The Granville papers do not contain any comparable series of letters exchanged with colonial governors for his period as colonial secretary, though his successors, Lords Kimberley and Carnarvon, seem to have carried on a very full private correspondence with the colonial governors.

Granville conducted in the intimate temper of an out-moded diplomatic freemasonry, was of particular importance in the months preceding the Black Sea Conference. The decisions that were ultimately recorded in the protocols were hammered out in private communication with Apponyi, Bernstorff, and Brunnow. Granville's correspondence with the under-secretaries shows some discrepancies of view both in Hammond's and Tenterden's time and, not perhaps unexpectedly, gives more evidence of their dissent from, than of their contribution to policy. It affords, too, useful technical material on the mechanics of conducting foreign policy.

Both these collections of private papers touch at every point the complex of changes that shaped the political history of the second half of Victoria's reign. The character of government was changing with the increasing importance in the administration of the reforming intellectual, such as Lowe, and of the expert. This latter tendency was reflected perhaps in the increasing use of the cabinet committee and the increasing frequency of references to the law officers. The character of party creed was changing. Gladstonian liberalism was the bridge between the political liberalism of the early nineteenth century and the liberalism of the twentieth with its social preoccupations. English liberalism also, under Gladstone's influence, shed the anti-clericalism that persisted among liberals on the continent. Conservative creed too was changing. Already in 1872 the conservatives sought to forge a link with the trade unions (no. 573). Under Disraeli's guidance they consolidated their new support by shaping a programme of social legislation. Foreign policy quickened in pace as it came under the influence of Bismarckian methods, increasing pressure of public opinion and speedier communications, while it was deflected temporarily into new channels by Gladstone's renunciation of the Castlereagh-Canning-Palmerston tradition. It is indeed impossible to compass in a single paragraph the variety of topics to which these collections are relevant.

III

Lack of space forbids publication in full. The choice then lies between selection by topic and selection by author. To select the two sides of a single correspondence, rather than to select the papers which bear upon a single theme, has the advantage of giving the most freedom to the documents to tell their own story and the least chance for the intrusion of the editor's hand. The two sides of a single correspondence make up a series of documents that can claim a natural completeness. The Gladstone-Granville correspondence was, at the time, distinctive among all Gladstone's letters owing to the exceptional personal relationship of the two men which was of considerable contemporary political importance. Lord Granville was Gladstone's closest political associate. From the union of these two dissimilar personalities sprang much of the harmony, such as it was, of the two first Liberal administrations: whether in their internal, parliamentary, or royal relationships. After Granville's death Acton wrote to Gladstone that he had watched this political friendship grow closer and easier ' in spite of much to separate you, in mental habits, in early affinities, and even in the form of fundamental convictions . . . I saw all the connections which had their root in social habit fade before the one which took its rise from public life and proved more firm and more enduring than the rest '.[1] Lord Granville's sense of perspective seemed to ease the tension in which Gladstone always worked ; the brevity and point in the one diminished a certain turgid quality in the other ; the flair which Granville had for practical steering gave fulfilment to Gladstone's intellectual grasp of a problem and its solution. Time and again Granville was called in to ease personal and practical difficulties. The correspondence, then, throws light upon the day-to-day working of the governmental machine by means of the intimacy of the prime minister with his leading coadjutor.

The method of selection by authorship has been adopted, but it has admittedly two patent disadvantages. In the first place, this correspondence was not an exchange of letters in the normal way. From February to August both men were in London and in daily contact. Granville's normal practice was to meet Gladstone almost daily, when both were in London, between one and two. This was a critical hour, for it came between the time when Granville saw the in-coming correspondence at the Foreign Office in the morning and his appointments with foreign representatives in London for which his normal hour was three.[2] During the tense days in August and September 1870, Gladstone was with Granville at Walmer for considerable periods, and they discussed ' the despatches as they came in '. Granville's practice of settling things with Gladstone in ' five minutes by talk, which it takes volumes of writing to dispose of ' [3] has severely denuded the correspondence for the historian. Only when Gladstone was at Hawarden and Granville at Walmer, or one or other in attendance at Balmoral, or on holiday in Scotland or France, was their exchange of letters full. When times were most critical abroad or in the House of Commons correspondence was apt to be scanty. Thus there is a break at the onset of the Franco-Prussian War and Britain's last-minute efforts to keep the peace are not recorded. There is nothing of real interest on the government crisis of March 1873. Things such as the Ewelme rectory affair or the Collier appointment left little or no mark upon it. A large number of letters were answered orally. There are weeks at a time with no or few letters. The story told by the correspondence is then always discontinuous.

The second disadvantage is that, despite Gladstone's thoroughness of exposition, much of what both wrote cannot be understood by the reader who does not share the knowledge that was their common property. The frequency of personal meeting, the considerable pressure of political business, as well as Granville's elliptical style, help to exclude the reader from full understanding. More important was the fact that much of Gladstone's and Granville's letter-writing was commentary upon other documents produced by royal, cabinet, departmental or parliamentary business.

These disadvantages have as far as possible been remedied by the footnotes. These contain references to the documents upon which the correspondents comment. Each man saw and commented upon some, though not necessarily all, of the other's letters to or from the Queen. These have been traced where possible and reference

[1] 20 April 1891, Add. MS. 44094, fo. 170. I have to thank Mr. M. R. D. Foot for this, and number of other references below.

[2] Cf. d'Harcourt to Granville, 5 Aug. 1872, G.D. 29/89.

[3] Granville to Lyons, private, 10 Aug. 1872, G.D. 29/109.

to them given. Some letters took their departure from cabinet discussion or from common knowledge of colleagues' opinions. It has sometimes been possible to reconstruct this background also from other parts of the Gladstone or Granville papers. References have been made, in order to enable the reader to recover something of the parliamentary knowledge that the letters take for granted, to Hansard, although *The Times*'s reports of debates had the greater authority in the Gladstonian era, and to the Journals and Printed Papers of both Houses, and to correspondence with Granville in his capacity as leader of the House of Lords. Dispatches and drafts, and telegrams, except those of a routine or trivial kind, most diplomatic private letters and sometimes copies of Granville's replies were seen by Gladstone. The prime minister's letters are frequently commentaries upon these documents. As far as possible they have been traced in the Foreign and (for 1868–70), Colonial Office records and the relevant part of the Granville papers, and so, to some extent, the departmental context of the correspondence given. Much of the information however that the letters assume is not recoverable by reference to a single document or documents.

The term political has been broadly interpreted. All the documents preserved in the Granville volumes of the one collection and the Gladstone volumes of the other have been printed except the following :—those which concern the private affairs of the royal family, give personal details of individual candidates for place or honours, make personal arrangements between the writers (such as Granville's note to Gladstone appointing a rendezvous for the Derby day of 1870), some enclosures, a few letters exchanged between the private secretaries, telegrams and drafts of telegrams, and a few letters from Mrs. Gladstone to Lord Granville. The omission of a letter written by Gladstone or Granville has been noted, where it occurs, in a footnote. Letters concerning promotion to the episcopal bench and to the peerage have been judged politically significant to ministries for whom the composition of the House of Lords was a prime consideration in their legislative careers. Letters concerned with Household appointments have also been printed ; for these acquired political significance from Gladstone's practice of using them to stimulate individual peers to active political work. Thus departments headed by commoners, such as the Board of Trade and the Board of Works, were represented in the Lords by holders of Household appointments.

So far as possible the personal idiosyncrasies of the two men have been respected. This is the explanation of considerable inconsistency in dating, punctuation and spelling. Yet each man had his own consistency. O.19.70 is as recognizably Gladstone's dating as Oct 9/70 is Granville's. 'Despatch', 'enquire', 'enclose', 'encrease', 'holyday', 'control' are as consistently used by Granville as 'dispatch', 'inquire', 'inclose', 'holiday', 'controul' are used by Gladstone. Granville writes normally 'favor', 'honor', and until 1872, Bismarck without the 'c'. He often wrote 'it's' and 'your's' and seldom finished the 't' in the abbreviation 'Govt'. His spelling of proper names and capitalization were erratic. He wrote most easily using the dash and the comma and a series of phrases, in contrast to Gladstone, who was most at home with the exactly punctuated, carefully and elaborately constructed sentence. The address is most often provided by the printed or embossed form at the head of the page, but '11 C.H.T.' or 'Bruton St' are reproductions of hand-written addresses. A place-name in square brackets has been supplied where there is good evidence to show where the letter was written. The superscription and subscription have not been reproduced. Granville most frequently wrote 'my dear G.' and signed 'yr's G.'. This has interest since Lord Granville was Gladstone's only political correspondent apart from Argyll and, after 1873, Bright to use this familiarity. Gladstone normally wrote 'My dear Granville' and signed 'Yours ever' or 'Ever yours sincerely'. The suppression of these forms does not really blur the distinction between the mere note and the more formal letter: the two lines of no. 380 have full address and signature while longer letters have neither.

The present volumes contain the correspondence down to 1876. The party history of Gladstonian liberalism during the period of the two great administrations divides conveniently at that year. The vigour and productivity of 1868–71 had been followed by decline. The legislative programme that united the party was exhausted. It had lost the confidence of the electorate and no longer commanded in full the support of its own members. In the autumn of 1876, with a new cause in the championship of the Christian subjects of the Ottoman Empire, the party achieved a fresh coherence and renewed its political vitality. Its history took a new departure. The present two volumes end when the Turkish question begins to dominate the correspondence. The first takes the party to the highest point of its achievement during the first administration. The first Irish legislation was completed and the Treaties of London and Washington signed. The correspondence in the second tells the story of thickening difficulties, and ends with the party not merely defeated and in opposition, but also deeply frustrated by the unreality of the leadership of Granville and Hartington as Gladstone, who had retired in 1875, began to resume command of the electorate.

It is unnecessary to enlarge upon the significance of the documents below. An assessment of their value or any attempt to use them as historical material demands the scope of a separate study. As the letters stand, they speak for themselves as a living day-to-day record of the impact of two personalities upon each other and upon the events they helped to shape. They kindle the formal departmental letters, parliamentary papers and cabinet memoranda into life and warmth by recalling the play upon them of human convictions and hesitancies. In short, the correspondence gives to the mass of government papers, which the historian normally uses, the enlivening touch, in Guizot's phrase, of that 'espérance pleine d'inquiétude et de travail' which Gladstone always brought to politics.

LIST OF ABBREVIATIONS

C.J. and *L.J.*	*Journals of the House of Commons* and *Journals of the House of Lords.*
D.N.B.	*Dictionary of National Biography.*
Fitzmaurice	Lord Edmond Fitzmaurice, *The Life of Lord Granville, 1815–1891* (1905).
F.O. and C.O. with index numbers	Foreign Office and Colonial Office papers in the Public Record Office.
G.E.C.	G. E. C[okayne], *The Complete Peerage* (revised edition (1910–).
Gleanings	W. E. Gladstone, *Gleanings of Past Years, 1843–78* (1879).
Guedalla	Philip Guedalla, *The Queen and Mr. Gladstone* (1933).
Hans. Parl. Deb.	Hansard, *Parliamentary Debates.*
Knaplund, *Letters from Berlin*	"Letters from the Berlin Embassy" edited by P. Knaplund, being the *Annual Report of the American Historical Association for 1942*, vol. ii (1944).
Letters	*The Letters of Queen Victoria.* Second Series, edited by G. E. Buckle (1926).
Mem.	Memorandum.
Min.	Minute.
Morley	John Morley, *The Life of William Ewart Gladstone* (3 volumes, 1903).
Newton, *Lord Lyons*	Lord Newton, *Lord Lyons* (1913).
Parl. papers	Parliamentary papers.
Tel.	Telegram.
Temperley and Penson, *Foundations*	H. Temperley and L. M. Penson, *Foundations of British Foreign Policy, 1792–1902* (1938).

Note : Since these volumes went to press, the Public Record Office has substituted the letters and figures P.R.O. 30 for the letters G.D. as the reference for the class of document to which the Granville papers belong.

ABBREVIATIONS USED IN THE INDEX

Ass.	Assembly.	Lib.	Liberal.
Att. Gen.	Attorney General.	Lieut.	Lieutenant.
Bd.	Board.	Min.	Minister.
Chanc.	Chancellor.	Nat.	National.
C.O.	Colonial Office.	Parl.	Parliamentary.
Col.	Colonial.	Priv.	Private.
Cons.	Conservative.	Rep.	Representative.
F.O.	Foreign Office.	Rev.	Revenue.
For.	Foreign.	Sec.	Secretary.
Gen.	General.	Sol. Gen.	Solicitor General.
Gov.	Governor.	Und.-sec.	Under-secretary.
I.O.	India Office.	W.O.	War Office.

THE POLITICAL CORRESPONDENCE OF MR. GLADSTONE AND LORD GRANVILLE

1. Mr. Gladstone to Lord Granville. [G.D. 29/29A]

Secret. Hawarden. Dec. 2. 68.

The Govt are certainly out.

Gen. Grey comes here with a letter from H.M. this afternoon. I write in anticipation. If I do not add, please to consider that I am off for Windsor tomorrow. And in that case I shall hope to find you in town on my return be it tomorrow night or be it Friday morning. Please send word to my house though if I can I shall call at yours.

Some circumstances of delicacy—not affecting me—have already arisen, which may require great nicety at the outset. They are personal.

Today I write to no one to be in town except you and Glyn.

I am of opinion that if H.M. chooses to accept the resignation now we have no right to decline on account of the great inconvenience which may arise to us in the vacating of seats.

I believe the case to be without precedent: I mean the formation of a Govt in the interval between the Election and the meeting.

2. Lord Granville to Mr. Gladstone. [Add. MS. 44165, fo. 218]

Private. Bruton Street. Dec 4/68.

In considering the arrangements for the Chancellorship of which you are thinking,[1] it is necessary that you should know what happened about a legal Peerage offered to Sir A. Cockburn.

Palmerston during the session preceding his death, submitted to the Queen the name of the Ld Chief Justice for a Peerage. H.M. objected, because Sir Alexander's character was not without stain, and had been the subject of much observation. Lord Russell agreed with the Queen.

Lord P. answered these objections, with the concurrence of Sir G. Grey, and one or two other colleagues in this way.

He admitted that Sir Alexander had been profligate in his youth, but he believed that for many years his life had exposed him to no public reproach. If the objection

[1] Roundell Palmer refused the chancellorship since he opposed Irish disestablishment; cf. Selborne, *Memorials, Personal and Political* (1898), i. 113–14, and Add. MS. 44296, fo. 133. Sir William Page Wood, Sir A. Cockburn, J. D. Coleridge, and Lords Westbury and Romilly were considered; cf. Granville to Gladstone, 29 Aug. 1868, Add. MS. 44165, fo. 174. Page Wood accepted office (4 Dec.), becoming Lord Hatherley, Add. MS. 44205, fo. 10. Cockburn declined a peerage; cf. Guedalla, i. 145.

however was valid, it was applicable to the appointment of Sir Alexander as Chief Justice (I believe the Queen had made some objections at that time) but that after having held high office for many years with great distinction, it would be an exception to the general rule, to exclude the Lord Chief Justice from the usual compliment of a Peerage; and the Common Law Judges already felt aggrieved that the Legal Peerages were exclusively held by persons who had held Equity Judgeships.

The Queen (I believe with some reluctance) signified to Lord P. H.M's consent—of which Lord P. informed Sir Alexander. He accepted the Peerage, but said as the session was so near its end, he would prefer being gazetted at the end of the year.

Lord P. died and Lord R. succeeded and was informed by a member of Lord Palmerston's family of what had passed. When I asked him what he intended to do, he said he should do nothing, unless Sir A. made a direct application to him, in which case he should fulfil Lord P's engagement.

Sir A. stated that Lord Russell had never forgiven him, when with Mr Lowe and nearly all the non Cabinet Officials in the H of Commons, he had signed a letter reflecting on Lord Russell's conduct after his return from Vienna—that he could not make a personal application to Lord R for that which had been graciously given him by the Queen on Lord P's recommendation—and so the matter ended.

3. **Lord Granville to Mr. Gladstone.** [Add. MS. 44165, fo. 220]

16, Bruton Street. Dec 10/68.

Will you, as a personal favor to me, submit to the Queen for Her consideration whether it would be agreeable to Her My. to have Lansdowne as a Lord in Waiting.[1]

He is young, but he has more manner, conversation, and general information than most men 10 or 15 years older. He knows French perfectly, and I believe German—but I have reason to suppose that H.M. would not consider me an authority on that point. The Queen would probably be well disposed to him, on account of his mother, and of his grandfather—& he would represent Ireland.

William Compton, brother to Lord Northampton, Lady Marian, and my poor sister in law [2] is anxious to have a small place about Court, but as he is not in Parliament, it is no use troubling you about it.

4. **Mr. Gladstone to Lord Granville.** [G.D. 29/29A]

Hatfield. Dec. 14/68.

Perhaps I had better put on paper the difficulty I was in about Enfield.[3] It seemed not improbable that Hugessen would decline the Home Under Secretaryship.

[1] He was offered and accepted a junior lordship of the Treasury instead; cf. Gladstone to Lansdowne, 15 Dec., Lansdowne to Gladstone, 16 Dec., Add MS. 44417, fos. 146, 155, and no. 5 below.

[2] Lady Marian Alford and Lady Margaret Leveson-Gower. All four were children of the second marquis of Northampton.

[3] The father, Lord Strafford, had complained about his son's exclusion from the government, Strafford to Granville, 10, 11 Dec., G.D. 29/22A.

In that case I meant (with Bruce's sanction first obtained) to propose it to Enfield. But Hugessen took it. There was then the Board of Trade. But this office under Bright seemed to *require* a man of special training like Lefevre. There was then the Poor Law Board, Enfield's old office. I really could not with propriety ask him to take this rather negative office again, and under Goschen a younger member of Parliament than himself. There was the Treasury which would have been subject to the disadvantage of re-election. There remained the Civil Lordship of the Admiralty. That is a decided step onward from the Poor Law : it is a thoroughly respectable & respected office : it is *the* office through which Childers Hartington & Stansfield have gone on to promotion. Glyn's belief was that Enfield's seat was safe. Of course none of us had a right to determine that he ought to vacate. But I really do not now see, what else I could have done : and I was greatly pleased by the kind manner in which he himself received the proposal though he could not act upon it.

Cowper declines.[1]

5. Lord Granville to Mr. Gladstone. [Add. MS. 44165, fo. 224]

Colonial Office. Dec 14/68.

Lansdowne after consulting Lowe has desired me to express his warm thanks to you for thinking of him. He will gladly accept the Lordship of the Treasury, doing its business in the House of Lords. He prefers in any case not to have any salary, or any Household place.

It is modern usage only which places the " Treasurer " in the Commons. He used always to be in the Lords.[2]

6. Lord Granville to Mr. Gladstone. [Add. MS. 44165, fo. 228]

Windsor Castle. Dec 16 [1868].

I am going to Johnny Acton some day about the 10th or 12th Jany. He says " Gladstone is under an old promise to come and refresh his mind among my books, but on the principle of the Duke of Orleans and the King of France, I suppose it is impossible now " " but I should like it extremely."

[1] A lordship-in-waiting offered 11 Dec. and declined 13 Dec. Gladstone's letter describes his use of Household appointments to strengthen the Liberal force in the Lords, Add. MS. 44417, fos. 78, 111.

[2] Gladstone revived the sixth lordship of the Treasury, abolished in 1847 ; see *Treasury Minute 28 Dec. 1868*. Parl. papers. H.C. 13 (1868–69). xxxiv, 621. In 1868 there were three senior and three junior lords : Gladstone, Lowe, Stansfield ; W. P. Adam, J. C. W. Vivian (answering financial War Office questions), Lord Lansdowne (unsalaried, answering for the Treasury in the Lords). In Oct. 1869 the third senior lordship lapsed, when Stansfield became a joint-secretary, but a fourth junior lord (W. H. Gladstone) was appointed. After 1871 when Vivian joined the permanent staff of the War Office, there were only five lords of the Treasury.

7. Mr. Gladstone to Lord Granville. [G.D. 29/57]

Copy. Private. Carlton H. Terrace. Dec. 16. 1868.

I wish to lay before you my views and to have the benefit of your opinion respg the vacant office of Lord Justice.[1]

In days when the principles of administration were more strict than they now are, I think it would have been the admitted duty of the person charged with the appointment, to ask himself whether there was any distinguished man of the legal profession, who had passed through great offices, and was at present unemployed, & who might possibly be disposed to accept the vacant seat. In a word to proceed on the principle applied in the case of Lord Lyndhurst [2]: to do this, before entertaining any question of promotion; and to leave it entirely to the person concerned to judge of all the nicer questions of personal rank and dignity of which in truth he would be the only person competent to dispose.

With these views I must call to mind that there are now in the House of Lords two Peers originally of the Equity Bar, & still in their full vigour, who have held the office of Lord Chancellor; Lord Westbury and Lord Cairns, and the question for me appears to be this—If it is possible, that Lord Westbury might be disposed to accept the Lord Justiceship ought not the power of taking it to be given to him?

Doubtless it may be asked, does the precedent of Lord Lyndhurst cover this case—and would he (Lord Westbury not Lord Lyndhurst) if it does not, be inclined to enlarge it. But (as it seems to me) there is no consideration of public interest which allows me to close these questions. [They are questions] (so to speak) for the other side.

Some men take as a friendly act and mark of regard what other men take in an opposite sense. If an offer of this kind were viewed *in malam partem* by any one, I could not help it. If it more justly deserves a better construction, this ought greatly to recommend it to the old Colleagues of Lord Westbury. Lord Westbury suffered heavily in 1866 [*sic*].[3] He became to a great extent a scapegoat. The vials of public virtue, a very acrid composition were discharged upon him. In 1868, it has been my plain duty, at a great crisis, to overlook former official relations, and to ask myself one question only—all circes taken as they are, what combination embracing the Chancellorship, would give most weight to a government, which will need every ounce it can get? But, this being so, I ought, and we all ought, to be the more desirous to pay to Lord Westbury every just tribute in our power, whether as an old Colleague, as a most distinguished Lawyer, or as a most remarkable man.

The upshot then of my thoughts is really this; that I ought in the manner most

[1] The lord justiceship of appeal in chancery, vacated by Sir W. Page Wood. Roundell Palmer refused the office, Selborne, *Memorials*, i. 113. Sir George Markham Giffard accepted it, 21 Dec., Add. MS. 44417, fo. 214.

[2] That the best man, whatever his politics, should be appointed. In 1831 Grey made Lyndhurst, who had been lord chancellor in the preceding Tory ministry, chief baron of the exchequer. Cf. to and from Hatherley, 14, 15 Dec., Add. MS. 44205, fos. 19, 20.

[3] The select committees which investigated the Leonard Edmunds and Leeds Bankruptcy Court cases found Westbury at fault and the Commons passed a vote of censure upon him, 3 July 1865, *Hans. Parl. Deb.* 3rd ser. clxxx. 1045–1138.

acceptable to Lord Westbury to find out whether an offer of the vacant Lord Justiceship would or would not be acceptable to him; and to ask you as Leader of the Govt. in the House of Lords, *and* as the man qualified above all others to answer the question, whether you can help me in this important business.[1]

Of course in any event this matter must remain strictly private until a later stage. I cannot but think the profession would think Lord W's acceptance a ***high minded*** act.

8. Mr. Gladstone to Lord Granville.[2] [G.D. 29/57]

11 C.H.T. D. 28/68.

1. Mr Oswald does not name his office—& I do not know if it is in my gift.
2. The Commrship of Inland Revenue is *dead*.
3. Vivian requires no comment.[3]
4. Camden (in a good letter) declines. I have written to Ld Carysfort.[4]
4 [*sic*]. Please to read & return the three inclosed.[5] Secret.
5. I have a paper [6] on the same subject to show you.

Early.

What would you advise about Mr La Touche's letter?[7]

On two of your inclosures I cannot at the moment lay my hand.

9. Lord Granville to Mr. Gladstone. [Add. MS. 44165, fo. 229]

[28 December 1868].

I presume C[hichester] F[ortescue]'s proposed general answer to La Touche will do.[8]

I doubt speaking to the Queen at all, till the Prince of Wales comes back.

10. Lord Granville to Mr. Gladstone. [Add. MS. 44165, fo. 230]

Private. Osborne. Dec 31/68.

I foolishly forgot to bring Dalhousie's letter with me, but I will write from London as to the spoils of poor Lord Belhaven.[9]

[1] Cf. Granville to Westbury, 16 Dec., and reply 17 Dec., G. D. 29/67. The upshot was the offer, also unsuccessful, of the vacancy to Cairns; cf. Gladstone to Cairns, 19 Dec., and reply 20 Dec., Add. MS. 44417, fos. 200, 207, and note on copy of no. 7 in Add. MS. 44165, fo. 226.

[2] Gladstone to Granville, 20 Dec., asking him to send no. 7 to Lord Cairns, G.D. 29/57, not printed.

[3] Gladstone comments on the several enclosures in an untraced letter from Granville.

[4] Relates to a lordship-in-waiting offered to Camden 24 Dec., and Carysfort 28 Dec., Add. MS. 44417, fos. 242, 267.

[5] Possibly included (i) Archdeacon Stopford to Gladstone, 26 Dec., on the Irish Church bill, Add. MS. 44417, fo. 257; (ii) Gladstone's scheme of the latter which had gone to Fortescue, 26 Dec., and was now sent, 28 Dec., to the Irish Attorney-General for drafting and to Granville.

[6] By William Atkins, dean of Ferns, Add. MS. 44417, fos. 203–6.

[7] 18 Dec., offering Harristown as a royal residence in Ireland, Add. MS. 44417, fo. 184; cf. Gladstone to the Queen, 6 Jan. 1870.

[8] Minute by Fortescue, 27 Dec., Add. MS. 44121, fo. 76, which Gladstone followed in letters to La Touche 30 Dec. discouraging, and 3 April 1869 rejecting, Add. MS. 44536, fos. 84, 139.

[9] Died 22 Dec. 1868 without direct heirs.

I return you the Archdeacon's most important letter. Even if he, the Bishop of Peterborough, and the Dean of Cashel get into a groove which does not suit you, their action must greatly disconcert those who propose to use the Irish Church as a political Engine—& better things may be hoped for from them—I keep the pamphlet by Mr Ditton, and I return to C[hichester] F[ortescue] the scheme, which at first sight I like much—Like some other documents in *your own handwriting* which has of late somewhat degenerated, one finds novelties on reading it a second time.

I am much obliged to you for this mark of your confidence and look forward to talking it over with you on the 18th.

11. Lord Granville to Mr. Gladstone.[1] [Add. MS. 44165, fo. 232]

Private. Osborne. Dec 31/68.

We took charge of Bright at Waterloo. He is rapidly becoming a very loose character. He flirted violently with my wife all the way down—describing to her his wife, his family, & his home—reading verses to her, and quoting similar passages in the older poets—Denouncing luncheons, and then eating enormously of Mayonaise, and drinking goblets of Claret, which he declared was so light, it must be "Gladstone's".

We had a fine passage—during which he left us to ourselves, and was mean enough, I am much afraid, to pump the openhearted captain on the extravagancies connected with the Royal Yacht. He was much pleased with the Royal footman who was waiting for us at Cowes, and asked whether they were really hired by the length. All went well till our entry at Osborne. He was really angry with the footman at the door for transferring his carpet bag to a man in an apron. In vain we pleaded the division of labour, the necessity of the former preserving his red coat, and his white stockings from the dirt of luggage. "If I had known the fellow was too fine to take it, I would have carried it myself." He staid [*sic*] in Lady G's sittingroom till past dressing time. Landseer came in. Nothing could be more striking than the contrast between the two men. Both a little vain, and with good reason to be so—but one so guileless in his allusions to himself, and the other showing it enveloped with little artifices, and mock humility—one so intrinsically a gentleman, and so ignorant of our particular society, the other a little vulgar, but a consummate master of the ways of the grand monde. The combined influences of Bright's connection with the press the platform, and the House of Commons, together with the great simplicity in which this combative and able man was brought up, and which he has maintained in his social and family habits, give his conversation a singular flavour.

He told us he only informed his wife two days ago of his visit here, and of her almost reproachful answer—"It seems strange you should be going, where I cannot follow."

I called for him at dinner time—his dress was irreproachable, after he had

[1] Printed Fitzmaurice, i. 539–40 (without the last sentence); see also G. M. Trevelyan, *The Life of John Bright* (1913), pp. 398–401.

readily agreed to take off a pair of bridal white gloves. He was rather pleased, quoted his tailor's approval of tights, and acknowledged he had promised to rehearse the costume before his wife and daughter.

The beginning of dinner was awful—the Queen with a sick headache and shy—Princess Louise whispering unintelligibly in my ear, and Lady Clifden shouting ineffectually into the still more impenetrable receptacle of sound belonging to Charles Grey. Bright like a war horse champing his bit, and dying to be at them. At last an allusion to children enabled me to tell Bright to repeat to H.M. his brother's observation "where, considering what charming things children were, all the queer old men came from." This amused the Queen, and all went on merrily. She talked to him for a long time, and the old roué evidently touched some feminine chord, for she was much pleased with him, and saw him again the next morning. Without unnecessary depreciation of our enemies, it is probable that she is not insensible to the charm of sincerity and earnestness.

We then retired to the Household at tea, and Bright was by no means dashed, when Alfred Paget addressed the company as if through a speaking trumpet. "Well I never expected to see John Bright *here*, winning his money at Blind Hookey."

If you ever get through this twaddle, you will believe in the neglect of your Colonies.

12. Mr. Gladstone to Lord Granville. [Add. MS. 44166, fo. 4]

[*Copy*]. H[aw]ard[e]n. Jan 6. 69.

1. The Ld in Waiting ought to be if possible, Irish [1]; I will write to whichever you think fit, after you have felt yr way. Ld Granard is an applicant for office.

2. I think Ld Southesk very good for the Thistle, & will write to him unless you dissuade me.

3. I think we have got the Bishop of Oxford right on the Irish Ch :—which will be rather material. I got two friends to write to him: of course not in my name.

4. Hearing of it from Spencer, Gen: Grey has mentioned the La Touche business to the Queen: a decided mistake, I think, on his part. Under these circs., probably I had better send her La Touche's letter.

5. Infinite thanks for yr acct of Bright's visit to Osborne: some day it will probably be history. Query—whether he is not a little hen-pecked.

6. I am deeply wounded by yr reflections on my handwriting.

7. It seems that Bruce really appoints the High Commr: will you ∴ communicate with him? [2]

8. I hope you have read Disendowment in the Bahamas. It is rich.

[1] Gladstone to Granville, 1 Jan., reporting Carysfort's refusal of a lordship-in-waiting (above, no. 8), G.D. 29/29A, Granville to Gladstone, 5 Jan., suggesting other names, Add. MS. 44166, fo. 2, not printed. Lord Lurgan was appointed. An undated mem. by Granville on the retirement of Lord James Murray, an equerry, Add. MS. 44165, fo. 238, also not printed.

[2] High Commissioner to the General Assembly of the Church of Scotland. Lord Stair was appointed.

13. Lord Granville to Mr. Gladstone. [Add. MS. 44166, fo. 5]

Althorp. Jan 7/68 [1869][1]

I have doubts whether it is possible for the Archbishops & Bishops to agree to conditions of surrender before the assembly of a Synod,[2] and whether it is necessary on our part to impose such conditions.

Once met, an empty declaration on their part that they objected to being eaten up, would not have much effect. In all probability they would not be unanimous, and it would be important for the Gov to have a tangible body with whom to communicate.

But if conditions are to be exacted, I am of opinion that a private communication would be the best at first.

I am sorry to say that in the discussion which took place on this subject in Palmerston's Cabinet, I remember Gladstone being disrespectful enough to apply the epithet "rotten" to that august Institution.

14. Lord Granville to Mr. Gladstone. [G.D. 29/57]

Copy. Private. Althorp. Jan. 7/1869

Please to read the enclosed confidential despatch from Sir John Young,[3] & the private letters [4] from Lord Monck & Genl Doyle.

Sir George Cartier & Mr Macdougall give similar opinions.

An opinion ought to be given without delay by HM's Govt., and I should be glad to have your permission to write in the sense advised by Lord Monck.

15. Mr. Gladstone to Lord Granville. [G.D. 29/29A]

Hawarden. Jan 8. 69.

I am entirely in the sense of Young and Monck. In one point I think Monck's sketch of a reply a little defective. It *seems* to mean, that if the Colonies were united in asking the repeal of the Act, we must therefore repeal it. I do not admit this, while I do not assert the contrary. But I do assert that the people of the United Kingdom are parties concerned in the Repeal, and must be heard if the case arose: as I think you will agree.

Here if any where finality is in place. If ever there was just & adequate evidence of a legitimate popular consent it was in this case. We I imagine are friendly bystanders to help in any work of conciliation, but no more. It will be easy to reserve the right of the British people, and yet to ground our refusal pointedly on

[1] Granville dates the letter at the end Jan 6/68 and at the beginning Jan 7/68.

[2] Relates to the Irish Protestant bishops' application to meet in synod, referred by Bruce to Gladstone, 31 Dec., and by him to Granville, Add. MS. 44086, fo. 10.

[3] No. 3, 12 Dec. 1868, asking for a statement from the new administration that it adhered to the British North America Act of 1867. Cf. J. A. Pope, *Correspondence of Sir J. A. Macdonald* (1921), 80, 83. For the dispatch and Granville's statement to Young, No. 13, 13 Jan., C.O. 42/671. Cf. Young to Granville, No. 728 confidential, 7 Jan., C.O. 42/675.

[4] Untraced. Lord Monck's letter, 23 Dec., enclosed General Doyle's; see note on no. 14.

the simple fact that we cannot dissolve a contract nor entertain the question of dissolving it at the wish of one of the parties.

P.S. You will doubtless bear in mind Mr Bright's [1] proceedings last year in the H. of C.

16. Mr. Gladstone to Lord Granville. [G.D. 29/29A]

Hawarden. Jan 9. 69.

1. I think it would be well if Lord Lurgan could be sounded. The Queen will get sick of giving permissions which are to end in smoke. I do not understand the reference to Camden.

2. I write to Southesk.

3. I am very sorry to hear of Hartington's malpractices in opening letters.

4. I am hard at work about this improper speech of Trevelyan's. It seems he said 'the Court' without meaning to say it.

5. As the view taken about the Memorial of Irish Bishops is not quite the same in all cases, & as circulation takes too much time, I think the question can stand over for the Cabinet, and in the meantime if I find there is no legal impediment I can perhaps manage the preliminary part without committing any one. We have not yet got far enough with Stopford to consult him on a point of practice.

6. What do you say to the proposal of the Fishmongers inclosed herewith? I rather suppose we ought to accept for the 9th. If you agree please to send a line to Glyn to save time.

7. Has it ever occurred to you to consider whether an honour ought to be tendered to John Mill?

8. I find Lyttleton would rather like to be P.C. He is entitled to it I think if he chooses.

17. Lord Granville to Mr. Gladstone.[2] [Add. MS. 44166, fo. 7]

Jan 11/68. [1869].

I have been in bed for two days—but am getting well again. It was a chill.

I send you a letter from Monsell about Fenians.[3] The seals of my two last letters from him had been tampered with.

Lurgan & Southesk will I think do.[4]

I have had a somewhat reproachful letter from Abercromby in consequence of a letter from you regretting you had not been made acquainted with his wishes.[5]

I am not surprised you did not remember my telling you so, which I did, without however any recommendation of his request.

[1] Moved for an enquiry into Nova Scotia's attitude to the confederation of Canada, but failed to carry it, *Hans. Parl. Deb.* 3rd ser. cxcii. 1658–96.

[2] Letter marked: 'direct if necessary to Aldenham, Bridgenorth'.

[3] Monsell to Granville, 6 Jan., G.D. 29/25A; cf. Fortescue to Bruce, 1 Feb., Add. MS. 44086, fo. 21, and Parl. papers. H.C. 72 and H.C. 125 (1868–69). li, 531, 533.

[4] For lordship-in-waiting and knighthood of the Thistle respectively.

[5] For lordship-in-waiting.

18. Mr. Gladstone to Lord Granville. [G.D. 29/29A]

Hawarden. Jan. 12. 69.

I really thought I had obeyed your exact directions, if not repeated your ipsissima verba, in writing to Lord Abercromby : but perhaps I made a confusion. Too old !

I have sent on Monsell's able letter to Fortescue—which I hope you will approve.

Archdeacon Stopford comes here on Thursday.

As I understand you, you think I may write to Lord Lurgan without fear of refusal.

19. Lord Granville to Mr. Gladstone. [Add. MS. 44166, fo. 8]

Aldenham. Jan 14/69.

Bessborough wrote to me in the first instance that Lurgan wished for Office. On getting your letter, I urged B. to sound him discreetly but so that there might be no mistake.

I know no one who has so strong a claim as Lyttleton to be P.C. if he wishes it. I am not quite so sure about J. Mill, merely on the ground that honors should go as much as possible with a general acceptance. Mill has failed as a politician for the moment, not so much from advanced views, as from errors of judgment and tact. I doubt whether at this particular moment it would be a very friendly act to Mill to persuade him to take an honor from the Crown—& of course an offer ought not to be made, which was likely to be refused. But of both these matters I should like to talk on Monday.[1]

If it were possible I should prefer the Fishmongers after the meeting of Parlt, so that the H. of Commons might have the absolute cream of your first ministerial statement.

I have written to Bright to explain the Nova Scotia matter.[2]

20. Mr. Gladstone to Lord Granville. [G.D. 29/29A]

Osborne. Jan 23. 69. 7 P.M.

I send you a letter from Spencer together with a very curious memorandum in which Roundell reports a conversation with the Abp of Dublin.[3]

The Abp shows no heat, nor malice : and is most righteous. But his management of the helm is not satisfactory.

He is keeping back with all his might the Bp of Oxford. I have written a

[1] Granville visited Gladstone at Hawarden, 18–20 Jan. ; see Granville to Gladstone, 21 Jan., Add. MS. 44166, fo. 11, not printed. This letter also proposed peers to move and second the address.

[2] See Granville to Bright, 14 Jan. His reply, 17 Jan., called the British North America Act ' a gross violation of all the principles ' on which we had governed the colonies for the last 25 years but did not press for cabinet discussion, G.D. 29/52. Granville circulated Bright's letter in the cabinet, Cardwell to Granville, 21 Jan., G.D. 29/53.

[3] From Spencer, 22 Jan., enclosing mem. by his private secretary C. S. Roundell of a conversation with the archbishop of Dublin, 21 Jan., on the intransigence of the archbishops of Dublin and Armagh, Add. MS. 44306, fos. 44–50.

letter in the opposite sense which is pretty stout: pointing out that his *private* good sentiments are after his operation of last summer, equal to zero.

If the Hawarden visit was not disagreeable on your side I can assure you the pleasure was reciprocated.

I have not yet seen the Queen but I am to see her tonight at 7–30. I see she wishes to have my paper to think over.

You will I have no doubt arrange the moving and seconding in the best way.

21. Lord Granville to Mr. Gladstone. [Add. MS. 44166, fo. 12]

Colonial Office. Jan 25 [1869].

I return Spencer's letter & Roundell's Mem.

As they mean to fight, I am not sure that it is a bad thing for us to have so little handiness in Dublin, and so little ability in Armagh.

22. Mr. Gladstone to Lord Granville.[1] [G.D. 29/29A]

11. Downing Street. Feb. 1. 69.

1. I think I gave you Bp of Peterborough's letter to Spencer to read. It is much wanted in Dublin: please to let me have it.

2. What do you say to Lady *Buchan* & her application?

3. What do you think of Mundella as Seconder in H. of C. The only possible objection to him that I know of that hypercritics might say it was for his triumph over Roebuck? You know his merits I have no doubt. They are real & great.

I bring a very good report from P[embroke] Lodge.

Do you dine here as I hope on Thursday? I have failed by defections in making it Cabinet—so will Lady G. come?

23. Minute by Lord Granville. [Add. MS. 44166, fo. 13]

16, Bruton Street. [1 February 1869].

I can suggest no improvement on the answer Mr G[ladstone] proposes to send to the Queen.[2]

H.M does not appear to be in very strong hands as to personal advice at present.

24. Lord Granville to Mr. Gladstone. [Add. MS. 44166, fo. 14]

14 S. Audley St. Feb 7 [1869].

The Queen says "she is ready to see the B[isho]p of Peterborough, but she must be able to state to him what the Gov proposes to do, and would be glad to know to what extent she may go in speaking of Mr Gladstone's intentions".[3]

I should like to send the answer by tomorrow's messenger.

[1] Gladstone to Granville, 28 Jan., G.D. 29/57, not printed.

[2] 3 Feb., on her refusal to open Parliament, Guedalla, i. 156–7; cf. Gen. Grey to Granville, 21 Jan., G.D. 29/32. No. 23 is minuted 'I quite agree E. C[ardwell].' The comment in its last paragraph was prompted by Jenner's conversation with Gladstone, 1 Feb.

[3] On the Irish Church bill, stated in mem. 21 Jan., communicated by Gladstone at Osborne during the weekend 22–23 Jan. (cf. Guedalla, i. 151–6), possibly developed by Granville, who was at Osborne 5–6 Feb.

25. Mr. Gladstone to Lord Granville.[1] [G.D. 29/29A]

11, Carlton House Terrace. Feb. 7. 69.

The case is peculiar & not free from difficulty. On the whole I think it would be wrong to place any limit upon the Queen's communications to the Bishop of Peterborough, except this that they would doubtless be made by HM to him for himself only, & that no part of them would go beyond him to any person whatever.

26. Lord Granville to Mr. Gladstone. [Add. MS. 44166, fo. 16]

Colonial Office. Feb 10/69.

It might be worth while to ask the Queen whether the reasons which prevented H.M to open Parliament, applied equally to what Bruce suggests.[2]

If so, you could probably do so in a light and airy manner in conversation, better than in a formal letter.

27. Lord Granville to Mr. Gladstone. [Add. MS. 44166, fo. 17]

Private. Mentmore, Leighton Buzzard. Feb 14/69.

I send you a letter from Ch. Grey.[3] If there is anything objectionable in my answer put it in the fire and I will write tomorrow to say that I had left to you to make the necessary explanations. If not, please lick, stick, and desire the Privy Council Messenger to deliver it on his arrival with your train. Ch. Villiers is here. At dinner he held the soundest party doctrines.

In the evening I heard him abusing Bright, taking for his text that which perhaps may meet your approval. "If a man takes the shilling, he is bound to serve."

Lady Airlie is very anxious that you should offer the Lord Lieutenancy to her father,[4] and equally anxious that he should refuse it on the score of health. She wishes the same course could have been taken about office, but admits that he would not have refused.

Rothschild hears that great efforts were made to get a Tory candidate for the City, but have failed.

Dicky Milnes goodnaturedly takes this pouch to London, but I am inclined to think rather likes the importance of carrying an official pouch.

28. Mr. Gladstone to Lord Granville. [G.D. 29/29A]

10, Downing Street. Feb. 14. 69.

Nothing can be better than your letter and I am well pleased to be the postman.

My impression is that we should make a great mistake if we were to yield on the point of time.

[1] Printed Morley, ii. 260. See the Queen to Gladstone, 12 Feb., for account of the interview, Guedalla, i. 160, Morley, ii. 261.

[2] That she receive in person at Buckingham Palace the addresses of the two houses in answer to the speech from the throne. See Bruce to Gladstone, 9 Feb., Add. MS. 44086, fo. 32, marked: 'Ld Granville what do you say W E G F. 10'.

[3] Gen. Grey to Granville, 13 Feb., and reply, 14 Feb., refusing to delay the introduction of the Irish Church bill, G.D. 29/22A; printed Fitzmaurice, ii. 7–9.

[4] Lord Stanley of Alderley. He refused the lord-lieutenancy of Anglesey 18 Feb., Add. MS. 44419, fo. 92.

It is not time which is wanted: we have plenty of time to deal with Bishop of P.s points so far as they can be dealt with at all.

Sir R. Palmer has been here today with overtures from persons of importance un-named. I think probably the Abp of Canterbury & others.

I will send you his Memm. I do not doubt that on the other hand they want time: for their suggestions are crude.

Palmer raised the question of the Ulster Glebes. I asked if his friends had considered the effect on the Presbns. He answered no, not at all. I suggested that they had better do it.

10 P.M. An answer from the Queen. She is pleased with the spirit of my letter.[1]

29. Mr. Gladstone to Lord Granville. [Add. MS. 44166, fo. 21]

10, Downing Street. Feb. 16. 69.

You will see from the inclosed that Mr Speaker is rather stiff about the Address.

I have seen him, & urged 1. That there is reason in the change, as the Queen declines what she feels to be beyond her strength, but exerts herself to do what she can.

2. That the connection between Speech & Address has not been invariably [*sic*] since often the one has been delivered, but the other not received, in person.

3. That the reception at B. Palace in person would please many.

I inclose also a short note from Glyn.[2]

Perhaps I ought to have consulted the Speaker first, but I had not an idea of difficulty *there*. There could be more awkwardness *now* in changing.

The Speaker does not think it would be popular.

It might be well to circulate these: & I inclose a Label for the purpose.[3] Our colleagues would I dare say kindly give their opinions.

30. Minute by Lord Granville.[4] [Add. MS. 44166, fo. 19]

[February 16?] 15/69.

The objections of the Speaker appear pedantic—and his precedents show that there is no perfect uniformity in the rule.

Any question of the dignity of the Houses could surely be met by the Courtesy

[1] Gladstone to Granville, 15 Feb.: 'All well today at Osborne', G.D. 29/29A, not printed.

[2] From the Speaker, 16 Feb., urging that as the Queen's speech opening Parliament was not to be delivered personally, the addresses should be presented by the privy council and not by members of the two houses to the Queen in person, Add. MS. 44261, fo. 275; from Glyn, 16 Feb., stating that the personal reception by the Queen was not expected, Add. MS. 44347, fo. 290.

[3] No. 29 must have been returned with the enclosures after circulation since Gladstone's papers contain the original and not a copy.

[4] On papers circulated in no. 29 and possibly misdated. Further minutes, in agreement, by Lowe, Argyll, Hatherley, Clarendon, de Grey, Childers, Kimberley and Bright follow. Minute by Bruce, Add. MS. 44086, fo. 34. See also Gladstone to the Speaker, 18 Feb., Add. MS. 44261, fo. 277. The ceremony was fixed for 22 Feb. but was later cancelled, Guedalla, i. 163–6.

of the Queen when thinking herself incapacitated from meeting the new Members in one way, endeavouring to do so in another way which does not *tax* her strength too much.

I cannot doubt that on the whole it will be popular with the H. of Commons, and it will certainly benefit the Gov to a certain degree. It will show a personal acquiescence of the Sovereign in the words which have been placed in her mouth.

31. Minute by Lord Granville. [Add. MS. 44419, fo. 110]

[22 February 1869].

Lord Rollo's case is very strong. I agree with all Mr Parker says excepting the danger of a little delay.[1]

I believe that Lord Rollo has given up the petition. Two of his supporters have flaws in their titles—those of his adversaries are all sound.

If all that is asked is (see Par 3) an intimation now that he may probably be called to the House of Lords by an English title, I see no objection.

But it is a matter requiring great consideration whether Mr G should make any exception to the rule of not creating Peers at present except in a professional case.

32. Lord Granville to Mr. Gladstone. [Add. MS. 44166, fo. 23]

16, Bruton Street. March 3/69.

Dizzy will give notice tomorrow that he will move on that day fortnight that our measure [2] (one of confiscation & bribery) be read that day six months. Hurrah.

Mrs Tait disapproves of our measure in toto.

The Archbishop said that it would be opposed, but that the great thing would be to improve the terms of the Commutation, & to try to get Post Reformation endowments.

33. Lord Granville to Mr. Gladstone. [Add. MS. 44166, fo. 24]

Confidential. 16, Bruton Street. March 3/69.

By something like a breach of confidence I have heard that the F.O are preparing a Memorandum for consideration whether they should prosecute the "Queen's Messenger" a disgraceful and scurrilous newspaper which has been attacking Lord Stanley in particular, and the Office Hammond & Clarendon in general.

Primâ facie this seems so foolish a proceeding that I wish you could make some enquiry, but you must not quote me, or my informant might be impeached.

[1] See Parker to Gladstone, 20 Feb., sent to Granville 22 Feb., urging that Lord Rollo, a Liberal, should be brought back into the Lords, Add. MS. 44419, fo. 108. Rollo and Lord Kellie (Conservative) gained an equal number of votes in the election of representative peers for Scotland and the latter took the seat, *L.J.* (1868–69), 5, 25–6. See below, no. 74.

[2] Irish Church bill.

34. Lord Granville to Mr. Gladstone. [Add. MS. 44166, fo. 28]

Windsor Castle. [7 March 1869].

Robertus Lowe, Robertus Lowe,
By name, and by Hugh Childers, so.

He is very unhappy at your having postponed the decision about the Law Courts.[1] He says if it is to be done every week is of importance. He is ready to take all responsibility on himself—and by his account he has gone most minutely into the whole case with Layard, Fergus[s]on and Hunt.

He would be exceedingly gratified if you would send for his box which is in circulation, & read his paper and the two enclosures. If you agreed to his proposal, there would be no doubt about the wish of the Cabinet.

The Queen was nervous to a degree about him, and sent me word before dinner not to make general conversation, or to do anything to draw him out—but she got on very well with him after dinner.

Confidential. P.S. I see that Potter is to ask Otway a question about the "Queen's Messenger".

If it has been suggested to him to do so, it is a pity.

Clarendon will of course take care to direct Otway as to the answer, but ex abundanti cautelâ had you not better see Otway?

35. Mr. Gladstone to Lord Granville. [Add. MS. 44536, fo. 12]

[*Copy*]. C.H.T. Mch 8. 69.

Lowe's box has not yet come to me: of course I shall read it, but I am already of opinion that his plan wld be an improvement on the present one which I have always disapproved. What weighs on my mind is the Parliamentary question, with the gravity of which I thought the Cabinet were not quite enough impressed; especially bearing in mind how important it is that at a moment like this we should not run any serious risks upon side issues.

Suppose Lowe's motion were met by a demand for a Committee—could we refuse it?

I have however asked Glyn to inquire about the prospects in the House.

I will speak to Otway.

36. Lord Granville to Mr. Gladstone. [Add. MS. 44166, fo. 31]

11, Carlton House Terrace. March 11 [1869].

If I do not hear to the contrary I will give the enclosed notice of a motion for Monday—& hope you will do the same.[2]

[1] In 1865–66 Parliament agreed that new law courts be built north of the Strand. Lowe favoured a site south of it. See Gladstone to Lowe, 1 Feb., on the difficulty of re-opening the subject, Add. MS. 44536, fo. 107; and note of the cabinet decision, 6 March, Add. MS. 44637, fo. 30. A bill for the acquisition of the southern site (Parl. papers. H.C. 113 (1868–69). ii, 117) introduced into the Commons, 10 May, was dropped. Cf. *Report of Select Committee on the New Law Courts*. Parl. papers. H.C. 381 (1868–69). x, 625. It was appointed, 28 June, and reported in favour of the north and present site, 30 July.

[2] See below, no. 38, note.

I will send you a mem.

Lansdowne who sat out the debate on himself,[1] wishes to know whether it would be agreeable to the Gov for him to resign,—a civil message from you would be better than an answer from me. Lowe tells me privately that he is doing his work admirably.

37. Mr. Gladstone to Lord Granville. [G.D. 29/57]

11, Carlton House Terrace. Mch 11. 69.

I am not sure what words are to form the *head* of this motion.[2] If you can let me know pray do.

I inclose a note for Ld Lansdowne [3]—please to read & forward unless you see objection.

Cardwell did his part thoroughly well but he was not enough *inside* the arrangement to say what might have been said about our proceedings in regard to these young Peers which I for one am ready to do battle for a [*sic*] l' outrance.[4]

I told H.M. today of the speeches of Reverdy and Cartier.[5] She likes C[artier] & will ask him to Windsor.

No sign whatever of uneasiness resp. Irish Church.

38. Mr. Gladstone to Lord Granville. [G.D. 29/57]

10, Downing Street. Mch 11/69.

May thinks I had better withhold my notice until your Committee is carried & announced by a message to us. I could then do it all on Tuesday.[6]

I think the Queen means to ask Cartier not in connection with his present business but as one whom she had at Windsor in the Prince's time.

Cartier also had the opportunity of paying great civilities to the Prince of Wales in Canada.

39. Lord Granville to Mr. Gladstone. [Add. MS. 44166, fo. 32]

House of Lords. March 11/69.

If you do not mind please take the first turn. Lord Russell, Grey, and Salisbury think it would be better.[7]

[1] The debate, 8 March, on the reorganization of the Treasury (see above no. 5 note) turned on the position of Stansfield (and the third senior lordship), Vivian (and War Office arrangements), Lansdowne (the principle of unsalaried office), *Hans. Parl. Deb.* 3rd ser. cxciv. 842–63.

[2] See below, no. 38, note.

[3] 11 March, deprecating resignation, Add. MS. 44536, fo. 128.

[4] Cardwell in the Commons' debate defended unsalaried office as economical. Gladstone, concerned to strengthen the Liberals in the Lords, saw it as an apprenticeship for young peers.

[5] At the inaugural dinner of the Royal Colonial Institute, 10 March.

[6] The committee proposed was a joint committee of the two houses. It was to consider parliamentary procedure, aiming at a better distribution of business between Lords and Commons. Granville's motion was carried in the Lords, 15 March. Six peers being then appointed, the Commons appointed their representatives, 16 March, *L.J.* (1868–69), 71, *C.J.* (1868–69), 84, 86–7. For the report of the committee, 2 Aug., see Parl. papers. H.C. 386 (1868–69). vii, 171, and below, nos. 200, 201.

[7] Granville in fact moved first.

I am much afraid about McDougall. He is very huffy, and imperious, and is aware that Cartier coalesced with me in forcing him to agree to the arrangements about the Transfer.[1]

Have you any objection to send my letter to [the] Queen,[2] or to my writing to H.M on the subject.

40. Lord Granville to Mr. Gladstone. [Add. MS. 44166, fo. 34]

Private. Colonial Office. March 11/69.

I am delighted to hear of the Queen's kind intention of asking Sir George Cartier, but I am afraid it would deeply hurt Mr William McDougall, if he had not the honor of accompanying Sir George.

Mr McDougall has had a much more difficult task than Sir George in acceding to our proposal for the Transfer of the Hudson's Bay Territory, and although they are Colleagues they represent two different parties in the State—the French & the English Canadians.

Mr McDougall is very quiet in his manner, and not likely to do anything which would be annoying to the Queen.

41. Lord Granville to Mr. Gladstone. [G.D. 29/57]

[13 March 1869].

The substance of two bills [3] which Ld Russell desires me to show to you, and any one member of the Cabinet, but to no more.

The first on Life Peerages he intends to lay on the table before Easter, anticipating Lords Salisbury & Carnarvon who talked of doing so—

The second he wishes to be moved by the Gov or the Archbishop.

42. Mr. Gladstone to Lord Granville. [G.D. 29/57]

Mc 13. 69.

1. I think any Bill about Bps' resignations must evidently come to us from the Bishops, to have a chance of success.

2. I am very glad Lord R. is disposed to stir the question of the Representative Peers and the Life Peers.

3. It will be for Lord R. to consider whether we should communicate with him fully on particulars of his Bill—or whether he should proceed without such communication. Either course has its advantages I think.[4]

I shd. have one or two comments [to] make on the Bps' resignation plan.

[1] *See Correspondence relating to the Surrender of Rupert's Land by the Hudson's Bay Company* . . . Parl. papers. H.C. 440 (1868–69). xliii, 373.

[2] No. 40 was sent to the Queen who replied 12 March, that she would ' see *both* ', G.D. 29/32. They went to Windsor 24 March, J. Boyd, *Sir George Étienne Cartier* (1914), p. 300.

[3] Russell introduced a bill to create life peerages, 9 April, which was shelved on the third reading, 8 July. The archbishop of Canterbury introduced a bill enabling bishops to resign on grounds of ill health, 5 July, which became law, 11 Aug.

[4] Cf. Gladstone to Russell, 16 March, G. P. Gooch, *The Later Correspondence of Lord John Russell* (1925), ii. 369.

43. Lord Granville to Mr. Gladstone. [Add. MS. 44166, fo. 36]

16, Bruton Street. March 17/69.

I am in the midst of a wrangle with the Treasury.[1] Would you kindly skim the enclosed correspondence. Do not give yourself the trouble of writing. I will call upon you.

44. Mr. Gladstone to Lord Granville. [G.D. 29/57]

11, Carlton House Terrace. March 24. 69.

1. Our division this morning even exceeded expectation & will powerfully propel the Bill.[2]

2. Consulting with Colleagues in the Commons I have put the next Cabinet for Tuesday Ap 6 instead of Sat Ap. 3.[3] We conceived that this would be certainly agreeable to the Peer Ministers.

3. It would not surprise me if prior to that date or at any rate to the Committee we had material communications from the Heads of the Irish Church.

4. I think you may safely answer Son Fairbairn as you propose, reserving a discretion for special cases of honours.[4]

5. You have hit the mark about Strzelecki with your usual precision.[5]

6. Sir J. Wilde will I think be Gazetted very shortly with Sir John Lawrence.

45. Lord Granville to Mr. Gladstone.[6] [Add. MS. 44166, fo. 42]

Walmer Castle. April 3/69.

I have recd the enclosed from Bright.[7] In ordering Dewey's execution, I did so upon the advice of the legal advisers of the Col: Office, and upon official information from Bruce that the Home Office would not commute the sentence in a similar case.

I wrote two days ago (hearing that I was likely to receive an application from Bright) to the Chancellor, but have had no answer.

The last paragraph in Bright's letter has nothing to do with my decision; I am bound to administer the law as it is, not as any individual however eminent may think it ought to be—but there is the question of feeling in the Colony.

[1] About a Treasury ruling on loans raised by colonial governments under the guarantee of the imperial government, correspondence 20–29 March, G.D. 29/66.

[2] The Irish Church bill passed its second reading by a majority of 118.

[3] For cabinets of 20 March and 6 April, see Add. MS. 44637, fos. 36, 37.

[4] Granville to Gladstone, 23 March, proposing a non-committal answer to T. Fairbairn's request for a baronetcy for his father, Add. MS. 44166, fo. 37, not printed.

[5] Cf. Strzelecki to Gladstone, 11 and 21 March, Add. MS. 44419, fos. 202, 260. Strzelecki claimed a money acknowledgement of his work in Australia. He was made K.C.M.G.; Gladstone to Granville, 29 March, G.D. 29/57, not printed.

[6] Instruction by Gladstone on the back of no. 45: 'Summon a Cabinet for tomorrow at one if Mr. Monsell from Lord Granville asks for it. Ap. 3.' The cabinet did not meet.

[7] 2 April, enclosing tel., 31 Nov., from the President and the Speaker of the Legislative Council of Prince Edward Island petitioning for the reprieve of convict Dewey, G.D. 29/52. Bright's last paragraph described hanging as 'unphilosophical and unchristian'. Granville refused the reprieve.

I have desired Monsell, or Rogers, or Holland to call upon you—and take your orders. I presume another respite would make execution impossible, but query whether as 28 Legislators, including the President and Speaker petition, a telegram should be sent to the President saying that in case he does not previously hear to the contrary, he may wait till he hears the decision of Tuesday's Cabinet.

It is a most painful thing for the first time in one's life to decide upon the life of a fellow creature, but I would not shrink from an adverse decision, unless there is sufficient authority against doing so.

There is direct telegraphic communication to Prince Edward's Island.

46. Mr. Gladstone to Lord Granville. [G.D. 29/57]

11, Carlton House Terrace. Ap.11.69.

A note I have just had from Manning [1] induces me to act at once without waiting for Monsell: and I inclose for your perusal the letter I have written to Argyll.[2] My messenger will take it on unless you see cause to stop it.

I think that you had better see Manning first—for I am afraid lest any thing be stated to him too incisively. If you agree will you send to him? I shall prepare him to hear from some one.

47. Mr. Gladstone to Lord Granville. [G.D. 29/57]

11, Carlton House Terrace. Ap 11.69.

Here is Argyll's answer.[3] I think he is taking in the difficulty by degrees. If you *could* be here when he comes it wd be the best thing. Hope Scott calls on me at 10. Evidently the R.C.s are full of the idea that they can fall back on effective support from the Conservatives who will consider them to be fighting the battle of the Church of England.

48. Lord Granville to Mr. Gladstone.[4] [Add. MS. 44166, fo. 49]

Colonial Office. April 14/4[*sic*] [1869].

A Scotch Roman Catholic Bishop has written to Dr Cullen to use his influence Parliamentary and otherwise, to support the Scotch Catholics against the Scotch Education Bill. If the Irish Roman Catholics come forward openly at this moment, they may lose all their Scotch Allies on some Important points of the Irish Church Bill.

[1] Manning to Gladstone, 10 April, on his wish to state the objections of the Catholic bishops of England and Ireland to the Scotch education bill, Add. MS. 44249, fo. 74.

[2] Urging the postponement of the committee stage, due 12 April, of the Scotch education bill, in order to give time for agreement with the Catholics on religious instruction in the grant-aided schools. The committee was postponed until 10 May. During a difficult passage the bill was amended by the Commons, and finally shelved by the Lords.

[3] 11 April, proposing to call on Gladstone on the morning of 12 April before seeing Kimberley and de Grey at the Council Office, copy, G.D. 29/57.

[4] Granville to Gladstone, 11 April, fixing a meeting at 11 a.m., 12 April, Add. MS. 44166, fo. 45, not printed.

I have therefore authorized Monsell to represent this to the Cardinal, telling him confidentially that a majority of the Cabinet see the harshness of the present proposal, and are considering how it may be possible to modify it.

49. Mr. Gladstone to Lord Granville. [G.D. 29/29A]

11, Carlton House Terrace. Ap.17.69.

I think you will not grudge the pains of reading the accompanying correspondence [1] which involves matter of delicacy and importance. I received the papers during the Cabinet today and I have written tonight the reply which I propose to send but which I hope you will fully criticise.

The papers within the band are put up in their order.

50. Lord Granville to Mr. Gladstone. [Add. MS. 44166, fo. 50]

Private. 16, Bruton Street. April 18/69.

I have carefully read the correspondence.

I approve of your answer with the exception of one irritating criticism. I doubt whether H.M. will be able to *read* it—but in that case Grey ought to copy it.

Clarendon seems to be perfectly in the right, & to have avoided a danger, of which I am always a little afraid, viz overstating our determination whatever it may be. It is very seldom necessary to announce a determination upon a hypothetical contingency.

The prejudice of H.M. against Clarendon is I am afraid not a decreasing one, but your letter will settle matters for a time. The beginning of it, exaggerates probably with intention, the Queen's concern at Clarendon being annoyed.

51. Mr. Gladstone to Lord Granville.[2] [G.D. 29/29A]

May 2 [1869].

Please return; with the Telegram.[3] I think that evidently H.M. could not have opened her boxes regularly.

I send my letter of Thursday that you may see the last Paragraph.

For your announcement I add a fabulous biography of my Father and myself. Wemyss Jobson is English & a consummate scoundrel. *If* refused his money.

52. Lord Granville to Mr. Gladstone. [Add. MS. 44166, fo. 52]

16, Bruton Street. May 3 [1869].

Satisfactory on the whole. I should think your conjecture about the order of the boxes disposed of by H.M. is worthy of a great critic.

[1] Between Clarendon and the Queen, 13–17 April, on foreign policy, *Letters*, 2nd ser. i. 589, 593. Cf. Gladstone to Gen. Grey, 17 April, Guedalla, i. 169–72; Gladstone to Clarendon, 16, 17, 18 April, Add. MS. 44536, fos. 144, 146, 147; Morley, ii. 316–18, Temperley and Penson, *Foundations*, pp. 317–18.

[2] Wrongly sorted with letters for 1872.

[3] The Queen to Gladstone, 1 May, withdrawing a demand, prompted by the case of the mayor of Cork, for firmness in Ireland, Guedalla, i. 172–4.

I can hardly concede the merit of "magnanimous" to your communication of your biography, although in point of accuracy, style, and argument it is far superior to an autobiography across which I once came.

I send you the continuation of the Grey Controversy.[1]

53. Mr. Gladstone to Lord Granville. [G.D. 29/57]

May 14 [1869].

1. I do not call the Power of Parlt. to call for the revocation of the Order 'Parliamentary Controul'.[2]

2. We have *got* a plan of controul for the Judges, & it is well. But if we had not got one, should we propose one?

3. Once within 120 years we have had a trouble of 2 or 3 days, & it has ended well. Does this show a very strong necessity for a General legislative measure?

4. Finally I lean not to think it *tanti*—subject to conviction.

54. Mr. Gladstone to Lord Granville. [G.D. 29/57]

H[awarde]n. May 20.69.

1. I send for your confidential perusal a curious account of the late *pourparler* in Dublin.

2. I also send a letter from Bury which has reference to an unpremeditated opinion let fall by me in conversation that, on certain suppositions, the Colonial Society might be an institution proper to be decorated with Her Majesty's name. But you I think would be the proper person to recommend it if you approve and if you do not it will fall to the ground.[3]

Please to supply me with an answer to Bury.

The Duke of Newcastle is smashed and Clumber will be shut up! Do not mention this sad business unless you hear of it otherwise.

On consn. I tell Bury that I will consult with you.

55. Mr. Gladstone to Lord Granville. [G.D. 29/57]

Hawarden. May 21.69.

1. I received, and dispatched again, the N.Z. papers last night: The Messenger

[1] Relates to Earl Grey's speech in the Lords, 26 April, *Hans. Parl. Deb.* 3rd ser. cxcv. 1545. The controversial point was the influence of the Fenian outrages upon the Liberals' conversion to Irish disestablishment; cf. Grey to Gladstone, 27 April, Add. MS. 44420, fo. 182, reply 28 April, Add. MS. 44536, fo. 152.

[2] During the debates on the bill to disable O'Sullivan, the mayor of Cork, from holding the office of mayor and justice of the peace (after his remarks on the attempt on the Prince of Wales's life, 27 April), a desire for legislation to give parliament control over the magistracy had been voiced, *Hans. Parl. Deb.* 3rd ser. cxcvi. 186 ff., 572–3, 576 ff. The order to hear evidence against O'Sullivan was revoked, on his promise to resign, and the bill withdrawn.

[3] Granville to Gen. Grey, 7 June, forwarded Lord Bury's letter to the Queen who gave her approval, G.D. 29/32.

should have delivered them about ten today. My minute was in decided affirmation of what you had done.[1]

2. Mackinnon wrote me a letter the other day which I could not understand: your note explains it.[2]

3. If Ld Russell were to say anything to me about Bright's scheme [3] I should answer that I believe we have thrown him over quite as much as Lord R. would have done, as a loyal gentleman & colleague, had he been in our place.

The chief mischief done by more feverish and fidgetty speeches in the H. of Lords has been not to us but to the questions, which they tend to embarrass, and to the House, which they tend to discredit.[4] The great possessors of property can surely not expect to act much upon opinion on behalf of property. And I own my view is that generally the House of Lords is by far stronger in a defensive than in an offensive position.

Johnny's moral sense is far from dead, and I think it pricks him. Think of *his* falling back upon the Times!

4. I think you would like to see the inclosed Correspondence with the Bishop of Gloucester: see what he says of the Second Reading.[5]

5. Perhaps Dalhousie ought to know that on *some* questions Moncrieff is thought to be losing his hold of the Scotch members by falling much short of them.

56. Mr. Gladstone to Lord Granville. [G.D. 29/57]

Hawarden. May 24.69.

I send for your perusal a letter from Bright about Irish Land with my reply.[6] His inclosure went back to him. It was in most unequivocal laudation of his plan. The Ex Mayor of Cork (who has most honourably redeemed his pledges) says he considers the Speech as a pledge to undo the Act of Settlement and hand back the land to the people of Ireland. It is most singular to me that Bright should strain at a gnat about Railways and yet should swallow without difficulty such a camel as the notion of making the State a great Land Jobber. Still he can hardly be held responsible for Mr O'Sullivan's misconstructions. Of these misconstructions themselves the probable source is to be found in the speeches delivered in the House

[1] See Granville to Bowen, No. 62, 21 May, refusing the New Zealand government's request to delay the departure of the last British regiment, C.O. 209/210 following Bowen's dispatch No. 30, 11 March; Parl. papers. H.C. 307 (1868–69). xliv, 483.

[2] Untraced, possibly concerned Mackinnon's claim to a peerage; see Meade to Gladstone, 9 June, Add. MS. 44166, fo. 67.

[3] Bright revived his scheme for land purchase in Ireland, first opened in a speech at Dublin, 30 Oct. 1866, in the cabinet of 14 May, Add. MS. 44637, fo. 58.

[4] Refers to the debate at Russell's instance in the Lords, 13 May, *Hans. Parl. Deb.* 3rd ser. cxcvi. 707 ff.; cf. Russell to Granville 1, 14 May, G.D. 29/57.

[5] Bishop Ellicott to Gladstone, 15, 20 May, Gladstone to Ellicott, 18 May, on increasing the episcopate and Ellicott's intention to vote against the second reading of the Irish Church bill, Add. MS. 44420, fos. 267, 283, 290.

[6] 21 and 22 May on land purchase, Add. MS. 44112, fos. 87, 89. Bright enclosed a letter from a Mr. Brown on the injustice likely to result from the sale of the Waterford estates. Cf. G. M. Trevelyan, *The Life of John Bright* (1913), p. 410.

of Lords: aided I admit by the penny-trumpet of J. Manners in the House of Commons.[1]

I also send what I presume to be the original text of Bright's plan.

57. Lord Granville to Mr. Gladstone. [Add. MS. 44166, fo. 53]

Private. Walmer. May 26 [1869].

Many thanks for sending me your correspondence with Bright. I agree in every word you say, and it is impossible for me to conjecture Bright's answer to your objections.

The D. of Devonshire when he succeeded, wished to sell all his Irish Estates excepting Lismore. He might have sold them on the plan proposed by Bright, making his own bargain with the Tenant. His credit being very nearly as good as that of the state—it would only have required a few years longer for the redemption, but He would have lost all chance of advantage, and lost none of the cares of superintendence, and of risk in case the Tenant deteriorated instead of improved his farm.

The Duke of Devonshire could do this better than the State, one or two agents would suffice for his purpose.

By Bright's plan not only would the State assume the responsibilities to the tax payer of a great land jobbing speculation but it would place itself in the odious position of a landlord exacting more than the average rent from the whole population. This question may break us up—Bright is thin skinned,—the attacks in the Lords ruffle him more than he chooses to admit. I cannot make out how far he likes office, the Cabinet, and his new position. It will be particularly disagreeable to him to have this plan, of which he is so much enamoured, and for which he has recd so much blame, and a little praise, snuffed out by the Cabinet—and yet how is it possible to avoid it, even putting aside the strong opinions of Lowe Cardwell & others.

My only hope is that you have got the germ of some larger & more comprehensive plan in your head, than has yet been developed. Clanricarde's bill,[2] Fortescue's changes in the law, facilities to Railways, extension of assessed taxes, & charging Police on the Irish with much more padding than I can think of, all jumbled up.

I come to town on Friday. This is the first Derby I ever missed voluntarily.

The Debate in the Lords is rather a nightmare to me. I saw the Archbishop yesterday, but he did not approach the subject, and I knew that he would tell me nothing more than he had told Lord Russell.

I will profit by your good opinion of A. Gordon,[3] and offer him as I had previously said to Rogers & Monsell, Mauritius. Rogers has a good opinion of him.

[1] Manners asked, 10 May, whether the government intended to introduce any measure for the better protection of life in Ireland, *Hans. Parl. Deb.* 3rd ser. cxcvi. 470.

[2] *An Act to simplify the Law of Tenure in Ireland.* Parl. papers. H.L. 36 (1868–69). vii, 279. Clanricarde introduced it, 5 April, and it passed its second reading, 20 April, but was shelved, 26 April.

[3] Gladstone to Granville, 15, 19 May, on Gordon's suitability for colonial employment, G.D. 29/57, not printed.

58. Mr. Gladstone to Lord Granville. [G.D. 29/57]

Private. 11, Carlton House Terrace. May 27.69.

One word to say that a conversation with Bright on the way from Chester today has comforted me greatly with respect to Irish land & given me good hope that no impediment will arise on his side of a nature not to be surmounted.

59. Mr. Gladstone to Lord Granville. [G.D. 29/57]

11 C.H.T. May 29.69.

It may be just worth while to mention to you that in January 1846 I wrote from the C.O. Instructions to Lord Cathcart as Governor General in Canada in which it was distinctly enough laid down that we did not *impose* British connection upon the Colony, but regarded its goodwill and desire as an essential condition of the connection.[1] I know not whether there is any thing still earlier to the same effect. Unless my memory deceives me these Instructions went to the Queen, and were returned with a rather decided expression of approval by the Prince.

This for the chance of being useful at a future stage when we resume the discussion.

60. Lord Granville to Mr. Gladstone. [Add. MS. 44166, fo. 41]

[1 June 1869].

I have added 5 words " are of a rhetorical character " to the P.S.[2]

I have sent it to Clarendon who entirely agrees.

61. Lord Granville to Mr. Gladstone. [Add. MS. 44166, fo. 58]

Confidential. Downing St. June 1/69.

I find myself in a proud position this evening, after your declaration of this morning, that you had only one secret from me.

Clarendon tells me that you would like to have my opinion on the subject of that exception.[3]

You must however take cum grano that opinion, as I believe my tendency is

[1] Gladstone to Cathcart, No. 14, 3 Feb. 1846, copy in G.D. 29/57. Cf. Granville to Young, confidential, 14 June, on the separation of Canada from the empire, C.O. 42/678 after documents of 11 Nov. See below, no. 195.

[2] See no. 61.

[3] Refers to Gladstone's relationship to John Motley, newly appointed American minister in London. Gladstone believed Motley to have virtually called him liar in his dispatch to Seward from Vienna, No. 8, Oct., which commented on Gladstone's Newcastle speech, 17 Oct. 1862, *Papers relating to Foreign Affairs, 1861–62*, pp. 571–3; sent home in Lyons to Russell, No. 495, 8 Dec., F.O. 5/839. Argyll intervened but failed to obtain any repudiation from Motley, Add. MSS. 44536, fos. 135, 136, 44420, fo. 180, and 44101, fos. 37, 45, 50–2. Clarendon also failed, Add. MSS. 44536, fos. 135, 136, 157, and 44133, fos. 215–21. Nos. 60–2 were the result of Granville's successful mediation. See also his exchange of letters with Clarendon, 2 June, G.D. 29/55.

not to be quickly alive to insinuations, even when they might appear to some to be offensive.

Clarendon has shown me Mr Motley's Despatch—particularly pointing out the passage in which Mr Motley compares your speech to the most perfidious part of Marc Antony's.

He tells me that you have always considered this as a direct attack upon your truthfulness, and to convey an imputation which stands in the way of the cordial relations which ought to exist between you as Prime Minister and the Minister of the United States.

There appears to have been some correspondence on the matter, and Clarendon tells me that Mr Motley told him today that he admits " he had been deeply hurt by your speech, and that he had written on it the more [*sic*] severe criticism in his power, and had endeavoured to mark the inconsistencies of different parts, but the idea of imputing falsehood to you had never entered into his head, that he was exceedingly pained at being accused of having accused you of such a thing ".

I have considered what in my opinion your course should be. In my own case, I should have thought that Mr Motley had not done much more in grandiloquent language, than Lord Derby did colloquially when he accused his Colleague of " dressing up a case " for the H. of Commons, or more than half our personal friends have done in public & private, when they declare that our professions on the Irish Church question are merely prompted by personal & party motives.

But I should have scruples about opposing my judgment to your's on a matter of construction.

What appears to me decisive, is Mr Motley's statement today. As soon as he denies the intention of doing that, which you think wounded your honor, the matter is at an end.

I remember Prince Albert saying that it was the duty of all whether on the throne or in Govt to lay aside all personal feelings even when they had been most painfully excited. If this is true, it applies with singular force to the present instance.

If you agree, I should suggest that the matter should drop, and that Clarendon should take an early opportunity of telling Mr Motley that ' bygones should be bygones '.

P.S. I have shown this letter to Clarendon, and we both agree that the passage in Mr Motley's despatch comparing your speech to that of Marc Antony is of a rhetorical character, and does not necessarily convey the imputation of falseness, even if any doubt were not removed by the assurance of Mr Motley, which I have quoted.

Clarendon will undertake to inform Mr Motley, that you have taken his and my opinion to the above effect, and that you will act upon it.

62. Mr. Gladstone to Lord Granville. [G.D. 29/57]

11 C.H.T. June 3.69.

Your opinion and that of Clarendon that Mr. Motley's words respecting me do not require to be construed as an imputation of falsehood will according to my pledge entirely over-ride my own: and in thanking you and him very sincerely for the trouble you have so kindly taken in a disagreeable matter I have only to add that I am sure Clarendon in informing Mr Motley that I have appealed to your judgments and shall follow them will say nothing to give him an impression that I was myself able to place your construction upon his language.[1]

63. Mr. Gladstone to Lord Granville. [G.D. 29/57]

11, Carlton House Terrace. June 3.69.

I propose to come to you in D. St at about 3.45 on the inclosed letter o the Archbishop.[2]

1. We cannot take any initiative of suggestion.

2. At the same time our knowledge of the Bill makes us by far the best judges what should be done.

3. We cannot accept the word "material".

4. It would be best for the Lords not to raise any point expressly ruled in the H of C. by a majority—seeing what the majorities were.

5. The Bp of Oxford is (I apprehend) the handiest man among the Bps: & we should make much more way with the Abp (supposing we 'tackle' him) if S.O[xford] were joined with him. But I do not say we should suggest this.

These are my first thoughts: *primissima.*

64. Lord Granville to Mr. Gladstone. [Add. MS. 44166, fo. 62]

16, Bruton Street. June 3/69.

Hayward [3] sent me a message to tell me that Cairns had yielded to the pressure of the extreme party.[4]

The Archbishop told Clarendon it looked bad. Grey told me that he was afraid there was a chance of the rejection, & that Salisbury to his surprise, had become shaky.

George Barrington told Delane that it was very serious.

65. Mr. Gladstone to Lord Granville. [G.D. 29/57]

11, Carlton House Terrace. June 4.69.

I send a letter from the Queen [5] on which we may have a few words.

I will then tell you about a little plan for a function in the City.

[1] Note by Granville that he had given this message to Clarendon who 'will conform to it', 3 June, Add. MS. 44166, fo. 65, not printed.

[2] Tait to Gladstone, private and confidential, 3 June, Add. MS. 44330, fo. 79, printed R. Davidson and W. Benham, *Life of Archbishop Tait* (1891), ii. 20; cf. Morley, ii, 267. Tait, at the Queen's instance, offered his help in negotiations with the Conservative leaders of the Lords, where the Irish Church bill was about to be read. He himself wished to pass the second reading, but to amend it materially in committee. Gladstone to Tait, 3 June, closed the door to direct negotiations for the time, Add. MS. 44330, fo. 83.

[3] See H. E. Carlisle, *Correspondence of Abraham Hayward* (1886), for this figure of Victorian society.

[4] For Conservative opinions on the treatment of the Irish Church bill in the Lords see Sir A. H. Hardinge, *The Fourth Earl of Carnarvon* (1925), ii. 9–10.

[5] 3 June, agreeing to entertain the Viceroy of Egypt, Guedalla, i. 177.

Other rills of intelligence yesterday about the course to be taken on the Irish Church Bill in the Lords conform but too exactly to your report.

It is a strange affair.

I send a copy of mine to the Abp.

66. Lord Granville to Mr. Gladstone. [Add. MS. 44166, fo. 69]

16, Bruton Street. June 9/69.

I executed your Commission with [the] Archbishop. I did not say the suggestion about Ball came from you.[1]

He was surprised, but looked pleased.

I had the same conversation with Carnarvon [2] as with the Archbishops. He has still some hopes of getting Salisbury to vote, and of persuading other peers, but he is always over sanguine in this matter.

It was a mistake on the part of Argyll to take this week as a good opportunity of delivering a good little essay on life Peerages, to throw contempt on Ld Russell's bill, and attack Salisbury & Carnarvon.[3]

67. Lord Granville to Mr. Gladstone. [Add. MS. 44166, fo. 71]

Col. Office. [10 June 1869].

I find on reflection that I did not take in your argument as to the equal treatment of Catholics & Presbyterians. Will you kindly put it on paper.

It is hard upon a church which does not see that the public good requires it to be disendowed & disestablished, but we smooth the change to individuals and to the future church, by giving full compensation to the former for all their vested rights, and to the latter 500,000 £ private endowments, some of which would bear but scant scrutiny, a power of commutation which if it were carried out as zealously as a similar boon was by the Canadian would yield a voluntary endowment equal to £ and we give them Churches, Church Yards, Schoolhouses, & glebe lands with the exception that we call upon the Church Body to repay only to a small extent the charges which the Commission would have to pay.

We create them a corporation by the bill, and we offer them every facility, which did not clash with the principle of Religious equality, to reconstitute themselves.

Are there any plums to add to this description.

68. Mr. Gladstone to Lord Granville. [Add. MS. 44536, fo. 174]

[*Copy*]. 15 June 1869.

In a report of a conversation with Sumner in N.Y. Times of 31 May which I have just seen the great Senator is made apologetically to condemn our John Bright in these words " with all the grandeur of his character, there is a very large residuum

[1] See below, no. 99.

[2] Hardinge, *op. cit.* ii. 10

[3] 8 June, *Hans. Parl. Deb.* 3rd ser. cxcvi. 1370–7; see above, no. 41 note.

of John Bull in him—with Cobden, there was not enough of this to hurt." Perhaps this may be useful in some strait after the Birmingham letter.[1]

69. Mr. Gladstone to Lord Granville. [G.D. 29/57]

11, Carlton House Terrace. June 17.69.

I think that you & I may both be pressed hard today on the point.

Do you or do you not adopt or approve the sentiments of Mr Bright's letter?

What do you think of declining to answer them wholesale or to debate the contents of the letter until they are made formally the subject of consideration by the Houses respectively.

About Windsor, I am fairly beaten.[2]

70. Lord Granville to Mr. Gladstone. [Add. MS. 44166, fo. 73]

Colonial Office. June 17/69.

I propose absolutely to decline giving the opinion of any Member of the Gov on Mr Bright's letter—but Bright cannot be in our house, and I shall state all the disclaimers of intention to menace, or to offend with which he has furnished me.[3]

As Bright means to be in the House tonight, you can settle with him, whether he or you should say [anything] on his behalf.[4]

I shall be glad to hear that you have not a debate, which is almost sure to do us harm tomorrow night.

I shall be in your house till five o'clock, and of course will shape my later course according to what you say.

The principal thing as far as the Lords are concerned is that you [and] I should declare that the letter was the individual & unofficial act of Mr Bright and that the Gov repudiates any notion of threat or dictation.

71. Mr. Gladstone to Lord Granville.[5] [G.D. 29/57]

House of Commons. 4.55 Pm. [17 June 1869].

It may be as well you should know that Bright was much pleased with my answer. I did not think it did him more than justice.

[1] Bright's letter to his Birmingham constituents, read at the meeting of 10 June, dwelt on the danger to the Lords if it rejected the Irish Church bill; cf. G. M. Trevelyan, *The Life of John Bright* (1913), p. 403. Granville used the quotation in answering Cairns, 17 June, *Hans. Parl. Deb.* 3rd ser. cxcvii. 10–17.

[2] Relates to a confused invitation to dine and sleep; see Gladstone to Granville, 16 June, G.D. 29/57, not printed, and the Queen to Granville, 16 June, G.D. 29/32.

[3] Bright to Granville, 15, 17 June, disclaimed hostile intentions but refused regrets, G.D. 29/52.

[4] Gladstone answered a question from Colonel North, but refused a debate, *Hans. Parl. Deb. loc. cit.* 121–2.

[5] Gladstone to Granville, 17 June, on honour for Mr. Fitzpatrick, G.D. 29/57, not printed.

72. Lord Granville to Mr. Gladstone. [Add. MS. 44166, fo. 79]

16, Bruton Street. June 22 [?21]/6 [*sic*] [1869].

I enclose young Sarum's answer to mine, asking his permission to propose to you that we should all three meet—saying that it would be difficult for us to initiate suggestions to him, but that your personal regard for him made me sure that a conversation would in some degree advance our common object.[1]

I am unluckily under a threat of being called as a witness all day.

Would six o'clock be possible for you, and if so, where?

73. Mr. Gladstone to Lord Granville. [G.D. 29/57]

11, Carlton House Terrace. June 21.69.

The letter is good and manly: but the prospect not very bright. If Salisbury is in consultation with Cairns, what hope have we that his conclusions can represent any thing, except the general result of the ideas & wishes of our opponents, and will not Cairns himself be the principal agent—not merely from the votes at his back but from the character of his mind compared to the others—in bringing these into shape?

It appears to me that we must throw upon Salisbury the task of questioning, & that our footing must be that of persons willing to give any information we lawfully may as to our own views & possibilities.

If we meet at six I suppose the Houses would afford the best locale and perhaps there would be no quieter spot than my private room?

74. Mr. Gladstone to Lord Granville. [G.D. 29/57]

11, Carlton House Terrace. June 21.69.

See the inclosed from Lord Kinnaird. We might now perhaps consider the case of Lord Rollo as ripe since the Proclamation has gone out which will seat his opponent and the Second Reading is passed.[2]

75. Lord Granville to Mr. Gladstone. [Add. MS. 44166, fo. 77]

Colonial Office. 21/6 [1869].

I should say that we are not sufficiently acquainted with the views of the different sections of the opposition to know whether they are inclined to meet us, but that you & the Gov Peers are glad to know that we may command his services.

Beg him to go over with Monck the details of the bill, to see whether they suggest any improvements for working it.

[1] See below, no. 99.

[2] See above, no 31. The royal proclamation of 18 June provided for a fresh election to the seat of representative peer for Scotland contested between Lords Rollo and Kellie, *L.J.* (1868–69), 447. After his defeat Rollo was created Baron Dunning, 29 June, in the peerage of the United Kingdom.

The Archbishop of York makes a great point (much I think to the disadvantage of the future Irish Church) of defining the powers of the Commissioners.

I forgot to tell you that York told me that Archdeacon Stopford had been sent by the Irish Church to open negotiations with you, but that you had repulsed him.[1]

76. Mr. Gladstone to Lord Granville.[2] [G.D. 29/57]

House of Lords. Jul 1 [1869].

About the commutation remember the new proposal in reserve on our side is that when four fifths (in value) of the Annuitants in any of the 12 Dioceses of Ireland are ready to commute, the Commissioners shall add 7 *per Centum* to the Commutation money.

Never mind the Clauses sent you: this is the pith.[3]

77. Lord Granville to Mr. Gladstone. [Add. MS. 44166, fo. 82]

16, Bruton Street. July 3/69.

Would it be very inconvenient to you & the rest of the Cabinet to meet here today.[4]

I should not like to miss it, and I am very gouty—besides having refused to go to Windsor, and to the Trinity House, I am afraid of its being announced that I could go out.

78. Lord Granville to Mr. Gladstone. [Add. MS. 44166, fo. 83]

16, Bruton Street. July 6/69.

Do you do more than acknowledge the rect of the memorial from the Reform League at Leeds.

Salisbury & Carnarvon will help me to reverse the date 72 to 71,[5] but the former says that they cannot give up Carnarvon's clause [6]—that he expects 1,200,000 £

[1] Note by Gladstone: 'Pray undeceive the Abp of York on this point W. E. G. Jû 22.'

[2] Gladstone to Granville, copy, 1 July, forwarding text of the Pensions Commutation Bill, Add. MS. 44537, fo. 1, not printed.

[3] Relates to the committee stage of the Irish Church bill in the Lords. Carnarvon moved and carried amendments to clause 23, despite the government's offer, on 1 July, to make compulsory the commutation of annuities (payable in compensation to the clergy) for a lump sum equal to 14 times the estimated aggregate value of the yearly income of all the clergy. See *L.J.* (1868–69), 422–3; *Hans. Parl. Deb.* 3rd ser. cxcvii. 940–1; Parl. papers. H.C. 27, H.C. 209 (1868–69). iii, 96, 203.

[4] The cabinet met in Bruton Street, Add. MS. 44637, fos. 75, 77.

[5] Lords' amendments to clauses 2 and 12 of the Irish Church bill moved the vesting date for the new commissioners from Jan. 1871 to Jan. 1872. Carnarvon moved to return to 1871 on the report stage, but the month was then altered to May. See *L.J.* (1868–69), 458, 460, *Hans. Parl. Deb. loc. cit.* 9 July, 1484–8.

[6] See no. 76, note.

from it—that money is the thing that he wants—that we are in a fool's paradise about the Clergy commuting, or the laity subscribing.

He also believes every day, with great regret that there is a decreasing chance of passing an Irish Church bill this session.

The last may be a diplomatic threat, but ça donne à penser.

I believe they will accept the 500,000 £.[1] Peterborough told me it would be madness if they did not do so.

79. Mr. Gladstone to Lord Granville. [G.D. 29/57]

11, Carlton House Terrace. July 6.69.

1. Carnarvon's Clause must be utterly blown to pieces in argument & no two shreds of it will hold together—in whichever House it be done. By fighting it against us I think the H of L. would expose itself almost to ridicule.

2. I hope the Lords will understand that the Commutation of Private Endowments for £500,000 means of course a Commutation paid at the date when the Private Endowments would come in or at 10 years from the date at which the lives are computed to run.

We have been discussing the matter this morning & find the *present* value would be £280,000: or might give 300,000 down.

3. I am sorry to think of any chance of a second Service.

4. I 'thank' the Leeds League.

Hancock will see you about the £500,000.

80. Lord Granville to Mr. Gladstone. [Add. MS. 44166, fo. 86]

16, Bruton Street. July 7/69.

I had prepared a perfect bouquet of fireworks for the close of the Committee—but this desirable moment was so long coming, that I began to doubt, & communicating with the Chancellor, de Grey, Argyll & Kimberley they each pulled a rocket to pieces, and ended by advising me to say nothing, and to give notice of the 500,000 £.

They all think that it is difficult to make a case for the withdrawal of that which I offered, and that it is important for us not [to] give even an indifferent reason to the House to complain of the conduct of the Govt.

I have therefore asked the Attorney General for the words, but I will not give notice of them without your sanction.

Prince Christian told me today that the Queen was not annoyed at your pressure.[2]

[1] I.e. as compensation for private endowments, a concession offered by the government on clause 29. See *Hans. Parl. Deb. loc. cit.* 5 July, 1123–5; Parl. papers. H.C. 27, H.C. 209 (1868–69). iii, 101, 211.

[2] Gladstone had urged the Queen to remain at Windsor until the Irish Church bill was passed, Guedalla, i. 185–7.

81. Mr. Gladstone to Lord Granville. [G.D. 29/57]

11, Carlton House Terrace. July 7.69.

I have read the Times' report in vain to obtain a key to the situation.[1]

I presume your meaning is, that you would propose to commute the Private Endowments for the sum of £500,000 *in the event of the withdrawal of the provision as to the Royal Grants.* Not having seen the Bill I am among pitfalls, but doubtless you mean an offer subject to conditions such that all other provisions in regard to private endowments of a nature to enlarge their scope shall be got rid of. The position would be ludicrous if the £500,000 were put in on your proposal and the other mutilations left.

To carry the £500,000 (*down*) on any terms will be a great demand on the patience of the House of Commons on account of its tampering so notably with the principle of the Bill: but this of course must be attempted up to the point which has been promised. It would be fatal to go farther.

Please send word whether you go to C.O. today. Not, I hope, unless you are better.

82. Mr. Gladstone to Lord Granville. [G.D. 29/57]

11, Carlton House Terrace. July 7.69.

With respect to the Surplus it occurs to me that we might devise words to satisfy the scrupulous who are afraid that 8 millions will be disposed of in Fortescue's room.[2] Might you not suggest the restoration of the Clause with a condition that if any Order in Council shall issue for the application of any monies before Parlt. shall have legislated further on the matter, it shall be laid on the Tables of both Houses and liable to be intercepted by Address. I do not remember the precise forms but the precedents could easily be found. Mr Lambert will see Mr Thring and consider whether any verbal improvements can be made in our Clause.

83. Lord Granville to Mr. Gladstone. [Add. MS. 44166, fo. 89]

Private. Colonial Office. July 8/69.

I have seen the Archbishop, and have settled that I am not to propose any amendment. He proposes to move that 500,000 £ be given instead of all private benefactions, and to retain the amendment as to Ulster Glebes which he has already carried.[3]

[1] This refers to the Lords' proceedings on 5 July. The archbishop of Canterbury carried an amendment to include royal grants since 1560 (Ulster glebes) in the land to be retained by the independent Church. This amounted to a rejection of the condition on which the government's concession of £500,000 compensation for private endowments was offered; see above, no. 79, and below, nos. 83, 84.

[2] Relates to the Lords' amendment which directed that the surplus should be spent under parliamentary control and not by authority of an order in council as provided in the preamble and clause 59 (later 68); see *L.J.* (1868–69), 443, 444; *Hans. Parl. Deb. loc. cit.* 1228–31, 1254–6; Parl. papers. H.C. 27, H.C. 209 (1868–69). iii, 114, 229.

[3] See *L.J.* (1868–69), 9 July, 461.

I hope I have frightened him about losing the substance for the shadow, & unless he is prevented by stronger men who see the advantage they may take of my clumsy words, there is a chance of his giving way. He will tell me more in the Lords.

84. Mr. Gladstone to Lord Granville. [G.D. 29/57]

10, Downing Street. July 8.69.

I am *very* glad that the Archbishop moves. This will leave you more free: and I hope you will feel at liberty to state, at least, that the Government have found the opponent all along contending that the Ulster Glebes were private Endowment of James I and that *they* therefore inseparably connect the excision of that amendment with acquiescence in or adoption of the £500,000.

I see the Ulster Glebe amendment *now* forms part of the *private endowment Clause.*

There will be some difficulties of execution in effecting the substitution of the £500,000: and I expect the Archbishop will make a hash of it.

85. Lord Granville to Mr. Gladstone. [Add. MS. 44166, fo. 91]

Confidential. Bruton St. July 11/69.

The Queen told me at dinner yesterday that the Archbishop of Canterbury had written to her that they (query) were decided (if they could not get 3,000,000 £ worth to float the church) to take the chance of what would happen by postponing the bill till next year. The Queen asked what could be done, that it was impossible to coerce the House of Lords, what did the Govt mean to do if the bill was rejected. I said that the Cabinet had decided, wisely in my opinion, not to discuss what they ought to do upon an hypothetical contingency, but that I thought it right to tell H.M., that there was no chance of their agreeing to postpone the bill for another year.[1]

She did not say any more, but asked me to see the Dean of Windsor.

Sir W. Jenner spoke to me in the evening, saying that the Queen had desired him to speak to me. . . .[2]

The Dean [3] on the contrary was as sensible, calm & moderate as possible. He sees C. Grey's faults, and says the Queen thoroughly distrusts him, but that his (the Dean's) position is a difficult one. I told him that the great thing to impress upon the Queen was not to commit herself, not to encourage the opposition, or threaten her ministry. He intends to advise her to adhere to generalities, to counsel moderation to both sides, to admit their respective difficulties, but to remind the Archbishop of the danger of delay, and to appeal to you to make all possible concessions. He admitted the Queen although she cared about the Irish Church,

[1] Cf. Morley, ii. 272; the Queen to Gladstone, 11 July, Gladstone to the Queen, 12 July, *Letters* 2nd ser. 616–18, Guedalla, i. 189–91.

[2] Part of the letter concerning the Queen's health has been omitted.

[3] Dean Wellesley.

cared more about her arrangements being disturbed, that she had threatened to break her promise to you & go to Osborne on Saturday, but he intended strongly to protest against this. I asked him whether he had any advice to give you in dealing with the Queen. He thought vivâ voce was desirable, and that when you wrote you should do so shortly with as few arguments as were necessary. She turned the best and most logical the wrong way.

The Queen saw me again, did not talk much, said she had exhausted all she had to say to the opposition, and complained bitterly that she had no friend left like the late Baron Stockmar. She complained of Grey meddling in things which did not concern him, and of his intense selfishness, but praised the Dean. I ventured to tell her that I could think of no one in whom she could better place confidence than in the Dean, for whom I added you had the greatest regard. I told her how much she had assisted the 2d reading, a step universally approved, and how much her influence might prevent a collision which would be most injurious to the Lords & to the Church of England.

And now I have a queer message to give you. Jenner has told the Queen, that the best precaution you can take before seeing her, is to send a set of clothes which have not been used by you, to Her residence, to put on when you see her. I have prepared the astonished Cowels for a parcel which may possibly be sent from you to him.

I left the Castle with a heavy heart.

86. Mr. Gladstone to Lord Granville. [G.D. 29/29, A]

Private. 10, Downing Street. Jul 13.69.

An admirably written article about you in D. Telegraph today has given me even more pleasure than one in D. News yesterday.

We *begin* [1] on Thursday at 4.15 with replacing the words in the Preamble. We expect an immense majority.

I am fearful that the vote of last night will create great excitement in the country. With a view to shortening its range, at a time when every day may add to danger, I wish that the House—whichever it may be—could if necessary sit on Saturday, were it only to give notice, so that a day might be saved.

Pray think of this.

We may I should think very well get through on Friday. But we are in the hands of the opposition. We shall however probably work from 4.15 to 2 Am on Thurs. & return at 2 Pm on Friday.

I saw D. yesty.

87. Lord Granville to Mr. Gladstone. [Add. MS. 44166, fo. 97]

July 13 [1869].

Many thanks for your note. I liked the Daily News better than the Telegraph.

[1] To consider the Lords' amendments to the Irish Church bill, which had passed the Lords, 12 July.

I am afraid the latter was a little ridiculous in its kind exaggeration, as Kimberley explained to me.

I have settled that the House shall sit as may be required Friday night and Saturday.

88. Mr. Gladstone to Lord Granville. [G.D. 25/57].

11, Carlton House Terrace. July 16.69.

It is probable that we shall finish the Irish Church Amendments before dinner today: reasons must then be drawn (in preparation this morning) and they may be agreed to this night.[1]

They did not divide on the *date*: and this, if the Lords like to insist, it will be easy to concede.

It is impossible for the Opposition to hold Carnarvon's Clause in argument. But they may urge raising the 7 per Cent to ten.

There is a feeling *unwisely weak* about postponement of the Surplus—Not more I think than this. It would be a very foolish measure. Were the Lords to insist strongly, they might possibly carry this—but then I am not sure that we could concede the three per Cent.

Kinnaird (Lord) has seen my son [2] and the inclosed mem. is the result—you will know best whether any thing can be made of it.

If you cannot turn tomorrow to account I hope nothing will carry you beyond Monday. We shall have the Queen in a state about her movements but she seems well disposed towards the passing of the Bill.

89. Mr. Gladstone to Lord Granville. [G.D. 29/57]

11, Carlton House Terrace. July 18.69.

With reference to the paper [3] shown me by you today, there are one or two points to be remembered.

1. There is not a word to be said in principle for any further pecuniary concession whatever. (The concession of 370 m to Curates & Rectors is to Rectors only—the Curates will not be one farthing the richer.) The best plea that remains to be urged, on the merits, is for expences of management; and you will recollect how that plea was received in the *Cabinet*. The whole question remaining is then, what can we recommend the majority to concede to the simple *will* of the House of Lords rather than lose the Bill.

2. My opinion is that though we may still use this plea for something say under a quarter of a million we cannot push it farther without incurring one or more of

[1] The Commons sat until after midnight on 16th. Reasons against some of the Lords' amendments were reported and agreed to early on the morning of Sat. 17th, *C.J.*, (1868–69), 334–8.

[2] W. H. Gladstone.

[3] Disraeli's mem. of proposals to settle the conflict between the Houses communicated to Lord Bessborough. Cf. Morley, ii. 274–7, and below, no. 99.

various dangers—especially the danger either of open schism, or of breaking up the moral union of the majority, which is vital to the completion of our Irish work.

I take it for granted we do not mean to carry this Bill against our friends by the votes of our opponents. That is an alternative quite possible, but plainly I think to be rejected.

3. Looking forward to the contingency of our having to bring in another Bill, the question arises in what points will such a Bill vary from the present one?

I do not see a single point in which it can be made more favourable to the Church.

In two points, at the least, I think it would be less so

(1) as to £500,000 *down* for Private Endowments

(2) as to the Glebehouses.

What is more serious is that Parliament might decline to trouble itself again with an elaborate scheme of commutation, which I believe is, and is known by the Church to be, worth [a] good two millions of itself.

4. Since we introduced the Bill, every material change made has been made in favour of the Church. Since it went to the Lords, absolutely nothing was done for any one outside the Church (apart from the Stanhope Clause) until we put in our substitute for the fourteen years Clause, which gives some £40000 or £45000 to the Presbyterians.

5. I did not say, even to the Dean, that we were prepared to concede any thing on *that Clause*. There we have them as in a vice. *Even with the seven per Cent, the Church would prefer our Clause as it stands to theirs as it stands.* Therefore, they are not in a position to fight for *any* addition to the 7 per Cent.

In the same way I think we can oust the Bp of Peterborough's amendment from the controversy altogether; as an amendment which teaches the Irish Congregations to throw the expences of their worship on the Representative body of the Church.

And we can oust the Glebehouse concession, as utterly damaged by the introduction in the House [of] Lords of the scheme of concurrent Endowment with a view to religious equality.

The ground therefore is extremely narrow upon which they can now argue for further concessions. It appears to me that when we come to the final stage of this woful huckstering affair, we shall have to say that in our view no case remains on any point—that all we can undertake to say is that the sum of £ does not so stultify the Bill as to be worth a quarrel, & that we will let them put that sum upon any head they please: when they will immediately, of themselves, choose the Commutation Clause.

90. Mr. Gladstone to Lord Granville. [G.D. 29/57]

11 Carlton House Terrace. July 20.69.

A note came from the Archbishop early this morning, and he will probably be here by the time this reaches you, *after* seeing Cairns, and with a meeting in view which it seems is to be held this afternoon at the D. of Marlborough's. What I want your opinion on is this—suppose the Archbishop comes prepared to accept concessions falling within the limit of the figure 3—shall I say yes at once or shall I send out for a flying Cabinet at 2? Perhaps this is due to our Colleagues.[1]

Suppose on the other hand that he makes an offer beyond 3 and will not reduce it—in that case I ought still to carry it to the Cabinet, but without holding out any expectations, I think.

When I speak of an offer I mean an offer which he is entitled and authorised to make by the leading coadjutors.

If you are minded to be here on the spot, instead of writing, pray come.

91. Lord Granville to Mr. Gladstone. [Add. MS. 44166, fo. 103]

11, Carlton House Terrace. [21 July 1869].

Cairns came to me again at 6.[2]

I told him I had found you not inclined to make concessions upon the basis which had been sketched which amounted to this. In order to induce him to look with favor on Carnarvon's indefensible clause, I was to propose a clause which was unacceptable to the Govt, and relieve the opposition from two amendments which were much in their way. I added that I had understood from him (Cairns) that his manner meant more than his words, although I could make no use of such a construction to you—I said you had gone carefully over all the amendments with me, and that if he would begin by telling me in the same perfectly confidential way that he would use his influence to prevent the Lords insisting on certain principal amendments, I did not despair of the possibility of an arrangement as to the other clauses, in which case we might discuss how the distribution of amendments & counter amendments should be made in the two houses.

I then asked him about the postponement of the surplus. He said that was the *only* point on which he could not enter upon with me. He did not know himself what course with reference to circumstances and to his party he should ultimately take—but that on all other matters he was ready to tell me his opinion in exchange for mine, but that I must remember that money was the real object.

I then broke off saying that with so capital a difficulty in the background, he must feel it was no use our showing our cards—He rather agreed, we parted good friends, and he expressed a wish that at any future time if either party wished it we might meet on the same ground.

I will call on you soon after two tomorrow.

[1] For Gladstone's record of the meeting with Tait see Morley, ii. 275; for Tait's, see R. P. Davidson and W. Benham, *Life of Archbishop Tait* (1891), ii. 40–1. The cabinet met Wed. 21 July at 11 a.m., Add. MS. 44637, fo. 90. The three concessions:—curate's amendment, Ulster glebes, free transference of glebe houses, clauses 15, 27, 29.

[2] Cf. Granville's two telegrams to the Queen before and after the Lords' debate, 20 July, G.D. 29/32. The meeting of Granville with Cairns occurred after the failure of Gladstone's negotiations with Tait; cf. Granville to the Queen, tel. 21 July, G.D. 29/32. Agreement was finally reached in the meeting of 22 July, described in no. 99 below.

92. Lord Granville to Mr. Gladstone. [Add. MS. 44166, fo. 98]

Thursday. [22 July 1869].

I send you some letters. Bulwer brought his own letter. He is quite unreliable but he declares that talking with MPs of different shades not one was for any course but a patient one.

Spencer gave the same account as to two hours during which he waited at Brookes.

Geo Grey says we shall lose the confidence of some of the best and staunchest of our friends in the H of Commons if we were thought to be the persons who broke off the chance of a peaceable passage of the bill.

On the other hand Mundella told Charles Bruce that the confidence felt in you by him & others enabled you to do what you liked, but that he thought you had already gone far in the way of concessions.

What shall I say to Charles Wood.[1] " That it is impossible in the present position to make any overture, that in *my* opinion the only person who could bring things right would be the Archbishop of Canterbury, & that he Halifax must not believe everything Cairns tells him."

I will call at noon on you but I have some previous appointments.

93. Mr. Gladstone to Lord Granville. [G.D. 29/57]

11, Carlton House Terrace. July 21[22].69.

These are good letters. I only differ from Halifax, I think, *if* in his last sentence he means that you should *state* that we do not stand on the preamble, or on the surplus. Your action tonight [2] will show that you do not stand on the Preamble —that is enough : it would be very unwise I think to *narrow* the ground on which in case of a rupture we may have to fall back.

I have written a letter this morning to the Archbishop which it appeared to me was necessary to make our case complete.[3] The amendment which I there accept is one suggested by Fortescue & approved by Sullivan, about which there could be no doubt among us. I inclose the copy for perusal—& for copying if you think fit.

The Archbishop not *knowing* what we can do, what do you think of sending Halifax to him ? I should *fear* telling H. our ultimatum. It could lead to further pressure.

This moment I have received your cover with Cairns's letter.[4]

You can judge best whether to see him. If you do I think your bill of fare for him will be as follows.

[1] See Halifax to Granville, 21 July, offering his services in the negotiations, G.D. 29/64.

[2] For the Lords' proceedings, 22 July, on the Commons' amendments to the Lords' amendments, see *L.J.* (1868–69), 518–20 ; for Commons' statement on which proceedings were based, *ibid.*, 504–7.

[3] See Gladstone to Tait, 21 [22] July, showing that there was nothing further to propose, the fate of the bill now lying with the majority in the Lords, Add. MS. 44330, fo. 98.

[4] Received 22 July, Morley, ii. 276, and below, no. 99.

1. Curates' amendment. Fortunately *he made much of this*.

2. Reduction of Clause 68 to an enactment in general words corresponding with the *later branch* in the Preamble—if they desire it.

3. Some *one* substantial, or perhaps it is better to say sensible, concession, which we could undertake to recommend to the House of Commons, for the sake of peace.

The amount I would not tell him: but, if you get so far, refer him to the Archbishop, not to learn at once what it is—for the Archbishop remains bound to secrecy—but to learn whether the Abp thinks it worth having. And *alors comme alors*.

94. Lord Granville to Mr. Gladstone. [Add. MS. 44166, fo. 107]

Private. Bruton St. July 23/69.

I had the pleasure of hearing your magnificent speech [1]—a fitting end to your great work.

I was deeply touched by the undeserved but most graceful compliment to the fly on the wheel of the wagon.

95. Mr. Gladstone to Lord Granville. [G.D. 29/57]

11, Carlton House Terrace. July 24.69.

You are very good to me: and much otherwise to yourself, in depreciating your own work, of which I can only in fairness confess, that I could not have done it.

Patched up for yesterday afternoon, I have had a roughish night and may perhaps be unable to attend the Cabinet today which so far as I know will be chiefly occupied with considering the abandonment of Bills, and the order of business.[2]

The doctor assures me that I am now practically out of it and by tomorrow I hope to be sound: but for today I must keep down *work* as much as possible.

You may I think mention to H.M. the articles in D. News & Star of today as showing that we went up to the line, which it would have been fatal to cross. Also she ought not to forget that we went up to it on Saturday last. Pray combine my thanks with your own for the powerful & valuable aid which she imparted through the Dean: always of course within the limits of the Constitution.

96. Mr. Gladstone to Lord Granville. [G.D. 29/57]

11, Carlton House Terrace. July 30, 4¼ Pm. [1869].

I am just arrived and at your command.

It is possible I may go up to Panizzi's for half an hour at half past eight, for we have most vilely broken an engagement to dine with him.

[1] On the passing of the Irish Church bill, *Hans. Parl. Deb.* 3rd ser. cxcviii. 564 ff.

[2] Granville, in Gladstone's absence, noted the topics of cabinet discussion, see Add. MS. 44637, fo. 93.

97. Mr. Gladstone to Lord Granville. [G.D. 29/57]

11, Carlton House Terrace. Aug. 2.69.

Please to look at Kinnaird's note,[1] *quoad* N. Zealand.

I want to jot down the particulars on our side of those anxious days from Sat. 17th ult. to Thurs. 22d.[2]

Will you kindly aid me by sending me the Disraeli & Cairns notes and memoranda —to be returned.

98. Lord Granville to Mr. Gladstone. [Add. MS. 44166, fo. 81]

16, Bruton Street. [4? August 1869].

I send you some rough notes.[3] You will probably be able to improve their accuracy, & I will then send you a fair copy.

Also Bessborough's list of Peers.

Also a letter from O'Hagan with enclosures,[4] and a copy of yesterday's minute.[5]

99. Memorandum by Lord Granville.[6] [Add. MS. 44166, fo. 111]

Colonial Office. Aug 4/69.

Before the second reading of the Irish Church bill in the House of Lords, I was asked by the Archbishop of York to meet him & the Archbishop of Canterbury. They said it was impossible for them to vote for the second reading in any case, but before they decided to abstain from voting against it, they wished to know how far the Govt would act in a conciliatory spirit. I made to them the same declaration which I afterwards made in the House—and after seeing you, I had another interview with the Archbishop of Canterbury. I told H.G. that it was impossible for the Gov to suggest amendments against themselves, but I gave a hint of the direction in which such amendments might be framed, and without mentioning that the suggestion came from you, I said that if H.G. would tell Dr Ball that he only wished to propose amendments which it would be possible for the Govt to accept, that learned gentleman would know better than others how it could be done. The Archbishop however seems chiefly to have made use of Dr Ball to supply him with arguments against the Gov. *After the Committee and before the report, the Archbishop as good as agreed to give up the Ulster Glebes, but he afterwards said it was impossible.

After the second reading the Dow Lady Salisbury told Lord Clarendon & Mr Delane that in her opinion a friendly communication might have great influence

[1] Arthur Kinnaird to Gladstone, 31 July, on growing disaffection in New Zealand, copy, G.D. 29/57.

[2] See mem. on 'critical days', 3 Sept., Add. MS. 44758, fos. 1–14.

[3] See below, no. 99.

[4] To Granville, 4 Aug., on Irish feeling about Church reform, G.D. 29/71.

[5] Minute of opinions on Princess Louise's marrying a commoner, 4 Aug., Add. MS. 44167, fo. 99; put with Gladstone's papers for 1870 but shown by drafts, G.D. 29/31, to belong to 1869.

[6] Printed in Morley, except sections starred, ii. 269, 270–1, 277–8.

on Lord Salisbury's course.* I therefore wrote to him stating to him why on public & personal grounds it was desirable that he should meet you. I said that although it would be difficult for us to initiate suggestions, yet from your personal regard for him such a conversation would advance matters. He consented, stating that he was in communication as to amendments with Lord Cairns, and the Archbishop. He was extremely desirous that no one should know of the interview.

You were of opinion that the interview had done good, and I wrote to ask Lord Salisbury whether he would like me to put dots on some of your i's.

He declined, & considered the interview had been unsatisfactory but gave me an assurance of his desire to avoid a conflict.

* I thanked him for the latter assurance, told him that my last letter was in consequence of the flattering terms in which you had spoken to me of him, and expressed a belief that he might perhaps be right as to our not meeting again while we pursued our separate but not divergent paths.*

On the 4th of July however I wrote again suggesting a compromise on Lord Carnarvon's clause.

He declined, that clause being the one thing they cared about. He ended by telling me his growing impression was that there would be no Church bill this session.

* Lord Cairns verbally proposed to call on me before the report, & suggested that I should replace the date of 1871, that I should propose a substitute for (I will talk this over with you). On the return of the amendments to the Lords, Lord Cairns in answer to my question—" I presume you have nothing to say to me ", said " No ". But on the 22d of July I recd the enclosed letter from him.*

After seeing you I met him at the Colonial Office. He offered me terms *—giving up everything excepting 1° a clause, which would have given double compensation to Incumbents, and their curates. 2° 5 per cent in addition to the 7 per cent offered by the Gov on commutation in consideration of the better lives of the clergy. 3° in lieu of Lord Salisbury's Clause, one which would have given to Incumbents their houses gardens and glebes at ten years' purchase.

I took these ad referendum, remarking however upon the arguments against a double compensation, and pointing out how untenable a ground his third proposal would be both for the Gov and the opposition, after debates in the House of Lords on concurrent endowment.* I also asked him whether in his opinion, he, the Archbishop and I could carry anything we agreed upon. He said " Yes, certainly ".

After seeing you, I met Lord Cairns a second time in his room at the House of Lords. I asked as a preliminary to giving any opinion on his amendments, how he proposed to deal with the preamble. He said, " to leave it as amended by the Lords ". I then proposed the words which were afterwards adopted in the 68th clause. He was at first taken aback, but admitted that he had personally no objection to them. He asked what was the opposition to be feared. I suggested some from Lord Grey. He believed this to be certain, but immaterial. I objected in toto to Lord Salisbury's clause or its substitute. He was unwilling to yield, chiefly on Lord Salisbury's account, but finally consented. We agreed upon the Commutation clause, if the 7 & the 5 per cent were lumped together.

On the Curates' clauses we could come to no agreement.

He proposed to see Lord Salisbury & the Archbishop, and to meet again at 4 at the Colonial Office. He spoke with fairness as to the difficulty of his position, and the risk he ran with his own party.

I again saw you, and asked the Irish Attorney General to be present at the last interview. I stated to him in Lord Cairns presence how far we agreed, & expressed my regret that on the last point "the Curates" our difference was irreconcilable. Lord Cairns said he hoped not, and proceeded to argue strongly in favor of his proposal. He at last however at 4.30 compromised the matter by accepting 5 years instead of one. I shook his hand, which was trembling with nervousness. We then discussed the form of announcing the arrangement to the House. We at once agreed it was better to tell the whole truth, and soon settled that it would be better for it's success that he should be the person to announce the details. I was afterwards apprehensive that this latter arrangement might be disadvantageous to us, but nothing could be better or fairer than his statement. I cannot finish this statement which I believe is accurate, without expressing my admiration at the firmness and conciliation which you displayed, in directing me in all these negotiations.

* There was a separate and important although abortive negotiation between Lord Bessborough and Mr Disraeli—the former communicated through me with you, but I have not got the papers.* [1]

100. Mr. Gladstone to Lord Granville. [G.D. 29/57]

11 C.H.T. Au 7.69.

Please to look at No 1.[2] Does it alter your view of the Southwell case? It has not yet changed mine.

No 2. The C[hancellor] of E[xchequer] writes as if the Office of Works were vacant.[3]

Do you think we have a case for asking Clarendon to appoint Layard to Madrid? He naturally dislikes stopping the promotion.

I cannot report well of myself: & I think I have now only to look to getting out of town & more away from business.

101. Mr. Gladstone to Lord Granville. [Add. MS. 44537, fo. 21]

[*Copy*]. 7 August 69.

I return your enclosures. Of Warburton I have heard too much; all in conformity with Lord Portsmouth's account. With Lord Portsmouth himself I have

[1] Bessborough to Gladstone, 19 Aug., on fate of these papers, Add. MS. 44421, fo. 289.

[2] Untraced. Lord Southwell claimed a United Kingdom peerage; see Southwell to Monsell, sent to Granville, 5 July, to Hatherley and to Gladstone, 17 July, Add. MSS. 44421, fos. 101, 168, 174.

[3] See Lowe to Gladstone, 7 Aug., proposing the appointment of A. S. Ayrton as chief commissioner of works, *vice* Layard, Add. MS. 44301, fo. 63. Gladstone sent Lowe's letter to Clarendon, 8 Aug., asking him to offer the Madrid mission to Layard, Add. MS. 44537, fo. 22; Gladstone to Granville, 9 Aug., sending him Clarendon's discouraging reply, G.D. 29/29A, not printed.

had heretofore the real pleasure of communicating about Irish Land, & I hope before our measure has been passed to enjoy that advantage again.

102. Lord Granville to Mr. Gladstone. [Add. MS. 44166, fo. 118]

16, Bruton Street. Aug 8/69.

Bright called at your house yesterday, but declined your servant's invitation to trouble you, & came here.

We had a long talk about the Peerage. He is strongly opposed to your making any more hereditary Peers. He thinks of making a speech soon about the House of Lords—suggesting that life Peerages are a mistake, & that an addition of Senators to the present body is what is required. He added ' Men like myself or Sir George Grey if we were appealed to might say " we are willing to give the five or six years that is left in us to the public service in this way."[']

Holding these views he thinks that manufacturers especially who have no business to make paupers of their younger sons, ought not to be asked.[1]

Getting on more practical grounds, these are his opinions of persons.

Sir Francis Crossley—He objects to, but says that his opinion must not be taken, as he has had a personal quarrel with him for 6 years.

William or James *Marshall*—unobjectionable, but is not sure that they are not Unitarians, in which case there would be no sympathy with them from other dissenters.

Thos Bazley—one son—very rich—Church of England—much too good—should be very sorry that he should accept, although it has been said that he has rather a hankering after great people (for which fact I (G) can vouch).

Titus Salt—perfectly silent in public & private—has wealth, has created a new manufacture—very liberal to his people—a dissenter, & friend of Miall—was a short time in the H of Commons and did not like it.

Sam Morley—first rate for our purposes—has wealth, brains and a great hold on Dissenters—He doubts whether he would be foolish enough to accept.

P.S. Aug 9.

I " render my esteem " to Bessborough who crossed from Dieppe to Brighton in a gale—says Salisbury is gone to Paris, but will come back.

Will the enclosed letter do for Layard.[2] It is not likely to be successful. Is not Ayrton at the Works rather a leap in the dark ?

103. Lord Granville to Mr. Gladstone. [Add. MS. 44166, fo. 123]

[9 August 1869].

The Queen is going on a lark at the beginning of September, & she leaves Balmoral on the 2d of November. This shortens the period to be covered by attending ministers.

[1] The first three paragraphs printed in Fitzmaurice, ii. 15.

[2] To Layard, 9 Aug., offering him the governorship of the Cape.

She proposes that you should come a few days later than the 6th—the 11th is a Saturday. Would the 11th or the 13th suit you.

Perhaps this will give us the immense pleasure of having you all as our guests at Walmer during the last few days.

104. Mr. Gladstone to Lord Granville. [G.D. 29/29A]

11, Carlton House Terrace. Aug. 10.69.

I see a great many reasons why, notwithstanding your kind offer our stay at Walmer should not be prolonged on account of the little change at Balmoral: and we will if you please consider the 4th of Sept. as the day not later than which we are to leave the coast clear of all except grateful recollections.

My ideal place for Temple would be St. David's or a Welsh See: that he might become what Bishop Thirlwell has failed to be. Wales is the point of danger & weakness; as we shall soon learn, & it requires a man who in addition to other gifts is fervently religious.

I do not mean that he would not *do* at Oxford: but he would have no special field: the *Bishop* is wonderfully barred out of the University. The present Bishop has coveted much to get in but has never been able. We go this afternoon I believe at 2 [to Walmer].

105. Lord Granville to Mr. Gladstone. [Add. MS. 44166, fo. 125]

16, Bruton Street. Aug 11/69.

I send you Layard's answer,[1] a bore for Clarendon.

I shiver a little at the thought of Ayrton at the Works.

I propose paying you a visit tomorrow for one night, as I may not arrive till 8 please do not wait dinner for me.

I am afraid Lady G took away most of the few books that were at Walmer. There is a good library at Deal Castle. Bobby Meade hopes you will make all possible use of it.

After consulting Glyn, I have written to Layard saying that I would take an opportunity of confidentially telling you & Clarendon what he says about Diplomatic Service.

106. Mr. Gladstone to Lord Granville. [G.D. 29/29A]

Walmer. Aug 16.69.

I am very obliged by your Memorandum upon the history of the private communications about the Irish Church Bill. To make my paper more complete I will ask Bessborough to be so good as to send me Disraeli's memorandum of the Sunday. I now return to you Cairns's note.[2] If there was a memorandum of his, as I had thought, I should be glad to see it.

[1] 10 Aug., declining the governorship of the Cape and referring to his wish for a diplomatic appointment, G.D. 29/99.

[2] See above, no. 99.

The Bishop of Winchester has just announced his intention to resign in October.

The Queen 's'avisera' about Peers: does not like making a lot at once: I have written, & put it that this is the best way of shutting the door. But there is no violent hurry.

107. Mr. Gladstone to Lord Granville. [G.D. 29/29A]

Most Private. Aug 18.69.

I send to you a note which through my stupidity has been unduly delayed. A few words on another subject.

The *personnel* of the Government generally has been proved by the experience of the Session to be good. But I think from my own observation and still more from the judgments & experience of others that one or two improvements might be made.

Ayrton has great talent and is a most pertinacious worker, with a good deal of experience and widely dispersed knowledge of public affairs. But he seems to be somewhat angular and better adapted for doing business within a defined province of his own, than in common stock or partnership with others, as his present office would require his business to be shared with Lowe and Stansfield. It appears also that they are strong enough to undertake the whole business of the Treasury by themselves, so that one place might be spared, which is much wanted for the War Department.

Again Layard, though he has great talents, remarkable powers of speech, and some special qualifications for his Department, has not succeeded in it with the House of Commons and does not seem very thoroughly to understand pecuniary responsibility and the management of Estimates. And there is no doubt whatever that in his department the present House of Commons will be vigilant and exacting: while the rapid growth of its expenditure certainly shows that it should be filled by some one capable of exercising controul.

At the same time it appears that Layard desires a diplomatic appointment; and the mission at Madrid for which he would be extremely well qualified is vacant. To this as I understand Clarendon would agree to appoint him.

All this personal detail is hardly fit for me to lay before the Queen in a letter. But as this will find you at Balmoral, I should be very glad if you would take an opportunity, without anticipating too absolutely Clarendon's judgment, to let H.M. have the sketch of these affairs and to know whether in the event of Layard's removal from the Board of Works the arrangement as to Ayrton, which would both positively and negatively improve the organization of the Govt in the H. of Commons, would meet Her approbation.

My reference to the War Department means that Cardwell finds it ought to be more fully represented in the House of Commons as was formerly the case under the Duke of Wellington's arrangement of the Board of Ordnance. The way to do this would be I believe to make Storks a political officer.[1]

[1] Done after the reorganization of the War Office under the War Office Act, July 1870, 33 and 34, Vict., ch. 17.

I suppose you have no answer yet from Westbury.[1] Mackinnon will lose nothing for want of asking.[2] We were quite delighted yesterday with a walk to St Margaret's at Cliffe, the S. Foreland lighthouse, & back by the bay and under the cliffs.

108. Lord Granville to Mr. Gladstone. [Add. MS. 44166, fo. 131]

Private. Balmoral. Aug 21/69.

I have spoken to the Queen about Layard and Ayrton. She did not object to Layard going from his office, or his being named to Madrid, if Clarendon does not, but she had already signified her approval of Charles Murray.[3]

She appears to be perfectly aware of Ayrton's character, and remembers his personal attack upon her.[4] She says that it is very important for Her to have a gentleman at the Office of Works, and one whose relations with her [are] of an agreeable character—that one of her reasons for disliking Windsor is the constant worry about little details, and this might be infinitely aggravated by a cantankerous person. I told her that it was an absolute necessity to remove Ayrton from the Treasury, and that it was very difficult to find a place for him, that I agreed with you in thinking that he (Ayrton) would be much better at the head of an Office, than a subordinate in one like the Treasury, that very often men of the class of Ayrton were more anxious even than others to make themselves agreeable to H.M. and that I had always found Ayrton in the few business matters I had had with him courteous to me. I also explained that economy was an absolute necessity for your Govt. She did not seem convinced, she begs you to consider whether some other place could not be made available for Ayrton. But I believe she would yield to pressure, unless Clarendon backs her up in her refusal.

The Queen made some objections to Sir H. Storks, not quite consistent or logical, but ended by acquiescing, with a hope that nothing would be done without informing the Duke of Cambridge.

H.M. has made no allusion to Peers or Baronets, but is very anxious that you should take care of yourself. She seems well and in good spirits.

I know your walk to St Margarets well, but being fat & lymphatic, I generally accomplish it on four legs.

109. Lord Granville to Mr. Gladstone. [Add. MS. 44166, fo. 135]

Balmoral Castle. Aug 23/69.

Do not feel too much elated at hearing from me on this goldheaded paper.

I am afraid Westbury must be sailing. I have had no reply.

[1] I.e. to the offer, made through Granville, of the lord justiceship of appeal in chancery vacant by the death of Lord Justice Selwyn, 11 Aug. 1869; cf. above, no. 7.

[2] Refers to Mackinnon to Granville, 14 Aug., on his claim to a peerage, Add. MS. 44166, fo. 127; cf. above, no. 55.

[3] For appointment as British minister at Madrid.

[4] In a speech to his constituents of the Tower Hamlets 1866, *D.N.B.* xxii. 89.

The Queen has written a philippic against the creation of Peers. I am inditing a Ciceronian reply.[1] You shall have them and the result, if any, tomorrow.

110. Mr. Gladstone to Lord Granville. [G.D. 29/57]

Walmer Castle. Aug 24.69.

Am I to gather from your letter that you think that the affair of the Office of Works should stand over at Balmoral until I come?

As respects making any *other* office available, I amafraid that matter has already been considered exhaustively.

There is however another scheme which I want now to test; one which I have often thought might be desirable on other grounds, that of getting rid of the personal relations between the Sovereign & the Office of Works by assigning either for life or for a term of years (this perhaps in the first instance) a lump sum for the maintenance and repairs of those Palaces, with their grounds, in which the Queen is personally interested. I have written to Childers and Lowe on this matter.

Glyn is coming down here today or tomorrow: we can once more cast a critical eye over the lists now with H.M.

The Bp of Winchester's announcement of a resignation to take effect two months hence will cause much speculation in the mean time: & the prominence of the figure of S.O[xford] on the canvas will lead to his being much more microscopically than goodnaturedly examined and criticised.

Dr Clark was here for a few hours on Sunday and made a very good report of me.

Yesterday I lionised the Deal Corporation over your beautiful lawn & grounds: they came with an Address: no politics.

We are always more & more obliged to your hospitality.

There is nothing stereotyped I imagine about times, as between 11 am & 3 pm, for me to arrive at Balmoral?

I fear, from the way in which she writes, that Lady Blantyre continues sadly out of health.

P.S. What about Westbury?

I incline to think it may be well, considering the grave matters the Cabinet will have to mature that we should meet in town before October is over? and after a while run down again if this should be found practicable. But I hope to see you in London when this crude idea can be talked over.

111. Lord Granville to Mr. Gladstone. [Add. MS. 44166, fo. 136]

[Balmoral]. Aug 24/69.

I send you Bouverie's answer.[2]

The Queen's note and the draft of my reply about Peers. I am glad C. Grey

[1] See the Queen to Granville, 22 Aug., Guedalla, i. 197–8; Granville to the Queen, 23 Aug., Add. MS. 44166, fo. 138, G.D. 29/32, part printed Fitzmaurice, ii. 16–18, fully printed Guedalla, i. 198–200.

[2] Bouverie to Granville, 22 Aug., reporting (i) the improbability of Moncreiff's accepting the governorship of the Cape, and (ii) Moncreiff's resentment at his advice being ignored on Scottish affairs, G.D. 29/25A; see below, no. 114.

is not here. Biddulph agrees with me, but doubts whether the Jew [1] will not frighten all " the old women ".

I wish it could be settled before the Prince of Wales comes on Thursday.

I said nothing about Baronets. It does not concern me like the other, though you were good enough to consult me. I do not know many of them, and after the meeting, & after your sending the list to the Queen Glyn & I (moutarde après dîner) rather agreed that the batch was large.

On the Peers, I consider myself entitled and bound to argue with my sovereign, and to preach to my chief (luckily a convert).

The weather is fine—the Queen starts for her expedition, which she flatters herself will be a perfect secret on the 1st.

Biddulph hopes there will be no political crisis during the time.

H.M is very well and gracious—the Household pleasant. Col & Mrs Ponsonby charming.

Christian the best and dullest of men and even Princes.

112. Lord Granville to Mr. Gladstone. [Add. MS. 44166, fo. 141]

Balmoral Castle. Aug 25/69.

The Queen sent me this answer before dinner yesterday.[2]

At that repast, H.M dying of laughter, made some allusion to the manner in which people *submitted* to her to do what she did not wish to do, and not to do what she wished to do.

She seems to expect me to open the subject in the evening, but unless she begins, I shall not do so till I hear from you.

I construe her assent to be given to everything but the Jew, eight now, three before the opening of Parliament. Biddulph says he does not know, but that he agrees with me.

I presume that you will not insist upon the Jew this year—in that case ought you not to get another commercial man in lieu of one of the others. You seemed to have an objection to K. Hodgson, but there must be some great city man.

I shall leave it to you to discuss in conversation whether it will be wise as a general principle for the future to treat R. Catholics with disfavor, in order to rescue the Protestant Religion.

The Municipal Corporation in the " state rooms " must have been an imposing sight. I am very glad you recd them.

The Queen hopes you are really resting yourself.

113. Mr. Gladstone to Lord Granville. [G.D. 29/57]

Walmer Castle. Aug 26.69.

You have done much: and I return the inclosed keeping copy. I should, however, subject to better advice—prefer postponing the whole batch until November,

[1] Baron Lionel de Rothschild, proposed for an English peerage.

[2] The Queen to Granville, 24 Aug., printed Guedalla, i. 200–1.

to taking 8 now and 3 or 4 in Decr. or Jan. What say you to this? By taking all at once, we can shut the door for a good while: and this will be an answer to claims—indeed I have already made good use of it in three cases. But a Postscript of three more Peers would destroy its validity and would I fear give rise to much offence.

Glyn is now able to announce himself here for Monday. I will therefore go to work to cut down the Baronets with him. The weakest case however is H.M.'s child [1]—and that I suppose must stand.

Do not suppose I object to K. Hodgson as a Peer—though I am afraid he would make some of our Baronets very jealous. The merit of Rothschild is that his position is well defined and separated. By my plan of delay, perhaps the Queen might give way? Her argument is null and void. If it be sound, she has been wrong in consenting to emancipate the Jews.

As at present advised I hope to go to Raby on the 7th and reach Balmoral on the morning of the 11th.

I do not like this business of the Porte and the Khedive. I write to Clarendon [2] in the sense of keeping close to France, unless & until she begins to develope a selfish policy.

114. Mr. Gladstone to Lord Granville. [G.D. 29/29A]

Walmer Castle. Aug. 26.69.

I return the Queen's letter with your most convincing statement in reply (keeping copies): also Bouverie's. I think as to the latter you could perhaps with advantage ask the writer to particularise. I am aware of no ground for the observation, but it is made in a friendly way. We have had many Scotch difficulties this year, but one of them arose from Moncreiff's having taken the line of the Radicals unexpectedly.

And I must say that excellent fellow as he is I think that reprint of the Education Bill,[3] done without my knowledge, was one of the most inexcusable blunders I ever heard of in Parliament.

Now as to the pending question of Peers and Baronets. In the main, we cannot recede. But I think we may cheerfully let the Peer matter stand over till Octr. or even Novr. if that will please the Queen. And the odds are they will not all accept.

As to the Baronets I think Glyn was the main cause of our lengthening the list. I do believe it will bear some shortening, and if that would be acceptable I will set to work with Glyn upon it.

I do not write to the Queen on these matters for they cannot be so well as in your hands. I am sorry to say also that I write once more from my (or rather your)

[1] None of the royal princes received an honour in the autumn of 1869.

[2] 26 Aug., Add. MS. 44537, fo. 38. The question arose from the Sultan's attempt to control the domestic administration and financial policy of the Khedive. It was settled by the firman of 11 Dec. 1869.

[3] Parochial Schools (Scotland) Bill, see above, no. 46. After the shelving of the bill by the Commons the Lords resolved, 10 Aug., to reprint the bill as amended by the Commons, *L.J.* (1868–69), 606.

bed but I hope to be right in a day or two. If the Queen expects any letter from me, perhaps you will say in general terms I was not quite so well today.

I send her however a recommendation [1] for the living of Brightstone. The man was put out of his Proctorship for publishing an able pamphlet in favour of the first part of our Irish Church Bill: being also excellent in other ways.

Thinking over Cambridge men, one who comes up is Lord A. Hervey. I am trying to learn what I can about his politics. Can you help me? Bath and Wells will want a Cambridge man. I am afraid Mrs Glyn's case is critical and may turn out very formidable.

My relapse is I believe fully accounted for by a *grouse* a little over-ripe.

115. Lord Granville to Mr. Gladstone. [Add. MS. 44166, fo. 143]

[Balmoral]. Aug 27/69.

The answer about the Board of Works will require either a letter from you or a delay till your arrival, but H.M. would yield if required, I think. I will not mention your endeavour to make an arrangement about the Palaces & grounds, lest it flaw her plan. She will however be much pleased by this mark of attention.

I am afraid Glyn will not encourage you about S. O[xford]. He told me, what is likely, that it would be very unpopular in Surrey.

I will allude to the 11th or 13th as if from myself. I presume that either day would do. She goes on her lark on the 1st. I go then or I hope the previous day, so that if you have any orders, they are sure to be late unless posted on Sunday evening at Walmer—& then would be too late if I get away on the 31st.

I hear also that poor Lady Blantyre is very ill, and much alarmed about herself.

Will it be convenient to you all to dine in Bruton St on the fourth, or any later day till the 7th, when we have little hope but a great desire of entertaining you at Walmer. Lady G. was delighted to hear that you all like it, but I regret to be informed that your wife speaks disrespectfully of my carpets.

116. Lord Granville to Mr. Gladstone.[2] [Add. MS. 44166, fos. 147, 145]

[Balmoral]. Aug 31/69.

I communicated your answer about Peers & Baronets to the Queen.

I told H.M that you were at work in order to submit a revised and reduced list of the latter.

I did not press the arguments about Baron Rothschild, because the Queen has evidently at present a strong feeling on the subject, as regards Herself and the Govt.

I gave your argument about the disadvantage of dividing the batch—and I told H.M how pleased you were with H.M's concession about numbers.

I find that I had misconstrued the Queen's sentence in H.M's previous letter —" that H.M would agree to 7 or 8 now, and 2 or 3 added later." The Queen did not mean an interval of two or three months, but a year—and the Queen would

[1] John Fielder Mackarness, rector of Honiton, 1855–68. [2] Printed Guedalla, i. 201–2.

like the whole number to be under 10. But I am now authorized to state that Her Majesty consents to the whole number with the exception of Baron Rothschild being created at once—but would prefer as you propose that it should take place at the beginning of November. She would like to have a promise for the future, but does not exact one as it will be your duty to advise H.M to the best of your judgment as the case arises. But the Queen wishes you to know Her feeling.

I am a bad negotiator on behalf of Her Majesty, as I have a strong conviction that every modification of the present unfortunate antagonism between the Lords and the Commons is good especially for the future of the House of Lords.

I have prepared the Queen for the probability of your submitting besides the omission of Baron Rothschild, the substitution of some other commercial representative for one of the other names.

The Queen approves this letter.

117. Lord Granville to Mr. Gladstone. [Add. MS. 44166, fo. 149]

Confidential. 16, Bruton Street. Sep 1/69.

I got your letter about Peers, and a note from the Queen (asking whether I had received one from you), on the same evening. The next morning I wrote a mem, of which I foolishly omitted to make a copy, but the précis in my enclosed letter to you is exact. I did not press her about the Jew, in consequence of Biddulph's advice, who said she was very strong on the subject.

The answer from H.M, probably written after seeing the Prince of Wales, took me by surprise and rather disconcerted me.

I therefore spoke to [her] after dinner, said that I trusted that she would not ask you for a pledge for the future, which it would be your duty to Her My to refuse. She immediately agreed, but said I might say so to you as from myself. I declined, telling H.M, that she must remember I was a bad negotiator on Her side in this matter. She then said that she should prefer the matter being postponed till November. All this was so vague, that I thought it better to write & read to H.M the enclosed letter to you.[1] She looked put out, but entirely assented to it. But she will expect you to write or speak to her. She would probably prefer the former, in order that the business may be closed before you meet. But we can talk this over.

Glyn tells me that only three of you can dine with me on Saturday.

118. Mr. Gladstone to Lord Granville. [G.D. 29/57]

Walmer Castle. Sept 1.69.

We shall be happy to dine with you on Saturday and as you have underlined all we shall not scruple to bring a daughter.

Our fashionable season here is now over; and our sons departed. We shall say goodbye to the old walls with regret, & with much thankfulness.

My arrangement stands for Balmoral on the 11th which will suit my sons best.

[1] No. 116.

Clarendon too is anxious that the Lisbon [1] Mission should be filled one way or another.

The rumour of Patten's death made Glyn & me (I am ashamed to say) extremely happy on Moncreiff's account.

As your books here are principally light, I shall drop a heavy one called "Juventus Mundi".

119. Lord Granville to Mr. Gladstone. [Add. MS. 44166, fo. 152]

No 2. Colonial Office. Sep 2/69.

I have just recd your letter of yesterday.

I am so very glad that you have liked Walmer, notwithstanding the addresses and the unfortunate housemaid.

Please tell Lambert the Porter to carry cards round to those who have called upon you.

I did not go through your emotions about Patten, as I heard of the contradiction before the announcement.

1000 thanks for "Juventus Mundi"—please write a suitable inscription.

I have a letter to give you on the part of the Prince of Wales,[2] but it is in a box in Bruton St, & will keep till we meet.

Johnny Russell wrote a violent criticism to me on my Colonial policy, in which he compared himself to Oliver Cromwell and Chatham, and me to Lord North & Geo Grenville. I rejoined much too good-humouredly, my private Secy thinks—& I have had a rejoinder, in which amongst other things he says "that which I wish to see is a Colonial Representative Assembly sitting apart from our Lords and Commons voting us supplies in aid for our Navy and Army, and receiving in return assurances of support from the Queen." [3]

Shall we immortalize your administration by proposing this?

120. Mr. Gladstone to Lord Granville. [G.D. 29/29A]

Walmer Castle. Sept 3.69.

Very many thanks for your letters. I send herewith

1. My mem. of the critical days.[4] It wants *B*, *E*, and *F*. The last I can supply. Bessborough cannot find *B*. If you have *E*, please to let me have it when I see you tomorrow evening.

[1] Read Madrid? This mission, vacant since Sir John Crampton retired, July 1869, would be filled either by transferring Sir Charles Murray from Lisbon or Layard from the Office of Works; see above, no. 108.

[2] Untraced. Granville to Gladstone, 30 Aug., G.D. 29/57, and Gladstone to Granville, 6 Sept., Add. MS. 44537, fo. 51, on the Herbert peerage (not printed), may relate to it.

[3] See Russell to Granville, 26 Aug., Granville's reply, 28 Aug., Russell's rejoinder, 31 Aug., G.D. 29/79.

[4] Mem. of negotiations 17–22 July on the Irish Church bill, 14 Aug., Add. MS. 44758, fos. 1–14. Cf. above, no. 97. B. was a memorandum of an overture from Disraeli to Bessborough, E. was Disraeli's rejoinder to the Liberal answer to his overture, and F. was Gladstone's letter to the Queen on the cabinet of 21 July.

2. A letter to the Queen [1] written in consequence of yours.

We can talk the matter over: but I think delay one advantage. I feel confidence that as the matter is thought over more, the Queen must see the breadth of the grounds on which we stand.

Keep my letter back, if you think it advisable. If not send it back to D. St, to be copied.

3. I see much difficulty in finding a substitute for Rothschild. Glyn thinks K. Hodgson would excite very great jealousy.

4. I return the Queen's letter.

5. Lord Russell's outburst is much to be deplored, and his plan makes it ridiculous. I was in hopes that at this time of year, his motto would still be the famous "Rest and be thankful". It is quite time that the questions involved in your Colonial Policy should be brought to a head: and I for one am sanguine about the issue.

I hope (or rather fear) to be at home at 2 tomorrow. You have I hope found Lady Granville as you would wish.

121. Mr. Gladstone to Lord Granville.[2] [G.D. 29/57]

Raby Castle. Sept. 8.69.

I am greatly pleased, as my wife will be when she arrives here after post time, to hear that the journey to Walmer was effected satisfactorily, and I trust Lady Granville will keep & gain strength under the more favourable conditions.

I have unfortunately shut up your letter to me where no one but myself can find it and I fear the matter must stand over till I get to Hawarden. But there is nothing urgent in it.

The Irish Land question is assuming an aspect of greater difficulty. Expectations rise over the water & I understand that a great part of the Conservative Press in Dublin calls for large concessions.

Spencer sends me an account [3] of a very satisfactory interview with the Bishop of Limerick who is now sanguine about the future of the established Church.

This Castle is a noble monument of antiquity and the hospitality warm and large.

The Greys among others come today.

Biddulph writes (on the 7th) that he does not know precisely on what day the Queen would return to Balmoral.

I hope the Porter's zeal may not have inflamed the clerical body of the neighbourhood. See the inclosed card.

[1] 4 Sept., agreeing to delay the creation of peers until Nov., printed Guedalla, i. 202–3. For proposals for peerage and baronetcies, 1869, see Add. MS. 44758, fos. 149–68. Gladstone added later here: 'I have a misgiving about having already sent you a copy.'

[2] Gladstone to Granville, copy, 6 Sept., on G. W. Dasent's application for the editorship of the *Gazette*, Add. MS. 44537, fo. 51, and Granville to Gladstone, 6 Sept., reporting return to Walmer, Add. MS. 44166, fo. 156, not printed.

[3] 3 Sept., Add. MS. 44306, fo. 130.

122. Mr. Gladstone to Lord Granville. [G.D. 29/57]

Balmoral. Sept 13.69.

1. I send the inclosed by H.M.'s authority. I explained that of course we should be too happy to find there was no barrier in the way of the original plan for Prince Arthur.[1]

2. It rains Bishoprics. My great difficulty is among the class of Churchmen called 'Low' to find men of sufficient calibre and weight: & their politics are for the most part very adverse. I am still inquiring about Lord A. Hervey of whom I have rather conflicting accounts.

I think you could learn for me something about a man of another school, Lord A. Compton. I know he is excellent, but I mean 1. as to his force, 2. as to his politics.

3. I have said nothing yet about Ayrton as I have not heard from Childers who seems to have turned sea-rover if not buccaneer and to be difficult to get at.

4. The Queen is very unhappy about Cullen and the R.C.'s. I pointed out that he has demanded nothing new and that his demand as to the higher Education comes to no more, perhaps to less, than the late Government volunteered to give him.

I hope Lady Granville has profited by the change of air.

Raby took my breath away: it is magnificent.

123. Mr. Gladstone to Lord Granville. [G.D. 29/57]

Balmoral. Sept. 14.69.[2]

Your letter to Westbury had been strangely delayed. He sends me a kind and good answer: chiefly to the effect that the appointment need not at present be filled up. I write to the Chancellor accordingly.[3]

The death of Lady Palmerston took me by surprise—she seemed so well when I saw her just before going to Walmer. I am afraid her later life was a good deal perturbed by household suffrage and Irish disestablishment. She is no inconsiderable personage in the memory of her time. Peace be with her.

Pray read Gerald Fitzgibbon's Land difficulty of Ireland. It is a sign of the times. You may begin at p. 25. All that comes before is gross abuse of us.

124. Mr. Gladstone to Lord Granville. [G.D. 29/57]

Balmoral. Sept. 14.69.

I think you should read Clarendon [4] on the Land question—inclosed.

I doubt whether he is fully aware of the state of affairs in regard to it.

[1] His journey to Canada was nearly abandoned owing to the Fenian danger; see Granville to the Queen, 28 July, and her reply, 29 July, G.D. 29/32. He began a tour of Upper Canada on 20 Sept.

[2] Copy in Add. MS. 44537, fo. 58, dated 13 Sept.

[3] 14 Sept., copy, Add. MS. 44537, fo. 58, enclosing Westbury to Gladstone, 12 Sept., refusing appointment as lord justice of appeal in chancery; cf. above, no. 107 note. The vacancy was not filled until 1875.

[4] To Gladstone, Wiesbaden, 11 Sept., Add. MS. 44134, fo. 11.

We shall need a great deal of nice steering, & the worst of it is that if we fail, much more will have to be done by others.

You should read the report of the Skibbereen dinner to MacCarthy Downing.

125. Mr. Gladstone to Lord Granville. [G.D. 29/57]

Balmoral. S. 16.69.

Our letters have crossed: but I am glad to have an opportunity of saying how glad I am to hear of Lady G's well doing.

For three days the Queen has not been well and the Royalties have dined with us. But she is out today.

You may have noticed an answer to some applicants for the release of the Fenians written by my Private Sec. in my name which was not very prudent. His letter was written on a minute of mine but unfortunately did not follow it.

The Bishop of " Honolulu " has written to me on the appointment of a certain Mr Stirling as Bishop [1] & his proceedings which appear to be very strange: but I imagine it was not done by the Govt. except formally & in any case I cannot interfere & have said so.

126. Mr. Gladstone to Lord Granville. [G.D. 29/57]

Balmoral Castle. Sept 18.69.[2]

I have sent in to the Queen (only last night) the inclosed Memorandum about Peers. It expands a little note I placed in your hands, and with which you concurred.

When you answer me about Lord A. Compton, please to let me know whether he partakes the faculty of his family for Art? He is young yet.

Nothing is formally settled about Bishoprics: but I have had a preliminary conversation with H.M. and no end of correspondence with the Archbishop of C., *the* Dean, & others.

Since I began I have had an approving answer from H.M. to my paper on Peerages.

127. Mr. Gladstone to the Queen. [G.D. 29/57]

Copy. Balmoral. Sept. /69.

Mr Gladstone presents his humble duty to your Majesty. He fully understands that nothing will be done in the matter of Peerages until the year is further advanced. But in order to aid in clearing the general question he has ventured to put on paper

[1] Of the Falkland Islands. The bishop of Honolulu forwarded complaints from British residents of Stirling's attempt to extend his jurisdiction to the South American coast; see Gladstone to bishop of Honolulu and archbishop of Canterbury, 16 Sept., Add. MS. 44537, fos. 62–3; cf. Granville to Clarendon, 15 Aug., G.D. 29/55.

[2] Granville's private secretary docketed this as dated 12 Sept., but Gladstone's figure was 18 and the letter is entered under that date in his letter-book.

several considerations which in the inclosed Memm he humbly submits for your Majesty's perusal with a confident hope that your Majesty will conceive them to be not devoid of weight.

Memorandum by Mr Gladstone on the Numbers
of the House of Lords.

1. Within the last ten years, the House of Lords appears to have declined in numbers by about 25, although 45 Peers or thereabouts, have been made. These figures seem to show a natural waste in the Peerage approaching 7 cases annually, or in other words to indicate that less than 7 creations in each year might not suffice to keep the Peerage up to its present No.

2. In the present year four seats in the House of Lords have been destroyed by the Irish Church Act.

3. The actual number of the House of Lords, after deducting Irish Bishops is 429. It may be difficult to say at what precise figure it would become inconveniently large for its purposes as a deliberative assembly. But certainly not until it was well past 500.

4. At present the House of Lords may be said to be inconveniently small. The greater part of its business is transacted, & the greater part of its Divisions are taken with numbers so very limited as to stand in marked contrast with those of the House of Commons, and somewhat to shock public opinion; and it can hardly be doubted that, within just limits, numbers are an element of weight.

5. While the real numbers of the House of Lords are small, the effective numbers of the House of Lords fall short of the real numbers; owing to the fact that its members sit for life, and therefore that it contains an unusual proportion of members incapacitated by old age and infirmity. Employments at a distance, & in the case of Bishops their episcopal duties, further diminish the effective attendance. And the rules recently adopted with regard to proxies reduces the numbers available for voting on the greatest and most critical occasions. The second reading of the Irish Church Bill in 1869 was decided on by a smaller number of Peers than the second reading of the reform Bill of Lord Grey in October 1831.

6. For many years passed [*sic*], the House of Commons has tended to outweigh the House of Lords in an inconvenient degree. There can be no doubt that the adoption of Household Suffrage has considerably added to the relative strength of the House of Commons; which more and more speaks for the nation, and not for any class or portion of it only. The crisis of this year was impatiently borne by the House: and there was an appearance of combustible temper which might easily have burst into flame. The greatest security of the House of Lords lies in its own prudence: but it is far from having any strength to spare. Its constitution after the reform Act of 1867, might readily be brought into controversy. But without doubt it is a cardinal object of good sense and good policy, to keep this, if possible, out of the category of debateable and debated questions. Now it is true that no great or signal measure can be adopted for giving greater relative strength to the House of Lords. The appointment of some Peers for Life may be desirable: but it is not easy to arrange, and it could not effect much. Reasonable and moderate

addition to the present numbers of the House, though it cannot effect any great results, appears to me to be desirable rather than otherwise. For if, with reference to any given end, the means of action are but moderate, it is the more important that they should not be overlooked.

7. A very large portion of the influence of the House of Peers depends upon, & indeed in one way represents the aggregate of the influence of its members individually. Every well conducted, nay even every not flagrantly illconducted Peer, is a distinct centre of influence on behalf of the House to which he belongs: of moral and social influence, over and above the mere weight of his property. In this view all such creations of Peers as do not degrade the order by excessive intrusion are real additions to the power of the House of Lords. And, besides their direct action, they tell in an important manner through elections to the House of Commons.

8. It may be said that Lord A. as a Peer fills the place which he formerly filled, under the name of Mr. A., as a commoner. But this is not the whole truth. For in this country, attached as it is to hereditary distinctions, more regard is paid, more influence accorded in the long run, and in the greater number of instances to an ennobled, than to an untitled family. And not only so, but beyond all doubt, as a general rule, the family itself by a natural & unblameable process, becomes when itself ennobled more attached to aristocracy by the habits of mind which the situation imperceptibly creates. This tendency, indeed, sometimes is developed to an inconvenient degree.

9. Is there, then, any fear, that the dignity of the House of Lords is likely, in present or in any probable circumstances to suffer through undue multiplication of its numbers? This could hardly happen, unless the number of Peers relatively to that of the Population were carried sensibly beyond the proportion which it has borne in former days. But if we compare these numbers (taken roughly) we find that there are in the United Kingdom. In 1869 about 14 peers for each million of the population. But in 1840 there were about 17 Peers for each million. Therefore we are not beyond, but within the proportion of former times and the country does not seem to be near the point at which any danger on this score is to be apprehended: while it has already been pointed out that for the simple purpose of transacting business the House of Lords needs not fewer but more members than heretofore.

10. It will be borne in mind that the whole of these topics are distinct from, and are over and above, the arguments which have been urged with much force by Lord Granville with reference to the position of the Liberal party in the House of Lords. They refer simply to the public interest involved in maintaining the power of that House as a great limb of the Constitution: although at one point the two lines of argument coincide, that namely, at which it may be urged that it cannot be for the interest of the House of Lords or for the interest which the country has in the House of Lords, that this assembly should stand in marked contrast with the steady and permanent judgment of the country which on every occasion since 1830 except one has returned a Liberal majority.

Sept. 14/69.

128. Lord Granville to Mr. Gladstone. [G.D. 29/57]

Walmer Castle. Sep 20 [1869].

Please read the enclosed,[1] and if you approve, obtain the Queen's sanction to it's being sent.

Bowen has taken upon himself to exercise the Queen's authority, and in an ordinary case it would be right to cancel the whole proceeding, but in the present state of our relations with New Zealand, it would be a pity to do an ungracious act,—there are few colonies in the same position as New Zealand is, and the danger of a precedent, even if it be important, is not great.

129. Mr. Gladstone to Lord Granville.[2] [Add. MS. 44166, fo. 158]

[*Copy*]. *Private.* Balmoral. Sept 22: 69.

I have received the inclosed from Fortescue.[3] It raises the question as to the mode of proceeding in the Cabinet, with res: espy to Irish Land. Should we open it early; & should we have a Committee.

Now this is a question arduous & critical within as well as without the Cabinet.

It fills the public mind in an extraordinary degree, & we can hardly avoid some early step towards making progress in it. A Committee keeps a Cabinet quiet.

It is highly necessary that we should be quite ready when Parlt meets, and yet there is so much mental movement upon the question from day to day, as we see from a variety of curious utterances (that of the Times included) that it is desirable to keep final decisions open.

Much information will be open, & this a Committee can prepare in concert with the Irish Govt.

It also, I think, affords a means of bringing men's minds together.

Upon all this I wish much to have yr opinion.

The upshot would be that we shd propose a Commee on the 26th Oct., when I think we may hold our first Cabinet.[4]

But I do not see how the Commee can have less than seven members of the Cabinet, even excluding Lowe (to whom, however, Cardwell, might *like* to give way) viz:—

Granville	W. E. G.	Bright
Kimberley	Cardwell	Fortescue.
Clarendon		

I expect to be at Hawarden abt the middle of next week. All continues to go well, I trust, at Walmer.

[1] Draft to Bowen, No. 115, 7 Oct., confirmed the policy of withdrawing British troops. Gladstone returned it with a pencil addition and the Queen's approval, C.O. 209/211. Cf. Parl. papers. [C. 83] (1870). I, 217–19, and above, no. 55, below, no. 141.

[2] The third, fourth, fifth and sixth paragraphs printed in Morley, ii. 288–9.

[3] 20 Sept., untraced. It looked to the drafting of the Irish land bill without further cabinet discussion; see Gladstone's reply, 27 Sept., and below, no. 132, note.

[4] For cabinet of 26 Oct., see Add. MS. 44637, fo. 102.

130. Lord Granville to Mr. Gladstone. [Add. MS. 44166, fo. 159]

Walmer Castle. Sep 23/69.

I return your admirable memorandum. It would indeed have puzzled our gracious mistress to answer it. Have you thought more of Mark Phillips [*sic*, read Philips]. It appears to me a very important element as to the strength of the House of Lords, to inspire a large & powerful class with the belief that they have a chance of belonging to it.

Clarendon's opinion about Irish land is a wish to have Clanricarde's bill and nothing more—and as sometimes happens, he has talked so loudly in that sense, that any other course is difficult for him. I did not think him looking as well as I should have hoped after his cure—but like other people to whom I can only darkly allude, he is apt to do too much work.

Have you been bored or amused at Balmoral.

I hope you agree with me in thinking the Ponsonby's pleasant.

131. Lord Granville to Mr. Gladstone. [Add. MS. 44166, fo. 161]

Private. Walmer Castle. Sep 25/69.

I am glad you have a cabinet on the 26th. I think you ought to mention land, and appoint a committee. The members are the difficulty.

I see none of the 7 you mention, whom you could omit. I doubt Clarendon and I being of much use. It appears impossible to omit Lowe, although he will not be quite a sweetmeat. Hartington will be a little disappointed but that cannot be helped—the Chancellor most useful.

Those who will take a purely Landlord view, I presume, are Lowe, Argyll, Clarendon Cardwell, & very moderately so, Hartington.

Is it best to have their criticism in the Committee or [at] a later period. None will break up the Cabinet.

All well here.

132. Mr. Gladstone to Lord Granville. [G.D. 29/57]

Most Private. Fasque, Laurencekirk, N.B. S.27.69.

1. Thanks for the report of Lord A. Compton. I am afraid the politics are fatal.

2. Mr S. Brooke is a man of ability, who should not be lost sight of, but he would create more alarm than Temple, or as much, and I do not know any thing of his administrative powers or other compensations. Clark is an able scholar and Tutor: no one has named him to me for high preferment: he is I imagine a stout liberal.

3. After much reflection, & prolonged inquiry especially about A. Hervey, I have recommended to H.M.

1. S.O[xford] to Winchester
2. Temple to Exeter
3. A. Hervey to B. & Wells.
4. Mackarness to Oxford.

Exeter would have been the best for Mackarness: but Temple desired it, and there would have been much more row at Oxford. Mackarness was known as one of the ablest Clergy in Convocation: but was put out on account of his Liberal opinions on the Irish Church. He is a sound but moderate High Churchman without any kind of follies.

I pondered much upon Fraser: but it would not have done to take three men all supposed to be touched with Broadism. He will stand I think *proximus accessit.* But if one more vacancy come it must be filled from Cambridge.

4. I write to Fortescue in the sense of your letter of Saturday. There is much *approximation* requiring to be wrought: and I think the first stage of it will best be effected in a Committee, or in an early Cabinet if the other cannot be managed. We must try to have the Cabinet *one* in spirit as well as form. I inclose copy of my letter to F.[1] for perusal.

5. The Queen holds out about Rothschild. But she is in such good humour (I think) at the respect with which she has been treated in the whole matter, that I have never formally abandoned him: taking into view that he stands so *much* better for the promotion,[2] than any one whom we can put in his place. On the other hand, if we finally withdraw him, the Queen is prepared for some one, which we will talk over. I always like Balmoral only my work this year was very hard, e.g. Peerage letters and Ireland. Mrs Ponsonby stands very high on the list [?], & is even better. Glad to hear accounts of Lady G.

133. Lord Granville to Mr. Gladstone. [Add. MS. 44166, fo. 163]

Walmer Castle. Sep 28/69.

I trouble you with this correspondence,[3] because if Lord Russell persists in giving up the Michael and George, I shall have to consult you how to deal with the matter.

I saw Lord Russell after his letter of the 31st Aug. The only thing with which I can reproach myself is not having answered the one of Sept the 3d.

Last Friday I wrote to tell him of the death of Mme de Galliera's sister, a friend of his, and on Saturday I recd a packet directed in his handwriting *to me,*

c/o Gairdner Esq
St Michael & St George Office
London.

There was no letter with it. I wrote an indignant answer, which I have burnt, and sent an answer of which I enclose a copy.

[1] To Fortescue, 27 Sept., Add. MS. 44121, fo. 175; cf. above, no. 129 note.

[2] The rest of the letter has not survived in the original and is taken from the copy in Gladstone's letter-book, Add. MS. 44537, fo. 73.

[3] Russell to Granville, 2 Jan., 26, 31 Aug., 3, 26 Sept., Granville to Russell, 5 Jan., 28 Aug., 27 Sept., G.D. 29/79. Lords Derby, Grey and Russell were made G.C.M.G. in March 1869. Russell meanwhile had opened a controversy with Granville on colonial policy. The insignia of the order, sent in by Russell in connection with his investiture, came to Granville by mistake. Granville hastily concluded that the controversy had caused Russell to resign. Russell to Granville, 30 Sept., cleared up the matter, G.D. 29/79.

134. Lord Granville to Mr. Gladstone. [Add. MS. 44166, fo. 165]

Confidential. Walmer Castle. Sep 29/69.

I like your bishops very much, always supposing that A Hervey will please the (reasonably) low Church.

The letter to Fortescue appears to be the common sense of the matter.

I have had two letters in rather rapid succession from Clarendon,[1] and one today from Lowe.[2] The position of the latter is a difficult one, but he is too strong to be bound by cobwebs, he likes his present office, and has a profound distrust (for the present) of caves. It will require firmness & mildness on your part but I have little doubt of your succeeding with him, unless you proposed something extreme which would alarm the rest of the Cabinet.

I am more puzzled about Clarendon. He is always a tall talker, and generally not very determined in action. His normal state is a passion for office, but for the first time I quite believe the sincerity of his declarations that the work is too much for his impaired health, & he warned Fortescue the other day, that the question might break up the Cabinet. Cardwell was the strongest in his language last year. I do not know but I should not think he was the man to break up the Govt.

My language has been to Clarendon, and will be to Lowe, that the settlement of this question requires much give and take—that this process will be especially required in the Cabinet, and that the danger to be apprehended is not only on one side.

To tell the truth, I am not sure that the language in Ireland is so alarming as it seems. They always ask for more than they expect to get, and they make allowance for exaggerations to which they are all prone. On the [other] hand, it may make the Landlords (at all events the Irish Landlords, less hostile to a tolerably strong bill from us. I fancied that Fortescue would not have suggested anything very novel. His old bill, with a retrospective effect, and a necessity for a very solemn form for a contract, which would have the effect of putting aside the law we are about to create. I am curious therefore to hear what is the sensational portion.

Is Clanricarde's bill, so far as it goes, as good as it is assumed to be. It is the work of Tighe who drafted Carnarvon's clause.

I open my letter to say I have just read Clarendon's speech [3]—good on the Lords, and not bad on the land, but the less Ministers speak on the subject the better.

135. Lord Granville to Mr. Gladstone. [Add. MS. 44166, fo. 169]

Walmer Castle. Sep 30/69.

I beg your pardon for having found such a mare's nest, and troubled you with it.

[1] Cf. 17 Sept., on the possibility of a cabinet split on Irish land, G.D. 29/55. No further letters have been traced.

[2] Lowe to Granville, 28 Sept., is missing from G.D. 29/66.

[3] At Watford, 28 Sept., mainly a defence of the House of Lords, *The Times*, 29 Sept., p., 7.

My only consolation is that I burnt my indignant letter—and it is also satisfactory to find Lord Russell has not behaved so oddly.

I shall be much humiliated if you have come spontaneously to the same conclusion.

136. Mr. Gladstone to Lord Granville. [G.D. 29/57]

Hawarden. Oct 1. 1869.

I am disturbed and consoled by the packet you send me. It is deplorable to think of Lord R., who has done such great things, & whom individually I have only known as a faithful & generous colleague, performing such petulant acts, and broaching such preposterous proposals. It is comforting to see the real tenderness as well as tact with which you treat him: you forgive him 'seventy times seven'. And I cannot wonder at your not answering the letter of Sept. 3: for there is always a hope that nonsense may evaporate of itself if it is let alone and not precipitated by the cold touch of scorn into the solid.

I may interpret wrongly the rather brief sentence with which your note concludes. But I gather that the packet was addressed to you on the outside—and that it contained the emblems of the order.

We shall see what your kindly expostulation produces.

Have you any Royalties already in the order? If not, one or two of them might be the best *plaister* for any folly of Lord R's.

I have no doubt your Colonial Policy will be discussed, and attacked, in Parliament. I hope we shall all claim it as *ours*, & give it no half-hearted defence. And it so happens that we are very strong in Colonial men of different kinds: Cardwell, Childers, Lowe, Fortescue, Forster.[1]

As regards my suggestion above, you will remember Mr Canning & the Admiralty of 1827.

I saw Patten yesterday at Warrington & discussed Irish Land with him. He may have some little influence, & will wish to use it well. I left him Fitzgibbon's and Campbell's pamphlets.[2]

Unfortunately our baronets, who I had hoped would roll in a broadside from the Gazette, have gone off in a sputtering fire of rather ludicrous effect.

Temple has accepted: but I want to announce S.O. & A.H. first—then the others a few days later.

P.S. Why did you not let me see your indignant letter? I remember once coming across, in some Gallery, a storm by Claude. This would have made a good *pendant* to it.

[1] For Childers' career in Victoria, Australia, see E. Spencer Childers, *The Life and Correspondence of Hugh C. E. Childers* (1901), i. 23–78; for Lowe's career in New South Wales, see A. P. Martin, *Life and Letters of Robert Lowe* (1893), i. 144–402: The other three had served in the Colonial Office.

[2] Gerald Fitzgibbon, *Land Difficulty of Ireland, with an effort to solve it* (1869); see above, no. 123, Sir George Campbell, *The Irish Land . . . Part I. A visit in the spring. Part II. A visit in the autumn* (1869).

137. Mr. Gladstone to Lord Granville. [G.D. 29/57]

Private. Hawarden. Oct 2. 69.

1. The Bishops to be have all accepted. Keep Temple & A.H. & Mackarness *secret* for a few days. My inquiries about A. Hervey have been infinite: and the general result is that the Low will be mildly pleased with him. He has *charged* rather strongly against their antagonists.

2. If you have a mind for more explanations about Irish Land, I can send you a selection of the letters & papers which throw most light on the subject. They may occupy an hour to read, & will I think explain more than I could convey in a letter.

3. I feel embarrassed by the communications which you have received about Prince Arthur, and which I now return. My own opinion of the American Fenians is so bad, that I should incline to act upon the safe side, as it is called. But the two strictly official advisers in the matter I conceive to be Young as Gov. General, and Macdonald as Minister of Police. Upon the papers as they stand I think the Queen would let him go forward.[1]

4. If you approve my plan of campaign is on meeting in the end of Octr. to try to lay the foundation stones of our greater measures especially 1. Land, 2. Education [2]: to let the Cabinet learn about this affair of the Sultan & the Khedive: to settle the question of the Fenian prisoners: and also to consider the applications which have been made with regard to division of Dioceses and the appointment of Suffragans.[3] To separate after Lord Mayor's Day: and to meet again towards Dec. 1 when probably the Estimates will be ready and we may make further progress in Land and Education.[4]

I return to you herewith what seems to be part of a rough draft.

I am very glad if Westbury was pleased: we must all feel for him.

138. Lord Granville to Mr. Gladstone.[5] [G.D. 29/57]

Copy. Confidential. Walmer Castle. Oct. 3. 1869.

I have received the enclosed from Lowe.[6] I should be glad to know what language I had better use with him.

I shall tell him (if he comes before I hear from you) that I am for compensation for past as well as future improvements. That I fear this will not be sufficent to give real contentment—that I therefore should be glad to hear if he you or Fortescue have any plan not open to very great objections by which the occupier's

[1] On his tour of Canada; see above, no. 122.

[2] Cf. Gladstone to de Grey, 2 Oct., inviting him to prepare for a meeting of the cabinet 'to lay the foundation stone of our Educational Measure for England', Add. MS. 44537, fo. 78.

[3] Cf. W. L. Mathieson, *English Church Reform 1815–40* (1923), pp. 116–17, R. P. Davidson and W. Benham, *Life of Archbishop Tait* (1891), ii. 53–7. See below, nos. 143, 181, 183, 186.

[4] For the cabinets of 26, 30 Oct., 3, 5, 10 Nov., 7 Dec., see Add. MS. 44637, fos. 102–15.

[5] Granville to Gladstone, confidential, 3 Oct., on the affairs of the Prince of Wales, Add. MS. 44166, fo. 172, not printed.

[6] Lowe to Granville, 2 Oct., is missing from G.D. 29/66. Lowe visited Granville at Walmer on 6 Oct.

distrust of the strength of his Tenure will be changed into confidence, if not into security. That although from different sources of information to which you have referred me, I have some notion as to your views, I do not know them, and may be quite mistaken and therefore had rather not mention my conjectures.

I sent you a Telegram which I found from Lady Jocelyn last night, & I now enclose a letter which you will be good enough to burn.

I also send you a letter from the Archbishop, in favour of Mr Watkins. His grace knows that I had a high opinion of him as an Inspector. I will find out if I can, what are his politics in order that you may add his name for consideration when you consider your list for Ecclesiastical dignities, not being Parliamentary.

139. Mr. Gladstone to Lord Granville. [G.D. 29/57]

Hawarden. Oct. 4. 1869.

I am pleased but not surprised at the inclosure from Lord Russell. I have never found it was in his nature to be rude. The great evil of the correspondence I fear remains.

I have made a note on the Telegram within.

I shall *try* to get A. Hervey to Carlisle for which he would I think be particularly well fitted: but it may be too late. (*Private*)

I doubt the wisdom of Clarendon's *voces ambiguae* on Irish Land at this moment. But there is no great harm.

140. Mr. Gladstone to Lord Granville. [G.D. 29/57]

No 1.[1] Hawarden Castle. Oct 5. 69.

1. I am sorry to say I have not the Herbert letter here and I know not how to get it until I come up to London.

2. Nothing can be better I think than the language you propose to hold to Lowe. In case however you should like to know all I can tell you I send in a separate packet (and box) a set of letters upon the question. Please to return them, read or unread. I doubt whether Lowe precisely appreciates the nature of the charges, to which he has in former times been subjected. But he has moved so far from the extreme opinions he once or twice stated in the H. of C. about Irish Land, that I have good hope he may come up to the needful point.

I doubt whether we shall take the question on the 26th; more likely I think about the 30th.

3. I will record Mr Watkins's name but I observe you give no opinion of a very specific kind. For Capitular appointments I have half a score of names any one of which it would be difficult to set aside. I wish I could make over some of the applications to the L[or]d Ch[ancellor] and the Ch[ancellor] of the Duchy.

[1] Gladstone to Granville, No. 2 secret, 5 Oct., on the affairs of the Prince of Wales, G.D. 29/57, not printed.

141. Lord Granville to Mr. Gladstone. [Add. MS. 44166, fo. 176]

Walmer Castle. Oct 6/69.

Lowe is here—apparently in a good and reasonable humour. His plan about Irish Land is to establish Courts of Conciliation, or rather a Chairman of Quarter Sessions (who I believe is paid by the Govt) to adjudicate without regard to law upon all cases of injury, whether by the Landlord against the tenant, or the tenant against the Landlord.

This is just one of those plans which would be good if there was any general agreement about the constitution of such Courts, but the Landlords and perhaps the tenants would object to a number of third rate lawyers deciding in their different districts questions affecting property without any regard to the present principles of law, and without any new principles being laid down for their guidance.

I have to thank you very much for your approval of the substance of the N. Zealand despatch, and for your suggested improvements.[1] It is provoking that the Regiment has been detained twice, once by a naval officer, & secondly by the General, both disobeying distinct instructions.

I quite approve of your plan of campaign. I wish I could see in it a little moment of rest for you.

I will return Fortescue's papers etc. tomorrow.

I send you a note from Portsmouth.

You will bear with fortitude the criticism in anticipation of your appointment of a Bishop.

142. Lord Granville to Mr. Gladstone. [Add. MS. 44166, fo. 180]

Walmer Castle. Oct 7/69.

I have told Princess Christian, that however anxious you might be to meet Her wishes, I believed from a note I recd from you two days ago, you would find it impossible.[2]

I have answered Lady Jocelyn.

I return the papers which I have read with great interest, and I think fruit. You are certainly seeing daylight.

I have given no opinion to Lowe excepting on his own plan. I do not think he has studied the question much since his speech, but he seems full of his finance, and fond of his office, & ready to stretch his conscience as far as it can legitimately go. He seems very anxious to know how the cat will jump in the Cabinet.

I think a little communication with him, without showing your cards, would do good.

Adderley is here for tonight—pleasantly sound about Colonial defences, but I am afraid not a very clear headed advocate.

[1] See above, no. 128.

[2] Relates to an effort to find Mr. Engleheart, private secretary to Princess Christian, alternative employment; see the Queen to Granville, 10 March, 3 June (2 letters), 20, 25 June, 5 July, Granville to the Queen, 8 June, G.D. 29/32; the Queen to Gladstone, 7 Oct., Guedalla, i. 203.

143. Mr. Gladstone to Lord Granville. [G.D. 29/57]

Hawarden Castle. Oct 8.69.

1. Please to read these from the Chancellor & Archbishop [1]: & then send them to 10 Downing Street for Circulation. The subject will keep till we meet. The Archbishop does not show close or accurate political discernment in this matter.

2. The extract given with the inclosed letter is eminently disagreeable.[2] I do not regard our position as well established until we have disposed of Irish Land. Were that once done it would I think be right to reflect carefully what we could do towards making the political importance of personal conduct and repute more practically felt than it now is.

3. Portsmouth in his PS. thinks he is writing as a witness but really writes as a party. And it is very desirable to know the impressions of all parties. But my experience has not shown me that there is much difference between High & Low properly so called with regard to Dissenters: nor is it so easy to say which way the difference lies. No man ever stood better with his Dissenters than Hook: I am not sure that I might not add, even than Bp Hamilton. At a place near Liverpool, where I have property, the Clergyman [3] an old friend of mine & one of the Lowest Low, wished me *not to let any villa to a Dissenter*. However this is all speculation in the particular case.

4. I do not see how, in the matter of Irish Land, any thing is to be made of Courts of Conciliation authorised to inquire and judge at the instance of one party. It seems to me that we should as far as possible aim at even a rather rough settlement by Act of Parliament, leaving over no subjects except points of fact & everyday use, rather than smooth down our own difficulties by passing what would either be a dead letter or else set every body by the ears.

5. I think this Fenian business should be disposed of soon & will try to get the materials.

144. Mr. Gladstone to Lord Granville.[4] [G.D. 29/57]

Hawarden Castle. Oct 11.69.

1. I incline to think, and Glyn who is here agrees with me, that I should gently try the Queen a little farther when she comes southwards about Rothschild: but if it fails, as it probably may, that it is not worth while to try to substitute any name of the commercial class, from the difficulty of getting one thoroughly effective & unexceptionable.

2. I return Princess Christian's. I have myself had a direct Royal correspondence on the matter. I find the Queen at present pays E[ngleheart] his salary for doing nothing so that it is desirable to find him an employment. I however am hardly aware of any thing in my gift that would suit him.

[1] Tait to Gladstone, 5 Oct., on increasing the episcopate, Add. MS. 44330, fo. 119. He returned Hatherley to Gladstone, 27 Sept., on the same subject, Add. MS. 44205, fo. 60; see above, nos. 55, 137, below, nos. 181, 183, 186.

[2] Unidentified.

[3] William Rawson of Seaforth.

[4] Granville to Gladstone, 10 Oct., on the royal princes, Add. MS. 44166, fo. 182, not printed.

3. I have written to Spencer [1] for the definitive judgment of the Irish Govt. about the Fenians and I presume that if he says further release would not be safe I may at once, so far as you are concerned, reply in that sense? I had wished to submit the matter to the Cabinet: but the delay would be rather long.

145. Lord Granville to Mr. Gladstone. [Add. MS. 44166, fo. 184]

Private. Walmer Castle. Oct 13/69.

In your place I should make Mark Philipps [*sic*, read Philips] or Kirkman Hodgson, and Glyn's advice in this one instance is rather "sujet à caution". He has a filial wish, not unnatural, and which may weigh with you, that any other commercial Peerage in the same line, would diminish the honor to his father—I am however a little afraid that in so large a batch the commercial & manufacturing Class being only represented by one man, will not be thought enough. Bright's opinions as to the feelings of that class is shown by a recent example not to be very accurate. He told me that Bazley was much too sensible a man to accept a Peerage. After his jump at the Baronetage, I doubt there even being a show of "nolo episcopari" if he ever has the chance of a Barony.

I also doubt pressing the Queen again about Rothschild this time. She will yield, but reluctantly, and there will be criticism enough reaching Her, to confirm her in her opinion that she was a better judge than her Govt, and make her more difficult on another occasion. But pray do not be biassed by me in this matter—my opinion is not very strong.

2. I offered a small Governorship to Engleheart, after ascertaining from Rogers that he was a fit person. I did so to enable the Queen to relieve Princess Helena from him. But after all, it is a strong order, for the Royal family to select their own households without any consultation with Ministers, and then to expect the latter to find places for them, if they are incapable, or fussy in manner.

3. If I were an autocrat I would release all the Fenians notwithstanding the bluster of their friends, but as you are not quite in that position, and have a very difficult task before you, you had better do nothing for them at present. If your land bill passes notwithstanding sufficient opposition to make it popular in Ireland, and you could release them before fresh demands were made, it would probably do much good.

I am released from giving evidence in the "Leonard Edmunds' Scandal" arbitration.[2] I hope you are.[3]

146. Mr. Gladstone to Lord Granville. [G.D. 29/57]

Grosvenor Hotel, Chester. O.15.69.

1. It will be time enough to speak about Rothschild when we meet on the 26th.

[1] 8 Oct., Add. MS. 44306, fo. 154.

[2] Leonard Edmunds, clerk to the patents, resigned with a pension after accusations of misappropriation of public money. He claimed compensation and a court of arbitration was constituted to try his claims, *L.J.* (1868–69), 469, 523. It decided against him.

[3] Granville crossed out a last sentence: 'Fetherstone and Dillon Bell will arrive in London from New Zealand in December [for loan negotiations]'.

2. If Engleheart declined an offer that he might fairly have been expected to accept, his claim is very weak whether on Queen or public.

3. I am framing a negative reply about the Fenians. You I think exactly hit the nail on the head.

4. All has gone enormously well here.[1] The Prince spoke about Herbert's affair (Muckruss) & seemed to think it had put *him* in a false position.

It is well that New Zealand is already covered by a decision which I suppose you will make known by Telegraph.[2]

Every body I am glad to say seems much pleased with Goodwin.

Temple writes [3] that he has had friendly letters from the Archbishop, & Bps of London Ely Oxford & Worcester, also Archdn Phillpotts & many clergy.

147. Lord Granville to Mr. Gladstone. [Add. MS. 44166, fo. 188]

Confidential. Walmer Castle. Oct 16/69.

Notwithstanding the injunction in the last para, I send you a letter from my brother which seems to me to be interesting.

Another violent letter from Lord Russell.[4]

" You adopt the arbitrary traditions of the Colonial Office—those derived from Ld Bathhurst, James Stephen and Henry Taylor are too arbitrary & despotic for my taste."

" What set my teeth on edge was your saying " etc.[5]

" If the Natives are loyal subjects you should give them protection and enforce fair terms. If enemies in arms against the Queen's Authority, you should assist a Govt set up by Pakington and me, and Parliament " (Ego et Rex meus).

148. Mr. Gladstone to Lord Granville. [G.D. 29/57]

Hawarden Castle. Oct 18.69.

I return Lord Portsmouth's of the 10th.

What I should like to know from him is his view of the *mode* of legislating upon " tenant right " in Ireland, if, as it seems, some legislation on that subject has become necessary.

I cannot see my way to making it by compulsion universal.

The Cabinet is fixed for *three* tomorrow week : and Clarendon will throw off chiefly by narrative our foreign affairs. I wish however that the aspect of the question between the Sultan and the Khedive may be better than it now is.

Fortescue wishing to make a short run, I have promised him not to go to Irish affairs until the end of the week.

[1] During the Prince of Wales's visit to Chester.

[2] See above, nos. 128, 141.

[3] 14 Oct., Add. MS. 44421, fo. 180.

[4] 15 Oct., on Britain's policy in New Zealand, G.D. 29/79.

[5] Russell continued, 'that Great Britain would be neutral between the British Colonists and the Natives'.

This evening my refusal of a further release of Fenians goes off.[1] I believe we are unanimous in that sense.

As I am wanted here on the 25th, I mean to go up on the morning of the 26th.

The Prince's demeanour at Chester was admirable to a degree, alike genial and dignified. And the old City behaved right well.

I feel confident that no great mischief can arise from the row about Temple.[2]

149. Mr. Gladstone to Lord Granville. [G.D. 29/57]

Hawarden Castle. Oct. 20.69.

1. I know that Cowie's merits are very great.[3] But it appears to me that the Dean of Ely to be should be Evangelical. Goodwin is no party man but with reference to Carlisle this is a great offence in the eyes of determined party men of that kind. The Record entirely declines to own Arthur Hervey. One of the artifices of theological party-spirit is to decline to give credit for a man at all, unless he is an out & out partisan, but an out & out partisan of any kind is just what I do not wish to be responsible for recommending.

2. The sphere of the anti Temple agitation will be narrow. The *congé* will issue immediately.

3. Thanks for your brother's interesting letters. Fortescue is apt to be tenacious. I have incited him [4] to draw out a plan for extending the Ulster custom over Ireland. It is early for details but I think the general scope of his notions is such as you would not disapprove: according to what I can yet see of them.

4. The Office of Works arrangement appears to be a brilliant success: Layard, Lowe, Stansfield, pleased: Ayrton in perfect raptures.[5]

5. From the inclosed of Lord R[ussell] you will see that I have come in for the sunshine—He likes a bantering letter.

[1] Gladstone to Henry O'Shea and others, 18 Oct., answering memorials for the release of Fenians, Add. MS. 44422, fo. 216. The reply was concerted with Fortescue; see correspondence 12, 17, 18 Oct., Add. MS. 44121, fos. 190, 204, 209. Cf. also Gladstone to Bright, 13 Oct., Add. MS. 44537, fo. 95. For Spencer's view see mem. and letter, 12 Oct., Add. MS. 44306, fos. 158, 164.

[2] Arising from both evangelical and high church opposition to his consecration as bishop of Exeter, owing to his contribution to *Essays and Reviews* of 1860, see correspondence in Add. MS. 44423, *passim*.

[3] Granville to Gladstone, 18 Oct., applying for clerical preferment for Benjamin Cowie, Add. MS. 44166, fo. 190, not printed.

[4] To Fortescue, 19 Oct., Add. MS. 44121, fo. 219.

[5] Layard went from the chief commissionership of works to the mission at Madrid, Clarendon to Layard, 4 Oct., and reply 11 Oct., Layard papers, Add. MS. 38997, fo. 6; Layard to Gladstone, 12 Oct., Add. MS. 44422, fo. 158. Ayrton moved from the secretaryship of the Treasury to the Board of Works, Gladstone to Ayrton, 13 Oct., and reply 15 Oct., Add. MS. 44422, fos. 168, 187. Stansfield replaced Ayrton as joint secretary to the Treasury.

150. Mr. Gladstone to Lord Granville.[1] [G.D. 29/57]

Most Private. Hawarden Castle. Oct 24.69.

Pray read the inclosed very secret letter from Maguire.[2]

I have inclosed to Sir W. Knollys a private letter to the Prince, to serve the purpose of the moment, if he should come to town.

Perhaps Bruce should arrange to have a confidential person sent down from Dublin to see Maguire?

I leave early on Tuesday.

The Temple agitation will not I think be very formidable. A majority of the Chapter will elect.

Dean Wellesley thinks there is a precedent for a Jew Irish Peer, Sir Sampson Gideon or some such name. If so surely he should draw in our Lionel.[3]

151. Lord Granville to Mr. Gladstone. [Add. MS. 44166, fo. 194]

Colonial Office. Oct 25/69.

I have read your letter and enclosure.

I can only return a like present.

If the Dean is right, I am all for insistance [*sic*].[4]

152. Lord Granville to Mr. Gladstone. [Add. MS. 44166, fo. 197]

Private. Colonial Office. Oct 29.1869.

I heard you tell Glyn the other day that you would not place your son [5] in the Treasury after having exercised so much pressure on Clarendon to make a vacancy for Ayrton—that if you did so, Clarendon would be of opinion that you exercised that pressure from a selfish object.

I thought you were mistaken, but said nothing, as I knew no more than yourself.

Yesterday however I committed an indiscretion, which I hope is pardonable. I told Clarendon confidentially what had occurred.

He at once said that he had disliked appointing Layard,[6] because it was unfair to the Corps—but that he had attributed your request exclusively to the difficulties created by Lowe and Ayrton, that he should still be of that opinion, if you were to appoint your son, and that he hoped I would tell you, to do what you thought desirable, without any fear of exciting an unfounded suspicion on his part.

P.S. Clarendon approves, & adds that what he said was perfectly sincere.

[1] Gladstone to Granville, copy, 21 Oct., on commissionership of customs, Add. MS. 44537, fo. 104, Granville to Gladstone, 25 Oct., on Prince of Wales and police protection, Add. MS. 44166, fo. 195, not printed.

[2] Untraced, but Gladstone's reply, 24 Oct., indicates Fenian threats as the subject and proposes as in the third paragraph, Add. MS. 44537, fo. 112.

[3] Baron Rothschild. For Sir Sampson Gideon, created Baron Eardley, see *G.E.C.* v. 1–2.

[4] Gladstone wrote on the back, 26 Oct., an instruction to verify the information about Sir Sampson Gideon.

[5] W. H. Gladstone, see above, no. 5 note.

[6] Cf. Clarendon to Granville, 17 Sept., on his yielding to Gladstone's pressure, G.D. 29/55.

153. Mr. Gladstone to Lord Granville. [G.D. 29/57]

10, Downing Street. Oct 29.69.

If you are so disposed I am sure there can be no harm in writing to Cook not to incite but to thank him.[1] He has behaved admirably.

Many thanks for your kindness about Clarendon. I give in.

154. Mr. Gladstone to Lord Granville.[2] [G.D. 29/57]

11, Carlton House Terrace. Oct. 31.69.

This is the very disappointing answer I have received from the Chancellor[3] to a suggestion I made that *if* all other expedients fail we might put ourselves fairly in a condition to keep Sullivan by pressure if we told him that he would be considered a qualified candidate for an English Puisne Judgeship (of course saving the claims of the Law Officers [])].

The truth is that the appointment of Mr D[owse] to an office of £5000 a year for life is little short of ludicrous; and the interposition of a man of six times his ability would if it had the effect of putting it a little back be a public advantage.

Bishop Magee was a great success[4]: but *that* is an open profession!

Failing other means I really do not know how to avoid returning to the charge. Perhaps you, if you agree in this view, can broach the Chancellor for me, if the case of need arise, which I shall know tomorrow.

155. Lord Granville to Mr. Gladstone. [Add. MS. 44166, fo. 203]

Private. Walmer. Nov 1/69.

I send you a good letter of refusal from the Duchess of Grafton.[5] I am glad you allowed me to sound her in your name. I will look over the list of Earls.

I send you a letter from Dr Cook. I have written to Fortescue. Please send Cook's letter to the Chancellor, or return it to me tomorrow for that purpose.

I am not much surprised at the Chancellor, but I agree entirely with you. If you remember I wished you to make Keogh an English judge in order to make a place for O'Loughlin [*sic*, read O'Loghlen].

I should think it would be easy to select 2 or 3 colleagues to argue with the Chancellor.

[1] Canon Cook contributed to still the opposition in the chapter to the consecration of Temple as bishop of Exeter; cf. Lingen to Granville, 29 Oct., G.D. 29/74.

[2] Granville to Gladstone, 31 Oct., on honour for Torrens McCullagh, Add. MS. 44166, fo. 201, not printed.

[3] Hatherley to Gladstone, 31 Oct., Add. MS. 44205, fo. 69. Sullivan wished to give up the Irish attorney-generalship and his seat in the Commons, but Gladstone considered him indispensable on Irish questions; he had drafted the Irish Church bill; cf. Gladstone to Spencer, 29 Oct., Add. MS. 44537, fo. 121; below, nos. 166, 175.

[4] In moving from Irish to English public life: he was dean of Dublin 1866–68 and bishop of Peterborough 1868–91.

[5] Relates to the mistress-ship of the robes vacated by the duchess of Argyll.

But keep Sullivan you must. It was impossible to open the question the other day in a more acceptable manner to the Cabinet, than he did.[1] How is Barry to succeed in England,[2] when E. Howard & J. Acton failed. Besides I am told by Monsell that although excellent on principles, he is not equally good on details.

I have asked Glyn to give me a dinner tomorrow.

156. Lord Granville to Mr. Gladstone. [Add. MS. 44166, fo. 205]

Colonial Office. 4/11 [1869].

A popular fête in the open air in November, is not attractive in itself.[3] But is it quite clear that the Queen ought to go in state to the City without any of Her Ministers being present.

It might be construed into a want of courtesy on the part of ministers, or on the part of the city—or as a proof of the indifference of the Queen.

Would it not be as well for West to make some enquiry *quietly* at the Home Office and Chamberlain's office, as to former precedents, and what the present state of the case is.

157. Mr. Gladstone to Lord Granville. [Add. MS. 44537, fo. 126]

[*Copy*]. 4 November 1869.

I strongly advise the circulation of Ld Portman's paper, wh: is a notable sign of the times. Though I do not suppose his plan in itself to be the right one, the question of the law of Distress must come under review whether for abolition or retention.

158. Lord Granville to Mr. Gladstone. [Add. MS. 44166, fo. 207]

Colonial Office. Nov 6/69.

The Duke of Leinster I hear once refused the Garter because he had before refused the riband of his own country.

159. Mr. Gladstone to Lord Granville. [G.D. 29/57]

11, Carlton House Terrace. Nov. 9. 69.

By the letter within you will see that Beaumont declines.[4] I suppose it would hardly do to press him: but I should be glad to know your opinion.

[1] For cabinet of 30 Oct. where Sullivan advised on the drafting of the land bill, see Add. MS. 44637, fo. 104; cf. Gladstone to Fortescue, 27 Oct., Add. MS. 44537, fo. 117.

[2] I.e. as a Roman Catholic representing an English constituency in the Commons.

[3] Relates to the Queen's opening of Blackfriars Bridge, 6 Nov.

[4] Beaumont on 8 Nov. declined the peerage offered on 6th, Add. MSS. 44537, fo. 130, 44423, fo. 34.

160. Lord Granville to Mr. Gladstone. [Add. MS. 44166, fo. 210]

16, Bruton Street. Nov 9/69.

If Leinster refuses, and you do not press Norfolk or accept de Grey, I think you might sound Bessborough for himself, the model Irish Landlord, the high officer of State, and the old household servant of the Queen.

He probably would refuse, then what do you think as the Queen does not like youth, of offering her old age—Stratford de Redcliffe, & St Germains.[1]

I would not press Beaumont. He would be a reed indeed to lean upon, if he came to the H. of Lords as a favor to the Govt.

As a substitute if you propose one how about Biddulph.

Beaumont must refuse from one of two reasons. Either he means to oppose us on the Irish Bill, or he is afraid of being so near his father in law,[2] when supporting our bill.

161. Lord Granville to Mr. Gladstone.[3] [Add. MS. 44166, fo. 216]

Confidential. Windsor Castle. Nov 21/69.

The Queen has said nothing to me about politics, excepting to express doubts of our Colonial policy, and strong objections against our economy. H.M's principal objections to the latter were 1° that England was being reduced to the state of a second rate power, and 2° that it would be disadvantageous to the Sovereign if all places available for old Household servants were abolished.

She told me in great confidence that the Peers are in great perplexity about a leader, that Cairns has positively resigned, that Salisbury is impracticable about Dizzy, and that Malmesbury is doing his best, but as yet without success to conciliate them. She thinks that it will end in Derby.

It may be convenient to you to know what some of our Colleagues are saying about land. Hartington says that as we have got beyond compensation for improvements, he agrees in the reasoning which brings us to Ulster tenant right. Clarendon is more violent than ever against it. He had passed an evening with Chi Fortescue, who " away from Sullivan, had nothing to say of any value in favor of his plan ".

Argyll says that he had rather break up the Govt than consent to anything so indefensible.[4]

Bright is for breaking up entails, & facilitating transfer of land, as a right thing to do, and for some plan like his own to please the tenants. But upon my

[1] Two garter vacancies were created by the deaths of Lord Derby and the marquis of Westminster. The Queen objected to the offer of one to the duke of Norfolk. On 8 Nov. it was offered to Lord Leinster who refused, Add. MS. 44537, fo. 132. Bessborough suggested to Granville, Lords Stratford de Redcliffe and St. Germans, 7 Nov., G.D. 29/71. It was offered to the former and accepted. The second was refused by Lords Portsmouth and Bessborough (to Granville, 22 Nov. *ibid.*) but accepted by de Grey.

[2] Lord Clanricarde.

[3] Granville to West, 15 Nov., on an advance in the peerage for Lord Saye and Sele, Add. MS. 44166, fo. 212, not printed.

[4] Such as ' Universal Tenant Right ', Argyll to Granville, 12 Nov., G.D. 29/51.

saying that my wish was to support you, he answered that that was exactly his feeling.

Dizzy succeeded Bright here—the last phrase I heard from him, was addressed to the K. of the Belgians " I will record it, Sire, in my heart ".

162. Mr. Gladstone to Lord Granville. [Add. MS. 44166, fo. 220]

[*Copy*]. *Secret.* Hawarden Castle. 21. Nov. 1869.

1. I have written to de Grey.[1]

2. Foley's death grieves me on every ground. Who should be appointed? Why should we not put on a young Peer maintaining the former understanding as to work [2]—either Morley or Camperdown & which?

3. As yet I can see my way to no better basis for Irish Land than this (on the nicely contested points) to lengthen the presumptive term of tenure (now a year) and of notice to quit (now 6 months) to secure to the tenant his own improvements, to legalize the Ulster Custom where it prevails, & to establish beyond that range an option as follows (a) tenant right presumed in all cases, with a materium for the good will of say six years of a fair rent.

(b) but this may be barred by the grant, or offer, from the landlord of a 31 years lease, at the old or a fair rent, with compensation at the end of it for permanent improvements. How does this look to you? or have you been able to work your way further into the " bowels of the " question? It does not wholly satisfy me but I see as yet nothing better. We are much grieved at the Archbishop's illness.

Proposed for Cabinets

Dec 7, 9, 10, 14, 16, 17, & again in Christmas week if necessary—Will this do? [3]

163. Lord Granville to Mr. Gladstone. [Add. MS. 44166, fo. 222]

Walmer Castle. Nov 23 [1869].

I attacked the Ailesbury's for having misled me as to Lord Normanton's politics —Their answer was that they have for years heard him fight on the liberal side against all his Tory Barrington relations, and that just before they asked me to put his name on your list,[4] they separately asked him about his feelings as regarded you—& his answer was " I have approved of everything he has hitherto done, & I have full confidence in him for the future ".

Who can write history? You however can make it.

[1] Offering the garter, 21 Nov., Add. MS. 44537, fo. 145.

[2] Lord Foley had combined the offices of captain of the corps of gentlemen at arms and second government whip in the Lords. Lord Normanby succeeded him in the Household office and Lord Cork and the duke of St. Albans jointly in the parliamentary, Bessborough to Granville, 27 Nov., G.D. 29/71.

[3] This programme was kept with the addition of 29 Dec., see Add. MS. 44637, fos. 115–34.

[4] For a baronage. He was created Baron Somerton, April 1873. Lady Normanton was the daughter of Viscount Barrington.

164. Lord Granville to Mr. Gladstone. [Add. MS. 44166, fo. 224]

Private. Walmer Castle. Nov 23/69.

I cannot say how sorry I am for Foley—one of the most straightforward, honorable men I know. In the House of Lords, the first to come the last to go, & with all that geniality of support which is so much wanted.

I should like to have a little time to think about his successor. Glyn would recommend Monson as a genius for whipping, but Bessborough would probably reject him as a low fellow.[1]

I should be glad if you were in the first place to sound Cowper whether he would take the place, coupled with official employment. He is now an important person, & much older than the 2 Household official Peers. As between the two, I think Morley should have the preference.

The Cabinets suit me to a day.

I will write again about Irish land.

165. Lord Granville to Mr. Gladstone. [Add. MS. 44166, fo. 226]

Walmer. Nov 29 [1869].

Rogers & the Canada Rose are here. You may have seen that McDougall the designate Governor of the Hudson's Bay Territory has been driven away from the Red River it is said by half breed Trappers with some Irish assistance—the Farmers twice the number being anxious for a settled Govt. It the Rioters are long successful, it may demoralize the Natives, & destroy the Trade. The Treasury only consented to the terms of the Guarantee two or three days ago—so that the transfer has not yet been made although the Barings have had orders to pay it on the first of next month.

In these circumstances the Canadian Govt, say they cannot accept the transfer until tranquility be restored. Rose forbids (by order from Canada) the money being paid. Hudson's Bay say they have a legal right to it, and if they claim their right to make the surrender, I do not see even if we wished it, how we could defer accepting it, and completing *in form* the transfer to Canada—the fix may be great. We could not force the Territory upon Canada if they put up their backs.[2] On the other hand Rose and Sir Curtis Lampson are sensible conciliatory men. The former is going to telegraph to his Govt to say that he has found me anxious to settle the matter, but that he appreciated my difficulties—and he will ask them whether they will accept the transfer at once, if I promise during one year only to use the Queen's name, which is all powerful with the Natives, and the use of one Company of Colonial Rifles, belonging to the Regiment about to be disbanded, on terms of payment to be settled between Canada, Hudson Bay Co, & us.

[1] Cf. Bessborough to Granville, 22 and 27 Nov., G.D. 29/71.

[2] The Act of Surrender of Rupert's Land by the Hudson's Bay Company to the Queen was signed, 19 Nov. The land was to be transferred to Canada on 1 Dec. Cf. *Proceedings* [*on*] *the Guarantee of a Loan to be raised by Canada for a Payment in respect of Rupert's Land.* Parl. papers. H.C. 315 (1870). xlix, 365–8. Canada refused to accept the transfer during the rebellion; see Young to Granville, tel., 26 Nov., C.O. 42/678, and below, no. 208.

I propose to ask the H.B to let me know what they wish as to surrender, but I do not at the present moment give them any advice.

If you can make head or tail of this statement, will you tell me whether I may promise the Company of Canadian Rifles, in case they are wanted some months hence. Rose believes the promise will be sufficient.

166. Lord Granville to Mr. Gladstone. [Add. MS. 44166, fo. 230]

Walmer. Nov 30/69.

Your note to Chich gratified my organ of destructiveness. My only fear is that he will neither show it, nor tell the substance of it to Sullivan, who may possibly be shaky.[1]

The two first paras of the enclosed letter are about the Lord Acton's Peerage —the remainder is worth your reading.[2]

I am afraid my post prandial letter to you about Red River was far from clear.

167. Mr. Gladstone to Lord Granville.[3] [Add. MS. 44166, fo. 231]

[*Copy*]. *Private.* Dec. 1. 69.

I send you a letter of Argyll's with my reply.[4] I do not think he has much studied or got up the subject of Irish Tenant right, and he is not unfrequently misled by the rapid facility of his active mind. His minute was warm [and] the temperature [of] his letter is not lower. I have my fears lest he should be the Rupert of debate in the Cabinet.

It is rather awkward to talk at this stage (as you reported) of breaking up the Government! And that is more easily said than done.

You may remember that when we projected our moderate bill of 1866, he was the most reluctant of all the then Ministers.

All these matters will require the utmost care. In the mean time I am desirous that you should know what is going on. In case you have any *good* opportunity of dropping a word in season.

I do not trouble you with the Gray correspondence.[5]

[1] See Gladstone to Fortescue, 27 Nov., answering Fortescue of 26 Nov., Add. MS. 44122, fos. 29, 25. Fortescue wanted to fill up the mastership of the rolls (Ireland). Gladstone wished to keep it free for Sullivan if, after six months' rest, he should still wish to resign the attorney-generalship; cf. Gladstone to Spencer, 1 Nov., Add MS. 44537, fo. 123, and above, no. 155, below, no. 175.

[2] Untraced, but may be Acton to Granville described by the latter to Clarendon, 4 Dec., as a 'philippic against Manning', G.D. 29/55; cf. below, no. 169.

[3] Gladstone to Granville, 1 Dec., answering no. 165 has not been traced though entered in the letter-book, Add. MS. 44538, fo. 8.

[4] Argyll to Gladstone, 29 Nov., deprecated 'heroic remedies' for Ireland and enclosed a minute of arguments against the extension of tenant right. Gladstone's reply, 1 Dec., enclosed a mem. of counter arguments; see Add. MS. 44101, fos. 90, 96, 104, and Argyll, *Autobiography and Memoirs* (1906), ii. 253–6. Cf. Morley, ii. 289–90.

[5] Cf. Gladstone to Sir John Gray, 28 Nov., on Irish land, Add. MS. 44423, fo. 233.

168. Lord Granville to Mr. Gladstone. [Add. MS. 44166, fo. 233]

Walmer. Dec 1/69.

I am inexcusable. I did not [1] send you the end of J. Acton's letter.

I am sorry to say that I have had two letters running from Clarendon [2] talking of the certainty of the Gov being broken up, " that no honest man could consent to the extension of Tenant right, even if he had not land in England, where tenants were watching what would come of the Irish agitation.["]

169. Mr. Gladstone to Lord Granville. [G.D. 29/57]

Private. Hawarden Castle. Dec. 2. 69.

I return Acton's most interesting letter. He sent a similar one to me.[3] I am warned not to write to him on such matters through the Roman Post Office.

Anxious & almost incessant consideration thus far go to convince me that Fortescue, though he had sadly underestimated his difficulties, and was thin & poor in the business of defending his plan in the Cabinet, was much nearer the rights of the case than any who were inclined to object to it.

My conversations with Halifax last week led me to encourage him to write a paper. It has just come & seems to me *satisfactory* in the main, which is important.[4] It will I hope reach you by Monday.

It *may* be politic to revive the idea of last year respecting him.[5] We shall see.

170. Lord Granville to Mr. Gladstone. [Add. MS. 44166, fo. 235]

[4 December 1869].

Thanks for the correspondence. I have written 8 pages to Argyll [6] which in a different way will have I hope a certain effect upon him. He is so well conditioned, and so much attached to you, that there is no danger of him in the last resort, but he [is] impulsive and fizzing, & fond of discussion and he might do more mischief with others than he would wish.

171. Mr. Gladstone to Lord Granville. [G.D. 29/57]

Hawarden Castle. Dec. 6. 69.

I shall hope to see you tomorrow forenoon in Downing Street where I shall be: I mean before Cabinet.

This note will indicate that I am come.

[1] A short passage crossed out here cannot be deciphered.

[2] 30 Nov., from which Granville quotes, and 1 Dec., to which Granville replied, 1 Dec.: ' we ought . . . to find the line . . . of doing not too much but enough ', G.D. 29/55.

[3] Rome, 24 Nov., on preparations for the proclamation of papal infallibility and Manning's plans to counter episcopal opposition, Add. MS. 44093, fo. 92.

[4] Halifax to Gladstone, 1 Dec., with enclosure, on Irish land. See also resulting correspondence, 2, 7, 8 Dec.; Add. MS. 44184, fos. 271, 275–85, 286, 288, 292.

[5] In 1868 he was offered a seat in the cabinet without office, Gladstone to Halifax, 12, 17 Dec., and replies 15, 18 Dec., Add. MS. 44184, fos. 240, 241, 247, 248.

[6] Confidential, 4 Dec., discouraging talk about breaking up the government on the Irish land question, copy, G.D. 29/51.

172. Lord Granville to Mr. Gladstone. [Add. MS. 4416, fo. 236]

16, Bruton Street. Dec 7/69.

Nothing could be more amiable & right than Argyll today during a 5 minutes conversation.

Hartington I think is not unreasonable.

Cardwell & Lowe agreed to the Chancellor's Mem [1] before it was sent to you.

173. Mr. Gladstone to Lord Granville. [G.D. 29/57]

11, Carlton House Terrace. Dec. 11. 69.

The menacing intimation you conveyed to me yesterday is but too fully confirmed by the inclosed letter.[2]

Without waiting to consult you I pray him to delay any thought of resignation, if he can contrive to do what may be indispensable in his office, until time shall show what course things are likely to take.

I return on Monday, rather late.

174. Mr. Gladstone to Lord Granville. [G.D. 29/57]

11 C.H.T. D 13/69.

Can you come to my house at twelve tomorrow, about Irish Land, for the redaction of brief propositions which may serve to bring the deliberations of the Cabinet a little to a head.[3]

175. Mr. Gladstone to Lord Granville. [G.D. 29/57]

11, Carlton House Terrace. Dec. 16. 69.

Sullivan came to me again yesterday to press for a final acceptance of his resignation.[4]

I told him the question was too important to allow me to act without the Cabinet.

Dowse is impossible; either Sherlock or O'Loghlen alone available. Either of them 'infinitely' inferior to Barry: but Barry cannot be brought in.

I told him I should state in the Cabinet that in my opinion two points ought to be considered and settled on one side before he took or pleaded finally any medical opinion.

1. What remission of Parl. labour we could arrange for him.

[1] On land tenure in Ireland, printed copy, G.D. 29/25A.

[2] Argyll to Gladstone, 9 Dec., offering to resign since his wife's illness prevented his coming to London, Add. MS. 44101, fo. 129. The Duchess recovered and the idea was dropped. Granville to Gladstone, 12 Dec., returning Argyll's letter and commenting on his exaggeration, Add. MS. 44166, fo. 237, not printed.

[3] For cabinet, 14 Dec., see Add. MS. 44637, fo. 130.

[4] Cf. Sullivan to Gladstone, 15, 20 Dec., Add. MS. 44423, fos. 312, 333, 343. The cabinet of 16 Dec. agreed to try to keep Sullivan, but in Gladstone's absence did not decide how to ease his work, Granville's note, Add. MS. 44637, fo. 131. Sullivan then resigned and became master of the rolls. Cf. above, nos. 155, 166.

2. What arrangement could be made *virtually* to hold over for him the Mastership of the Rolls.

On the first I think we ought to absolve him from all general attendance in H. of C.

On the second I have some ideas which I have talked over with West but they are crude: want of knowledge of the Irish Bench & Bar very much disables me. But I am confident something could be arranged if public spirit prevails.

176. Lord Granville to Mr. Gladstone. [Add. MS. 44166, fo. 239]

Dec 22/12 [*sic*] [1869].

I suppose you will recommend Annie Sutherland.[1] A Tory Dow Duchess would never do, and I presume you would not press her against her will to take the Duchess of Cleveland.

Had you not better write direct to the Queen, and to Annie.

177. Lord Granville to Mr. Gladstone. [Add. MS. 44166, fo. 240]

Walmer Castle. Dec 23/69.

I have a little more Irish Land gossip for you.

Bessborough says that he had been rebuked in London for having encouraged you to be in communication with Sir John Gray, but that in conversation with the Chancellor O'Hagan, the latter spontaneously said to him "the success or reverse of the Land Bill depends on the Freeman's Journal. If it says we accept this as fixity of tenure, every priest will say the same, and vice versâ." Bessborough adds "without going quite to that extent I agree in the view of the Chancellor, and think it wise to make a friend of the Mammon of unrighteousness. Gray is a rogue, and it would not do for Gladstone to put himself in any way in his power, but communication short of that is I am sure right."[2]

So much for the Irish view—now for the English. Lowe "oppressed by a feeling of heavy responsibility and an apprehension of serious danger", and writing to me to avoid anything like a contest with you, asks whether it is not possible to make some concession in order to relieve the position of those who will be driven to choose between their most serious convictions and their allegiance to their party, and the Govt of which they are members.

He says "the Minority of the Cabinet agree to compensation for improvements prospective and retrospective. To the reversal of the presumption of law as to the making of improvements. To the fixing of a limit of 10£ within which the right of the tenant to compensation for eviction shall be absolute. To the right of all new tenants at will to compensation on eviction. The issue is thus narrowed down to a single point. Will you insist on forcing the landlord under an existing lease at will where no custom can be proved, to pay a fine to his tenant on eviction otherwise than for [non-]payment of rent?"

[1] For mistress-ship of the robes, *vice* the duchess of Argyll. Cf. above, no. 155 note.

[2] Bessborough to Granville, 20 Dec., G.D. 29/71.

His arguments are those he used in the Cabinet.

I admit to him that he has a right to appeal to me for what help I can give in his very difficult position, because I have ventured to advise him to be moderate and conciliatory, and think that he has hitherto followed that advice.

I am not a lawyer or a practical land owner, and have not read or thought over one tenth of what Gladstone has on this question—what hope should I have of arguments availing in my mouth, which have not prevailed in that of his (Lowe) and of Cardwell's. I agree that if Bright and some half a dozen more of us had joined the minority it would have [had] considerable influence over Gladstone. But what was the state of the case etc etc. giving him the arguments the other way—telling him that [I] would write again in a few days.[1]

I suspect this is the last great effort, but his position is a difficult one, his amour propre is, and will be still more strongly, engaged. Can you send me a few lines which I would forward to him, not argumentation, but showing that you attach importance to his opinions, and would be glad to meet them short of producing a measure which would not suffice to grapple with the evil.

178. Mr. Gladstone to Lord Granville. [G.D. 29/57]

Hawarden Castle. Dec. 24. 69.

I am rather more staggered than you at the branch of the alternative which it is proposed to choose in the matter of the Mistress-ship of the Robes: and I have written confidentially to consult Argyll. Writing in the meantime to the Queen and telling her.

I send Lord C. Fitzroy's letter to her straight.

She has I suppose concluded that the Dss of Roxburghe whom I believe she likes greatly as Lady in Waiting is not in the running for the Robes.

I am sorry the Episcopal opposition to the Bishop of Exeter's consecration waxed so considerable in amount. Every Derby and Dizzy Bishop joined it, which looks a little political. *None* of the oldest Bishops Chichester St Davids St Asaph Winchester. The Daily News observed with some truth that it was a blow to establishment.

A happy Xmas & New Year to you & Lady Granville.

179. Mr. Gladstone to Lord Granville. [G.D. 29/57]

Hawarden Castle. Dec. 26. 69.

Please to read the accompanying letter [2] from Sir John Young & send it in an envelope to Lady Herbert at Wilton.

Tomorrow I hope to write to you about Irish Land in the sense you describe. Meantime many thanks for your letter.

Wishing you a happy Christmas time . . .

The passage I wish you specially to see is in p. 8.

[1] Lowe to Granville, 21 Dec., Granville to Lowe, copy, 23 Dec., G.D. 29/66.

[2] Young to Lady Herbert on the Fenians in Canada and America and Prince Arthur's journey forwarded by Lady Herbert to Gladstone; cf. Gladstone to Lady Herbert, 27 Dec., Add. MS. 44538, fo. 29.

180. Mr. Gladstone to Lord Granville.[1] [G.D. 29/57]

Hawarden Castle. Dec: 27: 1869.

The contest, so to call it, among us upon Irish Land has been no more than that twofold contest which is the best foundation of hope, and the only, or rather the indispensable condition, of success in difficult questions: first, rivalry in the desire to bring out fully, and from their root the difficulties of the subject, and secondly, a like rivalry in the endeavour to overcome them by patience and goodwill. No members of the Cabinet have shown more of the second, than those who have most keenly felt the first; and of this Lowe's letter to you is plainly a notable example. Of our 'Quinquarticular' basis, the difficulty now stated relates to *one* article: and the suggestion is that assuming our provisions about Improvements, Ulster Custom, and Custom beyond Ulster, we should, when we have passed this frontier, further legislate only to the extent that below a certain limit of rent, tenants shall receive compensation for eviction; but not above that limit.

The first question that arises is, what is that limit to be, or to represent?

If it is to represent the point at which eviction means in practice an addition to the pauperism of the country, I think such a plan must be admitted to rest on an intelligible principle.

It might represent something totally different; namely the point at which, in Ireland, we find the bidders for farms as independent, as much on a footing of equality in the market with the tenderers of farms for hire, as they are in Great Britain. If this were the aim of the limit, again I admit that such a plan, too, rests on an intelligible principle. It carries legislation as far as at first sight the facts of the Irish case require, and there it stops. It does not lay down a precedent for England and Scotland. The objections to it are entirely of a practical order. It runs the risk of offending men, few in number, but the select men, the natural leaders of their class: the gain to the Landlords as a body would be very small: the farm, which, in the hands of the Duke of Devonshire, would be a little under the line, in the hands of a Scully or a Leitrim would be above it; and the like.

I fear I must assume it is the former description of limit, not the latter, that we have to consider; and I turn to it accordingly. Now, no human wit can make the two identical: the limit for contingent pauperism is and must be very greatly lower than that which marks the line between normal and abnormal demand.

Now, if we are to provide damages for eviction in order to meet contingent pauperism, the question at once arises why should not such legislation go into England and Scotland? Special legislation for a country should go to meet its special and besetting evils. Is pauperism the special evil of Ireland? Quite the reverse. Ireland suffers from poverty, rather than from pauperism. I have not the figures before me, but I apprehend that pauperism has diminished, not increased, in Ireland; and that it is (probably) less than in Scotland, less than in England. So that if we make this provision for Ireland, *a fortiori* we ought to make it for the two other countries, where pauperism is more menacing. So far then, I find

[1] Written for communication to Lowe, see above, no. 177, and Granville to Lowe, 29 Dec., enclosing no. 180, G.D. 29/66. The version in Add. MS. 44166 is in Gladstone's hand. Granville received a copy signed by Gladstone.

that the proposed provision offends against that which I take to be among the first of the prudential rules that should govern the construction of our measure, namely to avoid as far as possible dragging England and Scotland, or even seeming to drag them into the fray.

But it may be urged that it is proposed to override existing leases, viz: leases from year to year. Now, Lowe's accute mind, and I think also Cardwell's, is satisfied to take away from the Landlord improvements which at present belong to him, on the ground that he has them by a technicality of law. But was there ever a technicality so technical, as that which in the case of an agricultural holding, absolutely requiring a twelvemonth for the completion of its ordinary processes, declares a covenant, determinable by either party at six months' notice, to be a lease?

But this technicality not only so declares: it favours the lease technically so called as compared with real leases. Holdings from year to year have been a curse to Ireland, not in all cases, yet too generally: leases for terms of years have been regarded as beneficial arrangements, which it was an object of public policy to promote. But under this legislation, the landlord with tenancies at will would at once receive a respite for one whole average generation, while the leasing landlord would have only the much *shorter* term of the residues of his 19 or 21 or even 31 year leases, before he should come under the sweep of the prospective damages for eviction. The man who has done what Parliament has desired would be treated worse than the man who has done what it viewed as in Ireland a public evil.

Again; it is admitted that while we recognise unconditionally the Ulster Custom, we are to recognise conditionally customs prevailing elsewhere. Two farmers are turned out from farms of the same rent. One proves the custom, the other does not. But the custom proved is that of payment (and this will be the common case) by tenant to tenant, not recognised by the landlord, generally not known to him, not liable for his arrears of rent. Why is this Landlord to be brought within the Bill, and the other not? It is totally impossible to contend that he is under a covenant, the very existence of which generally he does not know. Besides, if he is under such a covenant we must remove our *maximum*, and introduce the Ulster fancy-prices for cases beyond Ulster, where they may incidentally have obtained: nor may we limit the claim for payment in cases where the Landlord determines the tenancy. The ground of the covenant then cannot be held. And if it is abandoned, then as a matter of right the one Landlord has just as much claim as the other, and we cannot legislate against the one and for the other.

In all this long story, I have generally foreborne to argue the question on the grounds of History, of broad right, or of political expediency. On each and all of these I am for myself fully prepared to argue it. But my present purpose is only with those arguments which I think a maintainer of the proposition stated in your letter ought in consistency to admit. There is one argument at least of this kind which I must add. I ask for the admission that every measure, and especially every great measure ought to be in correspondence with its own ground, and its own end.

The end of our measure is to give peace and security to Ireland, and through Ireland to the Empire. How could we hope to give such peace and security by a

Bill, under which there might be large tracts of country, possibly even whole counties, in which it might be impossible to give judicial proof of those customs against Landlords thinking themselves deeply interested in disproving them, and where every tenant, say over £10, would find himself unprotected save as to improvements where the Landlord might traverse him by denying them to be for him improvements at all. Such tenants would find themselves not only excluded, but excluded by a rule to them wholly unintelligible. For the *ideas* of the Irish peasantry with regard to a certain permanency of interest in the soil are universal, though the particular customs in which those ideas are clothed are variable. And the worst of all is this: it will be found to a great extent that the custom (outside Ulster) has prevailed on the Estates of the mild landlords, but has been kept down by force as it were on the estates of the harsh. So that the legislation proposed would be distinctly legislation in favour of harshness, as against equity and consideration. Nor is it an answer to say the tenant's occupation value diminishes in proportion as he has been rack-rented. For the lower a man's means of livelihood are reduced, the more perilous, and the more severe it is to withdraw them, if he has no others.

Once more our measure ought to be consistent with its own ground. What is to be the *ground* of our measure? No one has answered this question more clearly than Lowe himself in his printed paper. I have it not at hand, and I shall do it injustice if I try to cite it. It is, I think, the second paragraph to which I refer. In substance, however, he founds the justification of our interference on the inability of the Irish people under past circumstances and present ones to make, except in certain cases, fair and equal contracts in that which is practically the only pursuit open to them. But his broad and true proposition is not limited to tenants under £10. It is not until we come to some amount difficult to fix, but many times £10, that the Irishman can be said to have that degree of choice among different pursuits necessary for the requisite degree of independence as to any one among them. I do not well see how it would be possible to acknowledge the ground truly described as the chief warrant for our measure, and then to pass by a very large portion of those who strictly fall within the definition of its objects.

If there be scruple felt as to present contracts, I am at a loss to conceive how it should fail to be removed by allowing the time necessary for their determination to elapse before the new law should in this point come into effect. That this would be illusory as a remedy for the Landlord can surely be no reason for giving him a life interest in a covenant which for his own purposes he has chosen to keep terminable at six months: terminable upon a notice given after the autumn seed is in the ground, and to be enforced before the crop has been gathered in.

I have omitted to comment on the extreme difficulty of a division so sharp in a matter so vital as I think the suggestion involves. But I own that even this seems to me to be an objection of no small practical weight.

It is difficult, when a new suggestion is tendered for a complex measure to take the place of a part which had been weighed in its relation to the other parts, to apprehend at once the whole of its effects. But the detail into which I have entered will I think have prepared you to find that the present leaning of my mind is unfavourable. We must indeed meet one another in every possible way. But we shall all feel that the sufficiency and consistency of the measure are indispensable. Unless it be weather-tight, it cannot live in the seas it has to navigate. My impression is that having unanimously left the old ground of improvements, we cannot now stop short of a plan which shall cover the *whole* of Ireland. By proposing such a measure now we may be able to rescue from great danger, and to render permanently defensible the position of the Irish Landlords. Either what we propose will be carried by us, or that and something more by our adversaries. We frame our plan then under an immense responsibility. Having once secured its adequacy, we should do everything to smooth and ease its passage by auxilliary adjustments. But I own it seems to me that the limitation I have been discussing, while it would strike a mortal blow at the first great condition, would and could conciliate none among those from whom opposition is to be apprehended, while on this side of the water it would actually raise new and grave objections.

181. Lord Granville to Mr. Gladstone. [Add. MS. 44166, fo. 258]

Walmer Castle. Dec 29/69.

Our post arrives ten hours after it is due, the road between Dover and Deal being blocked up by snow.

I wish you many happy and successful returns of the day.

I have read your excellent letter, which I shall forward to Lowe, and which must at least convince him that you do not wish to carry your measure in the Cabinet by brute force alone.

I am rather sorry to hear that Thring is to go over to Ireland, although not much surprised that they have not made much progress yet in Ireland with the bill.

I send you a letter from Lowe on a different subject,[1] also one from George Grey [2]—to whom I will write.

182. Lord Granville to Mr. Gladstone. [Add. MS. 44166, fo. 260]

Secret. Walmer Castle. Dec 30/69.

Argyll has written to tell me the advice which he has given you in re 'robes', but he has added what I am not sure he has told you that there is a possible chance of Sutherland not letting her take them. He, which the Q. luckily does not know, has cut his sovereign ! ! for reasons which it would be long to write.

The offer if you agree to make it ought in the first instance to be a confidential sounding from you (I think) to him, but not betraying any doubt.

183. Mr. Gladstone to Lord Granville. [G.D. 29/57]

Hawarden Castle. Dec. 31.69.

1. I have written to Grey.[3]

2. I inclose a letter from Argyll received today that you may see the

[1] 28 Dec., suggesting Dr. Scott for the bishopric of Manchester and Dr. Jowett to be master of Balliol in his place, G.D. 29/66.

[2] On the appointment of suffragan bishops; see above, nos. 137, 143, and below, 183, 186.

[3] 31 Dec., on the cabinet committee appointed by Palmerston to consider the question of suffragan bishops, Add. MS. 44538, fo. 34.

state of his mind. I send a reply [1] which I hope will tend to smooth matters.

3. Scott is excellent but would *not* do for Manchester. After lingering some time upon the claims of Archdeacon Durnford, by far the most distinguished Clergyman of the Diocese & a man who should have been made Bishop 10 years or more ago, I have, partly on account of age, & partly on account of the question of *Education* concluded that *Fraser* was the best man to be had for this particular see and have written to recommend him accordingly.

My wife has been laid up with a feverish attack & erysipelas in the head, which they say might have taken a typhoid character but for a strong constitution. Thank God has passed & she only wants a little time & moderate care now.

A happy New Year to you & Lady Granville.

I think Scott should be carefully borne in mind.

You will I hope be pleased about Fraser. It seems to me *the* see of all England for him. Barry would have done well. He will keep a little.

184. Lord Granville to Mr. Gladstone. [Add. MS. 44167, fo. 1]

[2 January 1870].

Lowe's answer [2] is as good as could be expected.

Is not Argyll's a bit of Dufferin's thunder? [3]

I cannot say how glad I am to hear of Mrs Gladstone's convalescence at the same time as of her illness. You must have had an anxious moment.

De Grey has taken Sandford from us—I have offered his place to Herbert. Was he not your private Secretary.

185. Mr. Gladstone to Lord Granville.[4] [G.D. 29/57]

Hawarden Castle. Jan 4.70.

Lowe always has a meaning and a clear one but in his note to you of the 1st I am sure I have not caught it. For we have already agreed upon 'introducing new terms into the contract' with yearly tenants by giving them improvements which under the contract belong to the landlord: and it is in order "to relieve from hardship and oppression under those contracts that exist" that we propose to say "you shall not inflict the supreme hardship, of expulsion *per se*, without giving a compensation for it". With less than this the Land question in Ireland will not be settled: I earnestly hope it may never require more.

Herbert was my Private Secretary but for an infinitesimally short time as we were put out: I should suppose it to be an excellent choice.

[1] Gladstone to Argyll, 31 Dec., sending a copy of no. 180, Add. MS. 44538, fo. 33.

[2] To Granville, 1 Jan., in reply to no. 180, on the sanctity of contract between landlord and tenant, G.D. 29/66, copy in Add. MS. 44167, fo. 2.

[3] For opinions on Irish land see A. Lyall, *The Life of the Marquis of Dufferin and Ava* (1905), i. pp. 155–87.

[4] Comment, 2 Jan., by Gladstone 'I like this' on an unidentified subject, G.D. 29/57, not printed.

186. Mr. Gladstone to Lord Granville. [G.D. 29/29A]

Hawarden Castle. Jan 6.70.

Here is the sequel on Suffragans. Do you think it might be well to circulate the correspondence? At any rate this letter of Sir G. G[rey']s and my reply.[1]

187. Mr. Gladstone to Lord Granville. [G.D. 29/57]

Hawarden Castle. Jan 8. 70.

To save time I send herewith copy of a letter I have written to Bruce (who is out of town) about the Commission [2] and the Bishop of London.

I also send a letter from Fortescue.[3]

188. Mr. Gladstone to Lord Granville. [G.D. 29/57]

Hawarden Castle. Jan 10. 70.

The inclosed [4] will sufficiently explain itself: please to advise upon it. I think, viewing the neuralgia, and other matters, it will be best to wait for ten days or a fortnight.

Fraser has accepted, in a letter full of modesty and of promise.

If you are in London on the evening of the 20th I shall hope to call upon you then.

189. Mr. Gladstone to Lord Granville. [G.D. 29/57]

Most Private. Hagley. Jan 15. 70.

1. I think that in a day or two I may write to the Queen and ask a purely conditional promise like that which she gave in the Bridge case, and which answered so well.[5]

2. I am concerned, but not surprised, at what you tell me of Cardwell. I do not abandon hope for the coming week, but fear rather predominates as to him & L[owe]. On the other hand I think for the first time that Argyll is coming to. Judge for yourself from the accompanying letter.[6] And I think my troubles with

[1] Grey to Gladstone, 3 Jan., enclosing copy of a memorandum by Palmerston with a minute by Gladstone July 1864; Gladstone to Grey, 6 Jan., G.D. 29/29A.

[2] The Ritual Commission. The vacancy created by the death of Archbishop Longley was filled by the bishop of London, Tait, the new archbishop being already a member. Bruce consulted Gladstone about Granville's view that this made the appointment of another lay member necessary, 6 Jan., Add. MS. 44086, fo. 68. Gladstone disagreed, 8 Jan., G.D. 29/57.

[3] To Gladstone, 7 Jan., on Lowe's obstruction over the Irish land bill and appointments, Add. MS. 44122, fo. 122.

[4] Gen. Grey to Gladstone, 8 Jan., on the likelihood of the Queen's refusing to open Parliament.

[5] On 6 July 1869 the Queen gave a conditional promise to open Blackfriars bridge which she fulfilled, 6 Nov., Guedalla, i. 188, 208–9.

[6] Argyll to Gladstone, 13 Jan., Add. MS. 44101, fo. 194, part printed *Autobiography and Memoirs* (1906), ii. 258–61.

Fortescue about the framework of the Bill are at an end: an explicit letter, as kind as I could make it, produced a perfectly satisfactory reply.[1] Thring is now in Dublin having passed a morning with me on his way.

Will you kindly let me 'eat mutton' with you in Bruton Street at 8 on Thursday —or else call on you say at 9.30—to review the situation. (This is cool, I do think, but it is an echo to your kind offer: pray deal, as Dizzy says, *frankly.*)

3. I have faithfully burned Monsell. Think of our appearing as, mediately, Suitors before the Holy Office!

4. Acton writes very serious letters from Rome.[2] They are now with Clarendon.

190. Mr. Gladstone to Lord Granville. [G.D. 29/57]

Hagley. Jan 16. 70.

If you think it well to send the inclosed [3] of this date to the Queen pray do so. In one form or another, the matter will have to be placed before her & this as matters stand is probably the best.

191. Mr. Gladstone to Lord Granville. [G.D. 29/57]

Most Private. Hagley. Jan 16. 70.

I have received your letter inclosing the Queen's of the 20th: but I send, *as* it had been written, mine of yesterday. For it expresses my conviction not founded on ordinary motives, nor having reference to ordinary circumstances. We have now to deal with the *gros* of the Irish question, and the Irish question is in a category by itself. It would be almost a crime in a Minister to omit any thing that might serve to mark and bring home to the minds of men the gravity of the occasion. Moreover I am persuaded that the Queen's own sympathies would be, not as last year, but in the same current as ours. To this great country the state of Ireland, after 700 years! of our tutelage, is in my opinion so long as it continues, an intolerable disgrace, and a danger so absolutely transcending all others, that I call it the only real danger of the noble Empire of the Queen. I cannot refrain from bringing before her in one shape or another my humble advice that she should *if able* open Parliament. The less formal manner in which the subject has now been opened if the least trying to the Queen will on that account be the most acceptable to me.

A contingent and free promise, like that in the case of the Bridge, is what I should pray.

[1] See Gladstone to Fortescue, 12 Jan., and reply, 13 Jan. Difficulties arose because Thring, drafting the bill in Dublin, diverged from the 'Memorandum of Instructions from the Cabinet' towards Fortescue's views on the recognition of customs other than the Ulster tenant right, Add. MS. 44122, fos. 129, 131.

[2] See below, no. 192 note.

[3] No. 191; printed without the first two and last two sentences, Morley, ii. 293.

192. Mr. Gladstone to Lord Granville.[1] [G.D. 29/57]

Hagley. Jan 18. 70.

Many thanks. I shall probably go alone to town on Thursday. We may have to talk about very private matters. Glyn however is an inner self, and never out of place.

I think Cardwell has made a great success with the Queen about his Department.[2]

I inclose Acton's two last letters, with one from Clarendon, as I think you will like to read them.[3]

Read D. Tel. of yest. on Ld Russell & Colonial Policy.

193. Lord Granville to Mr. Gladstone. [Add. MS. 44167, fo. 8]

Colonial Office. Jan 19/70.

I return with thanks J Acton's most interesting letters. The crisis must be of crucial importance to him and others of his stamp, & he says that if the Papal party succeed, all Catholics will become generally Tories & occasionally Revolutionists.

It is sad that so great a power as Roman Catholicism should be set against human progress, yet I am not sure that we have an immediate interest in shaping the course of Policy of the Council.

I never thought it was an object for Protestantism to get the Pope out of Rome, and I doubt it's being so to prevent the Council erring by extreme views,—which will by reaction probably loosen the hold of Rome on the National Hierarchies.

Our immediate & selfish object seems to be to cultivate good relations with whoever has influence over the Irish Bishops & Priests.

194. Lord Granville to Mr. Gladstone. [Add. MS. 44638, fo. 3]

[21 January 1870].

The Prince of Wales would like to have a talk with you about the Land Bill. I should think you could tell him the whole bill, and he would be quite unable to be indiscreet.

He wishes also to go to India.

195. Lord Granville to Mr. Gladstone. [Add. MS. 44167, fo. 10]

16, Bruton Street. Jan 25/70.

You will see by the enclosed mass of papers and particularly by a marginal note of Rogers in answer to a query of mine last autumn, that there is nothing of the

[1] Granville to Gladstone, 17 Jan., replying 'yes' to no. 190 and inviting to dinner, Add. MS. 44167, fo. 7, not printed.

[2] Cf. Gladstone to Cardwell 7, 18 Jan., Add. MS. 44538, fos. 45, 55. A bill for the reorganization of the War Office was introduced into the Commons, 15 Feb., *C.J.* (1870), 40; above, no. 107 note.

[3] Acton to Gladstone, 1 Jan., on Franco-British co-operation to influence the Oecumenical Council in an anti-papalist sense; 8 Jan., on a conspiracy against the Council, for communication to France; Clarendon to Gladstone, 16 Jan., on British and French resistance to the syllabus and infallibility, Add. MSS. 44093, fos. 102–11, 44134, fo. 134.

sort you want except what is to be found in your excellent despatch to Lord Cathcart. An extract from that despatch was the basis of a confidential despatch to Sir John Young which I desired him not to show to his ministers for fear of misconstruction but to use as a guide to his own language.

There is a phrase at the end of it, which would make it unwise to publish it at present.[1]

Sir John Young's answer shows that the almost unanimous opinion of the Dominion is against separation, at all events at present.

I will call on you before the Cabinet about the Red River.[2]

196. Lord Granville to Mr. Gladstone. [Add. MS. 44167, fo. 12]

Jan 29/70.

When you first talked to me on the subject of the Welsh Bishoprick[3] I was in favor, supposing the two things could not be combined, of a Clergyman possessing a practical hold on the feelings of the Welsh, rather than of one of a higher intellectual calibre.

On reading these letters I have rather changed.

I should be for Archdeacon Jones—as the one who would do most good.

Such a man would exercise a greater influence over the Clergy, than a mere popular Preacher in Welsh—& with his power of organization ought to be able to draw out a greater amount of service from the Howell's & Griffiths than any one of them could afford in the position of Bishop.

I should not say this, if the Archdeacon was not Welsh, and did not know Welsh.

197. Mr. Gladstone to Lord Granville. [Add. MS. 44167, fo. 14]

11, Carlton House Terrace. Jan 31. 70.

Do you think it necessary—I fear it is—that I should bring in the Irish Land Bill?

If you do, would you raise the point in the Cabinet tomorrow.[4]

[1] The dispatch to Young 14 June, following min. 27 Nov. 1869, C.O. 42/678, ended: 'You will also be good enough to bring to my notice any line of policy, or any measures which without implying on the part of H.M.G. any wish to change abruptly our relations, would gradually prepare both countries, for a friendly relaxation of them.' Cf. mem. by Gladstone, 19 Jan., and Granville's comments on it, Add. MS. 44759, fo. 1; see above, no. 59.

[2] For Red River rebellion see above, no. 165. In the cabinet of 25 Jan., no discussion on it was recorded, Add. MS. 44638, fo. 6.

[3] St. Asaph, from which Bishop Short had resigned. Joshua Hughes of Llandovery was nominated in March. For extensive correspondence on the subject see Add. MSS. 44423, 44424, 44425, *passim*; part circulated to the cabinet, 27 Jan., Add. MS. 44759, fo. 5.

[4] Returned by Granville minuted, 'I will.' He acted in the cabinet of 1 Feb., Add. MS. 44638, fo. 12.

198. Mr. Gladstone to Lord Granville.[1] [G.D. 29/57]

11, Carlton House Terrace. Feb. 2. 70.

I am very sorry we are not to have you.

Can you indicate a view on Fortescue's paper? Not perhaps a final one but your leaning or predisposition.

199. Minute by Lord Granville. [Add. MS. 44638, fo. 18]

[2 February 1870].

Fortescue's paper ought not to be lightly passed over. The facts he states are strong, the opinion of his professional advisers, and the formal declaration made on his behalf and that of Spencer are entitled to the most careful consideration. It is a great responsibility for the Cabinet to assume, if it disregards the advice of the Irish Gov on a matter affecting the lives possibly of many.

Beyond this, Representative Free Gov ought to be able to show itself as powerful as any other to maintain order, & repress illegal outrages.

A large portion of the Irish would rejoice at any measure of apparent vigor. Not only the Protestants and the Landlords, but the Catholic clergy.

But can any one say that such a measure would be successful. We have now as I understand nearly all the powers, which enabled Sir George Grey to deal with outrages, and these powers certainly are not of any use—& I hardly know what legislative measure can meet the cardinal difficulty, want of evidence—on the whole I incline to the trial of something such as Fortescue suggests, but I should be sorry to vote without hearing the discussion in the Cabinet.

200. Lord Granville to Mr. Gladstone. [G.D. 29/57]

Bruton St. Feb 7/70.

I agree with Dodson in thinking it impossible to carry out this year all the recommendations of last year's Joint Committee.[2]

I should be glad if you would allow me to encourage him to move the adoption of the 7th paragraph of the report.

I doubt whether it is desirable to have another joint Committee before the final change is proposed—those that we have had, have done admirably. It would be a pity to have a less successful one, and it would be in the interest of many people to make it fail, if it was supposed to be a test.

You will remember that I submitted the proposals of the report to the Cabinet, before proposing them to the Joint Committee.

[1] Granville to Gladstone [2 Feb.] regretting that influenza would keep him from the cabinet of that day, Add. MS. 44167, fo. 15, not printed. Cabinet discussed exceptional legislation to deal with Irish crime, Add. MS. 44638, fos. 14–16. Granville to Gladstone, 4 Feb., arranging for the cabinet to meet in Bruton Street, Add. MS. 44167, fo. 17, not printed.

[2] See above, nos. 36–9. Dodson wrote to Granville, 25 Jan., that the Commons would not accept the joint committees for private bills, recommended in the report, but that they might agree to waive their privilege in respect of rating clauses in private bills, as the seventh paragraph recommended, so that proceedings might begin in the Lords on some private bills, G.D. 29/73.

201. Mr. Gladstone to Lord Granville. [G.D. 29/57]

11, Carlton House Terrace. Feb. 7. 70.

I quite agree in the 7th Paragr. of the Report of the Joint Committee on Procedure & approve of its being proposed.

Should it be proved that 'parties' generally desire the adoption of the new system of Joint Committees on Private Bills might we not *then* proceed with it.

202. Lord Granville to Mr. Gladstone. [Add. MS. 44167, fo. 18]

Bruton St. Feb 13/70.

I beg pardon for having been misinformed about your despatch to Lord Cathcart having been published.[1]

The error arose from it's having been printed. It was not published.

203. Lord Granville to Mr. Gladstone. [Add. MS. 44167, fo. 19]

16, Bruton Street. Feb 15 [1870].

I wish you joy. I thought the statement most skilful.[2]

The Duke of Cambridge thinks it a moderate measure which will go down.

Harrowby entirely approves.

Delane says that all the people about him were delighted, and that your peroration was the best you ever made.

Bruce says that Maguire approves.

Our whole efforts must be directed to getting some landlords to object violently.

204. Mr. Gladstone to Lord Granville. [G.D. 29/57]

11, Carlton House Terrace. Feb. 16. 70.

I am very sorry to have missed you & the opportunity of thanking you for your note. The Irish popular party I understand are minded to accept though perhaps required to grumble a little. Upon the whole the appearances are so bright with respect to the measure that I tremble lest there should be a change of weather.

What a mess in Southwark; [3] Beresford came in!

205. Lord Granville to Mr. Gladstone. [Add. MS. 44167, fo. 21]

16, Bruton Street. March 2/70.

Many thanks for having killed & buried State aid to Emigration.[4]

[1] See above, no. 59.

[2] Introducing the Irish land bill, 15 Feb., *Hans. Parl. Deb.* 3rd ser. cxcix. 333–87.

[3] The Conservative won this by-election, caused by Layard's appointment to Madrid, as the Liberal vote was split between the official candidate, Sir Sydney Waterlow, and the working-man's candidate, George Odger; *The Times*, 17 Feb., p. 5, 18 Feb., p. 5.

[4] Gladstone's intervention prevented Torrens (Liberal) from carrying a motion against the government, to relieve distress by aiding emigration, 1 March, *Hans. Parl. Deb. loc. cit.* 1002–77. Cf. Denison to Granville, 2 March, G.D. 29/75.

Spencer tells me that he has written a very strong letter to C[hichester] F[ortescue] on the State of Ireland, which I presume you have seen.

Clanricarde has a motion on the subject on Friday, when we shall be closely pressed, and when a general answer will be difficult.[1]

Clanricarde would probably be willing to postpone his motion at my request, but it would be unwise to do so, unless we are pretty sure to have some proposal to make next week.

I shall be out tomorrow. Could you call a few of us together on the matter.

I believe Barry is coming or come.

206. Mr. Gladstone to Lord Granville. [G.D. 29/57]

Most Private. 11, Carlton House Terrace. March 3. 70.

I told you yesterday I had again urged the necessity of our being supplied with a full and careful statement of the Irish case. But I feel doubtful whether our Irish Government is at the present moment strong enough or calm enough to supply it. And it occurs to me that if we could get Kimberley to go over and confer with Spencer he would in a few days come back and report to us upon the 'situation' in a manner more effective and satisfactory than we seem likely to secure in any other manner.

Much allowance is to be made for Spencer, and I do not know what amount of masculine staff he has around him.

What I feel it necessary we should know, is what we should afterwards have to show. And chiefly perhaps.

1. The amount, circumstances, and effects of crime now, in relation to former periods.

2. The operation of preventive and corrective means to be similarly compared.

3. A careful tracing month by month of the history of the present crisis of crime to enable us to judge of the aggravation or mitigation of the disease.

4. A comparison of the remedies now proposed with those of former periods, with the reasons for duration when they durate.

5. An indication of the mode and degree in which it is to be expected that they will stop or abate the mischief.

If you are disposed to agree in the main idea of this note, perhaps you would either send it on to Kimberley or speak to him. I would then if he agreed speak to Fortescue and mention the matter in Cabinet on Saturday. Kimberley would in the meantime probably have made ready to go at once.

207. Lord Granville to Mr. Gladstone. [Add. MSS. 44167, fo. 25, and 44166, fo. 26]

Secret. 16, Bruton Street. March 4/70.

I like your plan of Kimberley—the only objection is the apparent slap in the face to Spencer—but I am sure he could not, and would [not] resent it, if it was

[1] Clanricarde postponed his motion, due in the Lords on 4 March, for papers relating to crime in Ireland, at the government's request, *Hans. Parl. Deb. loc. cit.* 1116.

put in this way that the crisis [?] was of importance, that it was impossible to ask Spencer to leave Ireland, & that Fortescue could not conveniently be absent from the House of Commons, that it was therefore convenient that a member of the cabinet should go over, & fully confer with Spencer, explaining the difficulties of the Cabinet, the points on which they wanted explanation in a manner which it was difficult to do in writing.

Once there Kimberley would not allow the grass to grow under his feet. He would put his nose into every hole—and one of the first things I think he ought to do would [1] be in communication with Spencer to find out the weak places in the administration, military, civil, & legal, and whether we could supplement these deficiencies by first rate adminiculating Royal Engineers such as Harness, Police Magistrates, like Sir Thomas Henry, & any eminent Solicitor skilled in criminal business. I am afraid Lambert is too ill to help in collecting such returns as you wish, & my impression of Hancock always was that he was an ass.

Of course Kimberley would see with Spencer how far the means in the power of the Gov have really been exhausted—& Kimberley might probably consult more freely than Spencer can Sullivan & some of the men not at present connected with the Gov.

I will speak to Kimberley.[2]

208. Mr. Gladstone to Lord Granville. [G.D. 29/57]

Private & Confidential. 11, Carlton House Terrace. March 6.70.

1. Has not an error been committed—now too far back to be recalled—in handing over the Red River people to the Dominion of Canada without their consent?

2. I presume that under the H[udson] Bay Company they had not any representative institutions and were governed absolutely?

3. The Plebiscite is not according to our fashion, but it is because we have something better in the vote of representative bodies.

4. Would it be safe—order being first re-established—to try the plebiscite in Red River?

5. The discussion of yesterday opened to me some new aspects of danger, for I had thought the armed force was intended only to subdue outliers not to overawe the community.[3]

6. *If* we cannot have the Plebiscite, can we found ourselves upon the document to which I referred as a covenant on the part of the Red River people, conditional of course according to the matter set out in it?

7. Is it too late to settle the matter by negotiation before May when the force moves?

[1] The rest of this letter has been bound as an imperfect document in the volume of Gladstone-Granville letters for 1869, Add. MS. 44166, fo. 26.

[2] Cf. Kimberley to Granville, 3 March [4 March], written against the proposal, after Granville had spoken to him, G.D. 29/55. Cf. J. L. Hammond, *Gladstone and the Irish Nation* (1938), p. 113.

[3] See Gladstone's note on the cabinet, 5 March, Add. MS. 44638, fo. 33; cf. *Correspondence relative to . . . the Red River Settlement.* Parl. papers. [c. 207] (1870). l, 293–526, and above, no. 165.

209. Lord Granville to Mr. Gladstone. [Add. MS. 44167, fo. 27]

Private & Confidential. 16, Bruton Street. March 6 [1870].

I have some doubt whether the Red Riverites ought to have been consulted, but they undoubtedly ought to have been managed, which probably would have been easy at first. We are to blame in not having seen to this, but the Dominion and the Company, who knew so much more than we did, seemed so certain of their business, that it never occurred to me, or as I believe to Rogers, that anything was necessary.

They were governed absolutely under the H. Bay Company, and it would have been and would be difficult and a farce to collect the votes by universal suffrage of a few hundred Europeans and ten thousand half savages scattered over this vast territory. (Not to mention the Indians.)

The Canadians are tolerably sanguine about delegates being sent to Ottawa, & this would be the best way of getting the assent of the people. The Canadians are fully alive to the extreme danger of bloodshed. I see no alternative to our standing by the Canadians, and if so the prompt assertion of authority is probably the safest.

I will look at the document you referred to, and let you know more about it tomorrow.[1]

The Queen was well—uneasy about military reductions.

210. Mr. Gladstone to Lord Granville. [Add. MS. 44538, fo. 93]

[*Copy*]. 7 Mch. 70.

I have not well expressed my idea wh: is (if & as far as may now be possible) to *isolate* the Red R. settlement, & deal with it as a separate plot of ground, not to recognize it as representing the vast territory on which it is a speck, nor to extend to the savages, or the dispersed groups of company's servants, throughout the territory, any similar recognition. To shut out effectually the title of the Red River people to claim in the name of country beyond their own limits, & especially of the zone between them and the United States which seems to be of great importance. To that zone they have no claim whatever beyond a right of way. Any recognition of them wd, I think, warrant dealing at once with all the territory except the spot they hold. To acknowledge their rights would be to limit them *ipso facto*. What I wish is that the American Filibuster should not when he crosses the dividing line be entitled to say, now I am upon the land of the people for whom I am going to fight. They are independent settlers. But they are settlers on their own ground only. I cannot help thinking something *might* be hammered out of this to improve the relative positions, & reduce the risks of future danger: unless the letter of the Act of Parliament presented a difficulty. I send for your perusal my report to the Queen of the Cabinet of Saturday.[2]

[1] Cf. Granville to Rogers, 6 March, sending a copy of no. 208 and asking him to find 'the covenant' mentioned by Gladstone, G.D. 29/57.

[2] 5 March.

211. Mr. Gladstone to Lord Granville. [G.D. 29/57]

11, Carlton House Terrace. Mch 14. 70.

I send herewith the description I propose to give of the repressive measure for Ireland.

In 1–4 you will find within inverted commas what was agreed on at the Cabinet.

But as the Bill is not to come in until Thursday I *think* it will be necessary to add to No 1 the sort of indication contained in the Postscript A.[1]

Please to let me know your view. I shall be in Downing St at 3.30.

212. Mr. Gladstone to Lord Granville. [G.D. 29/31]

Mch 21. 70.

1. Please to advise me, and to consult Bessborough, about the inclosed application touching several of the Hastings Baronies.[2] Perhaps I ought to mention the subject to the Chancellor: will you kindly send on the paper.

2. Who should be the new K.T. vice Ailsa?

3. There is also his Lord Lieutenancy of Ayrshire.[3]

4. Bessborough is strongly for giving the Ulster Tenant (which will carry the case of any other) the option of claiming under the scale, and says that Dufferin entirely agrees. I expect that the argument for this alteration will prove irresistible —Indeed I suspect that as the Bill stands if an Ulster Tenant simply disposes of his interest without (ostensibly) any price for it from the in-comer, that in-comer could not be evicted except under the scale.[4]

213. Mr. Gladstone to Lord Granville. [G.D. 29/57]

11, Carlton House Terrace. March 29. 70.

Next week we shall probably launch into a discussion of principles of Colonial Policy, on Tuesday evening Ap. 5. And I suppose the Cabinet will give us something like a Programme. Some time ago without any very special aim I put down the inclosed Memorandum, which I now send to you for the sake of raising the points.[5]

[1] For text of the description and postscripts see Add. MS. 44638, fo. 43, with note on cabinet of 12 March. It was drafted for answers by Granville and Gladstone to parliamentary questions. The Peace Preservation (Ireland) Bill was introduced on 17 March, *C.J.* (1870), 89, 90.

[2] For the falling into abeyance of the five Hastings baronies and the termination of the abeyance, see *G.E.C.* vi. App. D., 702. For mems. by Lady Loudoun and the Queen, 20 March, inclosed, see G.D. 29/31; Granville to Gladstone, replying to no. 212, *ibid.*, not printed.

[3] Lord Minto made K.T., 13 May; Lord Stair appointed to Ayrshire in June, see below, no. 227.

[4] For opinions on the question whether tenants might choose between relying on the legalized Ulster custom or resorting to the scale of compensation, to be established by the Irish land act, for areas where the custom did not obtain, see Gladstone to Dufferin, 22 March, Add. MS. 44538, fo. 105, and note on the cabinet, 26 March, Add. MS. 44638, fos. 52–60. The cabinet agreed to amend the bill to allow the choice.

[5] No mem. later than 19 Jan. has been traced, see above, no. 195 note.

214. Lord Granville to Mr. Gladstone. [Add. MS. 44167, fo. 31]

Confidential. Colonial Office. March 31/70.

O'Hagan called on me this morning. He began about his Peerage. Several persons had spoken to him about it. When he was first made Chancellor, he was strongly opposed to such an idea, but he would now like it, if you were willing to entertain the idea. It had been the constant practice almost till the appointment of Sir M Brady.[1]

Lord Mulgrave's Govt had been subject to violent attacks in consequence of the liberality of his administration. His Chancellor [2] was of the greatest use in defending the Policy in the House of Lords. H.M's Govt were now effecting a peaceful revolution in Ireland, and the same sort of attack was being renewed. A Peerage would strengthen his position in Ireland, and give him the opportunity which he much desired of defending himself against charges of Ultramontanism, partiality and weakness which were freely made. It was fair to Ireland, that the Judges should be represented in the House of Lords, at least to the extent that Scotland was.

On this point I gave him no answer at all.

He then spoke of his present position, and the way in which he had been treated by Chichester Fortescue. Nothing could be kinder than Lord Spencer, and they were on the best terms, but he could not forget that he had been chosen Chancellor partly on Political grounds—That he was supposed by a large portion of the Irish to have political influence. That the Chancellorship in Ireland was as in England, a semi political office. He thought I should be surprised to hear that he had never seen the land bill till it was introduced into Parliament—that he had never seen the Peace Preservation Bill, till I accidentally showed it to him on the afternoon of it's being introduced, and that he had never been told what was the policy of the Govt with respect to Party Processions, till he read the report of Chichester Fortescue's speech in the Times.

I told him that I thought he had better write in the first instance to Fortescue, stating what he had said to me. Upon consideration however he decided to write to Spencer.

215. Mr. Gladstone to Lord Granville. [G.D. 29/57]

10, Downing Street. Ap. 26. 70.

It occurs to me that at this moment the atmosphere of the Lords may be better than that of the Commons [3] for questions touching R.C.s & that we might introduce there our measure for cancelling the Ecclesiastical Titles Act. What do you say.

[1] Irish chancellor created a baronet and not raised to the peerage, 1869.

[2] Lord Plunket.

[3] On 29 March a motion was carried there against the government for an inquiry into convents and monasteries.

216. Lord Granville to Mr. Gladstone. [Add. MS. 44167, fo. 35]

Colonial Office. April 26/70.

I see no objection.[1] I reproach myself for not having kept notes of a bill which Cairns privately read to a Committee on the subject, & then withdrew. They will if I am not mistaken insist upon some preamble reserving the rights of the Crown.

217. Mr. Gladstone to Lord Granville.[2] [G.D. 29/57]

11, Carlton House Terrace. Ap 29. 70.

The medical report is that it would be highly desirable for me to go to Balmoral. On examining the times and seasons I find I could not exactly make the time; but if some one else took May 20 to June 1 I could take June 2 to 11 or 12. This would leave a vacant week. If you write to the Queen perhaps you will learn whether this plan would be satisfactory.

I am sorry to have bolted past yesterday morning. I did not know either of you till within some 5 yards.

218. Mr. Gladstone to Lord Granville.[3] [G.D. 29/57]

House of Commons. Ap. 29. 70.

I should not like to interfere with de Grey and I think his going might probably be more convenient to the Queen as his arrangements would be more elastic in point of time.

219. Mr. Gladstone to Lord Granville. [G.D. 29/57]

11, Carlton House Terrace. Ap 30. 70.

Mr Murdoch [4] explains very clearly the change in the 'situation'.

The murder of Scott,[5] if it be a murder, gives a great advantage to the Canadian Govt., and enables them to move not by way of political invasion but as punishers of crime.

If the Delegates do not come to 'reasonable' terms promptly (Murdoch's presence will be very useful in the interpretation of the Epithet) & if Canada has to move in consequence I hope that in her declarations she will turn this advantage fully to account.

[1] The cabinet, 27 April, agreed to the bill's being introduced into the Lords, Add. MS. 44638, fo. 67; introduced 19 May, *L.J.* (1870), 253.

[2] Granville to Gladstone, 25 April, asking at the Queen's instance whether Gladstone would go to Balmoral during Whitsuntide, Add. MS. 44167, fo. 34, not printed.

[3] Granville to Gladstone, 29 April, on the Queen's wish to have de Grey at Balmoral, Add. MS. 44167, fo. 36, not printed.

[4] He observed the negotiations at Ottawa between the Canadian government and the leaders of the Red River rebellion on behalf of the imperial government.

[5] Court-martialled and shot at Fort Garry, 4 March 1870, by the rebel government.

220. Mr. Gladstone to Lord Granville. [G.D. 29/57]

11, Carlton House Terrace. May 2. 70.

It occurs to me that in asking de Grey to go with the Queen you will have to bear in mind that the time when we shall have to consider & decide our course about the Education Bill [1] will probably be in the fortnight immediately preceding Whitsuntide and I am doubtful whether he would be able to go to Scotland before the short recess, for the matter is one that it may not be practicable to dispose of in a day.

221. Lord Granville to Mr. Gladstone. [Add. MS. 44167, fo. 46]

11, Carlton House Terrace. [6 May 1870].

The Queen spoke to me about the autumnal arrangements for Balmoral. She suggested you
The Chancellor
Goschen
Fortescue
or
Cardwell
&
me.

I told her that you had communicated with her & reported the substance of her letter.

She spoke in the most kind & flattering manner about you, and the importance you were to her and to the State.

She said she had hoped to see you in the Autumn, but that the one important point was to do that which was really most invigorating & resting to you. That she was going away from Balmoral for a fortnight during which time she would require no one in attendance.

That she therefore hoped that you would settle your plans in exact accordance to what you had written to me, if more convenient to you.

222. Mr. Gladstone to Lord Granville. [G.D. 29/57]

Private. 11, Carlton House Terrace. May 7. 70.

On further consideration as it is the Queen's wish to settle now the plan of the Summer campaign for Balmoral I do not see why it should not be done. From the lengthened period of escape which H.M. proposes I should think four Ministers would be sufficient, and I will withdraw from the list, as I am particularly pleased that the Queen should be desirous to have Goschen there. I think it is so very

[1] Introduced 17 Feb., and debated on its second reading, 14, 15 and 18 March. The committee stage, fixed for 1 April, was postponed on 27 April to 16 May, thence to 23 May and thence to 16 June, owing to the movement against leaving religious instruction, in grant-aided schools, to be determined by the local authorities. Parliament was in recess 1–9 June. Cf. note on the cabinet of 14 June, Add. MS. 44638, fo. 83.

important that she should take the opportunities that offer for acquiring ample personal knowledge of those younger members of the Cabinet with whom in the future her relations are likely chiefly to lie.

I think this will leave the matter easy to arrange.

223. Mr. Gladstone to Lord Granville.[1] [G.D. 29/57]

11, Carlton House Terrace. May 12. 70.

It is I suppose too late to discuss the question between the million & the half & no one would say the separation of a Colony ought to turn on so small a question.[2] But I hardly think it can.

I am to go to Windsor for the Council, on the 18th & unless the Queen then introduces the question of Balmoral with the expression of any opinion of her own, I will let the matter stand as in my last note. I do not think there will be *room* for more than four without cutting down the period of stay, which is not desirable.

Thanks for your suggestions on the Dinner List.

224. Mr. Gladstone to Lord Granville.[3] [G.D. 29/57]

11, Carlton House Terrace. May 23. 70.

The whole " Tale " of Peerages offered last Autumn was not accepted.

What do you think of my proposing now, i.e. before the Land Bill

O'Hagan—professionally & with a view to it

Eliot—son of an old & esteemed servant who considers himself disabled, & his Peerage unrepresented.

Milbank—Old M.P.
steady & staunch Liberal
large fortune high position
relation of his son to the Cleveland
Estates [4] great party services.

225. Mr. Gladstone to Lord Granville. [G.D. 29/57]

11, Carlton House Terrace. May 30. 70.

I am loath to trouble you with a quarter of an hour's reading but the subject of Education is so important & so arduous in regard to the " religious difficulty " that I am perhaps justified in attempting this infliction.

[1] Gladstone to Granville, 9 May, asking advice on the list of guests for the birthday dinner, Add. MS. 44167, fo. 39, not printed.

[2] New Zealand asked for the imperial government's guarantee for a loan of 1 million, was offered it for ½ million, but gained her object; see Lowe to Granville and reply, 9, 10 May, G.D. 29/25A, and *Correspondence with New Zealand Commissioners*, Parl. papers. H.C. 298 (1870). l, 281–92.

[3] Granville to Gladstone, 14 May, forwarding a note from Monsell, Add. MS. 44167, fo. 40, not printed.

[4] Milbank's first wife was a daughter of the first duke of Cleveland. He was not made a peer.

The inclosed paper [1] contains my view.

The next fortnight or three weeks will probably enlarge our means of judgment.

I have some thoughts of sending this paper to Sir G. Grey with whom I wish to communicate in entire confidence on the subject. Tomorrow I mean to see two or three of the hardest-headed Nonconformists and try to ascertain their real wishes.

226. Lord Granville to Mr. Gladstone. [Add. MS. 44167, fo. 42]

16, Bruton Street. May 31/70.

1. I have read with great attention your memo & like your plan, always subject to its being acceptable to your house.

The unsectarian explanation of the bill appears to me to be an absurdity, as a legal enactment, however successful it may be under the patronage of the British & Foreign Society.

The Catholics are an immense difficulty. I should like to provide for them out of the Privy Council Grants but I suppose some of the districts where local aid is required are exactly those where they are in large numbers.

I quite approve of confiding to the utmost in George Grey.

227. Mr. Gladstone to Lord Granville.[2] [G.D. 29/57]

11 C. H. T. June 8. 70.

1. I have seen Lord Stair and as the only solution have with his assent written to recommend *him* for the L. Lieutenancy of Ayr.

2. I send an interesting letter from Grey.[3] It indicates the difficulties rather than the solution: but it is written in the spirit you would expect, that of cordial helpfulness.

3. I send a letter from Spencer on Royal Visit and Residence in Ireland, with copy of my reply.[4]

4. I hereby solemnly convey to you all my right title & interest in a volume now at Walmer entitled 'The Letters of Sir Geo. Lewis'.

5. It weighs upon my conscience that you certainly paid at Epsom for a ticket virtually mine & we should be better friends if you would allow me to square this account.

With many more thanks for a delightful Whitsuntide.

Very hot here & little wind.

[1] Mem. on religious instruction in rate-provided schools, 28 May, Add. MS. 44759, fo. 104, sent to Sir George Grey, 2 June, Add. MS. 44162, fo. 318.

[2] Granville to Gladstone, 25 May, on Glyn's winnings at Epsom, and 31 May, arranging Gladstone's journey to Epsom to see the Derby, Add. MS. 44167, fos. 41, 44, not printed. Gladstone stayed at Walmer 1–6 June.

[3] 7 June, on religious difficulty in education, Add. MS. 44162, fo. 320.

[4] 6 June, and reply 8 June, Add. MS. 44306, fos. 285, 290. Gladstone stated that the rumours of the Prince of Wales's purchase of a residence in Ireland were untrue, and the Fenian danger made a visit from the Queen unwise.

228. Lord Granville to Mr. Gladstone. [Add. MS. 44167, fo. 48]

Colonial Office. June 9/70.

I return the correspondence with Spencer & Grey with many thanks.

Grey leaves us very much as we were, but is sure to help you as much as he can, when you have data enough to make up your mind.

My inclination is reading the bible with no comments (leave of absence being given to those desiring it), secular studies, and opportunities for various denominational religious instruction (some special grant for Catholics[)].

I am strongly for an Irish Residence for the P. of Wales, but as much as possible on the footing of Balmoral. I would avoid giving him any semblance of Vice Regal attributes. An Irish Court would have a very bad personal effect upon him—& he would certainly be urged, and would as certainly consent to meddle.

From the account Sydney heard yesterday, I am afraid the Queen is not unlikely to have a serious reason for postponing her expedition to Ireland. Prince Leopold seems to be very ill.

I delight in my accumulating Gladstonian library at Walmer, but the place seemed very still without you all, yesterday.

I should be glad to relieve your overburdened conscience, but I do not see my way. Rothschild hearing that you were going to the Derby gave me two tickets for his stand. I accepted for you, but declined for myself as I had my own place—the latter unluckily does not include admittance to the enclosure which your's did. It is hardly a case to refer to Bell's Life.

Johnny sent me the enclosed in a cover directed to me. I have profited by the address to send him a summons. You have probably a letter from him to me.

Pray tell Mrs Gladstone that Lady G said without fear Saturday.

229. Lord Granville to Mr. Gladstone. [Add. MS. 44167, fo. 52]

16, Bruton Street. [15 June 1870].

What was the tune the Duke of Wellington used to whistle?

I wish you joy of the Land Bill.[1] The worst of the amendments proposed seems to be the curtailing of the 31 years lease.

I presume we may agree about assignment.

They have hit a blot in the scale, but it is a very difficult one to correct, & we must of course resist any lowering.

I do not think it judicious of the Lords to propose to strike out the Cottage clause.[2]

Bessborough would like something to be done about Conacre.

[1] Granville moved the second reading of the Irish land bill in the Lords on 14 June, debate being adjourned to 16th and again to 17th, *L.J.* (1870), 298, 303, 308.

[2] Relates (i) to three amendments to clause 3 (compensation for disturbance), carried by Richmond, the first two, 24 June, the third, 23 June, and (ii) to clause 10, the cottage clause, which was not struck out. For the bill as it left the Commons see Parl. papers. H.C. 145 (1870). ii, 333, as amended by the Lords, H.C. 204 (1870). ii, 371. On the scale, see Kimberley to Granville, 22 June, G.D. 29/55.

Dufferin was very unhandy last night, and had no success excepting when answering me, but I hope you will not disapprove of my note.[1]

230. Mr. Gladstone to Lord Granville. [G.D. 29/57]

11, Carlton House Terrace. June 18. 70.

What do you think if you & nine other Peers were to meet Fortescue & me on Monday aftn say at 2.30? I think we could greatly narrow the ground. When would the discussion on the 24 points end in the Cabinet? [2] If you approve with or without the 2d Para, perhaps better without if you like it, please to *direct*. I am going to Cashiobury.

231. Mr. Gladstone to Lord Granville. [G.D. 29/57]

Cashiobury. June 19. 70.

Many thanks for the paper which I so stupidly left in my hurry.

De Grey asked me some days ago to get a Council at Windsor on *Thursday*, which I wrote for accordingly. On this account I did not name that day: but I am quite willing. We might meet at 11 a.m. perhaps?

Clarendon has got an invitation to meet the Peers of the Cabinet in D. St tomorrow at 2.30. Is not this too much or too little? I thought of a purely preliminary meeting, to narrow the ground by cutting off those points which clearly may be given or must be referred.

The toughest question is that of assignment.[3]

I expect to be in town by Midday tomorrow & shall be glad to concur in any arrangement you may think best for considering Lords amendements.

232. Lord Granville to Mr. Gladstone. [Add. MS. 44167, fo. 54]

Bn. St. June 29/70.

I had a talk with Hammond this afternoon.[4] Among other things he told me that for the first time in his life he had desired, & indeed made up his mind to leave the F.O, in consequence of Otway being under Secretary. From his account Otway is mauvais coucheur, conceited, jealous & perfectly incapable but he begs not to be quoted. Meade tells me that the same opinion is universal among the Clerks. My brother says that Clarendon ten days ago used still stronger language against him

[1] Granville to Dufferin, 15 June, deprecating his resignation after an unfortunate speech in the Lords on the second reading of the land bill, printed A. Lyall, *The Life of the Marquis of Dufferin and Ava* (1905), i. pp. 178–9; cf. *Hans. Parl. Deb.* 3rd ser. ccii. 60.

[2] Amendments to the Irish land bill to be moved when it went into committee in the Lords on 23 June were discussed in the cabinets of 18 and 23 June and in between by a meeting on Mon. 20th, Add. MS. 44638, fos. 88, 89.

[3] See correspondence between Bessborough and Gladstone, 21, 22 June, Add. MS. 44427, fo. 89–92.

[4] Lord Clarendon died, 27 June, and Granville was about to replace him at the Foreign Office. This and consequent changes (the Colonies to Kimberley and the privy seal to Halifax) were announced in the cabinet, 2 July, Add. MS. 44638, fos. 93, 95. Granville received the seals, 6 July.

at Cashiobury. Clarendon told me that he had been obliged to write out every answer Otway had given in the House.

Grant Duff would not do, and I know of no one as an exchange but Monsell, who probably would prefer me to Kimberley who is very anticatholic. In a sandwich Otway would be a very thin bit of meat between Kimberley & Rogers. Of men out of office I should be very glad to get

Whitbread
Arthur Russell
Henry Cowper
Enfield.

Don't trouble yourself to answer.

233. Lord Granville to Mr. Gladstone. [Add. MS. 44167, fo. 57]

Private. House of Lords. June 29/70.

Fortescue called on me today to ask about the Land Bill. On going away he asked me to give you a message. It was to the effect quoted in the beginning of his note,[1] & I repeating it, asked him whether that was what he wished me to say in case there was a question of my leaving the Col. Office.

234. Mr. Gladstone to Lord Granville. [Add. MS. 44167, fo. 60]

[*Copy*]. 10, Downing Street. 29 June 70.

I return Fortescue's letter. I am not aware, & could not admit, that anything passed between him & me on our taking the Govt, which ought to influence the disposal of the C.O. in the event of your becoming Foreign Sec. on the vacancy which our lamentable loss has brought about. I do not recollect any reference to a vacancy in the C.O. If there was such a reference, I probably said that there would be nothing to prevent him from urging his claim but I did not say & could not have said anything which could approach to a promise or to giving anyone an expectation. Fortescue has held his office with great credit and has done excellent & distinguished service. I am happy however to say that service of very high order has not been uncommon, during the short existence of the present Govt among its leading members; extending the phrase a little beyond the Cabinet.

His office is a very high one. From various circumstances it has while in his hands escaped entirely from the controul of the Home Sec. It has stood in *fact* not very greatly below a Secship of State. It has afforded greater opportunities of distinction than some of the Secships of State. It *may*, I do not say it will, rise even somewhat higher. I dwell more upon this: the work for which Fortescue took it is not yet complete, though I hope it may deserve that epithet next year. One of its branches, if the smallest not the least difficult remains untouched. Were the C.O. to go for service only, Fortescue has, it might be contended, one very formidable competitor in the House of Commons.

[1] To Granville, 29 June, on his claim, first made in 1868, to the colonial secretaryship if Granville became foreign secretary, G.D. 29/56, and copy, Add. MS. 44167, fo. 59.

But the occasion is one on which we must consider the relative strength of the Govt in the two Houses. It is plain to me, that the C. Secship should go to a Peer. If so those who are Peers already may be thought to have the first claim.

Of course it is not to be expected that Fortescue would take my opinion of what his fame requires, rather than his own. But nothing can prevent me from having an opinion & it is that his character & reputation have much more to gain by his remaining for the present where he is than by any transfer to any office whatever.

235. Lord Granville to Mr. Gladstone. [Add. MS. 44167, fo. 62]

11, Carlton House Terrace. [30 ? June 1870].

I have modified the answer to the N[ew] Z[ealand] Delegates, not insisting on their *asking* us to do that which we offer, but sending our offer simply as an answer to their proposal.

They have modified their Telegram a little—they recapitulate " their offer ", our rejoinder, which they will send, although they have warned us that it is not likely to be accepted by the Assembly. They hold out no hopes of further concessions on the part of the " Imperial Govt ".[1]

Verdon the agent for Victoria a sensible man tells Monsell that he is much alarmed about N.Z. that from what he hears here, and from what he is told from Melbourne he believes that they will separate.

Bobby Meade found his Sir George Grey closeted with the Delegates.

I have some doubts on reflection whether having consented to the 500,000 £ whether [*sic*] we were right in not accepting their offer en gros. Supposing the separation comes (which however I cannot believe) we shall have narrow ground to stand on.

236. Lord Granville to Mr. Gladstone. [Add. MS. 44167, fo. 64]

Bruton St. July 2/70.

Cairns & Richmond were here two hours.[2]

The latter assures me that he has the Peers in hand.

This is what was settled—(I had Barry in a back room.)

The change in the scale (subject to Kimberley's amendment) is to go to the Commons to be reversed by you.

Ditto the 21 years for 31.

The " Cottages " amendment to be adopted by you in the Commons.

Richmond is to move our words as to *Conacre.*

Richmond or Cairns is to move their amendment about '*special*' exceptions, as to a tenant in arrear. I am to admit that they have met half the case, but, giving reasons, to express doubts as to the Commons accepting the whole.

Cairns is to move an amendment preventing an Ulster Tenant getting com-

[1] See above, no. 223.

[2] In order to settle an accommodation with the Opposition for the report stage of the Irish and bill in the Lords, due on 5 July, *L.J.* (1870), 392–6.

pensation both ways. I have reserved some words, but Barry, & I believe Fortescue think Cairns is right.

I am to move a clause upon assignment, which subject to Cairns reading it again in a clear copy, will be agreed to.

I am to move to reinsert the clause on *presumption* with our provisos slightly extended. Where a Landlord can show that the practice on his estate has been to make the improvements the presumption as to a particular holding will cease. Where he can show that the practice is to assist, the presumption will be accordingly modified. They will both speak, express their hatred of the claims, but admit that it is so much improved, that they will not vote against, though they cannot vote for the Govt. They think they will take away sufficient votes, to give us a majority. No one, not even Ball, knows what they are doing.

They will help me over the style [*sic*], on the back of Barry's suggestion, as to my concession about the 20 years. I have told Bessborough to move as an Irish Landlord to cancel Salisbury's amendment.

I am bound not to tell what they said on the subject.

237. Mr. Gladstone to Lord Granville. [G.D. 29/58]

11, Carlton House Terrace. July 3. 70.

You must have had an anxious interview but I heartily congratulate you on the result of your labours. I think every difficulty is solved in your *projet de loi* and we have now only to desire that the evil angels may not fly athwart the light, & that the execution may correspond with the design.

The Queen lost no time in letting me know her fullest approbation.

Very grateful to you for your good steering I remain. . . .

238. Lord Granville to Mr. Gladstone. [Add. MS. 44167, fo. 68]

Bruton St. July 7/70.

Lavalette is sure that His Govt will have no possible objection to your decorating Lesseps.

I am rather provoked with the said Lavalette. He left me at seven in perfect good humour, and with no sort of complaint, and at 11 he complains to you of my more than coldness.

I read to him what I proposed to say, & I consider that my criticism on the strong language used at the beginning of the affair, and my reservation as to some of the arguments which he used as to the necessity of France going all lengths were absolutely necessary, before consenting to do that which he asked, i.e. using our influence with Prussia & Spain.[1] Bernstorf [*sic*] knew nothing of the matter, but

[1] Leopold of Hohenzollern-Sigmaringen's readiness to accept the Spanish throne was published on 3 July. France protested to Prussia and Spain, 4 July. Gramont made a provocative declaration in the *corps legislatif* and appealed to Britain, 6 July. For British action see Granville to Layard, tels. 8.10 p.m., 6 July, 2.25 p.m., 7 July, F.O. 72/1231 (pressure to abandon the candidature); Granville to Lyons, No. 14, 6 July, F.O. 27/1791, and private letter, Newton, *Lord Lyons*, i. 294–6; Granville to Loftus, No. 6, 6 July, F.O. 64/681.

said that the relationship between the King and the Hozenhollern's [*sic*] was one of 800 years ago, and that it was only an arrangement upon the father of the candidate being mediatized, that he was to have the rank of a puisne member of the Royal Family—this is a quibble, but it is very likely that the Prussians will hold the language that it is no business of theirs to sanction or to veto the choice of the Spaniards, because it happens to fall upon a Prussian.

I mean to have a talk with Cowley today.

239. Mr. Gladstone to Lord Granville. [G.D. 29/58]

11, Carlton House Terrace. 7/7/70.

A conversation with LaValette was unfortunately interrupted by Royalty. I want to send him a few civil lines, which I inclose—stop them if you see cause. I write them after reading what you have sent abroad. I concur in it, as the first step.

If you do not disapprove, let the messenger take on the inclosed.[1]

240. Mr. Gladstone to Lord Granville. [G.D. 29/58]

[7 July 1870].

If *necessary*, could you postpone the Richmond Amendment to a future night ?

Of course much better to go on if you can.

I think it is as ripe for decision now, as it will be.

But not for *drafting*.

241. Lord Granville to Mr. Gladstone. [Add. MS. 44167, fo. 71]

16, Bruton Street. July 7/70.

I had rather not forward this note,[2] without speaking again to you—there is a slight flavor of apology about it, and indeed it might have been written, if I had been indiscreetly cold yesterday—which I do not think I was. Cowley was here when it came, & without telling him what I thought, I asked him whether he thought it would do good or not to send it. He was of opinion that it was better not to send it. But of course I do not object, if you wish to do so.

Cowley is gone to Lavalette as if out of curiosity, & will let me know what [h]is tone is, & he probably would be able to reassure Lavalette about me, better than a colleague or my chief could do.

I had already written the enclosed.

[1] To Lavalette, 6 July, apologizing for abrupt end to a conversation that night and offering explanations if he had ' found Lord Granville reserved or sparing . . . of assurances ', Add. MS. 44427, fo. 172.

[2] For amended version of the note to Lavalette see *ibid.*, fo. 173, and Add. MS. 44538, fo. 158.

242. Mr. Gladstone to Lord Granville. [G.D. 29/58]

11, Carlton House Terrace. July 8. 70.

With reference to this new demand or suggestion from France,[1] I write to say that both Lowe & Cardwell, having seen your Telegram to Layard, thought it went rather far. I argued the case a little.

243. Mr. Gladstone to Lord Granville. [G.D. 29/58]

Jul. 8 [1870].

I am not quite certain at one or two points about the text of the draft to Layard.[2]

It does not seem to add any thing to your Telegram requiring delay, if it is material that the Messenger shd. go today (the same of the other).

I have put down one or two slight changes in pencil for consdn.

244. Lord Granville to Mr. Gladstone. [Add. MS. 44167, fo. 73]

16, Bruton Street. [8 July 1870].

I am so sorry to give you trouble, but please put on your hypercritical eye glass, as to substance form and language.[3]

245. Mr. Gladstone to Lord Granville. [G.D. 29/58]

11, Carlton House Terrace. July 8. 70.

1. I have just put in pencil such shadings as I had to suggest in the text of your proposed dispatch to Loftus.

2. I send herewith a proposed addition, for your judgment. The last point is cribbed from an able article in the Times of today, the earlier part, from Lyons.

3. I am doubtful whether this dispatch should go till it has been seen by the Cabinet, indeed I think it should not, & probably you mean this.

4. The Queen recollects being told something about this affair by Clarendon—without result—last year.[4]

5. I think Grammont [*sic*] exacts too much. It would never do for us to get up a combination of Powers in this difficult & slippery matter? [5]

6. I think we shall satisfy the Cabinet of the propriety of what you have done.

[1] That Britain should approach the Hohenzollern-Sigmaringen princes directly.

[2] No. 6, 8 July, F.O. 72/1231.

[3] Granville to Loftus, No. 6, 6 July, with Gladstone's addition, F.O. 64/681. It reasoned against the expediency of the candidature. It was held back until after the cabinet of 9 July which approved it, see Add. MS. 44638, fo. 99.

[4] Cf. Gladstone's instruction to his private secretary, 8 July, to search letters from Clarendon for references to Prince Leopold and Spain. West searched in vain, Add. MS. 44638, fo. 102. No. 245 is followed in Granville's papers by Ffrench to Clarendon, private, 1 Nov. 1869, describing Spanish ministerial discussions on candidates for the throne.

[5] Cf. mem. by Gladstone on desiderata for British policy at this juncture, Add. MS. 44638, fo. 103.

246. Lord Granville to Mr. Gladstone. [Add. MS. 44167, fo. 74]

16, Bruton Street. July 10 [1870].

What do you think of asking the Queen whether there is any one to whom she could write confidentially, with a view to persuade Hohenzollern to refuse.[1]

247. Mr. Gladstone to Lord Granville. [G.D. 29/58]

Chiselhurst. Jul 10./70.

1. I should think you could not do wrong in asking the Queen as you propose to procure if she can a refusal from Hohenzollern through some private channel. The letter of the Princess of Prussia [2] seemed to show that they might be well disposed & that they were friendly with the Hohenzollerns.

2. I suppose there could be no objection to sounding the Italian Government as to the Duke of Aosta.[3]

3. If in the meantime you have authentic accounts of military movements in France, would it not be right formally to ask their suspension if it be still the desire of the French Government that you should continue to act in the sense of procuring withdrawal.

248. Lord Granville to Mr. Gladstone. [Add. MS. 44167, fo. 75]

6, Bruton Street. July 10./70.

It was said yesterday, that you are going to poor Lothian's funeral in Scotland. I should not venture to write to you, on the subject, if it had not been the unanimous desire of the Cabinet that I should try to dissuade you.

It is impossible to argue on a question of strong feeling, but it cannot be a duty for you with your work and responsibilities to go so far. And Lothian's family must be fully soothed by your known wish & intention to do so.

It is a duty of a high order for you to do all you can for your health. Two nights in a Railway in order to be present at that which must be of a distressing character cannot do your health good, and may do it much harm.

You hardly ever are absent from the House without some screw getting loose.

I should write much stronger, if I did not feel that I had a strong personal interest in the matter. In so strained a state as Europe is now, the slightest thing may lead to great consequences, and it is possible that it may be a disadvantage to me & to the chose publique, if anything occurs during the 36 hours you are absent.

Pray excuse me for meddling in a matter so personal to yourself.

[1] Granville to the Queen, 10 July, and reply, 11 July; the Queen to the Count of Flanders, brother-in-law to Prince Leopold, *Letters*, 2nd ser. ii. 24–5, 27–8.

[2] To the Queen, *Letters, loc. cit.* 22; sent by the Queen to Granville, G.D. 29/32.

[3] See Granville to Paget, tel. 11.30 a.m., 10 July, F.O. 45/160; cf. Otway to Granville, 10 July, G.D. 29/107, and Granville's subsequent regrets, to Lyons, 13 July, Newton, *Lord Lyons*, i. 298.

249. Mr. Gladstone to Lord Granville. [G.D. 29/58]

Chiselhurst. Jul 10. 70.

Thanks for your most kind letter about the Lothian Funeral. The points are these. First—if this correspondence about the Spanish throne should at the time require it, I must give up the journey at the last moment. The other is the question of health & strength. Now there is really nothing weak in me, to my knowledge, except my *headpiece*, which would get rest rather than otherwise. The Supreme Court of Appeal, my wife, has considered this part of the case, and does not forbid or discourage my going. Then as to the House of Commons I think we shall have no difficulty in making a safe arrangement of business. I hope therefore you will not interpose a *veto*. It is Lady Lothian that I mainly think of.

I send you H.M.s answer to my last. We cannot release her quite so easily.[1]

250. Lord Granville to Mr. Gladstone. [Add. MS. 44167, fo. 79]

[12 July 1870].

The Rothschilds have recd a telegram.
The Prince has given up his candidature.
The French are satisfied.

251. Mr. Gladstone to Lord Granville. [G.D. 29/58]

H of C. July 12. 1870. 11.30 Pm.

I have seen, since Rothschild's Telegram, that of Lyons dated 7.55 Pm.[2]

It seems to me that Lyons should be supplied with an urgent instruction by Telegram before the Council of Ministers tomorrow.

France appealed to our support at the outset—she received it, so far as the immediate object was concerned—it was immediately & energetically given—it appears to have been named by the French Minister in public inclusively with that of other powers—under these circumstances it is our duty to represent, I think, the immense responsibility which will rest upon France if she does not at once accept, as satisfactory and conclusive, the withdrawal of the Candidature of Prince Leopold.[3]

It is not I suppose needful or desirable to tell her that by her rash and violent conduct she has already caused a strong revulsion of opinion against her. Pray consider this.

[1] From her promise to open the Thames Embankment, Guedalla, i. 234–5.

[2] F.O. 27/1806; the French held that Leopold's withdrawal settled the quarrel with Spain but not 'their complaint against Prussia . . . They will determine at a council tomorrow what course to take.' Gramont anticipated the council, tel. to Benedetti at Ems, 7 p.m., 12 July, R. H. Lord, *Origins of the War of 1870* (1924), p. 80.

[3] See Granville to Lyons, tel. 2.30 a.m., 12[13] July, F.O. 27/1791

252. Mr. Gladstone to Lord Granville. [G.D. 29/58]

11, Carlton House Terrace. Jul 13. 70.

Fortescue will explain to you about the Conacre Amendment.[1] All I need say is that we were most heedful of your engagement, as both he & I explained personally to Dr Ball—that we found a perfectly spontaneous & independent movement in favour of the distinction between white & green crops—that this extended to both sides of the House—& that I believe we should have been beaten by a large majority made up from both sides, had we been more punctilious.

253. Lord Granville to Mr. Gladstone. [Add. MS. 44167, fo. 82]

16, Bruton Street. July 13 [1870].

The improvement upon conacre is unlucky as it was part of the positive agreement between Richmond & me, and was wished by him to reassert his position with his party.

I have already explained to him what passed—& he said he would speak to Cairns—but if he wishes it, I must offer to decline agreeing to your amendment of our amendment.

I trust that you will divide against any alteration of the Assignment clause.[2] It would make a tremendous row in the Cabinet, & upset me as to the conduct of any bill in the Lords.

I have had a long talk with Lavalette.[3]

I see he has hopes, but says they are dreadfully frightened. He is going to telegraph my language to him.

254. Lord Granville to Mr. Gladstone. [Add. MS. 44167, fo. 84]

Confidential. F.O. July 13/70.

I intended not to answer your kind letter to me, as I saw how exceedingly anxious you were to pay honor to the memory of poor Lothian.

As regards your health it would be ridiculous to be more anxious than Mrs Gladstone, and as to the business of the House of Commons you are the best judge.

The Spanish question however is up to this time unsettled, the Prime Minister & the F.O. Secretary are responsible to the Cabinet for the conduct of pressing and important details. Questions may be asked in the Commons on very delicate matters.

[1] A Lords' amendment debarred tenants who let for a season land already cropped (i.e. 'in conacre') from claiming compensation under clause 3 of the Irish land bill, Parl. papers. H.C. 204 (1870). ii, 372. The Commons excepted land so let 'for the growing of potatoes or other green crops'.

[2] See *Lords' Amendments to the Irish Land Bill*. Parl. papers. H.C. 204 (1870). ii, 375. The new clause B, to be inserted into that part of the act excepting certain tenancies from the right to claim compensation for improvements, was accepted without a division by the Commons, 12 July, *C.J.* (1870), 323.

[3] See Granville to Lyons, 13 July, *Correspondence respecting Negotiations preliminary to the War*. Parl. papers. [C. 167] (1870). lxx, 45.

Hammond has heard from the Ker[r]s that you were going away for the funeral. It has made him extremely anxious, & he has begged me to speak to you. I own I do not feel that I have any right to refuse to do so, particularly as I think the public will be surprised at your absence at such a moment, even if no difficulty arises.

The case would be different if the funeral was that of a near relation.

Poor Lothian's mother told my sister how much they had all been struck by the extraordinary kindness & feeling you had shown in settling to go amidst all your work—this although it may be a strong inducement to go, also shows that they would not be surprised at your being obliged to give it up.

If you are of opinion that you still should go pray consider this letter as non avenue.

255. Mr. Gladstone to Lord Granville. [G.D. 29/58]

Immediate. 11, Carlton House Terrace. July 13. 70.

1. I think your note about Conacre has perhaps been written before receiving mine. I am sure you would yourself have done what we did.

2. Assignment, & every thing else I think, is passed just as agreed on.

3. As to my journey tonight, I am now entirely dependent on Foreign matters and live from hour to hour in hopes of hearing from F.O. that the Council of Ministers in France today has ended the whole affair.[1]

256. Lord Granville to Mr. Gladstone. [Add. MS. 44167, fo. 88]

37, Chesham Place. [14 July 1870].

I have seen Bessborough again. It is amusing, but also satisfactory and instructive to hear his talk.

The substance is the same, the tone as different as black from white [2]—from not expressed, but evident dissatisfaction with you.

257. Mr. Gladstone to Lord Granville. [G.D. 29/58]

11, Carlton House Terrace. July 14. 70.

You justly observed that we might have questions tonight. What are the answers to be?

That the candidature is withdrawn—that with this withdrawal we had hoped, & had a right to hope, that the whole affair would end—that as we are informed it is at an end between France and Spain, but that negotiations or communications are still continued with Prussia: what they are we do not know & are not able to conjecture. In duty to all parties we are bound to hope that the subject of

[1] Gladstone cancelled his journey when the Foreign Office heard, by 3.30, that, after the council, Gramont announced Leopold's withdrawal to the *corps legislatif* and added that negotiations with Prussia continued. A 9 o'clock edition of the *Norddeutsche Allgemeine Zeitung*, 13 July, carried the 'Ems telegram'. See Gladstone to Lord Schomburgh Kerr, Add. MS. 44427, fo. 193.

[2] Gladstone wrote here 'from what?' No. 256 may relate to Commons' amendments on Lords' amendments to the Irish land bill, and may be a note passed across in committee.

complaint having disappeared, the complaint itself & the danger to the peace of Europe, will disappear also.

I have put this down, in order to provoke thought as to the form of what is to be said. But there is another point.

What if you were to telegraph to Lyons to signify that we think it probable questions may be put in Parliament today: that having been called in by France itself we cannot affect to be wholly outside the matter: and that it will be impossible for us to conceal the opinion that the cause of quarrel having been removed France ought to be satisfied.

While this might fairly pass as a friendly notice, it might also be useful as admonition?

Please to consider.[1]

The claim in the Telegrams for more acknowledgment of the conduct of Prussia in Parlt seems to me to deserve consideration.

258. Mr. Gladstone to Lord Granville. [G.D. 29/58]

11, Carlton House Terrace. July 17. 70.

The case as to the provision for Ballot in the Education Bill [2] stands thus

1. Entirely & in every particular we disclaim the intent & construction which the Duke of Richmond attaches to it.

2. It is impossible for us to drop it; after having sat up till past five in the morning to carry it through fourteen divisions.

3. Any further contest on it in the House of Commons will lose public time, but will exactly suit our party purposes: the tenacity with which we have held to this point has almost atoned in the eyes of some of our supporters for the equal tenacity with which in some other matters we adhered to views which were agreeable to the Opposition.

259. Mr. Gladstone to Lord Granville. [G.D. 29/58]

11, Carlton House Terrace. July 19. 70.

1. I shall be sorry if in taking upon us the charge of the interests of French

[1] The cabinet was summoned at 11.30 for 12.30 to consider (i) answers to parliamentary questions and (ii) last efforts to preserve peace; see Add. MS. 44638, fos. 104, 105, and Granville to Lyons, tel. 2.45 p.m., 14 July, 'draft read and approved' in the cabinet but 'finally settled with Lord G. afterwards', F.O. 362/4, and Gladstone to the Queen, 14 July, Guedalla, i. 236–7, *Letters*, 2nd ser. ii. 32. Britain proposed an accommodation by which King William publicly sanctioned the withdrawal and France waived her request for a pledge that the candidature would not be renewed.

[2] The report stage in the Commons was due on 19 July. The provision for the election of the new school boards by ballot was attacked in committee; see Parl. papers, H.C. 167 (1870). i, 576–9, *Hans. Parl. Deb.* 3rd ser. cciii. 271–316. It survived but was cut out, except for the Metropolitan area, by the Lords. Richmond considered it a pointless piece of doctrinaire liberalism, *Hans. Parl. Deb. loc. cit.* 859.

subjects we have omitted any thing required by courtesy to Prussia. Doubtless her permission was an implied condition.[1]

2. May I answer the questions within as proposed—or amend as you think fit.

260. Mr. Gladstone to Lord Granville. [G.D. 29/58]

11, Carlton House Terrace. July 21. 70.

Respecting Ld Lyons No 811 and the advantage of obtaining an available written promise of neutrality from France.[2] It occurs to me that the following ground might reasonably be given, if the Belgians like, for asking it without fear of offence.

That the letter of L[ouis] N[apoleon] is in itself all they can desire—but that the relations between the Belgian Throne & Chambers are such as would not allow an equally binding character to attach to a reply in the shape of a letter from the Belgian King. But as the Belgian Govt could not rest satisfied without giving to France an effectual counterpart for her spontaneous engagement, & this could only be done by the proper minister, who could not presume to answer a personal letter from the Emperor, they would suggest a corresponding letter from the Duc de Grammont [*sic*], to which the Belgian Minister could reply & so the transaction would be complete.

Please to consider whether this is worth any thing.

I would propose 2.15 in my *room* in D. St for the small meeting we spoke of.

261. Mr. Gladstone to Lord Granville. [G.D. 29/58]

10, Downing Street. July 22. 70. 1 a.m.

We had to cram dishes of the Lords amendments down the throats of our men today; two points we altered. 1. We put in the £15 *valuation* according to the rule promised all through the Bill: secondly we restored "or character" with Balls full and distinct approval and according to our resolution in Downing Stree .

We have strained ourselves as well as our friends a good deal for the sake of peace: I hope the Lords will not tempt us any further.

I am unable to join in the compliments paid to their moderation, but I have kept silence thus far. They would have acted more wisely for the order as well as for the country, had they acted more liberally.

I hope the Bill will not come back: if it does our debates will I fear be of a different colour.

[1] Marginal instruction by Granville: 'Telegraph accordingly to Loftus. G.' Noted as done by his private secretary '19/7/70'. France had declared war on 15 July. Britain's last-minute offer of mediation having failed, she had taken measures to safeguard her neutrality.

[2] On the policy of asking assurances from France and Prussia to respect Belgian neutrality, see Granville to Lyons, private, 13 July, Newton, *Lord Lyons*, i. 297–8, King Leopold to the Queen, *Letters*, 2nd ser. ii. 30–2, and to Granville, 13 July, G.D. 29/83, Lyons to Granville, No. 811, 18 July, reporting a personal letter from Napoleon III to King Leopold, F.O. 27/1806. A dispatch to Lumley (Brussels) was drafted as proposed by Gladstone but cancelled, G.D. 29/58.

Both Disraeli and Ball spoke with prudence: indeed I am fully persuaded that they have by no means concurred in all the steps taken by your Opposition.[1]

262. Lord Granville to Mr. Gladstone. [Add. MS. 44167, fo. 90]

Confidential. Bruton St. July 25 [24?]/70.

I have had a bad taste in my mouth since yesterday's Cabinet.[2] I thought from your manner at the end of the discussion, that you were of opinion that I had not been respectful to you in my way of arguing. I need not say this was not my intention —and that I deeply regret it, if it were so. I have recd the enclosed this morning from Cairns. Nothing could be more reasonable than your requiring time, but if you could without inconvenience come to a decision before tomorrow morning, it would much facilitate matters. If you retain the Commons amendments, it would be difficult to explain the delay of a day, and would be discourteous to Richmond, who has his monster annual party this week.

If you yield, out of consideration for me, and to avoid the dead lock which would come, it would excite less observation, and work with less friction. The Commons clause was amended in the Committee of Lords, it was reamended on the report in order to meet one of our difficulties. You reamended the Lords amendment so as to meet the other difficulty. The Lords insisted on their view. You amended by certain words, which the Lords will accept, if "exorbitant" is substituted for "excessive" and "rent" for "valuation". I doubt whether this amount of give and take, would be much criticized.

You gave me Argyll's words, telling me you thought they would do, these were the words which I sent to Cairns. In my previous conversation with him I had said "valuation", and he objected on the ground of the excessive inequality in different parts of Ireland as to valuation compared with rent. I then sent him the words you had placed in my hand. He returned the amendment as written out by him —and Fortescue's statement in the Cabinet yesterday that he did not know where the words came from, or whose they were, was hardly consistent with his language to me before the change was made.

I am afraid from what Richmond said, that no mezzo termine is now possible.

I deeply regret the worry & trouble I have unintentionally given you, and wish I could help in finding some better solution.

The other question about "character" affects me a little, but the Chancellor more so.

263. Mr. Gladstone to Lord Granville. [G.D. 29/58]

Private. Chiselhurst. July 24. 70.

I will not deny that I *was* mortified, not by any language of yours, but by

[1] Relates to proceedings in the Commons, 21 July, on the Lords' amendments to the land bill upon which they insisted after the bill had been returned to them from the Commons.

[2] Gladstone notes a partial discussion of amendments on the Irish land bill in the cabinet of 23 July and decision, 25 July, to follow a course 'in accordance with Granville's views', Add. MS. 44638, fos. 108, 110. For further proceedings in the Lords and final yielding in the Commons, see *L.J.* (1870), 460, 464, *C.J.* (1870), 374.

some of the incidents of yesterday's Cabinet; but this, before receiving your kind letter of today, I had determined to put wholly out of recollection, and only to ask for an understanding between ourselves that when, amid the many & complex movements of the wheels, any one goes wrong, we two shall first talk it over together, for it is impossible for any man to talk over a difficulty with you & not to find himself nearer to a solution at the end than he was at the beginning.

I never knew the facts till yesterday, nor I suppose did you. When on Thursday I found the Registration Clause accepted, or at least affirmed by the Lords, with my own undoubting recollection (accurate or not) that the Cabinet had rejected it, I concluded without hesitation that you had *not* been making a treaty, & that we were bound by none. This was the key to my action, & a key without which my note of that day to you must have been an enigma.

The change of 'exorbitant' to 'excessive' was made, in haste I presume, without my knowledge; and I decidedly disapprove of it.

But that is not the point. Nor does the difficulty lie in any hesitation on my part to accept the Lords amendments rather than lose the Bill or expose you to suspicion. The difficulty is that I think the words used by me in debate may be construed strictly so as to bind me not to accept the substitution of rent for valuation. Immediately after the truce in the Cabinet, I asked Fortescue to find out how the acceptance would be taken by some specimens of that class of Irish member to whom I am under the deepest obligation. I think he will extricate me & sooth them if it can be done: and I write another note to him to beg him to be expeditious. I am to be in town at ten this evening.

I hope you will not think the request I have made unreasonable: I am almost ashamed to make any request of you, of whom all my recollections, were our political relation to end today, would be absorbed in one, that of your inexhaustible and overflowing kindness.

I quite agree that it is desirable to go on tomorrow.

Any further dark places in the facts I can explain at leisure.

I feel anxiety about the military question tomorrow.[1]

Please think of the Univ. Tests Bill if you can: we left it floating in the air.[2]

All is good here except the stationary. Cairns's note will have but narrow quarters.

264. Lord Granville to Mr. Gladstone. [Add. MS. 44167, fo. 93]

16, Bruton Street. July 25/70.

I cannot say how touched I am by the kindness of your note.

Let me know as early as you can, but in any case I will see you before the Cabinet.

[1] Cabinet discussion on the state of the army was postponed from 23rd to 25th, Add. MS. *loc. cit.*

[2] Partially discussed in the cabinet of 23 July, Add. MS. *loc. cit.*

265. Note by Lord Granville.[1] [Add. MS. 44167, fo. 204]

16, Bruton Street. [25 July 1870].

We had read the astounding document printed in the Times of this morning. We had no knowledge of how that document had been communicated to that paper.

From its nature it might be deemed incredible that such a proposal should have been made by one party, and in any way considered by the other.

We could not doubt that on the publication of such an alleged Treaty, both Govts will spontaneously hasten to inform Europe, either that the document is forged, or if genuine what were all the circumstances attending it.

266. Lord Granville to Mr. Gladstone. [Add. MS. 44167, fo. 94]

16, Bruton Street. July 26/70.

What do you think of my sending the enclosed note—please scan the statement, and the words.

The Report of what passed about the Irish Land Bill is inaccurate.

I tried my best in public and private to get Richmond & Cairns to get something out of the fire, but notwithstanding Halifax's assistance they stuck to their pound of flesh.

267. Mr. Gladstone to Lord Granville. [G.D. 29/58]

House of Commons. Jul 26 [1870].

I should be glad if the dispatch to Sir A. Paget [2] were a little more considered. It seems to me to go *further* against combined neutrality than the one to Lord Lyons.

268. Mr. Gladstone to Lord Granville. [G.D. 29/58]

11, Carlton House Terrace. Jul 26. 70.

The Telegram from Loftus,[3] while it removes difficulties as to disclosure, diminishes, does it not, the importance of our referring to previous communications with Bismarck? Had the Treaty proved a hoax we should have been compelled to tell.

I do not however see any objection to his [4] being informed that after what he

[1] Words settled in the cabinet, 25 July, for parliamentary answer about the project of treaty published that morning in *The Times*. Cf. note of the same words in Add. MS. 44638, fo. 111. Cf. Disraeli to Gladstone, 25 July, Add. MS. 44427, fo. 224. No. 265 is bound in the Gladstone papers as belonging to Dec. 1870. See also below, no. 268.

[2] No. 20, 25 July, on the Italian proposal to exchange pledges not to depart from neutrality without previous communication. A revised dispatch, delivered to the messenger in Paris, omitted the British view 'that no combination should be entered into . . . since it would carry with it the germ of an armed neutrality', F.O. 45/160. See also note by Hammond on Gladstone's letter, G.D. 29/58.

[3] 6 p.m., 25 July, reporting that a draft Franco-Prussian treaty of 1866, for the French acquisition of Belgium, was to be officially published, F.O. 64/689. It had already, 19 July, been communicated secretly by Bernstorff to Gladstone and Granville; Granville to Lyons, No. 130, 25 July, F.O. 27/1792. Published in *The Times*, 25 July.

[4] Bernstorff. Cf. Granville to Bernstorff, private, 26 July, G.D. 29/111.

said yesterday you take it for granted there is no longer any *secret* as to what passed between us: but I think I would make it shorter.

I am glad the issue is to be regularly raised at Berlin.

269. Mr. Gladstone to Lord Granville. [G.D. 29/58]

11, Carlton House Terrace. Jul 26. 70].

Might I not read out to the H. of C. at 2 today the Loftus Telegram? It touches matter of fact only: & I think would well vindicate our tone of yesterday.

270. Lord Granville to Mr. Gladstone. [G.D. 29/58]

16, Bruton Street. [26 July 1870].

I would not volunteer it—particularly as it only announces an intention.

I am quite happy about what we said yesterday, & we have vindication enough for it, but we must remember that all we have yet heard is from one side.

271. Mr. Gladstone to Lord Granville. [G.D. 29/58]

Jul. 26. [1870].

I shall not get off without questions, having had notice from Samuelson. I think to read it would save my making any other answer.

If you disapprove, *send* a word.[1]

272. Lord Granville to Mr. Gladstone. [G.D. 29/104]

16, Bruton Street. July 28/70.

I had begun a note desiring Hammond to put down his views in writing when I got the inclosed,[2] with which I do not agree.

I will try to get something into shape to consider.[3] What does Glyn say as to the way the cat is jumping about power to encrease the army.

273. Mr. Gladstone to Lord Granville. [G.D. 29/58]

Immediate. 11, Carlton House Terrace. July 29.70.

I think it worth while to observe how desirable it is that if we are to form Engagements about Belgium it should be done before any great battle takes place to alter

[1] No. 271 is written on the back of No. 270. Hammond noted that Gladstone was 'asked to read—if obliged—the substance not the whole as it came in cypher'. The document is followed in G.D. 29/58 by an extract from the *Newcastle Daily Chronicle*, possibly sent by Gladstone to Granville, on the form of the Belgian guarantee.

[2] Mem. by Hammond, 29 July, objecting to safeguarding Belgian neutrality by means of the proposed new treaties with France and Prussia, G.D. 29/104.

[3] I.e. at the cabinet, 30 July; see Add. MS. 44638, fo. 115. Cf. Granville to Lyons, No. 153, 30 July, F.O. 27/1792, and to Loftus, No. 55, 30 July, F.O. 64/681, proposing to record in a protocol or convention their intention to observe Belgian neutrality, and Lyons to Granville, private, 3 Aug., G.D. 29/85. No. 274 below is written on the back of no. 272.

the relative position of the two parties. I mean done as far as our proposals are concerned. I hope therefore all preparations, by conference with LaValette or otherwise will be carried as far as possible today so that the Cabinet if it approves may make you plenipotentiary tomorrow.

2. If you wish me to say more on Bulwer's motion than I said on Palmer's, please . . . . .[1]

274. Mr. Gladstone to Lord Granville. [G.D. 29/104]

C.H.T. July 29. 70.

1. Feeling much altered. Those who were strongly opposed to any measures, are now disposed to confide in the Govt. with respect to them. Those who before wd have confided in the Govt. & been *silent* are now speaking decidedly for measures to augment our force in one shape or other.

Glyn approves these words: though they are you see in Benedetti's handwriting.

I simply *report* without giving an opinion.

2. Hammond's Mem. I differ: as to what he rejects, & as to what he recommends.

Last night I spoke to Cardwell: On cons[ideratio]n he seemed to me well disposed to entertain the plan. (It would be well that you & I should meet him & Childers tomorrow at 2 before Cabinet ?).

Goschen seemed to like it.

275. Lord Granville to Mr. Gladstone. [Add. MS. 44167, fo. 96]

Confidential. [31 July 1870].

Lowe did not say what was accurate, when he declared he had never heard of the plan. I called on him on purpose to sound him. I am bound to say he objected. If he writes in a hurry, send for him, and be civil. I am sure all will go right.[2]

276. Lord Granville to Mr. Gladstone. [Add. MSS. 44167, fo. 97]

16 Bruton Street. [2 August 1870].

I only heard half your speech [3] which I thought excellent.

The debate reads well for us, and not encouraging for Lowe.[4]

Brunnow has an important communication to make from his august Master.

[1] Letter incomplete. For Sir Roundell Palmer's observations, 20 May, on the Greek massacres, see *Hans. Parl. Deb.* 3rd ser. cci. 1123; Gladstone's statement, *ibid.* 1152. Bulwer had given notice of a motion on the subject for 29 July, but postponed it, *ibid.* cciii. 1232, raising it on 2 Aug., when the House went into committee on supply, *ibid.*, 1412; Gladstone's statement, 1421.

[2] Relates to Lowe's opposition in the cabinet, 30 July, to fresh engagements on Belgium; see Gladstone's note, Add. MS. 44638, fo. 115. This is followed by an exchange between Fortescue, Gladstone and Granville on the possibility of Lowe's resignation.

[3] Answering Disraeli's observations on the war, 1 Aug., *Hans. Parl. Deb.* 3rd ser. cciii. 1300–13.

[4] Opinion on both sides of the House favoured action over Belgium which Lowe opposed.

277. Mr. Gladstone to Lord Granville. [G.D. 29/58]

Immediate. 11, Carlton House Terrace. Aug 2. 70.

I hope you will be able now to prosecute the Treaty with France full gallop.

There is an intense desire in the House that we should say or they should know something about Belgium. We are sure to be pressed again unless we speak, & every time we are pressed the demand for confidence will seem more exacting and supercilious.

Is it impossible that a draft should go to Lyons today for him to execute?

As to particular points

1. I think you cannot in the Treaty limit yourself to sea defence. In the joint engagement, there was a sort of rivalry of doing *much* between the two nations in 1854 & we need not fear that France will shrink.

2. There should I suppose be a Clause providing for the accession of other Powers.

3. As to the termination of the Treaty I suppose you will have precedents in the F.O. which are much better than suggestions. Otherwise what if it be made to last until a Treaty of Peace is ratified, & 12 months after to allow for settling down & disarming?

4. This followed up by an Article saving all the present obligations so that they might be resumed exactly as they are when they have ceased to be covered by the wider temporary engagement.[1]

This note is rather officious (in the English sense) but I am very anxious to keep things straight in the H of C *versus* Osbornes and Bulwers, both of whom did mischief.[2]

278. Mr. Gladstone to Lord Granville. [G.D. 29/58]

H of C. Aug 2. 70.

The difficulty in the case of Denmark seems to be that though neuter she has an unsettled controversy of territory with Prussia. It seems difficult therefore to do more, than join Russia in urging France not to drive Denmark from neutrality by pressure: and to urge Prussia to remove the cause of danger on the side of Denmark by making a fair arrangement of the matter as to territory now in difference. I do not know whether this would satisfy Russia.[3] It is desirable no doubt that we should do any thing in reason for the sake of working with Russia at the present juncture.

[1] For draft treaty with France (duplicated with Prussia) on Belgian neutrality, in three articles following Gladstone's outline, and for Gladstone's alterations, tending to dissociate the new treaty from that of 1839, see Granville to Lyons, No. 182, 3 Aug., F.O. 27/1792, and *Further Correspondence respecting the War*. Parl. papers. [C. 210] (1870). lxx, 198–200.

[2] I.e. in taunting the government for ineffectiveness over Belgium and for being surprised by the outbreak of war, 1 Aug., *Hans. Parl. Deb.* 3rd ser. cciii. 1321–6, 1354–9.

[3] For Russian proposal of Anglo-Russian representations to France against pressure upon Denmark, see Granville to Buchanan, No. 131, 25 July, F.O. 65/798, Brunnow to Granville, private, 12 Aug., G.D. 29/98, and reply 13 Aug., G.D. 29/115; for cabinet agreement to Gladstone's proposals, 6 Aug., Add. MS. 44638, fo. 119; instructions to Lyons, Nos. 237, 238, 15 Aug., F.O. 27/1792 cancelled after French defeats, No. 249, 17 Aug., F.O. 27/1793, Granville to Brunnow, private, 4 Sept., G.D. 29/115.

279. Mr. Gladstone to Lord Granville. [G.D. 29/58]

[*Copy*].[1] Aug: 3: 70.

The case contemplated by Lord Lyons in his dispatch [2] of Aug: 1, seems to be

1. That France should accept the Engagement, & Prussia decline it.
2. That Prussia should invade Belgium as a measure of war against France.
3. That we join in [*sic*] France in driving out the Prussian forces.
4. That either before or after this operation is effected France while acting under a distinct & recent alliance with us, shall traffic with Prussia in the independence of Belgium.

Even after the disclosures recently made can we regard this as a probable danger?

But then we must look to that on which Ld Lyons recommends us to rely. This is the fear of our displeasure. But this might & probably wd be a *sole* displeasure. How much would it be worth against a combination between France & Prussia for the absorption of Belgium?

How much wd it weigh in preventing such a combination?

In the absence of any positive measure such as we propose in order to heal the wound opened by the Project of Treaty, shd we not be compelled to intimate pretty distinctly that the displeasure impends? It must be remembered that in Parlt. we have referred to a *something* yet to be disclosed.

Would not this intimation when made, as I assume it must be, have a tendency to induce the two Powers to combine, if they are really set on the end of absorbing Belgium?

Is it not a great object to remove speedily the mistrust caused by the Project of Treaty, and would a declaration of our displeasure against any offender really satisfy Europe, or even this country after the first few days, that any new & real security had been taken?

Is there, in a word, any measure as appropriate to the 'situation' created by the recent disclosures, as taking a new point of departure, *and is there any new point of departure* so promising, as our taking pledges from the Belligerents at a moment when both are open to so many contingencies of danger, & when it is so much the interest [of] each (France especially I admit) to be well with us?

280. Lord Granville to Mr. Gladstone. [Add. MS. 44167, fo. 98]

16, Bruton Street. Aug 4/70.

I am very very sorry.[3] I presume you will make an unavailing attempt to keep him, & at all events ask leave to use your discretion as to the time of announcement.

[1] Gladstone's holograph in Add. MS. 44759, fo. 142. Granville's copy omitted starred phrase.

[2] No. 993, F.O. 27/1808. Cf. Lyons to Granville, private, 3 Aug., on Gramont's 'changed note' and his arguments against the proposed treaty, G.D. 29/85, underlined by Hammond to Granville, 4 Aug., G.D. 29/104.

[3] That Bright proposed to resign when the Belgian treaties were signed. See Bright to Gladstone, 3 Aug., sent to Granville, Add. MS. 44112, fo. 142. Cf. Gladstone to Bright, 4 Aug., Morley, ii. 342; 8, 10 Aug., Add. MS. 44539, fos. 6, 8. He resigned in November.

281. Mr. Gladstone to Lord Granville. [G.D. 29/58]

11, Carlton House Terrace. Aug 6. 70. 1 Pm.

M. de LaValette could not find you at home nor learn where you were. He came here. To save time I told him the purport of our conversation. I took down the words inclosed [1] from his mouth. He does not bind his government but he personally could recommend this basis for the conclusion of the affair.

I told him the Cabinet was to meet at two punctually & we would discuss this matter first. He has a copy of the words.

282. Mr. Gladstone to Lord Granville. [G.D. 29/58]

St. George's Hill, Byfleet. Aug. 7. 4 Pm [1870].

I have received & thank you for two Telegrams, last night & this afternoon.[2] They came quickly. The news stuns me. It is not merely a great action lost and won. It is the greatest blow apparently which France has received as a military Power for more than a hundred years, in the vital point of credit & reputation: and unless retrieved seems likely to depose her from the first place in that line. But further it raises the question whether it will be followed by a Revolution. If ever there was a Government-made War, it is this: & France may call the author to account. What is perhaps most of all remarkable is the stupid way in which France has managed the whole controversy.

If the Napoleon Government is alive I suppose they will make no more difficulty about signing with us.[3]

Tomorrow at twelve sharp I hope to be in C.H.T.

I count on having then to write to Bright: and I despair of stopping him. But it has occurred to me, that it may be well to keep his office open until November if it can be done without much inconvenience, which I suppose to be the case. The whole thing may be over, & he may be well. Should these happy contingencies unite he may come back. Should both or either fail the effect in the meantime will not have been bad. And all possible abstention in regard to filling his place is due to so eminent a man.

This is a charming retreat.

283. Mr. Gladstone to Lord Granville. [G.D. 29/58]

Telegram. [Walmer. 17 August 1870].[4]

Have received account Bernstorff's letter [5] and should like to have the power of referring to the original letters written from Berlin to or for Clarendon. Could you bring them to be used or not as may seem best.

[1] Proposed for the 'British explanation of their understanding of certain points' of the projected Belgian treaties, drafts by Gladstone and Granville, G.D. 29/68 and Add. MS. 44759, fos. 146, 150. The explanation met French objections. See Granville to Lyons, Nos. 203, 205, 6 Aug., F.O. 27/1792, and Add MS. 44638, fo. 119.

[2] Announcing the general French retreat behind the Moselle.

[3] The Belgian treaties were signed 9 Aug. with France and 11 Aug. with Prussia.

[4] Gladstone was with Granville at Walmer, 11–18 Aug.

[5] To Gladstone, 15 Aug., protesting against Gramont's account, 3 Aug., of Prussia's rejection

284. Mr. Gladstone to Lord Granville. [G.D. 29/58]

11, Carlton House Terrace. Aug. 20. 70.

I settled the inclosed Memorandum [1] with Childers yesterday evening, in conformity with what we had in view at Walmer. I have today seen Manning and have made known to him the substance in strict confidence. He is much pleased and thinks it quite sufficient. He understands it is for them at Rome to consider whether to make a communication to us on the subject of destination: but he seemed to think this had better stand over. He writes to the Head of the English College who he says will know how to make use of the information. He says he dare not send it to the Pope now, as H.H. would be so pleased that he would undoubtedly blurt it out to those around him, & they are not to be trusted & would trade in it with France or Austria.

Childers quite understood and will act upon our views about the fleet.[2]

From the look of my affairs here I am doubtful whether I can get down [to Walmer] before Tuesday.

Though it may be odd thus to act upon Manning's unofficial representations [3] I should think under the circs it is probably right.

285. Mr. Gladstone to Lord Granville. [G.D. 29/58]

11, Carlton House Terrace. Aug 21. 70.

This business about carrying French & Prussian wounded across the neutral territories has occupied me with Hammond & otherwise a good deal today, and Hammond sends you copy of a long Telegram which we send to Lyons, *he* Hammond feeling that he is sufficiently authorised on your part.[4]

This forenoon I saw Kusserow who told me that full 3/5 of the wounded to be conveyed would be French.

The urgency of the case is extreme, for the object is to prevent gangrene low fever & I know not what among thousands of men.

Kusserow believes that the killed & wounded of the two sides from Sunday to Thursday are full 70,000!

of Clarendon's secret disarmament proposals 1869–70 (revealed in *La Liberté*, 17 July) and reply 18 Aug., Add. MS. 44428, fos. 32, 43. Cf. the interchange of letters between Granville's private secretaries, H. Hervey and R. Meade, 13, 14 Aug., G.D. 29/107, min. by Granville on private letter from Lyons, 17 July, G.D. 29/85, and the Queen to Granville, 2 Aug., G.D. 29/32.

[1] Instructions to H.M.S. *Defence* to go to Civita Vecchia to protect British lives and property and to give shelter to the Pope if requested, copy, G.D. 29/58. The French evacuated Rome, 19 Aug.

[2] It was decided to recall the Channel and Mediterranean fleets from their Atlantic cruise 'for the sake of appearance'. Cf. correspondence between Granville and Childers, 18, 19 Aug., G.D. 29/54.

[3] Manning to Gladstone, 13 Aug., and reply, 14 Aug., Manning to Gladstone, 15, 18 Aug., and reply, 19 Aug., preceding a meeting with Manning on 20 Aug., Manning to Gladstone, 20 Aug., Add. MS. 44249, fos. 174–87.

[4] See to Lyons, tel. 5.15 p.m., 21 Aug., acquiescing in the Prussian project on the two conditions stated by Gladstone, F.O. 27/1793. Cf. *Further Correspondence respecting the War* . . . Parl. papers. [C. 244] (1871). lxxi, 33.

To me it seemed there were but two things to stipulate. 1. That there should be no armed men with the trains. 2. That the benefit should be for the wounded of the two sides alike.

Hammond went to Lavalette and he raised difficulties which I thought ill-timed & impolitic to a high degree.[1] He thought it should only be permitted, if all the Prussian wounded were put on the footing of persons forced into a neutral territory and disarmed there, and thereby incapacitated from serving during the war. In other words, this measure of humanity, equal for both parties, was to be turned into an engine for giving to the French a military advantage.

I could not be responsible for giving any countenance to such ideas, and I think France will raise a shout of indignation throughout Europe if unhappily she should adopt a like tone.

The telegram therefore goes to Lyons without any reference to these notions but signifies that any needless interposition of difficulties will entail a heavy responsibility.

I confidently believe you will approve the terms. By tomorrow doubtless we shall receive an answer from Paris. Meantime copies of the Telegram go to Prussia & Belgium, & I should think the Prussians will very probably act on their own responsibility.

The draft to Rome will I think be in perfect harmony with what I told Manning & what accordingly he will have written.

Hammond thinks the war will be long. I am beginning to waver, or at least to think it will be *less* long than I had supposed.

I shall see Halifax this evening and will tell him.[2]

I told H[ammond] I wd. explain to you.

286. Lord Granville to Mr. Gladstone. [Add. MS. 44167, fo. 102]

Private. Walmer Castle. Aug 22/70.

I like your telegram to Lyons. I presume time is so important that we ought to telegraph to Russia and Austria at once telling them what we have done.

I hope the Prussians will wait for a consent from France.[3]

287. Mr. Gladstone to Lord Granville. [G.D. 29/58]

11, Carlton House Terrace. Sept 6. 70.[4]

1. I see no objection to making known to Brunnow your instructions to Lyons.[5] Might we not add the expression of a hope that we should walk together in the

[1] Hammond to Granville, 22 Aug., describes this conversation, G.D. 29/104.

[2] Cf. Halifax to Granville, Balmoral, 29 Aug., referring to this conversation, G.D. 29/64.

[3] France consented, not to the original Prussian plan but to a later one for the care of the wounded of both sides *within* Belgium, which was executed.

[4] Gladstone was again with Granville at Walmer, 23 Aug.–6 Sept. During the gap in the correspondence the catastrophe had happened in France and the Provisional Government, with Jules Favre as foreign minister, taken power.

[5] To remain at his post communicating with, but not recognizing, the *de facto* government, No. 374 confidential, 5 Sept., F.O. 27/1793, Parl. papers, *loc. cit.* p. 59.

matter of recognition, without proceeding upon theory, but each being bound to recognise well-established facts.

2. I quite agree with your proposed instruction to Lyons for Jules Favre.[1] We are I take it, in intention, perfectly impartial, & must not think of the advantage to ourselves of obtaining the good will of one party or the other. This being so it is idle for us to think of good offices until we can tender them upon a basis which will not absolutely repel or exasperate either party. The fortunes of the war have not as yet been such as to indicate such a basis.

Jervoise is quite right I think in not encouraging the Pope to visit the Defence.

288. Mr. Gladstone to Lord Granville. [G.D. 29/58]

S. 7. 70.

See the accompanying.[2] I do not see *here* evidence of a *rule* that the appointments shall be non-political. If there is any record probably Sir T. B[iddulph] has it in his possession. To any special wish of the Queen's I should at once defer.

289. Mr. Gladstone to Lord Granville. [G.D. 29/58]

11, Carlton House Terrace. Sept 7. 70.

I am sorry to have to send you a letter from Chevalier and a draft of the sort of answer I propose to send it.[3]

I cannot say he is not justified, from our personal relations, in sending me this very sad letter, but it causes much pain with little profit. The appeal to our interests I feel to be weak.

I go out at half past eleven to the Agricultural Hall for the Workman's Exhibition. I should probably be at home at four.

290. Mr. Gladstone to Lord Granville. [G.D. 29/58]

Private. 10, Downing Street. Sept 8. 70.

This letter [4] induces me to say I hope Lyons will be very careful as to allowing the French Govt. to suppose we *adopt* their view as to integrity of territory which is clearly a demand out of proportion to the present distribution of good & ill fortune in military matters.

[1] Favre announced that France would welcome mediation if the mediator accepted French territorial integrity. The instructions to Lyons to refuse mediation were written privately, 6 Sept., F.O. 362/4, and were modified at once. Granville telegraphed, 1.50 p.m., 7 Sept., 'Give pith of yesterday's private letter and add [that Britain] would be happy to transmit any communication [from France to Prussia] which might lead to peace', F.O. 27/1793.

[2] A list of equerries since 1837 to show whether their politics were those of the government that appointed them. The Queen wished for the appointment of Lord Mt. Charles and Gladstone yielded; see correspondence between Granville and Biddulph, G.D. 29/32 *passim*, and Gladstone to Biddulph, Add. MS. 44539 *passim*.

[3] From Chevalier, 5 Sept., on France's need for England's moral support to prevent her dismemberment; reply on the uselessness of intervention without authority, Add. MS. 44127, fos. 74, 79. Cf. Morley, ii. 343.

[4] Lyons to Granville, private, 7 Sept., on France's desire for foreign aid to obtain an armistice, and his wish that Britain should not press France to give up territory, G.D. 29/85. Cf. Lyons to Gladstone, 14 Nov., Add. MS. 44428, fo. 200.

291. Mr. Gladstone to Lord Granville. [G.D. 29/58]

S. 11. 70.

I have made some very slight running suggestions.[1] But with regard to the passage in sheet 10 p 2 I should bring it down to the conclusion and to a certain extent soften & modify it, setting forth that we by no means seek to establish exceptional rights for ourselves & are prepared to enter into consultation with other nations as to the possibility of adopting in common a stricter rule, although our expectations of a practical result in the sense indicated by North Germany may not be sanguine.

292. Mr. Gladstone to Lord Granville. [G.D. 29/58]

11, Carlton House Terrace. Sept 11. 70.

I inclose a letter from Fortescue.[2] Should the Republican sympathy rapidly & painfully act on Spain & Italy it might be wise to regard it as an element in our case with the Fenians: but not, I think, otherwise.

To wait two months would run a risk of having the agitation raised at home: and I gathered distinctly from Motley that long before that time he would have to raise one of the cases on behalf of the U.S. Govt.[3]

293. Mr. Gladstone to Lord Granville. [G.D. 29/58]

11, Carlton House Terrace. Sept 13. 70.

I have just seen Thiers[4] and have left with him the copy I made of Bismarck's answer.[5] *Your* Telegram in copy reached me as I arrived there. I translated it to him as well as I could, which was very ill. I did not read to him however the last sentence, headed 'Private'.

He wishes you to give your moral support to the request to receive Jules Favre.

[1] On Granville to Bernstorff, 15 Sept., replying to Bernstorff's mem., 30 Aug., communicated 1 Sept., which opened the 'benevolent neutrality' controversy, F.O. 64/706. Granville's reply was sent to Gladstone with the injunction, 'Revise, correct and amend to any degree. Please'. Cf. Parl. papers, *loc. cit.* pp. 52–3, 91–5.

[2] 9 Sept., replying to Gladstone, 7 Sept., by suggesting two months' postponement, Add. MS. 44122, fo. 161. Gladstone first suggested to Fortescue and Spencer a further release of Fenians, 3 Sept., Add. MS. 44539, fos. 23, 25.

[3] For the conversations between Gladstone and Motley, when both were at Walmer, 3–6 Sept., see exchange of letters 7, 11 Sept., Add. MS. 44428, fos. 90, 96 and Gladstone to Motley, 18 Sept., Add. MS. 44539, fo. 31.

[4] For Granville's three conversations with Thiers, 13–16 Sept., see Fitzmaurice, ii. 52–8, Granville to Lyons, private, 13, 14, 16, 17 Sept., F.O. 362/4, and dispatches of the same dates, F.O. 27/1793.

[5] I.e. to Favre's question whether Bismarck would enter 'en pourparlers pour arriver à un armistice et une conférence sur les conditions de la paix et avec qui', Granville to Bernstorff, 10.30 a.m., 10 Sept. Bismarck replied by asking what guarantees the French could offer that the terms would be obeyed, Bernstorff to Granville, 13 Sept., F.O. 64/706.

I told him that—subject to the reserves stated in your Telegram—I was sure this was your desire.

He wishes to see you on this matter tonight & will go *to you* at whatever hour you name.

294. Lord Granville to Mr. Gladstone. [G.D. 29/58]

Copy. [Foreign Office. 13 September 1870].

I send you the Telegram as I have sent it in cypher.[1]

I will try to see Bernstorff as soon as he comes home.

I have seen Brunnow to whom I have told the answer of Bismarck to us. He thinks it a "fin de non recevoir" and asks with whom they mean to try. That not only does neither party seem to agree with one another, but they don't even honestly say what they want.

I have not told him of the proposed question to Bismarck as nothing is settled —but he stated that he thought Thiers had much better go to Head Quarters.

Beaulieu is in a fuss at having heard that in the city a most important member of the Govt. (meaning you) had mentioned Luxemburg as a possibly good solution.[2]

295. Lord Granville to Mr. Gladstone. [G.D. 29/58]

[14 September 1870].

What is the civilest answer to send to the D of Cleveland, who offers to go as Mediator.

296. Mr. Gladstone to Lord Granville.[3] [G.D. 29/58]

S. 14 [1870].

The best ansr. is the one you wd. desire for yourself.

I cd. tell him nothing better than that it is quite uncertain how much it will fall to our lot & perhaps little probable that we shall require extraneous aid but you are sensible of the kindness of his offer wh you will carefully weigh in case the occasion shd. arise.

297. Mr. Gladstone to Lord Granville. [Add. MS. 44539, fo. 29, and G.D. 29/58]

[*Copy*]. 15 Sept. 70.

I have read the enclosed with surprise. I am aware of no reason why it should have been written. I do not recognize any of the ideas to which it refers as mine,

[1] To Lyons, 6 p.m., 13 Sept., asking at Thiers's instance, whether Granville should inquire whether Bismarck would receive Favre at headquarters. Lyons's reply, midnight, 14 Sept., being favourable, the Ferrières negotiation followed, 19–20 Sept., F.O. 27/1793, F.O. 64/706. Cf. Granville to Tissot and Thiers, 15 Sept., G.D. 29/109, and Gladstone to Hammond, 15 Sept., G.D. 29/58.

[2] See Beaulieu to Jules Devaux, the *chef de cabinet* of King Leopold, 13 Sept., on England's proposing that Prussia should take Luxemburg instead of Alsace-Lorraine, and reply, 14 Sept., G.D. 29/83.

[3] Written on the back of no. 295.

& I am much concerned that if Baron Beaulieu was informed that we, or that I, had adopted the principle of the transfer of Luxemburg to Prussia & meant to propose it, he did not refer to me on the subject rather than report so strange a story to his government. How he could have been so informed, I am wholly at a loss to imagine. There are several considerable advantages which might attend such a transfer but there is much besides to be heard & considered before it could receive even a preliminary approval. I admired it as an ingenious idea which might deserve to be weighed but of the materials for that process I never supposed we were in possession. My wish would certainly be to ask Baron Rothschild for an account of this affair,[1] but I will do nothing to cause additional vexation.

P.S. Private

The worst part of the letter is in the very cool assumptions it makes about the interests of Belgium, which the writer takes upon himself to discuss. It is on this account that I have put so emphatic a disclaimer.

298. Lord Granville to Mr. Gladstone. [G.D. 29/58]

[16 September 1870].

Bernstorff has found out by our answer what a very foolish Memo he wrote. I hope you do not disapprove of my reply to his request.[2]

299. Mr. Gladstone to Lord Granville.[3] [G.D. 29/58]

S. 16 [1870].

Your reasons are irrefragable.
It was evidently impossible to agree to his request.

300. Mr. Gladstone to Lord Granville. [G.D. 29/58]

11, Carlton House Terrace. Sept 16. 70.

1. I very stupidly have always forgotten to ask you in what *shape* the Prussian idea of Napoleon as Emperor was communicated to you.[4] I cannot help thinking that we cannot with propriety receive the communication of that idea, considering the consequences it draws, without recording our objections to it.

2. I suppose we can hardly settle any thing about leaving town, until we know what may be Bismarck's answer, or no-answer, to the overture about Jules Favre's mission.[5]

[1] The letter from this point has survived in the original and is bound as an imperfect document in G.D. 29/58.

[2] That the mem. communicated on 1 Sept. (see above, no. 291) should not be published. Granville refused and the Prussian mem., with the British reply, was published in *The Times*, 19 Sept., Granville to Bernstorff, 16 Sept., G.D. 29/111. Cf. K. Ringhoffer, *Im Kampfe für Prussens Ehre. Aus dem Nachlass des Grafen A. von Bernstorff* (1906), p. 627.

[3] Written on the back of no. 298.

[4] Cf. from Loftus, tel. 5.20 p.m., 5 Sept., F.O. 64/697A; see below, no. 304.

[5] See above, no. 294.

3. I should like not to forget to tell you when we meet what is Strzelecki's doctrine respecting the feeling of Alsace. Lacaita, who says he has heard a good deal on the subject, says, very French in Strasburg & the low country, German in the Vosges.

301. Mr. Gladstone to Lord Granville. [G.D. 29/58]

11, Carlton House Terrace. Sept 16. 70. Midnight.

I am truly concerned to see that even in their present extremity the French cannot escape in principle from meddling in Italy.

It is ill advising folks as to the view they should take of their own interests, but the French will have to plead the sentiments of the people of Alsace while they put out of court the sentiments of Rome.

Does not this render it necessary that Jervoise & Severn should be instructed that they are not to interfere with any question as to the maintenance of the *temporal Power*, beyond the limits of the Italian offer but to report home on it.

Manning's letter [1] is inclosed. I have a letter *tonight* from my Sister, who is in Cologne, dated yesterday. Today's accounts from Brussels strengthen my apprehensions of meditated interference with the internal concerns of France.

302. Lord Granville to Mr. Gladstone. [Add. MS. 44168, fo. 66]

Private. F. O. Feb [September] 17/70.[2]

I have directed my telegram to Lyons to be forwarded for your approval, but as they tell me you have no cypher (which you ought to have) and as I feel sure you will approve, I have saved time by transmitting it at once to Lyons.[3]

Bernstorff encouraged me strongly to do so, but on a solemn promise not to betray him.

Brunnow was of the same opinion. Thiers sent for me again and got me into a conversation which was to be absolutely secret & confidential between ourselves.[4] After a philosophical, historical, eloquent address, he approached the subject of my position before an English H. of Commons, jealous of the honor of the country, and asked in various forms whether if Russia were to take the initiative in addressing [a] friendly remonstrance in favor of France, we should not feel bound to avoid being left behind. I told him that we were following the policy which the House of Commons had approved by votes of money and Legislative Acts—that I already had told him what that policy was, that I could give no sort of answer as to hypothetical cases, that I reserved complete liberty of action for the future, but that

[1] To Gladstone, 14 Sept., on the independence of the Pope, Add. MS. 44249, fo. 192; for replies, 15, 18 Sept., *ibid.*, fo. 196, and Add. MS. 44539, fos. 29, 32.

[2] The copy in G.D. 29/58 has the Sept. date. The misdated original is bound in the Gladstone papers as a letter of 1871.

[3] 2.40 p.m., 17 Sept., 'advise M. Favre to let you inform Bismarck that he is ready to go at once. . . .' Cf. Granville to Bernstorff, tel. 2 p.m., 18 Sept., announcing that Favre had agreed, G.D. 29/111.

[4] See above, no. 293.

it was fair to tell him that desirous as I am of acting in concert with Neutral Powers, I am not jealous of any action they may take which would lead to peace, but on the other hand I should in each step consider what England ought to do irrespective of any initiative taken by others.

It appears Brunnow had asked him whether he would not like to get leave to go through Prussia, (this is very unlike Brunnow's prudence) but when Brunnow asked Bernstorff, he got no encouragement.

Our telegram to Jervoise if it reaches him is perfectly safe. If it does not, they will not act without Instructions.

303. Mr. Gladstone to Lord Granville. [G.D. 29/58]

Hawarden Castle. Sept. 18. 70.

I think there could be no doubt about your Telegram to Lord Lyons.

I had better bring the cypher next time I come down.

The topics of your reply to Thiers seem to me thoroughly well selected.

When they talk to us about the House of Commons, there is a reply which but for proprieties would be the best: 'teach your grandmother to suck eggs'.

How could Thiers dream of going through Prussia.

In the inclosed letter, to my great regret, the Viceroy adheres to his view respecting the Fenians.[1]

Lord Russell is indeed propitious: rather German. Reeve has sent me a letter from Guizot which I venture to send for your perusal.[2]

I stand to arrive in London Tuesday 10.15 Pm.

304. Mr. Gladstone to Lord Granville. [G.D. 29/58]

Hawarden Castle. Sept. 20. 70.

I return to my old point, *a* [*sic*] *propos* of the Rheims communiqué [3]; which seems to be authentic.

It appears to me that, when a Government is totally dissolved, exercises no authority in any part of the country it had ruled, and has ceased to be acknowledged by any portion of the people, its recognition by a Foreign Power means and can only mean the authentic expression of an intention to effect a restoration.

The authority of the Emperor say the Germans is the only one existing legally for France. If it is the true Government of France, it will be competent no doubt to call a Constituent Assembly. But it will also equally be competent not to call one. So that once recognised, it will enjoy what is, as against the French people, a full and final re-establishment of the Empire.

[1] Spencer to Gladstone, 16 Sept., against a further release of Fenian prisoners, Add. MS. 44306, fo. 314.

[2] Cf. Reeve to Gladstone, 14 Sept., enclosing Guizot's letter which has not been traced, Add. MS. 44428, fo. 104.

[3] Issued from Prussian headquarters, 16 Sept., arguing that Napoleon was the only legitimate ruler of France; see Loftus to Granville, No. 321, 11 Sept., F.O. 64/691.

It appears to me that this is most grave. It embodies the doctrine that no country can have a new Government without the consent of the old one. Ought we to witness in silence the promulgation of such a doctrine, which is utterly opposed to the modern notions of public right though it was in vogue 50 years back, and though it was acted on with most fatal consequences by the Prussians of 80 years back.

Why should not the Germans recognise the 'Constituent' about to be elected ? [1]

305. Lord Granville to Mr. Gladstone. [Add. MS. 44167, fo. 104]

[23 September 1870].

I asked Forster whether he thought there was any necessity for a Cabinet in order to recognize the Republic.

He thought none, but that it was necessary to use that or some other excuse for having an early Cabinet.

Why not the 1st or second; if you agree, to the idea.

306. Mr. Gladstone to Lord Granville. [G.D. 29/58]

11, Carlton House Terrace. Sept 23. 70.

A Cabinet next week would suit me better than the week after but I own that I differ from Forster and think that the Recognition ought to be the work of the Cabinet, and it could not meet with any certainty for the discharge of that work in a regular manner *after the fact* [2] sooner than the 4th.

It might however meet before the fact and give an authority to act upon foreseen circumstances.

In that case I should like it to be on the 30th, which would be advantageous with reference to one or two other matters.

If you on the whole like the 30th please to Telegraph forthwith to West who will send out Summonses by tomorrow's post.

I think it well deserves consideration whether we ought to make any remarks upon Bismarck's bold paper about Alsace and Lorraine.[3]

307. Mr. Gladstone to Lord Granville. [G.D. 29/58]

Private. 11, Carlton House Terrace. Sept 24. 70.

I have asked West to send you a proof of my Paper for E[dinburgh] R[eview], which he will have for the purpose.[4]

I do this *ex majori cautelâ*, but at present the MS does not contain (I think)

[1] The decree of 17 Sept. had put the elections for the constituent assembly forward from 16 Oct. (date fixed on 9 Sept.) to 2 Oct.

[2] I.e. after the projected meeting of the constituent assembly, 2 Oct.

[3] Circular dispatch, 13 Sept., indicating the cession of Alsace-Lorraine as indispensable, communicated by Bernstorff to Granville, 22 Sept., F.O. 64/706, Parl. papers, *loc. cit.* pp. 103–4. Cf. Loftus to Granville, No. 295, 10 Sept., F.O. 64/691.

[4] See *Edinburgh Review*, cxxxii. 554–93, Oct. 1870, reprinted in *Gleanings*, iv. 197–257. Cf. P. Knaplund, *Gladstone's Foreign Policy* (1935), p. 56 note, and below, no. 310.

one word bearing on the conditions of peace, or on any question pending & for us to deal with.

The idea I had last night about silence on the Prussian circular is indigestible: it weighs on me today.

I go to Lord Wolverton's this aftn., to return Monday.

308. Mr. Gladstone to Lord Granville. [G.D. 29/58]

Stanmore Park, Great Stanmore. Sept 24.70.

It appears to me that a great importance attaches to the deposit by Count Bismarck with us, a Neutral Power, of a declaration of the intentions of Germany with regard to the terms of peace which she will exact from France; that it may entail embarrassing consequences; and that perhaps he ought to have an opportunity of considering whether he could withdraw the communication, and leave it *non avenu*.

It is easy to acknowledge it as an act of courtesy and friendship, and it would have been well if the matter could have ended there.

It might have so ended, had the paper deposited with us related only to what we may term details, or to any matters in which the two parties are exclusively concerned.

But it appears to me that Count Bismarck's paper raises questions of public right, in which all Europe has a common interest, and that it is impossible for us to receive in silence matter relating to such questions from the North German Government, if it is in itself of a nature to call for remark on its own merits. In such a case, silence, without *caveat* of any kind entered, is an approach to acquiescence.

If the paper be not withdrawn, it appears to me as at present advised, that we might examine it & comment upon it to the effect of the memorandum [1] herewith.

309. Lord Granville to Mr. Gladstone. [Add. MS. 44167, fo. 107]

Private. Walmer Castle. Sep 25/70.

I send you a note from Bernstorff, which differs from Lyons and the Moniteur. [2] I presume the latter is right. Also Manning's letter. [3] I hear he shows your letters, to which I presume you do not object.

To these are added some Royal twaddle—which I am desired to return after you have seen it.

I am like you—I itch to be at Bernstorff. I presume about French Imperialism, and forcible suppression of German opinions in favor of peace.

[1] See Temperley and Penson, *Foundations*, 324–7.

[2] From Bernstorff, 24 Sept., on the Ferrières negotiation, and the Prussian demand for Strassburg, Toul and Verdun before the signature of an armistice, G.D. 29/94; from Lyons, tel., 25 Sept., naming Strassburg, Metz and Mont Valérien (Paris), F.O. 27/1817.

[3] To Gladstone, 23 Sept., urging the settlement of the Roman question by a European guarantee of the Pope's temporal power, Add. MS. 44249, fo. 204.

I have great doubts however whether we should descend from our very strong position, to meet the enemy in the plain.

I will call on you soon after two on Tuesday, in order to discuss policy, and adopt identical post-prandial conversation for the evening.

Glyn told me that our friends approve much of our line up to the moment; and the speeches of Tom Baring and Carnarvon [1] show that the sensible Tories do not agree with the Standard.

The only weapon I know to oppose Bismark's possible insolence to us, is moral support to German liberalism, but it will require great discretion not to damage that cause and assist arbitrary chauvinism.

We as "intelligent foreigners" might easily do this.

Cas [2] & I were the only Churchgoers this morning. The rest being Catholics, Greeks, & Lutherans.

310. Lord Granville to Mr. Gladstone. [Add. MS. 44167, fo. 111]

Confidential. Walmer Castle. Sep 26/70.

I am dying for the proofs which have not yet appeared.

Your Manuscript [3] however arrived this morning. It seems to be an admirable argument the more so as it is the sort of thing Thiers ought to have said and did not.

I see however strong objections to making use of it at present. I will tell them to you on Tuesday. A caveat of a somewhat vague description might reserve the use of it for the time when it may be of practical use.

This stale circular which really teaches us nothing new is hardly a reason for doing that after the rupture of the negotiations, which the French would have liked us so much to do before Favre went. The imprisonment of the liberals is a great fact,[4] but it is not clear that our becoming their advocates would not more strongly excite German Chauvinism against them.

Then I rather doubt our suggesting any terms of peace, unless at the particular moment when both parties wish for a solution. Your plan is plausible, but I doubt whether it would meet the wishes of the inhabitants of Alsace & Lorraine. I imagine they would like best to be French,[5] next members of a great German Empire (not incorporated in any of the little German States) and lastly a sort of semi Belgians, an object of jealousy to both Germany & France.

Germany & France may be brought to such a plan, but they would not like it.

Bernstorff's offer to read the 2d circular, or his not doing so may give an opportunity of saying something to the following effect—

That of course when the opinions of the Prussian Gov are formally communicated to H.M's Gov, it relieves us from any delicacy in communicating our views in return

[1] Baring, 21 Sept., and Carnarvon, 23 Sept., approved the government's policy of not pressing mediation, *The Times*, 22 and 26 Sept.

[2] Lady Granville.

[3] Enclosure in no. 308.

[4] Loftus to Granville, tel., 24 Sept., announced the arrest of Dr. Jacobi for organizing the expression of public feeling against the annexation of Alsace and Lorraine, F.O. 64/697A.

[5] Gladstone wrote in the margin: 'So they would be'.

if we think proper to do so. But that I willingly acquiesce in his reply the other day, that it was not for the purpose of eliciting our views that he had been instructed to read the circular, because I saw no practical object at this moment for doing so—that circulars of this sort were not binding for the future—they were expressions of opinions at the time—that M. Favre had appeared to modify in a second circular the policy announced in a first—that the views of M. de Bismark, which M. de Bernstorff had communicated to me a fortnight ago, seemed to have been modified by the fact of M. Bismark's negotiation with M. Favre.

I could not then look upon this circular (or these circulars) as containing an ultimatum, which could not be influenced by free discussion in Germany, as to what their honor and interest required, or by the proposals which France might offer after the further trial of strength which has been unfortunately decided upon.

I would therefore postpone any observations for which the circular might call, till a more opportune moment.

To say as much as this would not move us from our present policy. Before we went further, I think we had better hear what the Cabinet have to say, in order to help our judgment.

I am in a puzzle, (a not unusual state with me) about Rome.

311. Mr. Gladstone to Lord Granville. [G.D. 29/58]

11, Carlton House Terrace. Sept. 26. 70.

Please to be not later than 2.25 tomorrow if you can help it.

The contradictions about the armistice are astonishing. Nothing will account for them except hard lying. If the Prussian version of the terms is true, they were *most* moderate and it was insane in the French Government to refuse them in terms of such outrage.

I return the letters; that of the Crown Princess: all things taken together, it is a noble one.

Yesterday I put down & sent off in great haste my thoughts about the deposited Memorandum of Count Bismarck: not that all of them are fit to be communicated. The question of noticing the paper is a grave one: but I still lean to the affirmative, & do not well see how to escape it if the document remains.

I do not think any mischief can come of my letters to Manning. At the same time I do not think him entitled to show them to persons who would report their existence to others.

I cannot help continually revolving the question of the Queen's invisibility.

312. Mr. Gladstone to Lord Granville. [G.D. 29/58]

11, Carlton House Terrace. Sept. 26. 70.

1. I much doubt the expediency, in any reply to Bernstorff about the Bismarck circular, of noticing the fact that it is not an ultimatum: for this sets him quite free (as far as we are concerned) to increase his demands.

It seems to me that the choice lies between indicating the points on which we feel obliged to read the Circular with certain assumptions and reservations, and, on the other hand, observing that as there are not now any actual negotiations for peace or armistice, we reserve the consideration of the Circular for a more practical opportunity should it arrive.

2. I do not think that in any case we can dispose of the question of the Circular without the Cabinet.

3. What do you think of asking Apponyi whether he has any information on the subject of the observation ascribed by Bloomfield to Beust that if Alsace & Lorraine were to be transferred to Germany 'the populations would have to be consulted'.

4. There is very great difficulty in seeing how to obtain an unbiassed expression of their wishes: but is not any thing better than simply handing them over as Chattels? This for rumination only.

313. Mr. Gladstone to Lord Granville. [G.D. 29/58]

10, Downing Street. Sept 27. 70.

I return Morier's pungent letter.[1] It seems to me Faucher's real idea is to prevent an intervention of the neutral powers in the sense adverse to [the] annexation of A. & L. by threatening Belgian troubles.

314. Mr. Gladstone to Lord Granville. [G.D. 29/58]

11, Carlton House Terrace. Sept 28. 70.

1. I am very glad the Draft [2] was gone, and I would *not* soften the letter.

On referring you will find that the King tried on a similar request during the Railway discussion with France, and that Clarendon utterly refused reply. So at least my memory runs.

The objection of the irresponsible nature of the question is of itself conclusive.

Please to say in the second page 'through' instead of 'by' Rothschild, as I have no means of knowing whether the twisting of my words was due to him or to some other person through whom the report may have passed.

2. I have recd. the proofs this morning and I hope they are with you also.

3. Thinking over the question of the sense of the inhabitants (a topic which seems to have been touched by Favre) of Alsace & Lorraine, it occurs to me that if the difficulty of getting at it were the only difficulty, that might be got over, by calling in the Agents of friendly Powers to superintend and conduct the process.

[1] Morier to Odo Russell, 19 Sept., according to a note by Granville's private secretary.

[2] To Lumley, No. 47, 23 Sept., an official reply to King Leopold's unofficial request for an assurance that England would honour her obligation to Belgium, tel. and private letter from Lumley, 22, 25 Sept., G.D. 29/83. The draft had gone when the Queen's protest against its coldness reached Granville from Ponsonby, 26 Sept., G.D. 29/32.

315. Mr. Gladstone to Lord Granville. [G.D. 29/58]

10, Downing Street. S. 28. night [1870].

This is indeed a strange tale [1]—and I fear I have no suggestion to offer. Indeed the appeal to you is scarcely legitimate. What have you or we to do with the matter.

As to the case itself, is it necessary for Bourbaki to go back to Metz? I imagine the Prussians have been taken in and all might be silent by consent.

If it is requisite for B. to go back I can suggest nothing better than what you have devised.

316. Mr. Gladstone to Lord Granville. [G.D. 29/58]

11, Carlton House Terrace. Sept. 30. 70.

This is my notion of the sort of thing [2]—

I am much oppressed with the idea that this transfer of human beings like chattels should go forward without any voice from collective Europe if it be disposed to speak.

317. Lord Granville to Mr. Gladstone. [Add. MS. 44167, fo. 120]

Walmer. Oct 2/70.

I send you Cole's plan. I have some Foreigners here. Azeglio does not say much probably balancing between Italian friendship to and Shaftesbury's hatred of France.

The Dutchman [3] evidently French.

The Bavarian, (a great goose) Hompesch, Salisbury's D. violent for territory, justifies transfer of inhabitants because this has been an unjust war on their part. Believes the supremacy of Prussia to be shaken by the war. The liberals will realize what they now say, Bismark makes the unity, but it is for us. He adds that Germany must force their conditions upon France in six weeks. Germany cannot afford to continue the struggle much longer.

Nesselrode, Russian, by way of being a great personal friend of Bismark, and extremely Prussian. He says defence of Paris is impossible—no discipline—no authority—utter demoralisation. But his moral is speedy peace. How is Prussia

[1] See Granville to Gladstone, 28 Sept., on Bourbaki's mission from Bazaine, in Metz, to the Empress Eugénie, Add. MS. 44167, fo. 117, not printed. Bourbaki had been tricked by an impostor, Regnier, see Fitzmaurice, ii. 58–61, Hammond to Granville, 9 Oct., G.D. 29/104, and cf. G.D. 29/73. See also Bernstorff to Granville, 30 Sept., 3 Oct., G.D. 29/94.

[2] Mem. of reply to the 'Appeal of the Government of National Defence to the Neutral Powers, Sep. 30 1870', Add. MS. 44759, fo. 166. It condemned both French obstinacy and the Prussian demand. The important cabinet, Friday, 30 Sept., decided the reply to the French appeal and the reply to Bernstorff's communication of the Alsace-Lorraine Circular (above, no. 306). It discussed 'alternative plans of Ld. G. and W. E. G. . . . Plan of Ld. G. adopted . . .', Add. MS. 44638, fos. 123–5. See also Granville to Bernstorff, 30 Sept., sent to Loftus and Lyons, F.O. 64/706, Goschen to Granville, 3 Oct., G.D. 29/54, Fitzmaurice, ii. 62, Morley, ii. 346.

[3] Baron Gericke, newly arrived Dutch minister in London.

to deal with absolute anarchy. How are they to get money out of a country ruined and disorganized. If he was Bismark, he would levy an immense pecuniary indemnity, raze Metz, leave Lorraine, and make a nice strategic boundary defending the Rhine.

Both he & Hompesch declare that if the Emperor had left Germany alone, it would have been impossible for Germany to have maintained the Prussian military organisation (to which the war has for a time reconciled the nation,) for another year.

The burden was too great—the three Parliaments, Prussian North German, & of Customs would have met with the secret but firm determination to change it.

318. Lord Granville to Mr. Gladstone. [Add. MS. 44167, fo. 126]

Walmer Castle. [4 October 1870].

I adopted all your alterations in the draft to Lyons,[1] and thought them improvements.

I have sent Bourbaki Bernstorff's note. I should not be surprised if he was manipulated at Prince F[rederick] C[harles's] headquarters.

Hayward I am told put the story into the Pall Mall, having heard it from Motley.

I go to town tomorrow to receive Marshall Saldanha.

Bernstorff writes

"I telegraphed to Headquarters and recd the following answer from Count Bismark about General Bourbaki. Prince Frederick Charles is instructed from here, to permit and facilitate General Bourbaki's return to his post at Metz according to the latter's wishes. Regnier makes the impression of being a swindler, but seems to have honestly wished to serve the Empress Eugénie in bringing Bourbaki to her."

319. Mr. Gladstone to Lord Granville. [G.D. 29/58]

Hawarden Castle. Oct 4. 70.

1. I return Cole's paper: I have not sufficient knowledge to judge if it has any value. I presume Cardwell has seen it.

2. Your observations on the proof sheets appeared to me most discriminating. I think I meet them all but one about our loss of an advantage through iron ships, with which I do not agree. One or two were due to errors of the printer.

3. I hope you have written to Elliot:[2] for the number and variety of symptoms that come up convey to me the impression that there is little time to lose. Every body at a time like this looks out for booty: it will be hard to convince Continental Europe that Turkey is not fair prize; and I think there is but the one card, which I have named, for him to play.

[1] No. 488, 1 Oct., postponing recognition until 'France having recognized a government for herself may justly expect its recognition by other Powers' (Gladstone's amended wording), F.O. 27/1794. The dispatch was held back until 4 Oct., but Tissot was told of it, Hammond to Meade, 3 Oct., G.D. 29/104.

[2] See to Elliot, No. 208, 6 Oct., on Britain's Turkish policy, F.O. 78/2120; cf. to Elliot, private, 12 Oct., G.D. 29/116. Buchanan to Granville, tel., 15 Aug., had foreseen a Russian denunciation of the Black Sea Clauses of 1856, F.O. 65/807. The Turkish ambassador also discussed it, to Elliot, No. 207, 6 Oct., F.O. 78/2120.

4. I sent Bright, for his information, my paper which the Cabinet declined.[1] You will see from his reply that he does not agree with me: nor with the Cabinet, but leans rather to the 'inviolability of soil': rather recalling the memory of his former words 'Perish Savoy'—

I am bound to own that I find the decision rather indigestible. Not on account of the reply to France, who has made the wrong appeal, and not made it on the right ground. What in *this* view I am most afraid of is that if, as seems to me not unlikely, France should collapse like the Southern States of America, she will make a sudden peace abandoning these people with the same indifference to their feelings as Bismarck seems to have professed in claiming them: & a most mischievous wrong will have been done and will be beyond recall, without a word from any body.

It would comfort me to find that the Alsatians were disposed to be German: I mean as a choice of difficulties, in present circs.

5. It appears to me that you might ask Bernstorff whether Bismarck admits the correctness of Jules Favre's recital.[2]

Thanks for your interesting reports.

About Alsace & L. the Duc d'Aumale talks to Mr Reeve, & Comte de Paris writes to Lady Waldegrave, very much in my sense.

320. Lord Granville to Mr. Gladstone. [Add. MS. 44167, fo. 124]

F.O. Oct 5/70.

I return Bright's letter. If we are to say anything, we ought to say what you propose. You see that Russia and Austria have taken no notice of the circulars. Whereas we have fully guarded ourselves against acquiescence.

I have just seen Saldanha, who began his interview by the most undiplomatic abuse of his own King—talked of his own victories, and then of his uneffectual attempt to persuade the ex King to accept the throne of Spain. He found in passing through France, that the people were favorably excited by Favre's last letter.

One of the canards is that a man just arrived at Metz saw Moltke in a dying state at Rheims, and that at the Prussian Embassy they are already beginning to say it would not much signify, but I don't believe a word of it.

321. Mr. Gladstone to Lord Granville. [G.D. 29/58]

Hawarden Castle. Oct. 5. 1870.

I received this morning the inclosed letter from the Queen: with which I send for your perusal the copy of my reply.[3] I felt it would amount to duplicity, if I received her emphatic comment on the decision of Friday without saying as much as this.

[1] Enclosure in no. 316. See Bright to Gladstone, 3 Oct., Add. MS. 44112, fo. 155. Bright was absent from the cabinet of 30 Sept.

[2] Report by Favre on the Ferrières negotiation, 21 Sept., enclosed in Lyons's dispatch 27 Sept., F.O. 27/1817, Parl. papers, *loc. cit.* pp. 114–24.

[3] From the Queen, 2 Oct., approving the decision of the cabinet of 30 Sept., and reply, 5 Oct., indicating Gladstone's view which it had overruled, Guedalla, i. 256–7.

I am very anxious to see Bismarck's comment on Jules Favre's report. 3 Pm. I have seen it. An able & characteristic paper. The *corvée* he does not question.[1]

The Emperor seems to me merely to have hit the point of what is fair and just *presuming* the A. and L. people to be anxious to remain French. Of course the demolition of the fortresses would admit of accompanying provisions in a similar sense. The question of military neutralisation might be settled by providing that the inhabitants of certain departments (i.e. those in question) should be organised locally like the Prussian *corps d'armées* and that no number of soldiers exceeding the local force should at any time be within the bounds.

I saw however a statement that the clergy (Protestant I think) of Strasburg assured the German Commanders that the large majority of the people of the town were German in feeling.

It appears to me that my Memorandum was too harshly concise, and would have required a softening development.

322. Mr. Gladstone to Lord Granville. [G.D. 29/58]

Hawarden Castle. Octr. 7. 70.

It occurs to me that you might with advantage instruct Lyons to use any proper opportunity of intimating, if he can do it without offence, to the Government of National Defence in France the fear that the Pouce and Pierre doctrine in its integrity cannot be maintained & that it is in the actual state of affairs prejudicial to the interests of France that the Government should be tied to it.[2] I do not think your doing this would be at variance with the views adopted last Friday.

I hope Hammond may be justified in the idea he has that the Napoleon manifesto though not genuine is a document intended to lead to a settlement on a basis milder than the absolute alienation. Saldanha will not I should think be well up in the wine duties and therefore can give Lowe little trouble.

I mean to spend Monday, from noon onwards, in Liverpool (care of Robertson Gladstone Esq).

323. Lord Granville to Mr. Gladstone. [Add. MS. 44167, fo. 128]

Walmer Castle. Oct 7/70.

I have taken the liberty of sending your Mem [3] to the Chancellor in case the Queen does not show it to him.

[1] This interpolated comment relates to Bismarck's circular, 27 Sept., on the Ferrières negotiation, communicated by Bernstorff, 8 Oct., F.O. 64/706. It had already been published and received from Loftus. Favre had reported Bismarck to have said of the hostile Alsatians: 'Ils nous imposeront une rude corvée ; mais nous ne pouvons pas ne pas les prendre.' Gladstone had referred to this in his mem. for cabinet of 30 Sept., see above, no. 316.

[2] Suggestion prompted by draft to Lyons, No. 489, 4 Oct., replying to the French appeal for neutral intervention, F.O. 27/1794. For instruction on which this was based, see G.D. 29/85, and for alterations, G.D. 29/104. The suggestion was executed in No. 508 to Lyons, 11 Oct., and tel. 7 p.m., 11 Oct., F.O. 27/1794.

[3] Enclosure in no. 316. Hatherley was at Balmoral and absent from the cabinet of 30 Sept.; cf. Hatherley to Granville, 2 Oct., G.D. 29/65.

The Queen has a very good judgment on Foreign Affairs, but in this case she is absolutely prejudiced.

On the particular point of difference between you & me, we cannot be biassed by any prejudice, as while our political feelings are for neutrality, I am personally better inclined to the French than you are.

My objection to doing at present what you propose is, that it is impossible according to my views to do so, without being considered to throw our weight into the French scale against Germany, with consequent encouragement on one side and irritation on the other.

Palmerston wasted the strength derived by England from the great war, by his brag.[1]

I am afraid of our wasting that which we at present derive from moral causes by laying down general principles, when nobody will attend to them, and when in all probability they will be disregarded.

We have reserved our full liberty of action, and can protest whenever we like. But there are symptoms of both sides wearying of the war, they may come to us at last, and it is not at all clear that we may not be glad to arrange a peace which would include a cession of some thousands of my " intellectual " Strasburgians, and the inhabitants of a narrow strategical line, without much reference to their wishes.

If Beaulieu is right whom I saw yesterday, & who says that Bismark has already sent five emissaries to Bazaine, that he has allowed him to get cattle, that he is going in for peace with the Emperor & Bazaine, and that he means to crush democracy,[2] then we shall want all our appeals to right and justice. In the meantime, I should be sorry to take the shine off them by brandishing them too soon.

French Diplomacy is getting very wild. You will see that not only have they asked us to give active support, but that being denied they have asked us to encourage the Italians to join the war.

I never saw any one so ashamed as Tissot, he went backwards & forwards so much that I was obliged to ask him to put (privately) on paper what he did ask.[3]

I do not think your Mem harsh.

I miss our discussions here over the despatches as they come very much.

324. Mr. Gladstone to Lord Granville. [G.D. 29/58]

No 1. Hawarden Castle. Oct. 8. 70.

I have read Dr Jacobi's speech. It has been printed in Germany. If you do not object, I strongly recommend that it be translated, & sent to our papers for publication.[4] It is really very good.

[1] This sentence was scored down the side, possibly by Gladstone.

[2] Cf. Lumley to Granville, No. 349 confidential, 3 Oct., giving the same information, F.O. 10/309.

[3] For account of this conversation see Granville to Lyons, No. 534, 18 Oct., F.O. 27/1794. The draft is followed by Granville's brouillon and a minute of Tissot's words in his own hand.

[4] Written here: 'Hammond. Can you get it and send it privately to the Pall Mall and Echo. G[ranville]. Done E. H[ammond].'

325. Mr. Gladstone to Lord Granville. [G.D. 29/58]

No 2. Hawarden Castle. Oct. 8. 70.

1. Your letter of yesterday, which incloses a Memm. I sent you from Lord Wolverton's on Sept. 24, seems to show some misapprehension. You say you have sent my Memm. to the Chancellor, "in case the Queen does not show it to him". But I have written no Mem. for the Queen, nor sent her any. The paper from Lord Wolverton's was sent to you, & has been seen by no one else. Your reply convinced me that we should do better not to give utterance to any sole opinion. What I afterwards proposed was an overture for a joint declaration: but that proposal also is in abeyance. Yesterday I made another suggestion to you, which rests upon another ground—namely the supposition that Ld Lyons may be upon such a footing with the Government at Tours as to be able to draw them back, without any formal recommendation, from their extreme claim. If he cannot do this I would not press him.

I need not say I agree in the general principles on which you found your opinion on the point recently disposed of. It is all a question of their application. In moral forces, and in their growing effect upon European politics, I have a great faith: possibly on that very account, I am free to confess, sometimes a misleading one.

2. What reply will you make to Wyke? If we have the *power* of helping his proposition,[1] it would be desirable?

P.S. The French proposal that we should urge Italy to join is really almost insane.

What do you think of the inclosed, from Max Müller?

You have a letter of the Queen's to return to me.

My mem. (submitted to the Cabinet) ought to have contained an *express* reserve for strategical necessities of frontier.

Lumley's of Oct 3 about Metz is most curious.[2] But a good many *canards* have come from that quarter.

326. Lord Granville to Mr. Gladstone. [G.D. 29/58]

Copy. W[almer C[astle]. Oct. 8/70.

I send you a letter from Kimberley with Papers respecting the purchase of Elmina from the Dutch.[3] The negotiations have lasted a long time and its conclusion will put an end to the deadlock in which things were—and which made it impossible for us to govern the Colony properly or to withdraw from it. There will be no difficulty in charging the revenues for the sum required to pay for existing stores.

[1] Relates to the hope of Denmark that England and Russia might help her to recover N. Schleswig from Prussia, Wyke to Granville, private, 7 Sept., G.D. 29/84, Granville to Otway, 29 Sept., returning a draft reply as unsatisfactory, G.D. 29/107, Granville to Wyke, 18 Oct., G.D. 29/108. Cf. above, no. 278.

[2] See above, no. 323 note.

[3] See Granville to Harris, No. 40, 24 Oct., for draft convention for the purchase of the Dutch Gold Coast settlements, F.O. 37/478.

It is estimated that the Colony could do it without difficulty, but the Dutch Government have a right to look for security to us, & I presume with no objection on your part to this being done.

For the first time in my life; I have got gout in both feet, but slightly.

327. Lord Granville to Mr. Gladstone. [Add. MS. 44167, fo. 133]

Confidential. Walmer Castle. Oct 8/70.

I presume the Queen has written to you the news.[1]

It seems to combine all the conditions which we thought necessary.

328. Lord Granville to Mr. Gladstone. [Add. MS. 44167, fo. 134]

Walmer Castle. Oct 8 [1870].

I send you two drafts on Turkey—one by Hammond, which I am so sure does not meet your views, & I have therefore sketched something, which fattened, & put into English might elicit an answer from Elliot which might be a basis for discussion in the Cabinet.[2]

I also send a confidential draft of a conversation with the Dutch Minister, which is worth your reading.[3]

I have given instructions for a short draft to Lyons, which I hope may meet your views about conditions of Peace, but you may think it too cautious.[4]

The gout has left one of my feet.

329. Lord Granville to Mr. Gladstone. [Add. MS. 44167, fo. 136]

Walmer Castle. Oct 9/70.

I have *not* done what you did *not* wish me to do, but it was gout and not intelligence which prevented my making the mistake.

I send you back your mem[5] & the Queen's letter.

I wrote to you by Messenger today to say that I have written an instruction for a draft to Lyons.

I had some talk with Brunnow about Denmark, but he was strongly of opinion that this was not the moment to begin about Denmark.

The way of doing the thing will not be difficult if the Prussians agree to the substance.[6]

Max Muller's letter is able, it does not convince me, but it shows the hardness of the rock we have to melt or break.

[1] Of the marriage arranged between the Princess Louise and the marquis of Lorne.

[2] See above, no. 319 note.

[3] Granville to Harris, No. 37 most confidential, 9 Oct., on Gericke's intention to work for closer Anglo-Dutch relations when he became Dutch foreign minister, F.O. 37/478.

[4] See above, no. 322.

[5] Enclosure in no. 316, see returned original in Add. MS. 44759, fo. 166.

[6] See above, no. 325.

Cartwright says all the Prussians talk of an understanding with Bazaine.

He says there is much Typhus and Diarrhoea, and the troops openly express their desire to be relieved from the siege.

330. Mr. Gladstone to Lord Granville. [G.D. 29/58]

Immediate. Hawarden Castle. Oct 9. 70.

1. The application of the Tours Government about Italy, absurd as it is, seems to me additionally to recommend my suggestion that Lord Lyons if he can without offence should expostulate a little with them upon their unreasonable view of the terms of peace, which must of itself be a great impediment to saying or doing any thing for them.[1]

2. I telegraphed to Hammond yesterday my concurrence with you about the Defence: but I presume it will be understood that Jervoise may at any time, if he sees occasion, fetch her back from Naples to Rome.[2]

3. I send you a letter just come from Manning, with my reply subject to your approval.[3] The PS is *nought,* for you.

4. Relatively to export of arms, some one has suggested to me what is ingenious, if the nations should be inclined to adopt it, though I am not *sure* that it would hold water. It is, to declare the export illegal, placing it on the footing of a private wrong, and giving to the Foreign State injuriously affected the power of proving and obtaining remedy in the Courts of the exporting country.

I wonder what the Prefects reported from Alsace & Lorraine?

Morier's reports[4] of Oct 2 & 3 are creditable to his power of impartiality, & important: will you not circulate them?

331. Lord Granville to Mr. Gladstone. [Add. MS. 44167, fo. 139]

Walmer Castle. Oct 10/70.

No 1. I hope by this time you have recd the draft to Lyons.[5] I can write a little stronger in a private letter.

2 The Defence was ordered to come back at a moment's notice.

3 On what does Antonelli found our readiness to mediate.

All I know of such an encouragement, is our telling Jervoise that Severn as Anglo-Italian Consul might (consulting with him) if asked transmit messages from the Pope to the Italian Gov.

Ought we to accept mediation without consulting the Italian Gov. and ought

[1] See above, no. 322. [2] See above, no. 284.

[3] From Manning, 8 Oct., referring to a letter from Antonelli and suggesting bases for British good offices between the Pope and the Italian government for the settlement of the Roman question. Gladstone to Manning, 9 Oct., did not reject British mediation. This was cancelled and a fresh letter sent, 12 Oct., rejecting mediation unless both sides asked for it, Add. MS. 44249, fos. 216, 218, 224.

[4] Private, on opinion in Alsace-Lorraine. Three further reports, 4, 7, 26 Oct., followed, G.D. 29/95. Cf. Granville to Morier, 22 Sept., 2 Nov., G.D. 29/112.

[5] No. 508, 11 Oct.; see above, no. 322.

you and I supposed to be the most Catholic members of the Cabinet to enter in such a delicate matter, without consulting our colleagues.

Otherwise I think your answer good—but I send it back to you for consideration.

I like the idea as to Neutrality, exportation of contraband of war, but I doubt it's working. Would you allow Tissot to prosecute Forster for exporting blankets to the German Army.

I will circulate Morier's letters.

The Bombardment weighs on my mind as much as the Alsatians weigh on your's. Some weeks ago I drafted a despatch on the subject and made Odo try another, but we both agreed the thing was impossible.[1]

It is very inconvenient that the whole Corps Diplomatique should be left in the shade at Berlin. How would it be to sound Brunnow as to a proposed move in that direction.

332. Mr. Gladstone to Lord Granville. [G.D. 29/58]

Liverpool. Oct 10. 70.

Hammond's draft to Elliot would have absolutely required enlargement but yours while shorter is far more comprehensive & to the point—I like it much.[2]

I have read the other drafts with interest: but among them I do not find any instruction to Lord Lyons.

I am very sorry to gather from your letter that you have had, & even have, the gout.

The news [3] of today affords more evidence against the military chances of the French.

You must have been much struck by the Duke of Baden's opinion about Alsace.[4] It did him honour.

I return to Hawarden tonight.

333. Mr. Gladstone to Lord Granville. [G.D. 29/58]

No 1. Hawarden Castle. Oct 11. 70.

1. I mentioned yesterday in writing from Liverpool that I had not yet received your draft to Lyons on the French view of the terms of peace.

2. The Russian judgment of opinion which you report as to Denmark is I should think a tolerably safe one for us to follow. It is not for us to act about Denmark as if we had some special interest of this country involved.

(Indeed for my own part I am prepared to throw overboard these special British interests. I do not believe in them, I mean as connected with the affairs of the

[1] See Russell to Granville, 31 Aug., enclosing his draft, marked 'Put by for the present. G[ranville]', G.D. 29/92. Cf. Knaplund, *Letters from Berlin*, p. 23. Granville's draft has not been traced.

[2] See above, no. 319 note. The draft to Elliot, No. 208, is in Granville's hand. Hammond's has not been traced.

[3] The French evacuation of Orléans.

[4] Given in Morier's second report, see above, no. 330.

European Continent. Take the one which comes nearest home, namely the hypothesis of a maritime aggrandisement of any of the Great Powers. That in my view cannot be formidable to us without being more formidable to others.)

3. But would it not be well that you should endeavour to ascertain the views of Russia as to the terms of peace, and especially as to the transfer of Alsace and Lorraine? Undoubtedly the decision of the Cabinet on the 30th was in some degree governed by the belief strongly declared by you that Russia would adhere to inviolability of soil but would not commit herself to any objection founded on the sense of the inhabitants. When that decision comes to be questioned, as it may, I think it will be very important that we should be able to show something about the actual views of Russia at this juncture. If you verify your opinion by communication with Brunnow, it will powerfully support the decision of the 30th ult. But considering that Russia is the only *substantive* among the Neutral Powers (besides ourselves) I think we ought not voluntarily to remain in the dark, but to learn all we can.[1] I had a vague idea that this had been understood between us: but it is probably an illusion of failing memory. I am glad that the gout seems to be mitigating its terms of peace with you. May Bismarck do the like with France.

334. Mr. Gladstone to Lord Granville. [Add. MS. 44539, fo. 49]

[*Copy. No. 2*]. Oct. 11. 70.

They have sent me a mass of papers without any precis or guide from the C.O. on the proposed cession of territory by the Dutch on the Gold Coast, but they do not as far as I can find contain the only thing material for me which is a statement of the reasons, why contrary to our general policy we are in this quarter (apparently) to extend our responsibilities.[2] I am therefore quite unable at present to give any opinion. But the question of the proposed payment or guarantee of £80,000 for the Stores & Fixtures is clearly one which will have to go to the Chancellor of the Exchequer.

335. Lord Granville to Mr. Gladstone. [Add. MS. 44167, fo. 143]

Walmer Castle. [11 October 1870].

I have advised the Queen by telegraph to communicate with some of the opposition before the news [3] is published in the papers.

I will send a note for West to forward to Delane, whenever he receives any instruction from you to communicate with the other papers.

I presume he had better let all know the fact.

I should think there need be no more delay than is required for you to give him instructions.

[1] See Granville to Brunnow, private, most confidential, 12 Oct., proposing confidential understanding between England and Russia on 'reasonable' peace terms, G.D. 29/115. See below, no. 341.

[2] See above, no. 326.

[3] Of the Lorne marriage; see Granville to the Queen, tel. 6.15 p.m., 11 Oct., G.D. 29/32.

336. Mr. Gladstone to Lord Granville. [G.D. 29/58]

No 1. Hawarden Castle. 12 Oct 70.

1. I am perfectly satisfied with the draft to Lyons [1] about the French terms of peace but have suggested by Telegram what is meant as an additional guard viz. to convert the *reference* to the *pouce & pierre* into a quotation.

2. I have agreed by Telegram to salute the flag at C[ivita] Vecchia.

3. You are quite right in stopping the letter to Manning.[2] My recollection was not quite clear as to the amount of our readiness expressed & this I trusted to you to rectify. I do not think the letter commits us to any thing beyond saying Aye or No upon a Roman proposition, which we cannot well help doing without it: but there is no sort of difficulty in writing to Manning on a different basis and this I will do accordingly: but direct to save time & as I think I now see distinctly the line to be observed which is *negative*.

4. I can more easily come up to your standard about Bombardment, than you to mine about Alsace and Lorraine: only I think the Prussians are not now looking to it, but to blockade, as their present resource; though this may change any day.

4 [*sic*]. The proposal made to me as to export touched arms only. I have by no means concluded in its favour: but it passes by a good many of the objections.

5. With respect to America it will be difficult I fear to bring all questions into one arrangement [3] because that of Canada is rather complex. But why should we not arbitrate on the Fisheries so far as the question is one of Treaty? I am quite prepared to add why should we not consider whether we shall make them a present of San Juan if we can thereby put forward the Alabama business? If we meant seriously to contest it we ought not to have allowed our proposal of an arbitration made 9 or 10 years ago to have slumbered all this time.

5 [*sic*]. I quite agree about the Corps Diplomatique and Berlin. It must have occurred to you, how defective are our means of communication with the French, since the Paris Government overrode that of Tours about the Elections.[4] It appears to me that special caution must now be had in all communication with Tours: and that Lyons should be reminded of this though he has probably thought of it.

6. My brother's chief working partner, a very able Aberdeensman, who has transactions of business with men of all nations, and is I should think profoundly impartial, told me on Monday that of the whole of them the Germans are by far the most slippery and grasping. Wo be to you, he said, if you have an agreement with a German & it is not on paper. This coincides rather remarkably with something said by Goschen, & with the habitual policy of Prussia: but it would rather astonish the Queen.

[1] See above, no. 322. [2] See above, nos. 330, 331.

[3] The fresh American overture, after Stanley's and Clarendon's failures to settle the several matters at issue between Britain and the United States, looked to the achievement of some bargain by setting the three kinds of question (Canadian, boundary and Civil War claims) off against each other. It was kept out of the official papers. See Thornton to Granville, private, 27 Sept., G.D. 29/80.

[4] Relates to Gambetta's balloon exit from Paris, 7 Oct., to enforce the veto of Paris upon elections decreed by the Tours Government.

337. Mr. Gladstone to Lord Granville. [G.D. 29/58]

No 2. Secret. Hawarden Castle. Oct 12. 70.

I quite agree with you about the coming event [1] which is full of interest every way. I presume it will remain for some time a secret. It cannot take place before the latter part of February.

338. Lord Granville to Mr. Gladstone. [Add. MS. 44167, fo. 147]

Walmer Castle. Oct 13/70.

I think my engagement to you was to encourage Brunnow to talk, which I have done abundantly but with no result on the particular points. I am afraid I argued in the Cabinet against the longer note to him of which I send you a copy.[2] Let me know if you have any criticism.

If anything was to come of it, we ought possibly to meet in London.

I have now been in bed for a week.

339. Mr. Gladstone to Lord Granville. [G.D. 29/58]

Hawarden Castle. Oct 14. 70.

I am very sorry to hear your attack of gout has been so serious. I ignorantly thought the departure from one foot signified an intention to depart speedily from the other.

1. No doubt you are right in your recollection as to asking Brunnow. But would there be any objection to mentioning to him the Chaudordy opinion (at any rate if, which I hope you will ascertain, it turns out to be that of his Government) and inquiring whether Russia has any particular view of the method of proceeding suggested? It is only, I think, when we speak of action that the matter becomes serious.

2. In your letter of yesterday, you speak of a draft as sent to me which has not arrived.

3. To put Italy forward, & this too as the Power which can best support its diplomacy by arms, is little short of ridiculous.

4. I most cordially sympathise with Lyons about the duality of the Government of Defence and about the postponement of the Elections.[3] The split between Paris and Tours is the greatest of all the incredible blunders which the French have made in this sad business.

5. My mind harps upon the old misgiving. We have no difficulty in answering the French Government (apart from its duality) as it has never made to us a reasonable proposal. But if the contingency happen, not very probable, of a sudden

[1] The Lorne marriage. The news, at the Queen's request, was published at once, 14 Oct., two tels., Granville to Gladstone, 13 Oct., G.D. 29/58.

[2] This sentence was scored down the side. See above, no. 333. Cf. Granville's draft tel. to Gladstone: 'Telegraph immediately to Hammond and to me whether you approve or object to my letter to Brunnow', G.D. 29/58.

[3] Lyons to Granville, private, 10 Oct., G.D. 29/85.

accommodation which shall include the throttling of Alsace & part of Lorraine, without any voice previously raised against it, it will in my opinion be a standing reproach to England. There is indeed the Russian plan of not recognising that in which we have had no part; but it is difficult to say what this comes to.

6. If we could sweeten the Alabama question for the U.S. by bringing in Canada, perhaps we might also sweeten the Fisheries question for Canada by paying her compensation for the charges of the Fenian Raid. It would perhaps be awkward to do this except as part of a final settlement with the U.S.[1]

7. I am sorry to see the Pope is likely to lose the Leonine City: but it is the natural consequence of the course he is pursuing.

8. What do you think should be our programme as to Cabinets? Shall we meet in the last week of this month, continue for a fortnight or three weeks, & then meet again early in December? The reason why I think we need not continue all through November & into Dec as sometimes happens is that the legislation of next year was principally prepared for last year & will not entail a great deal of Cabinet work. Of course this outline is subject to all possible change for Foreign Affairs. We may also have much military matter to consider. But it would be well not to take this too early.

340. Lord Granville to Mr. Gladstone. [Add. MS. 44167, fo. 149]

Private. Walmer Castle. Oct 15/70.

I send you an extract from the Globe of yesterday, and a letter from Bernstorff which I received this morning,[2] and I refer you to a passage in one of Walker's letters, in which he says the Crown Prince had complained to him of the hostility of England, and said that it would oblige Prussia to contract an Alliance with the United States.[3]

It all looks much as if Bismark wished to pick a quarrel with us. He has always hated the English, and at all events no confidence can be placed in him.

I do not know that I place much more in the pious King.

But I do so in the Crown Prince, who is an honorable straightforward man, of not much ability, led by his wife and inclined to like England.

We agree about the position of our Corps Diplomatique left in the cold at Berlin, with nobody at the Head Quarters to explain our position, or to detect plots against us. If we proposed to send the Berlin Embassy to Versailles, we should be refused civilly or uncivilly as the case might be—& even if they got there Loftus would only bore them all to death.

How would it do to invent some excuse (such as getting the residue of the Embassy out of Paris, or anything else) to send Odo to Head Quarters.[4] His know-

[1] For Granville's response to the American overture, see to Thornton, private, 13 Oct., F.O. 362/1. Cf. Rogers to Granville, on the Canadian side, 15, 23 Oct., G.D. 29/75.

[2] Private, 14 Oct., relating to mounting irritation in Germany about alleged British export of arms to France, G.D. 29/94.

[3] Cf. Lowe to Granville, 27 Oct., G.D. 29/66, and Granville to Thornton, 13 Oct., F.O. 362/1.

[4] Russell's mission to Versailles came to be associated with the Black Sea question, see below, nos. 343, 359 note.

ledge of Germany, and Germans would enable him to ascertain a little of what was going on, and certainly have influence with the Crown Prince, who I think I remember to have heard, was very fond of him.

I have asked Hammond to read this note, and to forward it with any remarks of his.

341. Mr. Gladstone to Lord Granville. [G.D. 29/58]

Hawarden Castle. Oct 15. 70.

I would observe on two propositions in this draft [1]

(1. That mediation is not to be offered except with the condition of its being acceptable to both parties

2. That advice is not to be offered except there be reason to believe it will be effective).

That I think we have laid down these propositions hitherto as applicable to the sole action of the British Govt, but have never bound ourselves to decide that the Neutral Powers or some combination of them should never offer mediation or advice except under precisely the same limitations.

In making these remarks, I do not consider them at absolute variance with the draft.

342. Mr. Gladstone to Lord Granville. [G.D. 29/58]

Hawarden Castle. Oct 15. 70.

(1.) Receiving this morning a copy of your letter to Brunnow dated 12th I perceive that my opinion on it is retrospective but I should only have had two observations to make on details while the main drift is very agreeable to my wishes and feelings.

1. I would have proposed to insert 'if so' as marked on margin of p. 2.

2. The words 'rectification of frontier for strategic purposes' are I think ambiguous—may mean

1. That strategic reasons show that the absolute limit of territory ought to be changed.

2. That what may be called the strategic not the absolute frontier ought to be changed. Many may admit 2 who would not admit 1 and I assume 2 to be your meaning.

I have telegraphed to you and Hammond on this subject as you have desired.

(2.) I hope I need not say that while you are laid up I am most ready to start

[1] Granville to Buchanan, No. 262, 16 Oct., with min.. by Meade, F.O. 65/799. This arose from sounding Brunnow on 12 Oct., see above, no. 333. Brunnow to Granville, 14 Oct., proposed Anglo-Russian agreement on two *démarches* to spare Paris and to investigate the 'strictly necessary' conditions of peace, G.D. 29/98. Private and official tels. to Buchanan, 4 p.m. and 8.45 p.m., 14 Oct., resulted, G.D. 29/114, F.O. 65/799. To Buchanan, tel. 11.30 a.m., 16 Oct., made the alterations suggested by Gladstone in no. 342. Instead of deprecating cession 'beyond what may be necessary for strategical rectification of frontier', Granville asked whether Germany would insist upon her full terms.

at a very few hours notice, at any time of day or night, to join you at Walmer upon any matter which you may find to require it. Indeed I could not properly or with comfort remain here upon any other terms, and I hope you will take this 'at the foot of the letter' as it is intended.

Meantime I have been sending Cardwell my lucubrations on Army affairs.[1]

The Chancellor says [the] Queen almost promises to open Parliament.

343. Mr. Gladstone to Lord Granville. [G.D. 29/58]

Hawarden Castle. Oct. 16. 70.

1. Lumley's dispatch of Oct. 9.[2] appears to me disagreeable, and the policy of [the] Belgian Govt. doubtful in regard to their intention of asking a special measure for restraint of the press. Will not such a measure make the Govt. thereafter responsible for everything they do not stop? And would it not be *more* safe for the Govt. to disavow by an explicit & public declaration the language of the Independance Belge, if, as I suppose, it is objectionable.

2. I send you Hammond's comments on the subject of sending a special person to the Prussian Camp.[3] I agree with most of what he says: & think your choice lies between transferring the Berlin establishment or part of it & sending no one at all.

3. I do not feel a great apprehension of Bismarck's wishing to pick a quarrel with us and fight us with the aid of the United States, who can do us a great deal of harm but can do him little good. If he means any thing of the kind, it can only be with a view to Belgium & Holland & we are in the dark as to his real intentions about these countries.

4. Having received in *clair* the long ciphered Telegram I see that the errors made little difference.[4]

As to the sentence I wished you to generalise, I quite agreed in what I suppose to be its main view viz. that Russia & we may co-operate in endeavouring to save Alsace & Lorraine from actual severance, while we should perhaps do it on different grounds, but I thought the closing words might be held to involve *some* absolute severance and I think it would be premature to commit ourselves to this, particularly as what we desire is to give Germany security in another form.

I find however that Strasburg was anciently separated from Alsace: and also that France agreed to dismantle it at the peace of Ryswick. I think also a similar stipulation was then made by the Duke of Lorraine with respect to Nancy if that was his capital.

5. Unless your message to Russia proves a flash in the pan, I presume it to be likely that we may require a Cabinet [5] before this week is over and when your gout

[1] See mem. on Army Questions, 13 Oct., Add. MS. 44759, fo. 169.

[2] No. 353 confidential, reporting Prussia's protest at the pro-French tone of the *Indépendance Belge* and the Belgian Government's project of law to check publication of matter dangerous to the state during the war, F.O. 10/309.

[3] See Hammond to Gladstone, 15 Oct., arguing against sending Russell or anyone uninvited to Versailles, copy, G.D. 29/58.

[4] See above, no. 341.

[5] For cabinet of 20 Oct., see below, no. 347.

permits. In that case, it may perhaps be well at once to draw the sketch of our legislative work and start the preparations for it instead of separating. Indeed if this proceeding takes at all, it will probably require more than one Cabinet to dispose of it.

6. It seems to me that Bismarck for once made a great mistake in his Starvation circular.[1] It was a kind of threat to the world, which never answers.

Then also the lapse of time is now in favour of the French; and you have apparently got a comparatively favourable opportunity for action. May it prove so in its results.

344. Lord Granville to Mr. Gladstone. [Add. MS. 44167, fo. 157]

Walmer. Oct 16/70.

1 I enclose a note from Forster [2] which he ought to have written to you. I presume there is no objection to the proposal for H.M to signify her approval of the Princess Louise's Marriage. Will you write to the Queen.

2. I have recd your telegram—& made the sentence about terms very general in the telegram to Buchanan.[3]

3 I propose to go to town tomorrow. Will you telegraph to me at the Foreign Office " yes " if you give me leave to summon you, or the Cabinet supposing any necessity should arise.

If Russia agrees to do something, it is a serious matter acting without the consent of our colleagues. On the other hand the communication ought to be made with as little ostentation as possible.

I should think we had better all write similar but not identic despatches—and Bombardment might be the handle. I shall see Bernstorff tomorrow at Betteshanger on my way to London.

Many thanks for your message giving me leave to send for you. How about the Cabinet.

Gout much better, but not gone.

345. Mr. Gladstone to Lord Granville. [G.D. 29/58]

Hawarden Castle. O. 17. 70.

1. I have written to the Queen in the sense of your and Forster's letters.

2. Have already written about Cabinet & now Telegraph Yes.

346. Lord Granville to Mr. Gladstone. [Add. MS. 44167, fo. 159]

Oct 17 8 PM [1870].

Brunnow declares he knows nothing more about the negotiations than that

[1] Ferrières, 1 Oct., describing starvation as the penalty of further resistance, communicated by Bernstorff, 11 Oct., F.O. 64/706, and Parl. papers. [C. 244] (1871). lxxi, 151–3.

[2] Minister in attendance at Balmoral. See Forster to Granville, 14 Oct., on the date of the meeting of the privy council, at which the Queen would assent to Princess Louise's marriage, G.D. 29/56; and Gladstone to the Queen, 17 Oct.

[3] See above, nos. 341, 342.

Wit[t]genstein got out of Paris 4 days ago, went to Versailles, and then to **Tours**, and is going back to Paris.[1]

I own I wish you could without great inconvenience come to town.

I have sent the Telegram to Buchanan to all the Cabinet Members asking each, whether if the answer is favorable, they wish me to go on carefully, or have a Cabinet, & to telegraph answers.

347. Lord Granville to Mr. Gladstone. [Add. MS. 44167, fo. 161]

F.O. Oct 18/70.

The Chancellor, Fortescue & Hartington do not wish for a Cabinet—Lowe is decidedly against it.

Childers was for it but has withdrawn his wish, being satisfied with what I propose writing—& he says Halifax would agree to the same, although he telegraphed for a Cabinet.[2]

Lowe had seen Cardwell, who would not dislike the line we have taken.

I am glad we asked Russia as Brunnow yesterday was inclined to take the line, of saying that it was Russia who had always been willing to move.

And I do not see how the enclosed draft can offend.

I am afraid that you will be annoyed with being called up, but all those whom I saw were so glad that I am comforted.

I send you a conversation with Tissot.[3]

348. Lord Granville to Mr. Gladstone. [Add. MS. 44167, fo. 163]

16, Bruton Street. [20 October 1870].

I presume we may answer that if the Duc d'Aosta is an acceptable Candidate to Spain we should hear with satisfaction that he has accepted the throne.[4]

349. Mr. Gladstone to Lord Granville. [G.D. 29/58]

11, Carlton House Terrace. Oct 24. 70.

The St Petersburgh Telegram is not very good.[5] It is not *now* a question of

[1] Cf. Granville to Lyons, No. 535, 17 Oct., passing on this information, F.O. 27/1794.

[2] Cf. letters to Granville, 18 Oct., from Goschen, G.D. 29/54, from Halifax, G.D. 29/64, from Hatherley, G.D. 29/65. The cabinet met, 3 p.m., 20 Oct., Add. MS. 44638, fo. 126. It agreed to (i) dispatch to Loftus, No. 226, 20 Oct., on Britain's having urged France to accept an armistice, F.O. 64/682, (ii) tel. to Lyons, 6.40 p.m., 20 Oct., F.O. 27/1794, (iii) dispatch to Buchanan, No. 267, 20 Oct., on British reliance on Russian support, F.O. 65/799. Russia had rejected the Anglo-Russian agreement (tel. from Buchanan, 18 Oct., F.O. 65/807) proposed 14–16 Oct.

[3] See Granville to Lyons, No. 537, 18 Oct., F.O. 27/1794, and Parl. papers, *loc. cit.* p. 170.

[4] Marked: 'I agree. W. E. G[ladstone] O.21.'

[5] From Buchanan, 6 p.m., received midnight, 23 Oct., 'there is an indisposition to employ diplomatic pressure against Prussia', F.O. 65/807. The change in Russia may have resulted from Thiers's presence in St. Petersburg. Russia offered mediation separately and convinced Granville that she was playing 'a double game', to Lyons, private, 2 Nov., F.O. 362/4, to Buchanan, 2 Nov., G.D. 29/114.

pressure 'against Prussia' at all, whatever it may be hereafter. Have we not a right to say we rely on the Emperor's words having acted in substance on them with respect to the French Govt.

Reeve assures me the Article [1] is profoundly secret. I told him about the ferret Hayward.

Bernstorff was here this morning—gave me the inclosed threatening letter, without asking any thing. He says he has had divers of them. I proposed to send it to Col. Henderson, as I have commonly done with my own. This brings them to a focus. Perhaps you will do it, if you approve, as B. did.

I send also a letter from Houghton.

350. Mr. Gladstone to Lord Granville. [G.D. 29/58]

11, Carlton House Terrace. Oct. 28. 70.

1. I am glad you approved my suggestion by Telegraph about Elections in A[lsace] and L[orraine] though it is rather impertinent to furnish Thiers and Bismarck,[2] like boys at school doing verses, with ideas.

2. As Bernstorff so distinctly refers to the offer through Burnside,[3] might we not ask him what it was. It is a material part of the *res gestae*.

3. Please to stop my letter to Hammond if you see cause.[4] I have just read Sir H. Elliot's No. 24[2] of Oct 1817 [*sic* 1870], and am glad that Ali Pacha is awakening, but he looks to military means (or threats of) only, and his case with regard to them seems to be deplorable.[5]

4. Having an old engagement to the Workingmen's Exhibition on Tuesday, I summon the Cabinet for Wedy.[6]—subject of course to an earlier call if need be. The hour will be 3.30 sharp, at the request of the Yorkshire Squad.

I think Lacroix's account of Nice one of the most curious papers of the whole war. Bismarck would think it a prize: it ought perhaps to be a warning.

[1] In the *Edinburgh Review*, see above, no. 307. The authorship was revealed in an article in the *Daily News*, Reeve to Gladstone, 4 Nov., Add MS. 44428, fo. 174.

[2] In negotiation at Versailles for an armistice, preliminary to elections for a constituent assembly. The problem arose, whether Alsace and Lorraine were to vote. Gladstone's solution was to allow the writs to run there without enforcing them, Granville to Lyons, private, 26 Oct., F.O. 362/4. The negotiation broke off on 6 Nov.

[3] See Bernstorff to Granville, 26 Oct., replying to Granville's notification, 25 Oct., of French wish for an armistice to enable an assembly to be convoked. Bernstorff answered that this had been offered through General Burnside and been categorically refused. F.O. 64/706.

[4] Follows no. 350 in G.D. 29/58; shows that the Crimean War policy of armed intervention on Turkey's behalf no longer held. It is marked 'suspended'.

[5] Elliot in No. 242 confidential, 17 Oct., received 27 Oct., reported a question from the Grand Vizier about military help from Britain if Turkey was attacked by Russia, F.O. 78/2125. The dispatch is minuted by Granville and Hammond.

[6] Cabinet, Wednesday, 2 Nov., discussed the legislative programme for the session, and 'Turkey. Treaty of 1856 . . .', Add. MS. 44638, fo. 127.

351. Lord Granville to Mr. Gladstone.[1] [G.D. 29/58]

Confidential. Walmer Castle. Oct 29/70.

Your letter to H[ammon]d seems a very good one—but I should be glad if you would keep it back till we have settled our Turkish policy in the Cabinet.

May I venture to make you a request, which does not come from any jealous feeling, although possibly from one of conscious weakness.

I imagine that the Prime Minister has an undoubted right to communicate directly either with our Representatives abroad, or with Foreign Ministers in London. But I think it is in his interest as much as in that of the Foreign Secretary that he should only appear as the Deus ex Machinâ

Both English & Foreign Diplomatists like the double communication, particularly when the Prime Minister is not only officially superior, but personally immensely so. Bernstorff once boasted to me that he liked going to you. "I like having two strings to my bow." They like checking what is said by one, by what is said by the other—& drawing inferences accordingly. They find you overflowing with original & large ideas, every one of which is invaluable for a despatch—they find very few ideas in my conversation, and those of a negative character.

On the other hand you are perfectly unreserved with me, and I am although not a powerful, a truthful exponent of your views.

After reading all this you will say, "What have I done?" and I should have nothing to answer—but I am glad to say what occurs to me on a matter likely to arise from your great zest for all public affairs, and from the interest & pleasure which Dips would derive from such communications.

352. Lord Granville to Mr. Gladstone. [Add. MS. 44167, fo. 164]

16, Bruton Street. Nov 3/70.

I told Bernstorff that I must formally request him to keep me informed of what was passing—that I should be glad that he pointed out to Count Bismark that I was obliged to make this request, as from the exceptional circumstances of the King commanding the army, & His Foreign Secretary being with him, HM's Gov had no channel of communication of a direct character with the Prussian Gov.

This telegram [2] may be the result. It somewhat confirms the news of a red Republic at Paris.

353. Mr. Gladstone to Lord Granville. [G.D. 29/58]

11, Carlton House Terrace. Nov. 5. 70.

1. What answer do you advise to the P.S.? The case is bad either way. The return at any particular date must be regarded as uncertain.[3]

[1] The original of no. 351 in the Granville papers is followed by a copy marked 'original within suspended'. Cf. Granville to Spencer, copy, 24 Sept., on the same subject, G.D. 29/77.

[2] From Bernstorff, private, 10 p.m., 3 Nov., circulated in the cabinet, announcing a break in the negotiations between Thiers and Bismarck owing to events in Paris, G.D. 29/94. For report, 2 Nov., of the fall of the Provisional Government circulated in the cabinet as untrustworthy, see G.D. 29/92.

[3] Concerns the Queen's continued stay at Balmoral and the attendance of a cabinet minister.

2. Could you not learn through Sir A. Buchanan [1] at *what time* it was—since we are now officially informed of the fact—that Russia expressed an opinion adverse to the severance of French Territory?

354. Mr. Gladstone to Lord Granville. [G.D. 29/116]

11, Carlton House Terrace. Nov. 8.70.

This draft [2] is I think excellent in all that it says, but it does not, in my view, embrace the whole case. In 'the whole case' I include not merely the removal of abuse, and the promotion of prosperity & contentment by just & equal administration, but the extension of self-governing privileges in municipal & local forms.

There never can be between the Porte and its European Provinces that closeness of relation which is either attained or attainable in European countries generally: and to obtain that attachment, necessary for zealous allegiance and defence, it seems necessary in a peculiar degree to decentralise the detail of government, that the people of the European Provinces may feel when Turkey is attacked that they are defending what is *their own*. This seems to be the best substitute, of which the case admits, for the true & pure spirit of nationality.

The *spirit*, which prompted the Porte in the case of Servia, is that which I should like to see it apply to the whole of its European dominions.

355. Mr. Gladstone to Lord Granville. [G.D. 29/58]

11, Carlton House Terrace. Nov. 9. 1870.

I thought yesterday that every thing as regarded us was at perfect rest: but Loftus's Telegram of yesterday about Gen. Allenkof's mission [3] suggests to me that we should further endeavour to learn from Lyons, Loftus, Buchanan, whether Russia is repeating the advice that French Territory be not annexed. For if she is, it raises the *question* whether we ought to be wholly silent on the terms of peace, as one for serious consideration.

We seem to be at present on this footing with Russia, that we are understood to communicate every thing to her, but without reciprocity.

356. Memorandum by Mr. Gladstone.[4] [G.D. 29/58]

[*c.* 10 November 1870].

The dispatches of Prince Gortschakoff dated 9th November 1870 declare on the part of Russia that the Treaty of 1856 has been infringed in various respects

[1] See Granville to Buchanan, tel. 3.45 p.m., and No. 298, 10 Nov., F.O. 65/799. He was told to 'antedate' the inquiry, see below, no. 355.

[2] Gladstone noted that the cabinet of 4 Nov. instructed Granville to draft a dispatch to urge Turkey to adopt any practicable means to strengthen the loyalty of her subjects, Add. MS. 44638, fo. 132. A draft in Hammond's hand, Nov., was suspended, G.D. 29/116, and no dispatch on these lines was sent, see F.O. 78/2120.

[3] Tel. 4.24 p.m., received 7 p.m., 8 Nov., reporting that Allenkoff was said to carry advice to the King of Prussia not to annex French territory, F.O. 64/697A.

[4] Printed Temperley and Penson, *Foundations*, pp. 331–3. Cf. to Buchanan, No. 301, 10 Nov., replying to the Russian denunciation of the Black Sea clauses of the Treaty of Paris,

to the prejudice of Russia and in one case that of the Principalities against the explicit protest of her Representative: and that in consequence of these infractions Russia is entitled to renounce those stipulations of the Treaty which directly touch her interests. It is then announced that she will no longer be bound by the covenants which restrict her rights of Sovereignty in the Black Sea.

We have here an allegation that certain facts have occurred which in the judgment of Russia are at variance with certain stipulations of the Treaty: and the assumption is made that Russia, upon the strength of her own judgment as to the character of the facts, is entitled to release herself from certain other stipulations of that instrument.

The assumption is limited in its practical application to some of the provisions of the Treaty: but as every Treaty in point of obligation is one and indivisible,[1] the assumption of a title to renounce any one of its terms is *ipso facto* an assumption of a title to renounce the whole.

The statement which has been made is wholly independent of the reasonableness or unreasonableness on its own merits of the desire of Russia to be released from the observation of the stipulation of the Treaty of 1856 respecting the Black Sea.

But the question now raised is, in whose hands lies the power of giving release from all or any of those stipulations?

It has commonly been supposed that that Power belongs only to the Powers who have been parties to the original instrument.

The dispatches of Prince Gortschakoff appear to proceed upon a different principle.

They [2] imply [3] that some one of the Powers who have signed the engagement may allege that occurrences have taken place at variance with the provisions of the Treaty, and upon that allegation, although it be one not shared nor admitted, by the Cosignatory Powers, may found not a request to those Powers for the equitable consideration of the case, but an announcement to them that it has emancipated itself or holds itself emancipated from those stipulations of the Treaty which it thinks fit to disapprove.

It is quite evident that the effect of such doctrine and of any proceeding which with or without avowal is founded upon it is to bring the certain authority and efficacy of all Treaties whatever under the discretionary controul of each one of the Powers who may have signed them.

That is to say. The result obtained is the certain destruction of Treaties in their essence. For whereas their whole object is to bind Powers to one another, and for

F.O. 65/799; *Correspondence respecting the Treaty of March 30, 1856*. Parl. papers. [C. 245] (1871). lxxii, 9–16. The dispatch followed Gladstone's mem. from the second line but added two paragraphs. One regretted the denunciation's effect on Anglo-Russian relations and came from a rejected draft reply by Hammond. The second, written by Granville, ended the dispatch by opening the door to negotiation. Cf. Granville to Buchanan, No. 299, 9 Nov., F.O. 65/799, Odo Russell to Granville, Wedy night, G.D. 29/92, cabinets 10, 11 Nov., Add. MS. 44638, fos. 140, 144. Granville to the Queen, tel., 11 Nov., G.D. 29/32.

[1] The clause 'but . . . indivisible' omitted, apparently at Granville's instance, from the dispatch.

[2] 'Proceed . . . They' omitted from the dispatch.

[3] Altered by Granville to 'assume'.

this purpose each one of the parties places a portion of his free agency in abeyance as regards himself and under the controul of others, by the doctrine & proceeding now in question one of the Parties in its separate & individual capacity brings back the certain subject into its own controul, and remains bound only to itself.

Accordingly Prince Gortschakoff has thought proper to announce in these dispatches the intention of Russia to continue to observe certain of the provisions of the Treaty. However satisfactory this may be in itself it is obviously an expression of the free will of that Power which it might at any time alter or withdraw, and in this which is the true point of view it is equally unsatisfactory with the other portions of his communication because it implies the title of Russia to annul the treaty on the ground of allegations of which she appoints herself as the only judge.

The question therefore arises not whether any desire expressed by Russia ought to be carefully examined in a friendly spirit by the cosignatory Powers, but whether they are to accept from her an announcement that by her own act, without any consent from them, she has released herself from a solemn covenant.

357. Mr. Gladstone to Lord Granville. [G.D. 29/58]

Hawarden Castle. Nov. 13. 70.

I return Odo. The doctrine about Egypt is rather rigid. As long as the Canal is not fortified I do not see much to fear. It would be a less strong measure to seize it in war, than to go to war about it: & this we ought always to be able to do. But never was there less danger or likelihood of our being overpowered in the Mediterranean.

I suppose the hint about Bloomfield may be worth thinking of?

Will there ever be another bit of angling for D[erby] himself? [1]

I think now that the tenor of the Chancellor's and A.-General's opinions will make it right to give the *interim* appointment [2] to Ld Aveland, expressly on the ground of the joint application.

I got the A[ttorney] G[eneral]'s opinion today.

358. Lord Granville to Mr. Gladstone. [Add. MS. 44167, fo. 166]

Walmer Castle. [15 November 1870].

I should have thought that appointing Lord Aveland on the ground of his having a *primâ facie* greater claim, was prejudicing the question to be tried by the

[1] See Odo Russell to Granville, Saturday [12 Nov., misdated on the docket 15 Nov.], stating that Derby, with whom he dined, 11 Nov., 'would go to war for the neutrality of Egypt but not for the neutrality of the Black Sea', and thought Bloomfield should have a peerage, G.D. 29/92. Bessborough to Granville, 24 June 1870, shows an effort to get Lord Derby on to the Liberal side then, G.D. 29/71.

[2] For the Gwydir and Aveland claims to the office of Lord Great Chamberlain, see *G.E.C.* ii. App. D, 607–9. See also Gurdon to Meade, 12 Nov., and mins. by Hatherley and Gladstone on the back of no. 358 in favour of Lord Aveland, and mem. by Gurdon, 22 Nov., with remarks by Granville, 1 Dec., and Gurdon, 2 Dec., G.D. 29/58.

House of Lords. Whereas appointing Lord Gwydir on the ground of his experience & knowledge does not do so.

I am perhaps biassed by Aveland being a rat from us—his father being a Whig creation, and Gwydir has promised his unexpected support.

359. Lord Granville to Mr. Gladstone. [Add. MS. 44167, fo. 168]

Private. F.O. Nov 16/70.

Hammond calculates that the answer from Buchanan will arrive on Monday.[1] I should be much inclined to have a Cabinet if you do not object on Wednesday.

The French are as was to be expected trying to get capital out of the Russian Circular. It would be everything to them to get up an armed coalition of England Austria Italy & Turkey.

Beust who can never keep his tongue or his pen quiet for a moment is mounted on his high horse and Apponyi tells me that Hungary very French, and anti Russian will exert much pressure to keep him there.

Bernstorff told Torrington that Bismark was as much surprised as he was at the circular but Buchanan's telegram shows that forced or unforced by the King, he is likely to support Russia.[2]

The Dips come flocking in for news, but do not bring any.

360. Mr. Gladstone to Lord Granville. [G.D. 29/58]

Hawarden Castle. Nov. 16.70.

1. The Queen sends through Ponsonby a strong approval of our reply (as described by me) to Russia.[3]

It is indeed deplorable that she should, for her own sake, have interposed such a bar to any effectual concert for restoring the peace.

Nevertheless I cannot but think the time is approaching when we shall have to say something on this question of annexation, which will alone cause the horrors of a war through the winter, and on which we find that Italy as well as Russia has given an opinion.

2. I do not know whether it is likely that you will want any one to examine the Fisheries' question on the spot.[4] If you do, Milner Gibson may be worth thinking of.

3. I return your very interesting batch of private letters.

[1] I.e. 20 Nov. A copy of the British reply to Russia's denunciation of the Black Sea clauses was carried by Odo Russell to Bismarck at Versailles, 13 Nov.; see Granville to Bernstorff and to Bismarck, 11 Nov., G.D. 29/111. See also Granville, private, 11 Nov., to Buchanan, G.D. 29/114, to Lyons, F.O. 362/4, to Paget, G.D. 29/112, to Loftus, G.D. 29/114, to Bloomfield, F.O. 362/2, 13 Nov., to Elliot and to Layard, G.D. 29/116.

[2] 4.30 p.m. received 10.30 p.m., 16 Nov., F.O. 65/807.

[3] See Gladstone to the Queen, 11 Nov., and reply by Ponsonby, 13 Nov., *Letters*, 2nd ser. ii. 81–4. Cf. Ponsonby to Granville, 14 Nov., F.O. 65/799.

[4] As part of the general settlement of difficulties with the United States, see above, nos. 336, 339. Cf. note on cabinet of 10 Nov., Add. MS. 44638, fo. 140.

Can Elliot [1] be right in calling the Black Sea an inland sea? No sea is inland, into which there is a passage for fleets.

4. I will refer your point about Aveland to the Chancellor, whom I feel obliged to follow.

5. I have written to Bright,[2] chiefly to *inform* him about Russia & our reply.

361. Mr. Gladstone to Lord Granville. [G.D. 29/58]

Hawarden Castle. N. 17. 70.

1. Together with your batch of private letters returned [herewith] I send you one from Manning [3] about Acton.

2. I suppose the day of the Cabinet need not be fixed till the answer comes & till you find it *is* an answer. I shall not be surprised if Gortchakoff's pen drives heavily. He has I think committed *both* the crime and the *blunder*. Gurdon will fix the Cabinet on hearing from you, at half past three on the day you name. Here I am like the Pope who you may remember proclaimed the day of his Council without fixing the year.

3. Pray let us see the dispatch to Clarendon which Buchanan mentions.[4]

4. And, if you have Palmerston's Life (very interesting) pray look at I, 224 on the rights of *Europe* in a war, and pp. 226, 236, on the conduct of Russia in 1828.

362. Mr. Gladstone to Lord Granville. [G.D. 29/58]

Hawarden Castle. Nov. 18. 70.

1. In reading the report made by Thiers to Lyons on the 10th [5] I am greatly struck by his having nakedly refused a Paris fort as equivalent and not proposed any thing else—although the pith of his negative reply rested on the word *Paris*. He might have proposed, for instance, Thionville (I suppose) without the garrison (not that the men are important but to save the indignity); or *something* at any rate. It is lamentable that in such a question the proceedings should not have been exhaustive.

[1] To Granville, private, 4 Nov., received 14 Nov., G.D. 29/102, supplements his official dispatch on the state of the Eastern Question in reply to No. 208, 6 Oct.; see above, no. 319 note, below, 365. The letter dwells on the importance of the neutralization of the Black Sea.

[2] 16 Nov., Add. MS. 44539, fo. 75; for Bright's reply, 17 Nov., see Add. MS. 44112, fo. 157.

[3] 15 Nov., on the 'impersonal' character of his controversy with Acton about the annexation of Alsace-Lorraine and Acton's political failure, copy, G.D. 29/58. For controversy see letters signed N.M. and Scrutator, *The Times*, 25 Oct. p. 12; 27 Oct. p. 10; 31 Oct. p. 10; 1 Nov. p. 10; 4 Nov. p. 12; 7 Nov. p. 12; 10 Nov. p. 9; 15 Nov. p. 15.

[4] See to Granville, private, 11 Nov., G.D. 29/97. When the reference could not be traced, Buchanan explained that he had erased the passage about the neutralization of the Black Sea not lasting long, from his dispatch to Clarendon before sending it, to Granville, private, 20 Nov., G.D. 29/97.

[5] On the armistice negotiations with Bismarck at Versailles, 1–6 Nov., enclosed in Lyons to Granville, No. 179, 13 Nov., F.O. 27/1820, *Further correspondence respecting the War* . . . Parl. papers. [C. 244] (1871). lxxi, 230–7. Cf. Granville to Lyons, private, 15 Nov., F.O. 362/4.

2. Cardwell has sent me (without approval) a proposal that *we* shall prepare to victual Paris on surrender. He will probably send you my reply which is adverse but makes certain suggestions.

3. Would it not be well that F.O. should prepare [a] memorandum showing the conduct, in the cases alleged as precedents by Brunnow's very clever letter, of the alleged repudiations? Nothing I think could surpass the way you met him, as detailed in your draft to Buchanan.[1]

4. Notwithstanding the stiff accounts from St P[etersburg] I feel confident in the strength of the position we have taken up.

5. Many thanks to you for sending me my wife; a Christian act.

Have you ever read (in Voltaire's Siècle, or elsewhere) Louis XIV's instructions to Philip V on going to Spain? Some of them which are excellent remind me strongly of you, & I shall try to learn them.

My youngest daughter is busy ciphering to you a telegram conformable to my *No 1.*

363. Lord Granville to Mr. Gladstone. [Add. MS. 44167, fo. 171]

Private. Walmer Castle. Nov 18/70.

I came here yesterday evening as much to avoid the Dips, as for fresh air. It is inconvenient being violently pumped by them what our next steps will be, and they tell one nothing. I shall go back on Monday.

What the next steps are to be must be determined by many circumstances.

I expect the Prussians will support the Russians, but suggest dilatory measures.[2]

I presume Gortchakoff without withdrawing from the circular, will profess to be peaceable, & ready to be conciliatory.

The French are getting bumptious. Tissot, (the most cautious of men) believes in the Army of the Loire.[3] They also think the Russian Circular has given them a hold upon us.

Musurus' notion is that we should say that we can do nothing without Turkey, that Turkey should say She can do nothing without the Powers, and if Russia does not withdraw from her circular that Turkey should say "these are words. We answer by words, you denounce the special convention we denounce all our treaties by which you have Consuls, capitulations, liberty for your commerce through the Canal of the Bosphorus. If you act upon your words, then we do the same."[4]

[1] No. 303 confidential, 13 Nov., summarizing Brunnow's letter and Granville's reply in the form of a conversation, F.O. 65/799. Granville argued that infractions did not justify unilateral denunciation.

[2] Cf. Loftus to Granville, private, 26 Oct., 5 Nov., 19 Nov., 22 Nov., G.D. 29/90.

[3] Under d'Aurelles des Paladines had resumed the offensive and taken Orléans by 10 Nov.

[4] See Granville to Elliot, No. 247, 17 Nov., No. 256 confidential, 28 Nov., both on conversation with Musurus, 16 Nov., F.O. 78/2120. The same argument reached Granville from Bismarck, private, Versailles 24 Nov., G.D. 29/94, and through Buchanan from Reuss, German ambassador in St. Petersburg, from Buchanan, private, 20 Nov., G.D. 29/97, and No. 474, 20 Nov., F.O. 65/805.

364. Lord Granville to Mr. Gladstone. [Add. MS. 44167, fo. 175]

F.O. [*sic*]. Nov 18/70.

I send you back Manning's letter. I presume there is no Protestant or Atheist, whom he dislikes more than Acton. I am however afraid he may be right about the latter's success in public life. If anything will spur him into action it will be the knowledge of Manning triumphing in his not having done so.

You have placed a hair trigger pistol in my hands about the Cabinet. I will not promise that I shall not summon it for Tuesday. There seems so much to consider.

I have asked for the despatch to Clarendon.

The despatch [1] of which the whole pith was your's, seems to have had a great success. I trust that our subsequent action will not come up to the Pall Mall standard of what we ought to do. But would not a little strengthening of the Mediterranean Fleet have a good effect, I mean an addition not a transfer. It would have an effect on Russia, who cannot wish for war, and would not compromise us.

The Prince of Wales has been more than usually unwise in his talk. He announced that " he had desired an interview with the Duc d'Aumale, to ascertain his views as to the proper conditions of peace—that he meant to tell him that it was an immense object for England that France should have a monarchical Govt, and that the Duc d'Aumale was the proper candidate, that as to the Comte de Paris, people must look out for themselves in these days."

365. Mr. Gladstone to Lord Granville. [G.D. 29/58]

No 1. Hawarden Castle. Nov. 19. 70.

1. I send you three letters from Bright, and copy of my reply.[2]

2. I think Elliot ought not to pass judgment in his Dispatches [3] on the cogency of the Ottoman Guarantee. His opinion may hinder, cannot help, and is wholly out of place, as anticipating in a public document, the judgment of those who are to instruct him.

3. My telegram of today [4] to you was founded on the idea that the ' situation ' would justify your going a little farther than you had done in pointing out to both Powers the impropriety of their standing still because neither likes to speak first.

Prussia is the worst because Bismarck discourages the use of a mouthpiece. It seems increasingly clear to me that we can *reckon on* no way out of the present horrors and complications, without a Constituent Assembly. I greatly doubt, for one, whether the capture of Paris will end the war, even if Bismarck set up a sham Govt. of notables, or obtain a terror-vote, in Paris, for cession as the basis of peace.

[1] See above, no. 356.

[2] From Bright, 17, 18 Nov., arguing that Britain should yield to Russia on the Black Sea question, Add. MS. 44112, fos. 157, 161, 163. Bright also asked that his resignation might now become effective. See also Gladstone to Bright, 28 Nov., Add. MS. 44539, fo. 85.

[3] See No. 254 confidential, 31 Oct., received 14 Nov., describing the state of the Eastern Question, and the necessity of Britain's honouring the guarantee, F.O. 78/2125.

[4] Led to fresh British representations to Prussia and France, see Granville to Bernstorff, private, 14 Nov., G.D. 29/111, and reply, 15 Nov., G.D. 29/94.

I trust Italy will not fail to say ditto to us: that we may make a good Chorus. The Turks seem to be temperate.

366. Mr. Gladstone to Lord Granville. [G.D. 29/58]

No 2. Hawarden Castle. Nov. 19. 70.

I have this afternoon received your letter of yesterday.

Being threatened with a cough, which I am anxious to coax away before it takes tight hold, I am rather alarmed at an idea of a Cabinet on Tuesday: but for other reasons I should be loath to have one before there is a real practical question to dispose of, such as the answer of Gortchakoff is likely to raise.

I *have* thought of the question whether we should strengthen the fleet in the Mediterranean but I own that for the time I am strongly against it. It would be an immense responsibility to take any military measure whatever at such a period, and one which I contemplate with very great disfavour. The tone of the press (though in some respects it may be useful) shows me that we have a highly inflammable and susceptible state of the public mind to deal with: one quite different from what it would be if war had not changed the temperature of the political atmosphere. Russia having nothing in the Black Sea an increase of force would mean the thought of attack: I think it would be premature, and I fear it might really prove mischievous as with many it would be popular.

Without pretending to a formed opinion, I do not see that it may not be right for us as the next move distinctly to challenge Russia to a formal examination of the *facts* upon which she professes to take her stand.

Your report of the P. of W., is wonderful.

What do we *know* of Russian movements of troops?

367. Lord Granville to Mr. Gladstone. [Add. MS. 44167, fo. 177]

Private. Walmer Castle. [20 November 1870].

I have asked Gurdon to summon the Cabinet for Wednesday.[1]

Tom Hughes is here. His language about the Americans is like that which Graves appears to have held to Hammond.[2]

Goschen is also here—although he does not admit it, he is rather Pall Mallish.

I send you a note from Lord Russell.[3] He proposes to us instead of going to war, to do that which we cannot do in time of peace.

Trevelyan's scheme seems out of the question. I agree with you in doubting whether we should go as far as the possible alternative which you suggest.

I suspect the Cabinet will be thirsty for talk about army and navy.

Our organization requires some overhauling.

Russell & Cardwell both say that Dover Castle cannot at this moment, although it is to be remedied, resist an Ironclad.

[1] 23 Nov., postponed to 25 Nov.
[2] Cf. Hammond to Granville, private, 19 Nov., G.D. 29/104.
[3] To Granville, private, 19 Nov., and copy of reply 20 Nov., G.D. 29/79.

Orders (cancelled the next day) were received by the Rifles on Thursday to cease recruiting.

There is a Troop of Cavalry at Walmer in the Marine Barracks—the two subalterns are on leave, & I am told but it may not be true that the Captain is so bored that he is always away.

I doubt whether these sorts of things happen in the Navy.

368. Mr. Gladstone to Lord Granville. [G.D. 29/58]

Hawarden Castle. Nov. 20. 70.

I rejoice that there should be a ray of light in this black Russian business.[1]

If Gortschakoff disavowing all intention to *act* on the Russian opinion offers to submit the claim to consideration in terms of your closing Paragraph,[2] it will not be easy for us to take effective objection to a Conference or Congress ?

I do not see the force of the objections reported by Lytton. It seems to me that Turkey would have four friends and Russia but one whether that one were France or Prussia.

It is very natural that the Turk should object even to discuss the Treaty, for if the discussion had any result at all it must be to diminish or take away the exceptional advantage she now enjoys.

I suppose it would be difficult to provide even by European Treaty that the Black Sea should be closed at all times and not only when the Porte is at peace, according to the present stipulation ?

It is difficult to deny Chaudordy's doctrine [3] that France must look out for herself, if he does not carry it to the extent (Forgive [4]: I write in bed) of claiming exemption from Treaties.

While it is not easy to find *smashing* objections to a Congress, it would be very desirable to see what could really be adopted as an arrangement equitable to all the parties.

The idea of the starvation of Paris affects me as that of the bombardment affected you seven weeks ago, and I am more & more anxious for a Constituent Assembly as the only starting point for a future (perhaps not an immediate) peace. You see Chaudordy admits the thing to be feasible.

369. Lord Granville to Mr. Gladstone. [Add. MS. 44167, fo. 180]

Private. Walmer Castle. Nov 21/70.

I asked Gurdon to summon the Cabinet for Wednesday before I got your letter —I will telegraph to you from London this afternoon.

[1] Buchanan to Granville, tel. 20 Nov., on the academic character of denunciation, F.O. 65/807 ; cf. no. 363. The conference proposal from Bismarck was not received until early on 23 Nov.

[2] Granville's addition to No. 301 to Buchanan ; see above, no. 356 note.

[3] Cf. Lyons to Granville, private, 17 Nov : 'If we do not help France she will take aid from any quarter she can get it, even from the Satanic Alliance (as Thiers calls it) with Russia', G.D. 29/85.

[4] An ink blot.

I am so sorry to hear of your cough, for I am afraid you ought not to stay away from London longer.[1] It is very hard upon you, but it is a topic which everybody appears to take up, and which of course will be used by our opponents. I must add that there are many things I should like to discuss with you, and which it is almost impossible to do in writing.

I have written to Bright, telling him that you had informed me most confidentially of his intention.[2] I like your letter to him very much. He is a great loss.

I have not Elliot's despatch, but I think it was "confidential" and written in answer to my request for his opinion. Did you remark that he takes the opposite view to Aali Pasha, of the relative importance of the conditions of the Treaty.

My hope is that we shall have a conciliatory despatch from Gorchakoff—that we ought to recognize its amount of retraction as strongly as the content will bear—that we should say Congress and negotiations are inexpedient, when Prussia & France are otherwise engaged, but state our readiness to study the merits of the case when the proper time comes.

Or we might as you suggest ask for a statement of facts.

How about our having saluted the Italian Flag at Civita Vecchia?

370. Lord Granville to Mr. Gladstone. [Add. MS. 44167, fo. 184]

Private. London. Nov 21/70.

I am very sorry to hear that you are not well—of course you must run no risk—but as soon as you can, you will, I hope, come up, and have a Cabinet.

Childers has been here. He tells me there is a perfect howl about the Ministers not meeting. He has been at Cambridge where residents and visitors were all in the same cry.

He is more quiet in his talk than I hear some of our colleagues are—But he says if there is to be war, every day lost is most injurious. I have told him that it is impossible to say that we may not be driven into it by Russia, or by other Foreign Powers, or by our own people, that we must take care of our dignity, but if there ever was a Cabinet which is bound not to drift into an unnecessary war, it is ours.

He is rather for a conference.

371. Mr. Gladstone to Lord Granville. [G.D. 29/58]

Hawarden Castle. Nov. 21. 70.

I am out of bed this afternoon, and though I shall be very glad if I find Gortschakoff will not allow you to load your piece by Wednesday I hope to make my appearance then if I find that you think best to adhere to that day. These coughs are I find very awkward customers if aggravated by neglect.

[1] Cf. Granville to Gladstone, tel. 11.15 a.m., 21 Nov.: 'I will telegraph about the Cabinet from London this afternoon. I am afraid you ought to come to town', G.D. 29/58.

[2] To resign, to Bright, copy, 21 Nov., G.D. 29/52, printed Fitzmaurice, ii. 28.

2. If we are really to entertain the affair of the Bahamas it will be needful to consider very carefully the *how* in all its particulars.

3. Read Reeve (herewith) from top of p. 4 and Guizot from 3½.[1]

4. The case [2] seems perfect as to the Principalities in form & substance, as to the ships in substance only. There was blameable neglect on the part of somebody in tampering with the letter of the Treaty and so giving Russia a shade of plausibility for her complaint.

5. Will she now say 'I have given you my opinion of my rights but such is my respect for Treaties that instead of setting it up against yours I will at once make the appeal you indicate ? ['] This I think would get her out, unless she too palpably shows that she is waiving her own course for the moment only.

6. I hope you have seen a query I sent you about Rome & the Pope. The day is probably coming when all factious R.C.'s will train off from us as we shall have no more justice to do them & cannot do injustice to others at their bidding.

372. Lord Granville to Mr. Gladstone. [Add. MS. 44167, fo. 194]

16, Bruton Street. Nov 22/70.

By a breach of confidence I have recd a copy of Lord R[ussell]'s suppressed pamphlet, but with the obligation of returning it at once.

It is twaddle. Abuse of our Colonial Policy. Strong strictures upon your review in the Edinburgh, exhortations to military defence, with many amusing anecdotes, defence of Prussia, & of the piety of Prussia's King, abuse of France & ending with proposals.

1. Strong army with a well qualified commissariat.
2. An embodied Militia of 120,000 men with 480 guns.
3. A garrison of British Troops with a brave General, in Quebec.
4. Advice to France to yield to Bismark's first terms (Alsace & Lorraine) and promise of assistance to Germany to obtain them.
5. Promise to unite with France to unite with her [*sic*] in resisting any further demands which imply dishonor or destruction.

373. Lord Granville to Mr. Gladstone. [Add. MS. 44167, fo. 189]

Confidential. F.O. Nov 22/70.

I think the Bahamas should be kept out of sight at least for the present.

I send you two memoranda one by Rogers,[3] the other by Tenterden.[4] They both make cases against the United States, which only encrease the difficulty of settling the questions in dispute.

[1] Missing from the letters of Reeve to Gladstone, which enclosed letters from Guizot, in Add. MS. 44428.

[2] Represented by Russia as an infraction of the Treaty of Paris, 1856, in the dispatches, 19/30 and 20/31 Oct., communicated 9 Nov., denouncing the Black Sea clauses.

[3] 'Questions at issue between Canada and the United States' by Sir F. Rogers, 18 Nov., marked 'circulated [in the cabinet] Decr. 5/70,' G.D. 29/68. Cf. Rogers to Granville, 15, 24 Oct., G.D. 29/75.

[4] 'Relations with the United States', 19 Nov., printed for the cabinet, 21 Nov., F.O. 5/1331.

I have had a long confidential talk with Rose. He says a pet object with Grant is to reduce their rate of interest from six to four and a half per cent, & that he is aware this cannot be done without a fair settlement of old scores with England.

He has doubts about the possibility at this moment of negotiating a reciprocity treaty.

He likes the idea of appointing Commissioners to discuss and recommend how each question in dispute could be best put in train for settlement. He had learnt confidentially from Mr Fish, that although no one could be so satisfactory to himself, Thornton had unluckily written home things which had been quoted—which had made Sumner his deadly enemy. (It is singular that although perfectly ignorant of this, in one of my first letters to Thornton,[1] I had suggested to him, that it might be as well not to treat Sumner as a national enemy, but to see whether he could not be approached by his weak side, which is vanity).

It would be necessary to sound Fish, & Macdonald, and if there was any chance of success, we might try a Commission.

My beau ideal of one would be—

Derby—Milner Gibson, & Sir John Rose—with Tenterden as Secretary.

If these were not to be had

Argyll Northcote

Cowper Whitbread

Dufferin or our Forster (who I am told is confident he could settle it.)

Devon.

I know of no Canadian who would do instead of Sir John Rose. If Rogers is about to retire, he might go, or Sir Clinton Murdoch.

Pray turn this over in your mind. No time should be lost.

374. Mr. Gladstone to Lord Granville. [G.D. 29/58]

Hawarden Castle. Nov. 22. 70.

1. I gather from Buchanan's Telegram that the Russian answer may be here by Friday [2] and I propose to come up on Thursday morning, so as to be at C.H.T. I hope before three o'clock. Should there be any thing urgent tomorrow I can on receiving a telegram from you come up.[3]

2. I have many things to mention but not until today any thing that would not keep. I send you a note from Bruce [4]—you will see that the idea of possible war for us has raised the pulse of the Fenians once more—I do not think we ought on this account to hold our hands as to the release with banishment?

[1] Copy, private, 13 Oct., F.O. 362/1.

[2] 25th. Buchanan's tel. 2 a.m. received 8 a.m., 22 Nov., announced the holding back of the Russian rejoinder to the British reply to the denunciation of the Black Sea clauses, for amendment at Buchanan's instance, but so that it should leave by the 23rd, F.O. 65/807.

[3] See Granville to Gladstone, tel. 6.15 p.m., 22 Nov., asking for a cabinet on 25 Nov., G.D. 29/58.

[4] 20 Nov., submitting reports on revived Fenian activities and advising release with banishment; cf. subsequent correspondence, 27 Nov.–28 Dec., Add. MS. 44086, fos. 157–79.

3. Among your very interesting private letters, that of Lyons [1] dated the 17th says the French Govt would do any thing to put us 'on their side morally or physically'. I should like very much to know whether these words may be taken *strictly* and whether the French Govt. are desirous of a moral support known to be such only. Not that I see an immediate importance in such knowledge, but the day might come, especially after the convocation of an Assembly.

4. I read with much pleasure in Loftus's letter [2] that Clarendon desired that other mode of dealing with the Black Sea which I recommended as preferable in the H. of Commons, because I now see that the authority of the Govt. was not really against me & am the more led to look upon this as one not unhopeful alternative for consideration.

5. I will frankly own that I am much disgusted with a good deal of the language that I have read in the newspapers within the last few days about immediate war with Russia. I try to put a check on myself to prevent the reaction it engenders. Your observation on drifting into war is most just: though I always thought Clarendon's epithet in this one case inapplicable as well as unadvisable.

I know however nothing more like drifting into war than would be a resort to any military measures whatever except with reference either to some actual fact or some well defined contingency. No such contingency as yet stands in my view. I am more sorry than surprised to see Lord Russell leading the mad, and making Shaftesbury stand by his side as the model of sober politicians.[3] I do not mean to imply that there is any thing palpably absurd in the opinion that war against Russia may be defensible by many arguments if she does not change her ground: but with the knowledge of particulars which we possess the case seems to me at present to be very clear against it.

6. Thornton's letter [4] seems to point to important practical issues which if possible we should not forego on account of the great pressure of European cares.

P.S. I do not quite understand your reference to C[ivita] Vecchia.

May the rumour about Chaudordy prove true.

375. **Mr. Gladstone to Lord Granville.** [G.D. 29/58]

Nov. 23. 70.

Hoping to see you tomorrow I shall be very brief today.

1. Of your list for a Commission I will say

1. I fear Derby could not be had.

2. Argyll and Forster disqualified by office.

[1] To Granville, private, Tours, 17 Nov., G.D. 29/85, and Granville's reply, private, 23 Nov., asking what France meant by moral support, F.O. 362/4.

[2] To Granville, private, Berlin, 19 Nov., recalling that before March 1856 Lord Clarendon was 'in favour of opening the Black Sea to all nations . . .', G.D. 29/90.

[3] Relates to bellicose letters from Lords Russell and Shaftesbury to *The Times*, 22 Nov. Cf. G.D. 29/79 for correspondence between Granville and Russell arising.

[4] To Granville, private, Washington, 1 Nov., on Fish's response to the British reply to his overture for the settlement of Anglo-American differences, G.D. 29/80. Cf. above, nos. 336, 339, 360.

3. Devon Dufferin Whitbread Cowper—strong & sharp enough for Jonathan? To Milner Gibson & Northcote I would add for consideration Sir F. Peel.

Derby, Gibson & Peel (+ Rose) would be excellent.

I do not know enough of Ld Lawrence to give an opinion.

Camperdown though young I think good.

The two memoranda you sent me are admirable.

2. I have had *half* an idea that it might be well I should see Brunnow either with you or alone. All know the mischief done by the Russian idea of Lord Aberdeen & the Opposition are in the habit of studiously representing me as his double, or his heir, in pacific traditions. This I do not conceive to be true, and possibly I might undeceive B[runnow] a little. But we shall see how the thing stands.

3. I inclose a letter of Cardwell's [1] with one from Palmer to him. The R.C.'s are bothering me about the Pope.[2]

376. Lord Granville to Mr. Gladstone. [Add. MS. 44167, fo. 196]

F.O. Nov. 23/70.

Telegraph whether you want a dinner, and when I shall meet you.

Do not appear as peaceable as you are to our colleagues or to the Foreign Representatives. I am come round to absence of warlike preparations, although there is much to be said for them.

One may take Odo's telegram [3] whichever way one likes. He [Bismarck] offers if we ask him to ask the Russians after the slap in the face which they have administered to us, to receive the whole of Europe in their capital in order with the assistance of Prussia, they may get all they want.

On the other hand Prussia has always thought this an unfair proviso, they owe Russia a debt of gratitude for keeping the Austrians quiet, but they wish to help a peaceful conclusion of the matter, and make a proposal which with certain modifications might be accepted.

377. Mr. Gladstone to Lord Granville. [G.D. 29/58]

11, Carlton House Terrace. N. 25/70.

These are the ideas [4] that occur to me with regard to a possible reply to Russia, if her answer prove to be such as must be taken in a bad sense.

Elliot's letter [5] wd be good to read to Cabinet.

[1] Untraced.

[2] See below, nos. 380 note, 389.

[3] Russell to Granville, tel. 22 Nov., received 23 Nov., announcing Bismarck's offer 'to take the initiative in proposing a conference at St. Petersburgh', F.O. 65/799.

[4] See no. 378, probably written on 25 Nov., but a fair copy sent to Granville was dated 26 Nov. The Russian rejoinder to the British reply to the denunciation of the Black Sea clauses, 8/20 Nov., was communicated, 25 Nov., F.O. 65/815; Parl. papers. [C. 245] (1871). lxxii, 32–4.

[5] To Granville, private, 14 Nov., G.D. 29/102.

378. Memorandum by Mr. Gladstone.[1] [G.D. 29/58]

[*Copy*]. Nov 26 70.

1. As regards the substantial justification of the proceeding, the Russian Government has alleged that breaches of the Treaty have already taken place which are of a nature to set her free from provisions she may wish to abrogate as injurious to herself.

H.M. Government must point out that it is the duty of the Russian Government to supply a particular account of these breaches. Such an account would have the advantage of being open to discussion, & it might be to confutation.

2. As regards what Prince Gortchakoff terms the form of the proceeding he alleges that it has been forced upon him by the failure of all attempts to bring about the meeting of Congresses: But H.M.'s Govt. must state in reply that they are not aware of any occasion on which Russia the party most interested, has proposed either through a Congress or Conference or without any such meeting her desire for a relaxation of the Treaty should be taken into consideration [*sic*]. The Imperial Government cannot allege in justification of their present proceeding, the failure of efforts which have never been made.

3. H.M.'s Government observe with satisfaction that Prince Gortchakoff considers the reply of Lord Granville to his circular as conceding the substance of the matter in question while differing only as to the form. For if that, which remains to be conceded on the one side or the other in order to an agreement [*sic*], be from the Russian point of view only a matter of form, it seems to follow that the Imperial Government cannot have much difficulty in making the concession.

4. They likewise notice with pleasure that Prince Gortchakoff describes the declaration which has been made by Russia as an abstract or "theoretic" declaration, without "immediate application". If these words are to be construed as an announcement that Russia has formed and stated her own opinion of her rights, but has no intention of acting in conformity with it on her own responsibility, they go far to close the controversy. But as they are capable of a different construction H.M. Government are not able to rely upon the interpretation just given without the explicit sanction of the Government of his Imperial Majesty.

5. If the favourable construction be disclaimed or not adopted, then Her Majesty's Govt. are obliged to say that if Russia announces herself to be discharged from certain obligations of the Treaty, such an announcement is for them of no value. It can have no effect whatever on the binding force of the Treaty: and any act done or to be done, which should be at variance with its covenants, would in their eyes be of precisely the same character, & would entail the same liabilities as if the circular of Prince Gortchakoff had not been written.

The despatch of the 20th appears to suggest that H.M.'s Govt. may ask for a

[1] Gladstone's holograph is in Add. MS. 44759, fo. 224. Cf. Granville to Buchanan, No. 326, 28 Nov., answering the Russian rejoinder to the British reply to the denunciation of the Black Sea clauses, F.O. 65/799. The dispatch drafted by Granville follows in substance paragraph 2 and the first two sentences of paragraph 4 and ends by accepting a conference. It was discussed in the cabinet of Friday, 25 Nov., and approved in that of Monday, 28 Nov., Add. MS. 44638, fos. 147, 150.

Conference, & that such conference may consider those portions of the treaty which are not included in the Russian disclaimers, but H.M.'s Govt. could enter into no conference which should assume any portion of the Treaty to have been already abrogated by the discretion of a single Power: and it would be wholly out of place for them under the present circumstances to ask for a Conference, as they are not the parties who desire to bring about any changes in the Treaty.

There might indeed be contingencies in which should the controversy be prolonged, it might be the duty of H.M.'s Government to consider of a step of that kind, but they would be of a description in which it probably would not be their duty to address themselves to the Russian Govt.

379. Lord Granville to Mr. Gladstone. [Add. MS. 44167, fo. 199]

Confidential. Windsor Castle. Nov 27/70.

Otway offered his resignation 3 months ago, in case I did not feel confidence in him, & hinted that his office was a bar to his political success.

Yesterday he tendered his resignation leaving the time to my decision on account of his disapproval of our telegram to Odo.[1]

Pray say nothing of it to any one till I see you—but I wish to be able to say I have already informed you, in case of a retraction.

Queen very sensible about Foreign Affairs.

380. Lord Granville to Mr. Gladstone. [Add. MS. 44167, fo. 201]

Windsor Castle. Nov 27/70

I beg your pardon—I believe you have already concocted an excellent answer.[2]

381. Mr. Gladstone to Lord Granville.[3] [G.D. 29/58]

Cipher Telegram. [? 2 December 1870]

I have learned exactly the Burnside terms.[4] Two days armistice for Elections, thirty days safe conducts of all kinds with other assistance to enable the assembly to meet and act: two days provision for Paris. Rejection was unpardonable. Thiers probably will not repeat it: but should not Lyons be informed of our deep regret. You will sufficiently understand this short statement.

[1] 8 p.m., 25 Nov., accepting Bismarck's conference proposal. For Otway's bellicose views on the Black Sea question see his mem. 11 Nov., sent to Granville, 19 Nov., and Granville's reply, 20 Nov., G.D. 29/107, and Otway to Gladstone, 27 Nov., Add. MS. 44428, fo. 224. Otway's letter of resignation has not been traced, but see Granville to Otway, 28 Nov., G.D. 29/107.

[2] To Edmund Dease, M.P. for Queen's Co., 30 Nov., replying to Dease, 15 Nov., on the temporal power of the Pope, Add. MS. 44428, fos. 205, 236, published in *The Times*, 8 Dec., p. 3.

[3] Granville to Gladstone, 30 Nov., on Bulwer's peerage and his income, and an undated note by Granville on precedence as between the King of Prussia and Emperor of Russia in signing a treaty, Add. MS. 44167, fos. 202, 206, not printed.

[4] See above, no. 350.

382. Mr. Gladstone to Lord Granville. [G.D. 29/58]

No 1. Hawarden Castle. Dec. 3. 70.

With respect to the intended release of the Fenian prisoners,[1] Fortescue properly observes that it would be well to have had the Congress *announced* when the release takes place: not the day but the intention to hold it. This may I presume be done when you have a Russian acceptance in satisfactory terms.

2. I think Elliot hits the point in his suggestion [2] that the Sultan should not resume an unbounded discretion but one to be exercised in case of menace, or to use our word in the Naval Reserve Act in case of 'emergency'.

3. I hear with regret of the taking of Champigny.[3] To my mind the Money Market is all wrong: it is a French success which is most likely to shorten the war.

The Bernstorffs come on Friday. Then or before or after should you, or better still you & Lady G. be moved to come hitherwards, great rejoicing will ensue.

383. Mr. Gladstone to Lord Granville. [G.D. 29/58]

No 2 Secret. Hawarden Castle. Dec. 3. 1870.

During the partial and momentary lull, I take this opportunity of writing to you on the subject, which we have sometimes touched lightly in conversation, respecting Royal Residence in Ireland.

For our time as a Government, and my time as a politician, Royalty will do well enough in this country, because it has a large fund to draw upon, which was greatly augmented by good husbandry in the early and middle part of this reign, and which is not yet exhausted.

But the fund of credit is diminishing, and I do not see from whence it is to be replenished as matters now go. To speak in rude and general terms, the Queen is invisible, and the Prince of Wales is not respected. With the Queen, who abounds beyond all necessity in private and personal kindnesses to those having relations with her, it is a matter of great and ever increasing difficulty to arrange for any part of those formal ceremonial duties to the public, which in an ordinary state of things would go as matters of course. These parts of business are among the most difficult, and are the most painful, of the duties of my place; and it would be a relief to me if I could lay the blame upon the unhandy manner in which I perform them. The Queen's reluctance grows, and will grow, with age. And even if it did not, her influence dwindles with the deaths of those who have felt it, & who are not replaced; while we live in a time in which the personal influence of the Sovereign is among the main props of the Crown. The Prince of Wales is now in his thirtieth year. He has, I think, that average stock of energy, which enables men to do that which they cannot well avoid doing, or that which is made ready to their hands:

[1] See above, no. 374.

[2] See to Granville, private, 18 Nov., on the abrogation of the neutrality of the Black Sea and alternative methods of protecting Turkey, G.D. 29/102. He favoured altering the closure of the Straits to allow Turkey to call up friendly fleets, before she was at war, as soon as an emergency occurred; cf. No. 293, 21 Nov. received 1 Dec., F.O. 78/2125.

[3] Prussian victory over the army of the Loire.

but he has not the rare supply of it, which enables a man to make duty, and so to win honour and confidence. When this negative position as to duty is combined with the highest activity of the appliances and stimulants of pleasure, the position is, for the formation of character, the most dangerous in which a human being can be placed; and perhaps, all things considered, we ought to be thankful even that matters are no worse than they are.

But the outlook for ten, twenty, thirty, forty years hence is a very melancholy one. And, in these circumstances, the only remedial measure of which I can think is, to try and frame some plan under which the Prince, before the habits of his mind and life become so to speak rigid, shall be provided with some fair share, not of political responsibility, but of public duty.

It would in my opinion not be impracticable to assign to the Prince the duty of representing the Queen in Ireland. While this plan worked, the Lord Lieutenancy would disappear: but there need not be of necessity any decision as to its ultimate extinction or survival. Residence in Ireland, during a large portion of the year, would be necessary: perhaps during half of it. The Salary of the Lord Lieutenant, and the sums assigned to his staff, would of course go to the Prince. He would make a sacrifice of personal freedom and pleasure: but he would be more than repaid, if repayment is wanted, in the general estimation which accompanies the discharge of public duty. I presume no difficulty can be thought to attend his taking over the ceremonial and external duties of the Lord Lieutenant: as I also presume there is no doubt that the measure would have, not only salutary, but also very powerful effects on the popular mind in Ireland. But what as to the political duties of the Lord Lieutenant, who is an officer of the Crown responsible to Parliament? My answer to this inquiry turns upon the fact that the Irish Government is subordinate to the English Government. After the change I have supposed, the Irish Secretary would be the only responsible agent, instead of having a joint responsibility with the Lord Lieutenant. But I see no reason why the Prince should not have a relation to the Irish Minister resembling in some points that of the Sovereign to the Cabinet; though without the final authority, which is not in fact represented in the Irish, but in the British, Government. As the Queen is now, apart from such authority, a kind of high impartial counsellor to the Cabinet, so the Prince would be made acquainted with the course of business, and have the opportunity of forming his judgment, and of advising, upon it. The tact, which this would demand on the part of the Irish Minister, would simply resemble that which every head of a great department of State requires in his *single* intercourse with the Sovereign. Meanwhile the Prince would obtain a very valuable political Education.

I now come to the proposal of Lord Bessborough,[1] that Parliament should vote a sum, say of ten thousand a year, for the charge of a residence in Ireland, whither

[1] In mem. for Gladstone enclosed in a letter to Granville, 13 Sept. The mem. has not been traced, but the letter was returned by Gladstone marked: 'Can we talk more on this and the kindred points? Or wait a little. W. E. G. Ja 18 [1871]'. No. 383 was sent to Bessborough, who returned it saying he considered Gladstone's scheme 'the wildest and most visionary . . . I ever heard of', 6 Dec., G.D. 29/71.

the Prince, or other members of the Royal Family, might repair for more or less of residence, the public only being responsible to the extent of the vote. Of this plan I would say

1. That, as respects effect on the people of Ireland, it would do part of the good that would follow the larger one.

2. That as respects the important purposes connected with the Prince himself, it would not embrace them.

3. That it would be valuable in itself as compared with the present state of things.

4. That it is not necessarily in conflict with the other, but might possibly be used as an introduction to it; and this would afford us some continuance of the valuable services of the present Lord Lieutenant.

5. But it is not free from difficulty as regards the comparative positions of the Prince of Wales (at least) and the Lord Lieutenant, unless the visits were of the most purely transitory character.

Please to think this matter over with much regard to the weighty subjects which I have touched in the earlier part of the letter. When you have had time to answer me I will consider whether to bring it under the notice of two or three of our colleagues.

384. Lord Granville to Mr. Gladstone. [Add. MS. 44167, fo. 207]

Private. Walmer Castle. Dec 3/70.

Dasent has told & shown me what makes me agree with him in thinking McColl a very slippery party.

I should think the more we can concert what is to be said to the Papers on F.O Affairs the better.

I sounded Rose,[1] telling him that I had no authority to speak. I asked whether he would go—whether his commercial business was of a nature which would make it natural for him to go, and whether there was anything in it's character which unfitted him to be employed by us.

To the first he asked for 24 hours to consider, to the second he answered in the affirmative, to the third in the negative.

May I continue the matter with him.

There seems no doubt of the conference.

He says that the Congress about to meet will separate at the beginning of March—that intrigues for the Presidential election will begin in the autumn, that it would probably be a disadvantage to delay.

The enclosed has just come in.

385. Lord Granville to Mr. Gladstone. [Add. MS. 44167, fo. 215]

Walmer Castle. Dec 5/70.

I should like a few days to consider your 'Secret' letter.

No 1. I go to town today, and hope to get a positive answer from Brunnow

[1] Whether he would go to Washington to prepare for official negotiations on Anglo-American differences. See above, nos. 373, 374, 375.

or Buchanan this evening.[1] I will telegraph to you, and to Fortescue when we can announce the conference. But there is a question whether we should do so, till we have an answer from France.

2. The best but most unlikely compensation we could get for concession on the convention, would be Prussia joining the tripartite treaty.

The next best and which would probably be as we choose, the restoration more or less complete of the Sultan's right.

If the Russians are to get back the whole sovereign right, it would be disagreeable to give to the Turk only a portion of his.

3. At this hour, the successes against the French do not seem decisive.

386. Mr. Gladstone to Lord Granville. [G.D. 29/58]

Hawarden. Dec. 5. 70.

1. Though I have never been intimate with McColl, I am surprised at the account you have received. I may have known him some 12 or 15 years, and all that time he has been a volunteer on my behalf fighting my battles at Oxford and everywhere else with untiring zeal, & never once asking any thing from me until quite recently I asked him whether there was any thing he wished for. All his writings have been conducted off his own hook, for he has at no time had from me any thing but generalities, and sometimes an old pamphlet. I mention this because you seem to be under the impression that he has had special foreign intelligence from me at times which is as far as possible from being the case.

2. My wife has cut out of the Motley fund [2] as far as personal activity is concerned and I suppose it will now proceed on a limited scale. In this view, I think it a mistake, though upon the larger plan I should have liked it much.

3. I am afraid you have not yet been able to take the dose administered in my Memorandum about Alsace and Lorraine.[3] But the French are now, in conformity with several passages of their ancient history, developing an energy of endurance (not to mention amended fighting) which makes me think we may be obliged, & that at short notice, some day or other to have an opinion on this subject which is now the sole pivot of the war. I frankly own I can see no plan wholly but I go so far with Mill as to be disposed to think it might not be the worst of all plans, if the fortresses were destroyed with no power to replace them for 20 years. I admit that at this moment we have no opportunity to speak.

4. The Bernstorffs announce that they give up their northern tour.

5. I inclose a letter from Mr Graves on the same subject as your Telegram which I answer by the hope that the Americans will move.

6. I think you may safely proceed with Rose.

[1] Odo Russell to Granville, tel. received 2.30 a.m., 1 Dec., reported a general acceptance of the conference proposal, which remained unconfirmed, F.O. 64/737.

[2] Began as a private gesture to reimburse Motley after a burglary, but grew into a partisan demonstration on his recall from London. Granville's persuasion caused Mrs. Gladstone's withdrawal; see her letters to Granville, 19 Nov., 1 and 9 Dec., G.D. 29/58.

[3] Further mem. on Alsace-Lorraine, Nov., with a letter from Argyll to Gladstone, 25 Nov., G.D. 29/58; mem. printed P. Knaplund, *Gladstone's Foreign Policy* (1935), pp. 270–9.

387. Lord Granville to Mr. Gladstone. [Add. MS. 44167, fo. 217]

16, Bruton Street. Dec 5/70.

Baron Brunnow asked to see me again,[1] and today he repeated his reluctance to go into a conference unless he knew how he was to come out of it.

He had proposed that Prince Gortchakoff should come instead of himself as Plenipotentiary—but in this he had been overruled—Prince Gortchakoff thought that Baron Brunnow's suggestion that he should come, if it had been approved by the Emperor would have placed him (the Prince) in a great difficulty. "In short" Baron Brunnow said "Prince Gortchakoff wishes to gain in Russia applause for the boldness of his circular and to put upon me the dirt of getting out of it in England. I do not like being between the hammer of public opinion in Russia and the anvil which England presents."

He had seen Count Bernstorff, and they had agreed that the more it was possible to avoid wrangling & protocolling in Conference the better. In the Luxembourg affair this had been avoided. He Baron Brunnow had been the go between with the Prussians and the French Ambassador and everything was settled among all the plenipotentiaries (what they were to say, and what they were to decide) before the Conference was opened. Baron Brunnow thought that one Plenipotentiary would be sufficient for each State.

This was the opinion which Count Bernstorff and Count Apponyi had already given me and in which I concurred.[2] Hammond is of the same opinion. I see by a telegram received today that Beust would like to have two. Baron Brunnow thinks I should issue the formal invitations, but not for a few days. He would be glad, as would M de Bernstorff, if everything was settled in conference before Parliament met.

He has had no instructions from St Petersburgh, and would prefer being without those which Gortchakoff has promised him. He has sent the enclosed statement for approval to St Petersburgh.

He presumes I should open the Conference with a short speech, that he should then follow. He would be glad to know what you and I think of his scheme of declaration.

He is desirous to know what are our views as to the issue of the conference, in order that he may decide whether he will continue to represent the Emperor. That he has a sense of his own dignity which makes him desirous not to play a ridiculous part. He had consulted his Doctor whether he could safely undertake a journey to St Petersburgh to give in his resignation. (He did not say what the Doctor had advised). He was perfectly aware that public opinion in England must be satisfied as well as that in Russia. He asked whether we had thought of any equivalents.

[1] Brunnow to Granville, private, samedi matin [3 Dec.], asking him to resume a conversation of 30 Nov. Granville saw him on Monday evening, G.D. 29/98. Granville to Buchanan, No. 342 confidential, 9 Dec., follows paragraph 3, part of paragraph 5 and summarizes paragraph 6 of no. 387 concluding with the advice not to withdraw from a useful task.

[2] Cf. Apponyi to Granville, private, 29 Nov., on agreement before the conference met, identic instructions to the representatives of the signatories of the tripartite treaty, and Anglo-Austrian co-operation, G.D., 29/82, and Granville's reply, 29 Nov., F.O. 362/2.

I replied by asking whether supposing that any grounds were found for conceding the request made by Russia as to the special convention, he had thought of any possible equivalent which could be satisfactory to this country, & to Turkey.

He said that there appeared to him to be only one—that to which Clarendon had given the preference, and which he had seen raised in some of our newspapers—viz the opening instead of the shutting of Black Sea, with a reservation of the Sultan's Sovereign power.

That anything like the proposal at Vienna of limiting but less strictly the number & tonnage of the vessels to be possessed in the Black Sea by Russia & Turkey would have the same disadvantages as the present arrangement.

He had no instructions from Home, & he did not know what the Turks would say, but the scheme he had suggested was the only one he could think of. He could not have assented to it a few days ago, at a time when Russia was only partially in possession of her portion of the shores of the Black Sea. But the people of the Caucasus had now retired from them. He pressed me to express my views.

I told him that the authority I held from you and from the Cabinet was only to enter the Conference on conditions with which he was acquainted and to listen with fairness to what Russia had to say.

That I could give him no further answer as to the ultimate decision whether he put the question as an Ambassador or as an individual to me. But if he spoke in the latter capacity I should venture to give him a piece of advice notwithstanding his great superiority in knowledge & experience.

He appeared to me to be quite right in not allowing Prince Gortchakoff to treat him as a passive tool in his hands. He was quite right to consider what was due to his self respect, and to the reputation he had acquired by such long and important services. But he would in my opinion fail in his duty, if in a great crisis pregnant with important issues for his own country, for the good relations which he valued between Russia and this country, and for the peace of a large portion of Europe, he shrunk from playing the part allotted to him, and which he was better fitted than others to perform. Although I could give him no assurance as to the result yet I thought he ought not to conclude that it was impossible by sense and moderation on both sides to come to a satisfactory conclusion.

He still pressed for further explanations, which he hoped I should be able to give after communication with you.

He talked with surprise of the hesitation of the French. "The Provisional Govt of Tours had been treated exactly in the same way as the Emperor of Austria. Both have been invited by England to join the conference and they are not wise enough to accept at once." I said it was not a question whether they were wise or not, but what we should do if by chance they refused to join.

Baron Brunnow was as might be expected against delay—Why did they not make peace. If we were to wait to settle this European difficulty till they had marched to Berlin it might take long.

I made no admission of this nature—but we parted in a friendly spirit.

388. Lord Granville to Mr. Gladstone. [Add. MS. 44167, fo. 233]

Confidential. 16, Bruton Street. Dec 6/70.

Pray let me know what you think of Brunnow's plans. His draft speech [1] if it is approved at home seems good.

He agrees to what appeared to us to be the principal equivalent we could think of. (I send you a memo from Layard [2] which is suggestive.)

There seems to be no doubt that Clarendon was for opening the Black Sea, but he had another and in my opinion an objectionable plan—that the Porte should allow *us* to make a Malta or Sebastopol of Trebizond.

Let me know whether I may communicate with Beust, as to the course we should adopt in Conference.

I see Apponyi today, but I will only ask him to get the opinions of his Gov.

389. Mr. Gladstone to Lord Granville. [G.D. 29/58]

Hawarden Castle. Dec. 6. 70.

1. I have written to Monsell,[3] sending him a copy of mine to Dease—and I have also sent this latter to the papers for publication.[4] I send you herewith a letter from Bp Gillooly, rather saucy, which I have answered.

2. Odo Russell's letter [5] is most interesting; but it contains matter which I regret to see in it. He speaks of Alsace and Lorraine as if the reason why we do not persuade France to surrender them is that she will not be persuaded. This however is inference only. But I am much concerned to see that he has won Bismarck by a representation about our going to war which really had not the slightest foundation.

3. As respects the King of Prussia's tone, I was not quite satisfied with his "versöhnlich", which I think (and I am borne out by such Dictionaries as I have at hand) means atonement or expiation quite as much as conciliation. "Versöhner" is used I believe for our Saviour. As to Bismarck, he may be very like Shakespeare, but some of his reported language is more like Bobadil.

4. Rose's Memorandum [6] seems to me very just, and very able.

5. In the 'Pontus' question I should say that a part of the Sultan's rights is

[1] Communicated to Granville, 5 Dec. The copy in G.D. 29/91 is headed *Annexe à no. 111 22 Nov./3 Dec.* (Brunnow to Gorchakov). It has alterations suggested by Granville, which gave it the form recorded in the first protocol of the Black Sea conference, *Protocols of Conferences . . . respecting the Treaty of March 30, 1856*. Parl. papers. [C. 267] (1871). lxxii, 122–3.

[2] See Layard to Granville, private, 26 Nov., on alternative security for Turkey after abrogation of the neutrality of the Black Sea, G.D. 29/99.

[3] About the letter of Bishop Moriarty to Monsell, 28 Nov., forwarded by Monsell to Granville, 1 Dec., and by him to Gladstone, G.D. 29/74. See also Granville to Monsell, 8 Dec., G.D. 29/77. The subject was the danger of the Liberals losing the support of Catholic Ireland for want of action to maintain the Pope's temporal power.

[4] See above, no. 380 note.

[5] Private, 30 Nov., missing from Odo Russell's private letters to Granville, G.D. 29/92, extract in Add. MS. 44428, fo. 245. Cf. below, no. 478.

[6] 26 Nov., on the settlement as a whole, of all questions at issue between the United States and Canada, and the United States and Britain, F.O. 5/1331.

more than the whole; as Elliot seems to think. He has a title to the whole: but if he cannot use them entire, and can use a portion, he may prefer the latter.

6. I do not see what you can do at present about an armistice: nor can I think the Defence Government is united in desiring one.

7. It would be awkward to delay our release of prisoners until the Session is coming near.

8. I send you copy of a letter I have written to the Chanclr of the Exchequer, with his which it answers.[1]

390. Mr. Gladstone to Lord Granville. [G.D. 29/58]

Hawarden Castle. Dec. 6. [1870]. 10½ Pm.

In the midst of the ball music within 3 yards or so (which does not worry me at all) I have written the inclosed short Mem.[2] on Brunnow's Paper.

I also send back your long and interesting account of your interview as you may require it.

His suggestion about the Straits is very well, but I own that Elliot's appears to me the most convenient & workable form of it. (See my letter of today.)

Your messenger ought to be in London again at nine tomorrow morning: or by half past six if he likes.

I think you are quite safe in continuing to communicate with Beust on the line you have already adopted.

391. Memorandum by Mr. Gladstone. [G.D. 29/58]

B. Brunnow's Annexe a No. 111 3 Dec. 70. Dec. 6. 70.

Par. 1. It seems quite proper that the Russian Plenipotentiary should give his own account of transactions which he thinks have partly altered 'the spirit & the letter' of the Treaty of 1856—but we ought not, I presume to be committed to the assertion that there have been such transactions.

(The change as to the Principalities, if it deviated from the letter, was I apprehend meant to give effect to the spirit of the Treaty, which projected I believe the meeting of popular Divans *ad hoc*.)

In Paragraphs 2–5 I see nothing which if proceeding from him in the Conference need call forth any controversial reply or notice.

The same remark will apply to Paragraph 6 (the last) but with some reserve. The Emperor expresses a desire that the changes to be made should be placed under the sanction of a general agreement. We hold that they can only take rightful effect in consequence of a general agreement. It might be enough if we take care that nothing in the documents to be drawn contravenes the proper idea: but I suppose we ought not to commit ourselves to the expressions used by Baron Brunnow in this Paragraph—which appear to have been adopted with a set purpose. Probably

[1] Copies of Gladstone to Lowe, 6 Dec., and Lowe to Gladstone, 5 Dec., on the introduction of competitive examinations for entry into the Foreign Office, G.D. 29/66.

[2] No. 391.

agreeing in the results to be obtained, you will doubtless find means of avoiding controversy on the prior question of right which is differently viewed by the two parties, and is quite separable from the active part of the business.

392. Mr. Gladstone to Lord Granville. [G.D. 29/58]

Hawarden Castle. Dec. 7. 70.

1. I have only received this morning the Italian Dispatches which arrived Nov. 29 [1]; and I am grieved to see that they confirm the seizure of the Quirinal, and also of the Journals containing the Encyclical.

Considering that a large Papal faction are pressing & will press us to interfere in Italy, I think we ought in some manner to make known to the Italian Government that our difficulty of resistance will be much increased if they restrict the Pope's liberty to rave at his pleasure, and if they confiscate his property which the seizure of the Quirinal would seem to imply if there has been no tender of confiscation [sic]. And if there has been such an offer, the King would do more wisely to hire the Europa, than to place himself in the Quirinal by violence.

2. I presume we shall make no difficulty about complimenting the King of Prussia on his becoming Emperor of Germany.[2]

3. If you do not expect to be *soon* able to fix the date of your Conference, and by soon I mean almost immediately, do not you think we had better proceed at once to the release of the Fenian prisoners? The public mind is I think entirely reassured about the Russian difficulty.

4. The Queen has desired an explanation about the D. of Norfolk, which I am sending. Have you any suggestion as to the Garter? [3]

393. Mr. Gladstone to Lord Granville. [G.D. 29/58]

Hawarden Castle. Dec. 7. 1870.

1. On your report of conversation with Tissot [4] respecting the position of France in the Conference, it seems to me that you might safely give the French Govt. a little more consolation. At least it appears to me that the proposal to France that she shall participate essentially involves her participating on a footing of equality. This, if I am right, would be the substance of the answer, & she would not be dependent on the compassion of other Powers. The only remaining question, in my view, would be the question of form, whether her participation would involve recognition of the Defence Government. Each Power would I suppose settle this for itself.

[1] From Paget, 26 Nov., F.O. 45/168.

[2] Cf. to Odo Russell, tel. 3 p.m., 10 Dec., instructing him to congratulate as soon as officially told the Empire was proclaimed, and Russell to Granville, No. 28, 19 Dec., reporting that he had done so, F.O. 64/737.

[3] The Queen refused to consider Norfolk for the Garter, Bessborough to Granville, 15 Dec., G.D. 29/71, and note by Gurdon, *c.* 9 Dec., G.D. 29/58. A vacancy was caused by Lord Hertford's death, 24 Aug., but was not filled until the nomination of Lord Zetland, Dec. 1872.

[4] Granville to Lyons, 6 Dec., F.O. 27/1796; Parl. papers. [C. 245] (1871). lxxii, 57.

2. Again as to the request for a prior sanction to an attempt by the French to bring the War before the Conference, and the Cavour precedent. I apprehend (but am not sure) that Cavour did this on his own responsibility without any previous understanding between him & this Country? If so, & if they quote the precedent, they should follow it. I agree with every word you said: but I should suppose you might add that in declining any compact beforehand you of course do not mean to bind yourself as to the course you might take upon an application to the conference itself with reference to that or any other question.

394. Lord Granville to Mr. Gladstone. [Add. MS. 44167, fo. 235]

Foreign Office. Dec 8/70.

The Chancellor, Argyll, Lowe, de Grey, Cardwell & Forster were all here yesterday.

I told them what had been done by you & me,[1] and [they] approved everything.

Argyll argued in favor of the Neutralization of the Black Sea, & Lowe wished for the annulling of the tripartite treaty, but all agreed on practical points. Form of invitation to Conference to define conditions[2]—my opening speech to do the same—Brunnow to follow with his declaration—and then to adjourn for a few days, when the pourparlers might take a more active form before the 2d sitting of the conference.

Our Colleagues seem to prefer the simple restoration to the Sultan of his Sovereign power as to the passage into the Black Sea, rather than Hammond's plan which I enclose,[3] or Elliot's.[4]

Pahlen tells me that Brunnow is in high force. He really did resign, taking high ground, and has been desired to remain, with all sorts of compliments from the Emperor.

I proposed a meeting today, but he prefers holding it tomorrow.

I shall tell him that we do not object to his making the declaration he proposes, but then he must expect an answer, that if he will modify it according to your suggestions then as far as I am concerned I shall leave it alone.

I shall decline telling him our views till after the first conference.

I am afraid our whole success has been owing to the belief that we would go to war, and to tell the truth, I think war in some shape or other sooner or later, was a possible risk after our note. In any case I would reassure nobody now. Promising peace is as unwise as to threaten war.

[1] In preliminary discussions with Brunnow, Apponyi and Bernstorff on the Russian speech in the forthcoming Black Sea conference, the invitation to the conference and the line of proceedings.

[2] The invitation containing a condemnation of the unilateral denunciation of treaties was ultimately dropped, see below, no. 410.

[3] See undated mem., received by Granville's secretary 12 Dec., recommending abolition of the closure of the Straits and regulation of the number of ships to be sent at any one time by the Mediterranean powers into the Black Sea, or by Russia into the Mediterranean, G.D. 29/104.

[4] See above, no. 382.

A sort of sentiment that the bumps of combativeness and destructiveness are to be found somewhere in your head has helped us much during the last five months.

I was sorry to hear Greville object strongly to any release of Fenians—but the sooner they go now the better—We are sure of our Conference.

Lowe has written to me about the compe[ti]tion. I will send you the answer I propose to write to him.[1]

395. Lord Granville to Mr. Gladstone. [Add. MS. 44167, fo. 240]

16, Bruton Street. Dec 8/70.

Halifax writes [2] that Childers has told him that the French would not be unwilling to sell a portion of their Ironclads to us, this is a strange story, but if true, he sees no great objection to it.

No more do I, if the French are willing to sell us ships of the class we want, and are about to build, equally good, and at the same or a lesser price.

With these conditions it would be rather popular here.

Has Childers said anything to you on the subject.

We go to Walmer and come back on Monday.

396. Lord Granville to Mr. Gladstone. [Add. MS. 44167, fo. 242]

[9 December 1870].

Invit. to Conf.

The enclosed is important, please read it carefully.

The Chancellor approves of [it] subject to his pencil alterations which I have put into ink.

397. Lord Granville to Mr. Gladstone. [Add. MS. 44167, fo. 243]

16, Bruton Street. Dec 9/70.

I have read your very able argument.[3]

I agree with you, but I own I am getting shaken about the case being so clear, as to warrant us in laying down the law on the subject, unless there is some political or practical object to be obtained by it.

If we could obtain a general sanction to the doctrine, it might be of use, but a brutum fulmen about Alsace would not help the other little nationalities much.

The telegraphic account [4] of the denunciation of Luxembourg Neutrality looks dreadfully like the Gortchakoff assumption of deciding for himself whether a Treaty has ceased to be obligatory.

Of course in a state of war, it is difficult for a Belligerent to wait for long diplomatic action but [5] the present state of the war gives no such excuse.

[1] See above, no. 389, and Lowe to Granville, 5 Dec., G.D. 29/66.
[2] From Halifax, Knowsley, 6 Dec., G.D. 29/64.
[3] On Alsace-Lorraine, see above, no. 386.
[4] See below, no. 405.
[5] The rest of no. 397 is taken from the copy in G.D. 29/58.

398. Lord Granville to Mr. Gladstone. [Add. MS. 44167, fo. 245]

Walmer Castle. Dec 9/70.

I improved my account of the conversation with Tissot [1] respecting his position at a conference, by the suggestion you made.

I have not altered the account of the other conversation about introducing the question of peace—1° because I had not said it to Tissot in the conversation, & it is inconvenient having two versions of the same talk.

2°. Lyons has already gone very far in a sort of tacit encouragement.

3°. That I have said nothing restrictive of my liberty of action.

4°. That Bernstorff has told me that he should be obliged to leave the room the minute the subject was introduced.

I have a sort of recollection that Cavour had obtained leave from France & England, but I will enquire.

As the end of the conference cannot be for some weeks, we shall have plenty of time to consider.

399. Mr. Gladstone to Lord Granville. [G.D. 29/58]

Hawarden Castle. Decr. 9. 70.

1. Hammond's middle term [2] does not smile on me. As for the question of partial or absolute restoration of the Sultan's power over the Straits, I should only prefer the former if the Sultan thinks it best for him, & in that case I suppose you would accede to it.

2. I quite agree that nothing can now be done to enlighten Bismarck about Odo Russell's representation: but would it not be well to admonish O[do] R[ussell] in what he says about peace to avoid giving any countenance to the transferance of populations against their will.[3] Silence is the best course, but I fear from his language that he may not have observed it. It involves a principle which can never have the general approval of the people of this country.

3. I do not understand Morier's P.S.[4] about our ignoring the German Liberals.

4. I have been reading Prevost Paradol's Nouvelle France,[5] and with extreme pain. It deepens one's impression of the responsibility of France in regard to the present conflict.

5. I write to Fortescue to urge on the Fenian release. If by Greville you mean Lord Greville, I join in your regrets.

400. Lord Granville to Mr. Gladstone.[6] [Add. MS. 44167, fo. 247]

Private. Walmer Castle. Dec 10/70.

I presume a programme to which Russia, Prussia, Italy & Turkey & probably

[1] See above, no. 393. [2] See above, no. 394. [3] See below, no. 401.

[4] To Granville, Darmstadt, 6 Dec., the PS. stating that Britain could have the game all her own way had she not ignored the liberal members of the North German Parliament, G.D. 29/95.

[5] L. A. Prévost-Paradol, *La France nouvelle* (1868), expounding the views of the liberal opposition to the Napoleonic Empire.

[6] Printed Temperley and Penson, *Foundations*, p. 333.

Austria & France would agree would be restoration to the Emperor of Russia of his sovereign rights in the Black Sea, ditto to the Sultan in the manner most agreeable to him—and a reaffirmation of all the remainder of the Treaty.

What further can we do. Possibly some declaration of the construction to be put on the clause forbidding Foreign Powers meddling with internal administration of Turkey.

But what sticks in my gizzard is the Tripartite Treaty. How very foolish it was of us to have concocted it. But there it is, with obligations as binding as were ever contracted. If Prussia who says she was never asked to join it, would consent to do so now, it would rather weaken than strengthen the obligations of England —and would act as a powerful check against Russia trying to put them in force —& be a real equivalent for the concession made to her in the Black Sea. But Prussia is almost certain to decline, and although she will declare as strongly as we like her sense of obligation under the treaty of March 1856, yet the fact will remain, that while six powers are bound by that treaty, two of them are not bound by the much stronger treaty of April.

If Odo ascertains that Prussia will not accede to the Tripartite Treaty, how would it do to ask her whether she would do so, if we made the same offer to Russia.

There would be something of the Belgian Treaty of last [*sic*] year in the principle.

It would have a deterring effect upon Russia and yet would rather release us.

If Russia denounced the remainder of the Treaty of 1856, and acted upon the denunciation, England, France Austria & Prussia would be too strong for her.

If Prussia played false to us, it would diminish the necessity of our putting ourselves forward alone, or with only half the other cosignatories.

What do you think of this.[1]

There is also a question whether when the conference is over, we should invite Spain to make a declaration in favor of the Treaty of 1856.

401. Lord Granville to Mr. Gladstone. [G.D. 29/58]

Copy. W[almer] C[astle]. Dec 10/70.

St Albans, Lansdowne, Kimberley G.C.B., Fortescue, Sefton, Lawrence [K.]C.B.

I should incline to the first, notwithstanding its being a little commonplace.

Some of Odo's letters appear to be extraordinarily gushing, till I remembered they came by the Post, so that I hope his head is not turned by the reception.

I have telegraphed to him [2] to be silent about conditions and that all I am pledged to is " not to offer mediation or good offices unless likely to be acceptable, or to be effective, & that I have left myself free to give advice.["]

Morier means that our R.R. have always turned a cold shoulder on the liberals, have refused to have anything to do with any but officials.

[1] Granville telegraphed to Russell, 8.15 p.m., 7 Dec. : ' Sound Count Bismarck as entirely from yourself whether Prussia disposed to accede to Tripartite Treaty ', No. 35 most confidential, 7 Dec., F.O. 64/737.

[2] 6.45 p.m., 10 Dec., beginning : ' It is most satisfactory to hear of your good position at headquarters. But take care not to commit yourself without instructions about conditions of peace ', F.O. 64/737.

Odo is already trying to get hold of some old friends of his influential liberals who happen to be at Versailles.

The Greville I quoted was the son.

402. Mr. Gladstone to Lord Granville. [G.D. 29/58]

Hawarden Castle. Dec. 10. 70.

1. The whole of your proposed invitation to the Conference [1] is I think in itself rational & sound—but I presume you do not mean it to become the occasion of a debate, and can you confidently reckon that it will not? Can you say as in p. 1 that Russia has expressed her " desire " for the reconsideration of the provisions respecting the Black Sea? Is it safe to *set forth* that the provisions " shall be deemed & admitted to be in full force " until altered by common consent? And if unsafe is it necessary? Have not we asserted it already, and ought we not to be content with tying Russia to it by implication through bringing her into the Conference (p. 4)?

Pray understand that I do not in the least object to the things said if you have reason to believe they will be innocuous, or if it can be held that they are absolutely necessary.

2. With respect to Alsace & Lorraine, there is no practical difference between us. Still inclining to regret that we did not indicate an opinion when Bismarck gave us a right to say he challenged one, I am far from thinking we should now say any thing on the subject. My sole desire is that we should sift it among ourselves and not be taken unprepared should it hereafter come up in a practical form. For while I more & more feel the deep culpability of France I have an apprehension that this violent laceration & transfer is to lead us from bad to worse, & to be the *beginning* of a new series of European complications.

3. Chaudordy's appeal to you to procure an armistice with revictualling & to secure Christmas from profanation is on one side touching—on another it approaches the ludicrous.[2] Odo Russell's telegram [3] respecting the strength of the Germans & unconditional surrender seems to supply an answer. It still appears that without an Assembly we do not know what France really means or wishes.

4. The Daily News had strictures on my letter about the Pope.[4] This is well as it may help to keep the R.C.s in order.

My wife is just leaving a full house to go to Eton where our youngest boy is sharply though not dangerously ill.

403. Mr. Gladstone to Lord Granville. [G.D. 29/58]

No 2. Hawarden Castle. Dec. 10. 70.

To purchase ironclads from the French seems to me dangerous.

1. It would be very difficult to ascertain the true value—very invidious to

[1] See above, nos. 394, 396.

[2] See Granville to Lyons, No. 788, 10 Dec., on Chaudordy's dispatch, 6 Dec., F.O. 27/1796.

[3] 3 p.m., received midnight, 8 Dec., ' . . . the position of Prussia is now so strong that no peace negotiations short of unconditional surrender will be entertained', F.O. 64/737.

[4] Dease letter, see above, no. 380 note.

criticise, & reject in case of need, their ships. I have always heard their iron is very bad.

2. There would be discontent in this country among disbanded Dockyard men, *and* among contractors, at our importing an article which they would say truly we manufacture better at home.

3. If we paid a low price the French people would say we took advantage of their necessities : if a full one, the Germans would say we were giving covert aid to their enemy who does not want ships & is out at elbows for money.

These remarks would I think apply to any considerable operation.

404. Lord Granville to Mr. Gladstone. [G.D. 29/58]

Copy. W[almer] C[astle]. Dec. 11/70.

If you think it desirable the private letter [1] to Paget of which I inclose a copy can be turned into a public or a confidential despatch.

405. Mr. Gladstone to Lord Granville. [G.D. 29/58]

No 1. Hawarden Castle. D. 12. 70.

1. Your Telegram to Versailles directing reticence as to conditions of peace was all, I thought that could be wished.

2. Bismarck's broad hint to the neutral Powers to advise the French to convoke the old Legislative was so repugnant to all English ideas that it should hardly have been received in silence.[2] Perhaps there was a modest protest, only one not reported for the reason you suggest viz. transmission by the post.

3. I am struck by Col. Fielding's account of the operations on the Loire. I do not mean as to its Frenchness which is very natural, but as to its (apparent) soldierlike capacity.

4. Max Müller, who is here, is very intimate with Abeken, a Prussian ex-Chaplain, who is now M.M. says, the very right hand of Bismarck, and writes all the state papers for him as he dislikes writing. His office corresponds with Permanent Under-Secretary. I knew Abeken well 30 years ago. He is an excellent man of open & liberal mind. I mention all this because some things might perhaps be conveniently said in course of time through this channel. Abeken is delighted with Odo Russell.

5. Burnside came here last Friday on his way to embarkation from Liverpool. I talked to him in a sense corresponding to your instruction to Rose : [3] about the discredit, in the face of the world, attaching to this prolongation of controversies ; our desire to deal promptly & liberally ; the deadlock to which America has brought

[1] 11 Dec., on the English Catholics' alarm lest the Pope suffer indignity, G.D. 29/112 ; it became dispatch No. 122 confidential, 19 Dec., F.O. 45/160. See also Paget to Granville, private, 22 Dec., G.D. 29/96.

[2] Cf. Odo Russell to Granville, No. 25 confidential, 14 Dec., recording an earlier telegram, F.O. 64/737.

[3] See Granville to Rose, No. 1 confidential, sent to Gladstone and returned with comments, 11 Dec., F.O. 5/1298.

us about the Alabama claims; & the disposition to remember in any settlement her wounded sentiment. He will probably report on the other side. He goes away in great good humour with England and is to return in January.

6. I should suppose it on the whole desirable to turn the private letter to Paget, about the follies in Rome, into a confidential dispatch as you suggest.

7. This letter must not close without my saying that while Max Müller made himself very popular personally his language to F. Cavendish & to E. Fitzmaurice about the intentions of Germany was most ominous when we consider his relations with Abeken & that Abeken sits so to speak in the mind of Bismarck. He announces a war with Austria *as a certainty*, by way of punishment for her having armed & concentrated on the Bavarian frontier at the commencement of this war. A war with Russia he thinks will come at a later date. He spoke to me about the Austrian arming but pulled up in a way which made me feel he had more to say & did not like to say it.

[P.S.]. 8. I hope there is no fire in the Luxemburg smoke,[1] of which I see you do not take notice in your letters.

406. Mr. Gladstone to Lord Granville.[2] [G.D. 29/58]

No 2. Hawarden Castle. Dec. 12. 70.

I quite agree that it is difficult to justify the Tripartite Treaty but as a practical question I am inclined to suggest looking at it from another point of view.

I incline to think that any action in regard to it, as for example the asking Prussia to accede,[3] would tend to rivet it upon us, and enhance our obligation.

On the other hand, stringent as it is in its terms, it does not appear to me to have much force as a covenant at present, when Turkey declares her own incapacity to fight except with (virtually) our money. Guarantees as such seem to me to presuppose the capacity of any guaranteed State to fight for herself; and then to supply a further auxiliary defence. At least I think it must be so in the case where nothing is expressed to give a different construction to the guarantee.

I am not sure that I know what you mean by making the same offer to Russia but I fear it would be futile to ask her to accede to the Tripartite Treaty. For my own part, I do not see that the Straits may not supply a sufficient compensation for the Black Sea changes: but I would urge the Turk to meditate as he smokes his pipe, and let us know what occurs to him in the way of compensations. . . .

I am *rather* against making Spain a party just yet: but things might look different a short time hence.

[1] Bismarck's circular to the signatories of the Luxemburg Treaty of 1867, 3 Dec., communicated 9 Dec., accused Luxemburg of breaking her neutrality, F.O. 64/707. A pencil note on a second copy: 'I propose telling Bernstorff that I wait for the reply of Luxembourg G[ranville].' See also *Correspondence respecting the alleged Violation of the Neutrality of . . . Luxemburg*. Parl. papers. [C. 246] (1871). lxxi, 655.

[2] Printed Temperley and Penson, *Foundations*, p. 335. Omission relates to his son's illness.

[3] Russell suggested Prussia's accession and Bismarck objected, to Granville tel. 3.25 p.m., received 6 p.m., 17 Dec., F.O. 64/737, and private, 18 Dec., G.D. 29/92, 21 Dec., G.D. 29/91.

407. Lord Granville to Mr. Gladstone. [Add. MS. 44167, fo. 254]

Private. F.O. Dec 13/70.

The Chancellor, Lowe, Goschen, Childers, & Cardwell & Forster came here at four.

They all wished to have a cabinet about Luxembourg (perhaps like the fox without the tail). They all advised doing nothing till it had met. The great object for us at present appears to be to avoid putting the conduct of the Prussians, on the same footing as that of the Russians, and to avoid admitting the justice of any demand upon Luxembourg, which might equally apply to Belgium.

It will probably be well to have a protest without threats against any attempt to lessen the rights of neutrals.

I sent a copy of my letter to you to the Chancellor, & forward his reply [1] which I got at the same time with your's. I have since recd Elliot's telegram.[2] I am sorry to say that my private letter to Tissot [3] was sent. The portion to which you object is only a repetition of what I said to Lavalette & every Frenchman.

If you can better your position do so, but if you do not expect to do so, have the moral courage to try to make peace. I did not commit myself as to terms.

I shall have time to stop the communication of the despatch recording my communication to Tissot, to the Provisional Govt when I get your letter tomorrow.

If you come up tomorrow please let me know.

I shall be at your orders for food & talk at any time excepting a tiresome dinner with the Turk on Thursday.

408. Mr. Gladstone to Lord Granville. [G.D. 29/58]

Hawarden Castle. Dec. 13. 70.

1. I telegraph [4] to you today to give you my address (by Telegraph) for the greater part of tomorrow—when I go to Liverpool for the marriage of a niece. I cannot but feel anxious about Luxembourg, my best comfort being that the story of Bismarck's having addressed the cosignatory powers on the 3d must be false.

2. I am also very uneasy about the reply which Odo Russell in his letter of the 6th [5] says he always makes to the Prussians about peace. It renounces a right which we possess: it implies what we do not think: and it expresses an intention which we have never expressed and do not entertain. I hope you will instruct him to make it clear beyond all dispute that he has in this answer given his own

[1] From Hatherley, 12 Dec., answering Granville's letter, 11 Dec., which enclosed copy of no. 400, and asked his opinion on Prussia's and Russia's joining the tripartite treaty. Hatherley approved but doubted the proposal's success, G.D. 29/65.

[2] To Granville, 11.30 p.m., 12 Dec.; see No. 353, 12 Dec., on his proposal to modify the closure of the straits (above, no. 382) and the Turk's desire that all the powers should adhere to the tripartite treaty, F.O. 78/2126.

[3] No copy in F.O. 27/1842 or G.D. 29, but see to Lyons, No. 788, 10 Dec., F.O. 27/1796.

[4] 2.40 p.m., received 3.47 p.m., 13 Dec., also expressed anxiety about Luxemburg. Granville telegraphed that he had 'asked some colleagues to talk over' Luxemburg at four that day (cf. no. 407), 13 Dec., G.D. 29/58.

[5] Missing from G.D. 29/92 and F.O. 64/737.

opinion and not your instructions. I am beginning to be afraid of him. How different from Lyons.

3. It will not in the least surprise me if you summon me sharply about Luxembourg. But God forbid.

Since I wrote this I have found among the papers of today—and I have telegraphed to you upon it at once as also upon a dispatch as follows—

" Have just read Circular of the third on subject named in my Postscript yesterday. Ought we not to meet in London. Also would you stop any action on yours of 10th [1] reporting a conversation with Tissot until you receive an observation which I have to make on the last Paragraph."[2]

The observation is

" This as it stands is capable of being construed, I think, as our advice to France to make peace upon the terms of the Germans."

Which I am sure is what you would not wish.

409. Mr. Gladstone to Lord Granville. [G.D. 29/58]

Hawarden Castle. D. 14. 70.

I write on the point of starting.

I feel anxious about the letter to Tissot—& I look on the Luxembourg affair as grave.

The Cabinet [3] appears not to have been called in the usual manner through me.

I can obey any call from you tonight say after 9.45.

410. Mr. Gladstone to Lord Granville. [G.D. 29/58]

Immed. 10, Downing Street. Dec. 15. 70.

1. It seems to me that the protocol sketched by Sir A. Buchanan is over severe, & deals too much in abstract declarations. Would it not be ample to say ' Whereas the continuance or change of the terms of any treaty, & of the obligations of the parties to it, must of necessity be matters for the joint consideration and controul of the signing Powers collectively ' ?

2. In your excellent speech I would suggest a somewhat similar conversion & say after *d'accord* ' that for the maintenance in full integrity of the law of nations it is requisite that each contracting party should submit any claim for release from the obligations to the other Powers.[']

I think you would lose nothing in force.

[1] Draft of No. 788, 10 Dec., F.O. 27/1796, has Gladstone's pencilled comment, 13 Dec., as repeated here and a consequent modification by Granville.

[2] Tel. 3.25 p.m., received 4.52 p.m., 1 Dec. Granville telegraphed that he had summoned a cabinet for three on Thursday, 15 Dec., G.D. 29/58.

[3] Cabinet, 3 p.m., 15 Dec. (Add. MS. 44638, fo. 153), considered and amended No. 372 to Loftus, 17 Dec., replying to Bernstorff's communication of Bismarck's circular of 3 Dec., F.O. 64/683, Parl. papers. [C. 246] (1871). lxxi, 660–1. Cf. min. by Hammond, 15 Dec., G.D. 29/104; Loftus to Granville, private, 17, 24, 31 Dec., G.D. 29/90; Granville to Russell, tel. 6 p.m., 15 Dec.; from Russell, tel. 11.30 a.m., 17 Dec., No. 33 confidential, 27 Dec., that the circular was not a denunciation of the treaty of 1867, F.O. 64/737.

3. In the draft of note my first point would be met by changing " having made known to the several Powers . . . his desire that the Provisions should be reconsidered "—" having brought under the notice of the several Powers . . . . the Provisions which it belongs to them collectively to reconsider."

I am not sure that this is good, but I think we cannot well recite as fact a desire which has not been expressed.

With regard to the second point, i.e. the *basis* resting in " admission " that all the provisions etc. are in force, would not the form be less choking, and the effect the same, if you recited with a *whereas* that they are all in full force except so far as they have been modified by common consent ? [1]

411. Lord Granville to Mr. Gladstone. [Add. MS. 44167, fo. 261]

F.O. Dec 20/70.

I *was* late for the train, which was ingenious of me.

I saw Cairns who thinks a bill will be necessary for the Bankrupt Peers.[2] He describes the House of Common's law on the subject to be most anomalous. I have written all he said to me, to the Chancellor.[3]

Brunnow has leave to sign our protocol.[4]

France has as you have seen agreed to join but foolishly proposes to send a Parisian Plenipo.[5]

I have telegraphed to Lyons suggesting Tissot. I have had a long talk with the latter who agrees in everything. He would particularly like to get rid of the tripartite treaty.[6]

May I have Rosebery & Clarendon as proposer and seconder.

412. Mr. Gladstone to Lord Granville. [G.D. 29/58]

Hawarden Castle. Dec. 21. 70.

1. Would it not be right to take the opinion of the Law Officers on the case

[1] Gladstone comments on 3 documents circulated to the cabinet by Granville, 14 Dec., before its meeting on 15th, G.D. 29/91. Gladstone notes no discussion of the Black Sea question in the cabinet before 17 Dec., Add. MS. 44638, fo. 154. The protocol condemning unilateral denunciation of treaties went through several changes. The first draft, abandoning Buchanan's wording, followed the words suggested here in paragraph 2 for Granville's speech, G.D. 29/91. The note referred to is the invitation to the conference. Cf. Parl. papers. [C. 245] (1871). lxxii, 75 ; [C. 267] (1871). lxxii, 122, 124.

[2] See J. G. Shaw Lefevre to Granville, 2, 8 Dec. ; J. Erskine May to Granville, 2 Dec. ; Granville to Richmond, 11 Dec., offering to concert a bill with the opposition, and Richmond to Granville, 13 Dec., proposing a meeting with Cairns, G.D. 29/78.

[3] To Hatherley, 19 Dec., and reply 20 Dec., G.D. 29/65.

[4] See Granville to Brunnow, personal and confidential, Windsor, 17 Dec., G.D. 29/115 ; Brunnow to Granville, 18 Dec., replying, 20 Dec., on his authorization to sign, G.D. 29/98 ; Granville to Buchanan, private, 21 Dec., G.D. 29/114.

[5] Cf. Lyons to Granville, 19 Dec., G.D. 29/85.

[6] To Lyons, tel. 4.20 p.m., 20 Dec., F.O. 27/1796. Jules Favre having failed to get out, France was not represented at the Black Sea conference until 3 March. Gladstone noted that the cabinet, 17 Dec., agreed to abandon the tripartite treaty if requested by the Porte, Add. MS. 44638, fo. 154.

of Mr Worth,[1] or else, as less formal, to communicate *first* with the Lord Chancellor upon it.

The resolution of the Prussians [2] seems to be only a brutal one as regards the French. But as regards the subjects of other countries it raises the question what liability is established by the analogies of international law for the case of balloons? *Primâ facie* it would seem to be little different from the case of running blockades, & not in the least like that of spies.

2. The plans of the Italian Government, within the Roman State, appear to be wise and liberal, except that it seems to be a pity they should have seized the Quirinal which gives a handle to the adversary.

On the other hand, *outside* the Roman State, I am amazed at their giving over into the hands of the Pope not only the nomination to the Bishoprics as spiritual offices, but a nomination which is to carry with it the temporalities of the Sees. They ought to know their own business best: but to me it seems that this is liberality carried into folly; and I know that some Italians think so. If they are not prepared with any other plan, they might give the (absolute) nomination provisionally: but it is difficult to see why they should not reserve the principle & power of controul.

3. Beust's advice to the French appears rather palpably selfish. He does not want North Germany to have a full purse at the close of the war lest she should empty it on him.

4. On hearing from Fortescue I shall be quite ready to make the admission which he or Frank [3] through him desires.

4 [*sic*]. I wrote to Enfield yesterday.[4]

So sorry about the train: I fear it was my fault.

413. Lord Granville to Mr. Gladstone. [Add. MS. 44167, fo. 263]

Savernake Forest, Marlborough. 23 Dec/70.

Lady Ailesbury has deluded us into passing our Xmas here, bringing with us Meade, and the two nurseries to a house full of children, with no grown up and a two hours' train to London at a mile from the House.

No 1 The Law officers gave an adverse opinion to Mr. Worth. I have sent for it to see how far it goes as regards B B (Bobadil Bismark's brutal threat[])].

2 Odo's letter[s] are very clever, and it is clear that his society is much appreciated. I cannot make [out] how much he is really under the charm.

[1] A British subject captured after leaving Paris by balloon and held by Prussia for trial as a spy.

[2] That all persons picked up out of balloons would be shot as spies, Granville to Loftus, No. 356, 12 Dec., F.O. 64/683.

[3] 'Countess Frank' or Lady Waldegrave, the wife of Fortescue who had been offered the Board of Trade in Bright's place, but asked for time to consider, 18 Dec., Add. MS. 44122, fo. 197. He wrote to Gladstone, 19 Dec., asking to be assured that acceptance would not spoil his chance of higher office, Add. MS. 44122, fo. 205.

[4] Offering him the parliamentary under-secretaryship at the Foreign Office *vice* Otway, 19 Dec., Add. MS. 44539, fo. 106.

There is occasionally some indiscretion or apparent indiscretion in what he says. I have enquired what he meant by asking whether Prussia could not be bribed into joining the Tripartite Treaty.[1]

3 There is a misunderstanding between the Turks and us about the cancelling the Tripartite Treaty.[2]

I hope they will still agree, but if they do not, how would it do for the three cosignatories to agree without reference to the Turk, who is no party to it.

4. I wrote to the Speaker saying what I thought which was much, but with tears in my eyes for you. I send you his answer.

I wrote this morning to Hartington.[3] I hope he will accept. What then.

If you think me wrong about Tenterden, pray telegraph to me, and I will recant.[4] The correspondence will be sent separately.

In another letter I mentioned two good men to him.

414. Mr. Gladstone to Lord Granville. [G.D. 29/58]

Hawarden Castle. Dec. 23. 70.

1. I know of no objection whatever to your proposal about mover & seconder but I expect Glyn tomorrow & may as well mention it to him.

2. Is Tissot of sufficient known weight to represent France in the Conference?

3. It seems to me that, for the greater satisfaction of Turkey, you might very well *work* the instrument by which you would have to renounce the Tripartite Treaty into such a notice of the terms of the more General Guarantee of the Treaty of 1856 as would have the effect of strengthening them, and accentuating the general adhesion: which would be perfectly fair.

4. I do not quite see why the conversations reported in Odo's most interesting letter of the 18th [5] should have increased his misgivings. In their general outlook they rather comfort me. But if Bismarck negotiates with the Imperial Government he will commit a great and perhaps fatal error.

5. I write to Hartington today: and telegraph to beg you to do the same. Spencer will follow suit.

Wishing you *all* a happy Christmas I remain. . . .

[1] To Russell, tel. 5.45 p.m., 24 Dec., and from Russell, tel. 2.46 p.m., and No. 32 confidential, 27 Dec., replying the 'bribe' was English help in gaining for Prussia the alliance of Austria, F.O. 64/737.

[2] Turkey understood that the British proposal was to insert the provisions of the tripartite treaty in the six-power guarantee of the Treaty of March 1856. See Granville to Elliot, tel. 17 Dec., F.O. 78/2120; Elliot to Granville, tel. 9.30 p.m., recorded No. 368, 20 Dec., F.O. 78/2126.

[3] Urging him to accept the Irish secretaryship *vice* Fortescue. See Gladstone to Hartington, 23 Dec., Add. MS. 44143, fo. 38. Cf. B. H. Holland, *The Life of Spencer Compton Eighth Duke of Devonshire* (1911), i. 80–1.

[4] See Lowe to Granville, 21 and 22 Dec., proposing that Tenterden be moved from the Foreign Office to the Treasury, and Granville's discouraging replies, 22 and 23 Dec., G.D. 29/66.

[5] See above, no. 406 note.

6. Bismarck's project for proceedings at the Conference appears very good. See O. R[ussell], No 23.[1]

7. Enfield's acceptance just received.[2] Glyn wishes it not to be *announced* publicly till we get Davison's.[3]

415. Mr. Gladstone to Lord Granville. [G.D. 29/58]

Hawarden Castle. Dec. 24. 70.

1. I return the Queen's letter. This is the first I have heard about the Treaty of Marriage: I will look to the subject. On the day of meeting, I will consult De Grey & those colleagues who are in town.

2. In some of Paget's dispatches he uses rather strong words about the Italian Government in its conduct to the Pope [4]—which [it] would not well do to print.

3. Dr Candlish the Free Church oracle writes to me (very kindly) about my letter to Dease, & prophecies movements.[5] I think I may be obliged to allow that to Dr Guthrie, or the main part of it, to be published.

4. I am much scandalised about Odo's account of the Newspaper correspondents, and about their being quartered on the French. It seems to deserve consideration whether the Govt. ought not to signify either at Versailles, or by a circular to the Proprietors of Newspapers, its anxiety that the presence of these gentlemen should in no case be allowed to add to the pressure of the burdens of the war upon French subjects, & that every thing they have had or may have in board lodging & the like should be duly paid for.

5. Your mover & seconder appear to be quite unexceptionable.

416. Mr. Gladstone to Lord Granville. [G.D. 29/58]

Hawarden Castle. Xmas D. 70.

1. I think that you are quite right in your correspondence with Lowe.[6]

A cleaner man about patronage than L. is not to be found.

Yet this is an odd proceeding. The office, of which he is disposing, belongs probably to me, certainly to me or Glyn! The C. of E. has *nothing* in the Treasury.

2. If you cannot merge the Tripartite Treaty by reason of the Turk's disliking such a measure, he will still more dislike any attempt to abate it by an agreement of the Three Powers. I should incline to let it alone, particularly as I feel that through

[1] To Granville, 14 Dec., reporting Bismarck's proposals: (i) that the Black Sea conference proceed as if the Russian denunciation had not occurred, (ii) that Russia open by requesting a revision of the Treaty of Paris, (iii) that Turkey speak next, (iv) followed by the other powers, F.O. 64/737.

[2] 22 Dec., Add. MS. 44428, fo. 297; cf. Enfield to Granville, 23 Dec., G.D. 29/107; appointment as foreign under-secretary announced 26 Dec.

[3] Of the office of judge-advocate-general *vice* O'Loghlen, offered 21 Dec., Add. MS. 44539, fo. 107.

[4] See No. 262, 14 Dec., F.O. 45/169.

[5] To Gladstone, 22 Dec., Add. MS. 44428, fo. 294. Gladstone sent Candlish his letter to Dr. Guthrie explaining the Dease letter. This was read at the Free Church Presbytery 28 Dec., see *The Times*, 31 Dec., p. 3.

[6] See above, no. 413 note 4.

the state of facts announced by the Turk himself, its inconvenient stringency is in great measure in abeyance.

3. No reply today from Hartington.

4. The little Reitlinger [1] is actually coming down here on Tuesday—he having requested an interview.

5. There is more noise in Scotland about the Pope: & I may be obliged to publish or allow to be published the Guthrie letter.

417. Lord Granville to Mr. Gladstone. [Add. MS. 44167, fo. 269]

S[avernake] F[orest]. Dec. 26/70.

I am afraid Bernstorff has encouraged Brunnow to fly away from his positive assent to the more stringent form of protocol,[2] but I shall see them both this week.

I do not see how we could admit the Sovereign right as to having a fleet in the Black [Sea], which is aggressive as well as defensive, and refuse Russia the right of fortifying her own territory.

But am I safe about the Cabinet on this point.

I will take care of Paget's despatches.

It was not necessary for you to consult the Cabinet about your letter to Dease,[3] but having done so, I should in your place be disinclined to go against their advice.

I will see what can be done about the Newspaper Correspondents.

Is it worth turning this private letter [4] into a confidential despatch, or had I better not send it at all.

418. Mr. Gladstone to Lord Granville. [G.D. 29/58]

Hawarden Castle. Dec. 27. 70.

1. The difficulty I feel about the letter to Odo Russell is that it reads like an indication of a strong opinion that France ought to give up the provinces which have been for some months demanded by the Germans, & that the Germans ought not to extend their demands. I think it doubtful whether we should unasked, give even the latter of these opinions: to any thing that can be understood to convey the former there are I think very strong objections. Whether with reference to the present and growing sentiment of this country, or to future good relations with France, or to the establishment of sound principles of policy for Europe at large, I think we should absolutely and rigidly eschew giving any sanction to such transfer of territory as is proposed. Even if France wished us to take the responsibility of recommending this to her, I should be inclined to demur, or at the least to pause; but unsolicited I would say nothing that was capable of being construed in that

[1] See F. Reitlinger, *Une Mission diplomatique en octobre 1870* (1899).

[2] See above, no. 410; Granville to Apponyi, private, 25 Dec., F.O. 362/2; Granville to Bernstorff, 26 Dec., G.D. 29/111. Granville saw both Bernstorff and Brunnow on 29 Dec. and agreed upon another text; see draft following Bernstorff to Granville, 28 Dec., G.D. 29/94.

[3] See Gladstone's note on the cabinet, 25 Nov., Add. MS. 44638, fo. 147.

[4] To Odo Russell, private, 24 Dec., original and copy in G.D. 29/110, marked by Hervey: 'Suspended by Lord Granville's desire'.

sense. I should think that if Odo Russell shakes his head, & shrugs his shoulders & delivers his *own* opinion about our aversion to all violent procedure & interference in French affairs it is perhaps as much as can be done at present.

I have not yet given up the opinion I hold about the probable military tenacity of the French and the possible effects of a prolonged, even if passive, resistance. But this opinion is in a woful minority, and I do not found upon it what I have before said.

In 1862 I made a gross blunder, with the best intentions, in forming and expressing an opinion that the Southerners had virtually established their independence. Since that time I have been very fearful of giving opinions with regard to the proper course for foreign nations to pursue in junctures, of which after all, I think, they have better means of forming a judgment than foreigners can possess.

Excuse this rather long disertation, but I did not like to seem peremptory when stating difficulties.

2. I am sorry to hear of any possible difficulty about proceedings in Conference: but I have not yet received the documents, to which your remarks appear to refer.

3. If I find occasion, I will send out another Mem. to the Cabinet about the Guthrie—Dease letter.

4. I send you a letter from de Grey.[1]

5. Hartington boggles [2]—but I hope to receive his assent tomorrow morning. Glyn thinks it requisite that P.O. should be offered to Stansfield, but in a deterring manner.[3]

6. Reitlinger expected but not come.

419. Lord Granville to Mr. Gladstone. [Add. MS. 44167, fo. 267]

Private. F.O. Dec 28/70.[4]

I wrote to Hartington twice—and he came up to town to see me today.[5] He is very strong against your offer. I believe I made some impression, but I got nothing out of him, but the promise of a postscript in which he asks whether you will see him notwithstanding his letter. Pray do so.

I have cheerfully given up my private letter to Odo.

I am curious to hear of your interview with Reitlinger.. He is as good as a play.

The weather here is tremendous. What it must be for the poor belligerents.

[1] To Gladstone, 26 Dec., on postponing the opening of Parliament to suit the Queen and on the negotiations on the Greek massacres, Add. MS. 44286, fo. 104.

[2] To Gladstone, 24 Dec., refusing the Irish secretaryship, Add. MSS. 44143, fo. 40; Holland, *op. cit.*, 81–2.

[3] See below, nos. 421, 425.

[4] Gladstone docketed no. 419: 'Christmas Day 1870'. Granville's figure can be read as 25. The date is fixed as 28 by the interview with Hartington. It must have been written after no. 416, announcing Reitlinger's visit, had been received.

[5] Cf. Hartington to Gladstone, 28 Dec., renewing his refusal of the Irish secretaryship after he had seen Granville but asking to see Gladstone again, Add. MS. 44143, fo. 46, Holland, *op. cit.*, pp. 82–3.

420. Mr. Gladstone to Lord Granville. [G.D. 29/58]

Hawarden Castle. Dec. 28/70.

M. Reitlinger came down here yesterday and in the evening we talked only of the general circumstances of the war. He is most sanguine as to the ultimate result: looks for a single victory as enough to change the relative position of the scales: thinks that upon a certain amount of success the spirit of the French would rise to such a point, as to lead them to refuse even an indemnity: without such indemnity the Germans would be in a deplorable position as to their finance. He dwells, & with a certain amount of justice I think, upon the approach to greater equality in the field, which has already been effected. Never until now, he says, have the provinces been thoroughly roused; but continued ill-success will only fortify their determination & aggravate the character of the war.

This morning he sat above two hours with me, and went over the ground he had traversed with you. As much was said on his side & not a little on mine, I wound up with observing that in the course of our conversation we had touched various points which were rather of personal opinion than of a nature to express the views of a Government, and I was desirous to know whether in any thing the representation of our position, as he might have gathered it from me, differed from the effect of your conversation. He answered no, not at all.

He began by representing the determination of the French *vaincre ou mourir*: of course it must be borne in mind that this & all he said last night must have had more or less of reference to the argument he was to make for our intervention in the fray. He then went to the question of the armistice and *ravitaillement*, but it is needless to go fully over this ground again. He put strongly the impracticability of holding Elections without an armistice as well as of an armistice without revictualling. I expressed some amount of doubt on both these questions, but with apologies, & with the admission that the French Government was the proper & only judge. I also admitted that the Government had gained, in point of moral basis, by the lapse of time, the practical adhesion of the country, and presumptions arising out of the Paris Vote. His main appeal was of course an argument in favour of either a material intervention at once, or of firm language, a cry of ' halt ' to the Prussians, accompanied by preparations, and by a determination to make use of them if needful. We were agreed that there was no place at present for a moral intervention: and whenever he fell back upon *Eh bien donc* you can do *rien* for us I always kept in view that the only substitute admissible at present for *rien* was our going to war, & this if not alone yet with the chief responsibility of initiation & action.

His arguments were chiefly that the war had changed its character: that it was now impious & immoral on the part of the Germans: that to stop it would be a dignified & noble act for a great nation: that in this act we should certainly have the assistance of Austria: that by a risk of war now, which he thought would never come to actual war, we should prevent a more terrible war hereafter: that Prussia with Russia, if they conquered France, would proceed to deal with England: that France, if she got the better, would bear in mind her abandonment by a Power, which she had thought bound to her by sentiments *de reconnaissance ou d'amitié*.

I put aside very decidedly the appeals to our apprehensions; giving my opinion, as *my* opinion only however, of the security and defensive power of this country, & not denying that we had a concern in continental affairs, sometimes from positive engagements, sometimes from regard to public right, or to friendship or to co-operation such as during our time we had enjoyed with France: observing, however, that our alliance with France was an alliance on behalf of public right and not an alliance against any Power or Powers.

With regard to what France would perhaps remember hereafter, I said there was already plenty of intimations that Germany was also to remember, as a wrong to her, that we had not intervened against France at the commencement of the war.

I admitted up to a certain point that the war had modified or altered its character, now that it was carried on by the Germans apparently for the sake only of a forcible annexation of French territory; but pointed out reasons why neutral Governments might hesitate to recognise the *changement complet* which he urged, including among them a reference to the French annexations of 1860, and to the undoubted intentions of the Imperial Government in 1870 to annex German territory, without any reference, as far as we know, to what the desire of the inhabitants might be. I could not admit that the questions of right were so cleared in favour of France from doubt, as he very naturally from his point of view considered them to be. But I stated that the difficulty of acceding to the demand for intervention was, apart from merely material considerations, a great moral difficulty. The proposition that any Third Power is morally entitled to interfere by force (and if not so entitled it is bound not to interfere) in the quarrel of two other Powers, on the ground that it thinks one of them to be in the wrong, is a proposition very far indeed from being self-evident; and an immense responsibility in many points of view attaches to the assumption of the office of Peace-Preserver for Europe. It was true that on this ground we might be held to have undertaken the Crimean War: but we went into that matter with the support of United Europe, though all the Powers did not think fit to accompany France & England to the last alternative of force. While not doubting that England had duties on the Continent, I said that we had been apt on some former occasions to accept too forward a position, and had thereby brought great sufferings on our own people.

I think I need not pursue this recital farther, except just to mention that I told him I thought the English nation had perhaps scarcely formed an opinion for itself on the Alsace & Lorraine demand, but I felt that their opinion when formed never could be in favour of a forcible annexation of provinces in such circumstances.

On a bye point, he expressed an apprehension lest there should be in England a strong focus of Napoleonic sympathies. I told him I thought not. The *coup d'Etat* was condemned here; the Imperial Government was first accepted by us, simply because it was the Government which France appeared to have chosen for herself; and afterwards because its policy appeared to draw the two nations closer together, an object we had much at heart. This appeared to give him some pleasure. He thinks Bismarck is deep in plans of Restoration. I said perhaps he only used them to terrify the Defence Government.

I told him I feared the question remained one for the sword; without abandoning the hope that at some juncture yet to arrive it may be possible to be useful. But so long as the present state continues, we had no right either to abate the spirit of France by counselling submission, nor to egg her on to a contest in which we were not prepared to bear a share.

Finally he hoped that you were not weary of the office of carrying any proposal to the Prussians, and I said I was sure you never would decline that duty where you might see a prospect of being useful. M. Reitlinger goes tomorrow.

421. Lord Granville to Mr. Gladstone. [Add. MS. 44167, fo. 271]

Private. F.O. Dec 29/70.

Forster has asked me to tell you that he reproaches himself for not having said more about Stansfield's being put in the Cabinet.[1] Not so much from his friendship for Stansfield as on account of the political feeling there is on the subject, and also the fact that although he feels confident of recovering the confidence of the Radicals, yet his being called up to the Cabinet was a reward for a success which had been displeasing to the strong liberals.

I stated some of the objections which occurred to me as to encreasing the number of the Cabinet, and the introduction into it of Mrs S.

He said that he had always told his wife that she had dragged him up as much as Mrs Stansfield had dragged her husband down.

His tone however was very earnest.

422. Lord Granville to Mr. Gladstone. [Add. MS. 44617, fo. 274]

F.O. Dec 29/70.

I had anticipated your telegraphic wish,[2] by dining and spending the evening with H[artington]—& I had exhausted my quiver to the bottom. The difficulty you will have is that while H. has a very strong innate sense of duty, he has been living in an atmosphere where the calls of pleasure and comfort are much preferred, and it is not easy to pitch the tone exactly in arguing that particular view of the question.

I was able to say more than you can about the motives that will be attributed to his refusal, but you will be able to work the duty of a political man to himself, and his colleagues with much more force although with not more reiteration than I did.

I think Brunnow will run straight after all—the Turk has not yet recd his instructions.

P.S. I was much interested with your account of the conversation with Reitlinger.

I am sorry you said as much as you did to him in his position, as to what would be the feeling of this Country, as to the annexation of French Territory. Everything else seems to me excellent.

[1] See above, no. 418, below, no. 425.

[2] Gladstone to Granville, tel. 10.15 a.m., 29 Dec., G.D. 29/58.

423. Mr. Gladstone to Lord Granville. [G.D. 29/58]

Hawarden Castle. D. 29. 70.

1. With reference to the dispatch of Paget No 281 and your pencil note upon it,[1] I remark that we perhaps may not have a Cabinet before the matter is to be decided, that I do not precisely recall the circs., probably special, in which you or we barred Paget's accompanying the King to Rome, and that his arguments appear to me to be exceeding strong.

2. I see the D. News letting fly at you, as they did at me about the Pope: meantime the Irish priests in Meath have extorted from Plunkett the Candidate a most extravagant pledge to oppose us in all things until we alter our Italian policy: which however I am quietly assured he will not keep!

3. Reitlinger is gone—we liked him very much, & I can tell you some rather amusing stories about him especially one about the meaning of the word *aplomb*.

4. I presume Hart[ingto]n will come tonight & I fear I must be very rude to him. I cannot think of any other member of the Cabinet, or even of Govt, who cd possibly be transferred. I conceive Forster to be excellent & most important where he is, but doubtful for Ireland.

424. Lord Granville to Mr. Gladstone. [Add. MS. 44167, fo. 277]

Savernake. Dec 29/70.

I am delighted to hear from West that you have prevailed with Harty Tarty.

I thank for the anecdote "aplomb".

425. Mr. Gladstone to Lord Granville. [G.D. 29/58]

Hawarden Castle. Dec. 30. 70.

1. I am not sure that I was right about Reitlinger in the point you object to. But at worst it was doubly guarded 1. as my individual opinion not that of the Govt., and 2. by my laying down very pointedly that we had no right either to encourage or to dissuade the French with reference to the struggle.

2. Hartington has behaved extremely well in overcoming an undisguised and strong repugnance. I am sure he will not have cause to repent of this sacrifice to duty and honour. Among other things, in our conversation, I touched upon the ulterior future.

3. I do not understand your faithful report of Forster's wishes to signify a change in your own judgment, and I write to Monsell offering the P.O.; to Stansfield, a letter of which copy shall be sent you for perusal.[2]

4. I also send a long & interesting letter from Max Müller; not *necessary* to

[1] 'Give me for next Cabinet' on No. 281 confidential, 21 Dec., F.O. 45/169. Paget asked for the withdrawal of his instruction (20 Dec., after cabinet, 17 Dec., F.O. 45/160), not to enter Rome with the King of Italy.

[2] Gladstone to Stansfield, 30 Dec., explained that he would not offer him the Post Office without a place in the cabinet, G.D. 29/58. Monsell accepted.

peruse. But I think he reflects through Abeken the Bismarckian mind, in the best light which it is capable of reflecting.

5. On your sending me a letter of the Queen's about the Treaty for the Marriage I went to work upon it & had a draft drawn in the Treasury which I sent two or three days ago to H.M.; and I await her directions. They will I hope clear up the confusion which has arisen, & easily settle the form. The curious point is as to the substance—What is the Duke to do?

6. I answer your Cipher Tel. as to Paget [1] 'Certainly in my opinion'.

7. You will be not a little surprised at the account of provisions carried on the Luxembourg Railway.[2]

426. Lord Granville to Mr. Gladstone. [Add. MS. 44617, fo. 278]

Private. Dec 31/70.

My letters of the 29th must have borne the mark of great haste—they were written in the intervals of perpetual interviews. I omitted to mention the most important work of the day, but of which you will see the import by the draft to Loftus,[3] concerning the sinking and firing upon the 6 vessels at Rouen. We got the Law Officers opinion only in time to draft the despatch and copy it. Hammond & I agreed that it would not do to let our regular messenger go without it. I took upon myself to soften the expressions of the Law Officers, but I hope I did not diminish the strength of our position. It will be very awkward if Bernstorff plays off this card against what he alleges are our breaches of neutrality—but his position is too stringent just at present to make this likely.

I trust the telegram in the Daily News is not true, and that Favre will not insist upon a formal recognition. If he does, I propose to tell him officially that I cannot admit of this compulsion—that the admission to the Conference is a great advantage to the Provisional Govt, and that I will guarantee M. Favre, as far as I can rely on the assurance of the other Plenipos that no objection will be raised to the informality of his powers, and that he will personally be treated with perfect respect—and I shall give him a dig about the neglect of our advice to call an assembly.

It is a question whether I might tell him confidentially and without committing myself that after the conference was closed I would bring the matter before the Cabinet, and ascertain whether in their opinion the time was come when we could with propriety send credentials to Lyons. This however would be a devil of a measure, if the Prussians behave well to us in conference, and about ships, if the war continues in their favor, and that there is no more chance than at present of the Provisional Gov becoming permanent, and that no chamber is called for the purpose of deciding the point.

[1] Granville to Gladstone, tel. 30 Dec., suggesting that Paget should accompany the King into Rome if the rest of the *corps diplomatique* did, and Gladstone's reply, 3.30, 30 Dec., G.D. 29/58.

[2] Gladstone enclosed a letter from M. Regray, manager of the Great Luxemburg line; translated extract in G.D. 29/58.

[3] No. 400, 28 Dec., protesting against the German sinking of six British colliers in the Seine. F.O. 64/683; *Correspondence respecting the Sinking of Six British Vessels . . .*, Parl. papers. [C. 250] (1871). lxxi, 374–5.

The delay in his arrival is very awkward, and I have taken advantage of the Turk and Cadorna not getting their full instructions, to couple that reason with Favre's absence to delay the conference for a few days—the delay will annoy all the Plenipos, but it cannot be helped.

By gross neglect of a F.O. Messenger, my letter entrusted to West, to be sent at the proper moment to Otway,[1] did not reach him till the day after the announcement in the newspapers of his successor.

427. Mr. Gladstone to Lord Granville. [G.D. 29/59]

Hawarden Castle. Ja 1.71.

1. Balloon men caught. It appears to me that the Law Officers have not taken notice of another point which is that the captives are not voluntarily within the Prussian lines but are brought in either by Prussian shot, or by atmospheric causes analogous to those which drive a ship by stress of weather into an enemy's port. This seems to me to strengthen the case further.

2. I watch the affair of the 6 ships with much anxiety. The country will be expectant, & not over patient. But I suppose you, rightly, are anxious to finish the Conference first.

3. With regard to recognition of the French Government, on general grounds I think them now pretty fairly entitled to it. But may you not point out to Jules Favre that even if the Cabinet were ready our recognising before the Conference would be no favour to them unless the other Powers generally recognised.[2] But what if the other Powers (except Prussia which *cannot* recognise as she cannot accredit) were ready? I see much awkwardness in doing it after the Conference.

4. I now begin to fear we made a mistake in recommending the Pope to remain at Rome where it seems to be his object to provoke violence & revolutionary disturbance with a view to reaction.

428. Mr. Gladstone to Lord Granville. [G.D. 29/59]

Hawarden Castle. Jan 2.1870. [*sic*, read 1871]

One thing seems to me perfectly clear about the Danubian Commission, & it is that we should *not* take the initiative which Stokes recommends. He founds himself on a principle altogether false, & one which exploded in the almost preposterous case of the Guatemala Road.[3]

It would be most mischievous to admit that we are the persons who should claim the lead in such a matter & the mischief is elevated into absurdity, when we

[1] Granville to Otway, 23 Dec., saying that Enfield had been offered the foreign under-secretaryship, G.D. 29/107. See above, no. 414.

[2] The subject was not pursued until reopened by the French, see below, no. 445.

[3] Colonel Stokes, British representative on the European Commission of the Danube, came to London on the eve of the Black Sea conference to urge Granville to secure permanency for the international control as compensation for ending the neutrality of the Black Sea. He argued that control of the Danube by the riverain powers would exclude English influence. See Stokes to Granville, No. 19, London, 29 Dec., F.O. 78/3226.

learn that this Danubian business is to be a compensation for abandoning the neutralisation of the Black Sea, i.e. that England is to claim a compensation for a supposed injury to Turkey.

Next I think there is great force in Hammond's objection to our running a risk of postponing the settlement of the neutralisation quarrel by tacking on to it any thing which can cause delay. If you can get a good thing done in the Danube without prejudice to what is politically so important, well and good.

As to the question of the two Commissions, it appears to me that Austria & Turkey ought to agree upon a plan & then you might consider it. If you bring before the Conference any thing to which Turkey is opposed, you play at once into the hands of the Czar.

Little Reitlinger has sent down three most lovely & fragrant bouquets for my three daughters. Angelic man.

429. Lord Granville to Mr. Gladstone. [Add. MS. 44168, fo. 4]

Private. 16, Bruton Street. Jan 3/71.

Otway is very angry with himself, and consequently with us.

His case against us is nil. He was justly surprised that he should have only heard from me, after the announcement had appeared in the papers that a successor was appointed.

My answer to this is that I wrote to him on the Friday,[1] that West not knowing till Sunday whether Enfield had accepted, sent my letter to be delivered immediately on Sunday morning, but that by gross negligence at the Foreign Office, and owing to Otway's omission to leave his direction the letter was only forwarded by Monday night's post.

He without reason complains that the Daily Telegraph announced the appointment of his successor without saying that Otway had resigned, and that the Daily News had given as a reason of his resignation a difference on Italian Policy. I told him that West had complied with my request, and had told the papers the resignation without giving any reason for it, which could only be explained by Otway himself. I offered yesterday to concert with him any mode of explanation either by a letter from me to him or a communication to the papers, or by a letter from him to his constituents—he took the night to consider of the course.

He then let a little bit of the cat out of the bag. He said he was the victim of circumstances.

I had objected to his going to Versailles, lest he should be supposed to have a mission. He yielded, and settled to go to Berlin. But I subsequently appointed Odo to go to Versailles. He thought my explanations why I had selected Odo were perfectly satisfactory, and he was quite of opinion that Odo was the best selection that could have been made.

[1] 23 Dec. Cf. 7 letters exchanged between Granville and Otway in Jan., Otway to Granville, 4 May and 25 Nov. (with pencil note by Granville on the back), G.D. 29/107. Granville to Gladstone, undated, sending part of this correspondence and withdrawing the suggested honour, Add. MS. 44168, fo. 14, not printed.

But Odo being at Versailles—He could not go to Berlin—He was obliged to remain at the office (which no one asked him to do) and so he became cognizant of the Conference, which if he had been away he might have ignored.

He said that the having kept the secret to oblige us had made him a disgraced man. The loss of salary & of a desirable office was a sacrifice to a poor man, but he had lost his good name. It was true that I, and particularly you had written him most satisfactory letters, but the public would think he was a disgraced man. He had been told that Layard was to have a home appointment, that Lumley was to go to Spain, and that he was to be offered Belgium. He told me in confidence that he should have declined the latter post, but that the compliment would have made every thing right, but he should now go without any acknowledgment of his services. He hinted at Privy Councillorship.

I reminded him that he had told me in the autumn that his office interfered with his political career—that I was sure you would permit him to publish your letter, as I was willing that he should publish mine—that the resignation was purely his own act. I did not press him much upon how perfectly illogical his arguments were.

It appears to me that "Right honorable" is perfectly out of the question. But how would our dear old friend the "C.B." do. I do not see much objection to it. He has served since you formed the Gov. He leaves us on no complaint on our part. His alleged reason is an honorable difference of opinion on an important and difficult question.

The honor would soften his feelings, and would lessen his position with the Radicals. It is worth thinking of, but I hope you will consider it well before you assent.

430. Lord Granville to Mr. Gladstone. [Add. MS. 44168, fo. 15]

Private. 16, Bruton Street. Jan 3/71.

There are some more hitches about the conference but which will not signify but one unexpected difficulty throws possibly alarming light on future contingencies. Bismark having told Odo that Brunnow must sign a protocol in which it is declared that to denounce a treaty can only be done with ["] the *assent* of the other parties" has instructed Bernstorff that if such a protocol is proposed he must sign it with a reservation ad protocolum that this does not bear on the case of a treaty having been broken by one of the parties. Now we do not pretend that it should, but that where there are more parties than one, one party alone cannot constitute itself sole judge of the infraction.

I have telegraphed to Odo to clear up the matter.[1]

But again Odo telegraphs [2] that he is afraid Prussian Troops will occupy Luxembourg, and at the moment when the telegram came, Bernstorff announced to me that

[1] 6.45 p.m., 2 Jan., proposing to add Bismarck's words to the draft protocol, and asking for Count Bernstorff's unreserved adhesion, F.O. 64/738. The final version of the protocol was settled with Brunnow and Bernstorff on 4 Jan., G.D. 29/91.

[2] 7 p.m., received 10.20 p.m., 1 Jan., F.O. 64/738.

he was about to bring to my notice the case of infraction of the Neutrality of Belgium by Franc Tireurs, who seized a Prussian Courier in Belgian Territory.[1]

I answered that I had seen an account of it, and the Belgians appeared to have behaved well, and done all that could be required of them. Bernstorff admitted this, but said yes but it was an infraction of Neutrality by the French.

This raking up of an old story, at the moment when the Prussians fear for their communications may be broken is significative [*sic*].

Shall I telegraph to Odo to do all he can to prevent troops being ordered to Luxembourg, but when they are there, to hold firm though civilly worded language, & intimate that in the case of Luxembourg alone, whatever angry discussions may arise, it was not likely as in other possible cases to do more.

I propose as soon as Bernstorff makes his complaint, to telegraph to Lyons to urge the F[rench] G[overnmen]t to lose no time in disavowing the Franc Tireurs, expressing regret, and promising to take measures to prevent a repetition of the event.

431. Mr. Gladstone to Lord Granville. [G.D. 29/59]

Hawarden Castle. Jan 3.71.

1. The answer of Bismarck about the ships is good [2]; but the reported intention of occupying Luxembourg is ominous. A Protest against such a proceeding is right in principle, if it is not thought to call for more: but a protest from this country against a war measure of the Germans, in the present state of public feeling, would place us within one step of war.

2. Prince Charles of Roumania seems to me self-condemned by his own clandestine proceeding. While he asks two for the judgment, he is it seems preparing the evidence! Is it not a great question whether his letter to the Queen [3] should be *received*?

3. What do you think will be the proper day for resuming *ordinary* or Session Cabinets? Friday 20th—Sat. 21st—or Mon. 23d?[4] If you have occasion for any intermediate meeting, the final one (so to call it) might be a little delayed.

432. Mr. Gladstone to Lord Granville. [G.D. 29/59]

No 2. Hawarden Castle. Jan 3.71

Your mode of meeting the difficulty likely to arise from the reserve proposed to be made by Bernstorff in the Declaration to secure Treaties against nullification

[1] See Lumley to Granville, No. 446, 12 Dec., reporting the incident, F.O. 10/310; to Lyons, tel. 7.25 p.m., 3 Jan., F.O. 27/1850.

[2] Russell to Granville, tel. 7 p.m., received 10.20 p.m., 1 Jan., and No. 4, 3 Jan., announcing German regret and readiness to pay full compensation, F.O. 64/738; Parl. papers. [C. 250] (1871). lxxi, 377–8; see above, no. 426.

[3] Described Prince Charles's difficulties. He wrote similarly to the rulers of the other guaranteeing states; see Green to Granville, No. 100, 9 Dec., and 101, 10 Dec. and enclosures, F.O. 78/2134. Cf. Granville to Green, No. 1, 9 Jan., saying the letter had been received, F.O. 78/2183.

[4] Cabinet met 19, 20, 25 Jan., Add. MS. 44639, fos. 2–4.

at the will of a single party, seems to me to be excellent. I have nothing to propose to add, or to take away.

2. With regard to the infraction of Belgian neutrality by Franc-tireurs, I have the same observation to make. Let the French Govt. disavow, & regret the act of their people. If there did happen to be a weak point in the Belgian prevention, it might be well to cover it by apology: but I should think it dangerous to admit any breach of duty in terms by way of civility & without real cause.

3. As regards the entry of German troops into Luxemburg, I in some degree anticipated your letter. As regards instructing Odo Russell to dissuade, all is so far clear. But if dissuasion fails, and if we have to protest, I should protest in terms which would neither distinctly threaten on the one hand, nor abridge our liberty on the other. Probably the language of Mr Canning with regard to the French invasion of Spain might be found to supply precedents. But I think it would hardly be dignified in protesting to signify directly that our words were words alone: and I am even afraid that such a course might practically be found to weaken our hands, & our ground, about Belgium.

3 [*sic*]. Possibly you may want a Cabinet on this. On Friday I have an engagement to meet a body of 70 tenants, chiefly small, with whom I have quite recently become connected. Please to give me the earliest notice you can, if you think we require to meet before or on that day.

433. Mr. Gladstone to Lord Granville. [G.D. 29/59]

No 3. Hawarden Castle. Jan 3.71.

Re Otway—I am very sorry you should have had to write at so much length but I think if the C.B is of use there can be no difficulty about it—& I freely leave it to you to publish my letter if on reading it you find it fit. I forget the contents.

434. Lord Granville to Mr. Gladstone. [G.D. 29/59]

Copy. F. O. Jany 4/71.

I really have no opinion about Cabinets. It would be agreeable to me to bore you between the hours of one and two every day at No 11—but I hardly know why we should meet this week.

Bernstorff recd this morning the same instructions as are reported in Odo's telegram.[1]

He has got out of Brunnow, he says with great difficulty, consent to a rédaction which appears to me to do all that is required for a protocol—I shall send it to Apponyi, and he will recommend it to Beust.

I presume we need not be in a tremendous hurry to rejoin to Bismarck's answer to our reply to his Luxemburg circular.

I had asked the same question about the Prince of Roumania's letter to the

[1] 11.50 p.m., 3 Jan., received 5 a.m., 4 Jan., describing Bernstorff's instructions to agree to any wording of the proposed protocol to which all would consent, F.O. 64/738.

Queen, but Hammond & Bergne said there was a precedent for the Queen receiving it.

Cardwell seems to have picked up spirits at Oxford.

I have never given any answer to Bulwer about Peerage—you had better settle what to do, and let him know.

I will write tomorrow about Otway. He has adopted the whole Pall Mall platform.

Lord Russell [1] says a pen & ink apology won't do for the colliers.

We must hoist the English Flag, and have it saluted by 21 guns. If this be so, I am very sorry that I thanked Bismarck for his answer.

435. Mr. Gladstone to Lord Granville. [G.D. 29/59]

Hawarden Castle. Jan 4. 71.

I have read Bismarck's reply [2] on the Luxembourg affair.

There is one point in the German case, I think, for which we may not have sufficiently allowed. It is this: that although Luxembourg may have been perfectly innocent in regard to the transit of French soldiers by reason of their disguise, still preventive measures may be allowable for the Germans.

They did not thus put the case but simply made a charge against Luxembourg.

But the plain flaw in their position seems to be this: instead of limiting their claim to the adoption of such provisional measures of security & prevention as the actual necessities of war may require—a matter in which their conduct would be subsequently cognisable by the Co-Signatory Powers—they claim to make positive and unrestricted use of Luxembourg for war purposes on the ground of their own allegation that this has already been done in certain very partial respects by their enemy.

And in the middle of all this the old King is to do the chivalry, without a blush, probably without even a suspicion.

I should think we might frame the answer upon or so as to include the following propositions in their substance.

1. No charge has thus far been substantiated against the Govt. of Luxembourg: the allegations stand for further cons[iderat]ion.

2. Prussia cannot be admitted to have a right even provisionally to take any measures except those of precaution against actual or bonâ fide apprehended injury.

3. A claim to make Luxembourg subservient to the operations of her army cannot in whole or in part be admitted. Taken at the best it would mean redress or compensation. But the title to this cannot be established by the declaration or opinion of Prussia *ex parte*.

4. The fact that this unwarrantable claim was contained in Count Bismarck's Circular, and at the same time that he referred without explaining them to further claims on the Duchy, & that he made no reference to the authority of the Co-signatory

[1] To Granville, private, 3 Jan., G.D. 29/79.

[2] Bismarck to Bernstorff, 24 Dec., communicated 2 Jan., F.O. 64/730; Parl. papers. [C. 246] 1871). lxxi, 685–6; cf. G.D. 29/94.

Powers, amply justified your reference to the Treaty of 1867: however glad you are to accept the assurances [1] now received respecting it.

These are my ideas, submitted for review, recast, or rejection.

It may be well to reserve your siege-guns, and only fire at present with a pea-shooter.

436. Mr. Gladstone to Lord Granville. [G.D. 29/59]

Hawarden Castle. Jan 5.71.

1. Though your ciphered Telegram [2] cannot be made out clearly, I take it to mean that I am not to write to Otway, & reply accordingly.

2. I quite agree that the real reply to Bismarck need not be hurried. Perhaps if necessary you can interject some query so as not to leave too long an interval.

3. Cardwell, after consulting Northbrook, writes to suggest whether a soldier & Peer should be substituted for him. I write back to dissuade strongly.[3]

4. What scandalises me in P[rince] Charles's letter is its shabby, intriguing, clandestine character. I hope it may be found proper & practicable to snub him. Trevelyan in his pamphlet [4] reports an immense material progress in Roumania: not very compatible with Prince C.s railing accusation against it. I think it a scandalous proceeding.

5. I think we must have a talk on Peerages.

6. Read my little balloon letter within. It is significant.

437. Lord Granville to Mr. Gladstone. [Add. MS. 44168, fo. 23]

Private. F. O. Jan 5/71.

1° Greece. I have sent you the despatches, and copies to the Chancellor and to De Grey before I draft anything on them.[5] It appears to me that we have a grievance now, whereas before we had nothing but complaints founded on inferences and suspicions. In its small way, it is as troublesome as any of the larger questions.

2° All the Plenipos here think we should proceed without a French plenipo—as it is their fault, & not our's, or that of the other Belligerent. I sent you a draft

[1] Granville to Bernstorff, 17. Dec., G.D. 29/111; from Russell, tel. 11.30 a.m., 17 Dec., F.O. 64/737; to Russell, private, 20 Dec. 1870 and 1. Jan. 1871, G.D. 29/110, printed Knaplund, *Letters from Berlin*, pp. 37, 39; see above, no. 409 note.

[2] For Granville's draft marked 'sent 3 p.m., 5 Jan.,' and Gladstone's tel. in reply, see G.D. 29/59.

[3] See Cardwell to Gladstone, 3 Jan., suggesting that Sir W. Mansfield should be made a peer and take the War Office in his place, Add. MS. 44119, fo. 191; reply, Add. MS. 44539, fo. 124, with which Granville strongly agreed, Add. MS. 44119, fo. 193.

[4] Charles E. Trevelyan, *From Pesth to Brindisi in the Autumn of 1869* (1870).

[5] See Erskine to Granville, Nos. 341, 342, 24 Dec., F.O. 32/409; *Correspondence respecting . . . Brigands . . . in Greece*. Parl. papers. [C. 249] (1871). lxxi, 561; Granville to Hatherley, 5 Jan, and reply 7 Jan., G.D. 29/65, on the suppression of evidence in the case of F. Noel, a British subject tried for alleged complicity in brigandage.

to Lyons [1] to go, if as I expect they decline to appoint any one but Favre, who has refused.

Reitlinger [2] has given me his word of honor that he will bring Favre out, if I can get him into Paris, but I told him I was afraid Bismark would not be as willing to accept his assurances as I might be.

I have telegraphed to Odo to let me know when my letter to Favre [3] will arrive, (Moran says that his despatches sent three weeks ago have not been acknowledged yet) and to take any means in his power to facilitate Favre's movements, if he changes his mind.

The Turk's instructions are moderate concession of non neutralization, return of Sovereign Rights to the Sultan, and confirmation of treaty of 1856. But he would like to add the particular condition of the Treaty of April, into the general Treaty. This would be worse than all parties entering into the Treaty of April.[4]—And Prussia would not consent, but Musurus thought there might be means of leaving out the fighting clause which appears to be the essential point. I will ask him to show me something in writing. He would like to get [rid] of the Capitulations, and he wishes to bring the Principalities before the Conference, which I told him was impossible, that I had said so to Prussia and Austria, in conformity with what Turkey had said to me.

He told me of an observation of Palmerston's, which I have put by for use.

If Beust will agree to the rédaction " that it is an essential principle of international law that no nation can free itself from the obligations of a treaty or modify its provisions, without a preliminary understanding with the other contracting parties,["] [5] our first day is landed. All the others agree.

I cannot say how grateful I am for the hints for an answer to Luxembourg.

The strong case for them appears to be the question what we should do ourselves in a similar case.

If we were in a death struggle, at the approach of a complete victory, but with a terrible danger of the communications of 3, or 400,000 men being cut off, and that by straining a point of international law, we could avail ourselves of a most useful bit of Railway communication, in a nondescript little country about which nobody cared, and nobody would fight about, what should we do? I suspect we should deal with it as we did with the Copenhagen fleet. The French in defending their consul, talk of the advice to many of the soldiers to take off their uniforms, but if they arrived in uniform, the opinion of all recent writers on International

[1] No. 19, 6 Jan., refusing to postpone the Black Sea conference further, F.O. 27/1850. Cf. Lyons to Granville, private, 12 Jan., G.D. 29/85. It was ultimately postponed to 17 Jan. for Favre's arrival, Granville to Lyons, tel. 12 Jan., F.O. 27/1850.

[2] Granville saw him on 5 Jan., Reitlinger to Granville, 4 Jan., G.D. 29/89.

[3] Copy, 29 Dec. 1870, on arrangements for Favre to go from Paris to the conference and its adjournment for a week, received by Favre, 9 Jan., G.D. 29/109; Parl. papers. [C. 245] (1871). lxxii, 79.

[4] See above, no. 413.

[5] The final version of the protocol condemning unilateral denunciation of treaties. Austria tried to restore the more stringent form of 29 Dec., but failed, Apponyi to Granville, private, 6 Jan., G.D. 29/82; Granville to Apponyi, private, 4, 10 Jan., F.O. 362/2; Granville to Lyons, private, 7 Jan., F.O. 362/4.

law is that they should not be allowed to go through a neutral country home to fight again.

As regards France & Luxembourg I am not sure whether if [*sic*] there be [or] no further right than that of repression & prevention in case of an infraction of neutrality on their part. As regards other powers, during the stress of war, it is long to wait for a congress to decide upon the facts.

Notwithstanding all this, I agree in the main with you, and I will look at Mr Canning's protest.

Telegraph whether we are to wait indefinitely for France or not.

438. Mr. Gladstone to Lord Granville. [G.D. 29/59]

Hawarden Castle. Jan 6.71.

1. I Telegraphed to you this morning that I quite agreed the Conference might go on, but I am sorry you have been taken through such a labyrinth of varying intentions.

2. I thought your side of the Otway correspondence excellent.[1] Of the Vice Consuls I know nothing: but I have some idea that Northcote Ex-Secretary of State is still C.B. & no more.

3. *Re* Luxembourg I observe on the Danish case that (1.) we always pleaded the existence of a domineering & omnipotent Napoleon—to which now there is nothing parallel unless it be on the German side. (2.) That I apprehend we never denied we gave a *casus belli* by our proceeding—which I do not suppose Birmarck would admit. (3.) of the cutting off of German communications no fear was alleged. (4) I think the present references to Longwy look most dishonest. What in the world can Luxembourg have to do with it. (5) Did you notice the paper I sent you about the 30 000 Tons sent to the Germans against 1200 to the French. But it is well to sift everything & take every possible point on the German side.

4. I would not give Bismarck over much time in the affair of the six ships.[2] What can he mean about compensation *if* requisite. Does he suppose you can scuttle a ship as a man tubs?

439. Mr. Gladstone to Lord Granville. [G.D. 29/59]

Hawarden Castle. Jan 7.71.

1. The Greek Government appears to be implicated in a gross breach of faith, & the subject matter in which it has been committed seems to be so important as to vitiate the authority of the inquiry.

2. Mr Noel's complaining of Erskine may be excusable under his peculiar circumstances, but I do not at present see that he has the smallest cause for it.

3. When do you intend the Conference to meet.

4. I return Otway's letter—the teeth are a little shown.

5. Correspondence continues about the Dease letter [3]—but nothing formidable.

[1] See above, no. 429; cf. Granville to Gladstone, copy, 6 Jan., G.D. 29/22A, not printed.

[2] See above, no. 431.

[3] Cf. resolution of the Edinburgh Reformation Society, 6 Jan., Add. MS. 44429, fo. 12, *et passim*.

440. Lord Granville to Mr. Gladstone. [G.D. 29/59]

Copy. F.O. Jan 7.1871.

Please look at the draft [1] founded on the Law Officers report and the Chancellors note [2] respecting the Luxembourg affair. If by chance you approve telegraph at once Yes.

441. Lord Granville to Mr. Gladstone. [G.D. 29/59]

Copy. F. O. Jany 7./71.

Otway has begged me to tell no one about the C.B. incident—so you know nothing of it.

I have sent you a stop gap despatch. I doubt your returning it [in] its present shape. It will come back longer or shorter.

I have telegraphed to Odo to hasten the Collier affair.[3]

I have threatened to break off confidential communication with Brunnow if Gortchakoff is to telegraph more or less exactly incidents connected with it to all Europe.

He has telegraphed a remonstrance.[4]

442. Mr. Gladstone to Lord Granville. [G.D. 29/59]

Hawarden Castle. Jan 9.71.

1. With reference to Thornton's letter of the 20th,[5] I have often racked my brains to think how we can make an ostensible approximation on the Alabama question to the Americans, without a surrender of substantial interests and principles: for I am one of those who do not admit our case to be bad on the Alabama question. Now the idea may be worth little, but I would just suggest whether when challenged by Schenck we might (without assuming an initiative) place before them the expediency of separating between the dry question of law & material interests on one hand, and that of feeling on the other: and confining the arbitration to the former of these. Possibly if they desire to recede from a rather false position, (and if the Tenterden plan does not work), this might afford them an opportunity.

2. I hope we shall hear of Rose [6] and the Commission in time to have something ready for the Queen's Speech.

3. There is a Council on Saturday when the meeting of Parliament will be

[1] To Loftus, No. 12, and to Russell, No. 15, 7 Jan., rejoining to Bismarck's answer to the British reply to the Luxemburg circular, 3 Dec., disregarding Gladstone's suggestions in no. 435, and acknowledging the Prussian disclaimers of hostility to the 1867 treaty, F.O. 64/714; Parl. papers. [C. 246] (1871). lxxi, 688–9.

[2] Hatherley to Granville, 7 Jan., discouraging further discussion, G.D. 29/65.

[3] To Russell, tel. 3.30 p.m., 7 Jan., F.O. 64/738.

[4] Cf. Brunnow to Granville, private, samedi matin [7 Jan.], G.D. 29/98.

[5] To Granville, private, Washington, 20 Dec. 1870, on the personality of General Schenck, and the popular opinion that he had been sent to London to settle the Alabama claims, G.D. 29/80.

[6] Left England with the proposal for the appointment of a mixed commission to examine Anglo-American differences, 21 Dec., and arrived in Washington, 9 Jan., Granville to Thornton, private, 17 Dec. 1870, F.O. 362/1; Thornton to Granville, tel. 9 Jan., F.O. 5/1214.

fixed. I suppose that to please the Queen we must adhere to the 9th, though there will perhaps be some dissatisfaction, which however might still exist if we adhered to the 7th which was first thought of.

I inclose a M. Post with a curious letter & article from the Débats.

443. Lord Granville to Mr. Gladstone. [G.D. 29/59]

Copy. Bruton Street. Jany 10./71.

Your idea about the 'Alabama' may and ought to be turned to good profit. If a pigeon takes the cattle disease from my farm to yours I can deeply regret it, without admitting your claim that I should compensate you for all your dead cows.[1]

I never understood why we should be squeamish about expressing regret in proper terms, on a fit occasion.

Thornton telegraphs that Rose is arrived, but it will be lucky if we have anything sufficiently definite to announce to Parlt.

I am glad you are coming to town. There are one or two things I shall like much to speak to you about.

444. Mr. Gladstone to Lord Granville. [G.D. 29/59]

Hawarden Castle. Jan 12. 71.

1. I cannot say that I like the language of the Turks or even Elliot's own language in No 394 about the Principalities.[2] The Turk does not & never will either understand or value freedom for its own sake but will, at his best, keep faith in tolerating it as a necessary evil until he can get a fair or plausible excuse for invading it. That the position of a man like Prince Charles should be untenable, is no reproach to the Roumanian people. I know of no fact yet shown against them except their persecution of the Jews i.e. their having much the same feelings as the people of England had about 130 years ago. What right can the Porte have to send in troops on a supposition that there will be disorder? What right has it to say the people shall not govern themselves as they please so long as they respect the Suzerain Power? They will not understand that the true & only way to make Roumania anti-Russian is to respect & cherish its internal freedom, not to be always nibbling and carping at it. I do hope that instead of the vague assertions & speculations which alone come to us you will call for some distinct and detailed report of *facts* to show what is really the state of that Country: indifferent, I doubt not, but, as I believe, better & not worse than it was before the Union.

2. I much liked your Telegram to Bloomfield, respecting Beust's rather unreasonable suggestions.

3. I propose to Cardwell to see him in C.H.T. on Saturday at 3.30 about his Estimates & the day for a cabinet which they will probably require. I think he

[1] Cf. Granville to Thornton, private, 14 Jan., F.O. 362/1.

[2] See statement, 'personelle et confidentielle,' communicated by Musurus, 9 Jan., on the need of armed intervention in the Principalities, G.D. 29/91; Elliot to Granville, No. 394, 30 Dec., received 11 Jan., on deterioration in the state of the Principalities, F.O. 78/2126; Elliot to Granville, private, 30 Dec., on the possible fall of Prince Charles, G.D. 29/103.

would wish for Tuesday. I hope to be at Euston [1] 2.30: but tonight's frost looks as if it would be sharper, and if we have a second severe bout probably the trains may be late.

4. Read the Echo of today on the recognition of the Provisional Government. I have long thought that the change of circs is material, but a recognition before the Conference would be awkward unless all the neutrals joined in it.

445. Mr. Gladstone to Lord Granville. [G.D. 29/59]

Hawarden Castle. Jan 13.71.

Probably I am wrong but I should not have supposed Kirby's complaint could have been put aside with an expression of regret as I gather from the pencil note.[2] (NB should directions for a dispatch be in pencil?) How can the right to make requisitions upon neutrals residing in a Belligerent country excuse insolence, personal violence, spoken abuse of the neutral flag, wanton luxurious indulgence, indiscriminate pilfering, & any abstraction of property whatever except upon account & receipt regularly rendered? If I am right a copy of Kirby's letter in the newspapers will go far to put the country in a flame. Perhaps Rosenberg and Co may tell another story: but that is a different matter.

I Telegraph to you at once in cipher to suggest a reference to the Law Officers. At least I could not help raising the question for your consideration.

2. I cannot but suspend my opinion, like Elliot, with respect to the genuineness, or authority, of the Russo-Khedive convention.[3]

3. I only became aware today that the French Government as far as Chaudordy represents it had already raised anew the question of recognition.[4] We shall see what Favre says.

We have thaw today. You would probably find me at 3 tomorrow.

446. Mr. Gladstone to Lord Granville. [G.D. 29/59]

11, Carlton House Terrace. Jan 20.71.

If you do not object I should like to send, or that you should send, the curious inclosure from Lord A. Loftus with the Address (not Petition) from the mass-meeting in America to some newspaper for publication—quite unofficially.[5]

[1] Gladstone interpolated here: 'What say you as to the Cabinet?'

[2] In Granville's hand on the back of Lyons to Granville, No. 18, 6 Jan., enclosing letter of R. W. Kirby, a British subject, whose property had been plundered by Prussian troops, F.O. 27/1854; Granville to Lyons, No. 35, 11 Jan., rejected his claim for redress, but, 13 Jan., Lyons was told to delay pending consultation with the law officers, F.O. 27/1850; Parl. papers. [C. 311] (1871). lxxi, 331–4.

[3] See Elliot to Granville, secret, 30 Dec., F.O. 78/2126, and private, 30 Dec., G.D. 29/103.

[4] Granville to Lyons, No. 43, 14 Jan., records Chaudordy's fresh appeal for diplomatic recognition, F.O. 27/1850; Parl. papers. [C. 244] (1871). lxxi, 264–5. Cf. Lyons to Granville, private, 20 Jan., G.D. 29/85. Granville to Lyons, No. 66, 26 Jan., refused recognition.

[5] Loftus to Granville, No. 38, 14 Jan., enclosing a petition and address to the Prussian *Landtag* from an anti-war meeting at New York, 19 Nov. 1870, F.O. 64/716. A note on the back of no. 446 states that the address was sent to the *Daily Telegraph* for publication.

I think the Prussian reply [1] is somewhat like the fire, as described by them, from the French forts; feeble.

447. Lord Granville to Mr. Gladstone. [Add. MS. 44168, fo. 30]

16, Bruton Street. Jan 21/71.

The Austrians have got a positive order to propose that 1° the Porte should be empowered to shut or open the straits 2° that an obligation should be imposed upon the Sultan to admit a certain number of vessels in proportion to the number kept by Russia in the Black Sea—and that a port should be set apart for such non-riverain ships.[2]

I persuaded Zeschen [*sic*, read Szécsen] & Apponyi to telegraph "the British Cabinet are unanimous against the proposed Port, and the proportionate number of vessels plan. They have decided to follow the initiative of the Porte.[3] Our instructions are to do so too. How close are we to adhere to them".

If they get a discretionary power, they would wish to restrict the right of opening the straits to the case of nonriverain [4] Powers in the case of the Sultan's security being threatened. Perhaps, but not certainly the Turk would agree to this, and possibly if much pressed the Russian would do so, in which case, I presume there would be no objection to our doing so.

Again the Austrians wish for a permissive encrease of the vessels at the mouths of the Danube. As long as it is permissive, and all parties agree to it, I presume we may do so too.

But our safe rule will be to stick to the Turks.

Favre and Bismark are too provoking.

Favre writes to me [5] that he wishes to come to London, that when he gets his safe conduct he will come out, if the state of Paris allows him to do so. Then instead of applying to the headquarters as he is told to do for what would be a military safe conduct, he applies to Bismark for a diplomatic safe conduct, perhaps intending to consider it as a recognition—& asks for a long list of family and friends.

Bismark makes use of this ridiculous question of form and refuses to send the Diplomatic safe conduct, and does not forward a military one.

I am informed *confidentially* by Bernstorff of these facts.[6] I have written a

[1] 9 Jan., to Chaudordy's circular on the excesses of the German army, communicated by Bernstorff, 16 Jan., F.O. 64/730; Parl. papers, *loc. cit.* pp. 266–71.

[2] Relates to Turkey's compensation for her loss of security when the neutrality of the Black Sea should end. See an undated summary in Granville's hand, docketed received 21 Jan., G.D. 29/91. This question was opened in the first sitting of the Black Sea conference, 17 Jan., and it was hoped to agree before its second sitting, 24 Jan.; see Granville's private letters of 18 Jan., to Lyons, F.O. 362/4, to Buchanan, G.D. 29/114, to Russell, G.D. 29/110.

[3] Then seeking compensation by recovering sovereign rights over the Straits, Ali Pasha to Musurus, communicated to Granville, 9 Jan., G.D. 29/91.

[4] Gladstone underlined 'nonriverain' and wrote 'meaning?'.

[5] 10 Jan., communicated 17 Jan., Granville to Lyons, No. 51, 17 Jan., F.O. 27/1850; Parl. papers. [C. 245] (1871). lxxii, 92–4.

[6] Private letters, 19 and 21 Jan. (with enclosures), G.D. 29/94.

scolding telegram half threatening a postponement of Conference, and a private letter complaining to Odo.[1]

You have got the Versailles papers.

448. Mr. Gladstone to Lord Granville. [G.D. 29/59]

11, Carlton House Terrace. Jan 22.71.

I think you are quite right in resisting the Austrian whim and I like the mode.

Do you by non-riverain Powers mean Powers not having territory on the Euxine? I think Russia might resist[2]: and if she agreed would it not be a remaining inequality, and a mark of jealousy, which might again at a future time give occasion for disturbing the Treaty. Please consider.

The affair between Bismarck & Favre is generally mesquin, and B.s arguments on the impropriety of F.s coming away little less than ludicrous.

449. Mr. Gladstone to Lord Granville. [G.D. 29/59]

Private. 11, Carlton House Terrace. Jan 23.71.

That is rather an unsatisfactory Telegram from America.[3]

Would it be possible for the U.S. to *buy* St Juan from the Colonists.

450. Lord Granville to Mr. Gladstone. [Add. MS. 44168, fo. 36]

16, Bruton Street. Jan 27/71.

I saw Derby this morning.[4] He was civil but argued against the proposal—that concession to the Americans was not [what] was wanted—it was firmness.

I then told him that our doubt had been whether he had not committed himself too much to like to argue the case against the Americans. He seemed to have entirely forgotten this. He was civil, would gladly avail himself of my offer to see the papers—would give me a positive answer in the evening—was afraid it would be in the negative—the personal inconveniences would be great, but he did not mind that—the interest of European affairs was intense at this moment—not that he had anything to do with them at present. It had never been his habit, nor would it be to create difficulties. He was very grateful for the compliment which we had paid him.

I thought it better to send Tenterden to him with the papers, & this is the note which he has sent me.

[1] Tel. 8.15 p.m., and No. 57, 21 Jan., F.O. 64/738. Copy of the private letter, 21 Jan., in G.D. 29/110, printed Knaplund, *Letters from Berlin*, p. 42.

[2] Cf. Bernstorff to Granville, private, 23 Jan., G.D. 29/94.

[3] Thornton to Granville, tel. 21 Jan., received 22 Jan., reporting that America would agree to the proposed mixed commission to examine Anglo-American differences provided Britain accepted liability for the Alabama claims and ceded San Juan, F.O. 5/1297.

[4] To offer appointment as one of the British commissioners to examine Anglo-American differences.

I wrote to George Grey after I had seen Derby, but previously to his confirmed refusal.

The enclosed came from Halifax this evening.

451. Mr. Gladstone to Lord Granville. [G.D. 29/59]

10, Downing Street. Ja 27.71.

The death of an aged Aunt, my last remaining relative in blood of the preceding generation obliges us to put off our journey to Osborne—and the dinner on Monday, which will be before the funeral.

I shall not have to leave London for the place is I think too distant (Dumfries) for me to attend at this time.

We can now put the Cabinet to Saturday which I should like.

Or it might go to Monday if you think that better.[1]

I hope the gout is going but assume that some postponement is desirable, & this is a very slack day [?] for matter.

Please answer about the day.

452. Mr. Gladstone to Lord Granville. [G.D. 29/59]

11, Carlton House Terrace. Ja 27.71.

Unless precedent both warrants and *requires* it I would not allow Gen. Walker or Captain Hozier to take part in any triumphal celebration.[2]

I should have thought it desirable for O[do] R[ussell] to avoid letting his departure seem to be a measure but if this can be managed not desirable for him to go into Paris.

I think this a far stronger case than the Te Deum: for here it is not the joy of the victors among their own people, it is flouting the defeat, in the bitterest form, in the very eyes & ears of the vanquished.

453. Mr. Gladstone to Lord Granville. [G.D. 29/59]

11, Carlton House Terrace. Feb. 1.71.

I see in the Times that they are eight days out in their calculations as to the food in Paris & of course on the wrong side.

What do you think of Telegraphing to Head Quarters at Versailles *and to* Jules Favre that on joint request by Telegraph or otherwise our stores and people are at their service if we can be of any use subject to no condition except that whatever we do must be done with the cognisance & approval both of a French & of a German Agent? [3]

[1] Cabinet met, Saturday, 28 Jan., at 2.30, Add. MS. 44639, fo. 6.

[2] See Granville to Russell, tel. 1.30 p.m., and No. 79, 28 Jan., instructing him and the two military attachés at Versailles to avoid the German entry into Paris after the armistice was signed (28 Jan.), F.O. 64/738. The entry did not take place until 1 March.

[3] Cabinet agreed 1 Feb., Add. MS. 44639, fo. 8; to Russell, tel. 1 Feb., F.O. 64/739. See mem. by Sir H. Storks on ways and means, 2 Feb., G.D. 29/59.

454. Lord Granville to Mr. Gladstone. [Add. MS. 44168, fo. 39]

16, Bruton Street. Feb 2/71.

I have had six hours of Plenipotentiaries [1]—more than enough.

Bernstorff is come back to the proposal which I showed you and others in the F.O Room. Brunnow has had regrets expressed to him that he had consented to the words 'non riveraines', but as he had done so, his Govt allowed him to sign them, and he will do so, with the additional words suggested by Austria. Italy & Austria will do the same.

I propose to open the sitting by reminding the conference of what passed at our unofficial meeting when it was proposed by some of the Plenipotentiaries that four articles which I will read should be examined at the next formal meeting. Musurus will then object, propose his draft, and argue for it. Austria will ask for the addition of her words "de la mer noire". Austria and Italy will adhere, so shall I, suggesting another article as to the Black Sea remaining open to the Mercantile Marine. Apponyi, (who knows that all the other powers object to the Austrian proposal of encreasing the Fleet at the mouth of the Danube, and has telegraphed to his Gov for permission to abandon it) will reserve his right to propose it. He will then propose his Austro-Hungarian plans about the Danube, & I shall propose the prolongation of the European Commission—which will be agreed to. I shall ask Musurus in the most deferential manner to refer home for further instructions.

Tissot has no instructions from his Gov, but says he sees very strong objections to the Turk's proposal. He has been good enough to correct the French of the Articles.

He says France was for the prolongation of the European Commission, and he has no reason to believe that there can have been any change of opinion.

455. Mr. Gladstone to Lord Granville. [G.D. 29/59]

11, Carlton House Terrace. Feb. 2.71.

I hope you have thrown off the enemy of yesterday. I have been caught in the chest & in bed all day without making any progress.

I cannot from your letter follow the *precise* course affairs are to take in the access question.

But if somebody *else* throws over the Turk, not we, I do not think it matters & I believe the redaction of your terms in the F. O. would in itself be quite satisfactory to the Cabinet.

To relieve—I think effectually—the anxiety you expressed yesterday I send you a letter from Max Müller.[2]

[1] On Turkey's compensation, still unsettled after the second sitting of the conference, 24 Jan. The third sitting was due, after postponement, on 3 Feb. For the article drafted on the eve of the second sitting, which Russia rejected, see private letters of 23 Jan., to Brunnow, G.D. 29/115, and to Bernstorff, G.D. 29/111, and Brunnow to Granville, confidential, 24 Jan., G.D. 29/98. For 4 articles drafted after the sitting of 24 Jan., see Brunnow to Granville, 26 Jan., G.D. 29/98. For 10 articles agreed to, 2 Feb., see *projet de protocole*, 2 Feb., G.D. 29/98, Granville to Brunnow, confidential, 2 Feb., G.D. 29/115.

[2] 2 Feb., copy in G.D. 29/59, reporting Delane's refusal of his offer to review in *The Times* A. E. Gasparin's *Appel au patriotisme et au bon sens* (1871), which recommended the neutralization of Alsace-Lorraine.

456. Mr. Gladstone to Lord Granville. [G.D. 29/59]

11, Carlton House Terrace. Feb. 3.71.

1. Did I not understand you were about to make Odo Russell deliver or proceed upon the dispatch [1] in which you inquired what were the German terms of peace?

2. With reference to Brunnow's overture on the same subject—I understand him to have said that in his opinion if England proposed a Congress it would be well taken at St. Petersburgh. On this I think we were both of opinion that we could hardly move in that direction: for a Congress would seem to deny the *primary* position & authority in reference to such a subject of the Belligerents themselves. But what if you were to inquire from & through Brunnow whether in case the proposed terms of peace when known should seem to be such as menace the future stability of peace in Europe Russia would be inclined to consider how far in concert with other Powers she might endeavour to exercise a mitigating influence?

The public mind in this country has been much excited by the terms of peace as reported yesterday from Berlin. They, i.e. the 400 millions, are hardly credible: & yet it is odd that we have as yet had no contradiction.

I think it will be justly expected of us to ascertain the disposition of other Powers as to pronouncing an opinion on any demands tending to endanger the future peace of Europe.

457. Mr. Gladstone to Lord Granville. [G.D. 29/59]

11, Carlton House Terrace. Feb 3.71.

As far as I can at present see we should name in the Queens Speech the following Bills

Army Organisation
Scotch Education
Secret voting, & perhaps
Rating

458. Mr. Gladstone to Lord Granville. [G.D. 29/59]

11, Carlton House Terrace. Feb. 4.71.

Please to recollect to send me back the letter marked 'Secret' (I believe) about Royal Residence in Ireland.[2]

459. Lord Granville to Mr. Gladstone. [Add. MS. 44168, fo. 43]

16, Bruton Street. Feb 5/71.

It is difficult to say what can be cut out of your excellent draft of speech, but it appears to me too long. I send you some crude notes on those parts with which I have to do.[3]

[1] No. 37, 20 Jan., F.O. 64/738. Russell to Granville, No. 38, 3 Feb., describes Bismarck's reply that the peace terms were still the same as in Oct. 1870, F.O. 64/739; copy, Add. MS. 44429, fo. 165; Parl. papers. [C. 244] (1871). lxxi, 272.

[2] See above, no. 383.

[3] Cf. the Queen's speech on opening Parliament, 9 Feb., *Hans. Parl. Deb.* 3rd ser. cciv. 1–9. It adopted Granville's suggestions 1, 2, 3, 5 (the word 'prompt' being omitted), 6, 7, 8

1

" More than common satisfaction " might be construed by the wags, as showing that the Queen rather liked the row.

Could you substitute some phrases, such as " importance ", " necessity ", " desirability ", " need of counsels " etc. etc.

2 & 3.

Very good. I should like to shorten it, yet my only suggestion is an addition something about the " maintenance of the rights of neutrals."

4.

I should omit. Qui s'excuse, s'accuse. Our case is *now* very strong.

5.

Appears to be all right—query, whether instead of referring to the prompt congrats, the Queen should not say " I rejoice ".

6.

query—substitute the following sentence—which will hit Luxembourg as well as the Black sea, and avoid overt allusion to Gortchakoff's note, which we have ignored in the conference—

" I have endeavoured in conjunction with my allies, to uphold the sanctity of Treaties, and to remove any misapprehension as to the binding character of their obligations."

I would omit reference to Prussia as the author of the Conference, on account of France to whom I have always said that it was not a Prussian Proposal, but a counter proposal to which we had agreed, and I should go on with the sitting of the conference, and the hoped for results of its deliberations.

7.

query substitute.

I greatly regret that my earnest efforts have failed to procure the presence at the conference of any representative of France one of the principal parties to the Treaty of 1856, and upon whose concurrence I rely to facilitate by a treaty the conclusions to which the Conference may arrive (or has arrived).

8.

Will require remodelling consequent upon Thornton's telegram.

9.

I think I should leave out the first eight lines and a half of the 2d page.

(to announce the joint commission to determine how to settle Anglo-American differences), 9, 9a (incorporating also a pencil suggestion by Gladstone) and 9b (dispelling anxiety caused by the Tientsin massacre).

9A.

query

The establishment of a Prince of the House of Savoy on the throne of Spain by the election of the Spanish Nation, will I trust ensure for a country which has so many claims on the goodwill of Great Britain, the blessings of a free and stable Gov.

9B.

Anything about China.

460. Lord Granville to Mr. Gladstone. [Add. MS. 44168, fo. 55]

16, Bruton Street. Sunday. [5 February 1871].

Geo Grey has refused.[1] I have asked Halifax. I presume you would not object to old Tom Baring if he would go with either Halifax or de Grey. Would Graves of Liverpool be a possible Tory makeweight.

461. Mr. Gladstone to Lord Granville. [G.D. 29/29A]

11, Carlton House Terrace. Feb. 5. 71.

I am not surprised about G. Grey.

Tom Baring, though a man of talents as unquestionable as his high character, is erratic to a degree. No man has so uniformly continued to be on the wrong side in that class of Parliamentary questions in which he has commonly taken the greatest interest. On Graves's judgment I should place no reliance. Horsfall, the retired member for Liverpool would be a better man. So would Sandon. So would Adderly though not wholly critical. So would Algernon Egerton, indeed I should think him decidedly good. Ld Overstone speaks very highly of Loyd Lindsay. *Mowbray* (Rt Hon) might also do. Sclater Booth I mentioned. Glyn will be able to tell you more.

If you are in want on our side I would mention F. Peel as well as Gibson for consideration.

462. Lord Granville to Mr. Gladstone. [Add. MS. 44168, fo. 57]

16, Bruton Street. Feb 7/71.

You will read the telegram from Elliot [2] saying the Turks refuse our article.

Which is the best of three courses.

1° to get the Turks to propose the Italian version which I enclose.[3]

2° to get them to propose to remain as they are.

or 3° To say that in this difference of opinion, we will wait for a French Colleague.

[1] Appointment to the joint Anglo-American commission, Halifax to Granville, 4 Feb., G.D. 29/64. Its membership (Lord de Grey, Sir John Macdonald, Sir Stafford Northcote, Montague Bernard, Thornton) and its instructions were approved by the cabinet, 6 Feb., Add. MS. 44639, fo. 10.

[2] Tel. 4.25 p.m., 6 Feb., received 7 Feb., F.O. 78/2173.

[3] See mem. by Cadorna, 6 Feb., secret, G.D. 29/96. The article on the Straits, adopted 13 March, broadly followed it. Cf. Gladstone's note on the cabinet, 11 Feb., Add. MS. 44639, fo. 11.

463. Mr. Gladstone to Lord Granville. [G.D. 29/59]

Immed. 11, Carlton House Terrace. Feb. 8. 71.

It seems to be coming rather clearly into view that there is a great change in the attitude & mind of the Turk relatively to us: in short that there is much truth in the communication from Pesth in the Times of the 6th [1] to which I called your attention.

Under these circs. I suppose what we have to do is to be very quiet & not affronted.

Of your three plans (I know no others) I would readily [?] favour the Italian version. It is the best towards the public as it shows a seeming equivalent—the best with reference to traditional policy as it really touches the non-riverain element, though without the word: & perhaps the best as coming from Italy, so that we are impartial about it.

464. Lord Granville to Mr. Gladstone.[2] [Add. MS. 44168, fo. 59]

16, Bruton Street. Feb 8/71.

Tissot only told me yesterday at 6-30 of an answer from Favre. I immediately sent the orders to the Admiralty.

I telegraphed to Odo about the Stores at Amiens.

465. Mr. Gladstone to Lord Granville. [G.D. 29/59]

11, Carlton House Terrace. Feb. 9.71.

1. At Windsor yesterday the Queen, strong for neutrality in general terms, started as a subject for possible consideration whether the Powers of Europe jointly might not hereafter find it their duty to give their judgment jointly on the war or the terms of peace.

2. Brunnow was here last night: expressed himself strongly against abstraction of territory, and also said rather decidedly he considered his Government by no means disposed to silence on the terms of peace if extravagant or menacing to Europe.

466. Lord Granville to Mr. Gladstone. [Add. MS. 44168, fo. 61]

16, Bruton Street. Feb 10/71.

Your speech [3] seems to me excellent.

In the Lords there was nothing but a feather bed to hit at.

Rosebery as good as possible.[4]

[1] *The Times*, 6 Feb., p. 12, on Turkey's resolution to free herself from European tutelage.

[2] Mem. of members of the Foreign Office and diplomatic service recommended for C.B. with mem. of policy in conferring the honour, 8 Feb., G.D. 29/59, not printed.

[3] 9 Feb., replying to Disraeli's attack on the government's foreign policy in the debate on the Address, *Hans. Parl. Deb.* 3rd ser. cciv. 96–114.

[4] In seconding the Address in the Lords, where Richmond was the only opposition speaker, *Hans. Parl. Deb. loc. cit.* 22–50.

467. Mr. Gladstone to Lord Granville. [G.D. 29/59]

Windsor. Feb. 12.71.

Lyons's longer letter of the 7th [1] is important on account of the expectation he expresses that the Assembly will appeal to the Neutrals, but more immediately because of his suggestion as to a prompt recognition of whatever Government the Assembly may choose. In this I should think we could hardly be too rapid: & if formal instruments are required would it not be well to have the preparations made as far as it can be done in our present state of ignorance as to particulars?

468. Lord Granville to Mr. Gladstone. [Add. MS. 44168, fo. 62]

F. O. Feb 13/71.

I asked Northcote.[2] His eyes twinkled through his spectacles. But he said he must ask his wife, and requested permission to consult Dizzy.

The former unlike Lady Grey & Lady Halifax consented—Ditto Dizzy—which looks well.

I have telegraphed to Thornton.

469. Mr. Gladstone to Lord Granville. [G.D. 29/59]

11, Carlton House Terrace. Feb. 14.71.

1. Otway has been here for explanations on my Speech of Thursday about the offers of other Powers to cooperate with us.[3] He went on to complain of you respecting 1. C.B.—on which I offered divers explanations—and 2. Versailles: but nothing new came out on his side.

2. With reference to Odo Russell's letter; [4] do you not think we should endeavour to investigate strictly the history of the Tower-marked Rifles? It is so important to separate in these matters clearly between real & unreal causes of complaint.

3. For the same reason, & not from any natural tendency to be over-civil, which is not my besetting sin, I am still disposed to write a note to Bernstorff about my passage on Bombardment.

4. Manning has left with me the inclosed statement [5] relating to the Propaganda and hopes we will intercede for it as far as we may.

a. as a working institution of the Church even if technically a *corpo morale.*

b. as an engine of literature, printing in all languages.

[1] See G.D. 29/85, and Newton, *Lord Lyons*, i. 361–3. Granville wrote on the back of no. 467: 'Prepare accordingly G.', and Hervey: 'Done'.

[2] See above, no. 460 note.

[3] In the debate on the Address, 9 Feb., Gladstone stated that 'no one Power in Europe' would have supported Britain in maintaining the neutralization of the Black Sea, which Otway had advocated to the point of war, *Hans. Parl. Deb. loc. cit.* 105.

[4] Untraced. Granville answered German allegations that British rifles had been found on French prisoners, in a dispatch to Loftus, 11 Jan., sent to Russell with instructions to communicate it to Bismarck, and give it publicity, No. 97, 17 Feb., F.O. 64/739.

[5] 1 Feb., follows no. 469 in G.D. 29/59.

c. as an institution teaching 100 pupils, one half of whom are of the English tongue. He says these youths make their best & most cultivated Ecclesiastics.

5. He also hopes you will intercede for the English College, again threatened. This he holds is a purely English institution, administered by or under himself & the other R.C. Bishops, though of course subject to the supreme jurisdiction of the Pope. I told him I would report to you on these two subjects.

470. Mr. Gladstone to Lord Granville. [G.D. 29/59]

11, Carlton House Terrace. Feb. 15.71.

On your debate last night [1] (in which I am so sorry you should have been troubled unfairly on my account), so far as I have read it, & on the speeches of the 9th, to which I have referred in the Times, I wish—though it is a day after the fair, to say as follows:

1. About Lord Clarendon I reported what you had told me—and this was the only passage in which I referred (though I am not satisfied in point of clearness with the report of the Times) to the *importance* of the neutralisation.

2. In citing my own declaration I named it as a personal difficulty not as a rule for the Government of this country.

3. In referring to neutralisation otherwise, I confined myself strictly to two points: that its importance was not exclusive, and that its character was that of a provision in its own nature almost of necessity temporary.

4. Disraeli attacked us for appointing the Conference, and for entertaining at all the question whether the Treaty should be modified. The whole course was wrong: we ought to have stood, he said, upon the neutralisation & told Russia she must take the consequences. We had fairly raised the question in the Speech by expressing an expectation that the Treaty would be modified: and I do not see how under such circumstances it was possible for me to remain silent. I told nothing, beyond what the Speech told.

In this sense I shall defend myself if the subject is raised in the House of Commons.

You said we should have refused to open the question: we did open it, & this was all I stated.

471. Lord Granville to Mr. Gladstone. [Add. MS. 44639, fo. 14]

[15 February 1871].

I hope you will meet Cairns and Salisbury [2] rather by a sneer at the attack behind your back & in your absence, rather [*sic*] than by any grave complaint of the Lords. It is very small hunting for passages in speeches made some time before,

[1] See observations by Cairns on Gladstone's statement in the Commons of 9 Feb., *Hans. Parl. Deb.* 3rd ser. cciv. 239 ff. He disputed Gladstone's assertion that Clarendon 'never attached value to the neutralization', and depreciated Gladstone's declaration of 1856 that neutralization could not be maintained.

[2] For Granville's reply to Cairns and Salisbury see *Hans. Parl. Deb. loc. cit.* 245–8.

but I am not clear that it is not legitimate referring to the statements made by the Prime Minister.

1. I thought I had told you subsequently that Cowley, & Villiers Lister did not agree—as to Clarendon's having changed his views.

2. I see no objection.

3. I assumed this in my reply.

4. Do. as to Dizzy. I agree with you about the Speech—which I forgot yesterday evening. I hesitated about saying that the acceptance of the Conference, implied revision as it clashed with "no foregone conclusion" and I refrained from uttering what came to my lips, that you knew we had arrived at revision in the Conference—because although we agreed to do so, it was on condition that we found a fitting equivalent, and we are still discussing what that equivalent should be.

472. Mr. Gladstone to Lord Granville. [G.D. 29/59]

11, Carlton House Terrace. Feb. 18.71.

I presume that when the French Comm[issione]r comes to the Conference if he tries to bring the question of the War before it he will be stopped, but that *most probably* either through him or through some other medium an appeal may be made to the Neutrals, of which the burden & stress will come chiefly upon us, to make an attempt to mitigate the German terms, and this at *extremely short notice.*

Bismarck has tied up the armistice so closely evidently (I conceive) with a view to frustrate such an appeal by time.

It would be an evil & a great scandal that it should be *so* frustrated, and worst of all if it were to fail because no preparation had been made for promptitude in the joint consideration of it.

Is not the time now come when you should lay the ground for quick dealing with the case in whatever sense especially with Brunnow since on the cooperation with Russia depends the possibility of being useful in the case should it arrive?[1]

473. Lord Granville to Mr. Gladstone. [Add. MS. 44168, fo. 70]

11, Carlton House Terrace. Sunday 5. P.M. [19 February 1871].

It was twelve before we got away from M[arlboroug]h House. I went very early this morning to see Brunnow.[2] He asked me the meaning in several ways of my letter.

I told him that it was not intended as a menace to Germany, that it did not go beyond what it said, the object was to save time, and that it was not intended that the matter should be brought before the Black Sea Conference.

I told him also what we meant by the necessity of it's being confidential.

[1] The problem was discussed for two hours in the cabinet, 18 Feb., and a letter to Brunnow framed, asking him to inquire whether Britain and Russia could examine a French appeal to the neutrals in common, Add. MS. 44639, fo. 16, G.D. 29/115, and Brunnow to Granville, 18 Feb., G.D. 29/98.

[2] See short mem. by Granville of this conversation, G.D. 29/115.

He said as regarded the last, he could not answer for it, that Gortchakoff was not the most discreet of men, that as for the Emperor he was completely under the charm of the King of Prussia, that Prince Reuss had a position now at Petersburg which no Ambassador had ever had before—that he had heard most curious details from Wittgenstein the Russian Attaché at Versailles, who had lately been at Petersburgh. He argued against the use of any joint action excepting military, for which he presumed Russia & England as they were both reorganizing their armies, were not prepared. He objected to the want of time, the unpopularity of negotiating on contingencies by telegraph etc etc.

I asked him at last to do one of two things. I had written an official though confidential letter to him, not as a mere fancy of mine own, but on the full deliberation of the Cabinet. I must have an answer, particularly as I was not sure whether Buchanan was in Petersburgh. He asked whether it was certain that my communication would never be known. He presumed not. He understood the exigencies of our situation, and that it would help us to have a refusal from Gortchakoff, but that I might take his word that Gortchakoff's answer would not help us in any way.

I said that he was mistaken in thinking we only asked in order to get a refusal—that we attached much more importance than he did to joint expressions of opinion—but I insisted upon his telegraphing or taking upon himself the responsibility of explaining the views of his Gov. He then said he would write me a letter, but he should like me to see it, before he sent it.

The letter [1] is longer than necessary, argues against doing anything, and describes the Policy of his Gov as that stated by Gortchakoff to Buchanan in the original despatch.[2]

After reading it, he said he was ready to telegraph to the Emperor, if I desired it—I asked whether I rightly understood that he thought such a communication would not be considered confidential, and that it would certainly have no success. He answered positively in the affirmative—upon which I said I saw no use in his doing so.

If however you think I am wrong, let me know, & I will ask him to do so. I will send you his letter anon.

474. Mr. Gladstone to Lord Granville. [G.D. 29/59]

11, Carlton House Terrace. Feb. 20.71.

The only thing which on reading the letters herewith now seems to me to remain for consideration [is] whether you should silently take Brunnow's wriggling letter as a reply in the negative, or whether you should tell him that you take it as such on the part of his Government through him.

I am afraid of his turning to account hereafter his appeal to you whether he should Telegraph or not, & saying the appeal was withdrawn.

[1] Brunnow to Granville, confidentielle, 19 février, G.D. 29/98.

[2] At the time of the *démarche* of Oct. 1870, see above no. 341, and Buchanan to Granville, 17, 18, 23 Oct. 1870, F.O. 65/804.

It seems to me it would be wise to 'establish' in black & white the effect of his letter: and *also* the circumstance indicated in your written recital of the conversation of yesterday, & mentioned by you to me explicitly, viz. that you might have to make known the step you had taken on the part of the Cabinet, & the reply.[1]

There is *curious* matter in the correspondence of the Daily Telegraph from Versailles today.

475. Mr. Gladstone to Lord Granville. [G.D. 29/59]

11, Carlton House Terrace. Feb. 20.71.

I think that *a propos* of the Commission in America, *this* is the time when we should supply them, through de Grey or Thornton, with the means of smoothing over any difficulties which may arise between us and *Canada* in the course of the negotiations by some undertaking on account of the expences of the Fenian Raid?[2]

Lowe did not like this, and if you concur in my idea it would be right to speak to him; but when it was partially discussed in the Cabinet I thought the *general* feeling was decidedly favourable. In money questions I am most commonly against the Colony: but the claim seems to me equitable, & my only fear was lest by a *premature* concession, i.e. one while matters were still unsettled with America, we should give these vagabonds positive inducement to repeat their marauding expeditions.

476. Mr. Gladstone to Lord Granville. [G.D. 29/59]

Entirely secret. 4.30 Pm Feb. 22.71.

Information has been given to me by a person very confident of being right that the terms of Peace have been agreed on—that they are what are called the Nevers terms.

Indemnity 120 millions. Metz *not* to be given up.

477. Mr. Gladstone to Lord Granville. [G.D. 29/59]

11, Carlton House Terrace. Feb. 24.71.

It will be right that I should answer Hoare's question,[3] as you suggest. But it occurs to me that I had better know, or not know, according as *you may advise* me at any time before the H of C. meets.

[1] For opinions of members of the cabinet on further action after Brunnow's letter of 19 Feb., see Add. MS. 44639, fo. 17. For record of the negotiation which was dropped, see Granville to Rumbold, No. 39 confidential, 22 Feb., F.O. 65/819.

[2] Cf. Granville to Kimberley, 20 Feb., asking him to propose to Canada a money compensation for damage caused by the Fenian raid from America, and reply, 21 Feb., and mem. by Kimberley, 22 Feb., G.D. 29/55. Cf. Lowe to Granville, commenting unfavourably, 1 March, G.D. 29/66.

[3] Whether the *Daily Telegraph* report of congratulations to the Crown Prince from the Queen, the Prince of Wales and the Duke of Cambridge on the German victories was correct. Gladstone's reply, 24 Feb., regretted the raising of questions personal to the royal family and denied that British neutrality had been compromised, *Hans. Parl. Deb.* 3rd ser. cciv. 866–8.

But, if I am not to know, I shall say I have abstained from inquiring, but that I can state my own full conviction that if congratulations were sent they were of a personal description, and not such as in any respect to compromise the character of neutrals.

It is plain that, within certain limits, Thiers or Jules Favre might felicitate the Prussians.

I return your skeleton hoping to get it back.

478. Mr. Gladstone to Lord Granville. [G.D. 29/59]

11, Carlton House Terrace. March 3.71.

Please to look at these papers together and consider whether Odo Russell's dispatch of Feb. 27 [1] should be presented, and whether any thing further should be said in connection with it, and what.

When I answered Sir John Hay's question,[2] I was not aware that the language of the dispatch, on which it was founded, differed from, and was much within, the language of the private letter to you [3] which I had in my mind.

I am sorry the passage was published, but the business of editing at the Foreign Office is of fearful difficulty, and I often think with wonder how well it is performed.

The case I take to be one of those, where the Envoy was perfectly justified in the language he used (as reported in the dispatch), but where we should have been highly to blame in instructing him to use it.

Hay's question was evidently put to implicate us in the statement.

Should I present the dispatch today as his own full explanation of the matter, repeat that I had already stated the Government did not think him open to the slightest blame in using these arguments of his own, & say that he was perfectly justified in using them as their employment by him was not open to the observations that might have been made upon them if directed by us.

He was also quite right in saying (Feb. 27) that he had not been instructed not to use them.

479. Mr. Gladstone to Lord Granville. [G.D. 29/59]

Private. 11 C. H. T. March 3.71.

The Queen seems not to like Lord Dufferin's explanations respecting the Duchy, I presume as reported. Was there any thing imprudent or exceptionable in them ?

[1] No. 64, 27 Feb., explaining his statement to Bismarck (reported in No. 5, 22 Nov. 1870, F.O. 64/737) that the Black Sea question was ' of a nature in its present state to compel us, with or without allies to go to war with Russia ', F.O. 64/739 ; Parl. papers. [C. 265] (1871). lxxii, 117, laid 7 March. Cf. Russell to Gladstone, 27 Feb., Add. MS. 44429, fo. 279. Gladstone to Russell, 25 Feb., 4 and 29 March, Add. MS. 44539, fos. 164, 170, 185.

[2] 16 Feb., whether Russell's statement was authorized, *Hans. Parl. Deb.* 3rd ser. cciv. 318–19.

[3] 30 Nov., missing from G.D. 29/92, extract in Add. MS. 44428, fo. 245 ; see above, no. 389.

480. Lord Granville to Mr. Gladstone. [Add. MS. 44168, fo. 79]

16, Bruton Street. March 7/71.

I telegraphed as you suggested to de Grey today.[1]

Halifax & Forster would like me to telegraph to him not to close about the fisheries, till he has made way with the Alabama.[2]

I have some doubts about perpetually bombarding the Commission with telegraphic instructions unless in reply to their questions.

I told Hammond that you would like my despatch to Buchanan [3] to be added unless he saw objections to it. As he was strongly against producing it unless upon a little pressure, and I was of the same opinion, I have authorized him to leave it out. The despatch to Broglie, and the one to Loftus tell the story pretty well.

I hear people are satisfied about Goschen.[4]

481. Mr. Gladstone to Lord Granville. [G.D. 29/59]

11 C.H.T. Mch 7.71.

I agree in the general rule you lay down about Telegrams but in the particular case I think Halifax and Forster are right in their suggestion if as I understood from Forster it is not only that the Comm[issio]n should not close upon the Fisheries before they discuss the Alabama but further that they should confine themselves as much as possible to general or hypothetical modes of proceeding so as to remain quite uncommitted.

Though I regret that your correspondence with Buchanan should not at once appear, I appreciate your reason for desiring not to volunteer it.

I would propose Thursday at two for a conversation on the Military Estimates.

482. Mr. Gladstone to Lord Granville. [G.D. 29/59]

10, Downing Street. Mch 9.71.

I would again suggest that we are so far as I know, wholly unsupplied with *facts* to warrant that idea respecting the internal condition of the Principalities, on the strength of which their ruler has been plotting against their liberties, & the Porte, in another way, seems to desire and meditate the overthrow of the existing arrangements. Could we not call for information ?

[1] In reply to de Grey, tel. 6 March, on Canadian wish to settle their fishery dispute with America for a term of years only. Granville advised a permanent arrangement but gave de Grey discretion, tel., F.O. 5/1300.

[2] See Granville to de Grey, tel., 8 Mar., F.O. 5/1300.

[3] Granville to Rumbold (Buchanan on leave), No. 39 confidential, 22 Feb., F.O. 65/819, not published. Granville to Loftus, 24 Feb., and Favre to Broglie enclosed in Granville to Lyons, 25 Feb., in Parl. papers. [C. 266] (1871). lxxi, 321–6; see above, no. 474.

[4] Appointed first lord of the Admiralty *vice* Childers.

483. Mr. Gladstone to Lord Granville. [G.D. 29/59]

10, Downing Street. Mch 9. 1871.

Some days ago Baron N. de Rothschild asked me my opinion about the Conference. I said that I considered the relations between you & Russia to have been satisfactory during the whole of the proceedings—that the state of the various questions in the Conference was such as not to suggest any shadow of fear as to the final issue—but that France had not yet taken its place, and that as a doctor says of a dying man while there is life there is hope, just *so*, it might be said of the Conference while it is still sitting there is fear.

Baron N. de R. asked me the question with a view to the financial operations then pending & since matured.

Today Baron Lionel is here and desires to know how far this is the view of the Government, & may be quoted as such. On these points I refer the Baron to you.

484. Minute by Lord Granville. [G.D. 29/59]

[9 March 1871].

Lord G[ranville] referred B[aro]n R[othschild] to the Statement he had made in the House of Lords on the first night of the session. He stated that the conference had pledged themselves to secrecy till the end of their sittings—that he could give no further information excepting that the French Ambassador had got his full power as plenipotentiary, and the Conference would meet again on Monday next.[1]

485. Mr. Gladstone to Lord Granville. [G.D. 29/59]

11, Carlton House Terrace. Mch 10.71.

I own it appears to me that the time has come, upon the receipt of these most unsatisfactory papers from Musurus, for admonishing the Porte as to its language and attitude with respect to the Principalities.[2]

Plans of forcible intervention, and the destruction of liberties obtained by the expenditure of Western blood and treasure, and established by the consent of Europe, are rashly put forward without the slightest attempt to prove the existence of the state of things which alone could justify their even being whispered.

Nothing has been proved against Roumania except the calamity of having an unfit and seemingly unprincipled man for its ruler. I do not take into account the treatment of the Jews: it is too exceptional, too easily accounted for by their position as money-lenders, too like what prevails elsewhere in the East, and what prevailed in England in the 18th Century.

[1] 3 March, for its fifth and penultimate session, having been adjourned from 7 Feb. France was for the first time represented. No. 484 is a minute of a verbal answer to Rothschild's question relating to a Russian loan.

[2] See Granville to Elliot, Nos. 65 and 70, 13 March, both altered by Gladstone, reminding Turkey that she could not occupy the Principalities without the consent of the guaranteeing powers, F.O. 78/2171.

Is the community of Roumania under terrorism like that of Westmeath? What have been the cases of revolt or organised resistance to public authority? Are the population quitting the country on account of the alleged anarchy? Are the finances in the dangerous confusion of those of Turkey? Do shipping & trade increase or decrease? Is Sir C. Trevelyan [1] right who notices the progress of agriculture in Roumania and contrasts it with stagnation in Bulgaria?

If a case is not made good against Roumania, it seems to me the Turks are committing a gross offence in this matter.

486. Lord Granville to Mr. Gladstone. [Add. MS. 44168, fo. 81]

[11 March 1871].

Roden told me that Goschen's appointment had given great satisfaction in his part of the House, & that Goschen was universally acknowledged to be a much stronger man than Stansfield.

On the other hand Countess Frank [2] says people are obliged to stop in the streets to laugh, the appointment is so ridiculous.

487. Lord Granville to Mr. Gladstone. [Add. MS. 44168, fo. 82]

16, Bruton Street. March 13/71.

Labouchere took the title of Taunton because he had sat for it.

Copley took that of Lyndhurst, because the name was pretty.

Poulett Thompson [*sic*] asked for St Lawrence, but was answered by Lord Melbourne "St Lawrence one of the largest rivers of North America I believe, Scipio Africanus—I don't think Pow we have done quite enough for that, eh?"

The Queen's pleasure would have to be taken I suppose about Sandhurst. I do not think there is sufficient ground for you to object, but it is a question whether you should not suggest that as a rule it is better to avoid taking a title to which many others think they have a claim.

488. Mr. Gladstone to Lord Granville. [G.D. 29/59]

10, Downing Street. Mch 17.71.

We cannot change the hour of the Cabinet [3] on account of H of C. proceedings today & perhaps tomorrow: but we may get rid of other matter before then, especially should there be a general concurrence.

The inclosed note from the Chancellor [4] relates to one which I wrote to him last

[1] See above, no. 436.

[2] Lady Waldegrave.

[3] Met at 2 p.m., Friday, 17 March, Add. MS. 44639, fo. 39. The Commons adjourned at 3.15 a.m., 17 March, but resuming the same day, concluded the second reading of the Army Regulation Bill soon after midnight, *C.J.* (1871), 91, 93.

[4] Hatherley to Gladstone, 17 March, suggesting that de Grey agree to the articles, as binding on the future but not on the past, Add. MS. 44205, fo. 175; see below, p. 228 note 1.

night after hearing the general result of your labours in 'redaction'. In debate, I should find the utmost difficulty in defending a simple *ex post facto* law. But I do not object at all [to] the words now proposed by the Chancellor.

This method of proceeding would I think considerably reconcile Lowe, who (reserving his objections to the Commission) approved of my note to the C[hancellor].[1]

489. Mr. Gladstone to Lord Granville. [G.D. 29/59]

11, Carlton House Terrace. Mch 22.1871.

Your box does not contain our answer.

I like Collier's suggestion [2] to deal with non-admittance rather than detention. At least I should not like to dismiss it without further con[sideratio]n—wh we might be able to give it at the Levee at 2 Pm.

490. Mr. Gladstone to Lord Granville. [G.D. 29/59]

11, Carlton House Terrace. Mch 24.71.

1. I should like to know the places where "the inhabitants pulled down the hated flag & put up the Pope's arms again".

2. Should not inquiry be made about the demonstration by a crowd under the Pope's windows.

3. I should much like to get all possible information about the Roman Plebiscite. The question may come to be of much practical importance.[3]

491. Mr. Gladstone to Lord Granville. [Add. MS. 44539, fo. 182]

[*Copy*]. 25 Mch. 71.

Looking cursorily over the letter from Sir G. Bowyer I should think it the kind of document which would form a *very* advantageous text for the Italian Govt to comment upon,[4] so as to confute his reckless allegations. I have merely told him I should not fail to bring the matter under yr notice.

[1] In the joint commission on Anglo-American differences, America insisted on laying down rules for the conduct of neutrals as a guide to the arbitrators on the Alabama claims. De Grey urged Granville to accept the version of 13 March as the best alternative to 'unrestricted arbitration'. The cabinets of 16 and 17 March made counter-proposals. Agreement was reached except on the fourth article after much private negotiation, 24 March. Granville accepted 3 draft articles, 31 March. The 4th article was dropped and the 1st article modified in America's favour, 4 April. See telegraphic correspondence to de Grey, F.O. 5/1299, from de Grey, F.O. 5/1300 and 1301 and G.D. 29/63. Cf. two notes by Granville possibly written during the cabinet, 16 March, Add. MS. 44639, fos. 37, 38.

[2] For wording of the fourth article.

[3] No. 490 comments on Lord Denbigh to Gladstone (with enclosure).

[4] Cf. Granville to Paget, No. 70, 26 March, asking, with reference to Bowyer's letter, whether Jervoise's reports from Rome had been communicated to the Italian government, F.O. 45/178.

492. Mr. Gladstone to Lord Granville.[1] [G.D. 29/59]

11, Carlton House Terrace. Mch 30.71.

1. I see no reason why if the negotiations succeed Macdonald should not be made a Privy Councillor.

2. The Chancellor may not get all these letters in circulation, but I am very desirous he should soon see the letter of M. Bernard.[2] In pages 3–6 it goes upon ground on which we conversed together yesterday. It seems to me that whatever concession we make beyond the words of our last Telegram ought not to be a simple addition to those words, but should be done by way of opening the construction of them. The form I am not well qualified to suggest but the following words would convey my meaning and would shut out the contention which prevailed (I believe) in the Alexandra case.

" It is understood that the word equipped is not absolutely and in all cases limited to the supply of things movable, and separate from the fabric of the vessel."

I can hardly see what legitimate object the Americans can have, from their own point of view, which would not be attained by words like these.

493. Memorandum by Lord Granville.[3] [Add. MS. 44168, fo. 84]

[30 March 1871].

Prussia

Has in my opinion acted fairly in this matter. Whether in her own interest or not, she has promoted a peaceful instead of a warlike solution of this problem.

She has never concealed her opinion (shared at different times as it appears by France, Austria & Italy) that it would be well to revise the stipulations as to the neutralization of the Black Sea.

Her regret and surprise at Prince Gortchakoff's [circular] was genuine, and she cooperated with us in obtaining a complete and satisfactory renunciation of the principles involved in it—& she equally cooperated with us in obtaining a due equivalent, and in the arrangements respecting the Danube. There is no reason to suppose that she is bound in any way to support ambitious designs of Russia against Turkey.

Alternatives to Conference

1 Complete acquiescence

2 Declaration of an offensive war deprecated by Turkey against a nation which

[1] Note by Gladstone : ' I incline to think the C[rown] Prince & Princess would be well received Mch 28.71 ', G.D. 29/59, not printed.

[2] To Granville, private, Washington, 16 March, received 30 March, relating to the rules on the conduct of neutrals, G.D. 29/71.

[3] Of material for an answer by Gladstone to Dilke. His motion deploring the British acceptance of a conference on the Black Sea question was debated, 30 March, as a vote of censure. The debate ended in anti-climax and Gladstone did not speak ; see *Hans. Parl. Deb.* 3rd ser. ccv. 894 ff. ; the Speaker to Granville, 31 March, G.D. 29/75 ; S. Gwynn and G. M. Tuckwell, *The Life of the Rt. Hon. Sir Charles W. Dilke* (1917), i. 121.

like ourselves has peculiar advantages for defence—a war which could only have been undertaken by finding money and arms for Turkey, and for an object for which in all probability no country would have joined us excepting France, who has had another object in view. (Nearly all the cosignatories of the Treaty of 1856 having said something in favor of revision[)].

3. The grand comprehensive scheme suggested to Lord Granville, of demanding from a victorious nation of 40,000,000 men (Germany) a categorical answer whether they were on our side or on that of Russia, and if the reply was not perfectly satisfactory, an offensive alliance with France, Austria, Italy and Turkey, which would with little risk of war check Russia in the East, and Germany in the West. See Despatches Nos describing what the Austrian Plenipotentiaries, and what the Italian Plenipotentiary said with regard to peace or war on the Black Sea question.

4. To wait—to say nothing has been done whatever may have been said—act if you dare and at your peril—this plan to which it might have been necessary to resort, would however have given an immediate triumph to Russia, and the power to her to act sooner or later as circumstances might dictate, in the mean time keeping England in suspense, destroying our commercial relations, and trying every joint in the complicated machine of the Turkish Empire.

Protocols of Conference

Give only a faint idea of the difficulties of the negotiation. It is not usual to produce the correspondence of a negotiation which is successful. Otherwise a mass of papers would show how difficult it was to come to an exact agreement upon the most important points. There were thirteen or fourteen versions of the protocol ad hoc before one was agreed to. (Lord G declined until that was signed to enter into any pourparlers with the Russian Ambassador on the subject of the Treaty—immediately afterwards he considered himself at liberty to treat in the same friendly way as with the other Plenipos[)].

There was however great difficulty in agreeing upon a proper equivalent to the concessions which were made.

Advantages to Turkey of present arrangement—a great cause of irritation removed. It is doubtful whether it would be in the interest of Russia to act much upon the permission now given. She would have to go to a great expence, before she would have a fleet (of no general use) equal to that of Turkey—& the latter has the advantage of being able to buy ships in all parts of the world, whereas Russia would only have her own yards in the Black Sea from which she could procure. It would be impossible for Russia to equal the allied force which Turkey might now bring against her in case of need. (See arguments in the Moscow Gazette.)

The prolongation of the Danube commission and arrangements for further improvements of the Danube, which have up to this time been opposed by Russia, a great boon for the Commerce of the world.

General conciliatory effects of the recent arrangement. If no just rights have been unnecessarily sacrificed, it is a positive advantage that Russia should be pleased with the removal of restrictions which appeared galling to its pride.

Charge of garbling papers

None of the Turkish & Austrian correspondence was omitted from the blue book, excepting *after communication with our Ambassadors* at Vienna & Constantinople, and *after the expressed opinion* of the Austrian & Turkish Ambassadors here in favor of the omission.

Otway

Soon after my appointment offered in a manner which appeared to me to be very honorable & considerate, to resign if I had not confidence in him. The post was an impediment to his political career, and an immediate separation from me could not be misconstrued.

I reminded him that although long acquainted, I knew him little, that Lord Clarendon had told me that he had been obliged to make a suggestion to him (not to be huffy and jealous of people in the office), but that I had found him up to that time very courteous & considerate to me—& the subject dropped.

It would be better to make no allusion to this, unless Otway was very pert & offensive.

But the day after the acceptance of the Conference had been approved by the Cabinet to my great surprise Otway resigned, on the sole ground as he assured me of that step, which he could not with sincerity defend in the Commons. He then broached the grand scheme, (which had previously been advocated in the Pall Mall, and which I have described as the 3d alternative).

494. Mr. Gladstone to Lord Granville. [Add. MS. 44539, fo. 186]

[*Copy*]. 31 March 71.

Please to look at these in the order in which they stand—& give yr opinion. I showed them to Forster last night in H of C & I think he approves the suggestion I have made in my letter to Northcote.[1] The operations of Dilke lost the country an evening but afforded a signal triumph to you & the Govt. I do not concur in the praise of the Dilke oration beyond the fluency clearness & order which he always shows, for he knows his own mind such as it is.

495. Mr. Gladstone to Lord Granville. [G.D. 29/59]

Ap [1871].

It seems to me that this dispatch[2] does not touch the point. It is not *possible* Count Bray should suppose that a limit is placed upon our liberty of action more than on his own. To reserve liberty of action is a form of speech having no small

[1] Gladstone to Northcote, 30 March, Add. MS. 44539, fo. 189; cf. Forster to Granville [30 March], G.D. 29/56.

[2] Howard (Munich) to Granville, No. 91, 25 March, answering Gladstone's complaint of his statement to Count Bray that Britain would dislike a European conference on the Roman question, F.O. 9/208. See min. by Gladstone, 22 March, on Howard, No. 83, confidential, 17 March, *ibid.*, and to Howard, tel. 4 p.m., 25 March, F.O. 9/207.

significance. Sir H. H[oward] shd withdraw altogether the personal opinion wh he (very incautiously) expressed & leave the field entirely open?

496. Lord Granville to Mr. Gladstone. [G.D. 29/59]

Copy. Private. W[almer] C[astle]. Ap. 4/71 2 p m.

I telegraphed this morning for the chance of your wishing to see me about the fisheries & the Principalities.

I have asked Rogers if Kimberley is absent to report on the previous question. Macdonald seems to have more to say for himself than his brother Comm[issione]rs admit, but he asks more than he has a right to expect.[1]

I see there is a telegram from the Principalities [2] announcing a revolution.

Odo [3] says that Bismarck always expected that Russia & Austria would divide the Principalities between them.

Russia is encouraging the Porte to interfere, which has always been her policy in order to make her unpopular but as the Turks desire to do so they are not unlikely to disregard our advice to the contrary and some awkward complications may arise.

If I do not get an answer from you in 20 minutes I cannot go to town today, which I shall bear with fortitude.

497. Mr. Gladstone to Lord Granville. [G.D. 29/59]

11, Carlton House Terrace. Ap 4.71.

1. I had not heard any thing about the Principalities nor had Hammond and I was unable to answer your Telegram until it was too late.

However I think our course is quite clear: to discountenance all intrigue and maintain the existing rights. Also to urge, almost insist, that there shall be no armed interference except in case of irremediable disorders, and to let it be known at Bucharest what will follow if they do not keep the peace. We have in truth, I think, a simply Conservative policy to follow.

2. Soon after your Telegram came the important one from de Grey [4] which led me to gather rapidly in Hammond's room all the available members of the Cabinet, nine in number. We were all of one mind to agree as Hammond under our directions has telegraphed to you.[5]

[1] Cf. de Grey to Granville, No. 53, 28 March, on fisheries agreement reached by the joint commission that day, with mem., 27 March, of Macdonald's objections. The telegram, 28 March, giving the substance, has minutes by Gladstone, 3 April, and Kimberley, 4 April, F.O. 5/1301.

[2] Relates to the riot, 22 March, provoked by a banquet at the German consulate in honour of the Emperor's birthday; see Green to Granville, tels., 23 March received 24 March, 24 March received 25 March, No. 25, 23 March received 3 April, F.O. 78/2183.

[3] Lord Odo Russell had resumed work in the Foreign Office.

[4] 3 April, received 4 April, on America's readiness to drop the fourth article (fixing liability for depredations upon the neutral which failed to detain a vessel joining in hostilities) in return for a modification of the first article, F.O. 5/1301.

[5] 4 April, proposing acceptance of the American offer and asking for Granville's assent, G.D. 29/104 and F.O. 5/1299. The draft of Granville's telegraphic assent is in G.D. 29/59.

3. We were also of one mind to hold a little with Macdonald about the Fisheries.

4. I think it impossible not to see that our excellent Commissioners, or the leaders among them, have an unconscious bias towards settling everything si possint, recte; si non, quocumque modo.

I go off at nine this evening and carry my cipher with me. But I do not think we ought to let ourselves be hustled about the Fisheries, much less about San Juan.

498. Lord Granville to Mr. Gladstone. [G.D. 29/59]

Copy. Private. W[almer] C[astle]. April 5.1871.

I was glad to hear from you. I entirely concur in the Telegram you sent about the Alabama.

In the fishery question it is awkward that one of our own Commissioners who I presume sees all our instructions should have an interest different from ours, but there seems ground for hope that the Commission will be a success.

I send you a note of Odo's.[1] I hope if Bismarck means to do anything about Luxembourg he will put it in a proper form. How far do you propose going in support of Holland if an attempt is made to squeeze her.

I see you are merciful about Cabinets.

It appears to me disgraceful if true, that English officers on full pay should be acting as Agents for the Emperor Napoleon.

499. Mr. Gladstone to Lord Granville. [G.D. 29/59]

Hawarden Castle. Ap. 6.71.

1. I have now seen the papers about the Principalities. What foul play there has been. A German Prince forces the Chamber and entraps the people into these ruinous engagements with swindlers who seem to smell of Germany, and who sell the Roumanian Bonds there, and in this state of things just when that Prince wants to bring about a political crisis to destroy liberty, a German commemorative festival is held as if to provoke the people into violence enough to justify before the world this most unprincipled ruler in enacting [?] his plot. I hope you will make known in some suitable manner the dissatisfaction which the whole of his proceedings are so well calculated to create: but especially that you will put the Roumanians on their guard against being inveigled into disorders, and the Turks against expecting any favour from us if they are fools enough to become the tools of Russia in knocking down the best barrier yet erected against her. I only wonder that such a people should not have run into greater excess but they ought to understand it is the plot of their enemies, and I really do not see who are their friends except ourselves.

2. Have we nothing but a private note from Brussels to establish the fact of the disquiet of Holland? To your question I am inclined to answer we never give opinions on hypothetical cases! But I would say two things: first if difficulty arise, Holland must [ask] herself whether she still has in her the old spirit of the

[1] Dated F.O. 4 April, enclosing a letter from Napoleon's agent in Brussels to Borthwick of the *Morning Chronicle*, G.D. 29/92.

17th Century: secondly it would not be bad if some military man *with brains* were to go and look about him there in order to be informed and to advise as to the real extent of our power to help.

3. The Cabinet of the 18th stands for ordinary i.e. Parliamentary business.[1] Till the Alabama Telegram of Monday it did not seem likely we could rest so long: but now perhaps the prospect is somewhat better.

This will I hope find you at Walmer—not Osborne.

A longish ciphered Telegram just arrived. 5 Pm.[2]

500. Lord Granville to Mr. Gladstone.[3] [G.D. 29/59]

Walmer Castle. April 6/71.

The Chevalier de Cadorna came here today to tell me that he was directed to speak to me on a matter of which M Visconti Venosta had heard rumors, and had lately had more detailed communication. At Paris it was said that the notion of a Conference was said to come from Vienna, that at Vienna it was said it came from Paris, but that at Berlin it was declared, with (as the Chevalier de Cadorna believed) more truth that it had its origin in Munich.

The object of such a conference was to be twofold " guarantees to the Pope " and " the question of Ecclesiastical Property at Rome "—that such a proposal, bringing Italy before the bar of all Europe was an impossibility for Italy to submit to—there would be no question of party, the nation would be as one man. Every one would become a Revolutionist, & rather than submit to a course which would be offensive and most injurious to the future of Italy—that the Italian Gov, who had refused to accept an amendment to the Bill which has recently passed the Chamber which amendment would have had the effect of preventing the Gov from negotiating with other powers; were quite ready to treat, and discuss with other Govts the arrangements to be made for the independence of the pope, but they would [wish] to inform the Gov of H.M of what has been said, and to secure our moral support in a matter of such vital importance to Italy.

M de Cadorna added many reasons against creating in Italy feelings of violence which do not now exist. He dwelt upon [the] moderate views of the Govts which have ruled in Italy for 20 years, both as regarded Home Affairs, and what concerned peace & order in Europe.

I told M. de Cadorna that I would answer for my Colleagues desiring the welfare and prosperity of Italy, that they rejoiced in its unity, and that it was contrary to their principles to see any population forced by external pressure to belong to a Gov which they [did] not like, that on the other hand they deplored the present tension of affairs between the Pope & the Italian Gov a state of things which was hurtful to the latter, and which excited alarm among the Catholic subjects of other

[1] The American negotiations caused the cabinet to meet at 12 and 2 on 17 April, and at 2 on 18 April, and parliamentary business was not taken until 19 April, Add. MS. 44639, fos. 48–56.

[2] See below, no. 501.

[3] Granville to Paget, No. 66 confidential, 17 April, was drafted from this account returned for the purpose. The dispatch puts the conversation to 17 April, F.O. 45/178.

nations. I told him that I was aware that at Vienna the clerical party were somewhat stronger than they had been, that some dissatisfaction had been felt there at the mode in which the Italian Gov had conducted matters recently as regarded the Pope, that some advice had been sent by Count Beust which was said to be in a friendly spirit to Florence.

I informed him that I had been told that the language at Paris was that the Gov was so absorbed by the pressing matters there, that they could pay no attention to other subjects, and that at Berlin Prince Bismark felt some embarrassment as to the policy he should pursue—that as an indication of our views he might tell M. Visconti Venosta confidentially that I had ordered before this conversation, a despatch to be drafted to Lord Bloomfield desiring him to take an early opportunity of telling Count Beust how averse we should be to any pressure being exercized with a view of transferring populations against their will to a Gov that of the Pope to which they were averse.

I would say no more at present, but would inform you & my colleagues of what M de Cadorna had said to me.

Please return this to me. I have been obliged to scribble it as hard as I could go, and it must be barely intelligible, but sufficient to show you the sort of appeal.

501. Mr. Gladstone to Lord Granville. [G.D. 29/59]

2. Immediate. Hawarden Castle. Ap. 6.71.

The ciphered Telegram [1] has been very difficult, & cannot be correct but I gather the general meaning.

I do not feel sure that the Italian Govt. is right in resisting outright a conference about the Roman question.

We should go there and should object to any forcing a Government upon the Roman people. Who would venture to do it, if we dissent absolutely?

If the Conference comes to a tolerable conclusion, Italy would hold Rome more peacefully & securely than in any other way.

If the matter is left to single action, any Power, & especially France, may intrigue in its own interest.

I am impressed with the notion that the danger to Italy lies in this single action and not in any thing that collective Europe could do.

I do not urge these as cast iron opinions especially if you disagree—the idea is rather new to me, but these are my impressions.

502. Mr. Gladstone to Lord Granville. [G.D. 29/59]

Hawarden Castle. Ap 7.71.

1. As I made an arrangement with Normanby [2] *direct*, I write to him to ask about the proper date.

[1] Granville to Gladstone, tel. 3 p.m., 6 April, announcing Cadorna's visit to Walmer to enlist British support against a conference on the Roman question, G.D. 29/59; cf. Granville to Odo Russell, tel. 6 April, instructing him to telegraph this to Gladstone, *ibid.*

[2] Resigned captaincy of the corps of gentlemen at arms and the charge of Board of Trade business in the Lords, on appointment as gov. of Queensland.

2. I suppose the resignation of Ld Lichfield [1] must be accepted? & that the Duke of Sutherland having already Sutherland (& Cromarty), can hardly be appointed?

3. I send for perusal a letter from the Queen. Please to send it on.

4. It seems to me that Bismarck instead of at once threatening an appeal to Turkey to intervene ought simply to have made his demand for redress and let the wait [*sic*] of it fall upon that misdoer Prince Charles.[2]

I find the view I took yesterday of the Bucharest riot supported by Consul Green in his dispatch of the 27th ult.[3] There is a great deal of foul play going on & I should like to see Consul G. encouraged to probe it.

503. Mr. Gladstone to Lord Granville. [G.D. 29/59]

Hawarden Castle. Ap. 8.71.

I wrote to you what occurred to me on the Italian question and I now return your interesting account of your conversation with Cadorna.

Notwithstanding his strong objections I still feel doubtful whether objection outright & *in limine* is their wisest course. It seems so difficult to deny that the question of the Pope is in some sort a European question. It seems to me their best reply to the invitation might be a call for a clear definition of the purpose of the Conference. Nothing could be safer I think than your language to Cadorna.

On the last Telegram from de Grey [4] respecting the *mode* of arbitration I replied this morning by telegraph with some misgiving because my objection did not seem to have occurred to you but yet I could not see how that can be an arbitration at all in which the two countries are each to reserve a *veto*. The Americans dare not I think break with us on such a point.

504. Lord Granville to Mr. Gladstone. [G.D. 29/59]

Copy. Private. W[almer] C[astle]. April 9/71.

I telegraphed to you yesterday [5] that I did not understand the objection to the English & American Jurists when app[oin]ted Arbitrators being allowed to overrule their Foreign Colleagues. I am inclined to think it a good provision as the latter might possibly hesitate to confirm a rule which we desire to establish for the future.

It was Bessborough who asked me to tell you of Normanby's wish. I am glad you have written to the latter.

I do not know whether Lichfield's resignation is in consequence of a quarrel in the county, or whether by chance it is dissatisfaction with Cardwell.[6]

[1] From the lord-lieutenancy of Staffordshire which he had held since 1863, Northbrook to Granville, 22 April, sending correspondence and mem. to explain, G.D. 29/74.

[2] Cf. Loftus to Granville, Nos. 268 and 283 most confidential, 25 March, F.O. 64/719.

[3] No. 28, 27 March, on the riot of 22 March which he said was arranged in order to justify a Turkish occupation of the Principalities, F.O. 78/2183; cf. above no. 499.

[4] 6 April, repeated to Walmer, 9.30 a.m., 7 April, reporting the American proposal that the court of arbitration to judge the Alabama claims consist of 5 members, its decision to be final only 'in any case in which its British and American members agree', G.D. 29/63, F.O. 5/1303.

[5] Granville's draft dated 8 April, but corrected to 9 April, and marked 'at night for tomorrow morning', G.D. 29/59.

[6] See above, no. 502.

I have sent the Queen's letter to the 3 you mention. I suppose there may be an advantage in huddling up as many cases as possible.

I will write again to you about the Principalities.

Another long cyphered message from De Grey arrived.[1]

505. Lord Granville to Mr. Gladstone. [G.D. 29/59]

Copy. Private. W[almer] C[astle]. Ap. 10/71.

I have telegraphed the change you suggest in the last paragraph of the Arbitration message.

I have told de Grey to look to the matter of "the other vessels". Hammond being away from the F.O. no one knows the facts so well as Tenterden.

If their telegram is correct the English Commissioners have gone further than Fish asked in including "other vessels"—but they may have done it on purpose, in order to make the regret apply to misfortunes which no one can pretend were their fault.

I have also suggested the words after escape "under whatever circumstances" as there can be no real objection to them.[2]

I will consult the Duke of Cambridge tomorrow (reviewing the troops at Dover) as to a safe man for a quiet visit to Holland.[3]

Our weather here is fine but very cold.

You will see that the Roman Conference is abandoned by France and Austria.

I had anticipated your views in favour of what might be said for a Conference and when I got your letter told him of its substance explaining to him that we only wished to discuss what would be most in the *interest* of Italy. Cadorna was firm, but had not the best of the argument, as people sometimes have, when they only think of what would be popular at the moment.

Auberon Herbert cannot be very wise.

506. Mr. Gladstone to Lord Granville. [G.D. 29/59]

Hawarden Castle. Ap. 12.71.

1. I received this morning de Grey's two Alabama Telegrams of the 10th,[4] and thereupon at once answered your inquiry (telegraphic) which came last night.

[1] 9 April, announcing the wording, proposed by the British commissioners, for the expression of regret in the preamble of the Anglo-American treaty, G.D. 29/63, F.O. 5/1303. Granville to Gladstone, tel. 9 April, asked for Gladstone's consent, G.D. 29/59.

[2] See Granville to the commission, tel. 10 April, (i) accepting the American proposal on the court of arbitration but allowing the British and American members jointly to withdraw any point from its cognizance; (ii) approving the wording of the British regret but so that it was expressed 'for the escape *under whatever circumstances* of the Alabama and other vessels', F.O. 5/1299. Cf. Gladstone to Granville, tels. 9.15 a.m., on (i), 10.50 a.m. querying 'other vessels' and Granville to Gladstone 11 a.m., and reply 12.45, on (ii), all of 10 April, G.D. 29/59.

[3] See above, no. 499.

[4] (i) forwarding an American proposal for a provision in the projected treaty directing the court of arbitration, if it decided against Britain, to fix a gross sum to cover all claims; (ii) forwarding a draft of the preamble, including the British regret, G.D. 29/63, F.O. 5/1302.

2. I propose to insert 'or duties' after 'duty', because there are several, and the 'gross sum' is a plan hardly applicable to a single case.

3. With regard to the Preamble, it designates the late War in America as "the rebellion". I do not think it is right for us now to adopt a mode of speech different from that, which we maintained throughout the struggle. Further, it tends to discredit our recognition of belligerency. And, if we declare it a rebellion, we have given an example available to be quoted hereafter for the dealings of a foreign Power with rebels, as belligerents. If on the other hand the Americans object to speaking of the "civil war" it is quite easy (so I think) to leave out the words "during the recent rebellion in the United States" altogether, and to say "in the year 186..": or even to begin 'whereas Her Britannic Majesty', perhaps inserting after "United States" "in respect of such depredations".

Further the word complaints ought to accompany claims all through and therefore to be inserted in the two places where the Preamble mentions 'such claims' & 'the said claims'.

4. With regard to the previous Telegram [1] on the composition of the Tribunal of Arbitration, I hope, and assume, that your construction of it is right, but if so the wording is most unfortunate, and I think inadmissible. To express that meaning, the words ought to be not 'their decision shall be final' but rather 'their ruling shall prevail'. From the text as proposed by the Comm[issione]rs the inference seems probably if not indisputably to arise that, where the British and U.S. Commissioners do not agree, the decision come to would want some confirmation or admit of some appeal. At the best it is a perilous ambiguity.

But I think that a wholly different form, without changing the substance, ought to be given to the proposition. A pretty effect it will have in *fixing* the international law of the future, if we make this arbitration an occasion for putting formally upon record conflicts of opinion between G. B. with the U. S. on one side, and the representatives on the other side of the three Powers whom we have chosen to arbitrate, and of whom one at least namely Italy (as Sardinia) is of high authority in international law. This inconvenience will be avoided, and the end gained (which is clearly a good one) by giving the *two* arbitrators power to withdraw any point or points from the cognisance of the tribunal.

5. I do not, after reading this morning de Grey's letters of the 27th,[2] feel at all more inclined to *concuss* (as the Scotch say) Canada into an arrangement about the fisheries. On the contrary I have fears lest our Commissioners, in their anxiety to settle all disputes, should virtually make the acceptance of some Fisheries arrangement virtually [*sic*] a British claim upon Canada. We ought most studiously to leave to Canada her own free-agency, only pointing out that the British people will of course exercise an equally free judgment on an acceptance or refusal in respect to all consequences which concern them. Similar principles should govern the

[1] Cf. Granville to Gladstone, tel. 7.30 p.m., 11 April, asking for assent to the proposal in (i) (see p. 237 note 4), and reply 8.30 a.m., 12 April, commenting as in no. 506, and Granville to Gladstone, 1 p.m., 12 April, agreeing to the objection to the preamble, G.D. 29/59.

[2] Two private letters, 27 March, G.D. 29/63. Cf. No. 3, 28 March, on Macdonald's objections to the proposed fisheries arrangement, F.O. 5/1301.

San Juan and other disputes. We ought not to let our own credit, or even that of our Commission, weigh a single hair in the balance. If *we* place a burden or an apparent burden upon Canada, we shall pay for it dearly, shall never hear the last of it, nay may perhaps tempt Canada to say ' if gifts are to be made to the United States at our expence, surely we had better make them ourselves, and have the credit for them '. I find the measure of our danger in the last sentence of the (not ' private ') letter.

De Grey however acted rightly on his own high principles of honour in refusing to proceed with Macdonald's prophecy of rejection in his pocket.

If the principle, or basis rather, of a money payment is to be abandoned, *let them be most careful to get it on record as between Macdonald and his colleagues that this is to suit his views not theirs.* We compromise in principle our policy of a generation, by exchanging property for Tariffs.

6. Northcote's letter [1] on San Juan seems at its close to bring the matter to a pretty rational upshot.

And now I think the account is clear to my present date.

Though I was not for refusal of a Conference on high ground by the Italian Government, I think they will stand on very good ground if the proposal after being made is (as it seems) spontaneously abandoned.

2½ Pm. I have your reply [2] to my telegram of this morning: and I am so glad that we are on the same lines about the Preamble.

507. Mr. Gladstone to Lord Granville. [G.D. 29/59]

No 2. Hawarden Castle. Ap. 12.71.

Though the salary seems rather a waste of money in Cowper's case while we have Peers such as Morley to whom it would be an object, I do not see how to escape the inconvenience, & I therefore accede to your opinion about Cowper and I write to him accordingly.[3]

I wish we could do something for Edward Clinton upon a suitable opportunity and I think we ought to stretch a point for it.

508. Lord Granville to Mr. Gladstone. [G.D. 29/59]

Copy. Private. W[almer] C[astle]. Ap. 12/71.

I do not like the proposed preamble. I have sent you an amended draft in which I try to make our regret appear to be less the ground of the Treaty, and to give a true character to the question which is to be decided by the arbitrators. Pray look at it very carefully, as it is important, & I have no one here to consult who has had experience in such work.

[1] Northcote to Granville, private, 26 March, received 10 April, G.D. 29/74, and reply, 22 April, G.D. 29/77.

[2] See Granville to Gladstone, 1 p.m. and reply 8.30 p.m., 12 April, G.D. 29/59.

[3] 12 April, to offer captaincy of the corps of gentlemen at arms, with charge of the Board of Trade business in the Lords, *vice* Normanby, Add. MS. 44540, fo. 2. Cowper accepted.

I shall come to town on Monday [1] on which day I suppose you will also arrive. Spring has at last arrived.

I have telegraphed to de Grey to insert "or duties" after duty.

509. Mr. Gladstone to Lord Granville. [G.D. 29/59]

Hawarden Castle. Ap. 13. 71.

Not departing from my point about 'rebellion' I think your wider objection to the Preamble quite sound,—and my suggestion to omit the first Clause as one mode of getting rid of the word will not do. On the matter touched by you, I think you turn the difficulty extremely well. But I have now put my comments and suggestions *seriatim* on the margin of your paper.

With many wry faces, I propose to reach Euston at 2.30 on Monday.

510. Lord Granville to Mr. Gladstone. [G.D. 29/59]

Copy. Private. W[almer] C[astle]. Ap. 14.1871.

This telegraphing work is despairing. It will be a mercy if we do not get into some confusion. But up to this time I believe we are all right. Three letters crossed from you, the Chancellor [2] & from Meade [3] objecting to the proposed preamble. I am concocting something out of your and the Chancellor's suggestions which I hope will be unobjectionable.

The Queen has telegraphed twice about Malets mediation.

I suspect she was backed up by the Chancellor, neither of them knowing exactly how the case stood.

I have therefore offered to telegraph to Lyons to delay execution of the telegram till further orders if it is not too late, and I have not yet received an answer. I thought it better to do this as you seemed to be rather reluctant, and altho' it is right, it is not likely to bear fruit.[4]

Pray telegraph tomorrow whether I may send the inclosed draft of telegram to de Grey.[5]

Halifax wishes [6] to substitute "injury sustained" for "depredations com-

[1] 17 April. [2] See Hatherley to Granville, Osborne, 12 April, G.D. 29/65.

[3] Cf. mem. by Meade on the careful avoidance of the word 'rebellion' during the Civil War, 18 April, G.D. 29/74.

[4] Malet, in charge at Paris while the British embassy was at Versailles, telegraphed for permission to mediate between the Paris commune and the French government, 11 April, G.D. 29/88. Cf. Granville to Gladstone, tel. 7.40 p.m., 12 April, and reply, 8.3 a.m., 13 April. He was authorized through Lyons 'to proceed cautiously if requested', 12.20 p.m., 13 April, F.O. 27/1851. For reprimands from the Queen, see three tels. 12 and 14 April, and reply 1.30 p.m., 14 April, G.D. 29/33, *Letters*, 2nd ser. ii. 127. Granville to Lyons, 7 p.m., 14 April, suspended Malet's authorization, F.O. 27/1851.

[5] Contained Granville's draft of the preamble, see above, no. 508. Gladstone to Granville, tel. 9.10 a.m., 15 April, approved, G.D. 29/59. Cf. Granville to de Grey, tel. 2 p.m., 15 April, F.O. 5/1299.

[6] To Granville, 12 April, on the preamble, G.D. 29/64. The phrase was modified in the telegram to de Grey.

mitted" but as neither the Chancellor nor you have objected I have not altered the phrase.

I inclose the two letters from the Chancellor & from Halifax. You will see that the Chancellor objects to the provision about a gross sum, and that Halifax suggests a change of words. Is it worth while retracting the consent we have already given ? [1]

The Chancellor's letter was illegible. I send you a copy produced after infinite pains.

511. Lord Granville to Mr. Gladstone. [G.D. 29/59]

Copy. W[almer] C[astle]. Ap. 14/71.

I received your note & enclosures in re preamble after I had sent you my letter.

I have had two reprimands from the Queen this afternoon, one disapproving of the message to Malet about Insurgents the other complaining of its having been sent without her sanction.

I have sent the enclosed answer. It would be a bad moment for me to wrangle with H M about being absent from London.

512. Mr. Gladstone to Lord Granville. [G.D. 29/59]

Hawarden Castle. Ap. 14. 71.

1. I volunteer a Telegram today respecting arbitration on the payment for the Fisheries [2]: and in conformity with one come from you I send the batch of Private letters on to H.M.

2. It appears as if Thiers had announced publicly for himself what at the same time he was encouraging us to convey privately for him.[3] This reminds me that according to the dates as now stated by Lord Lyons he appears to have allowed Broglie to make a very solemn appeal to us in his name on a matter which he had settled at the time when we first received it: and that he has never thought it necessary either to explain this or to offer any acknowledgments for our effort.[4]

3. Did I make any mistake about Austria in answering Baillie Cochrane [5] & shall I say or write any thing about it ? B. Cochrane accused you of interference

[1] Hatherley's objection and a suggestion how to meet it were passed on to de Grey in a second telegram, 15 April, F.O. 5/1299.

[2] Gladstone to Granville, tel.,12.30, and Granville to Gladstone, tel., 14 April, G.D. 29/59. They agreed to the way of settling the fisheries question proposed by de Grey, tel., 12 April, F.O. 5/1302.

[3] To the Paris commune through Malet.

[4] Relates to the appeal for Britain's good offices to reduce the indemnity, which Granville answered two days before the peace preliminaries were signed on 26 Feb., No. 74 to Loftus, copy to Broglie, Bernstorff and Odo Russell, 24 Feb., F.O. 64/714. Cf. Granville to Lyons, private, 15 March, instructing him to investigate, F.O. 362/4, and reply 10 April, G.D. 29/85.

[5] Moved in the Commons, 31 March, for British intervention to mitigate the peace terms for France, *Hans. Parl. Deb.* 3rd ser. ccv. 989–1000 ; Gladstone's reply, *ibid.*, 1002/13. No. 521 below quotes the offensive part in its variant wordings. Hansard reports the second variant. For Beust's complaints of Gladstone's reply, Bloomfield to Granville, private, 13 April, F.O. 362/3. Cf. Gladstone to Granville, tel. 14 April, G.D. 29/59.

against France as a hostile act—I replied that as a neutral and as a peace-keeper you could not do otherwise than let Austria know what Russia had threatened. I intended to say just enough to repel the charge, and less than was already printed in the Blue Book.

I see your accident reported in today's paper. I hope it is less painful than they report it.

Our Fishery Telegrams crossed.

513. Lord Granville to Mr. Gladstone. [G.D. 29/59]

Copy. Private. W[almer] C[astle]. Ap. 16/71.

I do not think you made any mistake about Austria, and I do not see what further explanation you can give.

Apponyi wrote to me a note [1] deprecating annoyance on my part at the publication by Beust of the Telegrams. I answered that I did not object to them.

I shall try to find you on my arrival in town today.

514. Mr. Gladstone to Lord Granville. [G.D. 29/59]

Immediate. 11, Carlton House Terrace. Ap. 17. 71.

To judge from the Telegrams of today the Canadians are rampantly unreasonable & our Commissioners want some support about the Fisheries.—What do you think of sending at once something like the inclosed,[2] which would not be quite final.

P.S. I had written this before getting de Grey's Private Telegram.[3]

515. Mr. Gladstone to Lord Granville. [G.D. 29/59]

10, Downing Street. Ap. 17.71.

It is quite fair as respects the Principalities that the Turk should expect from us a firm maintenance of the Suzerainty, and for my own part if assurances are necessary I should be most ready to give them, not of course as a new Guarantee.

But my view is that his interests and those of the Principalities are the *same* & that he does not sufficiently see this. He is tickled with the notion of interfering by force & asserting authority & seems to contemplate without much repugnance the possible disorders which are to supply him with a presumptive title. Now he is I think as foolish in this as Russia for her purposes is wise. She no doubt encourages this notion of Turkish Interference which will probably be a prelude to her own, and which is too likely to usher in afresh the Old Nick policy of territorial aggression and aggrandisement. What Turkey ought to do is to labour not only in good faith but zealously by a kindly treatment to arrest disturbance in the Principalities which in all probability will be the knell of her suzerainty there. If for whatever cause she is led to use forcible repression in Roumania, she will do it for the benefit of others not her own, & those who now favour her interference will as their next

[1] Private, 8 April, on publication in the *Gazette de Vienne* of material on the Black Sea negotiations, G.D. 29/82.

[2] Cf. Granville to de Grey, private, tel. 5.10 p.m., 18 April: 'Press strongly for free admission of Canadian fish. If you succeed in this we can back you', F.O. 5/1299

[3] Private and personal, 15 April, asking for backing against Macdonald, G.D. 29/63.

move in the game favour the resistance to it to show a case of anarchy & *her* unable to quell it. There will also arise the question who is to pay? and on the subject of finance I am amazed at the blindness of the Sultan and his advisers.

I do not think Sir H. Elliot really comprehends the point of view from which our warnings about Turkish interference in Roumania are conceived: and as I have had to do with prompting them, I may send him a copy of this letter if you think it can be useful.

As to the form of Government I fully admit his statement: but then too our policy & that of the Turk should surely be as he recommends conservative, in the best & also widest sense.[1]

516. Lord Granville to Mr. Gladstone. [G.D. 29/59]

Foreign Office. [19 April 1871].

Query

Express regret at not being able to take the step proposed adding that you have no official relations with the Commune, and you doubt whether any intervention on your part would be of service to the Eminent Prelate.[2]

517. Mr. Gladstone to Lord Granville. [G.D. 29/59]

11, Carlton House Terrace. Ap. 19.71.

With reference to Sir A. Buchanan's Nos 49 & 51 [3] I feel the subject to be delicate & difficult but I trust nothing has been or will be said or done to suppose that we have in any degree altered our original view of Prince Gortchakoff's dispatch & proceedings, though we have readily taken steps, & encountered misapprehensions at home & abroad, in order to avert or mitigate the mischievous consequences, & have rejoiced in the disposition of Russia to concur in the measures which received their completion in the Conference.

I mention what strikes me, but I dare say it has been all provided for.

518. Mr. Gladstone to Lord Granville.[4] [G.D. 29/59]

11, Carlton House Terrace. Ap. 21.71.

Why is there no numbering of Telegrams [5]? It is far more needful than with dispatches.

Taking de Grey's of Ap. 20 [6] in order of time

[1] Granville used Gladstone's argument in replying to Musurus, who had communicated a dispatch from Constantinople about the Principalities; see Granville to Elliot, No. 95, 1 May, F.O. 78/2171. Cf. Gladstone to Elliot, 9 May, Add. MS. 44540, fos. 26–7.

[2] Archbishop Darboy of Paris, held as a hostage by the communists. Granville to Lyons, tel. 3 p.m., 20 April, used the words in no. 516, but added 'and fear rather that any action on your part might be prejudicial to him', as suggested by Gladstone on the back, F.O. 27/1851.

[3] 7 and 8 April, recording Buchanan's remark, to the Tsar and Gorchakov, that the good understanding between Russia and England had not been impaired by the Black Sea question, F.O. 65/821.

[4] Two minutes by Gladstone, 20, 21 April, on de Grey's tels., G.D. 29/59, not printed.

[5] Granville to de Grey, tel. 3.25 p.m., 21 April, instructed the commission to number its telegrams, F.O. 5/1299.

[6] Three tels., F.O. 5/1303: (i) on American agreement to arbitration on the San Juan water

1. I am willing to abide by what you decide as to the Channels—and the arbitrator: not Russia.

It is a great matter to lay S. Juan aside.

2. They still say "free fishery". If this means Canadian fish free into ports of the U. States, I almost think that with Kimberley's assent you might authorise them to proceed—reserving the right of Canada—and if any reserve must be made for our Parlt., putting it in different form—query reserve of a *time* reasonable & sufficient for it to act in? If repeal of some Imperial Act is absolutely necessary, might it be sufficient to *ask* Comm[issio]n how they mean to deal with this point.

3. This seems good.

519. Mr. Gladstone to Lord Granville. [G.D. 29/59]

Private. 11, Carlton House Terrace. Ap. 28.71.

I am startled at your No 119 [read 19] [1] which I think should be suspended so far as I am concerned for it *commits* the Cabinet to give way on the word rebellion if the Americans continue in their outrageous insistance. The case is so bad that I cannot do less than ask that a full statement of it be placed in the hands of our Commissioners & the time for telling them we shall not break off upon it—a question never yet in our contemplation—if it is to come at all, should come only after our case has been made known.

It is only this moment that I have seen the Telegram No 119 [*sic*].

520. Mr. Gladstone to Lord Granville. [G.D. 29/59]

Immediate. 11, Carlton House Terrace. Ap. 29.71.

The Telegrams just come from America are very satisfactory.[2]

Wishing exceedingly to strain *nothing* beyond what is necessary, I write to say that so far as I am concerned the protocol plan of explaining the use of 'rebellion' in a protocol [*sic*] would remove all my essential difficulties.

521. Mr. Gladstone to Lord Granville.[3] [G.D. 29/60]

No 1. 11, Carlton House Terrace. May 1.71.

It was with surprise no less than regret that I learned that in my speech on

boundary with the Emperor of Russia, Germany or Brazil as arbitrator and the question confined to a choice between the Haro and Rosario channels; (ii) asking for permission to accept the fisheries agreement; (iii) asking for approval of the preamble's avoiding 'the late rebellion' to describe the source of Anglo-American differences. Granville replied in tel. No. 1, agreeing to the San Juan proposal but excluding the Emperor of Russia and agreeing to (iii) and tel. No. 2, replying on the fisheries as Gladstone proposed, both 21 April, F.O. 5/1299.

[1] To de Grey, tel. 27 April, saying he opposed the word 'rebellion, but we should not break off upon it'; to de Grey tel. 28 April, on the cabinet's not being committed, F.O. 5/1299.

[2] De Grey to Granville, 5 p.m. 28, received 4 a.m. 29 April, announced agreement on the preamble, excluding 'rebellion', and 5.5 p.m. 28, received 3.40 a.m. 29 April, announced agreement, with Canadian consent, on the fisheries, F.O. 5/1303.

[3] Granville sent a copy of no. 521 privately to Aponyi, F.O. 362/2. Cf. above, no. 512, and Granville to Bloomfield, private, 3 May, F.O. 362/2, and from Bloomfield, private, 11, 25 May, F.O. 362/3.

the occasion of Mr Cochrane's motion I had made some disclosure, over and above what was contained in the printed correspondence with regard to the relations between Austria and France at the beginning of the German War.

Nothing could be further from my intention. Nothing of the kind was noticed in Parliament, or, to my knowledge, in the public Journals. The point not having been prominently before me, I cannot undertake to state with precision the words I used. I have now referred to all the reports of them that I can find. In one I find "the correspondence shows that Austria leant to France". Another says "we were aware of a *given amount* of disposition on the part of Austria to *lean towards the side of France*". Another gives the same adding "had circumstances been favourable". The Correspondence on which I sought to found myself says "there were many circs that had created suspicion as to her neutrality in the minds of both the Russian & Prussian Governments". And of this, I do not understand that any complaint is made.

Now I cannot say the language imputed to me was used by me: but neither can I recollect verbatim what I did say. What, however, was *sufficient* for my purpose to say was, that we were aware not of a certain disposition but of a belief in such a disposition. And I shall be most ready, if it is desired, to take, or make, an opportunity of disclaiming both the report, and the language, so far as it goes beyond what I have described as the measure of sufficiency.

I return your draft; leaving it to you to send this note to Count Apponyi, or acquaint him of its purport, if you should see cause.

522. Mr. Gladstone to Lord Granville. [Add. MS. 44540, fo. 21]

[*Copy*]. *No 2.* 1 May 71.

On de Grey's telegram No 16 [1] respecting the Fenian raids I own that in my view, their connection with the present subjects is not so close as to warrant our pushing *à l'outrance* the demand for their admission into the Treaty now I hope about to be concluded.

523. Mr. Gladstone to Lord Granville. [G.D. 29/60]

Early. 11, Carlton House Terrace. May 2.71.

I take it for granted that our Commissioners are to come away from Washington before the Senate meets, but I do not recollect to have seen it distinctly stated, and I am very anxious that we should know it for certain: by telegraph if need be.

Of course this must be supposing the Treaty to be signed as I trust will be the case.

Northcote in a letter [2] which I send you (please return it & a former one) speaks of *May 21* in a way to suggest that he hopes then to be in England again. But since I wrote de Grey's letter [3] alarms me. If the Commn. remain it will surely be

[1] 30 April, on the danger of further pressure for the inclusion of the Fenian claims in the Anglo-American settlement, F.O. 5/1303.

[2] Cf. Northcote to Granville, private, 14 April, G.D. 29/74.

[3] De Grey to Granville, private, 18 April, G.D. 29/63.

a direct invitation to the Senate to reopen the whole affair & all our *ultimata* will be but starting points for new changes. This seems to me to be of great importance.

524. Mr. Gladstone to Lord Granville. [G.D. 29/60]

10, Downing Street. May 3.71.

U.S. Telegrams. On No 18 [1] I have fear of a trap, & conceive the object to be *reopening the discussion on the details* of the Treaty. Can our Commn. assure us that this will not be done? If they can let them do as they please: if they cannot they ought to come away.

Their point of view in the matter is really not quite the same as ours.

If you agree I hope you will Telegraph acc. to my first paragraph or to that effect.

525. Mr. Gladstone to Lord Granville.[2] [G.D. 29/60]

Most Private. 11, Carlton House Terrace. May 11.71.

It is now established beyond doubt by the letter of April 28 [3] that the recommencement for the fourth time of the amending process upon details has been in the contemplation of our Commissioners, & has in no degree disturbed them.

It remains then to me matter of surprise that no distinct notice has been taken of what I hope they have seen was a peremptory exclusion of any such proceeding.

Were I in your place I should *repeat*, under circs so strange. But if you are satisfied, I dare say it is right.

526. Lord Granville to Mr. Gladstone. [G.D. 29/60]

House of Lords. [12 May 1871].

May I send this letter [4] to Manning, and how do you direct to him? Read Johnny; & tremble.

[1] 2 May, proposed that the commission stay in Washington until the Treaty, signed on 3 May, had been ratified by Congress, F.O. 5/1304. No. 24, 3 May, authorized this provided negotiations were not re-opened, F.O. 5/1299.

[2] Gladstone to Granville, asking whether he should invite Prince Arthur to dine on the eve of the Queen's birthday and Granville's note of approval, Add. MS. 44168, fo. 96, not printed.

[3] De Grey to Granville, private, asking for instructions if the American senate proposed amendments to the Treaty, G.D. 29/63. Granville, tel. private, 11 May, replied that the commission was not authorized to discuss amendments.

[4] From Lyons, private, 16 May, on his powerlessness to save Archbishop Darboy's life, F.O. 362/4, Newton, *Lord Lyons*, i. 385. Cf. Manning to Gladstone, 19 May, Add. MS. 44249, fo. 258. No. 526 was returned by Gladstone marked: 'My only criticism on the letter is that I would not give the difficulty of commun[icatio]n with the Commune as more than a difficulty: for if we saw our way to doing good we should I think get over it.'

THE POLITICAL CORRESPONDENCE OF MR. GLADSTONE AND LORD GRANVILLE

527. Lord Granville to Mr. Gladstone.[1] [Add. MS. 44168, fo. 97]

Private. May 16/71.

I believe that I did not send you the enclosed. I answered it by saying that I thought it was a good arrangement for Dufferin to go to Balmoral, that he was a Privy Councillor, at the head of a department particularly connected with the Queen, and a safe and agreeable medium of communication between the Queen & you. I added that it would be affronting to him to make a change, after the Queen's commands had been forwarded to him. I added that you, de Grey, & Argyll liked a visit to Balmoral at this time of year, when circumstances permitted. But that most of the other Cabinet Ministers while they thought it a pleasure as well as an honor to attend H.M in the autumn, preferred making up the arrears of their offices, & remaining with their families during the short holydays of Whitsuntide.

As to the D. of Edinburgh's marriage my impression was that it was not desirable that he should marry a subject, or a daughter of the K. of Hanover, but that I should like to consult you before I advised H.M as to a marriage with a daughter of the Emperor of Russia.[2]

I believe Clarendon thought it undesirable, but if the Duke does not mind the difference of Religion, I do not think that the country object so much to the Greek as to the Catholic Church, and they prefer an exception to the perpetual German Alliances.

528. Mr. Gladstone to Lord Granville. [Add. MS. 44540, fo. 31]

[*Copy*]. 17 May 71.

I think it was a mistake to appt Dufferin but as H.M. has made it, I do not see that it can well be altered. I agree that so far as the public are concerned it would be less embarrassing for the Duke of Edinburgh to marry a Russian Grand Duchess than a subject or an ex-princess of Hanover.

I go to Windsor at 10.30 to return to D. St. in aft[ernoon].

529. Mr. Gladstone to Lord Granville. [G.D. 29/60]

10, Downing Street. May 22.71.

The Thornton Telegram [3] of today appears to me quite satisfactory.

[1] Granville to Gladstone, Friday, on the Queen's wish to see Gladstone at Windsor that week-end, probably 12 or 19 May as he referred to Dufferin's visit, Add. MS. 44168, fo. 94, not printed.

[2] Cf. Granville to the Queen, 14 May, printed *Letters*, 2nd ser., ii. 132.

[3] 21 May, on Fish's proposal to meet Roundell Palmer's criticism of rule ii in article vi of the Treaty of Washington, F.O. 5/1297.

530. Lord Granville to Mr. Gladstone.[1] [Add. MS. 44168, fo. 101]

Confidential. 16, Bruton Street. May 27/71.

I doubt about Portman. I do not think he has sufficient rank, or sufficiently important services—& he is not popular, or a very active supporter of our party.

I believe his great object has been to get an Earldom.

In Parliament he is an excellent objector to a clause in a Home Office bill, but I never heard such a mess as he made of an attack upon the late Bishop of Salisbury.

I rather like him personally, and he is always very goodnatured to me, but I would not if I were you make him a K.G.[2] without some concurrent opinion.

He wishes the Prince to make his son Edwin something under the Duchy, which if it is done would probably be a sufficient reward for his own Duchy services.

531. Lord Granville to Mr. Gladstone.[3] [Add. MS. 44168, fo. 105]

Balmoral Castle. [June 1871].

I am sorry to hear that you have doubts about the P.C. for Sir F. Rogers.[4]

What do you think of a compromise somewhat similar to the offer of an Irish Peerage made by Pitt in lieu of permission to drive through St James Park.

Rogers is of an old family.

He has none but a very high personal character—great knowledge of all political subjects.

I once heard that he spoke well.

A great compliment to the Civil Service, without creating a precedent applicable to many cases.

532. Lord Granville to Mr. Gladstone. [Add. MS. 44168, fo. 107]

Private. Balmoral Castle. June 3/71.

I am so sorry to hear about your indisposition, and that you have had to take care of yourself, instead of enjoying your short holyday.

We had a tiring journey to Perth, and a lovely day for the beautiful drive by road thence to this place, which I never saw in such beauty, snow on the hills, and the most delicate green below. We only saw the Queen for a moment the first evening, but were rewarded the next day by a ball, which lasted from 5–15 to past midnight, with a slight interval for a hurried dinner. It was the second in four days—Dufferin having left a great reputation as a dancer at the first. It may make Cockneys indignant at the Queen's preference to a Buckingham Palace ball, but there is a great difference. In both she sits on an elevated Dais, with great dignity, and

[1] Gladstone's request to be released from a promise to accompany Granville to the Derby, 23 May, G.D. 29/60, not printed.

[2] Not offered to Portman.

[3] Granville to Gladstone, June 1871, proposing Calcroft for receiver generalship of the Inland Revenue, Add. MS. 44168, fo. 104, not printed.

[4] Sworn P.C., 29 June, one of the earliest civil servants to receive the title. This date is the only indication of the possible date of no. 531.

watching every thing that occurs, but here the resemblance ends. At Balmoral it is in a tent open on three sides to the winds of heaven, and excepting a civil phrase to Lady G. and a kind warning to me that too much dancing might bring on gout, and an occasional whisper to the Duchess of Atholl, she speaks to no one, and merely names the dances which are to follow. She knows every man & woman, & their peculiarities, has the greatest interest in the success of the ball—& was seriously annoyed when she discovered next day at dinner that Lady G. had a more becoming gown than that she had worn for the dance.

It appears you were right about Dufferin, who absolutely declined to answer any question, or even to write to you—but he was thought pleasant.

I have had little to do in political talk—to discuss whether the Grand Duchess Marie would be a good wife—whether a judicious cross does not improve a Royal breed—to agree with you about C.B.s and to differ with the Queen about Cardwell not being sufficiently communicative with the D. of Cambridge.

I was very glad that she invited Bright to come here from today till Tuesday, and I am sure it will please him although I have just recd an answer, saying that he does not dare come here.[1]

He is very pleased with the American Treaty and surprised at the rapidity with which it has been transacted. In other respects, Army expenditure, Budget etc etc. he is critical as might be supposed. He says he [is] quite well again, but does not intend to work this summer.[2]

Can you get him back in the late autumn?

Our position with regard to refugees,[3] appears to be impregnable whether as regards French complaints, or Tory objections. I had the question to deal with during my two months previous occupation of the F.O.

I am sorry not to be in town to meet de Grey, but the Queen took advantage of her invitation to Bright to insist on our staying till Tuesday—& now will not let us off. I suspect at bottom she is conscience stricken as to her absence from England, and wishes to keep up appearances as much as possible.

The weather is rainy & cold today.

533. Mr. Gladstone to Lord Granville. [G.D. 29/60]

Private. Early. 10, Downing Street. Jun 7.71.

I talked over with de Grey yesterday the subject of honours for the Commissioners. I told him a Marquisate seemed to us to be the proper acknowledgment of his services. He thought a G.C.B. should be offered to Northcote immediately.[4] There did not seem to be any other honour that could properly be named.

[1] See to Granville, Inveraray, 2 June, G.D. 29/52.

[2] See to Granville, Inveraray, 29 May, *ibid.*

[3] See Gladstone to Granville, tel. 2 June, anticipating a French demand for the extradition of communist refugees, G.D. 29/60. Lyons had suspended negotiations for a new extradition treaty, expecting cases to arise after the communist insurrection, see Lyons to Granville, No. 678, 29 May, F.O. 27/1865. Cf. Parl. papers. [C. 565] (1872). lxx, 447, laid 13 June 1872.

[4] Offered but not accepted. It was accepted from the Conservative government in 1880.

These two may stand in some degree on special grounds. But we also thought
1. That P.C. might properly be offered to Bernard.[1] He is no inconsiderable jurist, & has done much public work. He would be no inconsiderable addition to the Judicial Committee?
2. That Thornton might be sworn P.C. on his visit next month.[2]
3. That Macdonald—either P.C. or G.C.M.G.—might & ought to stand over till his part of the business is completed.

I send a copy of this to Kimberley with special reference to the last head.

An immediate honour to Macdonald seems out of the question. And the others would not be given at once though H M s pleasure would be taken on all.

What about Tenterden?

Thanks for your interesting letter. I called today in B[ruton] Street.

534. Lord Granville to Mr. Gladstone. [G.D. 29/60]

Copy. F.O. June 8 [1871].

You will see by the enclosed notes [3] what R. Palmer says. I presume his questions are intended to be friendly, at all events to elicit answers which may liberate his mind, and enable him to speak for us.

The recent discovery of the objections raised in the Senate to the acceptance of the Bulwer Clayton Treaty makes it nearly out of the question to try a similar one.

There is another precedent, where we alone made the declaration.

De Grey will see Schenck in the morning before I see him at 3 tomorrow.

535. Mr. Gladstone to Lord Granville. [Add. MS. 44540, fo. 52]

[*Copy*]. 10 June 71.

If Blount's case is to be made known to Bismarck [4] (most properly I think) could not also that of the unfortunate man whose place & people were so ruined (I forget his name) somewhere in the direction of Orleans? I cannot but wish these things were published & opinion brought to bear upon them. Not that we could do this; especially when laying them before Bismarck. To me it is still a mystery why there is not as good a case for redress in matters of this class, as there was with respect to the ships sunk in the Seine.

[1] Sworn P.C., 29 June; appointed to the judicial committee 24 Nov. 1871.

[2] Sworn P.C., 19 Aug. Tenterden was made C.B., 23 June.

[3] Cf. Granville to Palmer, private, 8 June, on the interpretation of rule ii in article vi of the Treaty of Washington; approving min. by Gladstone, 9 June, both in G.D. 29/67; suggested replies to Palmer's questions in the Commons, Add. MS. 44168, fo. 114; and Gladstone's note on the cabinet, 10 June, Add. MS. 44639, fo. 63.

[4] For Blount's complaint of German looting on his French property, see Lyons to Granville, No. 688, 2 June. Hammond, on the back, wrote that England could only communicate the complaint to Bismarck, F.O. 27/1865. This was done; see Petre to Granville, No. 147, 24 June, F.O. 64/721. Gladstone's alludes to the comparable Kirby case, above, no. 445.

536. Lord Granville to Mr. Gladstone. [G.D. 29/60]

Copy. 16, Bruton Street. [12 June 1871].

A simple affirmative is sufficient for Sir R. Palmer's 1st question.[1]

For the second I send you the minute of the opinions of our Commissioners, and of General Schenck. Since then Northcote has added his testimony as to the opinions of Judge Hoar and Mr Sumner.

And General Schenck has furnished me with the following answer. He has given me nothing in writing, but has agreed and taken a copy of my minute of the conversation.

In the answer to the third question, you may say that General Schenck has informed me that Mr Fish is of opinion that in presenting the rules for adoption by other powers, the two Govts should agree to a declaration in the same sense.

537. Lord Granville to Mr. Gladstone. [G.D. 29/60]

[14 June 1871].

I must answer Bloomfield today. 1° I think in any case there is no doubt of accepting his offer to resign. 2° May I allude to the Peerage—and if so, 3 am I to say that I will mention it to you, or may I go further and 4° say that you have informed me that you will submit his name to the Queen 5° with an understanding that although there is no intention of requiring any political pledge from him, that you did so in the hope that he would not be in opposition to the present Gov.[2]

538. Mr. Gladstone to Lord Granville. [G.D. 29/60]

11, Carlton House Terrace. June 20. 71.

1. This is a good letter from Dudley. I suppose I should now write to Hatherton?[3]

2. I do not feel that I ought, under the very peculiar circumstances of public business, to give Adderley a day at present? certainly not if we can slip him in on some independent member's night. Every hour is now so much of our life-blood. I presume that the Treaty has been ratified?

3. I have put the meeting to 4.30 tomorrow.

539. Mr. Gladstone to Lord Granville. [G.D. 29/60]

Private. 10, Downing Street. June 26.71.

In the inclosed Mem.[4] you will find a record of my conversation yesterday respecting Royal Residence in Ireland.

Shall I circulate it to the Cabinet or only to those who were first spoken to?

[1] For questions, 12 June, on the British interpretation of rule ii, whether this was accepted by America and whether it would be put forward in presenting the rules for acceptance by other powers, and Gladstone's answers, see *Hans. Parl. Deb.*, 3rd ser., ccvi. 1903–5.

[2] See Granville to Bloomfield, 14 June, on his retirement and the submission of his name for an English peerage, F.O. 362/2. No. 537 was returned to Granville marked: '1–5. Yes W.E.G. Ju 14.71.'

[3] 20 June, offering the lord-lieutenancy of Staffordshire, resigned by Lichfield and refused by Dudley, Add. MS. 44540, fo. 59. Hatherton refused and Lord Wrottesley was appointed.

[4] Mem. of conversation with the Queen on the abolition of the lord-lieutenancy of Ireland,

540. Mr. Gladstone to Lord Granville.[1] [G.D. 29/60]

H of C. Jul 18.71.

I presume from what you said in D[owning] St that the question now is whether we shall dispense with the 12 months notice.[2]

Quite apart from the suicidal character of the policy which the French Government is now pursuing, it is evident that this notice assumes the nature of a positive covenant, for all practical purposes, not only with the British Government, but with manufacturers, merchants, & shipowners, engaged in the current transactions of trade.

Whatever we might do as between two Governments, I apprehend it is scarcely within our moral competence to agree to cancel what is really a charter & guarantee of individual interests.

Suppose there were a *law* in this country providing that a certain duty should not be altered without twelve months notice: no Government would under any circumstances be able (if it was disposed) to obtain an alteration without the full notice. If Parliament & the British Government would not assume this right, what is there in the nature of the case to enable them, in a moral sense, to dispense with a right they absolutely possess, to the prejudice of British subjects?

Without argument on the other side it is difficult to judge conclusively: but I do not *see* what more there is for debate in the question raised.

541. Lord Granville to Mr. Gladstone. [G.D. 29/60]

[20 July 1871].

I presume Corti the Italian proposed by Fish as the third Commissioner on British Claims[3] (we having objected to a third American) will do very well indeed for us.

542. Lord Granville to Mr. Gladstone. [Add. MS. 44168, fo. 118]

Confidential. [25 July 1871].

Although I do not care about the individual, I doubt whether some remonstrance should not be made either by you or by me, probably not by both, as to the principle

and the employment of the Prince of Wales as a royal resident, Add. MS. 44760, fo. 40. The cabinets of 24 June, 1, 5 July discussed this subject, Add. MS. 44639, fos. 67–70. Cf. further mem. circulating to the cabinet, Gladstone to the Queen, 29 June, 5 July and summarizing the Queen's temporizing reply, Add. MS. 44760, fo. 67. See below, no. 677.

[1] Exchanges between Gladstone and Granville on the former's period of attendance at Balmoral, 10, 13, 19 July, G.D. 29/60, not printed.

[2] Relates to the Cobden Treaty (1860) endangered by Pouyer Quertier's proposals of 12 June for increased customs duties in order to pay the German indemnity; see Lyons to Granville, No. 733, 13 June, F.O. 27/1865, and No. 43 commercial, F.O. 27/1883, and to Lyons, No. 28 commercial, 17 June, F.O. 27/1882, and Add. MS. 44639, fo. 64. For the French proposal of revision or denunciation, and Ozenne's project of revision, see Granville to Lyons, Nos. 35, 40 commercial, 1, 17 July, F.O. 27/1882.

[3] A mixed commission, consisting of Fraser, Corti, and Gurney, appointed under article xii of the Treaty of Washington, sat at Washington Oct. 1871–April 1872. Gladstone returned no. 541 with a note that the proposal was 'a very fair one'.

which the Queen lays down that it is too fatiguing for her to see Foreign Princes for ten minutes.[1]

543. Mr. Gladstone to Lord Granville. [G.D. 29/60]

House of Commons. July 28. 71.

Do you see any objection to the amended form of the motion proposed by Mr Rylands as to the use of Secret Service Money, which I inclose? [2]

544. Mr. Gladstone to Lord Granville. [G.D. 29/60]

Aug 2. 71.

Ld Lyons No 934.[3]

There is something to my mind rather suspicious in this long illness of Ali Pacha & the cessation of communications taken in connection with the Roumanian affair & the rumours abundantly afloat. I hope Sir H. Elliot is on his guard.

545. Mr. Gladstone to Lord Granville.[4] [G.D. 29/60]

Immediate. 11, Carlton House Terrace. [7 August 1871].

The inclosed notice,[5] though given by a man far from wise, reminds me to make a suggestion that to the sentence where you tell Broglie you decline, or do not desire, to negotiate on the details of Tariffs, you might beneficially, and with some effect of warning but without any aspect of menace, add " but would prefer to resume an unfettered liberty to deal with all articles of foreign commerce as fiscal interests or policy may require ".

or something of this kind—I commend this to your favourable consideration.

546. Lord Granville to Mr. Gladstone. [Add. MS. 44168, fo. 119]

Confidential. 16, Bruton Street. Aug 7/71.

I send you two letters, which do not look well, but I am not sure that some effect has not been made.

[1] May relate to a possible refusal to see Prince Oscar of Sweden, Granville to the Queen, tel. 11 July, G.D. 29/33.

[2] 12 Aug., that no payment out of secret service money should be made to members of the Foreign Office staff or diplomatic service, *Hans. Parl. Deb.*, 3rd ser., ccviii. 1515–17. An allowance had been made since 1824 to the permanent under-secretary. Granville wrote: ' no ' on no. 543.

[3] 30 July, recording his last official conversation with Favre, who spoke of Turkish designs on the autonomy of Tunis and Egypt and of a Russo-German-Turkish conspiracy for territorial changes, F.O. 27/1868.

[4] Gladstone to Granville, on a baronetcy for R. Wallace, 3 and 5 Aug., G.D. 29/60, not printed.

[5] From Sir T. Sinclair of a motion in the Commons for the raising of duties on French wine in retaliation for French duties on raw materials; text G.D. 29/60. The motion was not put. Cf. minute by Granville on wine duties, with note on cabinet 9 Aug., Add. MS. 44639, fo. 92.

The subject was avoided during a very long conversation—and I propose returning the letter [1] to Helps without any comment.

The Princess Royal was vehement for a minute of Cabinet,[2] but made no practical suggestion, and owned that she doubted it's doing any good. Ponsonby was sure it would produce no effect. The C[rown] P[rincess] abused Helps a good deal—said he toadied to the Queen immensely, and got money out of her.

I propose returning the letter to him without any comment—The Q. is not unlikely to revert once [more] to the subject.

The allusion to the Queen's departure is caused by her having asked me when Parl would be over. I said you had hopes of the 19th—She said that the 17th was her last possible day. I said I presumed that if her staying till the 18th removed the difficulty she would do so [3]—She half consented, but said it would be most inconvenient.

She spoke of a proposal of Cairns which she had mentioned to Halifax, to enable her to telegraph her consent. I said that I understood it was by means of a blank instrument which the Minister in attendance would have—and that necessarily implied there being a Minister. She settled that if Parl could not be prorogued till after her departure, I should go to Balmoral with the blank Instrument, but that if it was before her departure, I might as you kindly allowed take the first turn after Inver[ar]ay.

Do you know anything more of the probable day.

547. Lord Granville to Mr. Gladstone. [Add. MS. 44168, fo. 134]

Walmer Castle. Aug 14/71.

I forgot to speak to you about the enclosed letter,[4] which I recd on Saturday morning.

I answered that I had a bad habit, although it answered the purpose of the moment, of dismissing from my memory all those portions of a debate, which were not required for my reply—that I had listened attentively to what he had said

[1] The Queen to Helps, 1 Aug., written to be shown to Granville and sent to him, 2 Aug., on the Queen's desire for an explanation in Parliament of her non-appearance in public, G.D. 29/73; cf. Granville to Helps with Gladstone's revision, 3 Aug., G.D. 29/22A. Granville was at Osborne during the week-end 5–6 Aug.

[2] This instrument had just been revived (19 July) over the Army Purchase Warrant, *Letters*, 2nd ser., ii. 152–4, copy, G.D. 29/68. Cf. A. Tilney Bassett, *The Gladstone Papers* (1930), pp. 105-09, for earlier practice and note by Granville, 20 July [1871?], on the use of the cabinet minute, G.D. 29/22A.

[3] The session ended 21 Aug., and the Queen left for Balmoral with Granville in attendance 16 Aug., Granville to Ponsonby, tel. 15 Aug., G.D. 29/33. A mem. by Gladstone for Granville, 11 Aug.; Granville to Gladstone, confidential, letter and note, Walmer, 12 Aug., and letter, 13 Aug., and letters, Balmoral, 18, 19 Aug., on the Queen's health and arrangements at Balmoral, Add. MS. 44168, fos. 124–28, 132, 139, 144, not printed.

[4] Lord Lyveden to Granville, 11 Aug., explaining the phrase 'Orange Tory' applied to Gladstone by Lyveden in the Lords' debate on the second reading of the ballot bill, Add. MS. 44168, fo. 138. *The Times*, 11 Aug., p. 5, has that phrase, but *Hans. Parl. Deb.* has 'high Oxford Tory' (3rd ser., ccviii. 1277). Cf. Lyveden to Gladstone, 11 Aug., Add. MS. 44431, fo. 197.

about time, which had not appeared to me to be consistent that I thought his statement against ballot an able summary of the arguments on that side, that one phrase about you had grated upon my ear, but I did not think it contained the words in the Times report, or those which he substituted in his letter for it, that I had looked at the papers & found that all agreed with the Times, excepting the Standard which said " high tory " that I would speak to you, & that I would tell you that contrary to his habit he had been nervous, and that on sitting down he had spoken to me of the embarassment [*sic*] he had felt consequent upon speaking against his friends.

I have settled to go up this afternoon.

548. Lord Granville to Mr. Gladstone. [Add. MS. 44168, fo. 142]

Balmoral Castle. Aug 19/71.

The Queen is better today.

Jenner came to my room this morning, and I had it out with him [1]—so much so, that he said that my habits of Diplomatic controversy gave me an unfair advantage, & that he would put on paper what he meant to say. Pray for me that I may be equal to the occasion. I have telegraphed to ask your movements next week, and to request you to see Enfield or Odo before you go.

The French cannot complain of my absence as long as Broglie is away, & I shall be back in ten days.

Stansfield has been asked to remain till Wednesday, which seems to please him.

549. Mr. Gladstone to Lord Granville. [G.D. 29/60]

11, Carlton House Terrace. Aug. 19.71.

I have sent to inquire about Fortescue and have also invited Enfield or Odo Russell to call on Monday—on that evening or Tuesday morning I hope to go to 1 Crescent Place Whitby.

Yesterday & today for the first time I seem to breathe a little—having escaped from the ten hours a day in the H. of Commons.

Glyn is cut up about his brother. I do not quite understand this part of the censure.[2]

Please to let me know how the relays are now to stand.

You disappear, I suppose, from Inveraray ?—I follow you at Balmoral ? About the 4th or 5th of Septr ?

We got out of the Dublin riot [3] business better than might have been expected.

[1] Cf. Helps to Granville, 11 Aug., enclosing Jenner to Helps, 8 Aug., G.D. 29/73 ; reply, 11 Aug., G.D. 29/77 ; mins. by Gladstone and Hatherley, Helps to Granville, 29 Aug., enclosing Jenner to Helps, 27 Aug., G.D. 29/73.

[2] An Admiralty minute, 17 Aug., supplemented the judgement of the court-martial on the officers responsible for the stranding of H.M.S. *Agincourt* near Gibraltar. It censured other officers of the squadron including Capt. Henry Glyn commanding H.M.S. *Warrior* ; Parl. papers. [C. 444] (1871). xlii, 653.

[3] 4 Aug., when the ban on a demonstration for the release of Fenian prisoners was defied. It occurred during the visit of the Prince of Wales, Prince Arthur, Princess Louise and Lord Lorne, 31 July–7 Aug.

Dowse said ' we had a bad case ' : though he seemed to make a good one of it. The *law* broke down under us.

If after all that has happened the Q. would in your opinion like some one else to come rather than me, pray let it be arranged so.

550. Mr. Gladstone to Lord Granville. [G.D. 29/60]

1, Crescent Terrace, Whitby. Aug 23.71.

I arrived just after post yesterday and therefore could not answer your letter.[1]

The idea of your coming has created a lively & pleasurable sensation—You will find a *beautiful* railway drive from York, and here an interesting quaint place, with sea air & views good herrings & mutton to which will be added grouse and welcome. The place is crammed: but there will be *no* difficulty whatever about lodging you as we can make an exchange with our friend Dr. A. Clark who has taken a house for his family. No notice is necessary, though it may be slightly for your interest: and I think you will find, at least I found, flies at the station.

Glyn's brother together with another Captain is lightly censured for not having signified to the Agincourt that she was running into danger. I do not understand this. I should have thought it was the business of each captain to look to his own ship, & not to admonish his brethren, unless by informing them of something they could not naturally know. G G G[lyn] tells me that opinions in the Navy are divided on this subject.

I feel all to pieces, in mind more than in body, but I hope that if allowed to vegitate here for a little while mental life will return to me.

This day you are I suppose in high celebration: I trust that all will go off well, & especially that the Queen's change will be definitive.

The sight of the harvest yesterday down the Great Northern line was the most beautiful I ever saw; from the great range of corn land, and the colour so purely golden. The quantity seemed fair, sometimes very good. Most was cut, little led.

You see the Cabinet on review left in those most ethical portions of the Speech,[2] which the first rapid survey had menaced with excision.

We shall be anxious to hear about the Duchess.

551. Mr. Gladstone to Lord Granville. [G.D. 29/60]

Whitby. Sept. 4.71.

We leave Whitby this morning. I expect to be at Hawarden on Wednesday.

1. I think it is fortunate that the Austrians have taken the initiative and moved us about the Commercial Treaties with France: and your Memorandum,[3] returned

[1] Untraced. Granville stayed at Whitby, 29–30 Aug., on his way south from Balmoral; see Gladstone to Argyll and Lowe, 30 Aug., Add. MS. 44540, fos. 97, 98.

[2] The Queen's speech at the end of the parliamentary session; see notes on the cabinets of 9, 16 Aug., Add. MS. 44639, fos. 90, 99. Two notes by Granville on its references to foreign policy, Add. MS. 44168, fos. 129, 130, not printed.

[3] Of reply to an Austrian mem., 30 Aug., on co-operation among the powers affected by the new French tariff policy; see also Granville to Wolkenstein, 9 Sept., rejecting concert in the minute's terms, F.O. 7/792.

herewith, appears to me to supply an excellent foundation for a reply. The reciprocal communication of information will have the advantages without the disadvantages of a regular concert.

2. I am afraid few men of 74 can *learn* much in the sense of altering, and Thiers is not one of them. What a proof Mal[l]et's letter affords that the wise thing to do, & the only one, was what the Cabinet did, viz. to call for the new instrument in black and white & thus learn the whole truth, instead of being content with the morals which Thiers administers to us. I believe he has been endeavouring to hoodwink us all this time: but when the draft appears we shall have solid ground under our feet.[1]

3. You have I dare say already acted on Lyons's suggestion respecting the oil duties.[2] Our good stateable ground for vigorous pressure is this that our difficulties in making any concession will be much increased if questions of grievance and even of good faith under the Treaty have been previously raised. I presume you will take the opinion of the Law Officers on this case, or that you have done it already.

4. I found myself under a moral compulsion to hold a meeting, or rather to attend one, on Saturday. It was very crowded and enthusiastic. Our visit here has not been without political use, and yours I doubt not helped, although too short.

I hope you found Lady Granville going on well and I remain . . .

552. Mr. Gladstone to Lord Granville. [G.D. 29/60]

Hawarden Castle. Sept 10.71.

Bright's letter[3] does not advance us much. The opinions of the Industries should indeed as he says weigh, but not too much. They will naturally think half a loaf is better than no bread, & what applies to half applies to a quarter. The benefit of accepting a deteriorated Treaty is theirs, that of declining it is diffused over the whole field of the interests of Society. But the draft will show.

The letter does not I am sorry to say improve my estimate of Bright's health.

Macfies letter reopens a Customs controversy, which I can remember almost since I was in long petticoats; but which he names as if it were new. I have no doubt Fremantle could load several wheelbarrows with papers on it.

I inclose a letter from Sir Hamilton Seymour.[4] Was a more frivolously curious point ever taken?

[1] See above, no. 540. Sir Louis Mallet of the treaty department of the Board of Trade was commissioned to negotiate with Ozenne and to obtain a more definite proposal than that of 17 July. See Granville to Lyons, Nos. 42, 51, 65 commercial, 19, 29 July, 15 Aug., F.O. 27/1882; Granville to de Broglie, 5 Aug., F.O. 27/1887.

[2] Increased duties on mineral oils and other imports were enacted, 9 July. For the protests of British importers against a breach of the Cobden Treaty and Lyons's action on their behalf, see Lyons to Granville, Nos. 82, 92, 93, 127, 136, 150 commercial, 14, 21, 22 July, 23, 24 Aug., 2 Sept., F.O. 27/1883 and 1884. Granville to Lyons, No. 100 commercial, 21 Sept., instructed him after a reference to the law officers, F.O. 27/1882.

[3] To Granville, 5 Sept., after having read the Cobden Treaty papers, G.D. 29/52.

[4] See above, p. 253, note 4, and below, nos. 618, 619. Seymour protested against Wallace's title 'Sir R. Wallace of Hertford House'. For the relationship between Wallace and Seymour and their claims to the inheritance of Lord Hertford (d. 1870) see *D.N.B.*, xx. 559. See also Gladstone to Seymour, 10 Sept., Add. MS. 44540, fo. 105.

553. Lord Granville to Mr. Gladstone. [G.D. 29/60]

Copy. Walmer. Sep: 13./71.

I cannot conceive how the Baronetcy can damage Sir Hamilton Seymour in his cause—or the designation of Hertford House, although I suspect Sir Hamilton is correct as to the House in Manchester Square, and does it not belong to Sir Richard Wallace? There would be something in the objection, if he has been made Sir R. W. of Lisburn.

I wish you joy of your 2 speeches. I agree with you that Bright does not help us, but on the other hand he cannot find much fault with anything that we do. I hear Ozenne's draft of Treaty is nearly ready.

Broglie was here for 2 nights, but did not allude to the Treaty. He says Thiers is much knocked up.

Beaulieu is here, but has not even treated us to any Belgian political canards.

554. Mr. Gladstone to Lord Granville. [G.D. 29/60]

Hawarden Castle. Sept 19.71.

I have spared you lately; and I now merely send you Dufferin's written statement of his claim to the Earldom.[1] I incline to think well of the case and to consider that it might be *dealt* with, if need be, separately. I think too we might fairly accept the offer of his office. If you agree in these propositions I will write to him accordingly, and hold over the actual execution until any time between this date & the Session when it may be found most convenient.

What would you say to meeting in London by Oct 18 or 20 to hold a little Autumn Session of Cabinets until Lord Mayor's day or thereabouts and start the preparation of our Bills and Estimates so that they may be thoroughly matured and early.

This would not relieve us from a few further meetings, probably, before Xmas.[2]

555. Lord Granville to Mr. Gladstone. [Add. MS. 44168, fo. 146]

Private. 16, Bruton Street. Sep 21/71.

We have been a prostrate party at Walmer lately. Lady G. on her back on the Batteries—Vita confined to her room, but in full convalescence after measles of a mild character, and I in bed with cholerine, but we are all doing well and I came to town last night to wipe off some public & private business.

I agree about Dufferin and am glad to see that he offers to retire, as a thing that would be agreeable to himself. If he will condense a little, his history of Ireland is likely to be agreeable, and sure to be fair—and he will I trust turn out a superior

[1] Of Clanbrasil, revived for him, A. Lyall, *The Life of the Marquis of Dufferin and Ava* (1905), i. 150, 152-3; Dufferin to Gladstone, 13 Sept., copy, G.D. 29/60, reply, 23 Sept., Add. MS. 44540, fo. 119; see below, no 562.

[2] For cabinets of 21, 24, 25, 27, 31 Oct., 3, 6, 8 Nov., see Add. MS 44639, fos. 101–19; of 11, 14, 15, 18, 19 Dec., *ibid.*, fos. 124–39.

liberal Stanhope. In politics notwithstanding many qualifications I doubt his success. Did you ever move about Rogers.

Your plan of Cabinets would suit me perfectly, if it could be fixed, so as to give me the 19th and 20th at Manchester. As you are the cause of the difficulty, you are bound to help me a little in keeping my engagement.

A very bad account of the Queen's health from Princess Alice today . . .[1]

556. Lord Granville to Mr. Gladstone. [Add. MS. 44168, fo. 149]

16, Bruton Street. Sep 21/71.

I send you a letter from Mallet—who has had a long interview with Ozenne.[2]

I saw the latter today. He has made a table by which he shows that a small proportion only of the Anglo Franco trade is affected by the proposed reductions.

There is to be a meeting of the Chambers of Commerce at Plymouth and a resolution is to be proposed to make no concession with respect to the French Treaty, but the Chairman told Mallet that there was much more division between them than he had anticipated.

Gavard complained of the hostile tone of the Press on the subject, and that it was much to be regretted that the real state of the case could not be explained. I explained to him that it was not surprising that the public should not at once understand that the desire on the part of M. Thiers to retain the Treaty was owing to a wish to protect himself and his finance Minister against their brother protectionists—that with all his goodwill to England, M. Thiers would certainly think it a good thing, & the salvation of French interests if all English manufactures could be excluded.

M. Ozenne then gave me to understand that it was against Thiers & the violently protectionist Assembly, that men like Lefranc, Rémusat, and Broglie wished the status quo should be protected by the modifications which had been proposed. They are anxious for an answer, but I told them that we wished for no unnecessary delay, but that it was too important a matter to be dealt with without due deliberation.

I have authorized Mallet to communicate confidentially with some of the leading manufacturers again.

557. Mr. Gladstone to Lord Granville. [G.D. 29/60]

Hawarden Castle. Sept. 23.71.

1. Sir L. Mallet's letter gives us his conclusions but what I want to see and have repeatedly asked for is the old Treaty with the new draft in *juxtaposition* & some other matter that we may know what is to be taken & what left. I sent some

[1] A further sentence on the Queen's health omitted. These last sentences were copied as a postscript to no. 555 but are not with the original in Add. MS. 44168.

[2] To Granville, private, 21 Sept., urging acceptance of the French proposals, G.D. 29/74. See Gavard to Granville, private, 18 Sept., and Hervey's note on the docket, for Granville's conversation with Ozenne and Gavard, 20 Sept., G.D. 29/89. The negotiations, interrupted since the end of July, were resumed on the basis of a French draft of treaty submitted by de Broglie, 13 Sept., F.O. 27/1887.

time ago a description as clear as I could of what was wanted.[1] Sir L. Mallet I have no doubt understands the matter & gives his opinion, but we ought to have the means of judging for ourselves ; I feel this especially as I am for one unable to share in what appear to be his general views as to the system of Tariff-Treaties. For three or four years 1841–5 I was labouring at them almost incessantly and my experience left very unfavourable impressions on my mind.

Lord Lyons I observe has lately told us that the French free traders wish us not to make a retrograde step by Treaty. This if true I think very important : & their judgment would weigh with me quite as much as that of the English Chambers [of Commerce] especially where they are interested. I am glad however that your visit to Manchester will enable you to appreciate opinion there.

I wish that Mal[l]et had after seeing my letter explained the point on which I specially pressed for the explanation with which he says & I dare say truly that I am not acquainted.

I acknowledge the claim of France to dispatch, though there has been none on that side ; but it is impossible to proceed without knowing the case.

2. From what you say I gather that Cabinets on Oct 18 & 21 (Wed & Sat) will suit you and Gurdon will summon them accordingly unless after your receiving this he hears from you to the contrary. I think I ought to go to town about that time for the judicial appointments and other matters.

3. I am glad to see in your visit to town an indication of your having got well and I hope Lady Granville's condition is satisfactory.

4. Dr. A. Clark is here and I have mentioned to him the report you received from Princess Alice. He gave me his views—with reserve as founded on imperfect *data*—which I will *tell* you *vivâ voce*. They are noteworthy.

5. I will write to Dufferin.

6. I am to start on Monday and reach Balmoral on Tuesday evening, receiving the freedom of Aberdeen on the way.

558. Lord Granville to Mr. Gladstone. [G.D. 29/60]

Copy. Walmer. Sep. 25./71.

I hope you got the paper for which you asked the day after you wrote. I was promised that you should have it on Saturday. I have told them to forward to you all the papers which we have in print, in case you may not have them with you.

West in answer to my queries as to more detailed accounts of the views of the French Free Traders promised to send them in a few days.[2]

We must be on our guard against the bias which some of them will feel politically to Thiers, and we must remember how wrong Wolowski was as to possible free trade tendencies of the Chamber, but I should wish to be much guided by their opinion when sifted.

[1] To Hammond, 18 Sept., Add. MS. 44540, fo. 113.

[2] See Granville to West (in charge at Paris), 21 Sept., and replies 22 Sept., 3 Oct., enclosing mem., G.D. 29/88.

Ozenne pretends to be inspired by Remusat, Lefranc & Simon in their strong wish to receive help against the President and the Assembly in this matter. They, Gavard & Ozenne, have become reasonable about our requiring time.

I have asked Gurdon to fix the Cabinet of the 18th not later than 2 in order that I may get away by the 4.20.

I shall be very curious to hear Dr Clark's diagnosis.

You do not tell me about Rogers.

I gather that the Manoeuvres have been a success & I am particularly glad to hear that they will surprise the Public in their economy.

I have desired the Military Attachés to find out what the Foreigners really think.

Pray let me know what you find is really the Queen's state. It is becoming a terrible long affair.

559. Mr. Gladstone to Lord Granville. [G.D. 29/60]

Hawarden Castle. Sept. 25. 1871.

I should much like to know in due time how Lord Lyons regards the views put forth in Mr West's very interesting though painful dispatch No 54 of Sept. 22.[1] They have some bearing on the question how far it is expedient to go in concessions *as such* to the present French Government.

560. Mr. Gladstone to Lord Granville. [G.D. 29/60]

Balmoral Castle. Sept 27.71.

1. The Cabinet stands for Sat. the 21st as the Chancellor cannot come sooner.[2] But if you have occasion for an earlier day on F.O. business, this is no bar.

2. I wrote to Rogers as we agreed;[3] but he was abroad, and I have had no answer.

3. The feeling shown towards the Government at Aberdeen yesterday was most enthusiastic. I thought it right to touch the question of Home Rule; which I hope you will not disapprove. Huntly and Kintore attended, with many of the gentry. Huntly with whom I came up as far as Aboyne seems to be zealous active & intelligent as a landlord & country gentleman. Do you think it desirable I should sleep at his house? which he has invited me to do.

4. I have not received the copy of the French Treaty with the draft (details in outline only) in juxtaposition.

5. Send for & read Reynolds's Newspaper of last Sunday on the gambling at Homburg. These things go from bad to worse. I saw 'What does she do with it' advertised on the walls of the Station at Birkenhead.

[1] On political conditions in France, emphasizing Thiers's reactionary tendencies and the decline of political freedom, F.O. 27/1872.

[2] See exchange of telegrams between Gurdon and Hervey, 26 Sept., on Granville's agreement to 21 Oct. for the cabinet, G.D. 29/60. For note on this cabinet see Add. MS. 44639, fo. 101.

[3] Gladstone to Rogers, 1 Sept., offering a peerage, Add. MS. 44540, fo. 99. This was said to be the first peerage offered to a civil servant, *G.E.C.*, ii. 179.

6. I cannot help feeling very uneasy about the Missionary question in China,[1] & desirous that we should consider whether we cannot have some international proceeding in the matter to prevent imprudences & check excess by common action & so do what in us lies to avert disturbance.

7. The account of the Queen yesterday was decidedly good. I have not seen Jenner since he went to see her this morning.

8. We have much reason to be pleased, & to give credit to Cardwell & the Department, in connection with the Manoeuvres.

561. Lord Granville to Mr. Gladstone. [Add. MS. 44168, fo. 154]

Walmer Castle. Sep 29/71.

Thank God there is nothing Foreign requiring a Cabinet excepting the French Treaty. I do not know when you will be prepared for one on that subject. Any day will suit me excepting the 18th, 19th, & 20th. I have put my Manchester friends on & off so often, that I should not like to disturb their arrangements without necessity.

I send you another letter from Mallet.[2] He is too much a partizan, but has great knowledge on the subject. I have told him that he must not influence the Manufacturers whom he consults, and that Ozenne's Memo[3] (which I enclose) seems to me weak.

There is one point in it which is the self acting law upon which the French Gov would fall back, if Thiers really has courage to denounce the Treaty. I have desired him to send you a copy of it, if you have not got it.

I was delighted to see how enthusiastically you had been recd at Aberdeen. Your attack upon Home Rule was very powerful, and I believe opportune. Kintore is nearly an Idiot—Huntly intelligent & pleasing—with the self satisfaction natural to a goodlooking Highland Chief, who has married a fortune. I heard an excellent account of him as a Country gentleman. I should have been his guardian, had his mother died before he came of age, so I have a quasi parental feeling, & shall be very glad if you pay him a visit.

I will send for Reynold's Newspaper.

As to the Missionary question in China—Prussia & America have signified their concurrence with us. France is of course the danger. She has no commercial interest in China. She has 40,000 Chinese Catholics to protect. She has an elastic Treaty Clause which enables her to do so, and I take [it] the pressure to do so is very strong upon the Gov at home.

Jules Favre was apparently of our mind on the matter, Rémusat I should think is the same, & the Duc de Broglie notwithstanding his clerical tendencies is moderate, and promised me to use all his efforts with the French Bishops & Heads of Mission to calm them.

[1] See Granville to Lyons, No. 541, 11 Aug., favouring a separate rather than a joint Anglo-French reply to the Chinese circular of 9 Feb., F.O. 27/1852. Cf. Parl. papers. [C. 468] (1872). lxx, 152.

[2] To Granville, 28 Sept., again urging acceptance of the French proposals, G.D. 29/74.

[3] Enclosure in Sir L. Mallet's letter of 28 Sept.

We are all pretty well agreed as to the answer to be given to the Chinese Circular.

It has been a real pleasure to hear at last of an improvement in the Queen's health. I own I do not see how the very trying illness she has had bears upon the general question.

We are all well here.

562. Mr. Gladstone to Lord Granville. [G.D. 29/60]

Balmoral. Sept 29.71.

Please to read this letter from Rogers. I do not see in it any barrier—or at least any insurmountable one. Amberley is too peculiar & idiosyncratic to be used as a negative test I think. If you agree please to Telegraph *yes*.[1] In that case I may get it settled while I am here. And I might then as well submit Dufferin also ? [2]

According to present arrangements I should leave on Wednesday morning early.

The Queen continues to make satisfactory progress.

Disraeli has done her & the country a left-handed service, following suit to the Times.[3] The right aim is to keep her up to work : he has done all in his power to let her down.

The paper I asked for about the French Treaty has not appeared. I have seen nothing that brings the case *together* so as to be judged of.

563. Lord Granville to Mr. Gladstone. [G.D. 29/60]

Copy. Walmer. Octr 1./71.

Rogers' is a peculiar letter, and might mean anything, but he is so thoroughly conscientious, that he would be sure to feel the adverse reason as strong as possible. I am glad you are not deterred by it, and hope that in your answer to him you will accept the independence but conclude that he does not mean to take up his place on the X Benches.

You will see in West's letter[4] that Thiers does not press for an early answer, so we need not anticipate Cabinets.

The delay was provoking about the comparative statement. I asked Mallet the day I saw him to send it at once to you. He said he could not do so till the next day. It was some days ago when he sent it to the F.O., whence it was first sent to me. Please telegraph if you have not what you want.

[1] To Gladstone, 24 Sept., on the political difficulties in his accepting a peerage, G. E. Marindin, *Letters of Frederic Lord Blachford* (1896), pp. 312–14. Gladstone's reply, 1 Oct., took the letter as an acceptance, Add. MS. 44540, fo. 127. Granville answered 'yes' by tel. 1 Oct., G.D. 29/60.

[2] See Gladstone to Dufferin, 1 Oct., on the Queen's approval of the revival of the earldom and asking him to keep his office for the time being, Add. MS. 44540, fo. 127. See above, no. 554.

[3] A leader in *The Times*, 14 Sept., p. 9, expected 'remorse for the reflections . . . last session upon [the Queen's] comparative withdrawal from ceremonial appearances'. Disraeli at Hughenden, 26 Sept., spoke of the Queen's physical incapacity to perform her public duties, *ibid.*, 27 Sept., p. 6.

[4] West to Granville, private, 29 Sept., G.D. 29/88.

564. **Mr. Gladstone to Lord Granville.** [G.D. 29/60]

Balmoral. Oct 1. 1871.

I return the letter of Mallet and the Note. They are interesting, but they are, to me, Commentaries without a Text. Why Mallet has never supplied this I am at a loss to imagine. Doubtless he has the whole thing in his head, but we have other fish to fry all the time. As to other members of the Cabinet I know not but I hardly think they can be in a condition to act without some better general view of what we have & what we are asked to take instead of it than has yet been provided. The question is not only a very difficult one, but one on which we shall be obliged to bear almost the entire responsibility & Mallet who ought to be our guide appears to me one-sided.

I am surprised at his language about the Manchester Chamber: but it may have changed.

I am glad to hear of good dispositions in France about the Missionary question but if the Bishops there are in the last resort to decide little mercy and little good of any kind will come of it.

Weather here irregular: not two days alike. The Queen has continued in a satisfactory course of improvement: and I saw her today for half an hour.

The inclosed letter from Halifax [1] is I think in the right *frame* about the Treaty.

Dufferin & Rogers both agreed to.

But I think the execution of the former should stand over for a while. I go Wednesday *morning*.

565. **Mr. Gladstone to Lord Granville.** [G.D. 29/60]

No 2. Secret. Balmoral. Oct 1. 1871.

Besides that the Queen is thinner, & paler, her whole physical tone seems lower, and her voice weaker. Her appearance however is not at all unhealthy and I hope a moderate time may bring her up to her usual high level.

The repellent power which she so well knows how to use, has been put in action towards me on this occasion for the first time since the formation of the Government. I have felt myself on a new and different footing with her.

No doubt she considers it an offence at least so far as I am concerned that Parliament was not told authoritatively that she could never be for more than 3 days in London & the like.

It was certainly a matter which may call for explanation but that explanation it would have been cruel to offer at a time like this.

On account of her natural & constant kindness as well as of her position, I am grieved; & this much the more because of what is to come. For the question gathers in gravity, as we may judge from the visible signs which so frequently recur. And an instinct tells me, that much will have to be said about it ere long; more probably with reference to putting forward the Prince of Wales, than to forcing duty upon her against which she sets herself with such vehemence & tenacity.

[1] Untraced. It is missing from Add. MS. 44185.

Though she had sent to me for the Reynolds about the P. of W[ales], she did not name him to me.

I greatly doubt whether she has seen either of the two recent & remarkable articles in the Pall Mall & the Echo.

566. Mr. Gladstone to Lord Granville. [G.D. 29/60]

[Balmoral]. Oct 2. 71.

Without prejudice to further discussions on the French Treaty question,[1] I may say that I think *if* we go forward (as to which I am far as yet from being satisfied) we should ask to have our own entire liberty restored as to spirits, wine & exported coal.

In a good pamphlet got up by the Cobden Club, which gives some of the information which I think Mallet ought to have supplied long ago, I find that at any rate the Manchester Chamber *ought* to have their eyes open on this question for the exports of cottons (including Apparel) which were in 1859 294 m. were in 1869 1,560 m.

567. Mr. Gladstone to Lord Granville. [G.D. 29/60]

Balmoral. Oct. 3.71.

In anticipation of the paper I hope to receive from London showing exactly what we have and what is offered us, I have put into a Memorandum my view of the general argument. But I will not inflict it upon you until I have had the best means of judging, at least for myself, how far it may be modified by any of the actual circumstances of the case before us.

I had written to Rogers without the caution as to cross benches: but he may give us another opportunity, or you might perhaps do it, & would be sure to do it better. Off tomorrow to Aboyne Castle & so southward.

568. Mr. Gladstone to Lord Granville. [G.D. 29/60]

Aboyne Castle, Aberdeenshire. Oct 5.71.

I see West reports from Paris [2] that Thiers refers to our being out of town as a reason for his not asking a speedy answer about the Commercial Treaty. Lest this should at any time be made a pretext of complaint, would it not be well that West should say our being out of town is no impediment as we at any time can meet on 24 hours notice.

One or two of the Cabinet would like the meeting postponed to Tuesday the 24th but I am afraid of causing more inconvenience by a change.

The Queen is much vexed about the P. of Wales's proceedings at Homburg—and she will try to get the Chancellor to speak strongly to him. *That* part of the case, poor soul, she can discern well enough.

[1] In negotiation between Mallet and Ozenne, the British reply to the French proposals of 13 Sept. being still withheld; see above, no. 556 note.

[2] No. 68 confidential, 29 Sept., recording a conversation with Thiers, F.O. 37/1885.

I was astonished at her improvement between Saturday & Tuesday when I had a long conversation with her: but she did not leave it open to me to prolong my stay beyond the week she had prescribed.

Princess Louise despairs of her *ever* doing more in the discharge of ostensible public duty.

My host still improves upon acquaintance. He considers the young Lord Aberdeen as *gone* from our camp.

569. Lord Granville to Mr. Gladstone. [Add. MS. 44168, fo. 161]

Walmer Castle. Oct 6/71.

I was glad to find that the absence of the information which you desired was a little owing to you. I send you another letter from Mallet.[1]

Forster sent me [2] (as an able statement of one side of the question[)], a letter from Mallet containing the arguments, with which we are acquainted. Forster gives no opinion.

We are stumping so violently, that it is rather difficult to be posted up in all our respective speeches. I have another education speech to make at Margate on Monday—and at least one political one at Manchester on the 19th. I shall absolutely decline all opportunities between Manchester and Parliament.

Your Home Rule has had an effect.

How does the reproach strike you that not only no Royalties go to Ireland, but that no Minister condescends to do so.

I am dying to see your treaty memo.

570. Lord Granville to Mr. Gladstone. [Add. MS. 44168, fo. 163]

Secret. Walmer Castle. Oct 6/71.

I hope you are safely reestablished at Hawarden. Your secret letter was of deep interest, but not satisfactory.

It will be difficult to know how to deal with her. Nervousness alone would have made her manner repellent—but of course the retractations in the papers, and Dizzy's speech would have had some effect upon one less able to extract from everything [that], which she likes best to assimilate.

I expect you will find as much difficulty in persuading [her] to put the P. of W[ales] forward, as in doing what is necessary herself.

I read Reynold's paper. Has the Prince seen it.

[1] To Granville, 5 Oct., G.D. 29/74. See also his mem.: 'Commercial Changes in France . . . independent of those which involve a modification of existing Treaties', 6 Oct., Add. MS. 44432, fo. 28.

[2] To Granville, 4 Oct., enclosing Mallet to Forster, 2 Oct., of which an abstract follows, and reply, 6 Oct., G.D. 29/56.

571. Mr. Gladstone to Lord Granville. [G.D. 29/60]

23 Ainslie Place, Edinburgh. Oct 9.71.

With reference to Mr. West's Commercial No 10 of Sept. 25 [1] on the possible title of Third Powers to claim benefits temporarily accorded to Alsace and Lorraine I think it worth while to mention what may have escaped the memory of many, namely that a case which I *think* was strictly analogous in principle was argued in the House of Commons after the Ashburton Treaty of 1843 (I believe) which gave British privileges to the wood of the territory ceded to the United States. We, of Peel's Government, contended that the most favoured nation Clause would *not* entitle Third Powers to claim. This appears to be at any rate the *equity* of the case.

572. Memorandum by Mr. Gladstone.[2] [G.D. 29/60]

Copy. French Treaty. [3–9 October 1871].

An extraordinary responsibility is now cast upon the Government of this Country. France, which has been engaged from 1860 to 1870 in making Treaties of Commerce which involved a considerable approach from the former system towards freedom of trade, announces her intention to obtain if she can the abandonment [3] of these treaties by consent of the Powers with which they have been made; and commences with Great Britain, declaring by the mouth of her agent that unless she can begin by enlisting us in this course of policy, and making us parties to a new Engagement of a distinctly retrogressive character, she can have no reasonable hope of succeeding in her applications to other states.

2. One among the disadvantages of our position is this; that a free discussion of the subject with France involves more or less our passing or seeming to pass a judgment on the question what is most for her interests under her present peculiar & painful circumstances. Whereas, were we free, both sympathy and respect would prompt an entire silence on such a subject, where we could not give our concurrence to her proceedings. But this inconvenience is inseparable from the discussion which the French Government has pressed upon us: as we are asked to reverse our own course of action [4] by signing a retroactive instrument in order that France may improve her standing ground for striking other blows at the cause of free trade in other countries. In these circumstances, it seems quite impossible for us to conceal, though we may not offensively press, our conviction that the French Government,

[1] Relates to the projected customs treaty between France and Germany to establish a temporary special tariff for manufactured goods imported into France from Alsace-Lorraine and to the title of other powers to claim the same terms under most-favoured-nation clauses, F.O. 27/1885.

[2] Gladstone's holograph, dated 9 Oct., together with a sketch of reply to the French proposals of 13 Sept. is in Add. MS. 44760, fos. 103 ff. A printed copy annotated by Bright is in G.D. 29/52. Bright's comments, followed by his initials, are reproduced in footnotes below.

[3] France applies to us *first* because our Treaty has expired or stands only upon twelve months notice—& I think we should deal with the application without reference to other Powers.

We are in the hands of France as to *renewal*, as far as their original concessions are concerned. [J. Bright.]

[4] We make no retrograde step. France does, & asks us to remain as we are for a limited term. [J. B.]

acting on the principles of which M. Thiers & M. Pouyer-Quertier are distinguished advocates, is proposing what is not less injurious to France herself than to the other countries concerned.

3. It now becomes necessary to look back to the proceedings & discussions of 1860.

The arguments then urged against the Treaty were, so far as my recollection serves me, far from insignificant.

It was urged, & admitted that from a long experience of fruitless attempts to frame Tariff Treaties with other Powers, we had been led to adopt it as a fixed rule of conduct that such Treaties ought not to be attempted.[1]

That not only ought liberty of action to be preserved entire in all matters touching at all upon revenue, on the general ground that no one can say beforehand what necessity may require in the future, but that the French Treaty directly interfered with it in matters purely fiscal (as distinguished from what is protective); namely in the stipulations respecting the wine duty, the spirit duty, & the export of coal.[2]

That, France being divided between Protectionists & Free Traders, we made ourselves parties in her internal controversies by promoting a measure which evidently tended to help onward the cause of one of these parties, & to depress that of the other.[3]

Also, that we were assisting the Emperor Napoleon to escape the control of his Chamber.[4]

4. To the first & second of these arguments we replied, without denying their force, that we had carefully avoided that pretended balancing of concessions which was the usual & most grave vice of Tariff negotiations: that the provisions on our side, or rather the reduction of such provisions to the form of international stipulations constituted a great offering [5] made by us to obtain a measure abroad in the interest of Free Trade in France, which was important in itself, but even much more important because

(1) It would lead other states to follow the example of France.[6]

(2) It would induce France to take further steps in the same direction.[7]

(3) Every one of these steps made by France and by other states would, by augmenting peaceful [8] & friendly intercourse, strengthen the foundations of concord, & diminish the chances of war.

[1] An argument of force in former times, & used by Free Traders, but in 1860 used by Protectionists here against a partially Free Trade Treaty of no use *in this discussion*. [J. B.]

[2] This idea of 'liberty of action' is opposed to all Treaties. We do not desire liberty to do what we know is injurious to us. [J. B.]

[3] This is an argument wholly valueless. We dealt with her then Government based on a great majority of votes. [J. B.]

[4] A French question—not an English one. [J. B.]

[5] We made no *great offering*—it might seem so to the French—but we knew better. [J. B.]

[6] which it has done. [J. B.]

[7] Insecurity of the Emperor—& the late war & revolution are sufficient reasons why this expectation has been disappointed. [J. B.]

[8] No reason to suppose this has failed. England and France have been much more friendly since 1860. [J. B.]

As to the limitations on our fiscal freedom, they were not of primary moment; we could afford them.

As to the 3rd & 4th arguments, we contended that the thing itself being good, both for us & for France, these arguments were not matters for our notice at all, but for that of France herself; and that France was, as towards us, represented by her Government.

5. How strangely is the 'situation' now altered.

The arguments against the Treaty (except the 4th which we did not allow to have a *locus standi* at all) remain in their fullest force. The arguments for the Treaty are turned upside down.

We are now avowedly asked to a sign a retroactive instrument in order that, once more, other states may act in the same direction as France; but it is now the direction of restriction & preference, not of free trade.[1]

Are we not also asked to do what may induce or encourage France hereafter to ask of us further measures in the same sense?[2] If we are now to give up one half or one third of the ground made in 1860, by our own formal act, in order to preserve the rest for an unusually short term of years, why may we not again be asked to give up, for the very same reason, a portion of what we had thus retained? If the whole advantage be 100, & we now give up 30 in order to retain the 70, on what ground would a British Government hereafter refuse to give up (say) 20 out of that 70, in order to retain the 50.

And to all this we have to put our hands,[3] knowing that restricted intercourse means diminished security for concord & good will, & that the new Treaty will & must be a covenant for restricted intercourse.

6. Thus far it has been assumed that the process of assent will be a perfectly simple one, & that we shall (so to speak) gulp the French proposals. But if we are to enter upon the questions of detail, of a little more & a little less, it is to be feared that dignity might lose quite as much as commerce might gain, & that we might, as in some of the old Tariff negotiations, find that, in the process of doing good to one another, we were however unaccountably slipping into a hostile rather than a friendly attitude & leaving on one another's minds the impression of close & shabby contract.[4]

I assume on the whole that little is to be gained by endeavouring to patch the French proposals, & that in the main the question for us is between accepting & refusing them.[5]

7. It may be worth while to point out, as a part of the case, what has taken

[1] *We* are asked to make a new treaty or continue old one with 'changes'—because the term has expired. France is at liberty to propose this. [J. B.]

[2] This seems answered in subsequent Paragraph 10—& Mr Gladstone does not seem to believe his own argument! [J. B.]

[3] We do not '*put our hands*' as approving—the whole matter of the Treaty practically is one of *concession by France*—we concede nothing—but accept what she proposes to grant, not being able to obtain more. [J. B.]

[4] This if worth anything was an argument against the original Treaty for there were almost endless *details* in it. [J. B.]

[5] The suggestions in the Board of Trade Oct. 23 1871 are so reasonable that they may be accepted by France & some points might be *yielded* to us as ribbons, *plate glass*, etc. [J. B.]

place on the part of the British Government since 1860. In at least two very important instances, we have gone much beyond the Treaty.

We materially changed the Tariff of wine duties to the great advantage of the French Growers, from a portion of whom I myself, as Chanc[ello]r of the Exch[eque]r, received a direct application on the subject. And, at the instance of the French Government, we made an elaborate investigation of our duties on manufactured tobacco, & reduced them from rates almost prohibitory to those of simple equivalents, on the basis of a strict equality of trade as between British & Foreign manufacture.

I do not for a moment suppose that circumstances like these will be allowed by M. Thiers to weigh in the negotiations. His attitude towards us, when put into language, is this :—" We give you no credit for measures of free trade, because you think them good for everybody, yourselves included : & we expect & ask you to become parties to measures of restriction, although you think them bad for everybody, ourselves included."

8. Of arguments in favour of accepting the French proposals I can conceive these three.

(1) It is probable that, if we refuse, some of our own exporters will find [1] their goods taxed higher in consequence, & they will bitterly complain of us.

(2) France will (it may be said) apply to us her old tariff of prohibitions, & thus the cause of Free Trade will suffer more than if we by our own concurrence induce her to stop at an intermediate stage in her retrospective course.[2]

(3) We shall by refusal estrange the French Government & nation.[3]

9. Of the first I admit that it is likely to come true, & if it does it will be inconvenient to us as a Government. But it is not our business to consult the immediate interest of particular trades, at the expense of trade & of public policy in general.[4]

10. We must therefore pass to the second argument. And here I conceive it to be utterly unlikely that France will radically and violently alter the commercial system to which her people have now become accustomed, by going back to the system of prohibitions. On the other hand it may be probable [5] that she will move further backwards without us than she would do with us. We are invited then, to accompany [6] her in a bad & injurious movement, in order that she may not proceed so far in it as she would if she act alone.

Now, if she were to act alone to what point would she go ? She would go to the point which she might think to be required by her own interests ; even more than her acts under the new arrangement would prove her mistaking them. But she would mistake them on her own responsibility, not ours. She would not be able

[1] A great many will find this—& more than have yet given any *opinion* upon the question. [J. B.]

[2] She *may* & her difficulties in this may excite French *ill will* against us. [J. B.]

[3] Not so much on a/c of difference of duties—but that we have been obstinate in their great embarrassment and misfortunes. [J. B.]

[4] The Treaty was for all Trades—& its abandonment may be felt by all. *Public feeling* is now what it was in 1860—& the *general* interests of Trade remain the same. [J. B.]

[5] If this were certain, then the Treaty commercially will do neither good nor harm—but *politically* it may still be *good*. [J. B.]

[6] We do not *accompany* her—this is not *fair argument* in my view. [J. B.]

to point to our authority, nor to say 'see what England has already agreed to'. She would, according to the confession of M. Ozenne, lose the hope of inducing other states to give up their treaties in order to allow her at once to impose new restrictions upon trade. How are we to justify, for the sake of some (not certain) interest of this or that British Trade, strengthening the hands of France to enable her to do that which will greatly damage freedom of trade in many nations of the world.[1]

11. Moreover, is there not this fear in the case? By the hypothesis, France will, if we agree, stop short of what she thinks her own interests require. She will not do this in order to obtain an equivalent from us; for she is acting in the full belief that whatever happens she is sure on our side in fact of what she now holds by covenant. We know that she is really making this arrangement with us not in order to secure certain advantages in our ports, for of that she *thinks herself* sure: but to work through us on Foreign Powers. But this portion of the subject is kept underground. And she will never lose her ostensible right to say 'but for the desire to please and favour you, we should have proceeded further in the line of protection'; and thus we shall still be liable to be represented to French Protectionists (whom the French Government declare to be the bulk of the nation) as standing between them & their interests. She will still be able to point to sacrifices (in her own estimation) which she will have made to please us.

12. But as to the effect on the French Government if we decline. In my opinion there is little to be done in attracting or estranging Thiers, who will simply drive bargains & those Jews' bargains. Without doubt more or less complaint would be made in France. Would it be sustained by the general opinion of the world? If we, in very considerate language, restoring to France her liberty, declare that we so value our own, that nothing can induce us to waive it except covenants which she thinks adverse to her interests, and which therefore we cannot & do not ask, is it possible that she can find in such a course the subject matter of just, nay of real complaint? It is she who changes the *status quo*: & the presumable right of complaint is rather with those who would remain as they are, but are not permitted.

13. It is however really very material to consider what, if we agree, will be the effect of our conduct in other countries. I believe that Austria, Switzerland, Italy, & some other states, are in possession of Treaties which they consider highly advantageous to them, & which have yet some time to run. France has approached us with a certain proposal which they very well know to be made in order to improve her means of assailing or sapping the privileges they enjoy, & thus of bringing them into a position less advantageous than that which they now hold. If we accede, will not they have a very ready disposition, & moreover very good reason to complain of the prejudice done to them by our conduct? It is true we may reply that we do not interfere with their Treaty rights, & that France can only bring a moral pressure to bear upon them. But their rejoinder would be that power of moral pressure was the only power that it lay in our choice to put into the hands of France,

[1] We are to make or hazard a great sacrifice to enable other nations to maintain their Treaties with France!

Our friendly position with France is worth something to us—& other states must *act for* themselves. [J. B.]

& that it was a great power too.[1] The goodwill we might earn in France by concession, if any, would not have reason on its side, & would be outweighed, I fear tenfold, by the ill will which we should justly earn in other countries by the knowledge that with our eyes open we had put them, in a case too where we had a common interest, into a false & disadvantageous position.

14. For one, I cannot put entirely out of view the value of having our hands set free from the engagements of the Treaty of 1860: especially considering the outcry that is now made about our exclusive use of direct taxation. Whether the high values of the brandies of France ought to pay nothing more than the cheap spirits of Germany; whether the light wine of France ought to continue to enjoy the great advantages now accorded to it at 1/– per gallon in comparison with the strong wines, which France does not send us, at 2/6 [2]; whether we ought to be prevented by *Treaty* from imposing any export duty on coal: all these at least are questions on which it seems to me desirable, that we should be set free, though I do not assume any particular use as certainly fit to be made of our freedom.[3]

15. In sum. We made in the case of the Treaty of 1860 a great and marked exception to a well-established rule [4] for what we thought well defined & very strong reasons. (The Austrian Treaty was an addition, a supplement in miniature, to the French one.) We seem by this measure to have given considerable force to the Free Trade movement on the continent of Europe. When these powerful considerations are removed, and not only removed but reversed, is it not our safest course to fall back upon our old basis namely that the cause of freedom in commerce will, as a rule, be most effectively advanced by leaving each nation to consider the subject in the light of its own interest alone. Oct. 3:71.

P.S. I am not sure that I understand rightly the proposal which is now actually before us in its detail: and I now write subject to correction where I may be in error.

But as I take it, we are asked to begin by *giving up* the Treaty of 1860, & signing in its stead the draft transmitted (after very long consideration) by the Duc de Broglie on the 13th Septr: 71. Would not our position then be as follows:—

1. All our own concessions of 1860 (Art IV) would be revived & continue.[5]

2. The French concessions of 1860 would be largely [6] altered against us.[7]

[1] Our Treaty is at an end. Treaties with these states have some years to run. France offers a continuation of the Treaty on modified terms—better, *probably much better for us* than no Treaty at all—are we to reject this, lest other states should be importuned by France to make concessions before Treaties with them expire?

This argument seems to me beside the question, as regards the conclusions of an *English* Cabinet. [J. B.]

[2] We are not *bound by the Treaty* to charge Spanish wines 2/6 while France pays 1/–. This is an absurdity of our own doing. [J. B.]

[3] Why a duty on Coal more than on machinery or some other article? Is not the reference to this point some indication of the want of strength of other arguments in this paper? [J. B.]

[4] There was no *established rule* for the case had never arisen since we adopted Free Trade—the *reasons* were conclusive to all but the Protectionists & to pedants in political Economy, or to a few men jealous of Mr Cobden, or opposed to the Administration of the day & to Mr Gladstone in an especial degree. [J. B.]

[5] Rightly. [J. B.]

[6] 'Largely' queried by Granville in the margin.

[7] Not *largely*—see Board of Trade Paper Oct. 23 1871. [J. B.]

3. If the French Assembly agreed to the draft when made into a Treaty, we should enjoy it only until Jan. 1, 1877.[1]

4. During the term of (say) 5 years thus accorded, we should not be secured against seeing the goods of other nations imported into France on better terms than ours.[2]

5. If the French Assembly chooses not to authorize the President to proceed according to the instrument, what security have we for any tariff purporting to be provided by it, & what is to prevent France from setting up her old restrictive Tariff ?[3]

6. If she did so, should we not remain bound to our own stipulations of 1860 ?[4]

7. Contemporaneously with this draft is it not the fact that France by a new duty on shipping is striking a blow at sea trade as compared with land trade ?

8. And that she is also striking a special blow at English commerce under form of legislation respecting entrepôt trade ?

All this, taken together, is so absurd, I may almost say it would be so insulting, that it can hardly be true. But I am desirous to know exactly where, how, & how far it is not true.[5]

Even after large deductions, enough, I fear, would remain to leave on my mind a belief that we had better leave M. Thiers to himself in the execution of his designs against free trade, & national amity as connected with it. Oct. 9. 1871.

573. Mr. Gladstone to Lord Granville. [G.D. 29/60]

[Hawarden Castle]. Oct 14. 71.

1. Do you think this Wigan case[6] is one in which we, or I, can properly move the Queen to subscribe ? I do not think there is any claim. The only question is whether it is for her advantage *now* to let out more in this way as a sort of substitute for other ways ?

2. Col. Ponsonby wrote to me after my departure from Balmoral that my visit had worked well. But I fear this can mean little ; for of course, at such a time, I carefully avoided the sore subject. She talked however of the Homburg business ; and this was put in train for the Chancellor to take up.

[1] Good reasons for this as other treaties will expire then. [J. B.]

[2] Not likely. This might be guarded against without doubt. [J. B.] Marginal note by Granville : Yes we should be secured ?

[3] The Assembly is only too submissive—& even so our position would be no worse. [J. B.] Marginal note by Granville : then we fall back upon the present treaty till 12 months after its denunciation ?

[4] Seems to be impossible—or may be easily guarded against. [J. B.] Marginal note by Granville : Yes in the same way and to the same extent.

[5] The position of France—her calamities & her humiliation—should go for something with us. Unfortunate that Thiers and Pouyer Quertier are great Protectionists. It may seem necessary for them to gain popular support in some quarters. Five or six years hence there will be a new Government or President in France. *Then*, will matters be better or worse for us & for Free Trade if we now shut the door which even Thiers is willing to leave partially open ? I suspect much worse. J. B. Oct. 28. 71.

P.S. If the Treaty was thought so great a thing in 1860, can the proposed modifications make it worth nothing now ? I think not, & am sure the Board of Trade letter is sufficient proof of it. J. B.

[6] Colliery disaster, 6 Sept.

3. *We* certainly have over-stumped, or shall have over-stumped. But you cannot help it; nor can I. I have had much difficulty and *labour* in fighting off all manner of invitations. I think Glasgow cost me seven or eight letters.

4. Spencer is to come here tonight & spend Sunday, to talk over many Irish matters fully.

574. Lord Granville to Mr. Gladstone. [Add. MS. 44168, fo. 165]

16, Bruton Street. Oct 15/71.

I think I should forward two letters (not Mr Harvie's) to Ponsonby, but leave with him the responsibility of deciding.

I believe they have good traditions as to the Queen's charities, and unless it were a very strong case, it is not desirable that the Minister should interfere.

2. It was perhaps as well that you were not able to approach the important subject with the Queen. She would turn a very deaf ear to any advice at this moment, when she is in receipt of nothing but expressions of (real) sympathy with her in her illness.

I am like Princess Alice, desponding as to the future; and the best chance is some spontaneous movement when she is better.

3. I am glad you have Spencer with you for a time.

4. How much can I say as to attention to social questions from the Gov.

5. This coalition with the workmen,[1] which is probably exaggerated, will do Dizzy harm with his practical & sensible friends, and cannot have much political effect.

It perhaps explains Lichfield's insisting on his resignation as Lord Lieutenant.[2]

I was much opposed to my manager Roden coming into Parliament. I was afraid of his neglecting his business and of his sacrificing the interests of our business to those of his election. As far as I can perceive the only result has been to enlarge & improve his views as to the proper relations between Employers and their workmen.

575. Mr. Gladstone to Lord Granville. [G.D. 29/60]

H[awarde]n [Castle]. O. 15. 71.

£500 seems to me better.[3] But will not every one who reads it in the paper suppose it to be a donation of the Queen's own not of the British people? If it is recommended to H M should not the public fund at any rate only be pointed out as the source from which it may be defrayed if she prefers it? It seems to me, I own, hardly in the nature of a Secret Service.

[1] A group of Conservative peers was reported to have made contact with the trade union leaders, William Allan, Robert Applegarth and George Potter, and to have undertaken to support seven propositions drawn up by the workmen, see *The Times*, 16 Oct., p. 9.

[2] See above, nos. 502, 504. Lichfield, a Liberal peer, was known for his close association with trade union leaders.

[3] As a contribution to the relief of distress after the great Chicago fire. Granville had forwarded to Gladstone a letter from Hammond, 12 Oct., proposing to give £1,000 out of secret service in the Queen's name, G.D. 29/60.

576. Lord Granville to Mr. Gladstone. [G.D. 29/60]

Copy. Walmer Castle. Oct 15/71.

I have read your very able mem with great care. It is perhaps more of a pleading than a judicial summing up, but it is very difficult.

I think there are some mistakes in the P.S. as to the possibility of treating other nations more favourably than us, and also as to our position if the Assembly reject the Treaty, and I have availed myself of your permission to send the postscript to Mallet.[1]

577. Lord Granville to Mr. Gladstone. [G.D. 29/60]

Copy. Confidential. W[almer] C[astle]. Oct. 15/71.

Do not forget to send me some of the *personal* points we talked of at Whitby, and which I may possibly bring in at Manchester.

You have exhausted what is to be said on the general question, & I can only hope that the Quarterly Review which Dr Smith when at Walmer told me wd make a bitter attack on all the Departments of the Govt may supply some topics.

578. Mr. Gladstone to Lord Granville. [G.D. 29/60]

Hawarden Castle. Oct. 17.71.

1. I hope you read an able Article in the Standard of Oct. 14 on the French Treaty question. In case you should not, I send it herewith, begging it may be returned.

2. I pondered long upon the main question before writing, and do not doubt that my paper now seems what indeed it is, the expression of an adverse opinion: only subject to correction on better information.

3. I have duly racked my brain, but cannot recollect what are the "personal" points, talked of at Whitby, to which you refer.

4. I went over a multitude of Irish matters with Spencer—they will keep till we meet. She has nearly got rid of the traces of lameness.

This Manifesto,[2] Internationale & something more, ought to make some sport for us. Is it Dizzy? The brain that produced the India Bill of 59 might well have produced even this.

What you say of Roden involves a very high compliment.

579. Lord Granville to Mr. Gladstone. [G.D. 29/60]

Copy. 16, Bruton Street. Oct 18/71.

I am off to Manchester in half an hour. I have written a draft of a conversation with Leon Say [3] which contains nothing new. He is very pleasing. But after all

[1] Relates to no. 572; see Gladstone to Granville, tel. 10.30 a.m., 14 Oct., for permission to send the postscript to Mallet, G.D. 29/60.

[2] See above, no. 574 note.

[3] In London 17–19 Oct. to bring the thanks of Paris to the lord mayor and city of London for her revictualling after the siege; see Gavard to Granville, private, 10, 14 Oct., G.D. 29/89, *The Times*, 18, 19, 20, 23 Oct. Granville to West, No. 122 commercial, 20 Oct. (written 17 Oct.),

that has passed, it is not very civil bringing the Legion d'Honneur to the Lord Mayor.

[P.S.] Hompesch called on me to deliver his letters of recall. He said he had no instructions to explain to me the reason of the recall of the ministers at London, Paris, & Brussels. In conversation I gathered from him that they were all ultramontane, and anti Prussian. He said (which I do not doubt) that he would do his best to have the mission in London retained. He offered to come back to deliver his letters of recall in person to the Queen. I explained to him in civil terms that this would not be necessary.

I propose to recall Howard, and substitute Lytton as a permanent Chargé d'Affaires.[1] This will be in the spirit of the recommendation of the Diplomatic Committee,[2] and we shall have three most intelligent men in Germany to watch the progress of unification, and to report on the religious question, which has Munich for its centre. I do not think we ought to be without a representative there considering the presence of the R. R s of all the other Great Powers.

I shall be back on Friday evening.

580. Mr. Gladstone to Lord Granville. [G.D. 29/60]

Hawarden Castle. Oct 19.71.

I do not remember the exact recommendation of the Committee but your arrangement about Lytton seems in itself a good one.

Nothing can be more unsatisfactory than M. Say's say at the Mansion House about the French Treaty.

I hope to see you in the Train before this reaches you & remain . . .

581. Mr. Gladstone to Lord Granville. [G.D. 29/60]

10, Downing Street. [24 or 25? October 1871].

Coleridge *advises* applying to Palmer [3]; but would not himself remain. I think this being so we shall have to give up applying to P. who would not consent to displace C.

582. Lord Granville to Mr. Gladstone.[4] [G.D. 29/60]

[25? October 1871].

There must be a flaw in Coleridge's character or understanding. Do you remember the fuss he made about Collier.

recorded Leon Say's view that France wished to revise rather than to denounce the Cobden Treaty, F.O. 27/1882.

[1] Cf. Howard to Granville, private, 29 Oct., 4 Nov., G.D. 29/95. Lytton refused appointment and Morier was moved from Stuttgart to Munich.

[2] See *Report from the Select Committee on Diplomatic and Consular Services, Parl. Papers.* H.C. 238 (1871). vii, 204.

[3] To replace Collier, who had been offered, 16 Oct., appointment to the judicial committee of the Privy Council, Add. MS. 44540, fo. 136. Coleridge took Collier's place as attorney-general and Jessel replaced him as solicitor-general, Nov.; see Add. MS. 44432, fo. 159.

[4] Written on the back of no. 581.

It appears to me a little wanting in courtesy to Palmer to remove Collier without any communication with Palmer.

You applied to him in the first instance as the man with a preeminent claim.

He refused on account of one subject—on which he behaved well—I presume that Jessel, Harcourt, Denman & West cannot stand in comparison with R[oundell] P[almer] as a public servant.

Would not Coleridge yield, having such untenable ground, as he did before.

583. Mr. Gladstone to Lord Granville. [G.D. 29/60]

10, Downing Street. Oct. 26.71.

In part of your mem. yesterday (within) I think there must be some verbal error.

I doubt whether Coleridge's former yielding strengthens my ground for attacking him. He then stood upon a *personal* objection—he now stands on a rule of professional etiquette.

He once having taken this ground I am persuaded Palmer would not agree: & I think that in pressing Coleridge we shall violate a good general rule of official promotions, and even if we succeeded obtain a concession which has no grace & little value unless it be voluntary.

I have seen Glyn: he is strong in the same conclusion.

A word on Harcourt. His language was last night at *Goschen's House* that nothing would induce him to take office. And more of the same kind.

584. Mr. Gladstone to Lord Granville. [G.D. 29/60]

10, Downing Street. Oct 27.71.

I have got the Dasent letter [1] back & I understand you have kindly engaged to speak to the person principally concerned or to take some equivalent step. Your silence will mean consent.

585. Lord Granville to Mr. Gladstone. [Add. MS. 44168, fo. 169]

Walmer Castle. Oct 28/71.

I have just recd the news of your immense success. I am delighted, & wish you joy with all my heart.

I will see Doctor Dasent as soon as I get to town.

586. Lord Granville to Mr. Gladstone. [Add. MS. 44168, fo. 170]

Walmer Castle. Oct 28/71. 7 P.M.

How sorry I am for you all at this moment.

I ought perhaps to have volunteered to take your place, but it would have had a bad effect.

[1] Relates to the editorship of *Fraser's Magazine* which Dasent wished to combine with his work as a civil service commissioner.

I will administer your sweets and bitters to Dasent. I am not convinced that he deserves much of the latter. Ryan turned off Fred: Bruce as incapable of doing the duties of Secretary of the Railway Board—and I believe takes longer holydays than Dasent does—and I doubt Gurdon being right as to the coincidence of the Times' hostility with Delane's absence.[1] If it was so, my opinion of Dasent would be entirely changed. He would be a great humbug, of which I do not suspect him.

587. Mr. Gladstone to Lord Granville. [G.D. 29/60]

10, Downing Street. Oct 29.71.

The business on Blackheath yesterday involved some excess of physical effort and has left me voiceless or nearly so. This excess always disturbs memory & reason, & among other errors I forgot to say even a word of foreign policy. The multitude was vast, much the largest I ever spoke to in the open air. A knot of about twenty people, roughs from Westminster as I am told, were there to speak against me which they did stoutly except for about the last half hour. Glyn & Co are very well pleased and politically I think the affair was quite satisfactory: the enthusiasm at the break up was immense (perhaps from relief!).

I arrived here at six to a moment & had an hour with Ozanne [*sic*] & Tissot. O. seemed to divine the thing did not look very favourably & backed out of the statement about Thiers's not *himself* wishing etc. I tried not to indicate any thing. They added absolutely nothing to the argument.

Nothing new as to offices.

588. Mr. Gladstone to Lord Granville. [G.D. 29/60]

10, Downing Street. Nov 4.71.

1. Read the inclosed from Halifax.[2] I do not know for [whom] he is moved. I am *not* moved as to C[ardwell]. But as between the two *B*'s [3] I have had scruples from the first as to one of them, & these rather gain strength.

2. I have thought over your objections to my sketch [4] of an eventual reply about the Treaty: and, if we fail in doing what you want through Wolowski, I do not see that it is inadmissible. It spares the French Govt all labour as to details. It

[1] I.e. when Dasent took charge; see *History of the Times* (1939), ii. 498.

[2] To Gladstone, 4 Nov., on the possible choice of Cardwell as Speaker, Add. MS. 44185, fo. 208. Cf. an earlier letter, 31 Oct., *ibid.*, fo. 200, and Mrs. Cardwell to Gladstone, 22 Oct., asking him to persuade her husband to stand, Add. MS. 44432, fo. 74. An undated exchange between Gladstone and Granville on Cardwell's refusal to stand, Add. MS. 44168, fo. 174, not printed.

[3] Bruce and Brand. The latter was nominated Speaker, Feb. 1872.

[4] Dated 2 Nov., against further negotiation for the revision of the Cobden Treaty but offering re-consideration if other nations assented to the French terms, G.D. 29/60. For Granville's objections see his drafts of reply to the French proposals of 13 Sept. and to West, No. 133, 2 Nov. For the unfavourable but temporizing British reply see Granville to West, No. 132, 1 Nov., first draft 25 Oct., much revised by Forster, Fortescue and Gladstone, F.O. 27/1882. The negotiation was closed by de Broglie to Granville, *note verbale*, 30 Nov., F.O. 27/1887. France then published her intention to denounce the Cobden Treaty, 17 Dec., but to negotiate during the 12 months' period of notice.

imposes on them no new labour whatever. It only deprives them of our *authority*: and that is what, it seems to me, they ought never to have asked, & we never ought to give.

3. Bright proposes to come to Hawarden on the 13th.

NB. Monday 8 Pm, *exact*.

589. Lord Granville to Mr. Gladstone. [Add. MS. 44168, fo. 172]

Foreign Office. Nov 6/71.

I do not know what are the grounds of the change in Halifax's opinion.

I adhere as strongly as possible to the disadvantage to us of losing Cardwell.

I still think it injudicious of him to wish to change, but I understand better than I did his wish to do so.

If however Bruce is objectionable, as appearing to make a convenience of the speakership, I am afraid this will apply, (although unjustly) to Cardwell. Did you read the sneer in the Spectator yesterday.

Freddy Leveson to whom I mentioned the matter in complete confidence and on whose discretion I have full reliance, does not see the objection to Bruce—but apart from the convenience, which he fully appreciates, would personally prefer Brand.

590. Mr. Gladstone to Lord Granville. [G.D. 29/60]

10, Downing Street. Nov. 8.71.

I send you for your private perusal a mem. by Gurdon.[1] I have not asked him minutely but I take it that this Memm represents the sentiment of the office in its upper region.

I took as you did a favourable view of the letter of Mr Dasent: but I do not doubt it would be well to turn this opportunity to account for the purpose of conveying to his mind; (or at any rate of refreshing his impression on the point) that the office he holds is an office requiring what is termed the whole time of the holder, i.e. one leaving only odds & ends, fragments available through special strength & diligence, to his free disposal.

What I have suggested will I think help Dasent's case should it come into Parliament.

591. Mr. Gladstone to Lord Granville. [G.D. 29/60]

10, Downing Street. Nov. 10.71.

1. We were rather too slenderly represented at Guildhall last night. I thought that after Manchester you were entitled to beg off: but if we are in this time twelve

[1] 8 Nov., on Dasent's letter to Gladstone, see above, no. 584. It disapproved and again blamed Dasent for the hostility of *The Times*, G.D. 29/60. Cf. Granville to Gladstone, possibly written in the cabinet of 8 Nov., asking whether he might mention Gladstone's approval with which he agreed, Add. MS. 44639, fo. 123.

month, expect an attack from me. The audience was unruly but not so bad as the Times represents. The dinner & arrangements worse, I might say even worse, than usual. The Lord Mayor though a Tory good-humoured and fair to us. Having given a surfeit of Home politics at Blackheath, I put myself for the time into your Department.

2. Pray do not suppose I have formed an opinion adverse to Dasent. On him, & on many subjects, one is obliged to entertain & bear in mind, without accepting as proved. The likelihood of a stir in the H. of C. was a special reason for the wish that, without any reproach, we should state & he accept the proper official rule.

3. Cardwell's Financial Secretaryship is offered to Campbell. I suppose that if I fail with J. B[right] I ought to try to get Dodson either for the Duchy or the Judge Advocateship—but not until the business of the Speakership gets out. He ought to know, when the offer is before him that we have turned our eyes in another direction. Again as to Northbrook. Would the Duchy, without the Cabinet (as I think it must be) be a lift, or a compliment, to him? If it would, he ought to have the first offer. This I propound also to Cardwell.[1]

4. I propose when we come up again to have a long and serious talk about Royal Family matters—with a few, at all events.

5. Brewster accepts[2]: in handsome terms.

6. I met Broglie in Piccadilly yesterday & had a few words. He was in good humour but interpreted us as almost refusing about the Treaty. You see D. News follows in the wake of Standard & Times.

592. Lord Granville to Mr. Gladstone. [Add. MS. 44168, fo. 175]

Walmer Castle. Nov 11/71.

I shall be at your orders at this time next year, as at all times. In the meantime I do not recognize the paramount duty of each minister to render an account of his Department to the Lord Mayor in order that the Times may have a subject for several critical articles. I read your speech with much pleasure, and it required great skill to touch up the history of last year, to which luckily no new facts are being added.

From Glyn's account Campbell ought to be a catch.

I believe Dasent is to be at Deal Castle today. I will say to him exactly what you desire.

If J. B[right] refuses, as I presume he will do, something ought to be said to Northbrook either offering it to him, or saying that you abstain from doing so, on account of his much greater use at the War Office, with a hint that the one office will lead to higher things as soon as the other, circumstances permitting.

I did not know that Broglie was come back. I suppose he will come down here.

[1] Dufferin did not resign the duchy of Lancaster until he was appointed viceroy of Canada, March 1872; see below, p. 325, note 2. Dodson refused the office of judge-advocate-general, offered 19 Dec., Add. MS. 44541, fo. 18.

[2] Appointment to the royal commission to enquire into the loss of H.M.S. *Megaera*.

593. Mr. Gladstone to Lord Granville. [Add. MS. 44540, fo. 161]

[*Copy*]. Nov 11.71.

These papers [1] are disagreeable. I think Cockburn has behaved extremely ill. As to the proceeding itself I need not say that in all judicial matters of appointment I take the advice of the Chancellor & I believe I have never once departed from it, so I can look at this without being warped by prejudice in favour of a decision originally springing from me. But I really think there is no just cause to complain. We have appointed to the Court of Appeal, a man who by usage had had a title not only to be made a Judge, but to be made the head of a Court & a President over Judges. No one in the Cabinet was disposed to criticise. But there will doubtless to debate upon the matter [*sic*]. I propose to circulate the papers herewith, when you return them.

594. Lord Granville to Mr. Gladstone.[2] [Add. MS. 44168, fo. 178]

Walmer Castle. Nov 12/71.

I return this disagreeable correspondence. There can be no doubt that Cockburn *does* " act from an unfriendly spirit, and not from a sense of duty only ".

The Cabinet completely assented to the arrangement. Sufficient attention was perhaps not given to the technical point—For technical it only is.

You & the Chancellor have probably judged rightly in sending only a quasi acknowledgment to Cockburn's letter. It is however just a question whether to a protest from the head of the Common Law judicature, and a Member of the Privy Council some answer on merits ought not to be made. But of this you & the Chancellor are much the best judges.

I think you said at the Cabinet that Collier wished to have 3 months tenure of the judgeship—and that we agreed with you that that would have been only a sham.

595. Mr. Gladstone to Lord Granville.[3] [G.D. 29/60]

Secret. Hawarden Castle. Nov. 15.71.

Bright has been here for 48 hours of which we passed I think near a fourth in conversation on public affairs. Everything, in & everything out of, the Cabinet, I told him as far as my memory would serve ; and I think we pretty well boxed the political compass. On the whole I remained convinced of two things ; first that his heart is still altogether with us, secondly that his health though requiring great care is really equal to the moderate demands we should make upon him. The truth is I was quite as much knocked up with our conversations as he was : but then I had the more active share.

[1] Cockburn to Gladstone, 10 Nov., and reply, 11 Nov., on Collier's appointment to the judicial bench so that he might be made one of the four paid judges of the judicial committee of the Privy Council under the act of 1871.

[2] The second and last paragraphs printed, Morley, ii. 383–4.

[3] Printed by Morley with small omissions, ii. 381–2.

In the whole range of subjects that we travelled over we came to no point of sharp difference and I feel confident that he could work with the Cabinet now as harmoniously & effectively as before. In saying this I should add that I told him with respect to economy that I thought we should now again set our faces in that direction.

I told him that we should not expect of him ordinary night attendance in the House of Commons and that his attendance in the Cabinet was the main object of our desire.

He was pleased & touched with our desire & he has not rejected the proposal. He has intimated doubts & apprehensions but he reserves it for consideration & seemed decidedly pleased to learn that the question *might* be held open until the meeting of Parliament in case of need. I thought it well to give him all this length of tether but at the same time I pointed to the Cabinets of next month as the proper time for his joining our deliberations.

He said distinctly that if he felt sure as to his bodily strength he would not hesitate. I did not think it fair to put to him again the request by which I endeavoured to hold him in Decr. 1868 viz. that he would not determine in the negative without seeing me again: but I begged and pressed that he should in no case refuse without taking the opinion of a first rate London physician as these are the people whose wide experience best enables them to judge in such cases. Altogether my experience of him was extremely pleasant, and he was popular beyond measure in the House where the guests were one or two ladies, and for gentlemen Sir Geo. Prevost a High Church (but most excellent) archdeacon, John Murray the Tory Publisher, and Hayward whom to describe it needs not. One and all were charmed with him. In his character, the mellowing process has continued to advance, and whatever he may have been thirty years ago he is now a gentle and tender being.

Yesterday he had 5 hours of conversation with me; & much with others, also an hour & a half's walk in the rain which seemed to do him no harm whatever.

I will add but one word: he was deeply impressed with the Royalty question though disgusted with Dilke.[1]

Will you kindly send this to Cardwell that I may not multiply writings on the subject. I have sent a line to Halifax who was anxious to hear.[2] Details I will report to the Cabinet. He was not *keen* about the French Treaty question.

P.S. In reading Layard of the 8th [3] about Slavery I asked myself whether the degree of intervention in Spanish politics & home questions which it implied was quite warrantable or safe. This may be owing to my want of information. L. himself seemed to have no suspicion on the subject.

[1] He had developed at Newcastle, 6 Nov., the theme of excessive expenditure on the court already opened in the Commons, S. Gwynn and G. M. Tuckwell, *The Life of . . . Sir Charles W. Dilke* (1917), i. 139–40.

[2] Copy, secret, 15 Nov., on Bright's not having 'refused' to rejoin the government, Add. MS. 44185, fo. 221. Cf. note by Granville with Gladstone's note on the cabinet of 21 Oct., Add. MS. 44639, fo. 106.

[3] To Granville, private, G.D. 29/99.

596. Mr. Gladstone to Lord Granville. [G.D. 29/60]

Hawarden Castle. Nov. 20.71.

I am much concerned to hear of your sharp gout, but I hope you will rally briskly.

Pray meditate on the Royalty question: as I am doing, to the best of my power. You see Dr Norman McLeod has been at it. I think Disraeli and he are about the two greatest flunkies in the country, & it is right they should fall foul of one another.

The Paragraph in the Times today is founded on a note of mine to Delane:[1] except the cut in the last sentence at J. Favre, rather a cruel one.

I return Ayrton's letter.[2] It seems difficult for us to set him to work without an appearance of doublefacedness. If he can suggest any thing off his own hook as *amicus curiae* I suppose he may; owning that character explicitly.

There are indications of a storm about Collier: but I really think the Chancellor was right in the advice which he gave me, & for which I have made myself responsible jointly with him. An Attorney General may be appointed Lord Chancellor & sit in appeals alone—or Lord Justice, & sit in appeals with another Judge—or to Cockburn's own office & sit in appeals on this very Judicial Committee. Who can say that apart from breach of law the spirit of the law is contravened? There is no trace whatever of an intention to make a stricter rule for the future.

Read Standard of today on the Treaty.

597. Mr. Gladstone to Lord Granville. [G.D. 29/60]

Secret. Hawarden Castle. Nov. 22.71.

I send you herewith a letter which came from the Queen by this morning's post. The first I have had from her since I was at Balmoral. I also send copy of my reply[3] which I hope you will approve. You will see it is meant to open the way for something from a barrel of larger bore.

I cannot but be glad the opportunity for an opening has thus been afforded me.

Do not write if inconvenient as nothing presses for the moment.

598. Mr. Gladstone to Lord Granville. [G.D. 29/60]

Hawarden Castle. Nov. 25.1871.

1. From a letter of Bright's,[4] herewith, you will see that the matter is not hopeless.

[1] 18 Nov., denying that the plan to settle the Roman question by a European conference originated with him, Add. MS. 44540, fo. 169. This was alleged in Jules Favre, *Rome et la république française* (1871), p. 92.

[2] To Granville, Paris, 19 Nov., offering to negotiate with Wolowski and Chevalier for the revision of the Cobden Treaty, G.D. 29/71. Cf. reply, 22 Nov., refusing the offer, G.D. 29/77.

[3] See the Queen to Gladstone, 19 Nov., and reply, 22 Nov., on Dilke's Newcastle speech and 'republicanism', *Letters*, 2nd ser., ii. 164–9.

[4] To Gladstone, 24 Nov., mainly on the Education Act and the Liberal party, Add. MS. 44112, fo. 193; and reply, 25 Nov., *ibid.*, fo. 195; cf. Gladstone's mem. on the Education Act, 25 Nov., Add. MSS. 44760, fo. 125.

2. The inclosed from Sydney [1] will show it related to a preliminary question which I had put to him, with regard to E. Clinton as a possible successor to Lord Suffield who has resigned. Of course this will not go forward without your approval. I think however we are as likely to want votes in the Commons (where I hope he will be) as in the Lords.

3. I have from Childers a most flourishing account of himself.

4. Acting on Halifax's suggestion, I write to the Speaker about Brand.[2]

5. Is it time to write a farewell letter to Apponyi? [3] I would not put any question to you that you could not answer by another hand.

599. Lord Granville to Mr. Gladstone. [G.D. 29/60]

Copy. Secret. Walmer Castle. Nov 26/71.

You must have thought my answer to your telegraphic enquiry of today [4] that of a poor creature. But the fact is that I have never had such a licking from the gout. The general health is improving. There is nothing in the elbow & less in the knees & feet.

Beau Elice always preached that a long and severe attack was the best in the long run, but it is a bore while it lasts. My doctor, who knows no more than I do of what is likely thinks I shall not be able to go to London on the 4th or 5th, which I am particularly anxious to do, over and above the chance of meeting you which I trust your question indicates.

I have thought much of the Royal Question and very pretty sauce for the gout it is. The more I think the less (like cet imbécile de Wolowski) I find. Any plan good for its purpose appearing to me difficult to frame—the power of resistance very strong—the elements for carrying it out weak.

To begin an ineffectual struggle very disadvantageous.

From the accounts of today from Sandringham,[5] I think there is no real alarm.

600. Lord Granville to Mr. Gladstone. [Add. MS. 44168, fo. 182]

Walmer Castle. Nov 26/71.

This is a most painful question. The Queen's letter is not her own—there is hardly a single word underlined.

Your answer about Dilke is excellent. But I do not think it was quite prudent to give Her warning of what she will think means an attack from Her Ministers upon her, until you have made up your mind whether anything and what can be done.

[1] 24 Nov., that the lordship-in-waiting resigned by Suffield, 19 Nov., on going into the household of the Prince of Wales, might go to Clinton; see to Sydney, 21 Nov., Add. MS. 44540, fo. 172.

[2] See to the Speaker, 25 Nov., that the government would support the election of Brand as the new Speaker, Add. MS. 44540, fo. 177.

[3] See Gladstone to Apponyi, 30 Nov., Add. MS. 44541, fo. 2, and reply, 2 Dec., Add. MS. 44432, fo. 212.

[4] 10.40 a.m., 26 Nov., whether he was well enough to go to London within the week. Granville telegraphed that he could not go until 4 or 5 Dec., G.D. 29/60.

[5] On the illness of the Prince of Wales.

Although there are objections to Balmoral, there are conveniences connected with it. At Windsor I am afraid she will consult innumerable people, most of whom will give her bad and irresponsible advice. The best will abuse the Ministers, in order to avoid giving an opinion on her own conduct.

The Cabinet will be much divided. I am very anxious to talk the whole matter [over] with you.

The Queen's illness and Sir C. Dilke have both strengthened her position against beneficent advice.

601. Lord Granville to Mr. Gladstone. [Add. MS. 44168, fo. 184]

Walmer Castle. Nov 26/71.

Very pleasant reading indeed your conversation with Bright. Nothing can be more satisfactory—and I hope there is a fair chance of his agreeing to your proposal. The importance of his accession cannot be overrated.

Hayward who wrote to me for the sole purpose that " he had been at Hawarden to meet Bright " gave the same good account of his intellect, but a less good one of his body.

602. Mr. Gladstone to Lord Granville. [G.D. 29/60]

Hawarden Castle. Nov. 26.71.

The inclosed letter from Lowe [1] follows up one of the subjects included in mine of the 22d to the Queen, now in your hands.

It seems to me a nice matter to determine whether a Minister should now, outside of Parliament, answer Dilke in his own person, and I wish much to have your judgment upon it. There is a natural impulse towards concurring with the Queen's wish; but it ought not to be done to her detriment. I shall be able to come nearer a conclusion, when Lowe sends me all the information. At present I lean to think it imprudent & hazardous for him to handle the subject in detail unless the case is *complete & clean.* I am doubtful whether it may prove so: for about the payment of the Income Tax, which I had hoped would come out perfectly clear, it appears that there have been rules laid down for her benefit which are not allowed to subjects in general, & that there has been at least one palpable oversight committed by the Treasury in her favour. If there are holes in the case, this will happen: Lowe will make his speech, & be cheered no doubt; but Dilke will reply, and Lowe cannot reply upon him, or at least cannot enter on a war of words in the newspapers, & some of the dirt will *stick.*

If the case does not turn out thoroughly good, still 1. He might say at Halifax two things. First that people should suspend their judgments till the matter can be debated freely and fully in the House of Commons. Secondly that whatever has been done Ministers are responsible and not the Queen. (*We* must beware of treating the attack as an attack upon the Queen.)

[1] 25 Nov., on what he would say at Halifax on the civil list question raised by Dilke at Newcastle, Add. MS. 44301, fo. 217. Cf. further letter 27 Nov., *ibid.*, fo. 219. See above, no. 595.

2. We might put out the good parts of a reply, perhaps, in a pamphlet, by way of provisional answer. I mention this for consideration.

I will show this letter to Lowe,[1] and ask him to come here on his way to Halifax, or if it seems more likely to be effectual will come up to London myself & run down to Walmer for an hour or two—I must be here, if I can, on the 7th, and 10th.

My telegram of today has reference to this subject—I am truly sorry you are still suffering so much. The latest bulletin of the P. of Wales does not seem so good.

603. Lord Granville to Mr. Gladstone. [G.D. 29/60]

Copy. Walmer Castle. Nov. 27/71.

Bright's letter looks promising. It is of great importance that he should agree, but in any case you must be glad at having made the offer.

I should be glad that E. Clinton got something[2] and I know how anxious you are to help him. Otherwise I am strong against the thing. If these Household places are worth anything it is (under the present regime and non obstante Dilke) that they strengthen Govt for ordinary legislation particularly in the Lords.

The Queen often tries to break down the rule in favour of nonpolitical persons, & you & your predecessors have objected.

Do you suppose Childers is a candidate for Office.

Pray write to Apponyi. He will value it exceedingly.

604. Lord Granville to Mr. Gladstone. [Add. MS. 44168, fo. 186]

Walmer Castle. Nov 27/71. 9 P.M.

Your letter is just arrived, and the post is going out. I can therefore only scribble my first impression.

The Queen like all women, and most men when attacked, is in a great hurry to issue her defence, and she will resent as lukewarmness delay on the part of Her Ministers. But as you say it is their duty to take a businesslike view of what is the best course for her.

If the case, unlike most cases, is clear full and unanswerable a naked statement of it cannot do harm. But even then, I believe it would be better that it should be brought out in a sympathetic assembly, such as the House of Commons.

My inclination would be that Lowe should refer to Dilke without contempt or respect, but that he should condemn the *act* of bringing such a subject, which could only have one tendency before an audience, who could not possibly have the knowledge required to judge of the case—or to dispute any of the assertions—that he Lowe was not going to make the same error in a converse sense.

That the responsibility of such acts as Dilke had taken upon himself to state

[1] See Gladstone to Lowe, 28 Nov., inviting him to Hawarden and outlining a reply as no. 602, copy in *ibid.*, fo. 221.

[2] Not made a lord in waiting (see above, no. 598), but appointed to the commission to enquire into the property and income of Oxford and Cambridge Universities, 26 Dec., Add. MS. 44432, fo. 306.

as facts, would lay [*sic*] exclusively with the present or previous Ministries, and he looked forward to the time when on the meeting of Parliament he & his colleagues would be prepared to show in a place where every detail could be thoroughly sifted, how rashly & {falsely / inaccurately} the charges had been made.

I doubt about a pamphlet. What strength Dilke has is chiefly derived from the Press, where a rich possessor of the Athenaeum & part owner of the Daily News plays an influential part with literary men.

One night's debate in the House of Commons would shut up the question, if there are not many screws loose in it, better than anything else.

605. Mr. Gladstone to Lord Granville. [G.D. 29/60]

Most Private. Hawarden Castle. Nov. 28. 1871.

1. I see on a dispatch of Howard's about a Penal enactment against the Clergy in Germany the words 'approved by Ld Granville'.[1] I am not quite sure of their meaning. As to the dispatch, it appears to me to describe this law, in its first & second paragraph respectively, in terms that do not harmonise together. The description in the second Paragraph has the appearance of being chosen: and if it is correct I own I do not understand the objections taken by Howard to the law, especially considering the circs and methods which prevail in Germany.

2. I am sensible of the inconvenience you indicate as connected with my letter of the 22d to the Queen: and probably in the actual state of things I should have done better to confine myself to simple reply. But I have no doubt whatever on the question itself of a further representation for I think it impossible for me to allow, during even an indefinite time, things to proceed as they have gone this year, without making a serious representation and effort in relation to so grave a public mischief.

3. A Telegram direct from Sandringham has greatly relieved me this afternoon as to the Prince's illness. I hope too that your *paces* may mend.

606. Mr. Gladstone to Lord Granville. [G.D. 29/60]

Hawarden Castle. Nov. 29.71.

1. E. Clinton is a Candidate for Household Office. We also *hope* he may in February resume his seat for North Notts. I quite think the Lord in Waiting should be a Parliamentary Personage. I do not suppose we need make great haste about filling up.

2. The inclosed has been sent me by Spencer relatively to a wish he had expressed that Mr Macdonnell should be made a Peer.[2] It would be going very much beyond the Rogers precedent: in which there was the old family and Baronetcy, and the

[1] See Howard to Granville, No. 287, 22 Nov. The phrase is in the hand of T. F. Wetherell, initialled and dated by him, F.O. 9/211. No other dispatch in the volume bears this unusual comment.

[2] Spencer's letter untraced. Macdonnell was made a baronet in 1872.

prospect of active work. I declined Dr Lushington on account of his age, which however was more advanced.

3. Bright writes me a lengthened letter about Education.[1] I am pleased too with his *not* addressing his Constituents at present: it looks rather Ministerial. I am endeavouring gently to give the screw another turn; but must not be sanguine.

607. Lord Granville to Mr. Gladstone. [G.D. 29/60]

Copy. Walmer Castle. Nov. 30/71.

The Despatch from Howard was one of a batch which I read in bed, and which I told my private secretary to return to Hammond in due course. His "approved by Lord Granville" applied to Hammond's query "circulate", not to the substance of the Despatch, about which I agree with you, but as it only was Howard's opinion addressed to me, it is hardly worth while to argue with an ultramontane who has been recalled.

I send you a letter from E. Clinton's Mother in law aiming at smaller game.

I did not know that Kimberley had appointed Sir F. Seymour Governor of Malta. He is a great goose, with a pretty but silly wife.

I agree with Lord Grey that the Governor should be a civilian—an arrangement which might have enabled you to do a stroke of business.

608. Mr. Gladstone to Lord Granville. [G.D. 29/60]

Hawarden. Dec. 1.71.

1. I am perfectly content, & quite agree, about Howard's letter.

2. I know nothing of the appointment to Malta, and at first hearing it surprises me; qy Is it true?

3. From Biddulph's letter within I think the Queen has not taken as much alarm at mine of the 22d as might perhaps have been expected.

4. Lowe gives way handsomely after a hard battle[2] and comes here tomorrow with Mrs L. to talk over his speech for Halifax on Monday.

5. I cannot say the case of the Income Tax stands well for jealous debate—i.e. The Queen has paid a great deal, but there are holes I think in the case, beginning from a minute of Peel's in 1842. I have asked for an account of the matter to be prepared for the Cabinet, as I expect that in Ld Aberdeen's words to the Duke we shall 'hear of it'.

I do hope your cruel enemy is relaxing his grasp.

I do not know if Petre has any of the same leanings as Howard.

609. Lord Granville to Mr. Gladstone. [G.D. 29/60]

Copy. Private. Walmer Castle. Dec. 4/71.

Bobby Meade came here on Saturday evening. He knew nothing about Malta, so it must be a mare's nest of Lady Hartopp's.

[1] Rochdale, 28 Nov., Add. MS. 44112, fo. 199; see above, nos. 595, 598, and below, no. 738

[2] Cf. Lowe to Gladstone, 29 Nov., and reply, 30 Nov., Add. MS. 44301, fos. 225, 227. See above, no. 602.

The Lordship in Waiting does not press.

I am taken aback by the proposal to make Macdon[n]ell a Peer.

I doubt whether the Lingens, Hammonds etc would be valuable additions to the Peerage.

What are Tennyson's politics. How about Rothschild, Moncrieff [*sic*], and some rich country gentlemen of old family.

My health is much better but I am still most stupidly helpless.

Lytton (foolishly) has refused Munich—West does not wish for it.

Petre has the next claim. But I doubt its being a good thing to send another Catholic to Munich. I therefore propose to transfer Morier who desires it to Munich, and send Petre to Stuttgardt.

610. Mr. Gladstone to Lord Granville. [G.D. 29/60]

Hawarden Castle. Dec. 6. 1871.

I am disappointed with the part of Lowe's speech [1] which relates to the Queen. He went from here possessed as I thought with the programme founded mainly on your excellent letter, which he warmly praised: but his memory seems for once to have been treacherous. He said too much about the Income Tax, and if Dilke has sufficient resolution & sagacity to track it out, he will get Lowe into a scrape—on the other hand he seems to have omitted to insist upon that which is the safest of all grounds as far as the Queen is concerned, namely our exclusive responsibility. Her character was put forward as the defence.

How admirable his illustration of the star was.

2. I send you letters about the Speakership. My opinion remains as it was.[2]

3. I agree about Petre and Morier. Am very sorry Lytton declines: his talents seem quite extraordinary. I judge you thought he made a mistake in carrying that message to Andrassy.

611. Lord Granville to Mr. Gladstone. [G.D. 29/60]

Copy. Dec. 8/71.

I am sorry to have troubled you with a cypher,[3] which in any case will also be too late.

I am quite knocked down by the telegram of today. I was hardly aware of how strong my personal attachment was.

I am not a competent adviser about the Speakership. I see nothing to make you retract your offer to Brand. The only point, which is not a new one, is the having once been whip to the Liberal party.

I noted the omission in Lowe's good speech.

He had written me a short note rather contraverting the reticent doctrine.

[1] At Halifax, 4 Dec., *The Times*, 6 Dec., p. 3.

[2] In favour of Brand. Cf. Gladstone to Halifax, 6 Dec., Add. MS. 44541, fo. 7.

[3] 8 Dec. suggesting national prayer for the Prince of Wales. Gladstone telegraphed, 5.0 p.m., that he had not deciphered it. Granville then telegraphed *en clair*, G.D. 29/60.

I am as well as I can be without the power of motion. Unless I have a relapse I shall be in town on Monday.

612. Lord Granville to Mr. Gladstone. [G.D. 29/60]

Copy. Walmer Castle. Dec 10. 1871.

My doctor who is an old woman, and my wife who is a young one, which is worse, object to my going to town tomorrow. But I mean to do so. Would it be very inconvenient to you and the others to meet in Bruton Street. It would save me a good deal of transshipment.

If so will you let Hammond know. He will take means to warn those who arrive late in town.

613. Mr. Gladstone to Lord Granville. [G.D. 29/60]

11, Carlton House Terrace. Dec. 10.71.

1. I will move the Cabinet to Bruton Street.[1]

2. The £10 correspondence of Ld Russell's made me sad, this sadder.[2] It is like King Lear in the last stages. He knows not what he says; & vain it is that we present us to him. I do not see how your answer could be better: so it is of little account that I cannot read the word in which you suggest a misgiving about it.

3. Should not Elliot, if that £ 15,000 appear as an allegation against Dalling, instantly call for proof?

I tremble to open the next Telegram from Sandringham.

614. Mr. Gladstone to Lord Granville. [G.D 29/60]

Secret. 11, Carlton House Terrace. Dec. 13.71.

I have seen Cardwell and settled matters with him in a way which I hope will be satisfactory considering that these affairs can only be dealt with by reciprocal movements of approximation. He reduces 1 ¼ million, and 6000 men.[3]

615. Lord Granville to Mr. Gladstone. [Add. MS. 44168, fo. 192]

16, Bruton Street. Dec 13/71.

I am very glad that you have put up your horses together—and at no great sacrifice.

My doctor would not hear of my going to the University today, and has per-

[1] For cabinet, 11 Dec., held at Bruton Street on 'Collier appointment, Dilke Speech, Speakership, French Treaty,' see Add. MS. 44639, fo. 124.

[2] Russell to Granville, 8 Dec., on the dismemberment of Turkey, G.D. 29/79, and reply, 9 Dec., copy in G.D. 29/60 with covering note to Gladstone: 'Is his brain softening and is the enclosed proposed answer too pert'.

[3] Cf. Cardwell to Gladstone, 9 Dec., and reply, 11 Dec., Add. MS. 44119, fos. 286, 299; Gladstone's note on the cabinet, 14 Dec., which discussed the army estimates, held at Bruton Street, Add. MS. 44639, fo. 126; mem. by Gladstone, 12 Dec., Add. MS. 44760, fo. 126.

suaded me to avail myself of your kind offer to meet here tomorrow instead of Downing St.

Could you meet Beust here en petitissime comité, notwithstanding Brunnow saying that he (Beust) will make a point of inveigling you & me into some declaration about European politics of which he will make use en temps et en lieu.

616. Mr. Gladstone to Lord Granville. [Add. MS. 44168, fo. 194]

[19 December 1871].

Should I mention here [1] the question about a public act of Thanksgiving by the Queen ?

The only precedent, for an analogous matter, I have yet discovered, is that Geo III went to St Paul's in 1789 on his recovery.

617. Mr. Gladstone to Lord Granville. [G.D. 29/60]

Secret. Hagley. Dec. 22.71.

I hope you are peaceably lodged at Walmer and taking benefit from sea-air and comparative repose. You have had a hard time : & it will be a great pleasure to learn that it is over.

On Wednesday I had a long and very interesting conversation with the Duke of Cambridge ; which it was curious to compare and in some respects contrast with our *entretiens* on the Army Bill. He is warm, and even eager in the whole matter : but I think his views in the main are those of real sense and prudence.

We have arrived at a great crisis of Royalty : only it is a crisis which may be overlooked, because the issue is in a remote future. Not the less is it true that *this* in all likelihood is the last opportunity to be given us of effecting what is requisite.

I was with the Queen yesterday for an hour. No one can be a worse reporter than I am of conversations ; but I have put down some notes of this. I inclose the paper & beg you to return it. It will look as if written to show that I produced a considerable effect on the Queen's mind. But probably she had made it up to the effect of starting with *very* strong doctrine, so as to be able to part with some of it on the way.

About that republican business, I have sometimes thought whether, though I should not like to make a political splash of it, I could have a sort of talk to neighbours at Hawarden in the village schoolroom which might be reported. I should like to please the Queen in the matter, if I could do it without injuring her. The fear is reviving a controversy which probably for the moment is well laid : but which will revive of itself, unless we do something much beyond mere words to keep it down. If I did it I should avoid the polemical tone. If you favour this notion I shall at any rate think more of it. If not I shall abandon it at once.

[1] I.e. in the cabinet. For cabinets of 15, 18, 19 Dec., all held at Bruton Street, see Add. MS. 44639, fos. 128, 133, 139. Granville's reply was written below on no. 616 which was then returned : ' Better to mention it. Duke of Cambridge came this morning. He would like much to see you on this subject, and probably about things to be done in order to give the Prince employment. I do not like his particular idea, which is to keep him informed of all that goes on in the F.O.'

I trust Lady Granville & you will encourage one another in the matter of health and wishing you a most happy Christmas I remain . . .

What do you say, as we do not take E. Clinton, as to the Lordship in Waiting?

P.S. The Report [1] will go tomorrow.

618. Lord Granville to Mr. Gladstone. [G.D. 29/60]

Copy. Walmer Castle. Dec. 22/71.

I send you a good letter from Sir Richard Wallace. You will see it is a protest against my refusal to recommend to you Dr Cormack.

All the Paris people were thanked, and the letter published.[2] Wallace Blount & Malet had honours.

Lyons spoke to me of Cormack, and said that if additional honours were to be given he was the fittest. But he admitted that neither he nor any of them were inclined to let their reward be in their good work.

Pray let me know what you think.

Hugessen has written to complain of not being a P.C. and of his being a bad hand at asking.[3]

619. Mr. Gladstone to Lord Granville. [G.D. 29/60]

Hawarden Castle. Dec. 24. 71.

Sir R. Wallace has been perhaps a little misled by his own Baronetcy which was due to mixed considerations his conduct in Paris being one of them. Upon the whole I think you right in not putting forward Cormack but the weights in the scales are not very uneven & had you recommended I should not have opposed.

I do not comprehend either Hugessen's grievance, or his incapacity in the point referred to. What precedent can he allege? Into F. Peel's case I think some consideration of his Father's name may probably have entered. Certainly it was done early.

The Memorandum I promised is not quite ready.

I wish you & Lady G. a happy Xmas and New Year and I remain . . .

My wife has received for her Convalescent Home three anonymous donations of £1000 each through the same Channel. We are told by more than mere rumour though not with absolute certainty that this too is Sir R. Wallace.

620. Lord Granville to Mr. Gladstone. [Add. MS. 44168, fo. 197]

Secret. Walmer. Dec 24/71.

Many happy Xmas' to you—and your's and thanks for your good wishes about my health which is certainly making progress.

[1] See below, nos. 619, 620, 621, 622.

[2] Parl. papers. [C. 413] (1871). lxxi, 285.

[3] Not traced, but cf. Hugessen to Granville, 22 Feb. 1872, G.D. 29/73. He was made P.C. 24 March 1873.

I look forward to your memo.

I hope you are right about the effect produced—that some should have been produced is certain, by your strong & sympathizing expression of that which in her interest you have thought so much. But there is always the chance of her wishing to avoid the immediate contest, & to live to fight another day.

About the lecture at Hawarden. If you give it, I shall probably feel surprise that I ever had any doubts. On the other hand, my inclination is that you should wait for the House of Commons, where the debate on the address will give you the exact keynote of the feeling to which you must address yourself.

At Hawarden the very necessity of being judicial in your tone, may be misinterpreted in the present excitement. But I cannot say 'no', if it is to prevent your doing what on reflection you may think desirable.

I think Rosebery & Clarendon stand first for the Lordship, but as one never knows what pleases and what affronts, I would wait till the meeting, & *speak* to Rosebery.

621. Mr. Gladstone to Lord Granville. [G.D. 29/60]

Hawarden Castle. Xm D. 71.

1. Col. Ponsonby will by this time have sent you a noteworthy letter by young Knollys on the subject of the future avocations of the Prince of Wales. I now add one of Col. P's to me in reply to a letter of mine.[1] The Duke of Cambridge long ago expressed to me his conviction, which I took to be knowledge, of his readiness to go to Ireland.

If the Queen lived near her work as of old, and if the P. of Wales lived near her, and subject to the further condition of the Queen's willingness, something might be effected through Foreign Office business, *she* standing between the Govt. and him. But in the absence of all these conditions I do not see what can be done.

2. I now send you my slovenly memorandum [2]—and I well know the force of what you say—the Queen understands the *reculer pour mieux sauter*: and moreover though quite sincere in giving way she sometimes lets the original motives subsequently resume their force. Meantime, being my own Reporter, you will see that I give myself the best of it.

622. Lord Granville to Mr. Gladstone. [G.D. 29/60]

Copy. Walmer Castle. Dec 28/71.

I return the report of your most interesting conversation. It is impossible that what you said should not have had some effect. The Queen would not be insensible to such thoughtful advice.

[1] See Gladstone to Ponsonby, 22 Dec., and reply, 23 Dec., Guedalla, i. 320–3; cf. Granville to Ponsonby, copy, most confidential, 26 Dec., and reply, 28 Dec., G.D. 29/33, and Ponsonby to Granville, 1 Jan. 1872, G.D. 29/34.

[2] Mem. by Gladstone, 25 Dec., recording the conversation of 21 Dec., as occurring 'yesterday', Add. MS. 44760, fo. 129. It began with the plan of a public ceremony of thanksgiving for the recovery of the Prince of Wales, went on to the future of monarchy in England, and ended with the employment of the Prince of Wales.

Did you see the Dean of Windsor, & if not would it not be worth while to write a line to him.

623. Mr. Gladstone to Lord Granville. [G.D. 29/60]

Hawarden Castle. Dec.29.71.

1. I am not moved by the Belgian Rhetoric.[1] We did a very special act under very special circs and I should be very sorry if it were to become a precedent for every day; as I have no doubt you would also.

2. I omitted to thank you for your reply about a Village Discussion on Republicanism. I have given it up—& this without feeling certain that the subject will come up on the night of the Address, as however it readily may.

3. I am very much concerned not to hear of your at length throwing off your severe attack.

624. Mr. Gladstone to Lord Granville. [G.D. 29/60]

Hawarden Castle. Dec.30.1871.

Perhaps I am too fastidious about the matter of the presentations at Rome but Antonelli has asked Jervoise to undertake them "as being the Agent of H.M. Govt. in communication with the Holy See". It seems to me that Odo Russell's practice was quite right but he carefully kept it unofficial. Now Severn acted officially, and if we consent to this as a transfer from Severn, do we not get hooked into the Pope's principle of double representation which we have not accepted and with which we have no desire to mix ourselves.

It seems that Antonelli also said he wanted nothing more than the Certificate of an informed and credible person and on this ground, if it be explicitly stated, I suppose that Jervoise might continue to give introductions as O.R. gave them *simultaneously* with Severn's action & not as replacing it.

To make my meaning clear, I have put some suggestions in pencil on the margin.[2]

625. Mr. Gladstone to Lord Granville. [G.D. 29/61]

[*No.* 2]. Hawarden Castle. [30 December 1871].[3]

1. Without doubt Hammond hits a blot in the shape of an anomaly.[4] But my impression is that the Council never orders discontinuance: & if so it is left either

[1] Relates to a paper by the ex-secretary of King Leopold urging the signature of a separate Anglo-German treaty within the framework of the general guarantee of Belgian neutrality, enclosed in Beaulieu to Granville, private, 19 Dec., G.D. 29/83.

[2] I.e. of draft No. 1, 3 Jan., to Jervoise instructing him to conform to Odo Russell's practice in the presentation of British subjects to the Pope. It incorporated Gladstone's addition: 'especially in respect to the avoidance of any sign of formal or official intervention', F.O. 43/117.

[3] Date supplied from the copy in Add. MS. 44541, fo. 25. The undated letter was docketed as received for filing 14 Jan.

[4] Relates to the means of stopping the prayers for the recovery of the Prince of Wales ordered by the Privy Council.

to the Primate or the individual clergyman & the former seems an improvement on the latter.

The Archbishop made no communication to me: it struck me that something might have passed between him and the Queen.

2. I will write to Powerscourt.[1] Following you at a most respectful distance I have taken a touch of rheumatism. It is I suppose the nature of old limbs to crack.

626. Mr. Gladstone to Lord Granville. [G.D. 29/61]

Hawarden. Ja 1. 72.

What do you say to Friday 19th for a Cabinet—and to Tuesday 23rd for the Cabinet to dine with me? [2]

627. Lord Granville to Mr. Gladstone. [Add. MS. 44168, fo. 201]

Walmer Castle. Jan 3/72.

I send you a private letter from Lytton.[3] He is evidently a very able & clever fellow. Whether he may not have a little too much of that zeal, which Talleyrand dreaded in a Diplomatist is not certain.

I also send you the answer, which properly dressed up, I should be tempted to send to Lytton's despatch.[4]

I have just got the telegram from Buchanan desiring me not to send any answer till I hear from him, but I am not sure that something vague & friendly to Austria may not be desirable, in any case.

I have no doubt that there is some truth in what Andrassy says, that Prussia if she saw Austria & ourselves on really friendly terms, would be inclined to lean less on Russia.

Any agreement of any kind is quite out of the question.

I am sorry to say that I thought Buchanan [5] who paid me a visit here frightfully commonplace.

[1] See to Powerscourt, 31 Dec., offering the lordship-in-waiting resigned by Lord Suffield, Add. MS. 44541, fo. 26; see above, p. 284, note 1, below, no. 630.

[2] See notes by Gladstone on the cabinets of Friday 18 Jan. (*sic,* Friday was 19), Monday 22 Jan., and discussion after the cabinet dinner, 23 Jan., Add. MS. 44640, fos. 2–8.

[3] To Granville, private, Vienna, 26 Dec. 1871, F.O. 362/3; carried by special messenger together with his report of Andràssy's overture for an understanding with Britain, No. 108 most confidential, 27 Dec., F.O. 7/791. Lytton here emphasized the sincerity of the overture: 'no pledges or engagements on our part' were wanted; pledges were offered on Austria's part for 'the defence of our Indian Empire and our general interests in the East'.

[4] See Granville to Buchanan, No. 13 confidential, 16 Jan., rejecting 'prospective understandings to meet doubtful contingencies', F.O. 7/796; part quoted Temperley and Penson, *Foundations,* p. 344.

[5] On leave in London from St. Petersburg since 22 Nov., before going to Vienna; visited Walmer during the last week of Dec.

628. Mr. Gladstone to Lord Granville. [G.D. 29/61]

Hawarden Castle. Jan 3. 72.

1. By a series of mistakes I wrote first to Powerscourt and did not stop my letter though meaning to do so: I must now therefore take my chance.

2. I have recommended Mac Cormack [1] [*sic*] and return Wallace's letter.

3. The Queen would I think like the Virginian Lady's letter.[2]

4. Ponsonby sends me, by her desire, an account from Sandringham, a letter which without intimating any thing like actual danger, is less satisfactory than the Telegrams.

5. Please give me your opinion on the idea of a K C B for Jenner.[3] The Queen had first suggested C.B.

I should have liked to hear your malady was walking off—as mine seems to be —But it *was* a trifle only.

629. Mr. Gladstone to Lord Granville. [G.D. 29/61]

Hawarden Castle. Jan 6. 72.

I think your draft of reply to Lytton extremely good.[4] It avoids commonplaces, and avoids engagements. It would be ridiculous for us to place ourselves in the same degree of forwardness of position as Austria in those questions in which Austria is interested most. The compensation she offers as to India is illusory. No one can suppose that Austria would make war upon Russia in the event of her attacking India merely because she was in general harmony with us in questions of European interest. Speaking generally two things may be said—We seem to have no subject of controversy actual or probable with Austria and events in Europe may not improbably take a turn which may incline us—and her to the same course of action. But I can never forget that the people of Alsace & Lorraine may continue ardently French, and *if* that country shall become the Venetia of Germany, that will be a great perhaps an insurmountable bar to the effectual sympathy of England.

I cannot know enough to pass judgment on Buchanan or on Lytton but this I seem to see that more *ambassador's* work properly so called has been done at Vienna during the interregnum than in the previous $2\frac{3}{4}$ years of this Government.

I suppose that after Buchanan's request you will not fire off a detailed answer at once.

On the margin I have made one or two suggestions of a minor kind in pencil.

Many thanks for the Telegram & letter about Powerscourt, which relieved me —I have not heard from him yet.

I have been reading Lady Georgiana's Poems.[5] They have a marked & char-

[1] See above, nos. 618, 619. Cormack was knighted, 14 March.

[2] Enclosed in Thornton to Granville, private, 19 Dec., on the illness of the Prince of Wales, G.D. 29/80.

[3] Granville to Gladstone, 5 Jan., agreeing to K.C.B. for Jenner despite the rule that it should be awarded only to those who were already C.B., Add. MS. 44168, fo. 207, not printed. Jenner's acceptance, 12 Jan., Add. MS. 44433, fo. 47.

[4] Cf. the Queen's favourable comments, Ponsonby to Granville, 13 Jan., G.D. 29/34.

[5] Lady Georgiana Fullerton, *The Gold Digger and other Verses* (1872), pp. 102, 149.

acteristic charm. Taking design & execution together, and without any disparagement to 'Vita' I place 'Mary' first among those I have read, according to my own liking.

I think of being in London on the 16th.

If Powerscourt fail shall I write to Vernon?

630. Lord Granville to Mr. Gladstone. [Add. MS. 44168, fo. 209]

Walmer Castle. Jan 7/72.

I hope Powerscourt will accept, as Vernon though a very good little fellow is a wretched voter.

"'Tis a *bad* thing to have as brother in law,
A very magnificent three tailed Bashaw"

like Elcho.[1]

I am much touched at your selection among Georgy's little poems.

631. Lord Granville to Mr. Gladstone. [G.D. 29/61]

Copy. Private. Walmer Castle. Jan 8. 1872.

I presume that Andrassy sent the same message to Berlin & to London. If both had jumped down his throat, he would have gone on as a triple alliance which Lytton saw he was aiming at. But finding that it would not do at Berlin, and Buchanan being a wet blanket, he changed his language to us.[2] I think we may send the answer as it stands with a supplementary despatch, rejoicing that it appears that Andrassy is very much of our opinion, & promising not to talk of the matter to Beust, unless he is instructed to speak to me, or to any other person representing any Foreign power.

632. Mr. Gladstone to Lord Granville. [G.D. 29/61]

Hawarden Castle. Jan. 11. 1872.

1. I am now entirely satisfied by letters from Windsor that the Queen though she will not open Parliament (which I for one never expected) will sanction and share in the Thanksgiving at Saint Paul's.[3] I am now engaged in a smart action of Telegrams with Osborne about a visit we are to pay there—it may possibly come off on Saturday week. PS. No: Wednesday next.

2. I do not doubt your dispatch was perfectly safe as regarded Andrassy; but the *fact* of his receding from his own spontaneous & rather gratuitous language does not look as if he were very strong.

[1] Lord Vernon and Lord Elcho married two sisters, daughters of the first Earl of Lichfield. Cf. Granville to Gladstone, tel. 5 Jan., G.D. 29/61. It reported Biddulph to Granville, 3 Jan., on the Queen's wish for either Powerscourt or Vernon as a lord in waiting, G.D. 29/34; see above, p. 284, note 1, and no. 625, below, nos. 636, 637.

[2] Cf. Buchanan to Granville, private, 11 Jan., F.O. 362/3.

[3] Cf. Gladstone to the Queen, 10 Jan., and reply, 13 Jan., Guedalla, i. 324–6.

3. That is a horrible story of the ship Hope *alias* Anna [1]: and it raises a very grave question for us. That such things ought to be prevented there is no doubt; but I think it is Melbourne, which does them, that ought also to apply the remedy. Not merely because of the burden to John Bull. Not merely because of the difficulty of working naval police at the other end of the world. But because Victoria [who] is now demanding in high language some of the highest privileges of independence ought to be able to discharge its most elementary duties.

4. As at present advised I must go up on Monday night to try & get rid of a matter in dispute between Lowe (who is now fighting at almost all the points of the compass) and the Council Office.[2]

633. Lord Granville to Mr. Gladstone. [G.D. 29/61]

Copy. Walmer Castle. Jan 14/72.

I send you a correspondence of a very important character raised by a letter from Westbury.[3]

I hope you will not agree with him in thinking that we ought to speak at once without waiting for our counter case.

The 2d matter as to R. Palmer's attendance at Geneva,[4] & which can probably be satisfactorily settled. I believe Cockburn does not really care about the dual pleading (which wd be a farce) but about having Palmer by his side at Geneva in which he is perfectly right.

I hope to be sound by Friday. We go to town on Thursday.

634. Mr. Gladstone to Lord Granville. [G.D. 29/61]

Hawarden Castle. Jan 14. 72.

I very decidedly agree with you that we ought not to go out of the line of proceeding laid down in the Alabama case for the purpose of protesting. I have not seen

[1] See E. March (consul Fiji Islands) to Granville, No. 7, 19 Sept. 1871, received 8 Jan. 1872, reporting the share of this ship of Melbourne in the kidnapping of south sea islanders for work in Fiji or the Australian colonies, F.O. 58/129; see also Colonial Office to Foreign Office, 12 Feb., and enclosure, F.O. 84/1360. This slave trade disguised as legal immigration was checked by the act of 1872.

[2] Relates to the proposed publication, in the auditor-general's annual report to Parliament, of a Treasury letter to the Council Office blaming the defalcations of an accountant in the Science and Art department upon Henry Cole, the department's head. Ripon claimed that Cole was not responsible and that the Treasury letter should not be published without his reply. The latter was published, but Cole resigned Feb. 1873. See Ripon to Gladstone, 9 Jan., Add. MS. 44286, fo. 129, Lowe to Gladstone, 2, 8, 10, 11, 12 Jan., Add. MS. 44302, fos. 4–13. See also Forster to Granville and reply, 17 Nov., 2 Dec. 1871, G.D. 29/56.

[3] To Granville, 7 Jan., showing that part of the American case on the Alabama claims, which claimed on account of indirect damage, was not legitimate matter for the arbitrators to judge and urging an immediate British protest. Cf. Granville to Palmer, 8 Jan., enclosing Westbury's letter and his reply, and Palmer's reply, 10 Jan., and Granville's rejoinder, 11 Jan., G.D. 29/67.

[4] Together with Cockburn in order 'to supervise the statements and possibly to plead' before the arbitrators; see Granville to Palmer, 15 July, and reply, 19 July 1871. Palmer, 10 Jan., found that attendance in July would interfere with his professional duties. Granville replied that the timetable could be arranged with Cockburn, 11 Jan., G.D. 29/67.

the American Case [1] yet. But it looks to me as if, supposing it to be as it is described, all the bunkum and irrelevant trash might be handled in some degree as 'Americanism' due to want of knowledge of the world and of European manners. We cannot *in propriâ personâ* go far in this line: but I think much might perhaps be made of it in a pamphlet or some other unofficial medium, through which we might retaliate a little, show up their method of working foreign politics for home purposes, and allow that it was too much to expect from the President, who has got to be re-elected, with Sumner for an enemy, altogether to avoid reproducing Sumner's notorious speech,[2] although he must have known it could only do mischief to his case, if it did *any thing*, before a Tribunal of Arbitrators.

I am struck with the tone of Palmer's letter,[3] as to the public question I mean. But I never knew his original case against Arbitration. Some case he must have had; but what was stated in Lord Russell's dispatch was really no case at all.

I hope his attendance at Geneva will be secured.

I stand to be in town tomorrow evening & am glad you are certified to be moveable.

635. Mr. Gladstone to Lord Granville. [G.D. 29/61]

Hawarden Castle. Jan 15. 72.

I read Lyons's letter with misgiving, yours with comfort.[4] Pouyer Quertier may very well be more of a fox than Thiers, if he is less of a mule. He wants to get done that for which he does not want to be responsible. Our position about the Treaty is good & sound, & we ought not to compromise it by fidgetting. All they have a right to expect is that we should be ready to aid them as far as fiscal exigency is concerned, and I take it they know this already. Even here there may be difficulties as to what exigency is fiscal.

I send you the Queen's letter about St Paul's.[5] The Dean named to me an *hour* as the limit & it ought not to be narrower. Every thing shows (including even this letter of assent) that our position, after the illness of last summer, has become worse than ever as to combats in detail; & that accordingly it is more than ever desirable to think of some larger arrangement. In his Memoir of the Duc de Broglie, Guizot says "Dans la monarchie constitutionelle, la condition du lien entre le roi et le pays, c'est que la fidelité soit réciproque". Now is it less true that this fidelity lies in works as well as faith, and in visible & sensible works as well as insensible.

[1] See Parl. papers. [C. 476] (1872). lxix, 175; for the British case [C. 469], *loc. cit.* 1; see also Tenterden to Granville, 30 Nov., 2 Dec. 1871, G.D. 29/106, and for Gladstone's views, Hammond to Granville, 1, 6, 7, Dec. 1871, 7 Jan., G.D. 29/104.

[2] In the Senate, 13 April 1870, causing its rejection of the Clarendon-Johnson Treaty for the settlement of the Alabama claims.

[3] To Granville, 10 Jan., saying that he 'acquiesced' in arbitration rather than believed in it, G.D. 29/67.

[4] See Lyons to Granville, private, 12 Jan., on Pouyer Quertier's offer to come to England on the tariff question, G.D. 29/87; and discouraging reply, private, 12 Jan., G.D. 29/109. Cf. from Lyons, No. 57 commercial, 22 Jan., with Granville's min., F.O. 27/1936; to Lyons, No. 27 commercial, 26 Jan., F.O. 27/1934.

[5] To Gladstone, 13 Jan., Guedalla, i. 326.

636. Mr. Gladstone to Lord Granville. [G.D. 29/61]

10, Downing Street. Jan 16. 72.

I have seen Powerscourt and I find he is not afraid of the attendance at Court. But he has a fear and a wish. The fear is, of being obliged to spend the entire Session in London, to the prejudice of (useful and public-spirited) occupations in Ireland, and specially in Dublin. His hope would be, to be intrusted, like Morley and others, with the conduct of a Bill now and then.

I told him I thought he had better call to see you on Friday and learn how far these matters could be arranged.

All he has written and said increase my desire to get him into the Government. Believe me. . . .

637. Mr. Gladstone to Lord Granville. [G.D. 29/61]

Osborne. Jan 18. 1872.

1. I inclose a letter from Powerscourt [1] again declining, in kind terms. Please to consider whether you will still ask him to call on you. I think he has been a little precipitate, after agreeing to refer to you.

2. I also send a letter from the Queen, with my reply.[2] It affords new proof of the likelihood of increased difficulties of the future, and of the advantage which would attend any *comprehensive* mode of meeting them which might be found practicable: if we can venture to hope so much.

H.M. is well and cheerful—asks much about your gout.

Cardwell declines G.C.B.[3]

638. Lord Granville to Mr. Gladstone. [Add. MS. 44168, fo. 210]

16, Bruton Street. Jan 20/72.

May I ask Kildare, & Clarendon / Ilchester } to move & second.

I should like to consult Bessborough on the question of discipline before I asked Powerscourt to reconsider his refusal.

I thought your letter very good to the Queen, but I am not sure if when the time comes, that there would be much objection for the Queen if she would curtail the time, suddenly going to Germany to see her niece—& it would do her health infinitely more good than 3 weeks at Osborne.

639. Mr. Gladstone to Lord Granville. [Add. MS. 44541, fo. 52]

[*Copy*]. Jan. 24. 72.

1. What you told me last night has suggested my expressing to you the hope that

[1] 17 Jan., refusing the lordship-in-waiting and repeated refusal, 22 Jan., Add. MS. 44433, fos. 69, 81; cf. above, no. 630, below, no. 660.

[2] To Gladstone and reply, 18 Jan., on the Queen's proposed visit to Baden, Guedalla, i. 326–8.

[3] To Gladstone, 16 Jan., Add. MS. 44120, fo. 1.

proper arrangements have been made by or with De Tabley who is gone abroad for some months.[1]

2. The Japanese doctrine about Corea is horrible.[2] What Adams has said is very good & he is right in taking prudential motives for his base of operations, but might we not throw in a word to the effect that this would be according to our notions a gross iniquity & that we cannot believe they will ever perpetrate it. So that they may not hereafter say this was never stated to them.

3. Will it not be needful for you to make known independently of the action of Thiers, who will desire secrecy, our explanation or protest about Sur Taxes on raw materials & the compensating duties ? [3]

4. I was grieved at your letter about Severn [4] & you will be still more shocked when I tell you after considering the case that in my opinion the Treasury cannot properly go beyond £80 per ann ! But you will perhaps be relieved when I add that we will undertake to find him either £60 per ann fr. C.S.P. (which is less probable) or an annuity of £60 in the shape of the money which will buy that sum from the Special Service Fund of the Civil List.

5. I circulate an interesting letter from M. Chevalier.[5]

6. What do you think of Bury to succeed (Kenmare) Castleross[e] ?

640. Lord Granville to Mr. Gladstone. [Add. MS. 44168, fo. 212]

16, Bruton Street. Jan 24/72.

1 I have made no arrangement with de Tabley, & doubt whether Bessborough has. St Albans offered to resign, but I gave him leave under the sad circumstances.[6]

2 I will instruct Adams as you propose. I hope the Japanese will not ask whether Europe concurs with us.

3 Our despatches to Lyons were pretty sharp—& I have written a letter to the Bradford Chamber of Commerce. I will tell Lyons to communicate our remonstrances to some of his Free Trade friends. I should dislike any semi official announcement of what we have done, unless it comes naturally.[7]

[1] De Tabley resigned the treasurership of the household on arranging to stay in Rome until April, 5 Jan., Add. MS. 44433, fo. 19.

[2] See Adams to Granville, No. 121 confidential, 2 Dec. 1871, received 19 Jan., reporting a conversation with the Japanese foreign minister about the eventual conquest of Korea, F.O. 46/143. Adams's language was simply approved, No. 5, 20 Jan., F.O. 46/150.

[3] Part of the tariff changes, announced 12 June 1871 (above, no. 540), were shelved, 19 Jan., but finally enacted, 26 July. Thiers had represented Britain to the Assembly as favourable, 13 Jan. Britain then protested against the proposed internal taxes on raw materials and the compensatory import duties on British manufactures ; see to Lyons, tel. 18 Jan., No. 15 commercial, 19 Jan., altered in the cabinet, 19 Jan., Nos. 23, 24 confidential commercial, 24 Jan., F.O. 27/1934, Add. MS. 44640, fo. 2.

[4] Untraced.

[5] Missing from Gladstone's correspondence with Chevalier, Add. MS. 44127.

[6] Allowed to retain the captaincy of the yeomen of the guard and the position of second whip in the Lords when he went to the Near East, Nov. 1871–April 1872, Bessborough to Granville, 30 Sept. 1871, G.D. 29/71.

[7] Cf. Granville to Lyons, private, 27 Jan., G.D. 29/109 ; Lyons to Granville, tel. 28 Jan., suggesting an inspired article in the English newspapers, F.O. 27/1937.

4 I am glad to hear of poor Severn.

I think Bury [1] would do well.

Chevalier's letter is interesting.

The Belgians wish us to tell the French Gov that we acknowledge their right to denounce the treaty at any time (with a year's grace [)]—so that they may not have the excuse that it must be done by the 4th of Feby to force it down the throats of the Assembly.

Shall I tell Lyons to do so, and to communicate the facts to Chevalier, or leave it alone.[2]

I send you another letter of Westbury's.[3]

The Belgians as usual had no sort of proof of the Yankees bribing the Swiss, had only heard a rumor that it was probable.[4]

Bessborough suggests [5] Delawarr to second ?

641. Mr. Gladstone to Lord Granville. [G.D. 29/61]

Immediate. 11, Carlton House Terrace. Jan 27. 72.

I read the Treaty dispatches from Paris last night, and put down the particulars in the inclosed Paper for consideration & correction ; [6] not as an answer, but as a text for the sort of language we are to hold in Parliament.

I propose that you and I should meet on Thursday to consider the *foreign* Paragraphs of the Speech which will be the pinching part ?

642. Lord Granville to Mr. Gladstone. [Add. MS. 44168, fo. 216]

16, Bruton Street. Jan 27/72.

Mrs Gladstone is a great physician.

I am not quite up to the mark today. I will be in West's room down stairs at 2–30, in case you can come in just before you go to the Cabinet.

I think your draft would be excellent as a despatch to Lyons today. May I propose it to the Cabinet.[7]

Gwydir refuses. Ilchester has not answered. I might telegraph to Powerscourt to second ?

[1] Refused the vice-chamberlainship of the household, 4 Feb., Add. MS. 44433, fo. 126.

[2] The Assembly authorized Thiers to denounce the Cobden Treaty, 2 Feb. His success was clear by 25 Jan. The Treaty ran from 4 Feb. to 4 Feb. with provision for a year's validity after denunciation. Britain held that this year began on 4 Feb. following the denunciation ; France that it began on the date of denunciation. Britain accepted the French view, 27 Jan.

[3] 26 Jan., urging again an immediate protest against the indirect claims ; see also Granville's reply, 27 Jan., arranging a meeting, G.D. 29/67. See above, no. 633.

[4] Cf. Beaulieu to Granville, private, 24 Jan., answering Granville's enquiry, G.D. 29/83.

[5] To Granville, 23 Jan., G.D. 29/71. He moved the address, which was seconded by Powerscourt, 6 Feb.

[6] See Lyons to Granville, Nos. 74 confidential commercial, 75 commercial, 25 Jan., on the likelihood of the denunciation of the Cobden Treaty, F.O. 27/1936. Gladstone's paper, provided with a preface by Granville, became No. 29 commercial, to Lyons, 27 Jan., on Britain's readiness to ease French fiscal difficulties but her dislike of protectionist proposals though ' she did not close the door to them ', F.O. 27/1934. Cf. Granville to Lyons, private, 27 Jan., G.D. 29/109 ; see below, nos. 642–45.

[7] For the cabinet of 27 Jan., see Add. MS. 44640, fos. 13, 14.

I shall ask your leave to retire early from the Cabinet. But I do not wish it to be here.

I shall be at your orders on Thursday.

643. Mr. Gladstone to Lord Granville. [G.D. 29/61]

Imme. 11, Carlton House Terrace. Jan 28. 72.

1. I thought Lyons was to be in possession *today* of our view about dates of denunciation; according to what was settled yesterday in the Cabinet. I should think he could not communicate to a better man than Chevalier—who however is not, I think, in the Assembly.

2. I do not understand what agreement the Americans have broken, as is alleged in the main part of Westbury's letter. He states admirably the question of motive.

3. I know no reason against Ld Delawarr.

4. I wait to hear what you advise as to the Lord in Waiting and

5. I presume you will confer with Bessborough about De Tabley's tenancy.

644. Lord Granville to Mr. Gladstone. [Add. MS. 44168, fo. 218]

16, Bruton Street. Jan 28/72.

As you had seen the draft, I signed and sent the despatch yesterday evening. It contained our views of the denunciation. I have sent to enquire whether there was any hitch. I wrote at the same time a private letter to Lyons, telling him to give the substance of the despatch at once to the French Gov, and to do the same confidentially to his Diplomatic Colleagues and to opposition Deputies as the most efficient way of getting it known in time. If you think "confidential" too restrictive, I might telegraph to him to put a liberal construction on the word.

Westbury comes to see me today—at his own proposal—I shall listen.

He appears to me quite right as to the impracticability of going into motives, but I should have thought he laid down the rule too absolutely.

In a case of murder, would not counsel try to show that the accused was jealous of the victim, or that he would profit by his death.

I thought Tenterden's preface to the questions put to the Law officers [1] was good.

What do you think of Wenlock or Delawarr* for the Lord in waiting.

(* If we are not obliged to have recourse to him to move).

I have written to Bessborough about de Tabley.

645. Mr. Gladstone to Lord Granville. [G.D. 29/61]

11, Carlton House Terrace. Jan 28. 72.

I should think the word confidential rather tight when you want the matter to get out though without indication of the channel—discreet or careful use is I suppose the thing intended.

[1] On the British position in relation to the claims for indirect damage included in the American case for the Geneva tribunal.

I should incline to say in answer to your argument from jealousy in a case of imputed murder that here the matter is relevant because the juridical character of the crime does not depend upon the character of the act done only but on intention also, malice prepense as I believe they call it—but of this distinction international law knows nothing and looks only to the thing done or omitted in itself.

I will ask my wife about Wenlock but I should have supposed his character as a voter did not stand high & I fear he would not stand the restraint.

646. Mr. Gladstone to Lord Granville. [G.D. 29/61]

16, Bruton Street. Jan 31. 72.

The method of handling the Alabama question which is exhibited within [1] occurred to me this morning when the idea had lain for some time heavy & undigested. I mean for the *Speech* only a comparatively small though important matter.

Halifax who came in has seen & likes it as it now stands. But please to sift & ransack it pitilessly.

What we want I suppose is to exhibit watchfulness & lay solid ground for the future—not to inspire *alarm*.

Forster has written a Memorandum which he will circulate.[2]

I am really glad to miss you: it shows further progress on the right road.

647. Lord Granville to Mr. Gladstone. [Add. MS. 44168, fo. 222]

16, Bruton Street. Jan 31/72.

Is it quite right that the Queen should argue with the Yankee case. Would it not do to record all that has passed—the acceptance under the Treaty of Washington by the Emperor of Germany of the arbitration in the case of San Juan—the sitting of the court of Arbitration at Washington—the meeting of the Arbitrators on the Alabama Claims at Geneva—(I will get a correct form of what has been done.)—and then to continue as you propose.

"I have caused to be prepared and presented to the Arbitrators a preliminary statement of the British Case, upon the Alabama claims, and my Gov are considering the further steps which it will be their duty to take for the prosecution of the arbitration within the terms of the Instrument." [3]

The last words are very significant, & can be strengthened to any amount in debate.

I met the Chancellor Sir Roundell Palmer, the Attorney General, Tenterden and Bernard this afternoon.

[1] I.e. a draft for part of the Queen's speech at the opening of Parliament, returned to Gladstone, 31 Jan., together with no. 647 below.

[2] Not in the volumes of correspondence with Gladstone, Add. MS. 44157, or Granville, G.D. 29/56. Cf. Gladstone to Forster, 31 Jan., Add. MS. 44541, fo. 61.

[3] The first proposed paragraph was adopted, but the Queen went on to refer to 'the friendly communication' to the United States of the British view that the American case presented claims beyond the province of the arbitration; since by then Granville's note to Schenck, 3 Feb., had gone. *Hans. Parl. Deb.*, 3rd ser., ccix. 4.

Coleridge not knowing much about it, and at first doubtful as to their [*sic*] being anything in the protocols and treaty to preclude the Americans, but for an immediate protest. Roundell Palmer was very stout that the protocols & treaty did preclude their claims. Coleridge wished to put off the meeting of the law officers till Sunday, but I told him that we must have the opinion as soon as they could without undue haste present it. He promises to consider with Jessel some suggestions which were thrown out. Tenterden thinks the preliminary action might be through the agents.

The counter case must be presented in April. The Arbitrators meet in June. If notice is given in Parliament of our intention not to submit to an unlimited reference. . . .[1]

648. Lord Granville to Mr. Gladstone. [Add. MS. 44168, fo. 226]

[1? February 1872].[2]

Do you wish to see me before dinner today?

If so at what hour?

I think I like your first word 'reference' better than 'instrument'.

Query {" will take " / " are taking "} the further steps, instead of " have under their consideration ".

I quote from memory.

649. Mr. Gladstone to Lord Granville. [G.D. 29/61]

Imme. 11, Carlton House Terrace. F. 7. 72.

Can I see you? in Bruton St of course—at 5.30–6 or about 9.30 whichever you prefer.

I have had to make two rather large speeches [3] & wish to tell you the exact limits.

The Times, *alone*, put words, & meaning, into my mouth, for which I am in no degree responsible. I tried to draw the line clearly today but clearness will not do where the purpose of the critic is twisted.

I suppose it considers its honour pledged to a most feeble & inadequate treatment of our case, the reward of the great favour it received from you.

I am much pleased by the Telegraph within.[4] The 'pain' did it.

[1] The rest of no. 647 is missing.

[2] The date is suggested by the date when the Queen's speech was read to the cabinet.

[3] In the debate on the address, 6 and 7 Feb., on the British interpretation of the Treaty of Washington on the indirect claims, *Hans. Parl. Deb.*, 3rd ser., ccix. 73–89, 111–27; sections differently reported in *The Times*; *ibid.*, 85–6, 119–20.

[4] Possibly from the Queen, *Letters*, 2nd ser., ii. 190. Cf. Ponsonby to Granville, 7 Feb., G.D. 29/34.

650. Mr. Gladstone to Lord Granville. [G.D. 29/61]

Immediate. 11, Carlton House Terrace. Feb. 8. 72.

1. The Times of today improves the rather gross blunder of its own Reporter to make me say the direct reverse of what I said as to intention.[1]

2. I learn really for the first time that a man, who affirms that in his opinion a document is unambiguous in his favour, thereby affirms that one who reads it otherwise is dishonest.

However as this doctrine is held I am inclined to think it might be well if I were to publish an authentic text of the Speeches of yesterday and the day before?

651. Mr. Gladstone to Lord Granville. [Add. MS. 44168, fo. 227]

11, Carlton House Terrace. Feb. 9. 72.

Please to read the inclosed from Hartington about a Royal Residence in Ireland.[2]

I incline to think that question—which would have been found in any case to require much consideration in detail—is for the *present* scarcely to be extricated from the large question as to the future of the Prince of Wales.

I gather that the Prince of Wales is averse to the plan on account of the position in which it places him relatively to the Lord Lieutenant. But I will not say I know it for certain.

Please to send this on.

652. Mr. Gladstone to Lord Granville. [G.D. 29/59]

Immediate. 11, Carlton House Terrace. Feb. 11. [1872].[3]

Will you kindly learn from Thornton forthwith by Telegram as much as cannot be answered in the Foreign Office (where I remember there is some recent information) of the following questions:

1. Present Army Estimates of the United States, total amount
2. And number of men
3. Present Navy Estimates, total amount
4. And number of men
5. Changes in reduction or increase from last year.

I have a letter from the Queen [4] in the sense of the Telegram.

653. Mr. Gladstone to Lord Granville. [G.D. 29/61]

11, Carlton House Terrace. Feb. 11. 1872.

This seems to me something like the order of ideas in the U.S. business.

[1] See *The Times*, 7 Feb., p. 9, 8 Feb., p. 9. The second article came nearer to Gladstone's meaning but reported his having said that no view other than the British could be 'honestly attached' to the Treaty of Washington.

[2] To Gladstone, 9 Feb., Add. MS. 44143, fo. 156.

[3] Date supplied by Gladstone's copy in Add. MS. 44541, fo. 69. No. 652 is bound with the Granville papers of 1871.

[4] 11 Feb., partly printed, Guedalla, i. 335.

1. We contend [1] (a) that the *language* of the Treaty with the Protocols is clear and unambiguous.

(b) That we never consciously submitted the indirect losses to Arbitration.

2. The first step then seems to be to learn whether the Americans admit or deny our first contention.

If they admit, *cadit quaestio*: if they deny, what next?

3. The second step would be to find, that, opposite interpretations, of course in good faith, being put by the two parties on the reference, *quoad* Alabama claims, that reference must either fall to the ground, or be reconsidered with a view to mending it, or to a *tertium quid*.

4. Of these alternatives the latter seems evidently the right one.

5. But it implies a *hitch*—some delay must occur. During that delay, what is to be done as to the other three lines of operation? (Canada—San Juan—Washington.) Surely to push forward on them.

Not that we can hold the Americans bound to this.

But why should we not, at the proper time, propose it to them? If it were agreed to it would do much towards *rehabilitation*. I was at Schenck's last night. Everyone in good humour.

654. Mr. Gladstone to Lord Granville. [G.D. 29/61]

Private. 10, Downing Street. Feb. 13. 72.

I send you a letter from Argyll.[2]

To me Northbrook would seem a stronger & more eligible man.

655. Lord Granville to Mr. Gladstone. [Add. MS. 44168, fo. 230]

Private. 16, Bruton Street. Feb 13/72.

I agree with you. D[ufferin] is clever, charming and singularly what Morpeth used to call "well conditioned" but I should shrink from the responsibility of naming him Gov Gen. if I were you & Argyll.

I doubt his having sufficient stamina either of mind or body. If there is any necessity to distract him from his own wish to withdraw from political life, I should prefer seeing him the Constitutional Governor of Canada, or Ld Lieutenant of Ireland, if the place be not abolished.

Northbrook is a safe strong man, with indefatigable power of work. Cardwell knows his official qualities better than I do. I should be sorry to lose him in the Lords.

Napier of Magdala, (I thought the Duchess was talking of the other Lord Napier)

[1] Accepting the conclusions of Roundell Palmer; see mem., 7 Feb., on the construction of the Treaty of Washington, and note by Tenterden, both printed and circulated to the cabinet, 10 Feb., F.O. 5/1393.

[2] 13 Feb., on a successor to Lord Mayo in India. He favoured Dufferin; Kimberley was 'wasted at home'; Spencer was not quite able enough; Lords Lawrence, Napier, and Napier of Magdala were also possible, Add. MS. 44102, fo. 116. Cf. Dufferin's mem. of conversation with Argyll, 13 Feb., A. Lyall, *The Life of the Marquis of Dufferin and Ava* (1905), i. 153.

would be an experiment. He would put India in a complete state of defence, but at what cost I do not know.

I rate Spencer higher than you & Argyll probably do. He is not very clever, but he has a good deal of stuff about him—& a sense of duty & moral courage not often equalled.

Is Somerset out of the question. He has many qualities for it, & possibly might not dislike it.

He is the new leader of a very formidable cave in the Lords.

Kimberley would be excellent, but he could not be spared, and would not go. How he would talk, when he came back.

The present question about the Alabama puts Ripon out of the running.

656. Mr. Gladstone to Lord Granville. [G.D. 29/61]

Private. 11, Carlton House Terrace. Feb. 14. 72.

When I said Spencer was unavailable I was far from meaning incapable. I took it for granted at once that he would not go. Still I am not sure that he is as strong as Northbrook.

I agree about Somerset. But he is 68 : and on this account I had not thought of him. He is however wonderfully strong and wiry. His recollection of his son's death might be an impediment.

The inclosed note has just come from Halifax.[1]

657. Lord Granville to Mr. Gladstone. [Add. MS. 44168, fo. 234]

16, Bruton Street. Feb 16/72.

I have seen Cardwell, and find that his comparative silence in the Cabinet was caused by his agreement with the views which I and some others expressed.[2]

The declaration of your own strong views made it very difficult for me to reason on the matter, but the more I think of it the more convinced I am that it would create real dissatisfaction in the house, and outside the House if the announcement of a diminution of our effective army was laid upon the table of the House of Commons.

The difference of 100,000 £ will make no effect on either the friendly or the hostile Economists. I trust you will not think I am acting an unfriendly part, if when called upon in the Cabinet, I state as shortly and as moderately as possible what occurs to me.

You will probably send for Cardwell before the Cabinet.

[1] To Gladstone, 14 Feb., on Northbrook's willingness to go to India and his suitability, original in G.D. 29/61.

[2] See Gladstone's note on the cabinet, 10 Feb., for the discussion about the reduction of army estimates ; an exchange between Cardwell, Gladstone and Granville ; note on the cabinet, 17 Feb., Add. MS. 44640, fos. 21, 23, 30.

658. Lord Granville to Mr. Gladstone. [Add. MS. 44168, fo. 236]

16, Bruton Street. [16 February 1872].

I wish you & ourselves joy.[1]

The Chancellor's speech was admirable.

Argyll was very good, but too aggressive for the temper of the House, and made a mistake in turning round to the Duke of Somerset and calling him & others candid friends.

The Duke of S. looked furious, and at that moment would have voted against us, but told me he was converted by the Chancellor's speech.

It was a pleasure to look at the Chancellor after the division. One would not recognize the careworn old man of the later Cabinets.

Portman was wretched.

659. Lord Granville to Mr. Gladstone.[2] [G.D. 29/61]

[17 February 1872].

I imagine that the best bargain for this country would be to let the San Juan Arbitration go by default, on condition that the Americans gave up the Alabama claims of all sorts.[3] It would take away the grievance of the Americans, and we should give up what the Americans are sure to get in the end by fair or foul means, and what is of no use to us, and sure to be a cause of difficulty hereafter.

It is probable that the Law officers after seeing the cases and countercases, would come to the opinion that the words of the Bulwer Treaty are so vague, that it [is] almost hopeless to expect a fair Arbitrator to give a decision in favor of either party. I presume that if we were to take this course, we should be turned out, and branded as Traitors for the rest of our lives. I should not mind this so much, if I was clear that it would not be unfair to Canada.

660. Lord Granville to Mr. Gladstone. [Add. MS. 44168, fo. 238]

16, Bruton Street. Feb 18/72.

Bessborough & I think that Kenmare for the higher office, and Clarendon & Poltimore (a remarkably pleasing fellow) for the Lordship would be the best,[4] but we have not yet seen Glyn.

I presume you will let the Queen go.

[1] On the favourable division in the Lords on Collier's appointment to the judicial committee of the Privy Council, 15 Feb., *Hans. Parl. Deb.*, 3rd ser., ccix. 376–460. Portman moved the amendment to the opposition motion. See above, nos. 593, 594, 596.

[2] Mem. by Gladstone, 17 Feb., on the force of 'amicable settlement' in the Protocols and Treaty of Washington, G.D. 29/61, not printed. No. 659 was returned with Gladstone's comment: 'Let us talk of this. I do not much differ. F.17.1872.'

[3] Cf. no. iv of Schenck's four suggestions for overcoming the difficulty of the indirect claims which proposed to set British concession on the San Juan water boundary against an American admission that the Treaty of Washington excluded them; Granville to Thornton, No. 65 most confidential, 16 Feb., F.O. 5/1394, copies, G.D. 29/105, G.D. 29/81. Cf. Hammond to Granville, 16 and 17 Feb., G.D. 29/105.

[4] Poltimore took the treasurership of the household, resigned by de Tabley, 27 Feb., and Kenmare the lordship-in-waiting, 24 Feb., Add. MS. 44433, fos. 259, 233.

I should not dislike accompanying H.M in the independent way she proposes, and I hope Lady G. will have got over her troubles by this time, but it is impossible to say now whether the Alabama Claims will allow me to be absent from London.

661. Mr. Gladstone to Lord Granville. [G.D. 29/61]

11, Carlton House Terrace. Feb. 20. 72.

1. I suppose that the Queen now means to limit her Baden visit to about a fortnight—and that if this is so, whatever be the Easter recess, the best way would be to give it at once, especially as there may [be] serious matter to press hereafter ?[1]

2. You will doubtless let me know when you think we are ripe for any step touching the United States Correspondence.[2]

3. Please to look to Disraeli's question yesterday[3] which will require looking up the internal history of the F.O. as to the 'copies'.

4. Palmer did everything for us last night that man could do.[4] The other side all came up—we suffered heavily through Absentees.

5. The matter of the Household as you will see is urgent.[5]

662. Lord Granville to Mr. Gladstone. [G.D. 29/61]

Foreign Office. [20 February 1872].

1. I have already sent you a note saying I presume you would concur in the Queen's journey.

2. I think I had better see you tomorrow at any hour (excepting between 4 & 6 when I must be at the London University) which you will name.[6]

I will then ask the Chancellor to meet R. Palmer and the Law officers at the F.O.

3. You have the materials for an answer.

I am glad to hear that you have written to the Queen about the Household.

I have written to Col Henderson to ask whether [there] are not points at which the Cabinet could break into the line after it has been cleared.[7]

663. Lord Granville to Mr. Gladstone. [G.D. 29/61]

16, Bruton Street. [20 February 1872].

Shall I telegraph to Bright to let me show the American part of his letter to Schenck.[8]

[1] Marginal note by Granville: 'Yes'.

[2] The United States had not replied to the British note of 3 Feb.; see above, no. 647 note.

[3] Asking when the American case for the Geneva tribunal was received and circulated to the cabinet, *Hans. Parl. Deb.*, 3rd ser., ccix. 654; Gladstone's answer, 20 Feb., *ibid.*, 768–71.

[4] In the Commons' debate on the motion of censure on the Collier appointment, *ibid.*, 658–762.

[5] See the Queen to Gladstone, 19 Feb., asking that the three vacancies in the household be filled, copy, G.D. 29/61; see above, p. 302, note 1, p. 309, note 4.

[6] No. 662 was returned by Gladstone with the question: 'Will 1 suit you'. Granville replied 'I will be with you a little before one, and will wait if you are not ready'.

[7] Relates to arrangements for the thanksgiving for the Prince of Wales's recovery, 27 Feb.

[8] Relates to Bright to Granville, private, 19 Feb., suggesting an American declaration that the indirect claims were included as 'historic evidence' only, and the draft tel. to Bright, G.D. 29/52. Gladstone wrote on no. 663: 'I think so. F.20'. The letter went to Schenck, 20 Feb., F.O 362/1.

664. Lord Granville to Mr. Gladstone. [Add. MS. 44168, fo. 240]

16, Bruton Street. [20 February 1872].

Your speech was quite excellent—but your division bad.[1]

665. Mr. Gladstone to Lord Granville. [G.D. 29/61]

10, Downing Street. F. 22 [1872].

As I understand the points discussed yesterday[2] were four

1. Whether at once to lay before U.S. Government our argument on the meaning of the Treaty.

2. Whether to ask for an extension of time or to state our willingness to concur in one.

3. Whether to allow the arbitrators to entertain the question of their *competency*, under protest, so as to postpone as long as possible any risk of breaking off.

4. Which of the alternative modes of settlement would be *comparatively* least open to objection.

666. Lord Granville to Mr. Gladstone. [Add. MS. 44168, fo. 241]

Foreign Office. [24 February 1872].

I have got the minute about Morley.[3] He is an excellent man. But Halifax & Bessborough & I think that Lansdowne has greater claims, and is the stronger man. We put him above Morley, Camperdown, and Roseberry [*sic*].

You must take what *I* say cum grano, not only on account of my friendship for 3 generations but also because he has been my adlatus in the Lords, since I took the F.O.

Morley's claims have been acknowledged by Argyll's offer, which he declined.

667. Mr. Gladstone to Lord Granville. [G.D. 29/61]

[*No. 1*]. 11, Carlton House Terrace. Feb. 25. 72.

I think Northcote's letter[4] is valuable as to the room left for a gradual backing down.

[1] In the Collier debate, see above, no. 661, note 4.

[2] In conference between Palmer, Granville, Gladstone and possibly others, see Palmer to Granville, 24 Feb., G.D. 29/67. Cf. further discussion in the cabinet, 24 Feb., Add. MS. 44640, fo. 39.

[3] Marginal note by Gladstone: 'What?' and on the back: 'Mr Cardwell. This concerns your U. Secship—let us speak of it. F.24'. Cf. Cardwell to Gladstone, 24 Feb., with a post-script: 'Bruce has had a remonstrance from Morley against being passed over for Lansdowne'; 22 April, on Lansdowne's being the best appointment for the government, Add. MS. 44120, fos. 14, 26. Lansdowne took Northbrook's place as parliamentary under-secretary for war; cf. below, no. 688.

[4] See to Granville, 16, 24 Feb., on the indirect claims, G.D. 29/74; and replies, 16, 17, 25 Feb., G.D. 29/77.

He writes as if he had never heard of the Rathbone proposition [1]—which has sprung up in several quarters.

With reference to Palmer (Feb. 24) [2] p. 5 I take it that the Rathbone sum would lie about half way between a probable maximum & minimum—or thereabouts. As to p. 13 I do not see the difficulty of obtaining notice through our Arbitrator when the indirect claims were about to be imported—either as to competency, or as to justice.

Reflection on my low terms of yesterday for lodging the Countercase has not yet shaken me. Hammond's Mem.[3] appears to agree with them & to be very good generally.

668. Lord Granville to Mr. Gladstone. [G.D. 29/61]

[25 February 1872].

I wrote the enclosed note this afternoon [4]—but luckily found him at home.

He thinks the following telegram to Thornton [5] would be safe and that we should not be justified in asking for more. If you are of the same opinion, I will circulate the telegram, and request any Member of the Cabinet who objects, to ask you immediately to call a Cabinet for tomorrow.

669. Mr. Gladstone to Lord Granville. [G.D. 29/61]

No 2. 11, Carlton House Terrace. Feb. 25. 72.

As to the *matter* of the Telegram I have only to suggest softening request into 'urge'—and inserting words to allow for the chance that the American Government itself may be disposed to admit the force of our argument.

I have no objection to the course you propose for collecting the mind of the Cabinet. But is it not more advantageous to us to proceed through the American Minister here within arm's length of us, than through our Agent in the U.S. (of course informing Thornton what we do) and may not some confusion arise if we

[1] To avoid any increase in Britain's liability for damages resulting from the indirect claims by a preliminary agreement on the sum to be paid by Britain if the award was against her.

[2] To Granville, G.D. 29/67. P.5 objected to the Rathbone plan and to a similar proposal to fix the maximum and minimum limits of a possible indemnity. P. 13 objected to Cadorna's solution whereby the Geneva tribunal was to decide on the claim for direct losses first.

[3] See Hammond to Granville, 21 Feb., on keeping the timetable prescribed by the Treaty of Washington, G.D. 29/105; the British counter-case, without conditions imposed, to go in, 15 April; Britain's understanding of the tribunal's competence to be stated when arguments were presented, 15 June. Cf. Gladstone's note on the cabinet, 24 Feb., Add. MS. 44640, fo. 39.

[4] To Palmer, asking his opinion on a new proposal that Britain should not demand the withdrawal of the American case in its existing form on condition that the American agent at Geneva should withdraw the indirect claims when the tribunal met, G.D. 29/61. It resulted from Fish's appeal for a new suggestion, Thornton to Granville, tel. 24 Feb., F.O. 5/1394.

[5] Containing the new proposal. See draft, amended by Gladstone, G.D. 29/61, and tel., F.O. 5/1394. Cf. Schenck to Granville, private, 27 Feb., G.D. 29/81; reply, 28 Feb., F.O. 362/1; Palmer to Granville, 26 Feb., G.D. 29/67.

work indiscriminately through the two channels? I have a horror of our finding ourselves in the intolerable position which we held last year during the Treaty.[1]

670. Mr. Gladstone to Lord Granville. [G.D. 29/61]

10, Downing Street. Feb. 28. 72.

Here is the proposed letter to Schen[c]k.[2]

It will not take very long to read being written large on one side of the sheet only.

I am sorry to trouble you with it but I cannot send it without your approval.

It seems clear that I should send a letter of this sort, *if* it materially betters the position which I hold in the American 'Case'; for that position is a very bad one indeed.

On the other hand there is no use in sending it, unless I can make a sensible improvement.

On this I invite your judgment. Should it be decidedly adverse, I think I shall only have to 'grin and bear it'.

I also invite your criticism (in pencil) upon any words that you may think open to question.

671. Lord Granville to Mr. Gladstone. [Add. MS. 44168, fo. 243]

Private. Foreign Office. Feb 29/72.

Your letter is a complete refutation of the charge made against you personally in the case.

Could you emphasize the fallacy of confounding the expression of an opinion as to the probable course of events, with the desire that such such [*sic*] should be their course.

The thought is not necessarily the child of the wish.

Your humility is great but it perhaps shows in stronger relief the close reasoning which proves that there is no cause for apology.

I have marked a phrase in para 5, and pointed out on page 13 a very pointed sarcasm.

Whether, it be wise to send it now as a letter from you to Schenck with a view to publication, I doubt.

Lord Russell would immediately follow and probably in a different spirit.

[1] No. 669 is followed by the note: 'I agree. G[ranville] and I. H[artington]'. The similar opinions of Hatherley, Halifax, Bruce, Cardwell, Lowe, Fortescue, Forster and Ripon are in G.D. 29/69.

[2] To refute the 'chapter of motives' in the American case, which presented British hostility to the North, typified by Gladstone's attitude in 1862, as substantiation for their claim in respect of indirect losses. The cabinet decided the letter should not go, 2 March, Add. MS. 44640, fo. 45, but cf. Gladstone's mem., 2 March, of reasons against any other method of meeting the personal charges, Add. MS. 44433, fo. 264. The letter was ultimately sent, 28 Nov. 1872; see below, nos. 760, 765, 794, 796, 966.

In the critical mood of the press at this time, it would be much attacked & misrepresented.

What should you think of Abraham H[ayward] writing nearly the whole of it under one of his pseudonyms to the Times, or Tom Hughes doing the same with his name to one of the American papers having it reproduced here.

672. Lord Granville to Mr. Gladstone. [G.D. 29/61]

Foreign Office. [1 March 1872].

Query telegraph to Sir E. Thornton

I have no instructions to give you respecting the solution proposed by Mr Fish. Be as reticent as possible on any such point.[1]

673. Mr. Gladstone to Lord Granville. [G.D. 29/61]

11, Carlton House Terrace. 3 Mch 72.

We were prevented yesterday from exchanging ideas freely as to Hammond's minute against the reception of the Pope at Malta.

Without having any desire to see him there I see no sufficient reason for our taking objection should he desire to go. It will be easier, not harder, as I think, to deal with him should occasion arise, in an island which is virtually a garrison.

I am not sure what your mind was but I *rather* read your countenance in this sense.

I have been with the P. of Wales.[2] He looked quite a different being from last Tuesday. He will ask you whether he need take the first move in calling on Thiers. I thought not.

674. Mr. Gladstone to Lord Granville. [G.D. 29/61]

H of C. March 4. 72.

I am sorry to say that I think no *real* progress would be made by handling first in the Lords either the Licensing or the Commons Bill. At the same time I do not know that mischief would result unless in the very free handling they might afterwards receive in the Commons.

Glyn however as I am writing reminds me that there is already a rival Licensing Bill in the Commons & he thinks our proceeding in the H. of Lords would under these circumstances do real mischief.

[1] Fish proposed that both powers should present their counter-cases on 15 April without prejudice to the indirect claims, Thornton to Granville, tel. 26 Feb., Fish to Schenck, 27 Feb., communicated, 14 March, F.O. 5/1394. A note by Gladstone follows no. 672: 'I find the [Treasury] Bench not of one mind—and would therefore suggest waiting for the cabinet tomorrow unless there is haste'.

[2] About to go to France. An exchange of views between Gladstone and Granville, 6 March, on his proposed visit to Nice, G.D. 29/61, not printed.

675. Mr. Gladstone to Lord Granville. [G.D. 29/61]

10, Downing Street. March 7. 72.

Gen. Schen[c]k's object yesterday was as he told me to develop a proposition which he had laid before you, viz. his No 4 [1]; and which on consideration he was inclined to value more highly than at first.

He proposes to pair off San Juan against the indirect losses; and both on the same ground viz. that America in 1846 and England in 1871 fully believed that the respective subjects were not in question & that an admission to that effect by the other party, & consequent withdrawal of the matters from controversy, would be a graceful and generous proceeding.

In addition, he stated, to the matter in the Case, he would show that Mr Bancroft explicitly acquainted Ld Palmerston of the American interpretation of the Treaty (long after ratification I observed) and that no exception was taken to it.

I thanked him & observed, 'without prejudice' & in the quality of citizen, that two remarks were obvious.

1. The proposal was that Great Britain should in the San Juan case withdraw the whole matter in dispute: but that America should withdraw at Geneva only what she professed to consider as a *fringe* of little real substance.

2. That in the San Juan case a new party must be recognised in the person of British North America and that there might be a difficulty in finding a common measure for the interests proposed to be exchanged.

I also noticed, with reference to the basis of the argument, that its force would depend very much on the degree in which it could be developed into a claim of *honour*.

This I came to report yesterday but you had not come in. I told him I would report to you & presumed he would open the subject again to you.

After he left me I read the American & finished reading the British Case on San Juan. They do not answer one another's points: but taking them as they stand I would much rather argue theirs than ours.

At p. 18 of it however you will find two quotations from Grotius and Vattel respectively which are most valuable with reference to our argument on indirect losses supposing we are driven to the *lower ground*: and it is a question with me whether they should not be embodied in your proposed dispatch.

676. Lord Granville to Mr. Gladstone. [G.D. 29/61]

[8 March 1872].

May I quote you on thinking it undesirable that during the Alabama Crisis I should be absent from London.[2]

[1] See above, no. 659 note.
[2] Returned with the comment: 'Decidedly. W.E.G. Mc.8.'

677. Lord Granville to Mr. Gladstone. [Add. MS. 44168, fo. 248]

16, Bruton Street. [9 March 1872].

The difficulty of the case is immense.[1]

It is impossible to adopt any plan without the cooperation of the Queen & the Prince.

The former is evidently disinclined to do what old Lord Clifden called " taking off his clothes, before he went to bed."

The illness of the Prince has made him still more amiable and his manner still more charming. The Dean of Windsor says he does not see the slightest encrease of gravity.

I told you a little incident about the confidential papers which shows how little inclined he is even to read what is sent him.

All this does not relieve us from the consideration of what may be the plan which is likely to interest him, and induce him to work.

678. Mr. Gladstone to Lord Granville. [G.D. 29/61]

H of C. Mch 14–15. 72.

I have read the American reply [2] and it has also been read by all the Ministers in the Commons. They seem to think nothing can be done by the Cabinet before Saturday: and your people will probably employ the time in working up the reply for which the dispatch seems to give fit openings.

1. As to Confederate Loan, I told Schenck that when they appealed from our Agent at Washington we stopped his action (i.e. by our intention though defeated in time) & that now when we appeal from their Agent—for they make no secret that the case is a sort of pleader's work—if they will do the same the whole matter will be settled to our satisfaction.

2. After their reference to the strange ideas entertained here of the *amount* that might be claimed as indirect damages, I almost think we ought to have a short paragraph on the subject [3] simply compiled from their own statements.

679. Mr. Gladstone to Lord Granville. [G.D. 29/61]

10, Downing Street. Mch 27. 72.

It appears to me that the moment we declare to the United States that we will not proceed with the Arbitration unless upon a settlement of our dispute, we enable them

[1] On 8 March Ponsonby wrote to Gladstone on behalf of the Queen a letter which ' nearly killed ' the plan for the abolition of the lord-lieutenancy of Ireland and the residence there of the Prince of Wales (above, no. 539) which Gladstone had revived. Gladstone then worked to secure agreement on an alternative plan. Granville comments on Gladstone's mem., 9 March, recounting this, Add. MS. 44760, fo. 174. See below, nos. 727, 729, 730, 734, 735, 754.

[2] To the British note, 3 Feb. See Fish to Schenck, 27 Feb., communicated, 14 March, F.O. 5/1394; cf. above, no. 672 note.

[3] I.e. in the British reply. See Granville to Schenck, private, 21 March, F.O. 362/1; Granville to Schenck and Thornton, 20 March, F.O. 5/1395. It proposed a supplementary article to the Treaty of Washington. See also mem. by Tenterden, 16 March, Tenterden to Granville, 17, 18 March, G.D. 29/106; Hammond to Granville with a draft reply, 16 March, G.D. 29/105; Gladstone's notes of the cabinets, 16, 19 March, when the reply was framed, Add. MS. 44640, fos. 55–61.

to plead duresse and threat, and supply them with what I believe will be of great value to them viz. a reason for rejecting the arguments we have made on the meaning & on the intention of the Treaty.

And that, for this reason especially though not alone, we should make no threat of withdrawal until after (& in case) our reasons shall have been rejected.

Palmer's passage marked by me A in pencil on the margin is such a threat— & has all the inconvenience of a more positive declaration.

I should strike out A. and also B, near the end; substituting 'whatsoever' after rights, or if this be not enough "of withdrawal from the arbitration or otherwise".[1]

We go to Latimer tomorrow.

680. Mr. Gladstone to Lord Granville. [G.D. 29/61]

No 1. Read (2) first. H of Commons. Ap. 5. 72.

Lowe Cardwell & Goschen have had a conversation tonight the upshot of which they have communicated to me, and I now write to you on so much of it as concerns the form & matter of the Counter Case.

They conceive, and I imagine there is no doubt, that the decision of today implied that every thing was to be cut out of the Counter Case which touched either the Chapter of Motives, or the Indirect losses.

They think upon such inspection as they have been able to make that the Counter Case requires careful review in order to bring it into conformity with this decision.

If this is so, ought not Tenterden & Bernard who know it thoroughly, to go through it with the view of striking out at once whatever is plainly at variance with the view of the Cabinet, & they might mark by scoring any part about which they felt doubtful.

There are five pages on Fenian Raids against Canada & these naturally enough constitute an indictment against the U.S. Government & form part of the retaliatory statement which we have determined not to enter upon—Lopez & Walker follow.

Not having read the early part of the Countercase (which Ld Tenterden rightly says was sent,[2] but it was on the day when I was quite unequal to reading it, & I have not yet learned whether it was brought me or not) I cannot well judge but I am afraid there is much of it which will not stand with the Paragraph adopted today about the Chapter of Motives, as it is a detailed and sharp retaliation.

Independently of the bearing on the forbidden subjects Lowe & Cardwell think the tone too like that of a controversy in journals. I think however that this is not altogether avoidable.

[1] Relates to the protest to accompany the British counter-case to be presented 'without prejudice', 15 April. For two versions of it with comments by Palmer, 26 March, see G.D. 29/67. The second omits the threat of withdrawal. Cf. mem by Tenterden, 25 March, on procedure in presenting the protest, G.D. 29/106.

[2] Gladstone had complained to Granville in the cabinet that he had not seen parts i–v of the counter-case, Gurdon to Wetherell, 5 April, G.D. 29/61, and an exchange between Granville and Tenterden, 5 April, G.D. 29/106.

But we must take either one line or the other on the questions of principle whether we will notice the Chapter of Motives, & whether we will deal in any shape with the claims for indirect losses.

This will go by messenger; (if you do not come up tomorrow) as the subject ought to be brought at once to your notice.

I sent also a mem. succinctly drawn by Cardwell—which expresses rather an extreme view which I hope they will not adhere to.

681. Mr. Gladstone to Lord Granville. [G.D. 29/61]

No 2. H of C. Ap. 5–6 [1872].

The whole business of today [1] seems to have been conducted in entire ignorance of the Countercase—at least Ld Tenterden has been to me tonight to say it is physically impossible to alter the Countercase so as to bring it into conformity with the paragraph. If this is so I see no course except to summon the Cabinet on Monday at two in order to consider the matter, and to have Sir R. Palmer in attendance that he may if necessary explain his views. If you agree in this West will summon the Cabinet on hearing from you to that effect. Of course the paragraph adopted today cannot be given up except by the authority of our colleagues generally, and though there seems to be no choice yet they will have to decide. Tuesday would be in time however if we assume that the change must be made & harmony re-established in this way.

682. Mr. Gladstone to Lord Granville. [G.D. 29/61]

11, Carlton House Terrace. Ap. 6. 72.

A letter received quite unexpectedly from Lowe [2] this morning will explain to you a part of the imbroglio in which we have been involved—and I add my reply. They will be given to you here, or go to you, according as you may or may not come up.

683. Lord Granville to Mr. Gladstone. [Add. MS. 44168, fo. 253]

Holmbury, Wotton, Dorking. April 6/72.

I got a telegram this morning to meet Lowe & some of my colleagues to go over the case with Roundell Palmer.

I had no means of getting a fly, and having got an attack of rheumatism, I telegraphed that I could not come, but would agree to what was generally decided.

[1] The covering note was framed in a smaller meeting after the cabinet had decided on the counter-case. It adopted unawares a form that did not fit the latter; Hammond's mem. for Granville, 5 April, and min., 6 April, G.D. 29/105; Tenterden to Granville, 5 April, with drafts of an introduction to the counter-case to bring it into line; 6 April, describing his part in convening a second meeting to revise the counter-case, G.D. 29/106.

[2] To Gladstone, 6 April, on the revision necessary to the counter-case, Add. MS. 44302, fo. 35; cf. a second letter describing the alterations, *ibid.*, fo. 38.

I thought it was only to decide upon the exact wording of the passages which it was proposed to amend, or rather which had been amended yesterday.

I got your letter this afternoon—& I have asked West to summon a Cabinet for Monday at two as proposed by you.

I recd also the enclosed letter from Schenck,[1] of which probably Hammond has already sent you a copy. I have answered it to the effect that I understand from it that His Gov does not approve his suggestion to me which was that H.M's Gov should present the counter case without prejudice to the position it now maintains, nor his opinion that the Gov of the U.S. would accede to this understanding.

Cardwell's note does not appear to be exactly accurate.

I will call in Carlton Terrace at one.

684. Mr. Gladstone to Lord Granville. [G.D. 29/61]

10, Downing Street. Ap 8. 72.

Not having seen you I do not feel sure that I comprehend the grounds of your interpretation of General Schen[c]k's letter. Since he says " the rights of both parties will be the same after filing " the Countercase " as before " I should say that his Government accepts though not gracefully his position.

I am far from affirming Cardwell's Memorandum—but he spoke gravely about it. No one argues better: and I was therefore struck with what I thought his inability to shake the proposal to go forward up to June 15 and then challenge the Tribunal respecting the indirect losses.

685. Lord Granville to Mr. Gladstone. [Add. MS. 44168, fo. 260]

Foreign Office. April 8/72.

I sent you yesterday a copy of General Schenck's note of the 5th, and told you the substance of my answer. The General returned from Paris this morning, & has called upon me today. He says that in consequence of my note, which he could not understand he referred to a rough draft of his note to me, and compared it with the copy which Mr Moran had taken of the letter actually sent. He showed me the rough draft and pointed out a passage after the words " any position " (" they have taken nor affect any position "). He has requested me to cancel the 1st letter, and to substitute for it that which he intended to write out, and a copy of which I now send to you.

I called General Schenck's attention to the word confidential on the note which he had just handed to me. He explained that he had used it in consequence of the confidential character of our first conversation on the subject, but that he had no objection to my communicating it to my colleagues or indeed announcing it to. . . .[2]

[1] Private, 5 April. The letter was cancelled and an amended letter bearing the same date sent, 8 April, G.D. 29/81.

[2] The rest of no. 685 is missing.

686. Lord Granville to Mr. Gladstone. [G.D. 29/61]

Copy. Foreign Office. April 16/72.

I think in presenting the counter case tonight,[1] we had better say that we have reason to know that the American agent, Mr Bancroft Davis, has informed the Geneva Tribunal that as his instructions did not contemplate the presentation of any statement on behalf of HM's Govt., he has thought it necessary to reserve to his Govt. its full right hereafter to vindicate before the Tribunal the Authority which it understands the Tribunal acquired under the treaty in this respect.

I think we should add that when we are in official possession of this reservation of rights, we will present it to Parliament.

687. Mr. Gladstone to Lord Granville. [G.D. 29/61]

Immed. 10, Downing Street. Ap 16. 72.

1. There can I think be no objection to your asking Schen[c]k the question you propose about Fish's reply.

2. I will give the information you suggest as to Bancroft Davis's covering note.

3. I am much pleased at the prospect opened by Tenterden's Telegram.[2]

I have missed you twice.

688. Mr. Gladstone to Lord Granville. [G.D. 29/61]

D. St. Ap. 17. 72.

I have today conversed with Cardwell on the possible successors to Northbrook's office,[3] and have mentioned six names.

Cowper
Lansdowne
Camperdown
Morley
Rosebery

and Westminster—who has been rather confidently named in some quarters by report.

Cardwell and I both incline to think Westminster would be the best if he is to be had. But I have no idea of his inclinations. With your approval, I would ask Argyll.

Of the other five Cardwell is willing to take any; thinks Lansdowne would probably be the best for the *Government*: has heard such accounts of Rosebery as tend to show he would be very good for the department; which is my case also. But it would be *rather* violent promotion.

[1] See statements by Granville in the Lords and Gladstone in the Commons, *Hans. Parl. Deb.* 3rd ser., ccx. 1304–5, 1330.

[2] From Geneva, where Tenterden was British agent, 15 April, received 16 April. It reported the American counsel's proposal for the settlement of the indirect claims question by agreement between the counsel of both sides. Cf. Tenterden to Granville, private, 15 April, with the tel., G.D. 29/106.

[3] See above, no. 666 note.

689. Lord Granville to Mr. Gladstone.[1] [Add. MS. 44168, fo. 262, and G.D. 29/61]

16, Bruton Street. [17 April 1872].

You know my opinion that Lansdowne has the best claim, and would be the best Under Secretary, which is also Bessborough's view. He thinks it is hard upon both Lansdowne & Morley to be passed over. But we agree that if you & Cardwell wish it, and if Westminster has not enough to do at present, and is willing to take the place, he has a great position, is pleasing, and speaks agreeably.

What do you think of adding the following words to those upon which we agreed last night.[2]

" H.M.'s Gov have no doubt of the support which they will receive from Parliament in maintaining their position as to the scope and intention of the reference to the Tribunal of Geneva, but they believe that any Parliamentary declaration at this stage of the Diplomatic correspondence would not strengthen but weaken that position."

If you think them worth consideration, they might be circulated.

690. Mr. Gladstone to Lord Granville. [G.D. 29/29A]

10, Downing Street. Ap. 22. 72.

I passed yesterday in bed.

I feel confident Northcote would not endeavour to set up the Commissioners at the expence of the Government.

But it might be well to *deposit* with him in reply to his letter [3] some reference to the difficulties in which both Commn & Govt were placed by the method of communicatn forced upon us by the American Government & partly also by the circumstances of the case. It was impossible for the two parties to understand one another at each step as they would have done if they had exchanged their views in the ordinary manner. So they were astonished at things we did—and we at things they proposed.

One blunder you may remember we made: it arose in copying out. About the Museum (see the inclosed) do I understand that you agree ?

691. Lord Granville to Mr. Gladstone. [G.D. 29/61]

House of Lords. [23 April 1872].

We cannot announce any decision as to the Course we shall take about proceeding further with the Arbitration at Geneva until we know in what manner the

[1] There are two versions of no. 689, both in Granville's hand. That in the Granville papers, marked copy, and dated 17 April, has the last three paragraphs, after the signature.

[2] For a reply to a Commons' question, 18 April, why Britain had not insisted upon the withdrawal of the indirect claims before presenting her counter-case. Gladstone asked the House to forgo explanations, *Hans. Parl. Deb.*, 3rd ser., ccx. 1476.

[3] Northcote to Granville, 7 April, on the joint commission of 1871 and the indirect claims, G.D. 29/22A.

Govt of the U.S proposes to deal with the despatch of the 20th, the answer to which we understand to be on its way.[1]

692. Mr. Gladstone to Lord Granville. [G.D. 29/61]

10, Downing Street. Ap. 23. 72.

I feel the force of what you said yesterday about the almost certain necessity of much disclosure after the receipt of the U.S. dispatch if it is unsatisfactory.

Now, they have already made more than a half-confidence through the newspapers; and query whether if we do nothing before getting the answer & a great deal then they may accuse us of a surprise?

This thought has taken a form in my mind which I have expressed in the *imaginary* draft within.[2] There is something to say *for* a step of the kind: there may be more against it.

693. Mr. Gladstone to Lord Granville. [G.D. 29/61]

Immediate. 11, Carlton House Terrace. 24 Ap: 72.

With reference to Mr Rumbold's second or Te Deum Telegram [3] received today I had better mention that I received an application in the name of the Celebrators or some of them, two or three days back, seeking for my intervention to move you in behalf of Mr Rumbold's attendance. I thought it better not to interfere and made a minute copy of which I inclose.

You will be the best judge as to Mr Rumbold's attendance, I mean as to encouraging it, for I presume you would not force it or take the question out of his hands.

I should think it desirable, & conformable to precedent: Musurus was at St Paul's if I remember right. And you will recollect the recent proceedings on the Greek side at Patras, which went much farther.

694. Lord Granville to Mr. Gladstone.[4] [G.D. 29/61]

Buckingham Palace. April 25/72.

I had to introduce Lord Bloomfield to the Queen today. Biddulph took the opportunity of telling me that he had just recd the Queen's orders to speak to

[1] Draft for Gladstone's reply to a question, 23 April, asking for an assurance that further proceedings at Geneva would be suspended until the indirect claims were withdrawn, *Hans. Parl. Deb., loc. cit.*, 1679.

[2] Follows no. 692 in G.D. 29/61, copy in Add. MS. 44434, fo. 82. It was a warning that Britain might be compelled by parliamentary pressure to notify her intention to withdraw from the arbitration unless the indirect claims were dropped by 15 June. Cf. Wetherell's copy of Schenck's record of a conversation with Granville, late 24 April; Granville to Schenck and reply, 25 April, G.D. 29/81.

[3] Of 23 April, asking for instructions on the Greek patriarch's wish for his attendance at a *Te Deum* in Constantinople for the recovery of the Prince of Wales, F.O. 78/2216. Granville telegraphed, 26 April, leaving him discretion, F.O. 78/2213. The 'application' to Gladstone was from a Greek, Demetrius Aristarchi; for Gladstone's min. on his letter, see G.D. 29/61. Cf. Gurdon to Wetherell, 25 April, *ibid.*

[4] The original of no. 694 is in the Granville papers together with the envelope. According to the docket, a copy went to Cardwell and was answered by him, 27 April.

Gladstone as to whether it was not possible to compromise the young Guardsmen's question.

The Queen understood that the Duke of Richmond was likely to move and to carry an address to Her Majesty not to sign a warrant which Her Ministers recommended. The Queen felt it would place [her] in a somewhat embarrassing position and she would be glad if the matter could with propriety be arranged.

Biddulph would call on Gladstone, if it were necessary.

Bessborough told me the other day, that if it comes to a vote, some of our most steady supporters will vote against us.

695. Mr. Gladstone to Lord Granville. [G.D. 29/61]

11, Carlton House Terrace. Ap. 27. 72.

I would put the Telegram into cipher but not send it off before the Cabinet can see it: especially as the time is so near. I have suggested a few words to be added—*or* to be substituted for the words in red ink.

696. Mr. Gladstone to Lord Granville. [G.D. 29/61]

St. George's Hill. Ap. 28. 72.

That plaguy ship [1] has as you anticipated come in much too quick, and we must now trust to Schenck's discretion to give a little time for the real & practical communications in the question of the Alabama.

Reverdy Johnson said in a speech at Liverpool, which I heard, that he had settled the whole business with Stanley in half an hour: and it really has now reached a point at which it ought to be susceptible of that kind of treatment.

The judgment of the Arbitrators on "the abstract question" ought to resolve itself into their replying to the joint statement you propose by saying that they would not have regard to the indirect claims in their examination or award?

The only point of difficulty that I see remaining is how we are to put the pledges of the two parties into equipoise without entailing an application to the Senate at this critical moment. It just occurs to me to suggest for consideration whether we might get round the difficulty by saying first (as agreed) that we regard our language as laying down a rule for our future conduct, and as an independent declaration of policy, though of course it could not assume the character of a promise or international engagement except upon its being reciprocated. *They* however will very likely find some better way of solving this (I hope the last) problem.

I expect to be at Vauxhall tomorrow at 11.40 and at home by or about one.

I am superlatively delighted with Vita's speech in the dance reported by my daughter Mary.

[1] The American reply to the British rejoinder, 20 March, to the American answer, 27 Feb., to the British note, 3 Feb., on the indirect claims. The substance was telegraphed to Schenck, 28 April, who telegraphed to Granville, G.D. 29/81. Behind this exchange negotiations continued to supplement the Treaty of Washington.

697. Mr. Gladstone to Lord Granville. [G.D. 29/61]

H of C. Ap. 29. 72.

I think you must be prepared to see in the papers tomorrow surmises as to fresh communications from America, as the movements of the Cabinet Ministers to & fro in the H. of C. have been observed; &, as I stated publicly that the dispatch had not even reached General Schenck, probably the speculations will turn upon a substratum of telegraphic communications.

I got a query from L[evy] after seeing you this afternoon & thought I had better see him as I wished to press upon him the expediency of commending the *free* action of the judgment & feeling of the American nation, and the effect which this action seemed to be producing upon the tone & tendency of the Government. From the indications of the public telegrams and the evident movement in America I told him I thought he could hardly err in assuming it as a possible or probable hypothesis that the chances of settlement would not of necessity be confined to the slow process of the communications by post. He is a sharp fellow but I do not expect to see him sensibly ahead of his contemporaries tomorrow though he beats some of them & especially Delane in continually hanging about the Houses of Parliament & among us at least picking the brains of the likeliest people.

698. Mr. Gladstone to Lord Granville. [G.D. 29/61]

C. H. T. May 2. 72

For the utmost economy of time I think the best way will be to meet at your house if we meet.[1] But I am not sure whether your first note is recalled by your second. Please let me know & I will act accordingly.

P.S. I fear there is no chance of escape for me this evening.

699. Mr. Gladstone to Lord Granville. [G.D. 29/61]

11, Carlton House Terrace. May 4. 72.

I am not sure whether your Telegram to Thornton [2] as proposed is quite clear on account of the fact that the full stop at have would not appear. I suggest a few words at the end which it seems to me would remove any doubt & I think the message would be useful.

700. Mr. Gladstone to Lord Granville. [G.D. 29/61]

Immediate. 11, Carlton House Terrace. May 6.72.

I find the following Memoranda of Cabinets.[3]

"Friday Jan 18.

[1] On Fish's reply; cf. Hammond to Granville, 1 May, G.D. 29/105; Gladstone's notes on the cabinet, 2 May, Add. MS. 44640, fos. 87, 88; Granville's notes untraced.

[2] Draft with Gladstone's amendment, G.D. 29/61. It replied to Thornton's tel. 3 May, F.O. 5/1398. It gave him discretion to encourage a resolution in the House of Representatives for the withdrawal of the indirect claims.

[3] See Add. MS. 44640, fos. 2, 10, 17, 19, from which no. 700 made extracts.

Westbury's letter & advice. Approve the reservation to the Countercase."

" Jan 25. " Law Officers to see Chancellor on the question of the mode of preventing detriment through bringing illegitimate matter before the Arbitrators ".

" Jan 30. Alabama Case of the Americans. Proper course to take discussed. Adjourned."

" Feb 2. Communication to Fish discussed generally & outline agreed on.

Alabama Paragr. determined."

I thought it might be well for you to have them.

701. Lord Granville to Mr. Gladstone. [Add. MS. 44168, fo. 264]

Foreign Office. My 10 [1872].

I gave Schenck the note.[1] He grinned from ear to ear. I said " I suppose you have now got what you want." " Oh I can give no opinion. You have been several hours at work, & I have only read it once—but I think it certainly opens the way." I begged him not to talk of " opening the way." He answered " Oh I have told them that on Monday you will produce papers or make a statement ".

702. Mr. Gladstone to Lord Granville. [G.D. 29/61]

11, Carlton House Terrace. May 11. 72.

I am not in possession of any of the Telegrams or other documents since the date of Fish's last—I should much like to [go] over them before Monday.

703. Mr. Gladstone to Lord Granville. [Add. MS. 44168, fo. 266]

10, Downing Street. May 12. 72.

I mentioned to the Queen last night that I had failed with Childers.[2] She asked me what I thought of ; and my reply produced the rather earnest expostulation, a repetition of which is contained in the inclosed letter.[3]

As there is no great matter of duty or principle involved in making the offer, I am disposed to think we should give way to the Queen's wish.

She mentioned the Duke's book ; though not in the first rank of objection.

[1] 10 May, containing the British draft of the proposed article on the indirect claims to supplement the Treaty of Washington, F.O. 5/1398. Cf. Tenterden to Granville, 10.45 p.m., 9 May, G.D. 29/106 ; Schenck to Granville, 8, 9, 10 May, G.D. 29/81 ; to Thornton, Nos. 175, 176, 181–4, 6–9 May, F.O. 5/1398.

[2] See note by Gladstone, with his note on the cabinet, 6 May, that the chancellorship of the duchy of Lancaster, resigned by Dufferin, should be offered to Childers, Add. MS. 44640, fo. 90 ; Gladstone to Childers offering it with a seat in the cabinet, 6 May, Add. MS. 44541, fo. 123 ; and reply, Add. MS. 44128, fo. 225.

[3] Cf. Gladstone to the Queen, 11 May, abandoning his proposal of the duke of Somerset for the duchy, Guedalla, i. 348–9.

704. Lord Granville to Mr. Gladstone. [G.D. 29/61]

16, Bruton Street. [13 May 1872].

Schenck tells me that Fish has submitted our article to the President, who will submit it to the Senate.[1]

We think it better to say nothing but 'that we are more hopeful'.

705. Lord Granville to Mr. Gladstone. [Add. MS. 44168, fo. 267]

16, Bruton Street. May 14/72.

It has struck me that we could rectify the omission of R. Palmer's words, by putting them into the note of communication to the Arbitrators? [2]

The Queen told me what she had said to you about Somerset. I told [her] you had acquiesced.

She then asked me to whom you thought of offering the duchy. I said I believed you thought of sounding G. Grey.

She desired me to tell you such an appointment would be particularly agreeable to her—you might perhaps mention this to him.

I have told the Queen that you seemed much pleased by her thought of you about Blackheath,[3] but that there were some difficulties & that you requested to have 2 or 3 days consideration.

What shall I say about Fish presenting papers. I suppose *not* object.

706. Lord Granville to Mr. Gladstone. [G.D. 29/61]

[14 May 1872].

Schenck puts a little water in the wine as to the acceptance of the Senate—He says that his telegram (which he did not give me) was submit[ted] to the Senate for *their consideration*.

Please circulate this.

707. Mr. Gladstone to Lord Granville. [G.D. 29/61]

10, Downing Street. May 14. 72.

It occurs to me that you might say to Fish you are conscious the public presentation of the four notes will or may be in a polemical sense relatively disadvantageous to England as the U.S. will have the last word on that part of the question which they have argued; but that with the sense you entertain of the importance, for the honour as well as the interest of both nations, of a settlement, that you will on no account attempt to interfere with his liberty of action though he has kindly

[1] Cf. Schenck to Granville, Sunday morning, 12 May, G.D. 29/81.

[2] I.e. communicating the proposed supplementary article; cf. Tenterden to Granville, 15 May, G.D. 29/106.

[3] An offer of a permanent residence at Blackheath in his Greenwich constituency.

permitted it, lest you should restrict or impair his use of any instrument which he might deem conducive to the end in view.[1]

Lord Russell last night offered a spectacle melancholy to those who have known and admired him when he was himself. I presume you will say a few words to Schen[c]k, to prevent his taking the speech as that of a 'representative man'.

Dizzy was perfect.[2] I understand he was much pleased with my having called to inquire after Lady Beaconsfield a few days ago. Perhaps this helped a little.

Thanks for your other intelligence.

708. Mr. Gladstone to Lord Granville. [G.D. 29/61]

11, Carlton House Terrace. May 17. 72.

As the Telegram from Thornton[3] states that some days may yet elapse before the Senate decides, I mean to go to Hawarden this afternoon.

I have been reading a box of Turkey dispatches from Rumbold. If he is to be relied on, & indeed to some extent from his testimony as to facts, I cannot but think Andrassy is a great deal too meddlesome.[4] In the matter of the Bulgarian Church he is in my opinion simply playing the game of Russia (if Russia be guilty of all that is imputed to her), at any rate of the enemies of Turkey: and I feel uncomfortable at the idea of any thing like special relations of intimacy with him. Why has he not consulted you on this subject, since he was so desirous of universal & previous mutual consultation?

I declined Blackheath yesterday.[5]

709. Lord Granville to Mr. Gladstone. [G.D. 29/61]

Copy. Private. Deal. May 23/72.

I go to Holmbury Wotton Dorking, unless a telegram which I shall find at Dover from Hammond advises me to go straight to town.

I send you a correspondence which I have had with Schenck respecting a note

[1] Relates to Thornton's announcement, 13 May, that Fish proposed to present the correspondence about the indirect claims to Congress (British notes, 3 Feb., 20 March; American notes, 27 Feb., 16 April). Granville replied that he would not restrict America's freedom to publish, tel. 5 p.m., 14 May, F.O. 5/1399. The notes accompanied the president's message to Congress, 15 May, and were then published in the *London Gazette*, 17 May, and laid before Parliament after the recess, 27 and 31 May; cf. Parl. papers. [C. 545] (1872). lxix, 653.

[2] On 13 May, the eve of the Whitsun recess, Granville and Gladstone both made statements on the American negotiations and the supplementary article to the Treaty of Washington. Disraeli led the Commons in forgoing debate, but Russell sought to open one in the Lords, *Hans. Parl. Deb.*, 3rd ser., ccxi. 632–48, 654–65.

[3] Received 1 a.m., 17 May, F.O. 5/1399.

[4] Rumbold to Granville, Nos. 101–15, 23 April–1 May, on Turkish internal policy, the Bulgarian Church and Austrian policy; received 11 May and, except Nos. 107 and 108, sent together to Gladstone. See particularly No. 115 confidential, 1 May, on the 'categorical instructions' of the Austrian representative 'to exert himself strenuously in bringing about a schism between the Bulgarian Church and the Patriarchate', F.O. 78/2217.

[5] See above, no. 705, and Gladstone to the Queen, *Letters*, 2nd ser., ii. 206.

to the Tribunal [1]—Roundell Palmer having agreed with you and me that it would be desirable to obtain if possible the "shall not be entertained" into the note. He regrets the omission from the article, but says he adheres to the opinion which he gave in the Cabinet, that the words as they stand in the article are defensible in argument as sufficient.

From Schenck's last letter you will see that he prepares us for objections to anything but a simple communication of the article to the Arbiters.

It might be sharp practice on our part, but we might avail ourselves of the American alterations in the article to insist on the words "shall not be entertained" being inserted in the Article if they will not put them in the note—on the ground that the refusal does throw a doubt on the intention.

I think we ought to have a Cabinet the day after the news of the assent—there will also be some difficulty in deciding what papers we are to present at once.

710. Mr. Gladstone to Lord Granville. [G.D. 29/61]

10, Downing Street. May 27.72.

I wrote to the Queen [2] in the ordinary way of reporting all important Cabinet proceedings.

It did not occur to me to mention your reference respecting the wearing of a Foreign Order: or I, probably, ought to have done it—& will do so, if you think it desirable.

I am quite of opinion that, if baffled as to the opinion of the Senate in the matter of the Additional or Supplemental Treaty, we must not on that account bate any jot of heart or hope.

It is something to have Schenck with us: he is a stronger backed man than Thornton seems to be. I have rather altered my opinion of Thornton since he complained to me of his P.C. ship because Montague Bernard had one.

I thought it was material you should see Schenck; but, beyond that, am sorry you should be detained in town.

711. Lord Granville to Mr. Gladstone. [Add. MS. 44168, fo. 269]

B[ruton] St. May 29 [1872].

General Schenck (who has never seen a Derby) called on me at 9 A.M this morning, and informed [me] that he had recd in the night the following Telegram "Gov decline to agree to proposed alteration of supplementary Treaty. Holding to the opinion that the claims for indirect losses are admissible before the Arbitrators—the establishment of the principle embodied in the Article as assented to by Senate has been it's object in adhering to them, and the recognition of that principle by such supplementary Treaty will be the inducement for withdrawing them."

[1] See above, no. 705; Schenck to Granville, 18, 22 May, G.D. 29/81; Granville to Schenck, 17, 20 May, containing Granville's draft of the note of 22 May, F.O. 362/1.

[2] 27 May, *Letters*, 2nd ser., ii. 210. Cf. Gladstone's note on the cabinet, 27 May, which decided not to relax the rule against the wearing of foreign orders, Add. MS. 44640, fo. 99; Granville to Ponsonby, and reply, 25 May, *Letters, loc. cit.*, 208–10.

He also informed me that he had telegraphed last night the whole of the communications containing the additional observations I had addressed to him.

He expects no further telegram till tomorrow morning—when he will probably receive an answer to the proposal to extend the time for the Arbitration beyond the 15th of June—that answer he thinks likely to be favorable.

He believes he shall not have to trouble me before noon tomorrow.[1]

Congress have agreed to adjourn till the 3d.

712. Mr. Gladstone to Lord Granville. [G.D. 29/61]

11, Carlton House Terrace. June 2. 72.

1. I had a few minutes with Schenck last night and we spoke of the Telegram from Thornton [2] (not an answer to ours of yesterday) [3] which he had heard of from Lowe. I was struck by the manner in which he seemed to regard the Senate as a body foreign & extraneous to the American Government, one of the doings & dealings of which they were in no way as towards another State bound to render an account. He was anxious to be assured of the opinion of the Law Officers as to the power of the Arbitrators to adjourn which I said seemed to be the thread, now the single thread, by which the Treaty hung. We both hoped this one thread would be like the last of the three Horatii. No one could be more impressed than he was with the disgrace which would cover both countries if after settling apparently all questions of substance we should now break down upon difficulties of form & procedure.

2. I send herewith a letter from the Dean of Windsor.[4] Rather a 'large order'? Have you any information about the office?

3. Having now mentioned the Chancellorship of the Duchy in the Cabinet I am in a condition to speak to G. Grey.[5]

713. Lord Granville to Mr. Gladstone. [Add. MS. 44168, fo. 271]

16, Bruton Street. June 2/72.

Schenck spoke to me in the same sense. He was in high spirits. He told me that we had offered the olive branch.[6] I could not help thinking that he was somewhat surprised at [the] opinion of the Law officers.

[1] The Senate amended the supplementary article, 25 May. For new British proposal, see Granville to Schenck, 27 May, and to Thornton, No. 225, 28 May, and 'additional observations' to Schenck, F.O. 5/1400. No. 227, 29 May, to Thornton, reproduces the words of no. 711, *ibid.*

[2] No. 19, 31 May, received 1 June, a fresh American proposal: Britain should sign the Senate article on the understanding that a new convention nearer her views would at once be negotiated, F.O. 5/1400.

[3] No. 22, 1 June, a fresh British proposal: both sides to postpone the presentation to the tribunal of the arguments due on 15 June and the arbitrators then to adjourn; cf. note to Schenck, 1 June. For exposition of the legal construction of the Treaty on the matter of adjournment, see Granville to Schenck, 3 June, and following documents, F.O. 5/1401.

[4] 1 June, on the appointment to the office of Black Rod; see Gladstone to Dean Wellesley, 5 June, Add. MS. 44541, fo. 136.

[5] See above, no. 703.

[6] See above, no. 712, the British proposal. It was rejected by America, from Thornton, tel. No. 23, 4 June, received 5 June, F.O. 5/1401.

His manner would have been encouraging, if he [had] not been so often sanguine on former occasions.

R Palmer quite approves of the course we have taken.

He & Jessel whom I questioned, encouraged me to put to the Law Officers the question which Westbury advised me to lay before them.

I will try & find out something about Clifford's office.

714. Mr. Gladstone to Lord Granville. [G.D. 29/61]

H of C. June 4. 72.

Speaking roughly, the idea here is that, though we could probably array a majority of this House in support of a defensive motion on the Treaty of Washington, it is very doubtful whether a balance of advantage would arise. A large minority in this House would be arrayed against us, with a majority perhaps of independent and effective speakers. The Opposition Bench, which has hitherto been nearly silent, would be almost compelled to support their friends in the House of Lords. The mere preponderance of numbers there would be, but I doubt whether it would tell so much as the steady abstinence of the entire House of Commons and its implied approval in a general way of the objects & policy, if not of all the precise steps, of the Government. I send this, as expressing the impression of a few at the moment.[1]

715. Mr. Gladstone to Lord Granville. [G.D. 29/61]

10, Downing Street. Jun. 6. 1872.

A propos of Clanricarde: if you can rely on the indications given, might that section be encouraged to move some amendment of the nature of the sketch inclosed.[2]

716. Mr. Gladstone to Lord Granville. [G.D. 29/61]

11, Carlton House Terrace. June 6. 1872.

I think there is much in your point. It has indeed repeatedly crossed my mind during the discussions, but has escaped at the moment when it should have been present. Why should we not add ' or others inflicting injury ', or words to that effect, after belligerents. It would be only an amendment ' in furtherance '[3]— I assume Palmer's assent to something of the kind.

[1] Relates to the impolicy of a parallel debate in the Commons to that in the Lords on Russell's much postponed motion for the suspension of the arbitration until the indirect claims were withdrawn, 4, 6 June, *Hans. Parl. Deb.*, 3rd ser., ccxi. 1095–1190, 1262–8.

[2] Draft amendment to Russell's motion: approving the British declaration that the indirect claims were not within the scope of the arbitration, but refraining ' from any expression of opinion at this juncture ', G.D. 29/61.

[3] Relates to the wording of addition A. to the proposed supplementary article. It defined the term ' indirect losses '.

717. Mr. Gladstone to Lord Granville. [G.D. 29/61]

H of C. June 6. 72.

I conclude you will of your own authority refrain from pressing the Americans on point C, now that we have secured from them so thoroughly satisfactory an explanation as to the concluding paragraph of the Supplementary Article. In truth, even if the letter has gone as yesterday agreed on, I think Schenck should understand we do not press for a change in this part of the Article; otherwise there is a fear that A & B may be clogged with this additional demand.[1]

I find the five colleagues who are on the bench inclined to this course of proceeding.

718. Mr. Gladstone to Lord Granville. [G.D. 29/61]

11, Carlton House Terrace. June 7. 72.

With reference to the Thornton Telegram of today, in which Fish seems to take objection to the word belligerent, I think that if so disposed you might safely go so far at least as to say there would be no difficulty in enlarging it so as to meet Fish's very reasonable desire—and this without waiting for any measures of consultation home, in order to save time.[2]

719. Mr. Gladstone to Lord Granville. [G.D. 29/61]

11, Carlton House Terrace. June 10 [1872].

Bad! [3]

Cabinet summoned for 2.30.

I hope you will come here on your way.

It would be well to have Palmer before 2.30—here or in D. St as you please.

The U.S. Tel. contains one palpable error. The U.S. are not asked to be parties by understanding or in any way to our declaration as to the future.

Query point *this* out to Schenck *at once.*

720. Mr. Gladstone to Lord Granville. [G.D. 29/29A]

Secret. 11, Carlton House Terrace. Ju. 13. 72.

I have seen the Chancellor who is all in the right sense. He will see Cardwell tomorrow forenoon. K[imberley] it seems is not yet pliable.

[1] See Granville to Schenck, 5 June, which enclosed the British additions (A.B.C.) to the proposed supplementary article; Schenck to Granville, 6 June, explaining America's understanding of the article which made addition C. unnecessary, F.O. 5/1401.

[2] See Granville to Schenck; to Thornton, tel. No. 42, 7.45 p.m.; Palmer to Granville, 7 June, *ibid.* He re-worded the proposed addition A. to meet Fish's objection reported by Thornton, tel. No. 24, 6 June, *ibid.*

[3] Fish to Schenck, tel. 9 June, communicated 7 a.m. 10 June, *ibid.* He rejected Britain's proposal for a joint request for the adjournment of the tribunal and a British declaration, to be put in with her argument, 15 June, reserving her right to withdraw if the indirect claims question was not settled during the adjournment. The cabinet met 10, 11, 12 June, Add. MS. 44640, fos. 112–19. It was decided that Britain should ask for an adjournment and withhold her argument, and the British arbitrator, counsel and agent then went to Geneva. See Granville to Tenterden, Nos. 3–6, 12 June, F.O. 5/1402.

In conversation with the Chancellor we came upon this point—that there might with advantage be *ready for use at Geneva* in case of need a sealed revocation of the Commission of our Arbitrator. I do not know whether you have already provided this, or if it can be done.

All went off well enough with us.[1] Opposition Bench quite silent. I think they feel that Cairns's tongue has wagged too freely.

721. Lord Granville to Mr. Gladstone. [Add. MS. 44168, fo. 274]

Confidential. 16, Bruton Street. June 14/72.

Halifax was not in the House, so I called on him yesterday evening.

He was at first short as regarded himself, still more so as to others. I did not make much progress in the argument, till I appealed to him in the " man of the world sense " and then he came to the conclusion which he himself describes in the enclosed.[2]

I had some talk but with not much result one way or the other with Goschen, and Kimberley, but they were not under my charge.

I doubt the contingency arising.

722. Mr. Gladstone to Lord Granville. [G.D. 29/61]

H of C. Jun 14. 7 pm. 72.

I see nothing to object to in the draft [3] sent me in this box : but I do not know for what purpose it is intended, & I presume the critical review of it would be for our legal advisers here or at Geneva.

723. Lord Granville to Mr. Gladstone.[4] [Add. MS. 44168, fo. 276]

Confidential. 16, Bruton Street. [14 June 1872].

Sir John Rose has just recd this telegram from Governor Morgan an intimate friend of Grant's who has just left the President.

It seems to concede nothing—

The Secretary of the American Legation at Paris was told by Davis, " If the English will only let the Arbitrators meet for 48 hours all will be settled."

I send you back your draft which I showed to Halifax, who wrote the enclosed in his handwriting.

[1] On 11 June Granville and Gladstone reported the procedure proposed when the tribunal met at Geneva. Cairns in the Lords and Disraeli in the Commons spoke against the government, *Hans. Parl. Deb.*, 3rd ser., ccxi. 1562–82, 1589–1614.

[2] Halifax to Granville, confidential, 14 June, moving towards Granville's and Gladstone's view that the whole object for the moment was to keep the arbitration in being, G.D. 29/64. The cabinet was still divided on their course if the adjournment was refused ; see Granville to Palmer, 12 June, G.D. 29/67 ; Gladstone to Goschen, 17 June, Add. MS. 44541, fo. 139.

[3] Granville to Tenterden, tel. 14 June, authorizing him to give the secretary of the tribunal a sealed copy of the British argument, F.O. 5/1402.

[4] Gladstone to Granville, 14 June, on Foreign Office post for Herbert Gladstone and the deanery of Lincoln, and two notes, 15 June, G.D. 29/61, not printed.

724. Mr. Gladstone to Lord Granville. [G.D. 29/61]

11, Carlton House Terrace. June 17. 72.

It appears to me that the hint about a further short adjournment heightens the probability that U.S. mean to work the idea of ruling out.

The Evarts-Palmer Telegram [1] appears to call for some reply.

Acknowledgement & approval might be sufficient?

Might this be proposed in a Circulation box? With a note to the first dissentient to send it back that the Cabinet might be immediately summoned thereupon?

725. Lord Granville to Mr. Gladstone. [G.D. 29/61]

Foreign Office. June 20/72.

I think we had better *not* say that it is at the request of the Americans that the Tribunal has been adjourned—the mere statement of the fact of adjournment will be sufficient.[2]

726. Lord Granville to Mr. Gladstone. [Add. MS. 44168, fo. 278]

16, Bruton Street. June 28/72.

Although I was at first doubtful, I think Sir H. Howard's very long services, and his forced retirement owing to the abolition of his post entitle him to a move in the Bath.

If he has a G.C.B. there would be a K.C.B. available for Harris, who has successfully negotiated the 3 colonial treaties with the Netherlands,[3] and his C.B. would go to Jerningham to whom one was promised on his retirement, which takes place next month.

Last night was successful, and I am rather glad that Cairns showed the cloven foot.[4]

Il n'y a rien qui réussit comme le succès.

[1] Tenterden to Granville, 1 a.m. 17 June, solving the indirect claims question, F.O. 5/1402. On 16 June Evarts, the American counsel, and Palmer, the British counsel, agreed to a declaration by the neutral arbitrators against the indirect claims. See Tenterden to Granville, private, 15 and 16 June, enclosing a confidential mem. of the conversation between Evarts and Palmer, 16 June, G.D. 29/106. Granville to Tenterden, 1.20 p.m. 17 June, simply approved his proceedings.

[2] No. 725 was returned by Gladstone with the comment 'I wish we had discussed this—*all* the responsibility of these adjournments is now thought to lie with *us*. Cardwell rather agrees. W.E.G. June 20 4/20 Pm.' The short adjournments on the 15th and 17th were at America's request and separate from the British request of the 15th.

[3] 8 Sept. 1870, on coolie labour for Surinam; 25 Feb. 1871, transferring Dutch possessions on the Guinea coast to Britain; 2 Nov. 1871, settling relations in Sumatra; see Parl. papers. [C. 473], [C. 474], [C. 475] (1872). lxx, 557 ff.

[4] On 27 June Granville and Gladstone made statements on the settlement of the indirect claims question. In the Lords Cairns argued that Britain had been defeated since the tribunal had itself decided the scope and intent of the treaty. *Hans. Parl. Deb.*, 3rd ser., ccxii. 260–6, 293–301.

727. Mr. Gladstone to Lord Granville. [G.D. 29/61]

11, Carlton House Terrace. Jul. 1. 72.

1. I have made use of the liberty you gave me in striking out the *queried* part of the reference to the Arbitrators: the little compliment you have still left in the text *sits* I think perfectly well.[1]

2. I send the draft direct to Hammond—without the delay of Circulation.

3. I expect to be very free at the H. of C. for conversation about the Queen's letters [2]: if the H. of L. is equally kind to you.

My anti-Hanoverian opinion was not I think quite so strong as H.M. supposes. At any rate, it had reference to times and circumstances, which are in continual flux.

728. Mr. Gladstone to Lord Granville. [G.D. 29/61]

11, Carlton House Terrace. Jul 3. 72.

The Queen has approved the Bath Promotions.

I keep an extract from Cockburn's letter.[3]

The course marked out by the Cabinet in the *Sunday* Telegram was I think a much better one than that which he actually took; but I suppose it was not substantive enough for his taste. His method is less easy to defend against Cairnses and the like—if there be any body like Cairns; but all is well that ends well.

729. Lord Granville to Mr. Gladstone.[4] [Add. MS. 44169, fo. 3]

16, Bruton Street. [5 July 1872].

I beg pardon for the delay. It is impossible to state your plan more admirably.[5] You know that I have some doubts as to it's feasibility, even beyond the Question whether the Queen & the Prince will consent to it.

The sheets were somewhat shuffled, but I believe they are now right.

730. Mr. Gladstone to Lord Granville. [Add. MS. 44169, fo. 6]

10, Downing Street. [10 July 1872].

1. I have not an idea.

2. I have a feeling that my *letter* of Friday [6] may cause her too great a horror to make it humane for me to go. I should like to see my way a little further.

[1] See Granville to Tenterden, No. 26, 1 July, appreciating the several contributions to the settlement of the indirect claims question, with Gladstone's alterations, F.O. 5/1404.

[2] Not traced, possibly on the employment of the Prince of Wales.

[3] 30 June, missing from Cockburn's letters to Granville, G.D. 29/71. An extract, refusing, as arbitrator, to sanction a judicial decision that the indirect claims were outside the tribunal's jurisdiction, but offering to join in anything done extra-judicially, is in Add. MS. 44168, fo. 280. Cf. Gladstone's note on the cabinet, Sunday, 16 June, and an exchange between Granville and Gladstone, Add. MS. 44640, fos. 142–4. After the declaration the British application for an adjournment was withdrawn.

[4] Gladstone to Granville, 5 July, asking for the return of the draft letter to the Queen on the employment of the Prince of Wales, G.D. 29/61; an undated note by Granville asking to talk with Gladstone before he wrote to the Queen with a min. by Halifax or Hatherley deprecating a general discussion in the cabinet, Add. MS. 44169, fo. 5, not printed.

[5] On the employment of the Prince of Wales; see above, no. 677.

[6] 5 July, Guedalla, i. 351–8. For the Queen's reply, 12 July, see *ibid.*, i. 359–61.

N.B. Ponsonby by her desire has sent me a note promising her "earliest considn" which is all I could expect.

731. Lord Granville to Mr. Gladstone.[1] [Add. MS. 44169, fo. 6]

[10 July 1872].

I saw the Queen on Monday afternoon. She had received your letter—thought the difficulties great—did not enter into details.

I did not let out whether I had seen or not seen your letter, gave no opinion further than pressing the great importance of breaking the resumption of old habits. She talked civilly about your visit to Balmoral.

732. Mr. Gladstone to Lord Granville. [G.D. 29/61]

[*No. 1*]. H of C. July 12. 1872.

We are engaged in proposing and giving effect to the scheme for dealing with the Lords Amendments which we understood to have been agreed upon between you & the Duke of Richmond—and we hold ourselves bound to do our best to give effect to them exactly as they stand, except in so far as changes may seem irresistible, and then only if they are such as do not involve a departure from the spirit & substance of any material part.

However it is material to know whether these engagements are to be reciprocal. On the important point of the Declaration Sir M. H. Beach led the opposition, and Lord J. Manners & Mr Hardy have supported it.

It is not I think the first time that something of this kind has happened.[2]

733. Mr. Gladstone to Lord Granville. [G.D. 29/61]

[*No. 2*]. H of C. Jul 12. 72.

I wrote you a short time ago a note containing a complaint which related to the Ballot Amendments. The matter of the declaration has now been settled in a manner generally satisfactory—but this is in no degree due to the arguments or suggestions of the Opposition Bench, although (it having been received with great acclamation by the House) they accepted it.

I suppose the explanation is that Hardy & Co had not been apprised of the state of the case, through some default on the part of the leaders.

734. Mr. Gladstone to Lord Granville. [G.D. 29/29A]

10, Downing Street. July 16. 72.

For once I rather hesitate to accept your suggestion [3] & must consider farther. I have no wish to irritate: but I must consider how much the person in question

[1] Written below no. 730, which was returned to Gladstone.

[2] Cf. above, nos. 262, 263. For proceedings in the Lords, 12 July, on the Parliamentary and Municipal Elections (Ballot) Bill see *Hans. Parl. Deb.*, 3rd ser., ccxii. 1043–67. Cancelled mem. by Gladstone, 6 July, on policy if the Lords adhere to optional ballot, G.D. 29/61; Granville to Gladstone, 12 July: 'Richmond says "All right",' Add. MS. 44169, fo. 8, not printed.

[3] Not to press the matter of the employment of the Prince of Wales further.

has suffered, & the country through that person, from want of plain speaking. I must also consider that I am the only person who am under a definite responsibility, & bound in a peculiar & single way to take care that public interests do not suffer from this repression. I will however not act on any single subject: but I do not think my former letter, though it may have done enough to irritate, did enough to absolve.

735. Mr. Gladstone to Lord Granville. [G.D. 29/61]

10, Downing Street. July 17. 72.

I could not find time to put a scrap into your hand. A counsellor whom you can guess recommended some rather important softenings: with these, but without shortenings, it is gone.[1]

736. Lord Granville to Mr. Gladstone. [Add. MS. 44169, fo. 11]

16, Bruton Street. July 20/72.

I am going to Trentham for the coming of age.

The enclosed letters are not pleasant.

I should be glad if you would soon recommend Sir John Rose for the Baronetcy which was promised him as a reward for his success in the preliminary negotiations of the Washington Treaty. Thornton bears ample testimony to his great services during the last 6 months.

We asked him to submit to delay in consequence of Sir John Macdonald, but the latter has now asked for delay—& Sir John Rose's honor would be less remarked upon now, than later when we shall in all probability have to pay.

737. Mr. Gladstone to Lord Granville. [G.D. 29/61]

10, Downing Street. Jul 20 72.

1. I have written about Sir John Rose.

2. The account of C. of C. is disheartening: so is the Florida case; but it does not surprise me much, for in reading the original Case I thought that Nassau judgment bad, at least in a layman's eyes.[2]

3. Glyn tells me Morley is to have the Mines Bill.[3] You in the H. of L. know best: but I think that if the Cabinet Lords give over very important measures to very junior Lords, it will lead to awkward remarks, on the next Estimates, about Sinecure and quasi Sinecure offices.

[1] Rejoinder, 17 July, to the Queen's reply to the letter of 5 July, Guedalla, i. 361–6; see above, no. 730. The Queen's letter, 5 Aug., closed this correspondence, *ibid.*, 368–9. Cf. mem. by Gladstone, 6 Aug., circulating the letter of 5 Aug. to the cabinet and refusing to regard it as final, Add. MS. 44760, fo. 183. See below, no. 754.

[2] Relates to the proceedings of the Geneva tribunal resumed 15 July, after the stop of 27 June; see F.O. 5/1404 and 1405, and Parl. papers. [C. 688] (1873). lxxiv, 9.

[3] Morley managed the mines bill in the Lords, *Hans. Parl. Deb.*, *loc. cit.*, 1590.

738. Mr. Gladstone to Lord Granville. [G.D. 29/61]

Secret. 11, Carlton House Terrace. July 27. 72.

After two long and interesting conversations with J. B[right] I can say that the matter [1] is to stand over for a few days, but that it is at present *much* more yes than no, the difficulty of health being no longer in the foreground. I reserve details until we meet. No one in the Cabinet has been spoken to except Halifax and Cardwell.

I have written to recommend Spencer.[2]

739. Lord Granville to Mr. Gladstone. [Add. MS. 44169, fo. 13]

T[ren]tham. July 28/72.

I am delighted at the possible chance of Bright. He & Palmer (will the latter consent) will add great strength to your Gov.

I think you are right about Spencer.

740. Mr. Gladstone to Lord Granville.[3] [G.D. 29/61]

11, Carlton House Terrace. Jul 31.72. 2¾ Am.

Here is a sad letter from Bright—can any thing be done? Will you try your hand?

I am sorely puzzled about the Jervoise affair.

741. Mr. Gladstone to Lord Granville. [G.D. 29/61]

Copy. 10, Downing Street, Aug. 3 1872.

The subject of this letter from the Archbishop of Syra is curious, interesting, & important [4]: but not less difficult & complicated.

It suggests the possibility of drawing Turkey and Greece nearer together, in the sense of antagonism to Russian intrigues and to Panslavism.

What I should like with Ld Granville's approval would be to introduce the Archbishop to Sir H. Elliot—placing the letter in Sir H.E.'s hands if the writer permits it, & expressing a confidence that he would be alike able & disposed to treat the subject acc. to justice & good policy.

In doing this I would submit to the Archbishop the advantage of recommending moderate counsels; for if the Greek Church has an enemy in the Russian one,

[1] Of his rejoining the government, taking the duchy of Lancaster, see above, no. 606.

[2] For the lord-lieutenancy of Northamptonshire, 1 Aug., Add. MS. 44541, fo. 165.

[3] Granville to Gladstone, 28 July, on the duke of Edinburgh's marriage, Add. MS. 44169, fo. 14, not printed.

[4] To Gladstone, 15/27 July, on the schismatic Bulgarian bishops, whose superior the archbishop was, and British influence among them as a counterweight to Russia's; in German, Add. MS. 44434, fos. 314–31, translated, G.D. 29/61. Gladstone's reply, 13 Aug., Add. MS. 44541, fo. 179; cf. D. C. Lathbury, *Letters on Church and Religion of William Ewart Gladstone* (1910), ii. 304. The letter was sent to Elliot, G.D. 29/116, and to Musurus, Add. MS. 44435, fo. 130. See also Gladstone to Elliot, 16 Aug., sending his reply, Add. MS. 44541, fo. 178; Elliot to Gladstone, 26 Aug., 18 Oct., Add. MS. 44435, fos. 146, 256.

both have a more formidable and determined one in the Roman influence, which is sure to work in present circumstances in favour of both political and religious disintegration in the East.

742. Lord Granville to Mr. Gladstone. [Add. MS. 44169, fo. 17]

16, Bruton Street. Aug 3 [1872].

M. Ozenne [1] called on me this morning. He said he was glad to have an opportunity of informing me of the views of M. Thiers.

M. Thiers in the first instance, as a matter of course, desired to maintain the most friendly relations with England. As to commercial matters, it was not the intention of the President of the Republic to encrease the tariff at the expiration of the Treaty—and beyond that, as he believed that England held strongly to her late position as to the indirect navigation the President was willing to abandon the restrictions which had recently been imposed upon it.

It remained to be considered what means should be adopted for accomplishing the objects which were desired. A new Treaty seemed to the President to be unnecessary, probably an interchange of notes would be sufficient.

In these circumstances it would also be desirable to open negotiations on the duty upon raw materials (a very low duty) which had recently been voted by the Chamber. The two matters were linked together.

I told M. Ozenne that I would reserve any formal answer to what he had said to [me] but that I should [at] once state that I appreciated strongly the desire shown by the President to remove difficulties respecting commercial differences—which with one exception, which I hoped was on the point of settlement were the only questions of which I was aware which could lead to anything but the best feeling between the two countries.

I should be glad if M. Ozenne would describe a little more precisely the basis on which his Gov proposed to negotiate as to the duty on raw materials.

M. Ozenne gave me an account of what the law on raw materials was, in order to show that the measure was purely fiscal and not protective.

He promised to put in writing what he had said.

I asked him whether I understood the object of the negotiation to be to come to some agreement about the duty on raw materials, there now being a difference between H.M's Gov & that of France as to their applicability under the present Treaty. He said that that was his intention. M. Thiers was determined not to put differential duties adverse to England even after the Treaty expired, and it was also an object to him to begin revising the duties as soon as possible.

[1] In London as the French delegate to the sugar conference, 1 Aug. In Feb. Thiers had failed to re-open negotiations for the revision of the Cobden Treaty. France then denounced it, de Broglie to Granville, 15 March, F.O. 27/1947. In April France proposed to drop the taxes on raw materials if Britain agreed to the duties on foreign shipping and on indirect trade, enacted 30 Jan. This failed, and the raw materials' taxes were enacted, 26 July. Ozenne's proposal was telegraphed to Lyons, 5 Aug. See also to Lyons, No. 220 commercial, 3 Aug., F.O. 27/1935; private, 10 Aug., G.D. 29/109; from Lyons, No. 439, 4 Aug., F.O. 27/1942; Fortescue to Granville, 5 Aug., and mem. by Gladstone, 7 Aug., G.D. 29/70.

'43. Mr. Gladstone to Lord Granville. [G.D. 29/61]

10, Downing Street. Au. 3. 72.

I have read and return your Memorandum.[1] With this note I send a draft 'aragraph which I had sketched *last night*, of course before hearing of your con- 'ersation with Ozanne [*sic*], on the French Treaty.

Will you manipulate it as you think best with reference to circumstances as hey now stand. They seem to have improved, though the doctrine of a non- rotective duty on raw materials is moonshine.

44. Mr. Gladstone to Lord Granville. [G.D. 29/61]

Hawarden Castle. Aug 12. 1872.

1. As I was leaving town on Saturday I received your cover with the Queen's nessage [2] in a note from Ripon to you. Would you advise me to answer by accepting t literally, or to make a call there in passing, at such time of the day as she may ppoint ? I am a little puzzled as to the meaning. It may be that she only intends n audience for chat and commonplace. If it were really with a hope of making ny progress in the great business, I would gladly travel a long distance for it. As have put a question, I inclose the note for your further perusal.

2. I have not yet thanked you for the Memorandum you so kindly gave me bout my house.[3] I have no idea of leaving it while the Government lasts, but must do it when the wind up comes as it is much too expensive for me. The igure of those houses, even the medium ones, rather frightens when all is put ogether—& a variety of circumstances, by no means all of them unpleasant ones, ave combined to limit my fortune since the time when I bought it now 15 or 6 years ago.

I found them all here as well as I could desire after the heavy blow.[4] But here is a great deal to plan and execute. One of the first events has been that my on Stephen has had the offer of this large and important parish from his Uncle, which I think he may accept but with great misgiving and self-mistrust.

'45. Lord Granville to Mr. Gladstone. [Add. MS. 44169, fo. 26]

F.O. Aug 13/72.

I saw the Queen yesterday.[5] She was in high spirits, and acknowledged herself o be well, having derived benefit from a course of Carlsbad waters. She alluded o no subject of the least importance.

[1] No. 742. A copy by Hammond of Gladstone's comments and the draft paragraph for the Queen's speech at the end of the session anticipating an arrangement with France on the Cobden Treaty, and a complaint by Granville that Gladstone had not returned the mem. of conversation with Ozenne, G.D. 29/61, not printed.

[2] That the Queen would be glad to see Gladstone at Balmoral. Cf. the Queen to Granville, Aug., G.D. 29/34, and the Queen to Gladstone, 11 Aug., Guedalla, i. 371.

[3] Granville to Gladstone, 3 Aug., deprecating his leaving Carlton House Terrace, Add. MS. 44169, fo. 23, not printed.

[4] Mrs. Gladstone's brother, Henry Glynn, rector of Hawarden since 1834, died on 30 July

[5] On her way through London to Balmoral.

In the course of conversation she said " I have written to Mr Gladstone to ask him to pay me a visit at Balmoral although he will not be in attendance " I answered " That I had had a note from Lord Ripon and that I had forwarded it to you & that I presume as Your Majesty once invited Lord Aberdeen when I had the honor of being in attendance." She said " Yes ", & no more passed. If I were you I should go for two nights.

Johnny Russell bombards me with letters.[1] In one he wished me joy of the session being over, and [said] that you must be sick of it. In my answer I told [him] that I agreed you must be sick of it, although you must be immensely pleased with its great success. You had come in as a lamb, and gone out like a lion. His answer did not imply perfect acquiescence, but sent him into a long dissertation about himself, in which he made a rather touching allusion to his own poverty, and to the *impossibility of his accepting a seat in the Cabinet without a salary*.

I will discuss Carlton Terrace. I avoid counting the whole cost, I only investigate what additional rent including interest over & above Bruton St I shall have to pay.

The Japanese Minister, who seems intelligent arrived the day before yesterday at Liverpool. I had a man posted at Liverpool to bring him off at once, and landed him at Osborne at two yesterday the only time the Queen would see him. I shall receive the Japanese Embassy on Monday afternoon, and give them a dinner on the same evening.[2] On Tuesday I shall confide them to Hammond's tender mercies.

I have seen Ozenne & impressed on him that we can do nothing without full information.[3]

746. Mr. Gladstone to Lord Granville. [G.D. 29/61]

Hawarden Castle. Aug 17. 72.

1. I received a direct communication from the Queen about the visit to Balmoral on which I have written in the sense you advise.

2. Your account of Lord Russell is touching. He is the victim of infirmities, to which an energetic man yields with reluctance.

3. The Queen asks if it is necessary to make Hanmer a Peer. Of course I hold to it.

4. I have never thanked you, I think, for your great kindness and interest about my Priv. Secretaryship. It is settled very well. Capel, evidently an excellent man, takes an office under Stansfield. I get F. Cavendish with Gurdon, & as Third or Assistant young Mr Godley a very distinguished Oxford man, son in law to our friend Sir W. James.

5. I wrote to the Abp of Syra in a pacific or peacemaking sense, & sent a copy to Sir H. Elliot.

[1] G.D. 29/79.

[2] For correspondence concerning the Japanese embassy's reception, see G.D. 29/103.

[3] See above, no. 742. France made a formal overture to re-open negotiations on the Cobden Treaty, Lyons to Granville, No. 447 commercial, 9 Aug., F.O. 27/1942. They began, between Ozenne and Kennedy of the commercial department of the Foreign Office, on 13 Aug. ; see Granville to Lyons, No. 229 commercial, 13 Aug., F.O. 27/1935.

747. Lord Granville to Mr. Gladstone. [Add. MS. 44169, fo. 52]

[20 August 1872].

Many thanks for your note. I send you an interesting one from Acton. Paget has always appeared to be to be [*sic*] a grumbling Tory, but in Italian matters as Anti papal as possible.

Jervoise's letters are sometimes tinged by the more clerical atmosphere in which he lives, but I thought him very judicious & sensible in his conversation.

It is provoking having this Commercial Treaty question open at this moment of the holydays but I hope we shall get the points for decision clearly defined & limited in number.

I think Godley will train into an excellent private Secretary. All he wants, as you said, is knowledge of political men.

I am delighted to hear of your son's preferment.

748. Mr. Gladstone to Lord Granville. [G.D. 29/61]

Hawarden Castle. Aug. 21. 72.

I know of no circumstances suspicious about Paget's Italianism except this that Manning does not speak ill of him. But I think M. is a man of kindly nature except where he is poisoned by Ultramontanism, so that the point does not come to much. You might easily test Paget by *mentioning* the points suggested by Venosta. I am not sure that Jervoise would not be all the better for a hint from you. I saw him after he had been questioned in the H. of Commons,[1] and though he was disturbed at the circumstance he said nothing to purge himself. Possibly of course he felt himself innocent: but there is another possibility.

2. I think I mentioned to you that the Queen much to my surprise made a difficulty about Hanmer's Peerage. I certainly cannot recede: and if she perseveres I can put but one construction on it.

I return Acton's letter.

749. Mr. Gladstone to Lord Granville. [G.D. 29/61]

Hawarden Castle. Sept 1. 72.

I agree in Hammond's view that a present is better than a money payment to the Arbitrators. It would however be likely to become apart from the general question a cause of possibly an invidious debate, but if you could pay it out of Secret Service money I do not think there would be the same risk.

I am not much afraid of the debate on the 3 millions, though rather disappointed as to the sum.[2]

With respect to Cockburn I do not know that his former refusal of the Peerage [3] would bind him, or that Chelmsford's refusal of G.C.B. would be altogether in point but I think in the circs the less the acknowledgment is conspicuous the better for him and also it is a pity that lawyers so enormously endowed already should invade the Bath.

[1] See above, no. 740. [2] Damages awarded against Britain by the Geneva tribunal.
[3] See above, no. 2; below, p. 342, note 4, nos. 767, 802–5.

750. Mr. Gladstone to Lord Granville. [G.D. 29/31]

Hawarden Castle. Sept 1. 72.

This will find you I think at Balmoral. I send you in an inner packet a letter received from Halifax with my reply and communications to the Queen on the Irish Residence business.[1] I have had a vague idea of going abroad for a fortnight but do not yet know whether circumstances will permit. If I go I want to go anonymously—is there any objection? I should try to bring my sister back from Cologne where she has been living 4 years in an Hotel always intending to start on the morrow.

751. Lord Granville to Mr. Gladstone. [Add. MS. 44169, fo. 60]

Edinburgh. Sep 1/72.

This 3,000,000 £ & something more award will not be popular here—& will create an angry debate in each house. If the Arbitrators are right as to the Alabama, and their unanimity ought to be a presumption in their favor, I doubt whether they are wrong about the Florida and the Shenandoah although the last raises some awkward questions as to our Colonial liabilities. I see nothing to make me doubt the perfect good faith of the Italian & Brazilian. Cockburn has been a bad Arbitrator for us.[2] Adams most judicious and on the whole not unfair considering his position.

I am glad to see you are keeping your eye on the French Treaty. If we come to terms, and make no unnecessary concessions, the sooner we can do so the better. The only thing I care about is the friendliness of the Acts. The Chambers of Commerce who have answered [3] appear to be pleased. I suppose there will be a protest from Manchester.

I will write from Balmoral whither I go tomorrow.

752. Lord Granville to Mr. Gladstone.[4] [Add. MS. 44169, fo. 63]

Confidential. Balmoral. Sep 4/72.

The Queen commissioned Ponsonby to show me the 'P. of Wales question' papers. He told me that Halifax had advocated the plan, but had been convinced it was impracticable in the face of the objections of the Queen & of the Prince. (He P. said that the Prince had implored the Queen to take the matter upon herself, as a direct refusal from him would annoy you, and make you angry with him—

[1] Halifax to Gladstone, confidential, 25 Aug., on conversation with the Queen about the scheme for the employment of the Prince of Wales in Ireland. He had agreed with the Queen's objections, and said that the Prince should be put in touch with the India office; reply, 28 Aug., Add. MS. 44185, fos. 298, 302; Gladstone to Halifax, 3 Sept., Add. MS. 44542, fo. 4.

[2] He had pronounced a separate judgement; see Parl. papers. [C. 689] (1873). lxxiv, 419. In the tribunal he had violently disagreed with his colleagues, yet he welcomed the adverse award as an embarrassment to the government; see Tenterden to Granville, private, 18, 24 July, 28 Aug., G.D. 29/106; Granville to Cockburn, 20, 22 Aug., G.D. 29/77, G.D. 29/22A; reply, 25 Aug., G.D. 29/71.

[3] Granville to Chambers of Commerce, 20, 22 Aug., asking an opinion on the draft Anglo-French commercial treaty, F.O. 27/1950; replies, F.O. 27/1951.

[4] Granville to Gladstone, Balmoral Castle, after 2 Sept., on Ponsonby and the C.B.; 3 Sept., on presenting a snuffbox to Cockburn since the latter considered a peerage without the chancellorship an insult, Add. MS. 44169, fos. 24, 62, not printed.

this he told me as a secret.) He added that the Queen hoped when you came here you would not *talk* to her on the subject, that she dreaded controversy in conversation very much—that it had a great effect on her nerves.

I read the papers, & told Ponsonby that I should not have originated the greater Irish scheme, but that the great necessity of finding employment for the Prince, the complete absence of any other mode (for I did not believe in the office plan) made it impossible for me to oppose a scheme which the Prime Minister proposed with an earnest conviction of its necessity & its probable success. I said that I agreed with Halifax that it required the assent of the Queen & the Prince, and even the cordial cooperation of the latter. I observed on the absence in the Queen's letter of any allusion to your request to be allowed to place yourself in direct communication with the Prince.[1]

I think there is no objection to your anonymous journey, particularly with so good a family reason. I presume you would avoid Paris & Berlin, as your arrival would probably get out, and the question arise as to seeing the President or Bismarck, which you probably do not desire.

If you succeed, I may follow your example some calm day, on a furniture expedition to Belgium.

The P. of W's expedition to Trouville seems to have been a foolish affair.

753. Mr. Gladstone to Lord Granville. [G.D. 29/31]

Hawarden Castle. Sept. 6. 72.

I have your letter of the 4th, and I shall await the return of the correspondence, which I have sent you. Your answer to Ponsonby was I think all that it could be. Clearly the Queen was rather too many for Halifax, as I see also from her final answer to me. Of course it is idle to attempt to force her: and I do not think it would be right for me to resign upon the matter, as it would do more harm than good. I have told H.M. I will inform the Cabinet, will speak to the Prince if he speaks to me, will consult my Colleagues as to the Indian Council: & generally have endeavoured to avoid the appearance of mere ill humour. Her shielding the Prince is handsome, though there was nothing to shield him from. She need not be afraid of my pressing the subject in conversation, for I have always made it a point to act as far as I could in that sense—and at present I must say it will be a *great* relief and pleasure to me if she lets me off Balmoral altogether. I have had your Telegram this morning, and may perhaps have another.

My wife is desirous that we should go to Scotland, the region would be Inverness-shire, and this would probably drive me too late for the accomplishment of my little continental dream.

In my letter to the Queen today I shall make a mild effort to escape the visit.

754. Lord Granville to Mr. Gladstone. [Add. MS. 44169, fo. 68]

Confidential. Dunrobin. Sep 10/72.

1. The Queen showed me your letter,[2] and said she was sorry that you were

[1] Cf. Ponsonby to Granville, 2 Sept., and reply, copy, Balmoral, 3 Sept., G.D. 29/31.

[2] To the Queen, 6 Sept., replying to the Queen's of 2 Sept. which answered Gladstone's of 28 Aug. on the employment of the Prince of Wales, Guedalla, i. 374–80.

annoyed. I said that you were earnest in all matters that you considered of importance, that you believed a great responsibility attached to you in this matter & that you had full confidence in the plan you proposed, that it was therefore a sacrifice for you to give it up at H.M's wish, but so far from wishing to show ill humor, you had in a private letter told me you had taken care not to exhibit any. The Queen was civil, expressed real regret at differing from you, but said she had the strongest conviction on the subject, and when she had a strong conviction, she generally found she was right. She said nothing about the door (a well proportioned one) which you open to her to dispense with your visit. But I believe she is going to write to you.[1]

755. Mr. Gladstone to Lord Granville. [Add. MS. 44169, fo. 70]

Private. Dunrobin. Sep 10/72.

Hammond has ingeniously supplied you, Ponsonby & me with different cyphers, & I have been in agonies about your telegram of Saturday, which I only got on Sunday, which Ponsonby & I could not decypher, & which I could not get decyphered by Hammond, owing to the Golspie Telegraph Clerk having telegraphed to London that the Dunrobin Telegraph Clerk had made a mistake.

I was on the whole relieved by finding it was about Abyssinia,[2] because I have great doubts of the Viceroy intending war. I have desired Hammond to act upon your suggestion. But what can we do, if the Viceroy pretends he is attacked, & his soldiers murdered. Why may he not take the same redress, as we foolishly took for ourselves.

I had never seen this beautiful place—we leave it on Saturday, and go to Balmoral on Monday—the Queen having graciously but most inconveniently expressed a wish to have a visit from Lady G, & River's daughter, who is travelling with us.

756. Mr. Gladstone to Lord Granville. [G.D. 29/31]

Sept 15. 72.

1. I telegraphed to you this morning on the French Treaty.[3] 2. The course pursued with regard to Stanley having been so very marked, it will of course attract criticism no less special in the event of any awkward discovery but I entirely agree with you that the question of his birth is altogether irrelevant. If he raised himself from the condition of a pauper bastard, the more credit is due to him. On the finding of Livingstone I am not sufficiently informed to give an opinion.[4] 3. The Queen has kindly dispensed with my going to Balmoral. Last year I certainly was dis-

[1] See the Queen to Gladstone, 11 Sept., Guedalla, i. 380–1.

[2] See Stanton to Granville, tel. 8 Sept., on an Egyptian expedition against Abyssinia, F.O. 78/2229. The expedition ultimately went in Nov. 1875.

[3] Hammond had forwarded to Granville and Gladstone a mem. by Lowe, 7 Sept., against continuing the French commercial negotiations, G.D. 29/105. Granville to Gladstone, tel. 11.58. 12 Sept., advised going on, Add. MS. 44169, fo. 78. Gladstone's tel., 15 Sept., agreed and so did a mem. by Forster, 10 Sept., forwarded at the same time, G.D. 29/56. Granville then defined preliminary safeguards; to Gavard, 14 Sept., sent 3.30. 15 Sept. after Gladstone's sanction, F.O. 27/1947.

[4] Granville to Gladstone, 10 Sept., on the difficulty of Stanley's audience of the Queen owing to doubts cast on the truth of the Livingstone incident and to his birth, Add. MS. 44169, fo. 72,

satisfied with being asked to go there on a different footing as to time from my colleagues and though I did it then I would not do it again. At the same time, though I think it a pity that the Queen is gradually letting in intervals without the presence of any minister which may grow indefinitely, I think she has a perfect right to make her choices, and I am always glad of any thing which enables her to make play with those who are younger either as ministers or men. 4. I shall now write to Hartington telling him how the matter stands with the Queen and P. of Wales and referring it to him to mature with Spencer any plan they may think it desirable to submit with respect to occasional or periodical residence of members of the Royal Family in Ireland.[1] Halifax has sent me a very good sketch of what might be done informally in the India Office for inoculating the P. with a passion for affairs.[2] 5. I quite agree with you about the Abyssinian business that it would be difficult for us to adopt a peremptory tone. But the Telegram which I saw said the Viceroy had put 4000 men on the frontier. Perhaps the number may have been exaggerated but if it were not so it certainly bore an unfavourable aspect, and your friendly warning might be, I hope will be, of real use. 6. I trust your weather at beautiful Balmoral will be good: from Fasque on the other side of the mountains, not I think a more rainy district, my brother sends me a sad account. Here the harvest has been hit, the potatoes heavily hit. From Liverpool, I learn, on the best available authority, that the wheat harvest generally is calculated at 20 p.c., or thereabouts below an average. This must qualify the prosperity of trade and revenue, but perhaps not yet. 7. You see the Geneva payment is 3¼ millions. We need not pay until Sept. 73. But I should think Lowe would probably do well to take it out of his balances when they become strong in February next and get a fair discount from the Americans. 8. It seems hard to make out how they can be entitled to interest unless for the period before 67 when we were refusing arbitration; but we must not grumble, even if we may grin. 9. But I have administered a large dose and will close public matters with the French Treaty. I telegraphed this morning to you & Hammond my concurrence in your draft to d'Harcourt.[3] On Wednesday we start for an absence of about three weeks among the hills in Invernessshire, where I shall be ill to get at: and I should in no case desire or be well able to interfere about the French duties in detail as I have not the necessary knowledge at command. But I will endeavour to leave behind me clear expressions of my opinion on all the broader points.

757. Mr. Gladstone to Lord Granville. [G.D. 29/61]

Hawarden. Sept 16. 72.

I have put down in letters to Mr Hammond [4] nearly all that I can contribute to the consideration of the French Treaty, and have told him I was quite ready to come up for any consultation for which circumstances might be ripe, but no case

not printed. Cf. Rawlinson to Granville, 21 Aug., G.D. 29/75, and reply, 22 Aug., G.D. 29/77, on Stanley's presence at Dunrobin Castle during the Queen's visit.

[1] Missing from Gladstone's correspondence with Hartington, Add. MS. 44143.

[2] Missing from Gladstone's correspondence with Halifax, Add. MS. 44185.

[3] Read 'Gavard', who was in charge of the commercial negotiations in place of the ambassador. See Gladstone to Hammond, tel. 15 Sept., Add. MS. 44183, fo. 480.

[4] Not traced; but cf. Hammond to Gladstone, 13, 14, 16 Sept., Add. MS. 44183, fos. 478–83.

of this kind arising, I go off to Scotland on Wednesday: and as I shall be a long way probably even from the Telegraph I will sum up the little I have to say on the matter as it now stands.

I entirely concur in your disposing of the important points raised in your letter to d'Harcourt as preliminaries to negotiating, and not as parts of the negotiation.

2. It seems to me that of all things we should avoid complicating the process by any thing like, or capable of being represented as like, the gratuitous introduction of new points. The whole thing is a choice between the greater evil of offending & seemingly making light of France in the midst of her difficulties, and the lesser evil of agreeing to a Treaty which as far as it alters the preexisting state of things is retrogressive in its character: and it would be a practical solecism were we to attempt to give to this slippery arrangement the soundness of a perfect or normal work.

3. I am the more conscious that we should do nothing to add weight to the cargo, because I think France should clearly understand that to meet her views is our real and only motive for undertaking the voyage at all.

4. With Mr Hammond, I like less & less the form of separate denunciation.[1] I will accept your judgment upon it but I think that if we keep it in any form we must warn the French that, should policy lead them to diminish still further by using this provision the already diminished benefits of the Treaty, it will not be possible, so far as we can see, to refrain from setting ourselves free as to Wine, Spirits, and Coal.

5. As regards the particular rates of duty we are to agree to, we have now in a great degree I hope minimised the protective efficacy of the plan: and if upon a careful examination by competent persons this shall definitively [be] found to be the case, then I think it is better to stand for most favoured-nation treatment in a full and wide sense rather than to haggle upon details of duty.

6. It will indeed be formidable or at least awkward if the Law Officers shall in any degree sustain the doctrine of compensation for existing contracts.[2] If parties have even the least colour of warrant for such a claim the subject will be a very awkward one to deal with in Parliament. Have we not all along made it known, at and before the time of the denunciation, that the French Government contemplated, & that we had not excluded, further negotiation? Will it not however be necessary, if the case of current contracts is found in any way formidable, to except them from the augmentations of duty?

In writing to Mr Hammond the other day I forgot that the Board of Trade was now divested of all function as to Treaties.[3]

I shall be here on Wedy *till 3 Pm.* in any case.

[1] France proposed keeping the Cobden Treaty with the faculty granted to each signatory to alter his tariff in certain circumstances by denouncing separate parts of it, Gavard to Granville, 12 Sept., F.O. 27/1947.

[2] After the imposition of the duties on mineral oils in July 1871 the law officers had pronounced British importers, who lost money through being bound by contracts to a price fixed before the duties were enacted, entitled to compensation. Cf. above, no. 551.

[3] On Mallet's appointment to the India Council the treaty department of the Board of Trade was abolished and its functions transferred to a re-organized commercial department at the

758. Lord Granville to Mr. Gladstone. [Add. MS. 44169, fo. 80]

Balmoral Castle. Sep 16/72.

After the announcement in the Queen's Speech, we must not let the question of the East Coast of Africa Slave Trade sleep.

The Treasury having given way about the payment of a Resident,[1] although clogged with a proposal that would not act well, I should probably in the ordinary course have appointed Dr Kirk, of whom the F.O. has a high opinion. His reputation in the Indian Office does not stand so high, and the question has become more complicated by the Livingstone affair—the Dr has written strongly to complain of Dr Kirk, & Stanley's abuse of him has been violent. Argyll & Rawlinson are much inclined to believe Stanley in this matter. But a violent prejudice exists in Stanley's mind, probably never at any time a judicial one—even if his character for veracity is reestablished—and I should dislike giving any reason to Kirk's enemies to be triumphant before we know more of the matter.

In this dilemma what do you think of my sounding Sir Bartle Frere whether he would undertake the *job* of going to Zanzibar, to negotiate with the Sultan for a new Treaty, and to report as to the future arrangements to be made for the efficient suppression of the Trade.[2] He may object on the point of dignity, but having proclaimed the suppression of the Slave Trade as the great object of his life, he could only refuse with a bad grace.

His position as a former Indian Govr would give him weight with the Natives, and influence with the Indian Gov. His appointment would inspire confidence among the Anti Slave Trade people.

759. Mr. Gladstone to Lord Granville. [G.D. 29/61]

Invergarry. Sept 22. 72.

I received today your letter about Sir Bartle Frere and consulted Halifax upon it. He approved very much of the selection, subject to the supposition however that his acceptance is not to involve a long absence from his duties on the Indian Council—as this might give rise to objection from the D. of Argyll or in Parliament.

2. Your box came this afternoon and I found the papers rather a wilderness, not being sure as to some of them whether an opinion was sought from me—and on others what the real point at issue was. I have however written as well as I could on the question in the French Treaty business.[3]

3. With regard to Spanish wine I do not know what the real merits of the late change in the Spanish Tariff may be. For one [thing] I think the universal 1% duty

Foreign Office under Kennedy; see Enfield to Granville, 20 Dec. 1871, G.D. 29/107; memoranda by T. T. Farrer of the Board of Trade, 4 Jan., and Hammond, 9 Jan., G.D. 29/105.

[1] Treasury to the Foreign Office, 12 Aug., sanctioning the appointment of a Resident in Zanzibar but proposing separate representation of the Indian government, and minutes, F.O. 84/1386.

[2] Granville to Sir Bartle Frere, 24 Sept., sounding him in these terms. Cf. Argyll to Granville, 13 Aug., replying to Granville's question about Frere's fitness for the appointment, G.D. 29/51.

[3] See Gladstone to Hammond, 17 Sept., Add. MS. 44542, fos. 9–10.

would be a hazardous experiment, and any step in the further alteration of the Wine Duties requires much consideration.

4. I have written to *Palmer*, and have informed the Queen. I have not got his answer yet.[1] The arbitration being over, the time seemed to have arrived, the matter ought to be carried through at Balmoral on the occasion of the October Council.

5. About Cabinets I incline to think it would be well to have one somewhere about Oct 20 or 25. The questions of Irish Univ. Education, and of Local Taxation, are very difficult & grave, & it *might* be well for us all to look at them soon. Moreover I suppose you will want one for the French Treaty before concluding ? [2] Thanks for your account of H.M.

760. Mr. Gladstone to Lord Granville. [G.D. 29/31]

Guisachan. Sept 28. 72.

1. I am very sorry that Ponsonby has refused the C.B. If he objects to be *Sir* Ponsonby, he might *now* have waived off the K.C.B. But the matter is at an end. I return the Queen's letter.[3]

2. The recollection of my buried letter to General Schenck [4] on my unenviable position in the American Case has now revived and I am inclined to think that I should do well to publish it. Not only because I wish to get quit of what is really a misrepresentation ; but because I think it will tend rather to improve the position with reference to any discussion which the payment of $3\frac{1}{4}$ millions may suggest.

3. I have written to Hammond & asked him to send on what occurred to me on reading the answer of the Law Officers resp. Contracts under the French Treaty.[5]

P.S. I have written to the Queen to recommend Macdonald for the P.C.

761. Mr. Gladstone to Lord Granville. [G.D. 29/61]

Guisachan. Oct 2. 72.

You have not made any comment on what I stated about Cabinets, and accordingly I shall summon one for Tuesday the 22d at 3 P.m. unless my Priv. Sec. hears from you by Telegraph that this is inconvenient.

I had heard much of the beauty of this district but it even surpasses my expectations.

Private. I have recommended Mr Cowie for the Deanery of Manchester.

P.S. 11 Pm. Since writing have your Telegram [6] & reply through Foreign Office.

[1] Relates to his appointment as lord chancellor *vice* Hatherley. He accepted office and was raised to the peerage as Lord Selborne.

[2] See below, no. 761 note.

[3] The Queen to Granville, 19 Sept., G.D. 29/31. Ponsonby was made K.C.B., 12 March 1879.

[4] See above, no. 670.

[5] See Gladstone to Hammond, 28 Sept., Add. MS. 44542, fo. 15.

[6] 12.30. 2 Oct., asking with Lowe and Forster for an immediate cabinet. Gladstone asked for what purpose, 10 a.m. 3 Oct., and was told : 'It is about the treaty,' 1.50 p.m. 3 Oct., G.D. 29/61. The cabinet met on the French treaty on 10, 11, 12, 14 Oct., Add. MS. 44640, fos. 179–90.

762. Lord Granville to Mr. Gladstone. [Add. MS. 44169, fo. 91]

Br[uton] St[reet]. Oct 2/72.

In your place I should not publish your explanation of the expressions you used respecting the Civil War. But I admit that some of the grounds of my former objections no longer hold good.

763. Lord Granville to Mr. Gladstone. [Add. MS. 44169, fo. 88]

Br[uton] St[reet]. Oct 2/72.

I came to town on Monday. On Tuesday I had a long sitting with Hammond and Kennedy.

We settled a draft treaty to be submitted to you, and the rest of our colleagues.

I recd a note from Lyons [1] very unhappy about the delay and pressing us to lose no time.

I saw Forster who had had some discussion with Lowe about the Treaty, which ended in their both thinking from their different points of view that we ought to have a Cabinet as soon as it would be convenient.

Then came a Treasury letter [2] full of grave objections to the proposed Treaty. I saw Lowe in the evening, & said that I had come to the conclusion we must have a Cabinet. Lowe said that he thought the necessity of having one so great, that he had written you a letter demanding it, but which he had thrown in the fire owing to the strength of his expressions.

Forster says that whether we stop or go on the Cabinet ought to be held soon. He says the Cabinet will be useful to settle some points, but he believes no one but Lowe is adverse to a renewal of the Treaty, if the provisions can be properly adjusted.

I have this morning altered these so as to meet some of Lowe's strong objections and some further suggestions of Fortescue.

The draft Treaty will be sent to you tomorrow, together with the Treasury letter.

764. Lord Granville to Mr. Gladstone. [Add. MS. 44169, fo. 92]

16, Bruton Street. Oct 4/72.

Lyons is with me and has made a suggestion on the draft treaty which I think good. He wishes the treaty to be perpetual as to the most favored nation clause—and that the clause containing the most favored nation condition should stand by itself without exceptions—the exception being left in another clause.

I have asked him to send Kennedy the wording which would do this.

He is of opinion that the French will not accept the clause about Consuls—and

[1] 1 Oct., G.D. 29/87; cf. reply, 2 Oct., G.D. 29/109.

[2] 1 Oct., F.O. 27/1951; see above, p. 344, note 3; cf. correspondence between Wilson of the Treasury and Kennedy of the Foreign Office on Lowe's obstruction and neglect over the French treaty enclosed in Lowe to Granville, 19 Nov., G.D. 29/66. Granville, Lowe, Forster and Fortescue composed a cabinet committee for these negotiations. For text of the treaty signed, 5 Nov., see F.O. 93/80/97; Parl. papers. [C. 700] (1873). lxxv, 261. For the failure of the treaty see below, no. 817 note.

that they may object to some other extraneous matter, but he agrees with me that it may be as well to submit to them these clauses, which settle questions which have been long in dispute, although we need not insist on any.

Please telegraph, if you have previously sent away the draft treaty, whether you approve Lyons' suggestion.[1]

765. Mr. Gladstone to Lord Granville. [G.D. 29/61]

Strathconan. Oct 4. 72.

You will understand my having been puzzled a little about the Telegram I received on Wednesday[2]: for I own I think the time when a Cabinet was most called for was before the determination to negotiate with France was taken: but it did not appear to occur to Lowe while he was in Scotland. My perceptions probably became blunt as I got farther off.

But a question of that kind when it has arisen should always be decided in the affirmative sense.

I have taken for granted that Lowe knew we were proceeding.

I do not at all regret our having an opportunity of breaking ground on the question of Local Taxation: which at present seems to me to wear a very grave aspect.

If I hear from you tonight that you think next Thursday too late I will at once Telegraph to Gurdon to fix Tuesday.

Among other things I hope to talk over with you the question about my letter to Schenck. Certainly my feeling prompts me to send it: but my opinion on public grounds (as at present advised) is in the same sense.

As to Thiers and the Treaty my opinion is that his great objects are 1. to strengthen himself by a transaction with us 2. to improve his position for obtaining the consent of other Powers to changes in Treaties: and I do not believe time with reference to our Treaty only is much in his mind.

I have written to inquire about the 'letter from the Treasury' of which I know nothing.

766. Mr. Gladstone to Lord Granville. [G.D. 29/61]

Strathconan. Oct 8. 72.

A few hours after you receive this I hope to see you. Nevertheless I write to say with what dismay I find you were accurate in saying that your dispatch of Sept. 19[3] promised to annex a copy of the present British Tariff to the new Treaty.

[1] Gladstone wrote his draft reply on the back, 7 Oct: 'Am not sure I understand the suggestion of Ld. L. in all its bearings but it seems to me good. Also am averse to the introd[uctio]n of new points from this side unless for strong cause.'

[2] See above, no. 761 note.

[3] To Gavard, containing the British proposals for the new commercial treaty, F.O. 27/1947. It covered the main content of the Cobden Treaty, but departed from it in some particulars. A copy of the tariffs then in force was, for example, to be annexed and power reserved to both governments to make changes in their tariffs without thereby cancelling the treaty. Cf. no. 757, § 4.

I cannot say from memory whether I saw the draft of that letter before it went. If I did it was an unpardonable error on my part to pass over such a passage and I should be at a loss to understand my having done so: although I always consider that the review of the *form* of a Bill, or of a dispatch in which any thing is promised, is one of the most arduous labours, and hardly possible to be effected satisfactorily except in company.

Looking however to the exact words employed 'under the specific conditions', I suppose we may reserve a discretion over them. They are not stated in the dispatch. The words would perhaps equitably mean 'under such conditions as may be agreed on'—and if so, the difficulty can be surmounted without recourse to the extreme step of saying we have written in inadvertance and must ask leave to retract it.

The Customs Report [1] was I thought in the main unanswerable.

I start early tomorrow to travel all night & arrive 9.40 Am. of Thursday.

767. Lord Granville to Mr. Gladstone. [Add. MS. 44169, fo. 97]

F.O. Oct 17/72.

I told the Chancellor of my doubts as to the expediency of putting Cockburn (if he wishes it) into the Lords. The Chancellor takes your view. He agrees with me that on some questions Cockburn may take an adverse and disagreeable line. But he believes this objection may be mitigated by the offer itself, and by subsequent judicious communication. He thinks Cockburn's services justify a Peerage, that the Public expect him to get it, and that your's will be the *high* line in offering it.

I have therefore written a note, of which the enclosed is a copy.[2]

768. Lord Granville to Mr. Gladstone. [Add. MS. 44169, fo. 94]

Private. F.O. Oct 17/72.

Bergne made strong technical objections to our signing the treaty, and making the exchange of ratifications dependent upon the two Govts coming to an agreement.

The Law officers are scattered to the four quarters of the globe, & I was herefore glad to get the new Chancellor on his passage through London—he recommended that we should in the Treaty agree to ratify after the President had obtained the sanction of the Assembly (a provision already inserted) *and after the agreement of the Govts on the compensatory duties* [3]—I reckon on your approval.

[1] Of 27 Aug., enclosed in the Treasury letter, Oct. 1; see above, no. 763.

[2] Confidential, 7 Oct.: Gladstone 'would at once propose a Peerage to you, but he feels a difficulty in doing so owing to [your] refusal . . . on the formation of the present Cabinet', G.D. 29/77, Add. MS. 44169, fo. 99; see above, no. 2, p. 342, note 4.

[3] Under article xxi of the commercial treaty, 5 Nov., this agreement was to be negotiated by a mixed commission in Paris. For minutes of its proceedings and declaration and tariff, see F.O. 27/2011 and Parl. papers. [C. 821] (1873). lxxv, 341 ff.

769. Mr. Gladstone to Lord Granville. [G.D. 29/61]

Cloverley, Whitchurch. Oct 18. 72.[1]

I think, without prejudice, there is certainly great force in what you say of Sir K. Mackenzie. I will consult Glyn as to what *may* be in the other scale. The Gairloch family was a well known name to me in boyhood and youth.

I inclose for your perusal one of the most singular proposals that ever sprang from the mind of man, not to add of a man of splendid gifts.[2]

There *are* some things new under the sun.

Fancy making this suggestion to the Queen.

770. Mr. Gladstone to Lord Granville. [G.D. 29/61]

No 2. Hawarden Castle. Oct 18. 72.

1. I think your letter to Cockburn is the best possible.

2. I think Bergne quite right on the Treaty but see no objection to our new Chancellor's suggestion.

3. I forgot in London to tell you that at Guisachan I fell in with Hughes of Kirkonnell,[3] who strongly repeated to me, as within his certain knowledge, that Stanley was a bastard child born in a Welsh Workhouse. He said no evil of the man: who I hope has not denied the statement, presuming it to be a true one.

771. Lord Granville to Mr. Gladstone. [Add. MS. 44169, fo. 96]

Private. Walmer Castle. [19? October 1872].

I do not wonder at your surprise[4]—the objections which he mentions are strong, but what is the answer to those which he omits. The power of putting things in an epigrammatic way is certainly in many cases misleading.

772. Lord Granville to Mr. Gladstone. [Add. MS. 44169, fo. 101]

Private. Walmer Castle. Oct 20/72.

Brunnow gave me the enclosed[5] most confidentially. He said he could speak with no authority, as the Emperor was in the Crimea, and the Foreign Minister in Switzerland, that he was a bad Ambassador in the matter, as he thought his Gov attached too much importance in protecting their commerce which only amounted

[1] Gladstone's date has been read as Oct. 12 and the letter bound under that date in G.D. 29/61. The correct date is supplied by Gladstone's copy, Add. MS. 44542, fo. 24.

[2] The enclosure has not been traced.

[3] He had been the first to cast doubts on Stanley's finding of Livingstone and drawn attention to his birth; see Granville to Rawlinson, 22 Aug., G.D. 29/77, and no. 756 above.

[4] Possibly refers to the enclosure in no. 769.

[5] Westmann to Brunnow, dated St. Petersburg, 14 Sept., reporting his answer to Loftus's question about the Russian military expedition to Khiva then being organized, F.O. 65/874. Loftus reported the same conversation in No. 270, 1 Oct., *ibid.* Granville to Loftus, No. 205 confidential, 31 Oct., follows textually no. 772 but omits the allusion to Shouvalov.

to 4 millions of roubles in these countries, but at the same time it was impossible for the Russian Gov to allow Russians to be kept Prisoners without asserting their rights to recover them.

I said that I was struck by a passage in M de Westmann's letter, in which he quoted the example of England as to the difficulty of limiting the progress of a nation among barbarians.

I admitted the truth of this observation, but said that the drifting into such extensions of territory was a policy which I deplored.

That it could not be an important object to Russia to extend territory which was already so great, & that [there] were other considerations which merited attention. Both he and Prince Gortchakoff had constantly referred to a conversation on the continent between Lord Clarendon and Prince Gortchakoff as to the policy of both countries in Central Asia—that nothing was more satisfactory than the conclusions at which they had arrived. Any departure from that policy alarmed me for the future relations of the two countries. The British people were much alive to anything which could possibly excite alarm as to the Indian Empire—that nothing could be more moderate than the Duke of Argyll & Lord Northbrook on these questions—but that he (Count Brunnow) must have observed that peace at all price was not the special tradition of the Indian Govt.

I therefore hoped that while Lord Northbrook was giving judicious advice to the Asiatic Princes, Russia would not be led to take advantage of these causes of quarrel which always are so easy to be found with Barbarian Powers.

Count Brunnow spoke of the prudent personal policy of the present Emperor. He told me that Count Schuvaloff, the Emperor's confidant was coming to England. He hoped I should see him. He (Count Brunnow) did not know whether it was intended that Count Schouvaloff should succeed him or Prince Gortchakoff (the first supposition affected him to tears), but that he was bound to admit that I could have no more satisfactory person to deal with in either capacity.

773. Mr. Gladstone to Lord Granville. [G.D. 29/61]

Hawarden Castle. Oct 22. 72.

1. I do not see what more you could say to Brunnow: but it would be a good stroke if Northbrook could set himself to work energetically with the Khiva people and get the prisoners released. Till this is done our mouths are virtually closed: & I do not suppose that even a reference to our self-denial in Abyssinia would much touch these flint-hearted people. I am glad Westmann did not hear some part of the conversation in the Cabinet [1] about the annexation of Zanzibar: & I hope he did not hear, either, with what extreme difficulty we escaped through the blundering of the promoters a vote of the H. of C. last session, which was intended to force the annexation of the Fiji Islands.[2]

[1] See Gladstone's note on the cabinet, 12 Oct., where the instructions for Frere's mission to Zanzibar were agreed on, Add. MS. 44640, fo. 187; on the Zanzibar mission see below, nos. 781, 785, 836, 837 note.

[2] On 25 June a motion for an address to the crown favouring a protectorate over, or the annexation of, the Fiji Islands was defeated by 51 votes, *Hans. Parl. Deb.*, 3rd ser., ccxii. 192–219. See below, no. 842.

2. If as the Telegram says the 3 Emperors advise the Italian Government to give the Ex-King Francis his property, I hope they will guarantee that he shall not use it to create civil war or brigandage in the country.

3. I send you a copy of a letter from Sir Bartle Frere [1] about Livingstone's Vice Consulship which I have told him it is your affair to deal with in the first instance.

I have been laid up for 2 or 3 days but am about again.

How well the Times is writing about Irish Education.

774. Lord Granville to Mr. Gladstone. [G.D. 29/61]

Copy. Walmer. Oct. 23/72.

Although I hope the Duty on French Wines will not be raised, I presume that you are of opinion that the alterations suggested by Kennedy are out of the question. If you are of a different opinion please telegraph to me at the F.O.[2]

775. Mr. Gladstone to Lord Granville. [G.D. 29/61]

Hawarden Castle. Oct 24. 72.

I telegraphed to you today upon the Treaty with France. My impression is that the Cabinet if asked will not consent to convert the instrument into a Treaty of Tariffs. The French are not behaving in a straight forward manner.

I have received today a Protocol about the Commission [3] in which I see it is still proposed that *lot* shall decide which umpire is to act if two are chosen—or rather nominated. I thought we were to have our umpire nominated by the Governments before concluding.

776. Lord Granville to Mr. Gladstone. [Add. MS. 44169, fo. 107]

Private. Walmer Castle. Oct 25/72.

I send you a box with disagreeable matter,[4] which ought however to be settled by you the Duke & me.

It appears to me clear that the Imperial faith is pledged, and the hitch has been occasioned by the India Office sanctioning the draft Treaty, without communication with India. I only got the box this morning, and I have telegraphed to Enfield to get the Law officers opinion immediately, but if the India office agree with the opinion of the F.O. they should telegraph that the Imperial Gov has

[1] 19 Oct., G.D. 29/61.

[2] Gladstone's tel., received 5.35, 23 Oct., agreed in rejecting Kennedy's alterations, G.D. 29/61.

[3] See above, no. 768 note, and Granville to Gavard, 31 Oct., on the British view of the commission's function, F.O. 27/1947.

[4] On the Indian government's objections to the Anglo-Dutch convention on coolie emigration to Surinam, 8 Sept. 1870; see above, no. 726. Cf. Granville to Argyll, 22 Oct., and reply, 28 Oct., G.D. 29/51; Gladstone to Granville, tel. 26 Oct., on closer examination of the regulations before sending the proposed telegram to Northbrook, G.D. 29/61.

pledged it's faith, and the Governor General must be satisfied with the regulations which were provided for in the Treaty.

But Northbrook may answer " I was not committed about the Treaty. I am called upon to notify that the Regulations are sufficient, and I do not think they are so ".

In that case the mess would be complete.

I told Kennedy that I was at his orders either alone or with you, but he says there is no necessity at present for either of us to come.

I found the Delegates of the Manchester Chamber of Commerce, civil and amenable to reason.

You were more right than Odo about the San Juan award.[1]

777. Lord Granville to Mr. Gladstone. [Add. MS. 44169, fo. 112, and G.D. 29/61]

Secret. Walmer Castle. Oct 26/72.

I am rather annoyed at the report of the interference with the Emperor of Germany published in the American papers.[2]

It is impossible that Odo should have committed himself in the matter, but it is possible that he is cognizant of the C[rown] P[rince]ss having done so. At which I should not be the least surprised or at Bismarck having shown her up if she did so.

I do not know whether it would be wise to ask Odo privately or publicly for a denial.

Is it clear that the Americans would have accepted the award as to San Juan, if it had been given against them in the terms used.

I think they were justified at the time of the negotiation in insisting upon an arbitration & not a mediation,[3] but how far is it an award in an Arbitration to say " most " as the Emperor has done ? If so inclined, might we not ask the question " but is it or not in accordance with the Treaty ".

778. Mr. Gladstone to Lord Granville. [G.D. 29/61]

Hawarden Castle. Oct 30. 72.

I telegraphed to London yesterday for the exact terms of the reference to the German Emperor. There is no doubt that if his ' deliverance ' as the Scotch call it is not in conformity with these terms, it is no award. His recital appears to imply that he has proceeded according to the reference, but it is not perfectly clear. Unfortunately I have not as yet had an answer from the F.O. to my Telegram which may have arrived too late for last nights post but the question seems likely

[1] Cf. Russell to Granville, private, 24 Oct., on the German Emperor's award on the San Juan boundary which Russell had mistakenly expected to be favourable to Britain, G.D. 29/92, Knaplund, *Letters from Berlin*, p. 71. For the award, 21 Oct., see Russell to Granville, No. 272, most confidential, 23 Oct., F.O. 5/1473.

[2] See *New York Herald*, 23 Oct., alleging Russell's interference, enclosed in Thornton to Granville, No. 547, 28 Oct., F.O. 5/1473. The New York article was repeated in *The Times*. For Russell's denial see No. 300, 9 Nov., *ibid.*

[3] From here to the end the text is taken from the copy in G.D. 29/61.

to be a simple one. As however it is one of construction I suppose you will take legal advice.

With respect to the report of our having endeavoured to effect an irregular interference, I suppose your question if any would refer strictly and exclusively to the action of this Government or any one authorised by it and if so they could hardly with any decency drag in the Crown Princess. Again is it credible she should have committed such an act of folly as to meddle in the matter? I should think your safest course would be to inquire from Lord O. R[ussell] in the first place how the land lies.

If the answer of the Emperor does not correspond with the reference I think the Cabinet should meet to consider it without a moment's delay.

There is nothing in the popular objection taken to our having agreed to an arbitration only on the strict meaning of the Treaty. Taking that as the proposal of the Americans, how could we refuse it?

It seems to me that Odo Russell is needlessly disturbed [1] about the gold & that the Germans are making a gratuitous fuss and parade in that matter.

The Bank of England know perfectly well what they are about and will soon begin to give signs if they perceive any difficulty coming on.

779. Lord Granville to Mr. Gladstone. [Add. MS. 44169, fo. 114]

Private. Walmer Castle. Oct 30/72.

I have to make my excuses to you for having even raised a doubt as to the award.[2] I had not the Treaty, & had forgotten the terms of reference.

I asked Admiral Prévost to come here, & he appeared this afternoon. He wishes for two things—that we should ask for the reports on which the award was based, and that we should propose to the American Govt to agree upon an official map defining the Haro Channel.

The latter proposal appears to me quite right.

Of the first I have some doubt.

In the first place if we ask alone for it, it may appear like a cavil at the judgment, and may subject us to a refusal.

The same objection applies to joining with the Americans in the application. The Admiral thinks the public will desire it—but there does not seem to be much practical use in it.

If the Germans make out a strong case, it is somewhat of a slur on our previous conduct. If a weak one, it will encrease people's indignation. I guess from the Times that they think people are angry with us. I believe the decision to be of singularly little importance.

[1] See to Granville, private, 27 Oct., on the rumour that the Bank was buying gold in France and Germany's offer to withhold claims on it and buy gold elsewhere, G.D. 29/92, Knaplund, *Letters from Berlin*, p. 72.

[2] See above, no. 777. Cf. Gladstone to Granville, tel. 5.25 p.m., 30 Oct., on the German Emperor's award being within his terms of reference; Granville to Gladstone, tel. 30 Oct., that he had already written to apologize for his mistake, G.D. 29/61.

780. Lord Granville to Mr. Gladstone. [G.D. 29/61]

Copy. Walmer. Novr 1./72.

I have asked Kennedy to send you my correspondence with Gavard.[1]

You will see in a minute which I have written that I am inclined to insist not only on preservance of [the] most favoured nation clause but also on national treatment. The last point is one on which it is possible for us to yield, as the Cabinet only directed that we should try and get it, but as the French have once consented to it, it would be a pity to give it up.

Please telegraph your decision to Kennedy.

781. Mr. Gladstone to Lord Granville. [G.D. 29/61]

Hawarden Castle. Nov 1. 72.

I have read the Zanzibar papers [2] received this morning but am in some difficulty to know what is proposed.

I thought the Cabinet decided to expunge or limit by explanation the vague power to settle 'all questions pecuniary & political' & so forth. It is now struck out of the Foreign Office letter but it remains *in* the draft paper of instructions.[3]

In p. 6 of the Draft dispatch, the question [4] we discussed in the Cabinet reappears. You have put a note stating that all shipments from the coast to the Island should be stopped or our efforts will be useless. At the same time you have proposed to use the words adopted by the Cabinet; but they adopted no words which declared that these shipments were to be stopped. The words however in the text of the dispatch are "effectually put a stop to the exportation of slaves from his dominions".

If it is found that there is no way of permitting the passage of slaves from the coast to the Island of Zanzibar without affording a cover for the export then I presume every thing must bend to the main design. But it would be a very strong measure with reference to a country where slavery exists to say that under no circs shall slaves pass from one part of that country to another by the only means by which they can possibly pass, if the place to which they are going has a *bonâ fide*

[1] Gavard to Granville, private, 30 Oct., and reply, private, 31 Oct., on omission from the draft Anglo-French commercial treaty of the clause of article xxiii, which prescribed most-favoured-nation treatment between the two countries after the treaty had expired or been denounced according to the dates laid down in its first clause, G.D. 29/89; Granville's min., G.D. 29/61; Gladstone to Kennedy, tel. 2 Nov., indicating the relevant alteration, Add. MS. 44436, fo. 3.

[2] To Frere, Nos. 1 and 2, 9 Nov., instructions for his mission to the Sultan of Zanzibar for the negotiation of arrangements to suppress the slave trade on the East Coast of Africa; Foreign Office to India Office, 9 Nov., on the scope and purpose of the mission, F.O. 84/1385.

[3] The original draft gave Frere full power 'to adjust with the Rulers of Muscat and Zanzibar all pending questions pecuniary and political bearing on the Slave Trade on the coasts of Oman and East Africa', but this was omitted after minutes by Argyll and Granville.

[4] Whether the words calling upon the Sultan to co-operate to stop the export of slaves from 'his Dominions on the East Coast of Africa' covered shipments from the mainland to the island of Zanzibar; see mins. by Argyll and Granville on the draft; min. by Granville, 3 Nov., reserving the matter for supplementary instructions; Frere to Granville, 9 Nov., F.O. 84/1385; Admiralty to Granville, 13 Nov., F.O. 84/1387.

need & use for them. And only a clear & proved necessity will justify such a measure —(Do we prohibit the carrying of slaves from Cuba to Porto Rico & the reverse ?)

I cannot make out from the map the shortest distance of Zanzibar Island from the mainland. If it is a very short distance, probably a solution of the difficulty before us might be found in a distinction founded on the character of the vessel. The ferrying over might be permitted in open boats, or vessels not sea-going, and then the rule as to export might be made to cover all shipments in sea-going ships.

Perhaps some better suggestion may be made by those who know more but I offer what occurs to me.

P.S. I agree with you about the proposed application for the reports: and I do not feel sure as to our title to ask the Emperor for them. The Map is all very well, I dare say: but we had better be sure first that we are now entirely agreed with the U.S. on the whole question as to the Channel.

782. Mr. Gladstone to Lord Granville. [G.D. 29/61]

Private. Hawarden Castle. Nov 1. 72.

The Lord Mayor fired into me anew about his dinner and I replied in a letter [1] of which copy is sent to you herewith.

I hope the hint conveyed in the first words of it is not too strong. The only compunction that I feel is about your having to speak for the Government before an audience which, if it is as inattentive and even rude as it was last year, really does not give fair play. I know of *no* description of speech that more requires the speaker to be undisturbed by any discordant associations than a statement of that kind which ought to be thoroughly well balanced, & where the lines are not so to speak self-marked. But I think they are more apt to attend to Foreign Affairs, which have more dignity & mystery about them.

As to home matters I think there is nothing requiring to be said & very little which can be said with advantage. We have worked diligently in our youth as a Government, & shall do so in our old age.

Lowe's speech at Glasgow begins with a most graceful & pleasing Preface. The body of it might well have been dispensed with, and he is especially unfortunate about the Geneva business. Surely as we are to pay & pay cheerfully, it is not for us to set about narrowing the effect moral or legal of the judgment, in language which will very likely be quoted against us when we come hereafter to claim the benefit of it on our own behalf.

783. Lord Granville to Mr. Gladstone. [Add. MS. 44169, fo. 118]

Walmer Castle. Nov 3/72.

It was in a memo as to draft Instructions in which the objectionable matter as to "other pecuniary & political matters" was left. The draft letter is the official

[1] 29 Oct., copy, G.D. 29/61. In the opening sentence Gladstone hinted at the indifference of the Guildhall audience to the prime minister's speech.

document. I have asked Sir B. Frere to give me his opinion about the transit of slaves between the Mainland & Zanzibar. You will see that it is very decided against permitting it [1]—so much so that I assume it meets the case in which you allow me to instruct him to obtain the prohibition of it. If I am wrong, please telegraph to Enfield.

784. Lord Granville to Mr. Gladstone. [G.D. 29/61]

Copy. Walmer. Nov. 6. /72.

I have settled with Sir Bartle to leave the instructions in the vague way to which Argyll objected. He will do his best to obtain by permission the consent of the Sultan to the prohibition of the importation of Slaves by sea from the mainland, but fall back if necessary upon regulations.

In the meanwhile I am consulting the Admiralty and we can send definite instructions which can overtake Sir Bartle before his arrival.

785. Mr. Gladstone to Lord Granville. [G.D. 29/61]

Hawarden Castle. Nov. 7. 72.

1. I am quite satisfied with the footing on which you place the Zanzibar question, & I think we shall be agreed upon it. I do not want to forswear, but on the contrary to leave open, the question of the use of force, in any manner or degree which may be necessary for the suppression of the sea-going slave trade. Only I do not wish, except under an absolute & clear necessity for the main purpose, to take measures with respect to domestic slavery which in the case of a stronger power or one owned in the family of civilised nations we should not be prepared to take. Plainly if it can be done the test of sea-going & non-sea-going vessels is a far simpler and better one than a system of internal registration in Zanzibar the proposal of which I confess that I read with some misgiving. The Admiralty are pretty sure to have surveys sufficiently good to see whether a Ferry so to call it can be allowed: so that the slaves may be let pass if they can go as they would have gone with Charon over Styx or something so far like it as to be a method of transit broadly distinguished from that of sea-voyaging. If it cannot, I have no doubt Sir B. Frere will see what can best be done. If he allows men to carry over slaves *bonâ fide* acquired for their own uses that surely should be enough. But very possibly he may induce the Sultan to take the fence at once, & I hope this will be so.

2. The last letter of Sir H. Elliot [2] on the curious question of the Bulgarian heresy throws a rather new light upon it, and explains something written to me by the Archbishop of Syra. It seems they do not ask an independent administration for Bulgaria, but for Bulgarians—wherever they may go, it seems to follow, and wherever they may abide. This demand pushed to extremities is a plain violation of the first principles of unity in any religious society. Their complaint was that Greek Bishops were thrust into Bulgaria and with the complete removal of this grievance they ought it would seem to have been satisfied.

[1] See Frere to Granville, 3 Nov., enclosed in no. 783, text in Add. MS. 44169, fos. 120–23.
[2] Elliot to Gladstone, 18 Oct., Add. MS. 44435, fo. 256; see above, no. 741, and below, no. 806.

3. I send for your perusal a very good note from the Duke of Cambridge.[1]

4. I hope you read your political Biography in the Daily News. It was I thought not only clear but generally good though the word subacidity, or any other acidity, was wholly out of place in it.

5. You will find much interesting matter in Stockmar's Memoirs. There is a short but terrible & rather one-sided description of Lord Derby—" a light-minded aristocrat for whom mischief-making finds occupation and sport ". A long article on Peel's death seems to me as if it had been written not from an inner inspiration but to please the Queen and Prince. He is not at all fair to Palmerston. Altogether, his heart was abroad, and I do not think much of his appreciation or knowledge of British institutions: but on foreign policy he is very instructive. I speak from an incomplete perusal, chiefly in the latter half of the book. He saw the false position of the Peelites, but does not seem to have seen that it was due to Peel himself and to the unwillingness of Lord Aberdeen & Graham to follow any other path than that in which he had walked with such a set purpose from 1846 to his death in 1850.

It is rather a strong measure to print bodily (except with certain liberties in the German rendering) William IV's memorandum on political affairs. A paper which I presume he did not *write*.

You remember Bismarck's blood and iron speech. What says Stockmar? Ch. 25. " Force will in the end cut the knot."

There is more to say on the book.

786. Lord Granville to Mr. Gladstone. [Add. MS. 44169, fo. 124]

Walmer Castle. Nov 7/72.

I had intended to send you a sketch of what I should say [2] on the Washington Treaty, and the Commercial Treaty with France.

But what with the difficulty I have in writing out an intended speech, & my unfortunate difficulty in getting the steam on, till the near approach of the fatal necessity, I have failed in sending you anything.

It must be very common place—the obvious arguments in favor of arbitration, without attributing to it the merits of a specific—& defence of the three rules, & a dignified tone about the two awards. Of the French Treaty, I think I shall say nothing of which you would not approve—& I suppose I may wind up by a balanced statement, that there is nothing incompatible between a determination not to meddle with that which does not concern, or to create unnecessary points of honor, with the firmest defence of our interests & honor.

If there is any point on which you wish a few words to be said, pray let me know by return of post.

Bernstorff is here, but utterly uninstructive.

[1] Confidential and private, 6 Nov., on the employment of the Prince of Wales, Add. MS. 44436, fo. 6.

[2] At the Guildhall dinner, 9 Nov., where he deputized for Gladstone; cf. above, no. 782.

787. Mr. Gladstone to Lord Granville. [G.D. 29/61]

Hawarden Castle. Nov. 8. 72.

I have just received your note on the speech of tomorrow—there could not I think be a better outline and I have nothing to add or criticise.

What is the last word about Bernstorff?

Cardinal Cullen & Lord Granard's application to interfere with the Italian Govt. about the Convents has come from you without any mem. or minute—and *zero* seems to be about the proper answer.

How the Cardinal romances in his letter.

I think it is quite right to hold our hand a little about Ripon.

788. Lord Granville to Mr. Gladstone. [Add. MS. 44169, fo. 128]

Private. Br[uton] St[reet]. Nov 10/72.

We were four. All well received—the Chancellor's short good speech listened to by all—Lowe's & mine by about ¾ths of the audience—Bovill by ¼th—Goschen the Lord Mayor & the rest by no part excepting the reformers. I thought some of the talk intentional but am not sure. I am ashamed of how much it prevented my expressing what I wished to say.

I read the Daily News Character—Lady G. & I thought the lard just of the sort, which provokes criticism—the reproof as to acidity, did not touch a very bad sore.

I return the Duke's letter a good and fair one.

I will read Stockmar. Clanwilliam is much interested in it. The Bernstorffs said that they heard that the Queen did not like it.

What is your programme. Cabinets in "close order" or at intervals.

789. Lord Granville to Mr. Gladstone. [Add. MS. 44169, fo. 130]

Walmer Castle. Nov 11/72.

Gavard asked me I presume officially for our good offices with other Powers with respect to their commercial Treaties.

I told him that I could give no answer at once, that he had always told me that our example would be sufficient to determine other countries, that those who thought we were right, would require no spurring from us, that those who thought we had made unwise or unnecessary concessions might think we were interested parties in the matter. He mentioned Belgium as a Country on whom our advice would have a great effect.

It is difficult to know what to do. On the one hand it is in our interest that other Powers should agree to make the same concessions as ourselves—on the other it is disagreeable to recommend others to make concessions in a retrograde sense which they are not like us obliged or quasi obliged to make, and it is clear that no advice will make Austria under Prussian influence yield—But again this adverse pressure ought perhaps to be met by us.

790. Mr. Gladstone to Lord Granville. [G.D. 29/61]

Hawarden Castle. Nov 12.72.

1. If there is a real ambiguity in the Treaty or the proceedings, which can give fair ground for misapprehension, I see no objection to a draft [1] such as that (returned herewith) which exhibits your course with regard to the proposal for altering Tariff upon notice. But if otherwise is it desirable to write such a Draft on account of an erroneous statement in the Times which rarely has an article reciting matters of fact without one? Some other newspaper will assuredly in discussing the Treaty fall into that or other errors—is there to be another explanatory dispatch?

NB. I observe in the prior draft that the penultimate Paragraph has not been cut out: but probably it was done in the dispatch itself of Nov. 4.[2]

2. Thanks for your account of the Guildhall Banquet. *You* are the person to whom I really owe an apology. I have felt it before, and especially last year when I had to speak of Dilke & other matters: it is impossible to make a ministerial statement (& such is the speech of the man who returns thanks for Ministers) properly under the double condition of 1. noise among the audience & 2. great physical effort, which that hall requires. Can we not do something to procure a reform? At *no* other dinner are such things tolerated as that half the company shall leave their seats & become a mob.

I inclose a statistical return [3] which I took for the *longer* Govts. It shows 3 absences in 20 years fewer than I had expected & two *of* them Peel's.

3. We go to Oxford tomorrow to visit Edw. Talbot and his wife—forward to London on Thursday when I dine with the Templars. My idea of the work is that the first solid & heavy bit should be Irish University—some of this may require to be done in Cabinet—when we have got that into shape I should be for taking to the yet stiffer work of Local Taxation—most of the Cabinet take a personal interest in this: I think it will require immeasurable talking over—which might be done chiefly in an open informal Cabinet—before binding Resolutions are taken.

But I propose to let Palmer have his say (general) on Friday about Law Reform.[4]

4. The more I read of Stockmar the more I am dissatisfied with the son. Instead of "O 'tis love etc. that makes the world go round", it really was old Stockmar that made the world go round for the first 20 years of the Queen's reign. I think the Queen has very good reason to be offended, whether she is so or not. Both the reviewers Ed[inburgh] & Quart[erly] give the young Baron a little rub: but it is plain to me that neither of them had read the book or they must have com-

[1] 11 Nov., submitted by Kennedy; denying an assertion in *The Times*, 11 Nov., that under the proposed new Anglo-French treaty, tariffs could only be altered on a year's notice. The draft was adopted and sent to Gavard who agreed, 19 Nov., F.O. 27/1947.

[2] See Granville to Gavard, 4 Nov., concluding the negotiation of the commercial treaty, signed next day, *ibid.*

[3] On attendances of prime ministers at the Guildhall dinners from 1835; follows no. 790 in G.D. 29/61.

[4] The series of cabinets on the French treaty ended, 14 Oct. Meetings were resumed, 15 Nov., when the judicature bill and Irish education were discussed, and continued 18, 20, 22, 26, 28, 30 Nov., 3, 5, 7, 10 Dec., Add. MS. 44640, fos. 194–227. Exchanges between Granville and Gladstone, *ibid.*, not printed.

mented more sharply on the total want of tact taste and insight which mark it. It glorifies Germany as against England, the Prince as against the Queen, Leopold as against both, Stockmar as against all. Except in one or two passages, the Queen appears rather like a dummy. I should rather like to write a review of it but that is quite out of the question.

The book will draw great notice.

791. Mr. Gladstone to Lord Granville. [G.D. 29/61]

Hawarden Castle. Nov. 13. 72.

I do not see what you can well do in the way of rendering good offices as requested by the French. For

1. It is a complete novelty, to me, for a Third Power to interpose in a commercial negotiation between two other Powers; and I think it tends to give such negotiations a distinct political character, which is not expedient as a rule.

2. We are interested parties—& on that account our intervention is objectionable. We are the fox without the tail.

3. Our taking such a course would give the Germans some colour of reason in their charging us with French proclivities.

4. If we ask Austria to ' scratch ' us in this matter & she agrees, we shall have to scratch her in some other.

3. Lastly I recollect most unwarrantable language, amounting to menace, used by the French Envoy at Brussels to the Belgian Govt. about these commercial negotiations [1]: and I should be very sorry to be associated in any way with such proceedings.

792. Mr. Gladstone to Lord Granville. [G.D. 29/83]

N. 14 [1872].

I do not see any harm in his arranging for a more direct superintendance over the doings of the Irish Priests [2]: but at a time like this they will hardly get fair play, strange as it may seem, from the Pope, whose whole proceedings are directed to the subject of the temporal Power. In this view he must show himself to be the grand supporter of law & order everywhere. I am not really afraid of their being ill treated but I think Mr J[ervoise] should be very cautious about getting any thing like a favour from the Pope for some payment might be expected for the position of affairs is much changed since an intimation of this kind was asked by Peel in (I think) 1844 against O'Connell's agitation.

[1] See above, no. 640.

[2] Relates to Jervoise to Granville, private, 6 Nov., asking for authorization to take private steps to ensure that the doings of the Irish Clergy ' be brought under the eye of the Pope himself and of the Propaganda ', G.D. 29/83.

793. Mr. Gladstone to Lord Granville. [G.D. 29/61]

11, Carlton House Terrace. Nov. 17. 72.

I agree.[1] I have suggested a slight addition on p. 2.

The conduct of the Portuguese Govt amply deserves the menace. But there is a weak point in the case (I think) which had not occurred to me when I previously saw the papers. It is this, that I suppose a doubt may be raised whether it is right to break off *official* relations on account of a subject matter which is confessed not to lie within their range ? Whether this be so or not the Queen's writing is an improved form of proceeding.

794. Mr. Gladstone to Lord Granville. [G.D. 29/61]

10, Downing Street. Nov. 19. 72.

1. Please to look at the inclosed letter from Lowe on my proposed communication to Schenck.[2] I abandon all idea of controversy. But it would be a satisfaction to me to tender my explanation, avowing at the same time that there the matter would end, It seems to me this might do good, and could not do harm. It would only be if it proved acceptable to the American Govt (of course as a matter wholly unofficial) that any one could come to know of it.

2. The letters [3] respecting the Zanzibar strait completely dispose of the idea of a negro-ferry.

795. Lord Granville to Mr. Gladstone. [Add. MS. 44169, fo. 134]

Foreign Office. Nov 19/72.

No 1. I agree with Lowe, as I believe I have already said, that the question of sending your letter is become a purely personal one, & I admit that people are generally extravagant of their advice to others not to defend themselves, when they have a good case. But I continue to think, that [if] I were in your position I should not send the letter.

No [2] In re Instructions to Sir Bartle Frere, as one point is settled, it might be better to leave the other to be discussed by Argyll & Lord Selbourne [*sic*].[4] I quite agree with you respecting A. Kinnaird's officious proposal to make Sir B.F a P.C before he begins his work—& besides the obvious objection, it would delay his departure.

[1] To Granville's letter to Ponsonby, 17 Nov., deferring to the Queen's views, G.D. 29/34. See also Granville to Saldanha, draft, 14 Nov., threatening to break off relations unless Portugal answered representations on the Lindsay case, F.O. 63/1073 ; Ponsonby to Granville, 15 Nov., on the Queen's objections and proposal of a private letter from herself to the King instead, G.D. 29/34.

[2] Gladstone to Lowe, 15 Oct., asking him to re-consider his opinion against the proposed letter to Schenck (above, no. 760). Lowe's reply, 16 Oct., stood by his view, but said that it was now a case for Gladstone's ' own feeling and discretion ', Add. MS. 44302, fos. 69, 70.

[3] Admiralty to Foreign Office, 13 Nov., and enclosure, F.O. 84/1387.

[4] Frere was to have supplementary instructions on (i) the method of preventing the traffic between the island and the mainland, settled by the Admiralty letters on the negro ferry, and (ii) proposed arrangements to prevent the slave trade among subjects of protected states ; see above, nos. 773, 781, 785, below, 836.

796. Lord Granville to Mr. Gladstone. [Add. MS. 44169, fo. 136]

Walmer Castle. Nov 25/72.

Although I retain my instinctive feeling that if I were you I should not send your letter, I have read it again with admiration.

I withdraw my objection to pages 12 & 13—as you are (not unnaturally) loth to part with them.

I do not quite like the phrase that as an individual it is open to you [to] adopt the tone of simple apology or explanation (see new page between old pages 6 & 7.)

As to the precise time of publication, you are aware that Fish has published a pamphlet or rather a collection of ' pièces justicatives ' against Northcote. I hear that Northcote is writing a reply.

797. Mr. Gladstone to Lord Granville. [G.D. 29/61]

11, Carlton House Terrace. Nov. 30. 72.

Here is a letter from Lord Russell [1] which it is really mournful to read.

Will you advise and inform me as to the first point (Fish) which I do not fully understand.

The others will be properly looked up. In no case will I give him other than a soft answer, but I am not sure it will ' turn away wrath '.

798. Lord Granville to Mr. Gladstone. [Add. MS. 44169, fo. 138]

Walmer Castle. Dec 1/72.

Mournful indeed! I understand point no 1 relates to the Counter case, & the chapter of motives. If so, it was decided by the Cabinet that it was more dignified not to take any notice. But it may mean Fish's general charge of a want of due negligence [*sic*, read diligence]. When the Tribunal was sitting, Lord Russell wrote to me to express a hope that his personal conduct should be defended. I forwarded his letter to Lord Selbourne [*sic*], who promised to do so if he had a further opportunity, which at the time Lord Russell wrote, he doubted having, but he said he had communicated with Cockburn, who had promised to do what was desired. I informed Lord Russell. But if you go into this point, it would be better to speak to Lord Selbourne [*sic*].

I lately strained a point with the Civil Service Commissioners to get an intelligent son [2] of Lord Russell's into the F.O. I am very sorry to say the poor boy is obliged to resign on account of his eyesight.

Ripon has the selection of the place which Villiers Lyster [*sic*] desires to have—& is not unlikely to give it to him, but properly does not commit himself.

[1] Russell to Gladstone, 29 Nov., blaming Gladstone, with Lords Ripon and Granville, for leaving him ' undefended against the calumnies of Mr. Fish ', and accusing him of persistently disregarding recommendations for patronage, Add. MS. 44294, fo. 234. For Gladstone's replies, 30 Nov., 4 Dec., *ibid.*, fos. 238, 240. See also below, nos. 798, 807.

[2] Lord Rollo Russell.

799. Mr. Gladstone to Lord Granville. [G.D. 29/61]

Secret. Sandringham. Dec. 1. 72.

I inclose for your private perusal a letter which I received today from Hartington and with it a copy of my reply.[1]

The party here breaks up tomorrow.

800. Lord Granville to Mr. Gladstone. [G.D. 29/61]

[4 December 1872].

The Japanese are very anxious that the Queen should say a few words in answer to their speech to H.M tomorrow morning. If the Queen does not object I see no objection. I've no objection to Her complimenting them on the progress which they have made during the last 20 years—& express her desire that there should be unrestricted intercourse between the two nations, and her wish that the progress in civilization which Japan has already made will be crowned by the establishment of religious liberty in that country.[2]

801. Mr. Gladstone to Lord Granville. [G.D. 29/61]

D. 4. 72.

I quite agree: but I do think that any thing she says to the Japanese on Religious liberty should be very mild; we may by pressure drive them upon changes which might bring about civil war & bloodshed. This religious freedom is a *late* triumph of Christian Civilisation, & if we recommend it as an initial proceeding to the Japanese it surely shd not be without acknowledgment that there may be difficulties in the way of wh we cannot presume to judge, but we wish to make known to them our own happy experience.

At the same time I admit that any qualification will not be popular.

802. Lord Granville to Mr. Gladstone. [Add. MS. 44169, fo. 142]

Private. Chatsworth. Dec 17/72.

In the conversation I had with Cockburn he said that several of his friends had expressed to him their regret that the Gov had done nothing to mark their sense of his services, & that he had of course made no allusion to the communication which I had had with him.

On mentioning this to the Chancellor who regrets that Cockburn has not

[1] See Hartington to Gladstone, 30 Nov., on difficulties about the resolutions of the cabinet on Irish university education, Add. MS. 44143, fo. 208; and reply, 1 Dec., that the resolutions were not final, Add. MS. 44542, fo. 50.

[2] Cf. Ponsonby to Granville on the Queen's desire to speak to the Japanese in favour of religious toleration. No. 800 was sent, with Gladstone's answer, no. 801, written on it and a draft of the reply which the Queen might make to the Japanese speech, to Ponsonby on 4 Dec., G.D. 29/34.

accepted, he thought it was desirable that I should ask Cockburn whether he had any objection to its being quietly let known that it was Cockburn's act & not your's which had prevented a public acknowledgment such as a Peerage would give. He thought it better for the Gov, & for Cockburn.

There are two sides of the question. Pray let me know what you wish me to do.

I was glad to hear from Glyn of your satisfactory conversation with C[ardwell].[1] He is so essentially well conditioned, that I was sure a little talk would settle the matter.

We are ankle deep in snow.

803. Mr. Gladstone to Lord Granville. [G.D. 29/29A]

Hawarden Castle. Dec. 19. 72.

1. In my opinion the offer made to Cockburn is not private and cannot but be made known after the meeting of Parliament. Would it be worth while to ask if he would like G.C.B. ? There is nothing else I suppose that can be proposed. Pray offer G.C.B. if you think fit—or hint to him eventual publicity.

2. I was alarmed at Mr Hammond's heroic style but your manner of looking at the subject reassured me. It fairly frightened Lowe whose business it was & not mine nor did I desire any communn to be made though I quite approve of it. I am glad to see there is no practical question remaining for us & it is for the Americans to say whether they wish or do not wish to effect what is a pure cash transaction & not one as H. seems to think *inter apices* of diplomacy

3. I observe you do not say any thing about Fortescue. *Apropos* to the case of Amory I send Portsmouth's letter to Glyn. (I am glad to say Ld Wolverton has been much better.)

4. The Cardwell matter is I hope well over: a few words on it when we meet; but I need not say his conduct was all that could be desired in point of honour and feeling.

804. Lord Granville to Mr. Gladstone. [Add. MS. 44169, fo. 145]

Private. Capesthorne, Congleton. Dec 23/72.

It would not be inconvenient to me to go up for a cabinet, but I think it would make some of our colleagues very angry to be summoned. I have therefore desired a despatch to be written agreeing in everything but the question of the taxe d'entrepôt.[2] Our refusal cannot at once destroy the treaty; & Thiers ultimatum against Kennedy, may not hold against us. If it does & everything else is settled, it will be time to consult the whole or portion of the Cabinet.

I will see Cockburn again at the end of the week. I am almost certain that

[1] On the reduction of army estimates; see Glyn to Granville, 14 Dec., G.D. 29/25A.

[2] See Granville to Kennedy, British commissioner in Paris under the Anglo-French commercial treaty of 5 Nov. (see above, no. 768 note), No. 36, 26 Dec., F.O. 27/1944.

he would refuse the G.C.B, and am not so sure that he would not be affronted unless it were done in the most gingerly way.[1]

What a brilliant speech you appear to have made at Liverpool.[2]

805. Mr. Gladstone to Lord Granville. [G.D. 29/61]

Hawarden Castle. Dec. 24. 72.

1. My letter to you on Sunday night was written under the belief you were in London: when I found from the messenger before his departure that you were not, it did not seem worth while to open & alter, as I knew you would perfectly understand. I was very sorry to find the argument (in my view) lying that way; and I should be glad if Tenterden, or some one else, would knock it over. I think you have done quite rightly.

2. The G.C.B. could only be mentioned to Cockburn I conceive as a sort of thing we should offer if he were likely to take it rather than that he should have nothing at all.

3. I rather turned against the Plate when I found the high figure, especially as it is not high enough (£1500 or even £2000), I think, for a service. But a very fine telling lot of old really ornamental plate may be had for that money or less by judicious selection in the old Plate shops.

4. I am very glad you liked the Liverpool address, which I framed not without the distinct advice of the people interested in & best informed about the Institution.

A happy Christmas!

You are I am afraid too far south now to think of turning back northward; & indeed my brother in law has in his mourning had hardly any one here except his family, so that though most welcome I fear you would have found it dull.

I have just sent on your messenger with some suggested alterations in the Draft.

806. Mr. Gladstone to Lord Granville. [G.D. 29/62]

Hawarden Castle. Jan 2. 1873.

1. I telegraph to you this forenoon my assent to the rather absurd surtaxe d'entrepôt.[3]

2. Yesterday I sent you a private letter which Elliot had written to me about the Bulgarian Schism.[4] I cannot help fearing that that schism may become a source of political danger as it will bring in Russia to meddle in the religious concerns of the Turkish Empire under the plea of ecclesiastical communion. Being thus

[1] Offered to and accepted by Cockburn, 1 Feb. 1873, Add. MS. 44542, fo. 79; see below, p. 375, note 4.

[2] At Liverpool College speech day, 21 Dec.; see *The Times*, 23 Dec., and Add. MS. 44436, fo. 161.

[3] See Granville to Kennedy, No. 9, 4 Jan., extending tel., 'altered according to Mr. Gladstone's telegram', agreeing to a French duty on English imported cotton goods of 60 centimes on 100 kilos, compensating for the *surtaxe d'entrepôt* to be levied under the French law of 30 Jan., F.O. 27/2011. See above, no. 742 note.

[4] Elliot to Gladstone, 20 Dec. 1872, on the consequences of the patriarch of Constantinople's declaring the Bulgarian Church schismatic, Add. MS. 44436, fo. 154. See also above, nos. 741, 785.

langerous it is also if I am rightly informed a quarrel without any fair ground of lifference; as I understand that the Patriarch of Constantinople who was wrong at the outset has been willing for some time to grant the Bulgarians their independence of his ordinary jurisdiction, but asks some territorial delimitation of the Bulgarian Church & its inmunities. If this be the case the demand is so reasonable hat I am at a loss to conceive how it could be evaded:. on its being granted, or agreed to be granted, the excommunication ought to be rescinded & peace re-established. Sir H. Elliot's language & conduct seem to me most reasonable. An attempt at an accommodation may be regarded as lying beyond his ordinary attributions. But I wish something could be done.

3. I have read your letter to Paget [1] about Borneo & the Italian Prison proposed o be founded there. I am rather behindhand in my information but I did not know that we had properly speaking territorial rights in Borneo. The plan may be bad but if they think it good it would seem that *somewhere* they ought to be able to do that which France & for all I know other countries are still doing, & which we n my opinion were obliged to abandon only because we had so ludicrously overdone it.

In the inclosed tract, sent to me by Sir E. Freshfield, you will find an interesting account of the Bulgarian affair.

807. Mr. Gladstone to Lord Granville. [G.D. 29/62]

No 2. Hawarden Castle. Jan 3. 73.

I think Kennedy's references home in the matter of the French Treaty are either a little over or a little underdone. This morning I had a draft [2] about woollen duties with a request to reply 'approve' or 'wait' while the box is marked 'Pressing'. In the explanatory paper I find no material whereupon to found a real judgment. It seems to me that where he and the Delegates from the Chambers are agreed he may safely proceed—& that where they are not agreed the *degree nature* and *reasons* of the difference between them should be clearly stated & that reference without this is little better than futile in matters which are not of policy or principle but of the purest technical detail.

2. I send you herewith for perusal a letter from Biddulph on H.M.'s behalf about Prince Leopold, and copy of my reply.[3]

3. I also send Lord Russell's two last.[4] You will see that he has in some degree relapsed. I had asked him, in view of probable discussions on the Alabama business, to let us know generally what line he would suggest our taking about himself.

[1] Granville to Paget, No. 223, 30 Dec. 1872, recounting an explanation to the Italian minister of the reasons for withholding 'the assent' asked for by Italy to her proposal, draft by Granville, F.O. 45/196.

[2] Granville to Kennedy, No. 7, 3 Jan., F.O. 27/2011. The draft was marked by Tenterden: 'This is the Draft about which I am in difficulty'.

[3] Not traced.

[4] Russell to Gladstone, 20, 24 Dec., pursuing his complaint of the government's failure to defend him against American accusations arising from his policy during the civil war, Add. MS. 44294, fos. 246, 251. See above, no. 797, for the beginning of the attack. Russell to Gladstone, 7 Dec., had withdrawn his accusations about patronage, *ibid.*, fo. 242.

808. Mr. Gladstone to Lord Granville. [G.D. 29/62]

Hawarden Castle. Ja 3. 73.

1. Audience question with China.[1]

I have read much about its postponement or its acceleration, & about what we or others should do on it; but I never recollect to have read a reasoned statement of the merits of the case *pro* & *con*, and especially of the arguments which are or might be made by the Chinese against it. The very first thing for us to do I think is to get this. The question is not one of the self-evident class and among other things may be borne in mind—

a. That the dignity of Foreign Powers may be impaired rather than promoted, if the forms of presentation should assume a certain character. I observe that prostration is contemplated by Mr Wade as a part of them.

b. Considering that this matter seems to be regarded as a first class question in China, I rather hesitate to agree to Mr Wade's demand that we should decide simply whether the audience is to be pressed for, and leave the manner to the joint action of the Ministers there. Mr Wade himself deserves much confidence I believe, but as to the diplomatic corps at Pekin I am not so sure.

b [*sic*]. The danger of being tripped up by the Russians is I think grave. If they have a territorial question alive with China in all likelihood it is much more important to *them* than this matter of the Audience, and they will work accordingly, and *sell* the common demand for the particular advantage of which they are in quest.

c. Mr Wade describes the matter as urgent but I do not see why—We surely have very little to complain of as a nation in the conduct of the Chinese through a series of years. It is not the practical conduct of business that seems to be in question but some sort of symbolic manifestation. This surely will bear at least the lapse of time sufficient to let us know what is to be pressed for, & why.

In conclusion I must say that I do not quite appreciate the frightful grievance that all these diplomatists appear to have suffered in having the announcement of the Marriage conveyed to them *together* with the request that foreigners should not come into the line of the procession. It *may* have been wrong: but for all I can see there might have been a counter-grievance, if the marriage had been announced & the intimation reserved for a separate and subsequent communication when the Chinese might have been told they had forfeited their right to restrict the free movement of foreigners by not exercising it at the proper time.

809. Lord Granville to Mr. Gladstone. [Add. MS. 44169, fo. 147]

Jan 5/73.

Schouvaloff who arrived last night, has desired Brunnow [2] to find out as he

[1] The marriage of the Emperor and the end of the regency gave occasion for raising anew the claim of the western ministers plenipotentiary to the ordinary privilege of access to the ruler denied to them in China; see Wade to Granville, Nos. 179–88, 13–25 Oct., received 31 Dec., F.O. 17/632. See also below, no. 912.

[2] Brunnow to Granville, dimanche, 3 heures [5 Jan.], G.D. 29/98. Cf. Gladstone to Granville, tel. 4.15 p.m., 7 Jan., thanking for the message and offering to come to London; Granville's reply, tel. 8 Jan., that the interview was satisfactory and Gladstone's coming unnecessary, G.D. 29/62.

cannot remain long, what it will be " convenable de faire tout en ce qui regarde les devoirs de Cour, qu'en ce qui pourrait être desirable par égard envers M. Gladstone personellement ".

If I see him before I hear from you, I shall say that I am not prepared to give an opinion, as you are getting all the holyday you can, and your house in the Country is in deep mourning.

810. Lord Granville to Mr. Gladstone. [Add. MS. 44169, fo. 148]

Walmer Castle. Jan 8/73.

Schouvaloff came here yesterday, goodlooking civil & intelligent. As pleasant a Russian as I have met.

He came from the train to our dining room in evening dress, with his grand cordon on, & his hat in hand.

He taught us Russian whist, & was droll about his interview with Thiers. He went to Versailles by invitation—he was alone—the Huissier did not ask him his name but seemed glad that there was a visitor. He found Thiers, Mme Thiers and Madle Dosne—all asleep, in different attitudes which he mimicked. Thiers woke up, and started at once on politics. Schouvaloff had seen something of Emperors and Kings, he had never heard one talk in the same way of " my armies, my fleets, my excellent soldiers, my brave sailors [”]. I asked what he gathered were Thiers' political aims. He answered—Absolutely none, but to conserve himself.

At midnight he gave me a personal message from the Emperor, of which Hammond will send you my report.[1]

The pith is that he promises not to take possession of Khiva, or even to occupy it, and that we may say so to Parlt.

That with regard to the Boundary of Affghanistan there may be difference of opinion in our respective Chanceries, but the Emperor is determined that it shall not be a cause of difference between the two countries.

Schouvaloff left Walmer at 2 AM, in my landau & fat old pair of horses to meet the Dover Mail train. He had so many Fournisseurs to see this morning. He goes away on Saturday.

He had seen the Prince of Wales yesterday.

811. Mr. Gladstone to Lord Granville.[2] [G.D. 29/62]

[Hawarden Castle]. Jan 10. 73.

1. Your account of Schouvaloff and of his communication is very agreeable. I am sorry to miss him.

2. I can see no objection to your asking Clarendon and Vernon—or Aberdeen

[1] Granville to Loftus, No. 8 confidential, 8 Jan., F.O. 65/875; draft by Granville, 7–8 Jan., G.D. 29/98; cf. Granville to Loftus, private, 1 Jan., G.D. 29/114. Shuvalov was announced for 4–11 Jan., but stayed until 14 Jan.

[2] Granville to Gladstone, 8 Jan., proposing Lords Clarendon and Vernon to move and second the address with Aberdeen and Breadalbane as alternatives, Add. MS. 44169, fo. 152, not printed.

in case of need. He has entered the Carlton but as I understand on an assurance from G. Hamilton that it meant nothing political!

3. I hope measure will be observed in talking about the poor Emperor's fidelity to England.[1] It was a matter of policy; and of feeling subordinate to policy. *How* subordinate it was we had proofs enough; most of all the Benedetti business, which no one wished to bring into the notice it deserved, and of the disgrace of which certainly France & I presume therefore Napoleon bears much more than half.

4. Those interesting but most sad letters from Spain[2] suggest one or two observations. They are strangely unfortunate in having to bring in so to speak their Puerto Rico Bill & then adjourn for three weeks. In this country, when matters were in our small way critical, we should regard this as certain death to a measure & a ministry. Again what can be more left-handed than to provide that the emancipation shall take place at a certain time *after* an event of which they may not be masters viz. publication in the Island Gazette. The date of legal freedom ought to have been fixed absolutely with reference to the passing of the Act in Spain.

I wish it were possible by any slight complimentary act to give a token of good will to King Amadeus.

I am just off to a rent-dinner & must say no more today.

812. Mr. Gladstone to Lord Granville. [G.D. 29/62]

Hawarden Castle. Jan 11. 73.

1. With regard to Ld O. Russell's letter[3] on the anti English feeling at Berlin. He seems to found it on the preposterous charge about Arms, in which it seems they think they have a case. Why should we not invite a general conference of nations, either including America or without her if she would not sit to discuss the question without prejudice—to have submitted to it the cases in which during the recent wars complaints have been made as to the supply of arms and to inquire whether any impediment ought to be placed in its way. I do not see that inconvenience could well arise from such an international commission so to call it, while there would I should think be decided advantage in our proposing it, if the Cabinet thought fit.

2. I read Gen. Walker's report inclosed in the Dispatch with greater interest than any one I have ever seen from him. Of course it will go to Cardwell. I have always understood that our Staff Arrangements and Appointments were by far the most expensive in the world. Lowe told me the other day he found there were three Colonels over Netley Hospital! As to details Cardwell has been a great

[1] Napoleon III died at Chiselhurst on 9 Jan. Cf. the Queen to Granville, on Napoleon as a 'faithful ally'; G.D. 29/35.

[2] Layard to Granville, Nos. 408, 409, secret, 30 Dec. 1872, received 4 Jan., describe the precarious state of the dynasty, F.O. 72/1313; cf. Layard to Granville, private, 14, 19, 30, 31 Dec., G.D. 29/100. The bill abolishing slavery in Puerto Rico was submitted to the Cortes before it was adjourned, on 25 Dec., until 15 Jan. It provoked hostile demonstrations.

[3] Untraced. Gen. Walker to Russell, No. 134, was enclosed in Russell to Granville, No. 12, 4 Jan., F.O. 64/766, and was forwarded to the War Office. Cf. Col. Reilly's report to the surveyor-general of the ordnance, Dec. 1872, W.O. 33/25.

deal too much & too well employed in great matters to be responsible for all that was done in the strange business called our Army reorganisation in 1855 & the subsequent years. I can hardly suppose General Walker right in his facts: if he were so it would be a sad disgrace to us. As to the German invasion it would pull down that nation very much, at least in my opinion, if they thought of it as a practical or practicable business except in the case of some combination of all Europe against us which is not an easy one to conceive. But they are quite right to include our little country in their exercises. I dare say it will not make you very nervous if some energetic pupil demonstrates the mode in which even Walmer Castle might be taken.

3. The Parliamentary aspects of the central parts of our Irish Univ. plan rather improve to my eye as I gradually try to acquire a closer acquaintance with this very large subject.

4. I think of calling the Cabinet on Wednesday 22d, which I shall assume to suit you unless you telegraph by Monday to the contrary.[1]

813. Lord Granville to Mr. Gladstone. [Add. MS. 44169, fo. 153]

Br[uton] St. Jan 12/73.

I send you the enclosed from the Queen.[2]

1⁰ If upon after thoughts She thinks the Russian Marriage more undesirable than She did eighteen months ago, She may avail herself of the apparent break off last summer, to alledge some reason or other for not renewing the question, but I do not see how the Political & Ecclesiastical questions are changed from the time when she was rather hot upon the subject.

2 The Queen & the Prince of Wales had determined that he and all the Royal family should attend the funeral of the Emperor.

The desire to pay respect to fallen greatness and to a person who had been very kind to most members of the royal family was very natural. But I ventured to advise against doing so.

It will be a fatigue for the Prince coming up for it from Sandringham and going back again in four & 20 hours as he proposes.

He has been demonstrative already. He postponed the theatricals at Rothschilds, he has postponed his ball, he went in person to Chiselhurst yesterday.

There are crowds of Imperialists of all sorts at Chiselhurst. Although Bassano and Lavalette oppose it, and are to a certain degree backed up by the Empress, Plon Plon,[3] Rouher, Fleury etc are determined to have a demonstration.

Fleury asked Sydney whether we could not send troops, which Sydney said was out of the question.

Pictu answered some one who asked after the Prince Imperial "You mean the Emperor".

[1] The cabinet met on Wednesday, 22 Jan., and on 24, 27, 29, 31 Jan., Add. MS. 44641, fos. 2–18.

[2] To Granville, tel. 11 Jan., announcing Shuvalov's overture to the duke of Edinburgh on behalf of the Tsar for the duke's marriage to the Grandduchess Marie, G.D. 29/35.

[3] Prince Napoleon, son of Jerome, cousin of Napoleon III.

It would be annoying if the Princes were present at a great acclamation of the new Emperor, which is not impossible.

Our attitude with regard to the future Gov of France ought to be perfectly neutral. No Frenchman would consider the presence of the Princes as otherwise than a demonstration of the Constitutional Royal family of England in favor of Despotism.

(It is not an object to provoke the assembly just before the discussion of the Treaty.)

Luckily it has turned out that the Royal Family did not attend the funeral of Louis Philippe—& I have made no objection to the Queen & Princes sending persons of their Household to attend.

I hope you approve.

814. Mr. Gladstone to Lord Granville. [G.D. 29/62]

Private & Confidential. Hawarden Castle. Jan 12. 1873.

I do not quite gather from your note received today or from the accompanying draft (or copy) [1] how or in what shape the question of the Duke of Edinburgh's marriage to the Czarewna has revived. But this is not very material. The fact being so, I agree that the balance of reasons against any attempt to interfere with it still subsists. Indeed it is strengthened by the fact that the Duke himself is now by three or four years farther advanced into manhood so as to have passed beyond those periods of life to which any thing like restraint except in the form of advice is principally applicable. It is further strengthened, as far as appears, by the circumstance that a *greater* amount of difficulty attends any other course than was at the former period in full view.

I should not feel the smallest hesitation in arguing the case for the grant before the House of Commons if the arrangement now apparently in contemplation should take effect; and no Parliamentary obstacle could arise unless it were in a state of things little likely to prevail where empty and shallow pretexts are through foregone purpose made to perform the work of reasons.

815. Lord Granville to Mr. Gladstone. [Add. MS. 44169, fo. 160]

Foreign Office. Jan 14/73.

I send you a report [2] of what passed between Schouvaloff and me—the Queen wished to have it in writing. I do not trouble you with the arguments which I used with the Queen, but she soon saw that some of the objections, whether good or bad, could not be made at this stage of the proceedings.

Whatever may be his objects, the Duke of Edinburgh is dying for the marriage, & I quoted your note to Her with great effect.

The P. of Wales whose power of talk appears to me much encreased, was first

[1] Granville to Loftus, private and confidential, 14 Jan., telling him Shuvalov's mission was concerned with the royal marriage as well as Central Asia, G.D. 29/114.

[2] Granville to the Queen, 13 Jan., G.D. 29/35.

impartial about the funeral, then wished to go, then told everybody I was against it, but that he meant to go all the same, then said that he had unwillingly yield[ed] to my refusal backed by the Queen—& some of his conservative friends have put the last version into the Standard—She only puts in a discourteous way, what ought to have been represented as a mere adherence to precedent.[1]

You will see what passed between d'Harcourt & me, by my private note to Lyons.[2]

816. Mr. Gladstone to Lord Granville. [G.D. 29/62]

Hawarden Castle. Jan 15. 73.

1. I am truly glad you were able to throw over the plan for the Prince's attending the Emperor's funeral; and I must say I am rather surprised that the Queen should have given in to it. In the Prince it does not surprise me: for it is account[ed] for by his good points and his weak ones; his love of movement and excitement, his real good nature and sympathy, and his I fear total want of political judgment either inherited or acquired.

2. The odds seem now to be much in favour of the Russian marriage after the turn which matters have taken.

3. Does Bismarck make a fool of Bancroft or Bancroft make a fool of himself in supposing that the Yankees intend to be the catspaws of Germany or any other Power?[3] If Bancroft makes himself too conspicuous in this kind of activity his Government may serve him as they served Catucazy for minding other peoples' business instead of his own.

817. Lord Granville to Mr. Gladstone.[4] [Add. MS. 44169, fo. 164]

Walmer Castle. Feb 1/73.

I find I made a mistake yesterday[5] about the French Treaty. They can reject it in toto, but if the Assembly insist on the complete execution of the Pouhier [*sic* for Pouyer] Quertier clause, then the treaty remains, and we should only pay

[1] Cf. Granville to Gladstone, tel. 14 Jan., that the Prince would not attend Napoleon's funeral on 15 Jan., G.D. 29/62.

[2] 14 Jan., urging that Rémusat should not make difficulties about signing the protocol, which became the declaration of 29 Jan., with the tariff negotiated by the mixed commission annexed to replace that annexed to the treaty of 5 Nov., G.D. 29/109. See above, nos. 768, 804, and below, no. 817.

[3] See Odo Russell to Granville, private, 11 Jan., relating 'Bancroft's offer of American assistance to occupy the attention of England while Germany is fighting France', G.D. 29/93; printed Knaplund, *Letters from Berlin*, pp. 83–5.

[4] Granville to Gladstone, 30 Jan., announcing Cockburn's readiness to accept the G.C.B. (conferred 12 Feb.), Add. MS. 44169, fo. 163; correspondence on Breadalbane's replacing Huntly as lord in waiting, 1 Feb., *ibid.*, fo. 165, on the back of no. 817; an exchange in the cabinet of 29 Jan. on reduction of judicial pensions, Add. MS. 44641, fo. 16, not printed.

[5] Relates to Lyons to Granville, No. 55 commercial, 30 Jan., on the submission to the Assembly of the recently signed commercial agreements, F.O. 27/2002. The treaty of 5 Nov., the declaration of 29 Jan., with the amended tariff submitted, 8 Feb. The Assembly was hostile and they were not ratified. A new treaty of 23 July revived the Cobden Treaty and annulled the denunciation of 15 March; Parl. papers. [C. 822] (1873). lxxv, 627. Granville refers to

duties on the articles specified in the column in Annexe I headed " import duties " minus the duties in that column leviable on raw materials. The practical effect would be that we should go on as we are now under the treaty of 1860.

818. Lord Granville to Mr. Gladstone. [Add. MS. 44169, fo. 166]

Foreign Office. Feb 5/73.

I recd a note from Brunnow this morning, telling me that he had recd the answer,[1] of which he gave me a copy, but that privately & personally he was bound to tell me that there was a postscript which he could not read.

I telegraphed to Biddulph in cypher to tell you of this, & that you had better obtain the Queen's assent to alternative passages.[2]

I then went to Brunnow. He abused Gortchakoff's despatch as not half civil enough—said the Postscript was in a cypher, which was giving his attachés much trouble—that he would let me have it as soon as it was made out. I said I would wait, upon which he rang for an attaché, who brought in a decypher, in great confusion, verbs & nouns being bracketed as possible meanings. It began—this incident is closed, & then apparently gave explanations why the Russian Gov adhered.

Brunnow called later at the F.O. with the Postscript complete, marked confidential, and he said he did not communicate it to me—but I might look at it, as it contained nothing but ' des bétises '. It gave the reasons for agreeing—1° that the question was of no importance to Russia 2° that the assurance to exercise our influence with the Ameer was as good as a guarantee—3° that they were glad to do what was agreeable to the present charming Gov of the Queen.

819. Mr. Gladstone to Lord Granville. [G.D. 29/62]

10, Downing Street. Feb. 5. 73.

I had no communication from you at Osborne which we left about 2.40 : but I suppose from your letter that we go on as we are notwithstanding Gortchakoff's P.S.

820. Lord Granville to Mr. Gladstone.[3] [G.D. 29/62]

[before 6 February 1873].

Van de Weyer gave me today a confidential message from the K of the Belgians, and told me that positive reliance could be placed on the information.

a clause in the law of July 1872 enacting the taxes on raw materials. The cabinet met on 31 Jan., but Gladstone does not record discussion on the French treaty, Add. MS. 44641, fo. 18. See above, nos. 742, 745, 768, 804, 815.

[1] Gorchakov to Brunnow, 19/31 Jan., without the PS., F.O. 65/876. It answered Granville to Loftus, No. 22, 24 Jan., laying down the British view of the Afghan boundary, F.O. 65/875. Russia now accepted the British demarcation and at the same time recorded a British engagement to prevent Afghan aggression. See above, no. 772.

[2] I.e. for the Queen's speech for the opening of Parliament, 6 Feb.

[3] This was not apparently reported officially or privately to Lumley. No. 820 is marked by Gladstone : ' This intelligence rather tends to lower my estimate of the *acumen* of the King of the Belgians '. The date is suggested by a pencil note of Granville's secretary that he received it on 7 Feb. Cf. Granville to Odo Russell, 5 March, on a Franco-Russo-British understanding, G.D. 29/110.

There is a perfect understanding between Russia, Germany, France & the United States in case of a quarrel between the first power, and England on Asiatic matters. Bismark's remark to Schouvaloff was—" We shall see the eggs we broke at Sedan paid for by England.["] Thiers was the most " acharné " and assured Schouvaloff that he could land 500,000 men in England.

I said that I could understand Russia wishing for Allies—& that Thiers with all his desire for a military splash should like the idea, if backed up by such powerful Allies, but what do the United States want now, and how would Bismark like, much as he might approve of seeing us & France on bad terms, desire [*sic*] to see the latter in possession of all our resources. He announced that I might be perfectly convinced of the fact—however extraordinary it might seem, but the King was most desirous that nobody should know the quarter from whence the information came, as it would close the channel of communication. Van de Weyer asked me whether the Belgian Govt had not been able to give us useful information during my stay at the F. O. I readily acknowledged the amount of information which M de Beaulieu had given, but was obliged to admit that much of it had turned out to be perfect mare's nests.

821. Lord Granville to Mr. Gladstone.[1] [Add. MS. 44169, fo. 170]

Foreign Office. [14 February 1873].

Hammond tells me of the Memo he has sent you through Enfield, stating his opinion that a Cabinet Minister should answer Ryland's question. But I do not agree. Enfield will say all that is prudent & sufficient to meet Rylands, and if the latter brings on a Debate, it is infinitely better that you should hold yourself in reserve for bigger guns.[2]

I wish you joy with all my heart of your plan and of your great speech.[3]

822. Lord Granville to Mr. Gladstone. [G.D. 29/62]

Copy. Private. F.O. Febr 15/73.

I hope I have not said more than I ought.[4]

Do you think it would be well for Lyons, to communicate that I have taken advantage of an occasion offered me, to give a hint to the Spanish Govt.

[1] Granville to Gladstone, 12 Feb., expressing readiness to do all he can on an unidentified subject, Add. MS. 44169, fo. 169, not printed.

[2] On 14 Feb. Rylands moved that the French commercial treaty and all future treaties should be laid before Parliament before ratification. Lord Edmond Fitzmaurice answered him. But Gladstone spoke too, though Enfield wound up the debate; see *Hans. Parl. Deb.*, 3rd ser., ccxiv. 448–90.

[3] Introducing the proposals for the extension of university education in Ireland, 13 Feb., *ibid.*, 378–426.

[4] To Lyons, private, 7 p.m., 15 Feb., and No. 99 confidential, 15 Feb., F.O. 27/1974, reporting, for communication to Thiers, a conversation with Moret, the Spanish minister in London, G.D. 29/109. Granville had warned Moret, in answer to a question, that Britain would not be indifferent to a Spanish attempt to annex Portugal; see Granville to Layard, tel. 7.15 p.m., 18 Feb., No. 31, 19 Feb., F.O. 72/1334, to Murray, No. 15 confidential, 19 Feb., F.O. 179/196; cf. Temperley and Penson, *Foundations*, pp. 341–3, and Gladstone's note on the cabinet, 15 Feb., Add. MS. 44641, fo. 37; Granville to Lyons, 19 Feb., private, G.D. 29/109.

823. Mr. Gladstone to Lord Granville. [G.D. 29/62]

11, Carlton House Terrace. Feb. 16. 73.

In reading your letter to Lyons my only scruple is about the word 'obliged' lest it should be quoted against us—I do not very well know what to suggest—could it be put "under which we had formerly defended Portugal from external aggression; and the disposition of the people of this country in such a case might probably be much what it had been before." But I am not particularly enamoured of this.[1]

I am confirmed in the disposition towards *reserve* by noticing that Thiers is at his old tricks and talks of the United Peninsula just as he used to talk of United Italy and United Germany.

824. Mr. Gladstone to Lord Granville. [Add. MS. 44542, fo. 87]

[*Copy*]. 19 Feb. 73.

I see in this intelligence no obstacle to the prosecution of the design. What Loftus reports[2] makes her to be all the better woman & perhaps not the worse Princess.

825. Mr. Gladstone to Lord Granville.[3] [G.D. 29/62]

11, Carlton House Terrace. Mch 14. 73. 10 Pm.

Will you kindly read these[4]—revise with your most critical eye—and see me here in the morning (or I can come to you) as soon after ten or 10.30 as you can make it convenient.

826. Mr. Gladstone to Lord Granville. [G.D. 29/29A]

Secret. 11, Carlton House Terrace. Mch 15. 73.

In consequence of a command through Ponsonby I have been at the Palace—not for any very distinct object, but partly to fill the blank before the public.

[1] Gladstone's alteration was not adopted, but the phrase 'which obliged us', used in relation to the treaties of alliance with Portugal, was marked 'omit' by Granville in the copy of the private letter and was not used in the dispatch; cf. also Ponsonby to Granville, 28 Feb., reporting the Queen's views, G.D. 29/35.

[2] Loftus to Granville, private and secret, 5, 13 Feb., on the *affaires de cœur* of the Grandduchess Marie, G.D. 29/31.

[3] Granville to Gladstone, 2 March, on Breadalbane for the lordship in waiting, and 6 March on Lord Lurgan's wish to resign his lordship in waiting, undated (i) on Prince of Wales's regret at his presence at a theatre where Gladstone was burlesqued, (ii) Mrs Grote's impression of Gladstone's speech, Add. MS. 44169, fos. 174–5, 177, 178, not printed.

[4] The government was defeated in the Commons, 2 a.m., Wednesday, 12 March, on the Irish universities bill; see Gladstone to the Queen, 2.45 a.m., 12 March, Guedalla, i. 394–5. After two meetings of the cabinet Gladstone resigned, about 3 p.m. the next day. Parliament was told and adjourned until 17 March. The Queen then saw Disraeli, who declined to form a government. Ponsonby communicated this to Gladstone early the same evening. No. 825 sent parts of Disraeli's refusal and an exchange with the Queen on ambiguities in it and the 'long letter' referred to in no. 826. This was drawn up late 14 March, but dated 15th after Gladstone had met Granville and Ponsonby on it. See mem., Cliveden, midnight, 16 March, outlining these events, Add. MS. 44761, fo. 100.

H.M. was in perfect humour. She will use the whole or part of my long letter by sending it to Disraeli: she seemed quite to understand our point of view: and told me plainly what shows that the artful dodger *did* say if it came back to him again at this juncture he would not be bound by his present refusal. I said 'But Madam that is not before me.' 'But he told it to me' she said.[1]

827. Mr. Gladstone to Lord Granville. [G.D. 29/62]

16, Bruton Street. Mch 17. 73.

I miss you on my way from Paddington home.

If you will read the inclosed [2] (& please send or bring them) you will come up to the present state of the transactions.

Disraeli as usual escapes the real point and argues against a proposition which I have nowhere stated or implied viz. that the Opposition are unconditionally bound to take office.

828. Lord Granville to Mr. Gladstone. [Add. MS. 44169, fo. 176]

16, Bruton Street. March 18/73.

I think it better that you should look at the passage double marked in Spencer's letter,[3] before I answer him.

829. Lord Granville to Mr. Gladstone. [Add. MS. 44169, fo. 181]

Foreign Office. [4 April 1873].

I had nothing particular to say, but glad that you are taking care of yourself.

It may be as well to send the enclosed. Please turn the label round, & send box to Wetherell

I hope you will have the Cabinet at your house tomorrow.[4]

[1] The Queen saw Gladstone, Saturday afternoon, 15 March, but Disraeli had not yet answered the communication of the 'long letter'. He adhered to his refusal and Gladstone was re-called late the same day. Gladstone's statement to the Commons, 17 March, showed that Disraeli would not form a government, but his own resumption of office was not announced until 20 March. Cf. Guedalla, i. 394–408; Morley, ii. 446–56, 652–3; W. F. Monypenny and G. E. Buckle, *The Life of Benjamin Disraeli* (1920), v. 207–18; Add. MSS. 44641, fos. 63–73, 44761, fos. 102–11; Granville to Odo Russell, 19 March, G.D. 29/110, Knaplund, *Letters from Berlin*, pp. 95–6.

[2] Gladstone's mem., 16 March, Add. MS. 44761, fo. 100; the Queen to Gladstone, 16 March, enclosing Disraeli's reply to the communication of Gladstone's 'long letter', printed Guedalla i. 402–6.

[3] Untraced, but probably on his possible resignation of the lord-lieutenancy of Ireland. Cf. Spencer to Granville, 23 March, on his readiness to remain for the time being, G.D. 29/75. See below, nos. 868, 871–8, 882, 889, 900, 901, 903–6.

[4] For cabinet, 5 April, at 11, Carlton House Terrace, see Add. MS. 44641, fo. 92.

830. Mr. Gladstone to Lord Granville. [G.D. 29/62]

10, Downing Street. Ap 8. 73.

The Telegram from Thomson [1] today about the R[euter] R[ailroad] from the Caspian to Teheran is sufficiently sensational if not alarming. But has Persia freely given this Railway Concession? If she has upon what pretext could we object to it? There may be here matter for consideration but I write my first impression.

I sent the letter to Baxter [2] as it was after showing it to Glyn & F. C[avendish].

831. Lord Granville to Mr. Gladstone. [Add. MS. 44169, fo. 182]

Private. 16, Bruton Street. April 9 [1873].

She was in great spirits—did not get within 100 miles of *the* subject.

She praised you—*so* kind about everything—complained of Clarendon having been uncivil, & said she was always afraid of his saying something disagreeable in conversation.

832. Mr. Gladstone to Lord Granville. [G.D. 29/62]

Hawarden Castle. Ap. 13. 73.

1. I found the Queen in excellent health and humour. I tried to comfort her about the Advent of more Eastern Sovereigns, as not immediately probable: and I also advised that if she wished such a personage not to entail charge upon her she should beware of inviting him herself to the Palace. It is however not bad policy all things considered that he should come & she should pay something: it will tend to keep the Londoners content to see the Palace used, & used at the Queen's charge.[3]

2. You will have observed that much notice has been taken of my dry answer about the Carlist subscriptions.[4] I had no idea that there was any shadow of doubt about the law: and I think it would be very advantageous if you would direct a *précis* to be prepared of the legal opinions & the transactions, at any rate in recent times, on and about the subject. We shall hear more of it. It is full of difficulty. But certainly the case which has occurred is a scandalous one: & so was that society for promoting war in Italy, to which I some time ago referred.

[1] 7 April, announcing that the building of the railway, for which a concession had been granted to Baron de Reuter, would mean 'Persia's ceasing to be an independent power', copy G.D. 29/62. No. 830 is marked by Granville: 'Put by'. Cf. Hammond to Granville, 8 April, deprecating an alarmist opposition, G.D. 29/105.

[2] Gladstone to Baxter, 7 April, reprimanding him for leaving London when the budget debates were due and Lowe needed his parliamentary help, Add. MS. 44438, fo. 160 Gladstone submitted the letter to Granville, who wished to strengthen it by a plain request for Baxter's resignation, *ibid.*, fo. 162.

[3] Cf. the Queen to Gladstone, 3 April, on the entertainment of the Shah of Persia during his proposed visit, Guedalla, i. 410.

[4] Gladstone stated that the law had not been broken by an advertisement in the *Westminster Gazette* asking for subscriptions to the Carlists who had renewed their struggle on the proclamation of the Spanish republic, 16 Feb. Gladstone replied to a question from J. Stapleton; *Hans. Parl. Deb.*, 3rd ser., ccxv. 633–4. Cf. Foreign Office mem. for Gladstone's reply and Moret to Gladstone, 28 April, Add. MS. 44438, fos. 224, 226.

3. I should be very glad if the Foreign Office would give or get us some recent and trustworthy map of the Central Asian district. I suppose Arrowsmith & other Atlases which one would naturally refer to are out of date.

833. Lord Granville to Mr. Gladstone. [Add. MS. 44169, fo. 184]

Private. Walmer Castle. April 15/73.

I will have the précis prepared you wish to have.[1]

At the Cabinet on the 5th, I sent a minute to Hammond to desire him to furnish you with an answer to Stapleton, based upon the Law officer's opinion, with a sentence in addition marking that the Carlist subscriptions had nothing Governmental or National in their character.

I send you now a disagreeable correspondence with the Attorney General,[2] and a minute of mine to Hammond. The latter came into the Office twelve years before any one else in the office, and nine months after Lyndhurst's opinion was given. He is enquiring into the facts, but Herslett [*sic* for Hertslet] is unfortunately out of town.

The idea of Twiss, who has come back to seek a livelyhood, and who is a near relation of Delane came into my head before I received Coleridge's last letter. The Attorney General had justly been very severe upon him.

834. Lord Granville to Mr. Gladstone. [G.D. 29/62]

Copy. Walmer Castle. April 15/73.

I send you three letters (and one enclosure) from Argyll.[3] I have asked him to send some which I sent him.

Lord Derby's view seemed to be of a different kind from that of either Beust or Rawlinson.

He believed that the concession was so great that the Persians would never keep their word, & that possible Shareholders should be warned.

835. Mr. Gladstone to Lord Granville. [G.D. 29/62]

H[awarde]n. Ap. 16. 73.

With reference to the inclosed notice,[4] I have asked Mr Stapleton to postpone until Thursday.

[1] See Granville to Hammond, 15 April, instructing him to send to Gladstone a *précis* of transactions on the support of one side or the other in a civil war, G.D. 29/105.

[2] Coleridge to Granville, two letters, complaining of the publication in *The Times* of Lyndhurst's opinion, as a law officer of the crown, 1823, on British subscriptions to the Carlist cause, not traced. The correspondence and the minute and no. 833 were enclosed in Granville to Hammond, 15 April, for forwarding to Gladstone, G.D. 29/105; cf. mem. by Tenterden, 15 April, on the publication of law officers' reports, G.D. 29/106.

[3] 9, 12, 14 April about Persia's political independence and the building of the railway from Teheran to the Caspian, G.D. 29/51. Rawlinson to Argyll, 13 April, in favour of the railway was enclosed. Beust had asked for British support in opposing it. See above, no. 830 note.

[4] Stapleton moved for legislation to forbid the collection of money in Britain calculated to foment the Spanish civil war, on Thursday, 24 April, *Hans. Parl. Deb.*, 3rd ser., ccxv. 896–9.

The practice is I think objectionable; but in some cases extremely popular. I do not know even whether we could prohibit associations & public appeals. The prohibition would be evaded by asking the money for Carlist wounded, or Polish wounded?

Would it be worth while to have a *précis* of the Suez Canal & judicial reforms case made for the Cabinet.

836. Mr. Gladstone to Lord Granville. [G.D. 29/62]

Hawarden Castle. Ap. 17. 73.

I have read Sir Bartle Frere's letters.[1]

There are two points on which I should like to have full information when we come to consider the question.

1. How far does the position of France as co-Guarantor of the Sultan's independence affect our right of sole coercive interference in Zanzibar.

2. What does Sir B. Frere propose to do with regard to ships suspected of carrying slaves but carrying the flags of countries which have not conceded to us the right of search?

837. Mr. Gladstone to Lord Granville.[2] [G.D. 29/62]

H of C. May 12 [1873].

We are between two fires on Wedy of early & late Bills but I will say 3.15 which means 3.30 for *work*.[3]

I go to Windsor tomorrow (at 12 from P[addingto]n).[4]

838. Lord Granville to Mr. Gladstone. [Add. MS. 44169, fo. 188]

Confidential. May 12/73.

The Duke of Edinburgh's affair seems to be going on quite well—the excuse of the fever was according to his account quite valid, and he is invited to meet them again in June in Germany. The discouraging telegram was badly transmitted

[1] Frere to Granville, No. 25, 10 March, No. 26 confidential, 12 March, No. 27, 12 March, all received 7 April, F.O. 84/1389. He reported after visiting the southern Zanzibar ports Mozambique and Madagascar. He recommended coercion to stop the slave trade of the southern ports by breaking off their trade with British Indian subjects. See also Granville's mem. for the cabinet, 29 April, G.D. 29/103. A cabinet committee was appointed on Zanzibar, Add. MS. 44641, fos. 101, 106. See also above, nos. 773, 781, 785, and below, no. 837 note.

[2] Gladstone to Granville, 4 May, reporting the living of Whittlebury already filled, Add. MS. 44542, fo. 116; Wetherell to Gurdon, 8 May, on Granville's agreement to a 'careful answer' to the Spanish Minister's thanks, 28 April, for Gladstone's answer on the Carlist subscriptions, G.D. 29/62, not printed.

[3] The cabinet on Zanzibar and parliamentary business was altered to 3.15, 14 May. It decided the form of slave trade treaty with the Sultan and Granville took a minute of the decision, Add. MS. 44641, fo. 110. For the treaty, 5 June, see Parl. papers. [C. 889] (1874). lxii, 917.

[4] See Gladstone's note, 13 May, of proposed heads of discussion with the Queen, Add. MS. 44761, fo. 127.

—a change of figure which altered " I am very much satisfied " into " I am *not* very much satisfied ". The Queen has written a civil & firm letter to the Empress.

839. Mr. Gladstone to Lord Granville. [G.D. 29/62]

11, Carlton House Terrace. May 22. 73.

Lowe and I have heard the Sugar Refiners in the presence of the Customhouse authorities about the agreement lately signed at Paris. It appears to me as at present advised that they make out their case, but I am going to discuss it with Lowe, who rather differs, in the presence of Cardwell, who thoroughly understands the matter. This will probable [*sic*] be in my room today at the H of C. but if you would like to come we could appoint some other time & place.

840. Mr. Gladstone to Lord Granville.[1] [G.D. 29/62]

Chatsworth. June 1. 73.

If there be a question of an instruction to Jervoise about the place of the Papal election, I should for the moment, incline to confining it to his recommending, as far as he can, that it be held in Rome.

One step farther it might be right for him to go, but only I think after we have fully considered it—namely to point out the difficulty we should feel as to Speeches & Addresses publicly delivered in British Territory by so high a personage as a Pope, of a nature contemplating not only moral resistance but *voies de fait* against an Allied Government.

I am not sure what ground we should have for objecting to the election of a Pope in Malta particularly: it is of course the likeliest place in the Queen's dominions.[2]

841. Mr. Gladstone to Lord Granville.[3] [G.D. 29/62]

11, Carlton House Terrace. June 8. 73.

The L. Lieutcy of Essex was *offered* to Petre in 1869, and seemingly declined, though no letter of refusal can be found.

Under these circs perhaps you, or Bessborough, or some other suitable person, could sound him, before I commit myself a second time in a formal manner ?

If pressure *can* be applied, it would be useful.

[1] An exchange between Granville and Gladstone during the cabinet, 17 May, on Gladstone's visit to the Empress Eugénie, 18 May, Add. MS. 44641, fo. 122, not printed.

[2] Gladstone's letter was prompted by newspaper conjectures that the election of the next pope might take place in Malta. See Granville's min., 4 June, for the drafting of an instruction following Gladstone's first paragraph, but forbidding any initiative ; and Granville to Jervoise, No. 2, 6 June, F.O. 43/120.

[3] Correspondence, 31 May–6 June, on the lord-lieutenancy of Essex, vacant by the death of Sir T. Western and filled by Fortescue's appointment, 26 July, G.D. 29/62 ; Gladstone to Granville, 7 June, reporting Russell's wish for the calling of his son to the Lords, and Granville's reply agreeing, Add. MS. 44169 fo. 190, not printed.

842. Mr. Gladstone to Lord Granville. [G.D. 29/62]

10, Downing Street. June 10. 73.

I have seen Captain Goodenough, and liked him much, as far as a single interview goes. He sails tomorrow morning.[1] Kimberley sent me, by him, the Memorandum [2] herewith which sets out a great deal, & very well, in small compass. I think *No 2* should become *No 1*.

843. Mr. Gladstone to Lord Granville. [G.D. 29/62]

10, Downing Street. June 11. 1873.

The First Lord of the Treasury presents his compliments to Lord Granville, and begs to call attention to the following Minute of the Cabinet [3] recently adopted. 'The Cabinet desire that when it is proposed to include in any Bill, which is to be introduced into Parliament on the responsibility of the Government, or of any of its officers, any charge on the local rates, notice of such intention be given beforehand to the Cabinet, and its authority obtained for the same, before the introduction of the Bill.[']

844. Mr. Gladstone to Lord Granville. [G.D. 29/62]

Private. 10 Downing Street. June 12. 73.

After the loathsome account [4] of the Shah, can any thing be done to give the wretch a hint as to his behaviour?

Could not a very mild paragraph be made to appear in some Brussels paper on European & Eastern manners & then copied into the English newspapers?

Keeping back O. Russell's dispatch from the Queen will not diminish her annoyance if the conduct at Berlin is repeated in London.

[1] The problem of the continued labour traffic to the Fiji islands (above, no. 632) was partly met by the appointment of a new consul, E. L. Layard, with stronger instructions, to Layard, No. 7, 29 Sept., F.O. 58/135. At the same time Capt. Goodenough was associated with him in an enquiry preliminary to more effective measures and a decision on the islands' application for annexation, Colonial Office to Foreign Office, 31 July, F.O. 58/140. The cabinet decided to send Goodenough, 7 June, 'subject to a satisfactory discussion with him', Add. MS. 44641, fos. 124, 128. The islands were annexed, Sept. 1874. No. 842 is marked by Granville 'answd', but no answer has been traced.

[2] On four possible courses: (i) to confer magisterial powers on the consul, (ii) to recognize the existing Fiji government, (iii) to proclaim a protectorate, (iv) to annex, Add. MS. 44225, fo. 45.

[3] See decision on 'circular on local charges' in cabinet of 7 June, Add. MS. 44641, fo. 128; for cabinet minutes see above, no. 546 note.

[4] The Shah of Persia's visit to Berlin ended on 7 June. Russell reported the difficulties created by the Persians' disregard of European manners. A minute by Granville on the dispatch noted Russell's wish that it be withheld from the Queen; Russell to Granville, No. 306 secret, 7 June, F.O. 64/772.

845. Mr. Gladstone to Lord Granville.[1] [G.D. 29/62]

10, Downing Street. June 21. 73.

This note [2] embodies a request made to me orally by Ld R. Grosvenor.

There seems to be a little mixture of the two questions

1. How far new means of communication are desirable.

2. How far we are to give an opinion as between this & other modes of providing them.

On the second question it is for us to say as little as possible. Still it occurs to me that the Tunnel is free from an objection to the Ferry plan viz. that it might give an excuse for a great naval harbour on the French side at the narrowest point of the Channel.

But on the first question I suppose we really while renouncing all interference regard with a friendly and lively interest all schemes framed with this object and open to no just objection, which is the case of the Tunnel.

I presume this to be as much as Ld R.G. desires—would there be any harm in writing it?

846. Mr. Gladstone to Lord Granville. [G.D. 29/62]

11, Carlton House Terrace. June 25. 73.

1. The proposed presentation of a Persian Bible to the Shah can only be taken as a kindly and becoming act.

2. As to addresses pressing him about Toleration, they seem to me much more questionable. It is like getting a man into your own house, & then hustling him. This even if there are grievances; of which I know nothing one way or the other. Such addresses ought surely not to be presented in a Church.

3. Though St Pauls is so much less interesting, it might be much more effective & impressive for the Shah, than the Abbey? But this may I suppose take its course. The offer is, again, a kindly and becoming act. I return the papers.[3]

847. Lord Granville to Mr. Gladstone.[4] [G.D. 29/62]

[26 June 1873].

Hammond & Rawlinson think the Star of India the right thing for the Grand

[1] Gladstone to Granville, 13 June, on accommodation of members of Parliament at Portsmouth for the reception of the Shah and the bad state of the Zanzibar question; and 21 June, on the gift of a horse offered to him by Lord Marjoribanks, G.D. 29/62; and Granville to Gladstone, 22 June, replying, Add. MS. 44169, fo. 191, not printed.

[2] Grosvenor to Gladstone on the channel tunnel scheme, untraced. Hervey wrote on the back of no. 845: 'Ld. G. wishes to know the facts of this case'.

[3] Correspondence between Granville and the archbishop of Canterbury, 25 June, sent to Gladstone with a note from Granville that the Persian minister saw no objection to his broaching it, Add. MS. 44169, fo. 199.

[4] Gladstone returned no. 847, having written on the back: 'It is I suppose the first rank of the Order. I am ill able to judge but see no cause to dissent. You may have to do the same for Japan & other countries. W.E.G. June 26 [1873]'. The Grand Vizier to the Shah of Persia was made G.C.S.I., 1 July.

Vizier—Argyll at first objected on account of the Statutes, but I believe was convinced by the example of Lesseps.

If he does not object, do you approve, & may I sound the Queen conditionally today.

848. Lord Granville to Mr. Gladstone. [Add. MS. 44169, fo. 193]

18, Carlton House Terrace. June 28/73.

You will see by the enclosed memo,[1] that the F.O. & Lord Lyons have hitherto followed the line you describe as the right one, respecting the two questions 1° How far new means of communication are desirable & 2° How far are we to give an opinion as between Lord R. Grosvenor's scheme & others.

It must however be borne in mind that the project for improving the Harbour at Dover sanctioned by the Cabinet [2] does to a limited degree compete with the Tunnel scheme.

849. Lord Granville to Mr. Gladstone.[3] [Add. MS. 44169, fo. 206]

18, Carlton House Terrace. [5 July 1873].

The Archbishop sent me a copy of his letter to you.[4]

I answered by ack[nowledgin]g it, and said that you would probably mention it to your colleagues.

The objection of the Archbishops is that the Clergy would set at defiance the decisions of a lay Tribunal in matters of doctrine, more easily than those of a tribunal constituted as at present.

850. Mr. Gladstone to Lord Granville. [Add. MS. 44542, fo. 135]

[*Copy*]. July 7. 73.

It is unfortunate that the circuln Box on the Lord Mayor's Dinner affair did not reach me until after the Cabt. on Sat.[5] With a considerable number of our

[1] Mem. by J. G. S[tavely] on the Grosvenor channel tunnel scheme, 23 June, Add. MS. 44169, fo. 195.

[2] The decision to proceed with the Dover Harbour Bill was taken in the cabinet, 21 June, Add. MS. 44641, fo. 135. The bill was then being amended in committee in the Commons. The committee stage ended, 3 July, and the bill passed as amended, 8 July.

[3] Granville to Gladstone, possibly 1 July, suggesting a baronetcy for Mr. Drewe, chairman of the N. Devon Liberal association, Add. MS. 44169, fo. 200, not printed.

[4] Tait to Gladstone, 5 July, urging 'that the Court of Appeal shall in Ecclesiastical matters be advised by the presence of Ecclesiastics', Add. MS. 44331, fo. 105. It related to clause 18 of the Supreme Court of Judicature Bill. Gathorne Hardy warned Gladstone, midnight, 3–4 July, of his amendment to transfer ecclesiastical appeals to the new court. Gladstone consulted cabinet colleagues of the Commons, wrote to Tait, 4 July, and raised the matter in the cabinet, 5 July; memoranda by Gladstone, Add. MSS. 44761, fo. 160; 44542, fo. 134; 44641, fo. 145. The amendment was accepted by the government.

[5] Gladstone accepted, 8 July, the Lord Mayor's invitation to dinner on 30 July, Add. MS. 44542, fo. 136. On 26 July he excused himself on account of illness, *ibid.*, fo. 141, and Selborne spoke for the government.

Colleagues anxious to accept I probably ought not to throw him over, but I think the inconvenience of my having to make a political speech at the close of this session wd be serious, & I am not inclined personally to attend, nor do I see any reason why unless so inclined you shd do so. Two City Dinners with the Lord Mayor in one Session for the first time—take it as you will it is a very bad precedent.

851. Mr. Gladstone to Lord Granville. [G.D. 29/29A]

10, Downing Street. Jul 7.73.

I understand from your note that the Queen now invites all the Ministers who are to attend at Balmoral for " weeks ".[1]

This being so I shall be happy to take my turn (it is likely enough to be the last), and if, as I suppose, it would fall somewhere about the last week of August, to take the first turn.

852. Mr. Gladstone to Lord Granville. [G.D. 29/62]

11, Carlton House Terrace. 7.45 Pm. Jul 8 [1873].

I see no better plan than that of the separate Bill—but in the Commons or the Lords as you think best.

I am utterly at a loss to comprehend the ' privilege '.[2]

853. Lord Granville to Mr. Gladstone. [Add. MS. 44169, fo. 207]

F.O. July 9/73.

The addition of snub [?], which I have suggested, is infinitesimal.

I have put " occasion " instead of " opportunity " at the beginning because at the end I suggest the insertion of " opportuneness ".[3]

854. Mr. Gladstone to Lord Granville.[4] [G.D. 29/62]

18, Carlton House Terrace. July 16. 73. 11¼ Pm.

The suggestion in Col. Ponsonby's note appears to be that Parlt shd present 100,000 crowns or some analogous sum to the Grand Duchess.[5]

[1] Cf. exchange between Granville and Gladstone with Gladstone's note on the cabinet, 5 July, Add. MS. 44641, fo. 147.

[2] Relates to Cairns's speech calling the Lords' attention to amendments, in the Commons committee, to the Supreme Court of Judicature Bill, to transfer Irish and Scotch appeals to the new court. Cairns argued that the Commons infringed the judicial privilege of the Lords, *Hans. Parl. Deb.*, 3rd ser., ccxvii. 10–24. Granville asked Gladstone's advice through Glyn ; see Glyn to Gladstone, 8 July, Add. MS. 44348, fo. 241. Selborne's advice to drop the amendment was followed, but the separate bill to deal with Scotch and Irish appeals was postponed.

[3] Relates to the draft of the Queen's reply to the address of the Commons on the settlement of international disputes by arbitration, see Granville to the Queen, 11 July, G.D. 29/36.

[4] Granville to Gladstone, 15 July, on the procedure for publishing the Queen's assent to the duke of Edinburgh's marriage, Add. MS. 44169, fo. 208, not printed.

[5] For Parliament's financial provision for the duke and duchess of Edinburgh, see *C.J.* (1873), pp. 402, 407.

This would be a departure from the arrangement made in the time of Lord Palmerston and approved by the members of the Opposition. It would destroy the whole argument from authority. Every one would be free to take a new starting point for himself as to the whole subject. We could not plead before the House the weighty assents wh the existing plan had received.

I saw at Lansville

Argyll Bruce
Kimberley Goschen
Cardwell

None of these saw their way to a departure from what was formerly arranged.

Anything sent to my House will find me for reply if need be before you go in the morning.

855. Mr. Gladstone to Lord Granville. [G.D. 29/62]

10, Downing Street. Jul 17. 73.

I have got the Telegram of yesterday from Sir H. Elliot [1] threatening the failure of your plans with respect to the Shah's visit to Constantinople.

He takes offence it seems at the defined term of 3 months. Why not make it a suspension during pleasure? The Turks could not object to this? And if the Persians did it wd be so unreasonable as at least to acquit us of responsibility.

It is singular that this acute man does not sufficiently see the vital importance of a thorough union with the Ottoman Power.

I have written this to save time.

856. Lord Granville to Mr. Gladstone.[2] [Add. MS. 44169, fo. 211]

18, Carlton House Terrace. [19 July 1873].

Is not this [3] rather in the "unprotected female" line—if one may say so without disrespect.

It is very natural that the Queen should wish to see her future daughter in law, but it is rather a large order insisting upon the Emperor of all the Russias bringing her over to be looked at.

And as to the religious question, surely if her children are to be brought up as Protestant, the Grand Duchess herself ought to have all the conveniences for her own religion.

But Brunnow told me some time ago that she would not require a chapel in the house.

[1] The Shah had agreed to end his European tour in Constantinople. Turkey suspended her regulations on the admission of Persian subjects for three months. Elliot telegraphed, 16 July, that the Shah was not satisfied, but the difficulty was overcome, F.O. 78/2269. Granville explained Turco-Persian relations in the cabinets of 21 and 28 June, Add. MS. 44641, fos. 135, 138.

[2] Granville to Gladstone, 19 July, giving a train time, Add. MS. 44169, fo. 210, not printed.

[3] The Queen to Granville, very private, 18 July, insisting on a visit from the Tsar and the grandduchess before the marriage, and objecting to her having a private Greek chapel, G.D. 29/36; see also letters of 19 and 20 July, *ibid.*, and G.D. 29/31. The chapel was allowed in the Marriage Treaty, 22 Jan. 1874, Parl. papers. [C. 901] (1874). lxxvi, 155.

857. Mr. Gladstone to Lord Granville.[1] [G.D. 29/62]

Private. 11, Carlton House Terrace. July 23. 73.

When I encouraged your discussing on all sides with the members of the Cabinet, I need hardly say I meant as to the more general & obvious likelihoods of the Reports of the several Committees,[2] not as to the contingent intimations conveyed to me by Glyn about supposed leanings or intentions of colleagues.

858. Lord Granville to Mr. Gladstone.[3] [Add. MS. 44169, fo. 220]

18, Carlton House Terrace. [6 August 1873].[4]

Monsell proposes to write a letter to Mr Gladstone, at once, stating that from information which he has recd, he believes he could not be returned for the County of Limerick again without a fierce contest, which he is not prepared to undertake, after the almost unanimous support he has hitherto received.

This communication to be considered " confidential " for the present.

He proposes to go to Ireland tomorrow, to arrange that an influential deputation should call upon him stating their regard for him, but asking his opinion as to Home Rule.

He will state his opinions to them, but decline to have a " desperate contest with old friends—this they will see will involve the necessity of placing his office at the disposal of the Prime Minister."

He has the strongest desire for the sake of his own character, that the Peerage should immediately follow.

Seen by Monsell.

He would like to keep the office till October.

859. Lord Granville to Mr. Gladstone. [G.D. 29/62]

Holmbury. Aug 7/73.

I send you a disagreeable correspondence.[5]

I hope I have said nothing wrong.

[1] Gladstone to Granville, 22 July, and reply, on the Queen's enquiry about the grandduchess's dowry, Add. MS. 44169, fo. 213, not printed.

[2] I.e. of the committee of public accounts. They revealed that the post office revenue and savings bank balances had been used for capital expenditure on the telegraph services without parliamentary sanction. For the debate see *Hans. Parl. Deb.*, 3rd ser., ccxvii, 1189–1232. The post office and Zanzibar contract scandals and Ayrton's unhandiness over the public parks caused ministerial changes. W. P. Adam replaced Ayrton at the Board of Works, Lowe moved to the Home Office, Baxter resigned the joint secretaryship of the Treasury, and Ripon and Childers resigned for personal reasons ; all announced, 7 Aug. Monsell resigned the post office, Nov.

[3] Granville to Gladstone, on the Zanzibar contract written in the cabinet, 25 July, Add. MS. 44641, fo. 174 ; Gladstone to Granville, 26 July, asking him to note the decisions of the cabinet of that day under named headings, *ibid.*, fos. 177–86 ; Granville to Gladstone, 6 Aug., enclosing a promise to Monsell of a peerage after his retirement, Add. MS. 44169, fo. 217, not printed.

[4] No. 858 was marked by Gladstone : ' Accepted by me Aug. 6, 11½ P.M.'

[5] The Queen to Granville, 6 Aug., protesting at the ministerial changes, 6 Aug., reply 7 Aug., G.D. 29/31. Cf. the Queen to Gladstone, 5 Aug., objecting to the appointment of Ayrton as judge-advocate-general, Add. MS. 44761, fo. 170. Gladstone wrote at the end of no. 859 : ' Excellent I think. The letter to me was similar. I send copy of reply for perusal. W.E.G. Au. 7.' Cf. Guedalla, i. 420–6.

860. Lord Granville to Mr. Gladstone. [Add. MS. 44169, fo. 225]

18, Carlton House Terrace. Aug 8/73.

Notwithstanding Mr Scudamore's promises to give particular orders about my telegraphic messages both your's arrived in one cover at 2 o'clock.

Lowe has been in the highest spirits and most agreeable—very complimentary to you.

I had a note this evening from the Queen. Everything serene, excepting regrets about Ripon's retirement.

I am anxious to hear whether Ayrton accepts.[1]

Please telegraph again if you wish me to come to London before Monday.

861. Lord Granville to Mr. Gladstone. [Add. MS. 44169, fo. 227]

Confidential. [9 August 1873].

Lowe has returned [2] in a more irritable state.

Whether owing to the fatigue of the journey, to the fresh attacks of the press, & to the want of cordiality on the part of the Queen I do not know.

He seems dissatisfied with the colleagues (excepting yourself) whom he met at Osborne—" Ripon affectionate & sentimental, Bruce exuberant in spirits. Every-one thinkin of himself and of no one else ".

I had given up the hope of giving any advice, but managed to do so this morning. He recd it admirably and with complete concurrence. But his self delusions about his own faults & merits, are extraordinary—praising and condemning himself in wrong directions.

He calculates there will be a surplus of 3,500,000 £ which will enable you to deal with local taxation, take off the sugar duties, and a penny off the Income tax.

He harps much on Dodson's appointment,[3] founded on Goschen's report of his bitterness during the Committee.

862. Lord Granville to Mr. Gladstone. [Add. MS. 44169, fo. 229]

Private. Holmbury. Aug 10/73.

Lowe has given me your message respecting the difficulty as to your seat.[4] I trust that the Law officers will be able to set the matter at rest—as it would be almost impossible for you to go back now.

It is hardly possible to conceive that the construction put by the Solicitor of the Treasury can be correct.

I hope to see you tomorrow, but if you are gone, I presume that I may deal

[1] Ayrton to Gladstone, 8 Aug., accepting the office of judge-advocate-general ' revived in its old form ', Add. MS. 44439, fo. 281. Sir R. Phillimore, admiralty judge, had held the office since Davison's death in May 1871, pending a re-arrangement of its duties. Ripon was replaced by Bruce, made Lord Aberdare, as lord president.

[2] From Osborne, where he had gone to carry through his change of office.

[3] As joint secretary to the Treasury *vice* Baxter.

[4] For considerations bearing on the question whether Gladstone's acceptance of the additional office of chancellor of the exchequer obliged him to seek re-election, see Morley, ii. 466–72.

with Count Munster, who has instructions to see me, in order that the Germans & ourselves may settle our joint instructions on the principles we have already laid down with respect to rebel Spanish vessels.[1]

I send back with many thanks your excellent answer to the Queen.

863. Mr. Gladstone to Lord Granville. [G.D. 29/62]

Hawarden Castle. Aug. 13. 73.

1. I take these four dispatches [2] of Sir A. Paget's (on their way back to the F. O.) almost at random as examples in which the dockets are to (you or) me quite useless for their main purpose, i.e. enabling me to judge whether I need read the paper. I have daringly added words to show my meaning—not as the best, for I hold that docketing is an art, & a practised docketer would do it much better.

2. I think it would be a convenience if you had lithographed forms for all *mere* covering letters, such in colour or otherwise that they might be recognised on the outside. The covering letters sometimes contain in a few words the point of the whole thing & are like a good docket to the paper inclosed. Then they are *most* useful. But one has to open & read in order to see whether they are of this class, or *merely* covering: and sometimes this is not discovered, such is the diffusiveness of forms, until over the leaf. All this is important to men who only get through their business by acting on this version of an old rule—" take care of the seconds, & the minutes will take care of themselves ". There would, if this suggestion were adopted, be an economy of manual labour.

864. Lord Granville to Mr. Gladstone. [Add. MS. 44169, fo. 231]

Private. Foreign Office. Aug 13/73.

I had a long conversation with Delane after dinner yesterday.

He acted great sympathy with the Gov. He made as good a speech about your personal merits, and " your place in history ["] as the Chancellor could do.

He lamented over Lowe's defects. Could not forgive him for having turned that great Governmental institution, the answering of questions in the House of Commons, into an element of weakness for the Gov. He was wroth at his not having made the slightest use of his great memory, or of his undoubted ability to prepare a decent budget speech.

He thought Ripon no loss, Bruce a gain at the Council Office, & in the House of Lords.

[1] Yelverton on the *Swiftsure*, protecting British lives and property in the Spanish ports, acted with Kommodore Werner of the *Frederic Karl* and seized two Spanish ironclads, which had gone over to the rebels of Cartagena. For conversation with Münster in which Granville prescribed the surrender of the ships to the Madrid government, see Granville to Adams, No. 41, 11 Aug., F.O. 72/1392. For discussion in the cabinets of 30 July, 2, 6 Aug., see Add. MS. 44641, fos. 187, 189, 191.

[2] Nos. 280, 281, 2 Aug., 283, 284, 4 Aug., all received 10 Aug. Nos. 280, 281, 284 bear Gladstone's additions to the statements of subject on the dockets, F.O. 45/219. Granville issued a circular dispatch to all representatives abroad on the importance of a clear docket about the content of a dispatch, see Granville to Thornton, No. 245, 22 Aug., F.O. 5/1429.

He thought a mistake had been made in playing the game of the last ten days in not comprehending Bouverie in the arrangement.

I asked him whether he thought it was of good example to buy a man of no extraordinary though good ability, who had tried to make himself as disagreeable as possible to a Gov.

He thought it would be easy to get him through Brand to give some striking proof of adhesion. He professed not to like him personally, but believed that the fact of his whig name, high character, large fortune, and a certain following among the radicals, would make him a useful accession to the Gov.

He was discomposed at my asking him what Dizzy thought of the new arrangements.

I cannot tell whether his gush meant gratitude for having recd information of the changes, and not having been left in the cold as he deserved to be—Whether it meant that on the whole it would be expedient for the Times to be on good terms with the Gov during the recess—or whether it was only a way, of giving me an opportunity (of which I did not avail myself) of giving him hints as to the character of the future minor changes.

He recommended James for the Solicitor Generalship.[1]

P.S. I have telegraphed that the Queen expects you on the 20th instead of the 18th.

I sent her a rota, & she postponed by two days the arrival of you, of Hartington & of me.

I hope this will not be inconvenient.

865. Mr. Gladstone to Lord Granville. [G.D. 29/62]

Hawarden Castle. Aug 14. 73.

1. The postponement of my journey to Balmoral is rather a convenience. I hope to be there on Wednesday morning.

2. Many thanks for your interesting account of the conversation with Delane. I have no vow recorded against Bouverie: but his value would be chiefly negative —and we have no room.

3. The question about my election is a disquieting addition to my present plurality. Yet I cannot but feel rather hopeful about the argument, which goes before Jessel tomorrow.[2] Lambert, who at first was adverse, has I think come to my side.

4. Fred. Cavendish's triumph [3] is a real pleasure. The Duke writes in great delight.

[1] Appointed solicitor-general, 26 Sept., *vice* Jessel who had become master of the rolls. For other changes see above, p. 389, note 2.

[2] See Jessel's opinion, 15 Aug., on Gladstone's seeking re-election at Greenwich, Add. MS. 44439, fo. 300.

[3] Cavendish was appointed a financial or extra lord of the Treasury since the offices of first lord and second lord (chancellor of the exchequer) were about to be held together by Gladstone. He vacated his seat and stood for re-election in the North-west Riding. The Conservatives announced they would not contest the election, 13 Aug. Cf. above, no. 5 note.

5. Lowe's mind is more than ever incomprehensible to me. I have written to him a very free letter.[1] I think you wise to do the same. If you care to see mine I will send it you. He has *rushed* now into the adverse opinion about Greenwich, having started in the opposite view: much too rapid, though he may prove right.

6. I hope the Commander of the Swiftsure will give, & if needful will be desired to give, a complete account of his proceedings, which seem to have gone a trifle beyond the mark.[2]

866. Mr. Gladstone to Lord Granville. [G.D. 29/62]

Hawarden Castle. Aug 15. 73.

1. On receiving your Monsell papers today I have telegraphed to you as follows.[3]

'I have received your envelope cannot agree to postpone announcement or to accelerate in any degree what is to follow after the performance of the act agreed upon for the beginning of October.'

In other words announcement, resignation, peerage, must all stand in the relative order & at the times fixed for them.

He really has pottered with this matter too much & too long; and the only alternative will be a sharper method of proceeding.

I hold his letter to me as *non avenu* till I hear again—it had better I think be with you.

2. I send you a letter which has just arrived from Hartington and copy of my reply.[4] I hope for *his own sake* he will retract.

3. It is a curious point which has been raised in Germany about taking German sailors and will require the very best advice.

4. The question about the seat *looms* larger & deeper: but through with it I go, come what may.

5. I inclose my letter to Lowe, in case it may remind you to do what you can to keep him straight.

I go on Tuesday to Balmoral.

[1] Gladstone to Lowe, 13 Aug., a highly personal analysis of Lowe's character, his intellectual impatience, and his selectivity in work, Add. MS. 44302, fo. 144. See below, nos. 866, 880, 882.

[2] See above, no. 862 note. Yelverton failed to execute the orders sent to him, 11 Aug., to surrender the Spanish ships; see below, no. 891.

[3] See Monsell to Granville, and enclosure for Gladstone, 11 Aug., asking that the peerage promised to him should be conferred at once so as to precede his resignation of the post office, G.D. 29/74; Gladstone to Granville, tel. 15 Aug., G.D. 29/62.

[4] See Gladstone to Hartington, 12 Aug., assuming that Spencer would retire from the lord-lieutenancy of Ireland in Dec., and that Hartington would not then stay as chief secretary, and asking whether he would return to the post office in Oct., Add. MS. 44542, fo. 149; Hartington to Gladstone, 14 Aug., putting his office at Gladstone's disposal but refusing the post office, Add. MS. 44144, fo. 110; Gladstone to Hartington, 15 Aug., arguing in detail against his total retirement, *ibid.*, fo. 112. Cf. B. Holland, *The Life of Spencer Compton, Eighth Duke of Devonshire* (1911), i. 123–6.

867. Lord Granville to Mr. Gladstone. [Add. MS. 44169, fo. 238]

Walmer Castle. Aug 16/73.

The enclosed letter of the Chancellor's [1] is in answer to queries which I sent him.

If you agree, I will send instructions accdgly and write to the French.

I do not agree with the Chancellor as to identical instructions with the French, even if the Germans do not concur.

The Germans have concurred, and the French who know our instructions, but have never sent theirs to us, have laid down the same principles.

All that remains to be done is to disapprove as mildly as possible of the past seizure of the vessels, and to strengthen the instructions we have already given against seizing them for the future.

868. Mr. Gladstone to Lord Granville. [G.D. 29/62]

Hawarden Castle. Aug 17. 73.

I was stupid about your first Telegram of today: it oddly happens that the Barba Rossa and the great Library in the Midland Counties apply in a degree to both. Your second came after post: and I can hardly answer by wire.[2] This letter will be in London tomorrow afternoon by 3.

Spencer's claim to retire appeared to me very fair. I have no doubt he has been sorely missed in Northamptonshire. Hardly any one has been so long Lord Lieutenant of Ireland. All withdrawals of good men are rather injurious to the Govt under present circs: but our fate must be decided by much bigger causes one way or the other than this. So that I did not feel entitled to remonstrate. Thus viewing it as a fact I connected it with Hartington's changing his place, and this again with Forster's replacing him. This last circumstance is not immaterial. Indeed it is very much indeed the reverse in the view of Bright: and I think any change in this respect might bring into question the fulfilment of the engagement, as the expectation of this change in the Educn Dept was mentioned when that engagement was entered into, and he attached much importance to it. This I think is the whole matter so far as I am concerned.

[1] See Granville to Selborne, 14 Aug., and Selborne to Granville, 15 Aug., agreeing that it was a mistake to have seized the Spanish ships (see above, nos. 862, 865), and urging joint action with France as well as Germany, G.D. 29/67; France did not co-operate, Macdonell to Granville, No. 120 confidential, 1 Sept., F.O. 72/1393; but the instructions to surrender the ships were strengthened, 20 Aug., F.O. 72/1392. See also Gladstone to Granville, tel. 17 Aug., agreeing with Granville 'on all points', G.D. 29/62.

[2] (i) Granville to Gladstone, tel. 10.8 a.m., 17 Aug.: 'The brother [Hartington] of Freddy and Eddy [Cavendish] has telegraphed his visit here today. Barbarossa of the great library in the Midland Counties [Spencer] has written to me for advice as to his final letter to you. What are your wishes'. Gladstone replied, tel. 2.20 p.m., 17 Aug.: 'What most strikes me is that under present circumstances it would be a very great mistake for himself [Hartington]. I told him I had directed my reply to be sent to you. Pray see it. You probably know Wolverton's opinion.' (ii) Granville to Gladstone, tel. 5.40 p.m., 17 Aug.: 'I have no doubt about my visitor [Hartington]. It was about his nominal chief [Spencer] I desired to know whether you wish that he should adhere to his proposal [to resign] or withdraw it.' Gladstone replied, tel. 9.5 a.m., 18 Aug. referring Granville to no. 868; all in G.D. 29/62. See also Spencer to Granville, 15 Aug., asking his advice how to proceed after mentioning resignation to Gladstone in June, G.D. 29/75.

Sir G. Jessel declares decidedly that my seat is not vacant; as decidedly, that have taken an office of profit.

About Delane another day.

69. Mr. Gladstone to Lord Granville. [G.D. 29/62]

Hawarden Castle. Aug 17. 73.

With reference to your question about the Cabinets, my impression is that hey will depend mostly on the state of the Ashantee business; but I should think he time would be about the 5th October, or soon after.[1]

70. Lord Granville to Mr. Gladstone. [Add. MS. 44169, fo. 244]

rivate. Walmer Castle. Aug 18/73.

I wrote to Monsell after the receipt of your telegram, and again after the receipt f your letter—adding to your words a civil expression of your regret that your rrangements prevented your meeting his wishes.[2]

In my last note I told him that I had informed you that I had his authority o send you his letter.

(But it may perhaps be as well to wait for a day or two before making use of it.) I thought it safer to clench the matter.

Wolverton writes suggesting that Monsell's Peerage should be postponed and ccompanied by others.[3]

I presume you will wish to keep the engagement on both sides—but the 2d uggestion appears to me good. Say James or Mellish (I presume you would consult he Chancellor) to fill up Westbury's place, and another excellent candidate if you an find one in your list. Have you a good Scotchman. Such a man plus a fortune, character, and real public service would be invaluable.

Please look at the list, or have it sent to me.

I can think of no one diplomatic, or Colonial.

Admiral Milne, Sir Bartle Frere, Hammond would not be of sufficient calibre.

871. Lord Granville to Mr. Gladstone. [Add. MS. 44169, fo. 31]

onfidential & secret. Walmer Castle. Aug 18/73.

My clumsy attempts at ingenuity have been complete failures.[4] You have vidently understood "the brother of Freddy & Eddy" and "Barbarossa of the reat library in the Midland Counties" as the same person, whereas the first was ntended for my visitor Hartington, and the second for Spencer who had written ne the enclosed letter, which I send you confidentially.

When you spoke to me in London, I considered, & you evidently considered

[1] The cabinet met 3 and 4 Oct. and 10 Nov., Add. MS. 44641, fos. 193–209; see below, nos. 890, 904, 906.

[2] See above, no. 866, and Granville to Monsell, two notes, 17 Aug., G.D. 29/77.

[3] Wolverton to Granville, 17 Aug., G.D. 29/73; cf. Wolverton to Gladstone, 22 Aug., Add. MS. 44348, fo. 267. Glyn had succeeded his father as Lord Wolverton, 24 July.

[4] See above, no. 868 note.

that Spencer's resignation, and Hartington's decision not to remain without him were "accomplished facts"—whereas, by Spencer's letter, he still seems to have doubts whether he ought to resign or not. Hartington on the other hand is evidently sore, that an obiter dictum of his to his brother on a contingency which he did not know was likely to occur, has been so readily taken as a means of quitting a place for another of his colleagues. But on the other hand he is evidently averse (after the proof which he thinks he sees that you would prefer to have Forster in Ireland rather than himself) to remaining thus. The Post office is exceedingly distasteful to him. He readily accepted it on the reconstruction of the Gov. He considered that he had been pitchforked into the War office, & that it was quite natural that he should have a lower office, but after having been so much pressed against his will to go to Ireland, and not being aware that the little which has been done in Ireland was owing to any fault of his, he has the strongest repugnance to go to the G.P.O.

(He may also feel although he does not mention it, that Monsell jumbled him up with himself in the neglect for which Monsell was turned out.)

He argues that his retirement in consequence of a change of Lord Lieutenancy is as good a reason for his retirement from office altogether, as his transfer.

I used every argument in my power as to the personal disadvantage his retirement would be to him at such a moment as this. I said some very disagreeable things, which he took admirably. I told him what a loss I thought he would be to the Gov. (which I suspect I was able to do with more *sincerity* than you could) and I believe myself to be right.

Nothing could be more honest, more candid, or shown better feeling towards you, than he did, but the effect of my oratory was small.

This morning I told him that I had reflected on the way of putting his case forcibly before you, and that I found it impossible.

We went over the whole thing.

I have been much embarrassed by not knowing whether you consider Spencer's resignation & its consequences as final. I shall know this evening but he will be gone.

Hartington & I agree that Spencer's reason has taught him that it is wise and expedient for all the reasons he gives to go, but that at least he is sorry to do so.

The difficulty of a successor is great.

Hartington says that the 'season' costs Spencer twenty thousand pounds.

Dufferin might accept it, as his folly about money matters amounts to insanity, but would Lansdowne, Cowper, or Lorne do so, who could not reduce the expenditure as in their case they would have to provide the outfit, which Kimberley says it is impossible to recoup excepting in two years.

The result of this morning's interview was a note, which you will probably receive with this letter—asking permission to see his father before giving his final answer.

If Spencer remains, or if the Gov of Ireland was put into Commission, and you could write to Hartington that although it would have been convenient to give the Secretaryship to Forster, you were satisfied with Hartington as an Irish Secretary, & wished him to remain, I think notwithstanding his disclaimers he would stay.

He would I believe have taken Ayrton's place. It appears to me that his objection to the Post office is insuperable, excepting by a personal interview with you. He is going to Bolton Abbey tonight.

Your second letter to him was excellent—the first was rather short, & not unlikely to produce the effect which it appears to have done viz that you were rather glad to get him out of the Irish office. With his rather brusque ways, he is more sensitive than one would suppose.

872. Mr. Gladstone to Lord Granville. [G.D. 29/62]

[On the rail]. Aug 19. 73.

I return Spencer's letter.[1] I have just received, *on the rail*, your telegrams of this morning [2]: but you will be clever if you catch me again before Balmoral.

I imagined Spencer to have settled the matter rather more than he seems to have thought but am quite content either way. Only I think a change in the Secretaryship desirable.

Ld Strafford's note is more flattering I fear than just: I can only plead hard work towards deserving it.

I am so glad of the good opinion of so consummate a judge about my letters to Lowe.

I cannot admit Hartington's right to be sore. There have been so many *obita dicta*: to me, &, as I learn, to Spencer, and not only to F. C[avendish]. A man has no right to put himself in the position of being able to say " I gave you clearly enough to understand I should go " or at his choice to say ' my place was not vacant & you had no right to think or speak of it to any one '. You will observe that I have only dealt with it contingently & have given Forster no pledge whatever.

Hartington has many good & fine qualities besides his birth: but I am tempted to say he sells them rather dear. I earnestly hope he will not go, & especially will not go in a huff—I am *altogether taken by surprise*. I assure you I am not without the fear of Bright's bolting.

I am past all matter of fear in a case like H[artington]'s, for I think the fate of the Govt will depend upon bigger things.

But your letter has been of great use to me & I send you a copy of one I have written to him.[3]

873. Lord Granville to Mr. Gladstone. [Add. MS. 44169, fo. 42]

Confidential. Walmer Castle. Aug 19/73.

I send you confidentially two letters which I have recd from Spencer yesterday

[1] Spencer to Granville, 15 Aug., G.D. 29/75; see above, no. 868 note.
[2] Acknowledging Gladstone's letter, no. 868, G.D. 29/62.
[3] Gladstone to Hartington, 19 Aug., two letters, the second more cordial, agreeing to his delaying his decision, Add. MS. 44542, fo. 158; see above, no. 871.

evening and from Bessborough this morning. Neither of them intended for your perusal—also a copy of my answer to Spencer yesterday evening.[1]

Your letter of yesterday only reached the F.O. at past 8 o'clock, & I recd it this morning.

My first letter which crossed Spencer's was merely [a] note saying "I hardly knew whether to be glad or sorry but I believe the former" and sounding him as to a visit before he left the Throne.

I am afraid the withdrawal of Spencer & Hartington with a nasty taste in their mouths, would be a great shake to the Gov.

The messenger is going. I will write again, but it will merely be verbiage.

874. Lord Granville to Mr. Gladstone. [Add. MS. 44169, fo. 44]

Private. Walmer Castle. Aug 19/73. 1 P.M.

When I saw you in London, I was delighted to see the relief you felt at your difficult arrangements having been made.

I am vexed now at being the channel through which more annoyance reaches you.

I had only a minute at least as regarded one letter to consider whether it was fair to the writers to send you Spencer's & Bessborough's letters.

I agree however with what Bessborough says about the difficulty of replacing Spencer. Although I am not so strong against Cowper, who is clever though absent, and can make very good splash speeches, is rich & a grand Seigneur—& moreover has a "pratiche [*sic*] frau"—but I admit he would not be good.

As for Lorne, the appointment would be popular, & She would be excellent. But I am afraid it would be the finishing stroke for him, who as it is is drifting into being a Prince Teck. But I conceive there would be an impossibility for Lorne or his father to find the money for the start—unless he intended to go on under a Tory Gov, which would be neither good for him or for us.

I am not sure that it would be possible now to keep Spencer & Hartington in their offices but it would make a vast difference whether they went out discontented, or under a strong pressure from you to remain.

The argument about Forster's removal is strong, and much strengthened by Bright's wish. But much as I like & respect Forster, I never saw any particular qualification in him for Irish Secretary excepting his supposed skill in arranging Educational questions which would no longer be available.

Rather odd to say, Hartington has been very civil to everybody in Ireland, and there is no doubt that with their temperament the Irish prefer the son of a great landed Irish proprietor of high rank, to a Yorkshire manufacturer with rough manners.

If the Post office is out of the question for Forster would Bright insist, if he knew all the circumstances of the case.

[1] Spencer to Granville, 17 Aug., on his having now settled to resign, G.D. 29/75; Bessborough to Granville, 16 Aug., regretting Spencer's supposed resignation, disapproving of Cowper as successor and suggesting Lorne or Lansdowne, G.D. 29/71; Granville to Spencer, draft and copy, 18 Aug., on his talks with Hartington and Spencer's mistake in thinking Gladstone had accepted their resignations 'with alacrity', G.D. 29/77.

I had an amiable letter from him this morning [1] and should be ready to write to him on the subject, though I should not be the best person to do so. I much doubt, pleased as he might be at the arrangement made for Forster, whether he would wish to squeeze out the other two.

On reading over this letter I am afraid that I may convey the erroneous impression that I think you have been behaving ill to Spencer & Hartington. As regards Spencer, he has no real case. If a man talks at two different times of the necessity of his resignation, and argues for its being made obligatory on him by other duties, he cannot complain if he is taken at his word. Hartington has perhaps more reason to complain that a declaration made to his brother upon an hypothesis of which he knew not the probability, should have been construed as a message to you, & acted upon without any enquiry. But his case is again weakened by his previous reluctance to remain in.

875. Mr. Gladstone to Lord Granville. [G.D. 29/62]

Balmoral Castle. Aug. 20. 73.

1. One thing I omitted to say yesterday in writing about Hartington—I feel he has been unjustly dealt with as to the G.P.O. Monsell seems never to have bestowed a thought in this matter upon any body but himself—and I considered that his return to the G.P.O. (which as I have told you I supposed would be otherwise agreeable—& this explains the succinctness of my words in writing to him) would be the most emphatic assertion on our part at least that he had been wholly free from blame in his administration there.

Had I dreamed of his preference for the B. of W. I should not have closed that door so speedily.

2. I have sent for the list of possible or intending Peers. I think your suggestion good.

3. I arrived this morning, in most brilliant clear cold. Ponsonby tells me *you* follow. On what day do you (or the second man) stand to arrive? There must it seems be a Council for me to take the Oath.

4. I postpone acting about Monsell till tomorrow—but the time is running on.

876. Mr. Gladstone to Lord Granville. [G.D. 29/62]

Balmoral Castle. Aug. 20. 73.

Many thanks for the inclosures. I do not see what you could have said more or better than you have said. We are in truth surprised all round. I will not discuss any question about complaint. The question is what is best to be done. Circular correspondences on these matters are difficult to conduct satisfactorily to an issue. I think that the best way will be to let these matters lie over until the October meeting and that this had better follow Oct. 1 as closely as may be.

I regret Bessborough's strong language about Cowper; and even more about

[1] Bright to Granville, 17 Aug., on Granville's suggestion of his return to office, the burdens of office and the difficulties caused by the Conservative majority in the Lords, G.D. 29/52.

Forster. Cowper's antecedents are certainly far better than those of Abercorn: and to call Forster a gorilla simply shows unacquaintance with him, & with the secret of his strength, for strength undoubtedly he has.

It would be very unfortunate, & would indeed be a strong measure, that Spencer & Hartington, if they go, should go at the same moment like Siamese.

If you agree about postponement perhaps you will work in that sense. In personal nearness there will at any rate be less risk of the rather ridiculous misunderstandings which have marked this last series of proceedings. My only desire in the matter is to act for the best. No man willingly makes a fool of himself, when things draw near a final wind up.

What a strange Mem. of P. about Bismarck. I should like a copy of it for record. One would rather have anticipated a more sympathetic view?

I am afraid that were I off my own hook and by letter to retract about S. and H. I should expose myself to stronger & more warrantable complaint in other quarters.

877. Lord Granville to Mr. Gladstone. [Add. MS. 44169, fo. 247]

Walmer Castle. Aug 21/73.

What answer shall I send to this good letter of Spencer—[1] query—ask him to wait till October?

Tell Ponsonby that the Queen has a rota from me in which Hartington is to be at Balmoral from the 3d of Septr instead of the 1st.

I am to go on the 19th instead of the 15th.

878. Lord Granville to Mr. Gladstone. [Add. MS. 44169, fo. 54]

No 2. Walmer Castle. Aug 21/73.

I have just got your letter, & will therefore write at once to Spencer to suspend action till October, telling him that it will be the most useful course for you.[2]

I wrote to Hartington yesterday,[3] telling him that I hoped he would follow your suggestion of delay—that it appeared to me that triangular communication from different parts of the Ud Kingdom was impossible.

879. Mr. Gladstone to Lord Granville. [G.D. 29/62]

Balmoral. Aug 22. 73.

It has been fixed that we shall have a Council here on Saturday the 30th when I am to complete the formalities of my change in office.

I sent your congratulations to the Queen.[4] It does not appear that the swimmers

[1] Spencer to Granville, 19 Aug., is missing, but cf. his letters of 21 and 22 Aug., agreeing to postpone any final decision till Oct., G.D. 29/75.

[2] There is no copy of Granville to Spencer, 21 Aug., in G.D. 29/77.

[3] Cf. Granville to Hartington, 19 Aug., Holland, *op. cit.*, 127. There is no copy in G.D. 29/54, but cf. also Hartington to Granville, 31 Aug., on his readiness to wait as long as necessary, *ibid.*

[4] See Granville to Gladstone, tel. 21 Aug., asking Gladstone to do this, G.D. 29/62. Prince Arthur and his *aide de camp* had been caught by a current while bathing off Trouville, 20 Aug.

were exhausted: but they seem to hint they were glad of assistance. The Queen evidently means him a jobation.

The Queen is very desirous now that the ex Duke of Brunswick is dead that progress should if possible be made in the matter of securing that succession to the son of the King of Hannover by way of compensation for the titular succession to his Father which he would resign. Bismarck as the incarnation of evil seems to be the impediment, with the Crown Prince and Princess behind him. It is a great misfortune if he is governed by a mania of centralisation and absorption. The Queen is quite satisfied with Lord Odo about this matter. She is on the other hand afraid of her daughter's views in politics & in religion. There may be some resemblance between this question in Germany, and that of the native princes in India: where I for one am on the side of those who wish not to absorb.

I have written to Monsell,[1] & have disposed of the 'early intelligence' according to your suggestion.

880. Lord Granville to Mr. Gladstone. [Add. MS. 44169, fo. 248]

Private. Walmer Castle. Aug 22/73.

Good as I thought your letter, I am not sure that this is not better.

From Lady Lansdowne accepting for Edmond Fitzmaurice, Lowe's private Secretaryship.

"Instead of having to persuade, I found myself pointing out the objections, some of which he admitted the force of, but he thinks the advantages to *himself* far outnumber them, and he hopes that in time he may learn to be useful to you.

He is very hardworking, very painstaking, & like his brother discretion itself.

I think he would write an essay better than a letter, a letter better than a note. I do not know that he would *smooth* down a ruffled deputation (you see I am supposing that you have ruffled it in the first instance)."

On this hint I spoke, and returned Lady L's letter with the enclosed.

881. Mr. Gladstone to Lord Granville. [G.D. 29/62]

Balmoral Castle. Aug 23. 73.

I send you very privately an interesting letter from Granville Vernon.[2] He is I apprehend a faithful relator.

I have not yet before me a complete list of Peerables (papabili). Rothschild is one of the best I know, and if I could but get from him a Mem. of certain services of his father as to money during the war I think it wd carry the case over all difficulty. But though I have begged & they have promised for about 4 years, I have never been able to get this in an available form.

I hope you have not thought me fractious on one of the subjects of our late correspondence.

[1] Gladstone to Monsell, 21 Aug., noted but not copied, Add. MS. 44542, fo. 160.

[2] Untraced, but see Gladstone to Granville Vernon, 23 Aug., replying on his published address to the Hawarden people on the provision of local infant schools, Add. MS. 44542, fo. 162.

The Chancellor recommends James for Sol. General. I suppose he may be the right man: but will hear what the A[ttorney] G[eneral] has to say.

Is Dizzy affecting to play Bismarck in speech?

P.S. I refer to you a letter just come from Ebury: & copy of my reply.[1]

882. Mr. Gladstone to Lord Granville. [G.D. 29/62]

Balmoral Castle. Aug 24. 73.

Spencer's letter is indeed just like himself & comforts me much.

Your recommendation to him is the right one. At the same time I know of no reason that would justify me in hesitating to say at once that if his view is altered as to his resignation, I hope he will stay. If I feel the delay till October to be desirable as to Hartington, it is from no dissatisfaction, but because though unpledged there are considerations of policy which may give that case a somewhat different aspect.

I write in haste for the messenger has been delayed by an accident, happily a harmless one.

I have just received with regret the inclosed letter from Cowper.[2] Please consider whether to remonstrate. It is odd that it should come just at the moment when his name had been in question for a high place. It is not wise.

I return your letter to Lowe which I frankly think much more likely to be of use to him than mine.[3]

The Council here will be early on the 30th: I leave after it. I will give your message to Ponsonby.

As the French are so obstructive in the Egyptian question, I do not think it will be bad for them if they get a lesson.[4]

The basis of the old *entente* or special alliance with that country is gone.

But what has become of the intense anxiety of the Austrians to be in all things one with us? [5]

883. Lord Granville to Mr. Gladstone. [Add. MS. 44169, fo. 250]

Walmer Castle. Aug 25/73.

I return G. Vernon's curious letter. It would have been a curious sight to see the two Bobadils trying to humbug one another, one so clumsy, the other so subtle in that art. I believe the Queen is quite aware of the process, but cannot resist it's viciousness, & suspect there is nothing which he does not try upon her, and upon her surroundings.

[1] Ebury's letter untraced, but see Gladstone to Ebury, 23 Aug., replying, on an evangelical alliance and the encouragement of religious liberty abroad, Add. MS. 44542, fo. 162.

[2] Cowper to Gladstone, 23 Aug., resigning the captaincy of the Corps of Gentlemen at Arms, not traced. No. 884 was docketed: ' under sec. ship of the Board of Trade ', by mistake, which caused Gladstone to write as in no. 886. He had charge of Board of Trade business in the Lords.

[3] There is no copy of Granville's letter to Lowe in G.D. 29/66; for Gladstone's see above, no. 865 note.

[4] For French policy on judicial reforms in Egypt, 1867–77, see F.O. 78/2742–52. For British policy on the Spanish ironclads and the French refusal to co-operate see Granville to Lyons, No. 402, 20 Aug., F.O. 72/1392; Granville to Lyons, private, 23 Aug., G.D. 29/109.

[5] See above, nos. 627, 629, 631, 632.

I (ignorant) should be inclined in favor of James.

I am for Rothschild being made a Peer—and in one sense his Peerage would be a complement to that of the Catholic. But for this especial purpose I should prefer some one to whom neither the Queen nor any one else could object.

No—I have not thought you "fractious".

You have rather puzzled me with Ebury. I presume the Queen would be well inclined, and that it would be popular. But if she begins patronizing one of these associations (which are generally composed of foolish men,) how can she refuse others. I will take a day to consider. I am not sure that I shall not send the correspondence to Ponsonby, who knows better what the practice has been than I do.

I have just seen the papers & presume that D E added much of his own.

884. Lord Granville to Mr. Gladstone. [Add. MS. 44169, fo. 56]

Secret. Walmer Castle. Aug 27/73.

I cannot pretend I am very sorry about Cowper, who is a very great friend of mine. I was wrong in persuading him to take the office in the Household, with the duties attached, which he has failed to discharge. I am sorry to say that two thirds of the business have been done for him in the Lords by Halifax, Kimberley or Morley, & he was most unhandy in explaining or working a bill. I do not see that if there are no other objections, why his resignation should prevent his having such an office as the Lord Lieutenancy. But he could not be serious in thinking his claims to be equal to those of Morley, who has had five years work & who like Lansdowne had done his business in the most complete & workmanlike manner. I should certainly not push him to go on, but tell him what is true that he ought to take a larger share in debate, and you might ask him not to announce his resignation for a few weeks.

In the meanwhile might I offer it from you to Morley, but I am not sure that he will accept.[1]

885. Mr. Gladstone to Lord Granville. [G.D. 29/62]

Balmoral Castle. Aug 28. 73.

1. I am not aware of any intention or disposition to delay acting on the vote of the House of Commons in the case of Dover Harbour: but I will send your note to Dodson with a minute in that sense.

2. You were right in supposing that my communication to D[elane] was confined to the case of M[onsell]. I do not think his appended speculations conveyed much daylight but they were not ill meant.

3. I have had a good letter from Bright about Education.[2] I have told him that I think it must be for the present to a *certain extent* an open question among us.

[1] Gladstone to Morley, 15 Sept., offering him the captaincy of the Corps of Gentlemen at Arms *vice* Cowper, Add. MS. 44440, fo. 66. Morley refused, Clarendon also, 5 Dec., and Ilchester took office, Jan. 1874, Add. MS. 44441, fos. 175, 182, 245; see below, nos. 937, 940, 943, 945.

[2] Bright to Gladstone, 25 Aug., refusing to rejoin the government if that should lead his Birmingham constituents to expect concessions on the Education Act such as Gladstone was resolved against, Add. MS. 44113, fo. 64; Gladstone's reply, 27 Aug., *ibid.*, fo. 68. Bright returned as chancellor of the duchy of Lancaster, Oct., below, no. 905.

886. Mr. Gladstone to Lord Granville. [G.D. 29/62]

Balmoral Castle. Aug 28. 73.

Please to send Cowper's letter to Downing Street. I write to him as you advise.[1] But the office is I am sorry to say pre-engaged—to the House of Commons. Our official staff there is very low and we cannot afford to weaken it by transfer to the House of Lords.

I go Sat. afternoon—to reach Hawarden Thursday—Naworth Tuesday.

887. Mr. Gladstone to Lord Granville. [G.D. 29/62]

Balmoral Castle. Aug 29. 73.

1. I have been examining the Russian counter-project of Marriage Treaty and comparing it with some old ones. My observations on it are in a paper of which H.M. has been in possession & which will doubtless come to you. I do not see, after long conversations with the Queen, that it is likely to present any insurmountable difficulty as to the substance, but it raises a number of points which will require careful handling both to clear the meaning & to set the expression right, besides some real amendment. It seems to me, and the Queen is strong in this sense, that the matter is not likely to be readily adjusted except by personal conference between well qualified people. I suppose the first thing will be to let the lawyers see it: and then to proceed with the materials which may be in hand. It would be well settled between you & Brunnow but I do not know whether this is possible.[2]

2. The Queen makes much difficulty about the Army Complaints Commission. I have not at all given in as to the argument but have said probably it would be well that the Cabinet should again be consulted. She expressed an opinion that you were in some way more favourable to her views.[3]

Please to consider the case of the Maharajah (see the inclosure): & give me your view of it as a House of Lords matter.[4]

888. Lord Granville to Mr. Gladstone. [Add. MS. 44169, fo. 254]

18, Carlton House Terrace. Aug 31/73.

The Queen wrote to me [5] to ask me to press you to add two military men to the Commission. I said in reply that I could not do so, as the Duke of Cambridge had impressed on me twice that there should be no soldier on it, and I had informed the Cabinet accordingly.

[1] Gladstone to Cowper, 28 Aug., asking him to delay announcing his resignation until Oct., and hoping that he would be more active in the Lords, Add. MS. 44542, fo. 167; see above, nos. 882, 884.

[2] Relates to the arrangements for the duke of Edinburgh's marriage. Cf. the Queen to Granville, 28 July, tel. 31 July, 4, 30 Aug., G.D. 29/36. See above, no. 856.

[3] Cf. Gladstone to Cardwell, 29 Aug., on the Queen's pressure for the appointment of Lord Grey and Sir G. Grey to the commission, Add. MS. 44542, fo. 167.

[4] Biddulph to Gladstone, 28 Aug., proposing Duleep Singh for an English peerage; see below, nos. 892, 903 note, 907, 972, 974. 975.

[5] The Queen to Granville, 27 Aug., G.D. 29/31.

889. Lord Granville to Mr. Gladstone. [Add. MS. 44169, fo. 255]

18, Carlton House Terrace. Aug 31/73.

I send another letter from Spencer.[1]

I think you have been misled by the docket on Cowper's letter, which appeared to be not quite correct.

Cowper is Captain of the Gentlemen at Arms, and Gold stick. (I believe these appointments are always held by a Peer.)

Holding this office he represented the Board of Trade in the Lords.

890. Mr. Gladstone to Lord Granville.[2] [G.D. 29/62]

Naworth Castle. Sept 3. 73.

I now learn from Kimberley [3] that the probable period for further consideration of our plans about the expedition against the Ashantees will not be till the close of November. This being so, *that* cause for a Cabinet at the beginning of October no longer exists.

I think I might perhaps manage the matter of the Army Grievances Commission in writing with the aid of what you have done.

Could you contrive to take Hawarden on your way northwards or southwards? The former of the two would be far preferable, as sooner: & also because I think Bright will soon be wishing to fix the terms of his Address. Should I try to get him to meet you? I should like you to be in possession of the most exact knowledge of his position with reference to the question of Education.

My fear is that that question will eventually either split the party, or fatally cripple it for a time in regard to Parliamentary action. I personally have no fear of the secular system: but I cannot join in measures of repression against voluntary Schools. The present question however is what we are to expect from Bright whose return to office we are making use of as a means of at least temporary reconciliation. We must not therefore omit to consider on what terms we can expect him to arrange matters with his constituents. I return Spencer's letter.

891. Lord Granville to Mr. Gladstone. [Add. MS. 44169, fo. 259]

Private. C. H. Terrace. Sep 5/73.

My answer to the Queen was verbatim what I sent you, but I preceded it by saying that I did " not know how the commission was composed—that it had been

[1] Spencer to Granville, 29 Aug., on his hope of leaving Ireland by the end of the year, G.D. 29/75.

[2] Granville to Gladstone, 31 Aug., congratulating on Agnes Gladstone's engagement, Add. MS. 44169, fo. 253, and reply, 3 Sept., G.D. 29/62, not printed; Gladstone to Granville, 31 Aug., on the proposal to make Coleridge P.C., Add. MS. 44542, fo. 169, and reply, 3 Sept., agreeing, Add. MS. 44169, fo. 257, not printed.

[3] See Kimberley to Gladstone, 1 Sept., on Wolseley's instructions, Add. MS. 44225, fo. 87. His mission arose from the Ashantee attack on the Gold Coast. The cabinet was to decide on his report whether to send reinforcements. This was expected mid-Nov. if he left England by 11 Sept. The cabinet met and agreed on the aims of operations against the Ashantees, 3, 4 Oct.; considered Wolseley's report and agreed to send white troops, 17 Nov.; approved instructions on policy and peace terms, 21 Nov., Add. MS. 44641, fos. 192–7, 204–6, 218–28. See above, no. 869.

proposed to consist of two judges of high standing and Lord Derby, and if the latter refused, then Ward Hunt.

I presumed she had calculated to [*sic*] a more favorable answer to her commands, or that she alluded to my having, when reporting the decision of the Cabinet held at your house, said I thought it was a wise decision not altogether to refuse the Commission.

I heard from Munster that the Russians were much pleased " (and probably I dare say much surprised) " at finding from the Khan of Khiva's papers, that our language to him had been what was reported by us.

I shall be delighted to go to Hawarden. What would suit me best geographically, would be to go to you on the 30th on my return from Balmoral, but if more convenient to you I could pay you a visit on Friday next the 12th.

I am not competent to give an opinion on the Maharajah Peerage from the Indian point of view, but otherwise I see no objection. I think the offer ought to be accompanied by the expression of a wish that H. H. while retaining his perfect independence, does not go into the House as a decided partizan.

Yelverton appears to have been in a most unaccountable fidget to act against his instructions. Why did he not remain satisfied with the Status quo. Carthagena is the place, where his fleet is of more use than anywhere else at this moment.[1]

892. Mr. Gladstone to Lord Granville. [G.D. 29/29A]

Hawarden Castle. Sept 7.73.

I must begin, in a very unbusiness-like manner, by thanking you for your beautiful gift to Agnes, and still more for the letter with which it is accompanied. I am so glad, after a domestic crisis of this kind, to find myself back here with my wife & all my children.

It was with compunction that I sent you yesterday a Tel. proposing the 12th as preferable to the 30th. But I feel it will be advantageous to consider with you, if you can come, earlier than the 30th, the position of Bright, the question of changes in the Irish Government, the time for a Cabinet, besides the Greenwich seat, the Maharajah, & perhaps some other minor matters (though the G. seat *might* grow out of that category).

Shall I ask Bright to come on the 12th ? You will I hope stay as long as you can. There is some question of the Odos in the offing. My brother in law I am afraid will not be here, on account of a visit to Chatsworth.

I hope you will 'think thrice' before agreeing to other than moral protection, or at least to protection involving the *use of force*, for Austrians & Swedes.[2]

[1] For Yelverton's instructions to surrender the ironclads see above, no. 865. He had sent the ships to Gibraltar, 3 Sept., and evaded both the Cartagena rebels and the Spanish admiral from Madrid ; see Admiralty to Foreign Office, 1 Sept., and mem. by Hammond, F.O. 72/1393.

[2] Macdonell to Granville, tel. 5 Sept., received 6 Sept., reporting the request of the Austrian *chargé d'affaires* for the protection of the British navy for Austrian and Swedish subjects in Bilbao, F.O. 72/1342.

893. Lord Granville to Mr. Gladstone. [Add. MS. 44169, fo. 263]

Capesthorne, Crewe. Sep 7/73.

I will be with [you] on Saturday the 13th please.

I have got another letter from Goschen in a state of enthusiastic admiration of Yelverton & his fleet.[1]

I have answered by stating the reasons why, although there is always something pleasant & popular in a splash, which shows spirit & dash, the conduct of the naval men are [*sic*], like the sun, not without a speck.

I forgot to return the enclosed letter from Ponsonby.

I have got a little gout, the result of a wet walk and a cold drive—but hope to [go to] Halifax, Hickleton, Doncaster tomorrow.

894. Mr. Gladstone to Lord Granville. [G.D. 29/29A]

Hawarden Castle. Sept 9.73.

Lowe's speech at Sheffield is really too bad, &, free as I believe it is from all evil intention, it illustrates the incurable solecisms of his extraordinary mind.

1. He begins with half a column on a wonderful meeting of elderly gentlemen at the inception of the Government. It is pure romance.

2. He says no C. of E. before him did Treasury business but left it to a subordinate official. Pleasant for Stansfield, Baxter, Dodson! Wise, to depreciate & disparage perhaps the most important secondary office of the Government! Consistent when he was incessantly complaining Baxter would not do the Secretary's work, & threw it upon him! Also wholly untrue. Some have done more some less. No one probably more than Lowe, but some as much. I did less, perhaps much less. But I hold that the first duties of C. of E. are outside the Treasury. One of these is to look after & controul the great expenditures & Estimates. In this duty I am sorry to say he was wretchedly deficient: yet he coolly takes to himself the credit of Army & Navy reductions which is due to Cardwell & Childers (who in his admirable speech did not say a word, I think, for himself) and with which every member of the Cabinet had about as much to do as he had. I can speak from experience for I know what it has been to have had cast upon my shoulders the most important & most offensive duty of the Finance Minister. I must also say he has been most unsatisfactory in another capital duty, that of attending the H. of C. on questions of expenditure.

3. Take even his Thames Embankment question—Unless my memory deceives me I had to use some effort to keep him up to the mark and prevent his receding & giving up the point!

I think it well to deposit this explanation with you—with no one else. This exorbitant boasting is very foolish. He has ample merit to stand on, in a great amount of patient labour done, & generally well done & with good results, for the public. Much

[1] Goschen to Granville, private, 1 Sept., F.O. 72/1393, and Thursday evening [4 Sept.]: 'Yelverton . . . has got out of the imbroglio . . . with great credit and éclat . . . It is really refreshing to find a man who does not shrink from taking upon himself tremendous responsibilities', G.D. 29/54. Granville's reply, untraced.

of the unpopularity is unjust : a little patience would set all right. I am afraid this speech may provoke attack or criticism, and these will be formidable if they come from competent men—in or out of office.[1] I have been telegraphing hard to Hammond today about the Austrian & Swedish request (where I want to generalise the answer more) [2] & about Deerhound as bearing on the case of the Ironclads.[3]

895. Mr. Gladstone to Lord Granville. [G.D. 29/62]

Hawarden Castle. Sept 9. 73.

I have thought it best to send through Hammond by wire a suggestion which occurred to me that the conduct of the Spaniards in the case of the Deerhound might afford us a fair plea for holding our hands in the case of the Ironclads—& thus open a way of escape from a serious though I hope a temporary difficulty.

Before I got the facts about the Deerhound I had been inclining to the following conclusions.

1. Loyalty (*loyauté*) binds us to restore the ships if the Spanish Govt is really able or presumably able to receive them.

2. That being so it would be unworthy to be deterred by rebel threats at Carthagena.

3. These threats should be met by sending to that place *all* the British Naval force we can collect for the occasion.

896. Lord Granville to Mr. Gladstone. [Add. MS. 44169, fo. 265]

Hickleton, Doncaster. Sep 10 73.

If you approve, will you send the enclosed [4] to Hammond, with any alterations that occur to you. We have laid before the law officers all the information that we officially receive, and they continue to say that they have not enough data to give an opinion.

We ask information from our Chargé d'Affaires, our Consuls, and from the Admiralty.

[1] Lowe spoke at the Cutlers' feast, 4 Sept., boldly defending the government, *The Times*, 5 Sept., p. 3. The remainder of no. 894 is part of the letter in Gladstone's copy, Add. MS. 44452, fo. 175 ; but is an undated document, marked by Hervey as received for filing, 25 Sept., in G.D. 29/62 separated from the rest of the letter in G.D. 29/29A.

[2] See above, no. 892 ; and Gladstone to Hammond, tel. 9 Sept. : 'Why not answer we are not prepared to enter into any engagement, but civil and naval functionaries will undertake irrespective of nationality to fulfil any duties of humanity which their more immediate & direct obligations may allow them to undertake also adding explanations', Add. MS. 44183, fo. 500.

[3] See Gladstone to Hammond, tel., that the Spanish seizure of the *Deerhound*, 18 Aug., 'would be warrant for holding our hand' in surrendering the ironclads, *ibid.*, fo. 499. See also Hammond to Gladstone, 9 Sept., *ibid.*, fo. 501, and to Granville, tel. 3.30 p.m., 12 Sept., reporting his communications with Gladstone, F.O. 72/1393. The *Deerhound*, an English ship, was alleged to be carrying arms for the Carlists.

[4] Granville to Macdonell, tel. sent 11 a.m., 11 Sept., instructing him not to discuss the surrender of the ironclads until the *Deerhound* was restored and her crew released, and hoping that Spain by delay would not 'destroy all appearance of spontaneity', F.O. 72/1430. Cf. Granville to Goschen, 10 Sept., G.D. 29/54.

In the meanwhile these Englishmen are in Prison, & there would have already been an immense explosion, if they had been liberals instead of Foreign Carlists.

Not only Sir R. Peel, but Lord Penzance was a good deal excited about it yesterday.

Halifax approves the enclosed draft.

I have sent a copy to Hammond. If you agree please telegraph. If you make alterations please send them on by the messenger.

à Samedi—I have told Hammond to hold his hand about Swedes & Austrians.

897. Mr. Gladstone to Lord Granville. [G.D. 29/62]

Hawarden Castle. Sept 10. 73. 11.45 Pm.

Receiving your Messenger & proposed telegram at 11.30 P.M. I send it on by Messenger during the night to Hammond and do not telegraph to him at this hour.

I only altered 'destroy all' into 'impair the' (appearance of spontaneity).

I would telegraph to Yelverton, I think, that on account of new circumstances on which it is not necessary to enter he is absolutely to hold the vessels until further orders? [1]

I had no idea until yesterday of the scandalous character of the case of the Deerhound.

I hope you will be able to give us a pretty liberal length of visit.

No time for answer from Bright yet—Wolverton is also asked—Jim Wortley here, a bachelor.

898. Mr. Gladstone to Lord Granville. [G.D. 29/25A]

Hawarden Castle. Sept. 18. 73.

I learn from Forster [2] that I am perfectly free as regards him and therefore Hartington is quite welcome to remain where he is if he likes.

I have laid to heart your words on parting; which have given me food for reflection because I think I have been as civil to him as I can honestly be: having a high opinion of his gifts, but being dissatisfied with the manner in which he uses them with reference to the business of the Government in the House of Commons.

Under these circumstances, and as he (very properly) called you into council, I should be glad if you would carry on this matter with him, and perhaps you might not dislike it.

[1] Done, F.O. 72/1393. For surrender of the *Deerhound*, 20 Sept., see Macdonell to Granville, tel. 20 Sept., F.O. 72/1342. Assurances of indemnification if British property suffered at Cartagena were then asked from Spain and the surrender of the ironclads promised in return, to Macdonell, tel. 24 Sept., F.O. 72/1393. For the surrender of the ships, 26 Sept., Admiralty to Foreign Office, 26 Sept., *ibid*. See below, no. 899.

[2] Forster to Gladstone, 17 Sept., answering Gladstone's note, 15 Sept.: he was 'quite right in supposing that I do not *wish* to go to Ireland', Add. MS. 44157, fo. 84.

899. Mr. Gladstone to Lord Granville. [G.D. 29/29A]

Hawarden Castle. Sept. 19. 73.

You will have received my Telegram.[1] I hope it was in time. The main points are the two first.

1. As to Peerages please to read Wolverton's letter within.[2] I do not say we ought permanently to stay our hand; but he is always well worth hearing. I write to C. Howard.[3]

2. Cardwell & Kimberley wish me to agree to the purchase for £30000 of 15 miles of Railway for the contingency of our deciding to invade South Africa. I had already stated the need of information about this business for the Cabinet as well as myself—we have never had any I think except a few sentences *vivâ voce*. And I have told Cardwell that if it be necessary to proceed in this matter now, I do not feel able to do it without a Cabinet.[4] At such a Cabinet Bright should if possible be present—and I *may* therefore have to ask you to get an earlier day fixed for the Council than we had contemplated.

3. The Chancellor evidently took the right point about the Deerhound but it is fortunate for us that the Spanish Government are so unreasonable. From the way they behave I am now thankful that we have something to hold against the Deerhound.[5]

[P.S.] Hammond might come separately a while after if thought right.

I had almost forgotten Wolverton's mention of my son. There is I think more than one conclusive reason against moving him at present.

900. Lord Granville to Mr. Gladstone. [Add. MS. 44169, fo. 84]

Balmoral Castle. Sep 20/73.

I have recd your letter this evening. I found a telegram last night—& have not alluded to the Council, or to Hammond. I suppose the last sentence " consider

[1] See Gladstone to Granville, tel. 19 Sept. : ' Please delay fixing Council or doing anything about the honour for H[ammond] which we discussed also consider vacant Lord Lieutenancy ', Add. MS, 44169, fo. 267. Hammond's retirement at the end of Sept. occasioned the offer of a peerage, conferred Feb. 1874. Cf. above, p. 261, note 3; see below, nos. 905, 972.

[2] Wolverton to Gladstone, 17 Sept., doubting the popularity of the proposed peerages: Howard, Moncreiff, Monsell, James, Erle and Milbank; suggesting the transfer of W. H. Gladstone from the Treasury to the Board of Trade, Add. MS. 44348, fo. 275. The first three were made peers, Jan. 1874, but Coleridge represented the legal profession instead of James or Erle. For Monsell's peerage, see above, nos. 866, 870, 875, 879, below, no. 911.

[3] Gladstone to C. Howard, 19 Sept., proposing a peerage for his brother, Add. MS. 44542, fo. 183. Admiral Howard became Lord Lanerton.

[4] Gladstone to Cardwell, 19 Sept., Add. MS. 44542, fo. 182.

[5] See above, nos. 896, 897; see also Macdonell to Granville, tel. 17 Sept., received 18 Sept., reporting Spain's evasion of her undertaking to surrender the *Deerhound*, F.O. 72/1342. This prompted Gladstone to Hammond, tels. 16, 18 Sept., demanding an apology for the misuse of the British flag by the Spanish vessel capturing her and urging that Macdonell should refuse everything till she was released, Add. MS. 44183, fos. 506–8; Gladstone to Hammond, 20 Sept., F.O. 72/1393.

the Lord Lieutenancy vacant" means that you have heard from Spencer, who elects to go. Is this so.[1]

I am afraid you misunderstood my words as an indirect attack upon you in re Hartington, whereas I meant them in a different sense. He is a little of a spoiled child, as who would not be in his personal & social position.

But he is an excellent straightforward fellow, and with all his rather brusque & downright manner, is the reverse of self confident. Anything like coldness from you would cut him to the quick, whereas the effect of a few kind words *from you*, I know to have an immense effect [*sic*].

I agree with Wolverton that the less changes we have at present the better, and I believe that Hartington remaining would be good for us all, and especially for himself.

I will write in the sense you indicate, as soon [as] I hear what Spencer has done.[2]

The Queen told me last night that she had never known you so remarkably agreeable.

901. Mr. Gladstone to Lord Granville. [G.D. 29/29A]

Hawarden Castle. Sept. 21. 73.

I send you a letter from Spencer [3] which I received this morning: I hope he will remain.

I also send a letter *to* Goschen which may lead to an application to you about a Council.[4] I trust you will not think me over fastidious: but I think that in London they have in zeal & anxiety about the thing itself proceeded rather far upon their own authority, as will sometimes happen.

Please send my letter back through *Halifax*, who should see it.

902. Mr. Gladstone to Lord Granville. [G.D. 29/29A]

Hawarden Castle. Sept. 22. 73.

I am very well pleased that I had not inadvertently given Hartington offence. My view of him is I think the same as yours. There is every likelihood that he may yet have to pass from 10 to 20 years in the House of Commons; and his rôle there ought to be a very important one with his excellent brother F. to back him.

I hope my Telegram was in time this morning to remove the misapprehension

[1] See above, no. 899, note 1; Gladstone to Granville, tel. 9.0 a.m., 22 Sept., replying 'no' since he had meant the lord-lieutenancy of Cambridgeshire not Ireland and adding that he was puzzled about the British title to interfere in Morocco, G.D. 29/62.

[2] Granville to Hartington, 22 Sept., untraced. It induced Hartington to agree to remain in office if Spencer did so, to Granville, 24 Sept., G.D. 29/22A.

[3] Spencer to Gladstone, 20 Sept., blaming himself for Gladstone's thinking him resolved to resign and offering either to remain, especially if Hartington did so, or to go, Add. MS. 44307, fo. 171. See below, no. 904.

[4] At the Council held at Balmoral, 30 Sept., Goschen's proposal for increasing the number of lieutenants retiring from the service under the Order in Council, 4 Aug., was approved, *London Gazette*, 10 Oct.

into which I had misled you. It also expressed a scruple of mine about Morocco but perhaps our warning is to be on behalf of British Jews & Christians.[1]

From what is going on in London I presume we shall have a Cabinet some 10 or 12 days hence. If Hartington remains, as I expect, there will be the G.P.O. to fill. Perhaps this had better be reserved until we meet.

The Queen is very kind. I hope my manners will continue to mend: also, that she will not change her mind when she finds (today) that I am obliged to thwart her about a Winchester canonry for which she wants me to recommend a respectable man of no calibre, Mr Phipps. I really think my own relations as good as Sir C. Phipps's, and I have never put them forward. I had recommended Dr Lowe a man of very eminent services to Middle Class Church Education, and a valued supporter also of Dodson.[2]

I am glad to find we are to see your brother here tomorrow.

903. Lord Granville to Mr. Gladstone. [Add. MS. 44169, fo. 268]

Balmoral Castle. Sept 22/73.

As soon as I learnt the meaning of the phrase in the Telegram about the Lord Lieutenancy, I wrote to Hartington, & believe that the letter will find him in London.[3] This evening I found the enclosed letter from Spencer.[4] I wish he had saved you the trouble of another letter, but a very few words from you will settle the matter.

I have spoken to Ponsonby and to Biddulph about the Maharajah,[5] and I am told the Queen quite understands now the difficulty about Whitby, which she had not previously done. Biddulph has never had an answer to his letter, enquiring from Col Oliphant what was the state of the case. It was a cautious letter, & I believe he will write another, saying that it is not necessary to answer his first.

904. Mr. Gladstone to Lord Granville. [G.D. 29/29A]

Hawarden Castle. Sept. 24. 73.

1. I propose to fix a Cabinet for Thursday in next week if I find that you can be present.[6]

[1] See above, no. 900 note. On the death of the Sultan, 11 Sept., Hay summoned a warship from Gibraltar and issued a strong warning on the protection of British lives and property in case of disorders, to Granville, tel. and No. 54, 18 Sept., F.O. 99/155. Gladstone related his proceedings to earlier instructions on Jewish persecutions, to Hay, No. 23, 26 Aug., F.O. 99/153.

[2] Dr. E. C. Lowe accepted the canonry of Ely, 2 Oct., Add. MS. 44440, fo. 140; F. J. McDougall, that of Winchester, 27 Sept.. *ibid.*, fo. 115.

[3] See above, no. 900 note.

[4] Spencer to Granville, 21 Sept., G.D. 29/75.

[5] See above, nos. 887, 891, 892. It was rumoured that Duleep Singh intended to stand for Whitby in opposition to W. H. Gladstone at the next election. He published a denial; Gladstone to Biddulph, 29 Aug., and to Ponsonby, 7 Sept., Add. MS. 44542, fos. 168, 174. The honour was postponed, Gladstone's mem. of points agreed on with Granville, 3 Oct., Add. MS. 44641, fo. 199; below, nos. 972, 974, 975.

[6] The cabinet was summoned, 26 Sept., for 3 Oct.; see above, no. 890. See also Gladstone to Goschen and Cardwell, 23 Sept., refusing further preparations for an expedition against the Ashantees without the cabinet, Add. MS. 44542, fo. 185; Gurdon to Granville, tel. 25 Sept., G.D. 29/62.

It is rather urgent on account of War Office & Admiralty preparations for movements on the Gold Coast against Ashantee. I have not been able to sanction without the Cabinet all that Cardwell & Goschen wished.

2. Will you kindly consider the inclosed [1] & let me have an answer as soon as you can. If you are able to speak by Telegraph call him Hurst and I shall understand.

3. A letter from me which Spencer would receive yesterday will I hope have settled the business of the Lord Lieutenancy.[2]

It is a little difficult, even with that excellent man, to hit the right point between wind & water.

Your brother is here but I am sorry to say inenviably goes tomorrow.

H.M. has behaved right well & kindly about the Canonry.

905. Lord Granville to Mr. Gladstone. [Add. MS. 44169, fo. 270]

Private. Balmoral Castle. Sep 24/73.

I got your telegram about the Council—& one from Bright—& telegraphed to you in Downing St that it would be held on Tuesday the 30th.[3]

Does it mean an early Cabinet. I should like to know as soon as possible please.

The Ashantee war perturbs me a good deal.

Goschen must begin to think there is some limit to his sentiment that it was so refreshing in these times to find people ready to act on their own responsibility.

The proceedings of the naval officers on the Cape Coast seem to have been most imprudent.

I have asked Hammond to ascertain from the Admiralty the facts about the Albertina the American Barque.[4] I have some doubts whether they are justifiable.

Dover [5] is an unpleasant addition to our list.

Forbes had been somewhat distasteful to the liberal party, & many of the lower sort were not likely to vote without being paid, but on the other hand the head of the liberal party there told me that he would have no difficulties raised by the Education, or by the Licensed Victuallers' question.

I send you back Wolverton's letter—also Hammond's answer to my letter,[6]

[1] Not traced.

[2] See above, no. 901; Gladstone to Spencer, 21 Sept., on his 'remaining over the winter', Add. MS. 44542, fo. 184; Spencer to Gladstone, 26 Sept., written in Hartington's presence, agreeing to remain and closing the incident, Add. MS. 44307, fo. 174. Cf. Spencer to Granville, 26 Sept., G.D. 29/75.

[3] See Gladstone to Granville, tel. 23 Sept., that he had asked Bright to tell Granville whether he could take office as chancellor of the duchy on 'Monday or Tuesday', G.D. 29/62. Bright took office at the Council at Balmoral, 30 Sept., *London Gazette*, 3 Oct.

[4] Relates to a ship seized by the naval commander off Cape Coast on suspicion of landing supplies for the Ashantees, see Colonial Office to Foreign Office, 19 Sept.; and minute by Hammond that the matter was 'unintelligible' and by Granville that he had seen the Admiralty dispatches and ordered a reference to the law officers, F.O. 84/1382.

[5] E. W. Barnett, the Conservative candidate, defeated J. S. Forbes by 326 votes in the Dover by-election, 22 Sept., caused by Jessel's vacating his seat when he became master of the rolls.

[6] For Wolverton's letter see above, no. 899. Granville to Hammond and reply have not been traced.

in which I did not mention a peerage, but according to Agreement quoted your answer that Hammond's claims were so high, that you should not object to recommend to the Queen any honor which I recommended, and asked whether he could give me a light as to wishes.

I walked myself on Sunday into a slight attack of gout, but am nearly well. But it is provoking losing such an opportunity for exercise.

I do not know yet the final result of the correspondence with Spencer.

906. Mr. Gladstone to Lord Granville. [G.D. 29/29A]

Hawarden Castle. Sept. 27. 73.

1. Perhaps you have informed H.M. that the matter of the Lord Lieutenancy of Ireland is at rest, or if not please to do so before you leave Balmoral.

2. I know of no reason for more than one or two Cabinets: at any rate I would not now propose to begin a series until Lord Mayor's Day comes.[1] The ministerial manifesto of that day will be a queer affair.

3. Undoubtedly I think our friends in London, in their anxiety to make due & full provision for emergencies on the Gold Coast, have not been sufficiently alive to the question by what authority certain acts were to be done. I have myself under pressure gone farther than I could have wished in giving Treasury sanction to a part of the order for a Railway in order that time might not be lost: but I acted for the best.

I do not telegraph about the Cabinet as I have no doubt you will get today the regular notice. You will see that there is no necessity for your being in town on Thursday.

I am much concerned to hear you have not had the advantage of the Balmoral air. It did me great good, now as always: & I am just getting out of old shoes—those dear old friends.

I am so glad you arranged to have B. & C. as guests.

907. Mr. Gladstone to Lord Granville. [G.D. 29/62]

Hawarden Castle. Sept. 28. 73.

1. What do you think now as to the Maharajah. See Gurdon's Mem. within.[2]

2. And what do you recommend as to Cowper's Office? The offer to Morley has done good.[3] But should you not dissuade him from giving over the business he has hitherto managed.

3. Hammond's case might be dealt with when he goes & therefore I suppose a little after the contemplated Peerages.

[1] The autumn cabinets met 10, 12, 17, 21, 28 Nov., 1 Dec., Add. MS. 44641, fos. 209–40.

[2] 25 Sept., on the impolicy of ennobling 'the largest game preserver in Norfolk' at that moment, with note by Gladstone, 27 Sept., that he referred to Duleep Singh, G.D. 29/62. See above, nos. 887, 891, 892, 903.

[3] See above, nos. 882, 884, 886.

4. Remember we have the P.M.G. ship to deal with.
5. You give up the D of Leeds for Cambridgeshire ?[1] I think he was named.

908. Mr. Gladstone to Lord Granville. [G.D. 29/62]

Hawarden Castle. Oct. 15. 73.

When I was at Balmoral, the Queen observed as I thought with great force that large as was the fortune of the Grand Duchess there might be *gaspillage* which would much reduce it on its way. I suggested that in the preliminary practical arrangements for the marriage it would be well to lay down some precise plan for the transmission of the money at a certain & precise charge, or with a maximum, subject to which it should be payable in London, or else to some agent of the married couple in St Petersburgh. I did not say quite so much to the Queen but spoke to this effect. Since then I have had the inclosed communications from Ponsonby,[2] the latter of which desires me to call your attention to the matter.

909. Mr. Gladstone to Lord Granville. [G.D. 29/62]

Hawarden Castle. Oct 17. 73.

1. I send you a Mem. on the Yemen question.[3]

2. Dizzy has indeed made a mess of it.[4] Among other reasons for my gratitude, he has furnished me with a good additional reason for shirking political demonstrations in the West & elsewhere, lest I should put a counter-reproach into the mouth of the adversary.

3. I am very sorry to say Whitbread declines, and Wolverton (by Telegraph) seems to hesitate about Baxter whom I thought you & he agreed in recommending, or approving, for No 2. Whitbread writes as if pleased.[5]

4. So are Howard & Moncreiff about the Peerages. But both ask for time to consider. The Admiral is unwell.

5. I hope to remain here till the 4th & spend the week until Lord Mayor's day in visiting the Sneyds, & the Spencers.

[1] Gladstone agreed with Granville, 3 Oct., to offer the lord-lieutenancy of Cambridgeshire to the duke of Bedford, and then to Lord Dacre, Add. MS. 44641, fo. 199. On their refusal it was offered to the Speaker, M.P. for the county, 20 Oct., Add. MS. 44542, fo. 201 ; on his refusal to C. W. Townley, 9 Dec., who accepted, Add. MS. 44543, fo. 23 ; see below, no. 940.

[2] Ponsonby to Gladstone, 8, 14 Oct., on the possibility of peculation in regard to the Grand-duchess Marie's fortune and the Queen's wish for preventive measures, G.D. 29/62.

[3] The Turkish pasha at Jedda claimed authority over the tribes behind Aden. Granville had instructed Elliot to remonstrate, 30 Jan., 11 March, 15 May. When the government of India urged the establishment of a British protectorate over the tribes, Granville minuted that the Porte would be told of the proposal but given a further chance to abide by its assurances, F.O. 78/2753. A copy of no. 910 below follows Granville's minute.

[4] See Disraeli to Lord Grey de Wilton, on the Bath electors' leading public opinion in ending the government's career of 'plundering and blundering', *The Times*, 8 Oct., p. 3. On its part in causing the defeat of the Conservative, W. Forsyth, by Capt. A. D. Hayter in the Bath by-election, see Gladstone to Hayter, 11 Oct., Add. MS. 44542, fo. 195.

[5] See Gladstone to Whitbread, 10 Oct., offering the postmaster-generalship which Monsell was about to resign, Add. MS. 44542, fo. 193 ; Whitbread's refusal, 13 Oct., Add. MS. 44440, fo. 193 ; see above, p. 393, note 3, and below, p. 416, note 2.

6. I have thought a good deal over the questions of legislation for the coming year & think I can see pretty well what our programme should be. On the large subject of County Suffrage I believe our best course would probably be to encourage Trevelyan to come forward on a very early day, and to give him at least individually such aid as we can.

910. Memorandum by Mr. Gladstone for Lord Granville. [Add. MS. 44542, fo. 198]

[*Copy*]. 17 October 1873.

I entirely concur in Ld Granville's Mem just received. There is every imaginable objection to the proposed Protectorate. It involves the most indefinite obligations. It binds us to support those over whose conduct to others we have no controul. It threatens to impair & that chronically our good understanding with Turkey wh. is so necessary to the peace of the East. Nothing but absolute necessity can warrant our interference & then only within the limits, moral & local, to which that necessity extends. What we are fairly entitled to ask is that Turkey shall commit no act of aggression agst those chieftains & this we have every reason to believe we can obtain fr. our general experience at Constantinople. It wd be unpardonable to make another Gold Coast of this.

911. Mr. Gladstone to Lord Granville.[1] [Add. MS. 44542, fo. 199, and G.D. 29/62]

[*Copy*]. Hawarden Castle. Oct 18. 1873.

Pray tell Monsell that the delay in the appointment of his successor which I much regret has been due to causes beyond my controul. But I am aware of no reason why, if he is desirous to accelerate the proceeding, he should not at once execute his resignation by a letter. I write however rather at a venture on this point; he will know whether for his statutory duties an absolute continuity in the office is required.

I rather gather from his letter that he expects the Peerage will *accompany* the retirement. This could not be, as the union would lead to serious misapprehensions. It can only be *after* his retirement: but no very long interval need separate the two. I return the letter.

P.S. I send you Wolverton's letters about Baxter. They are much at variance with my recollections of his conversation with us. Baxter is not very good, but what can we do better?[2] Most seats (not B.'s) are in danger. I think W. Cowper would be better than Massey—but Hampshire?

[1] A copy of no. 911 without the postscript is also in G.D. 29/62, but dated by the copyist, 13 Oct. The original was sent to Monsell; see Hervey's docket on Granville's copy. See also Monsell to Granville, 15 Oct., asking when the arrangements for his resignation and peerage would be executed, answered by no. 911; 26 Oct., on his readiness to remain until his successor's appointment, G.D. 29/74.

[2] Baxter refused the postmaster-generalship since he was leaving for Italy, Add. MS. 44440, fo. 285; see also below, nos. 913, 914, 916, 917. Wolverton to Gladstone, 16 (two letters), 18 Oct., answering Gladstone's request for his opinion on Baxter's appointment, giving reasons for his objections, and excusing himself for having raised them, Add. MS. 44348, fos. 300–7. Playfair was appointed, 18 Nov.

912. Mr. Gladstone to Lord Granville. [G.D. 29/62]

Hawarden Castle. Oct 18. 73.

I have received this morning a box of papers respecting the Tunis Bank.[1] They do not include the Prime Minister's letter of concession. And I am very far indeed from comprehending the whole question. But there are many points which suggest to me misgiving. I think the great object for the moment should be to obtain time if possible for a thorough examination.

1. Mr Wood's case is not fully before me. I do not know his character, & much depends upon this. Upon the surface, his language to the Bey savours as much of dictation and pressure, as any thing we *know* of the French agents.

2. De Broglie alleges that he sought the concession originally for himself. Is he now free from all pecuniary interest in the matter?

3. The remonstrance is stated by the Bey of Tunis in his note to have been addressed to him by the Consuls generally and the Traders of the place. This statement from such a source tells strongly against peremptory action of any kind.

4. I cannot say that the words 'Banque Privée' cover a *société anonyme* with limited liability so as to enable us to argue high the question of good faith.

5. I find nothing in the papers to explain the strange stipulation for 'preference' to this English Bank. It is an ominous and inauspicious word on which it would seem that almost any claim might be founded.

For all these reasons I am very glad that by the Telegram of the 17th you have directed Mr Wood to press for time.

One point of difficulty seems to be the determination of the degree in which the letter of the Prime Minister pledges the Government or rather the Bey. This would be plain enough here.

Mr Wood speaks of the Bey & Tunisian Govt as under coercion but the tone of their documents is that of resistance to him.

If we have to go farther into the matter perhaps a F.O. précis will be advantageous.

It is delightful to hear that the Audience question is for the present at an end.[2] I hope Wade will not be emboldened by your approval, which I suppose could scarcely be withheld, to assume too much. I am not greatly pleased at the satisfaction expressed by the missionaries and especially the Romish missionaries.

[1] The London Bank of Tunis began operations, 5 Sept., on a concession of 19 May, Wood to Granville, No. 12, 31 May, F.O. 102/122. It became a diplomatic issue between Britain and France, who tried to stop the enterprise. The documents sent to Gladstone were: Lytton to Granville, No. 199, 10 Oct., reporting representations to de Broglie; private, 14, 15 Oct., on the probable French reply; Granville to Tenterden, 17 Oct., commenting on de Broglie's insinuation that Wood was financially interested and on the third point of the concession stipulating 'preference' for the English bank and ordering the delaying tel. to Wood; see note by Gladstone on the last, *ibid.*

[2] See above, no. 808. The Emperor granted an audience to the foreign representatives when he received the Japanese embassy, 29 June; see Wade to Granville, No. 175, 20 Aug., received 17 Oct., F.O. 17/655; decipher misdated 12 June, received 9 July, F.O. 17/654.

913. Lord Granville to Mr. Gladstone. [Add. MS. 44169, fo. 274]

Private. Walmer Castle. Oct 20/73.

I got your telegram,[1] & hope I have not misconstrued it in thinking it was an offer to my brother of the Post Master Generalship.

He is perfectly delighted with the compliment from you. I should be very glad to see him in office—& I believe that with very little practice, he would become a good official speaker.

We both think that as he has taken little part in the House, it would be better for him (though rather old for a subordinate place) to take one such as Huguesson's [*sic*] than at once to be placed over the head of all the present officials. I should think Sandwich was safe for a single election.

We have another feeling which is, that with your kindly bias to him & to me it would be desirable that you should consult some one besides his brother.

914. Mr. Gladstone to Lord Granville. [G.D. 29/62]

Hawarden Castle. Oct 21. 73.

1. I shall await Wolverton's verdict with much interest.[2] I was not warmly for Baxter, but I do not quite understand W.s reasons against him. Your brother would certainly be the best Post Master General of the three: & I think Baxter the next. So undoubtedly he would be a wiser Under Secretary for the Colonies —but then he would not with his views be able to talk the Bunkum in which, on that subject, the House too much delights. He would I am sure deliver very sound Ashantee & Gold Coast doctrine.

2. Chancing to hear from some authentic source an excellent account of Erle's recovered health, I wrote to the Chancellor, and I inclose his reply, which I interpret as meaning that E should now be No 1 for the legal Peerage.[3] Do you agree?

3. Reading your Draft [4] on the Three Rules moved me to put down in a short memorandum what I have to say on the subject—It has reference to future stages of the matter.

We expect to be at Althorp (probably) on the 6th.

[1] See Gladstone to Granville, draft tel. 20 Oct: 'I wrote to you on Saturday about choice of men. I shd like best one who wrote to me thrice from Walmer about Mrs Grote [F. Leveson-Gower]. Wd you and he consent', Add. MS. 44169, fo. 273.

[2] Gladstone replied to no. 913, tel. 9 a.m., 21 Oct., objecting to Hugessen, holding to Leveson-Gower as the best candidate with Baxter next, but asking Granville to consult Wolverton. Granville telegraphed that he had written to Wolverton; both tels. in G.D. 29/62.

[3] See Gladstone to Selborne, 11 Oct., enquiring whether Selborne knew of Erle's recovery when he advised on the proposed legal peerage, Add. MS. 44542, fo. 195; Selborne to Gladstone, 19 Oct., approving the choice of Erle, Add. MS. 44296, fo. 325; but see above, no. 899 note.

[4] See Granville to Schenck, draft by Granville 15 Oct., final draft 25 Oct., F.O. 5/1570; Schenck on 14 Oct. had revived the matter of presenting the three rules of article vi of the Treaty of Washington for the acceptance of the maritime powers. The draft was not altered by Gladstone's memorandum, which had no practical bearing since negotiations on the form of covering note were not reopened, see Granville to Thornton, 18 Feb. 1874, recounting the whole subject, *ibid.*, see above, nos. 534, 536.

MEMORANDUM ON THE THREE RULES

1. It appears to me that the submission of the three Rules to the Maritime Powers, besides being generally required for the dignity of the two Contracting Parties to the Treaty of Washington, is greatly for our interest, in this sense and to this extent, that if they were at this stage renounced or allowed to drop, such an issue would throw great discredit on the British share in the negotiations. The idea when these negotiations were in progress I think was this; that America might derive some special advantage from them in the impending arbitration, but that in the long run their operation would not be prejudicial, nay on the contrary that it would have a tendency to establish a construction of law somewhat favourable to the probable interests of England. Thus there was something in this stipulation of the nature of give and take; give now, and take hereafter. We have actually given, and we ought not now to be shut out from the take. I am here speaking of popular impressions rather than of the substance of the case: but I have said what seems to me to show that it would be most disadvantageous to us, as matter of opinion and repute, were the Three Rules to remain a dead letter.

2. Having been called upon to deliver my opinions in the House of Commons I am in some degree bound by the record if a correct one. As far, however, as I recollect, I should see no reason to change them. And I cannot doubt that as is stated in Lord Granville's draft of October 1873, in the presentation of the Rules comment will be necessary.

a. I presume that the word 'open' will disappear from the Rule respecting arms: and the history of its insertion and its removal will have to be told.

b. Evidently the Propositions enunciated not very considerately by the Arbitrators at Geneva cannot be passed by. So important a circumstance, occurring between the formation of the Rules and their presentation, deserves notice, and requires it.

But I would put it for consideration whether *this* notice should not be purely negative. We do not mean or desire, I take it, to embody any part of the Geneva propositions in the Rules. And I think it plain that to them no authoritative comment should be attached: i.e. that if they require authoritative comment such comment should take effect in an alteration of the text. My impression as to the Geneva propositions is that what we have to do is to put them aside: to state that we neither accept them, nor reject them: the Rules have received neither addition nor deduction, but stand just as they did. Again I say if there is need to affix a sense to the Rules, there is need, exactly in the same measure, to amend the Rules. The force of judgments under them, and the force of comments by Judges, might be left to the future. These have been measured, & might be measured again: but the force of an extraneous joint comment on the Rules, which is to explain them yet not be adopted with them (for then it would become part of them) who could measure.

c. One statement historical in its nature, and not obnoxious to the objection I have pointed out, might be worth appending, as it would tend to obviate or soften jealousy on the part of the Maritime Powers. Namely this, if as I believe it is correct. That the Rules embody & express what according to the American view [1] was

[1] Amended in pencil by Granville: 'recent statements of the view now entertained in the United States'. Cf. Selborne to Granville, 25 Oct., G.D. 29/67.

international law before they were made: and that although Great Britain did not accede to this proposition, yet we hold them to express what we had thought it fit to embody in our own Municipal law, and to endeavour to carry into effect through the action of that law, at a time when the Rules did not yet exist. Therefore, it would remain for inference, they do not constitute the formidable and selfish innovation which some Powers might think to be found in them. W.E.G. Oct. 21.73.

915. Lord Granville to Mr. Gladstone. [Add. MS. 44169, fo. 277]

Private. Walmer Castle. Oct 21/73.

I sent the papers respecting greater security for the payment of the Grand Duchess's fortune, saying that in my opinion the two cases were different, that we could not do more in the treaty, than provide for the payment of the interest at a certain rate half yearly.

I send you his answer & the pith of it to the Queen.[1]

916. Mr. Gladstone to Lord Granville. [Add. MS. 44543, fo. 3]

[*Copy*]. *Private.* Oct. 24. 73.

Wolverton [2] has set out the reasons *for* in the case of Hugessen; I am sorry to say they do not at all satisfy me. 1. Nothing but *necessity* should lead us to open a ministerial seat to which any doubt can attach. W. gives a favourable opinion but with "I think". 2. The P.O. with its huge & growing estabt requires a real economist. I own I have never seen a sign of this in H. 3. He is a good fellow, a clever fellow, a very good speaker; but he has had the P.C. given him very lately—another step wd now be quite gratuitous, & he like Baxter has never earned a reputation as a hard worker. 4. A gratuitous promotion in his case is the more questionable, because he very needlessly ran amuck at the Dissenters. 5. Two important appts are voided by a Scot & an Irishman—it is hardly desirable to make upon this two important appts both of Englishmen. In or among these considerations I find more than enough reason for a negative after thinking the matter over. I send a copy of them to Wn [3] & I telegraphed to you both this morning—I send his letter.

917. Lord Granville to Mr. Gladstone. [Add. MS. 44169, fo. 279]

Private. Walmer Castle. Oct 24/73.

I am very sorry as I told Wolverton that I incautiously showed Freddy your telegram,[4] before fully discussing with you the offer in it.

[1] See above, no. 908, and below, no. 918.

[2] Wolverton to Gladstone, 22 Oct., agreeing with Granville, who had sent him Gladstone's offer of the Post Office to Leveson-Gower, that the appointment would cause trouble, suggesting Hugessen and proposing the under-secretaryship of the Board of Trade for Leveson-Gower, Add. MS. 44348, fo. 308.

[3] Gladstone to Wolverton, 24 Oct., adding that he would write to Baxter, Add. MS. 44543, fo. 3; cf. Gladstone to Baxter, 27 Oct., *ibid.*, fo. 5, and above, no. 911 note, below, nos. 919, 921.

[4] See above, no. 913 note.

He was immensely pleased, and to have nothing now would be a disappointment to him. He entirely agreed with me as to the answer which I sent to you, and would I am sure cheerfully acquiesce in any decision of your's of any kind.

I feel myself in a delicate position towards him, as I have always been sensible that my official position was a disadvantage, whereas he was much better fitted for office than I was excepting perhaps in the thing of pushing.

I believe though it would be somewhat against the grain, that he would give vent to the moderate amount of buncum Kimberley might desire.

I am not competent to give an opinion upon Wolverton's change of opinion as to Baxter. The result of our conversation in Carlton Terrace certainly placed him second to Whitbread. But I know nothing of the exact position he holds in the House.

918. Mr. Gladstone to Lord Granville. [G.D. 29/62]

Hawarden Castle. Oct. 25. 73.

Your cover which reached me today covered two letters dated the *21st.*[1] On one of the subjects I have already written.

With regard to the other, the Russian fortune, you will judge better than I can whether there should be any thing in the Treaty. But it does not seem to me out of the question. Whatever is given in a marriage settlement should be placed at the ready and easy command of the married pair, and the G. D.'s fortune should be as accessible as the dividends on the Russian Funds, subject to any reasonable charge, if there be occasion. But at any rate I should think full subsidiary provision should be made contemporaneously with the Treaty.

I have named the 10th at 3 for the Cabinet.[2]

919. Mr. Gladstone to Lord Granville. [G.D. 29/62]

Hawarden Castle. Oct. 29. 73.

Having no answer to my Telegram of Monday morning I sent off yesterday from London an offer of the P.O. to Baxter. There may I fear have been some mischance in the dispatch of your reply which came here today (Wednesday) afternoon.

Nothing could be more unfortunate than the breaking up when we were separated of the understanding arrived at *vivâ voce* with Wolverton; for it is almost impossible, in nice cases, to settle these things properly by letter, & for us, under present circumstances, every case is a nice case.

I am afraid the Monarchists in France are mad: they seem to have hitched themselves into a position when it is a disgrace to recede & disaster of the highest order to advance.[3]

[1] Only one letter traced, no. 915 above, but see exchange between Godley, Wetherell and Nicolson, 25 Oct., on the reasons for its delay, G.D. 29/62. Nicolson thought that it was due to Granville's habit of holding back letters after sealing them for post.

[2] For cabinet of 10 Nov., see Add. MS. 44641, fo. 209, and above, no. 890 note.

[3] Hopes for agreement on the restoration of the legitimist line, represented by the Comte de Chambord, revived when he did not deny the 'concessions' which Chesnelong in Sept. reported

We shall not be at Althorp till Friday of next week.

I could hardly hope that the Sec. ship of B. of Trade would have any attractions for your brother, remarkable as I know his modesty to be.

920. Lord Granville to Mr. Gladstone. [Add. MS. 44169, fo. 283]

Walmer Castle. Oct 30/73.

I am not surprised at Forster being a little sore, and he probably did not sufficiently make allowance for the difficulties of Bright's position. Your letter appears very judicious.[1]

921. Mr. Gladstone to Lord Granville. [G.D. 29/29A]

Hawarden Castle. Oct 31. 73.

I am I assure you extremely concerned at the failure of my little plot against your brother: & he 'heaps coals of fire on my head' by the way in which he takes it. I did not change my mind about the suggestion, but only gave way to his modest unwillingness. On the other hand it is really necessary, in the present state of Civil Service agitation for increase of pay, to put a man firm in such matters to the P.O. and such I think Baxter will be—but I have no idea whether he will accept.

I have not yet heard from you whether you accept *Erle* in lieu of James—it appearing that his health is quite adequate, & the Chancellor having on this ground altered his preference.

What a letter of Chambord's, and what an explosion of a grand conspiracy against liberty !

922. Lord Granville to Mr. Gladstone. [Add. MS. 44169, fo. 284]

F.O. Oct 31/73.

I am shocked to remember that I have not answered you about Erle. I gather from the Chancellor's letter, that Erle deserves a Peerage, that it would be popular in the profession, and that he would probably be able to do judicial work in the Lords.

I do not know whether he recommends him as *additional* to James, or as a substitute for him.

The Chancellor's letter about James was very complimentary—& my idea is that he would be much more useful in Debate than Erle. But if the Chancellor prefers Erle, I cannot object.

My box with the Chancellor's letter will come from Walmer this evening.

him ready to make. His letter to Chesnelong, 23 Oct., destroyed the fusionist cause, for it insisted on unconditional return. Chesnelong sought its modification before publishing it. After a week's tension, it was published, dated 27 Oct., unchanged, 31 Oct ; see *The Times*, 27 Oct., p. 9, 31 Oct., p. 5 ; cf. Lyons to Granville, No. 887, 24 Oct., No. 902, 31 Oct., F.O. 27/1994.

[1] Gladstone to Forster, 30 Oct., commenting on Forster's letter to Bright (taking up points in the latter's speech at Birmingham on the Education Act of 1870), which Forster had sent him, Add. MS. 44543, fo. 7.

923. Lord Granville to Mr. Gladstone. [Add. MS. 44169, fo. 286]

[?31 October 1873].

I do not think Lefevre one half as strong as Morley—and Cowper has always complained of something not being done for the latter.[1]

But a good man with a safe seat in the Commons would perhaps be better.

924. Mr. Gladstone to Lord Granville. [Add. MS. 44543, fo. 7]

[*Copy*]. Hawarden. Nov. 1. 73.

Having recd today a draft of a Slave Trade convention & yesty one of a Commercial Convention [2]—all in due course—I am reminded to suggest what I think wd be an useful rule for the F.O. to adopt in forwarding papers of this class to the First Lord [of the Treasury]. In all such cases the substance is one thing & the wording another. The wording should have a close & careful consideration all through, apart from the substance. This considn it is impossible for him to give, nor can he be generally speaking the most competent person to suggest or review questions which are of wording only. Neither does he know, when he receives these documents, what are the points of policy or substance for which they are referred to him. I suggest that it wd be well if in all such references his attention was called, either by a short Mem or by markings on the draft, to the points which it is desired to bring under his notice. This would make the whole transaction more real & effective, as I think.

925. Mr. Gladstone to Lord Granville. [G.D. 29/62]

Hawarden Castle. Nov 1. 73.

A strange fatality has attended this G P O business. Baxter's letter gives a reason for his refusal (not I think quite strong enough) of which it is pretty plain we never should have heard but for the unfortunate delays which have postponed the offer to him.[3]

I am really for the present at my wit's end : but it is better to wait a while than to act badly.

I cannot say a word against your final answer which has reached me by Telegraph.[4]

I inclose a copy of a letter I have written to Wolverton.[5]

[1] Cf. Granville to Gladstone, draft tel. 29 Oct., proposing Mauleigh [disguise for Morley] for the post office, G.D. 29/62 ; Gladstone to Wolverton, 1 Nov., proposing Lefevre, Add. MS. 44543, fo. 8.

[2] See *Engagement of the Jemadar of Shur for Abolition of Slave Trade in his Dominions, 17 Nov. 1873*. Parl. papers. [C. 985] (1874). lxii, 931 ; *Convention between Her Majesty and the French Republic supplementary to the Treaty of Commerce and Navigation of 23rd July 1873, signed at Versailles, 24 January 1874*. Parl. papers. [C. 888] (1874). lxxvi, 115.

[3] See above, no. 911 note.

[4] See Granville to Gladstone, draft tel. 1 Nov., reporting that Granville and his brother had agreed with the ' Lord of the station ' [Wolverton] against Leveson-Gower's accepting the post office, G.D. 29/62.

[5] Gladstone to Wolverton, 1 Nov., on the difficulties of the post office appointment, Add. MS. 44348, fo. 313.

The name (' Morley ' I think) was sorely mangled in a late Telegram from you.[1] But that would be such a blow to another that I almost think if it were done something else must go to the Lords along with it : & would he keep down the demands of the P.O. servants ?

926. Mr. Gladstone to Lord Granville. [G.D. 29/62]

Most Private. Hawarden Castle. Nov. 3. 73.

1. I have received and read today Paget's dispatch of Oct 23 with the article from the Osservatore Romano on Home Rule in Ireland.[2] I dare say you are considering the subject of it. My first impression is that we cannot pass it over. I do not think we should be silent on a similar declaration by the Organ of any European Government ; & I presume & believe there is no doubt that this impudent declaration must be considered to have the direct sanction of the Vatican until it is directly disavowed.

2. I pass to a yet more private matter. The death of Bovill of course leads to an offer of his place to Coleridge, who without doubt will accept it, and James I conceive will be Attorney General. Who is to be Solicitor ? Watkin Williams has the best legal position. Harcourt by much the best Parliamentary position with no legal position (as I understand) whatever. I think him objectionable on various grounds, but they are such as tell more against seeking him, than in favour of thrusting him aside when circumstances put him in the way of having something. But I feel the greatest objection to investing a man who has no position at the Bar, on political grounds, with a title of succession in series to the principal Judgeships, under the Chancellorship, of the country. I think however there is much to be said in favour of an alteration of rule, and of laying it down clearly that now & henceforward the presumed rights of succession should be abrogated or modified. You see we have already been engaged in making changes 1. as to the incomes of the Law Officers 2. as to the Privy Councillorship of the Attorney General, which of itself places a wider interval between him and the Solicitor than heretofore. I do not now enter into details, which I reserve until we meet.[3]

Harcourt's best claim is in the purely political line : and I do not know that as matters now stand it might not be advisable to offer him our P.M.G. ship.

Wolverton answers my inquiry about Lefevres seat by saying he thinks there could be little or no risk.

We go to Keele on Wedy.

[1] See above, no. 923 note.

[2] Paget to Granville, No. 318, 23 Oct., F.O. 45/220. The article praised the work of the Irish Catholic clergy for the ' autonomy of Ireland '. Granville did nothing through Paget, but Jervoise communicated the public statements of Irish clergy in favour of home rule to Antonelli and was assured of his condemnation of the movement ; see Jervoise to Granville, tel. 28 Nov., private letters, 17, 20, 31 Dec., G.D. 29/84 ; see also above, no. 792, below, nos. 927, 961.

[3] Coleridge became lord chief justice of common pleas ; James attorney-general ; Harcourt solicitor-general (20 Nov.). The cabinet, 10 Nov., agreed to end the prescriptive right of the attorney- and solicitor-general to succeed to certain judgeships, Add. MS. 44641, fo. 209. Cf. Gladstone to James, 11 Nov., Add. MS. 44441, fo. 38 ; to Harcourt, 12 Nov., Add. MS. 44543, fo. 12.

I never read a better description than Layard's late dispatch on political prospects & the state of parties in Spain.[1]

927. **Mr. Gladstone to Lord Granville.** [G.D. 29/62]

Hawarden. Nov. 4. 73.

I return Dufferin's letter[2]: and while I do not think we ought to restrain him or his local Government from making. through their R.C. Ecclesiastics any arrangement with the Pope which he & they may like, I am of opinion that it would be a mistake for us to interfere. Indeed the proceedings of the R C Clergy & Bps in Ireland about Home Rule—which 4 years ago Cullen used to ridicule as the bubble of a moment—taken together with that impudent declaration in the Pope's newspaper make me think there is a turn in the old gentleman's proceedings towards governments other than the German.

928. **Mr. Gladstone to Lord Granville.** [F.O. 102/122]

Keele Hall, Staffordshire. Nov 7.73.

I have read the Memorandum on the Tunis Bank[3] and I fear the case is full of doubtful points and to require much caution.

1. The concession seems to have been not made nor promised, and the Prime Minister's letter to describe what it *would* contain.

2. A question difficult for foreigners to understand is raised upon the validity of a Minister's promise in Tunis without some formal act of the Sovereign to back it.

3. The third Article seems to me quite indefensible. A promise of preference to a particular Bank, in vague terms, lays ground for all manner of disputes hereafter, and seems at once to place any confuting instruction at a disadvantage. Mr Wood's explanation as to the word assistance is not quite satisfactory, as no one Bank, or foreign resident or body of residents, ought to receive aid in the recovery of debts which is not granted to others.

4. The question of Private Bank & Bank Anonyme if arguable on our side seems to be perhaps even more arguable against us.

5. And then comes the engagement implied by the signature of the British Delegates, and

6. the point, probably verbal, which I raised as to the terms of Mr Wood's answer respecting his personal position.

I have only named difficulties and have not much to suggest but I should suppose it well worth the while of the parties to surrender or alter the third article if that would avail to smooth their way.

[1] Layard to Granville, No. 462 confidential, 14 Oct., describing an improvement in the political situation since July when he went on leave, F.O. 72/1342.

[2] Dufferin to Granville, on the nomination of Catholic bishops in Canada, has not been traced. It was sent to Jervoise, who was on leave in England. He later urged on Antonelli the arrangements it recommended; see Jervoise to Granville, private, 2 Dec., G.D. 29/25A.

[3] See above, no. 912 note.

929. Lord Granville to Mr. Gladstone. [G.D. 29/62]

Foreign Office. [14 November 1873].

Ponsonby writes [1] " that the Queen wishes to know what is my opinion with respect to the order given by the Pope to the R.C. College in Dublin empowering them to grant degrees.["]

We have heard nothing of it in the F.O.

I will write to Spencer if you know nothing on the subject.

930. Mr. Gladstone to Lord Granville. [G.D. 29/62]

11 C H T. Nov 14. 73.

It was a power possessed & exercised by the Popes in the Middle Ages and I believe inherited from them by the Archbishops of Canterbury. I apprehend it has been long in disuse and the revival of it is a *measure*. I think it wd be quite right to have the exact facts ascertained. If the degrees have no distinctive mark, of an unexceptionable kind, it is a question whether they should be allowed. I know not what lawyer we have now who would be perfect in this learning, as Hope Scott was—Phillimore would know something : perhaps Acton & Döllinger more : Selborne would advise.[2]

931. Mr. Gladstone to Lord Granville. [G.D. 29/62]

10, Downing Street. Nov. 18. 73.

I shall be glad to hear further, in due time, about the Papal degrees in Ireland. Without disputing any of the statements in the Chancellor's letter, I do not think it supplies conclusive grounds for the course of acquiescence, on which I suspend my judgment, especially until we know the facts from Ireland, and whether civil or secular degrees are included. It is one thing for a private person to perform a mountebank's trick, it is another for a body to assume a title which is in the nature of a testimonial, under the authority of a foreigner, who has not renounced the character of a temporal Sovereign.

I hope the teeth do not misbehave today.

932. Mr. Gladstone to Lord Granville. [G.D. 29/62]

N. 30. 73.

Here is the " authorised version " : a manifest improvement.[3] I go to Windsor on Tuesday.

[1] Ponsonby to Granville, 13 Nov., G.D. 29/36.

[2] Granville to Selborne and reply are missing from G.D. 29/67. The subject was also raised in the cabinet, 21 Nov., Add. MS. 44641, fo. 222. No. 930 was written on the back of no. 929.

[3] On 29 Nov. the Queen telegraphed a protest against the fixing of a meeting of the Privy Council on Wednesday, 3 Dec., to Sir A. Helps. She had already appointed that afternoon for audiences of the French ambassador and Saxon minister ; see Ponsonby to Granville, 24 and 30 Nov., G.D. 29/36.

933. Lord Granville to Mr. Gladstone.[1] [Add. MS. 44169, fo. 287]

18, Carlton House Terrace. [30 November 1873].

She has always been huffy at days being fixed for her, instead of leaving it to her to choose—but I am afraid that she must be in a state of unusual irritation. I think your reproof will be the same, if you leave out " extraordinary " and " pleased to ".

She obviously is [*sic*] that she has appointed the 3d for the audience of the Saxon Minister.

934. Mr. Gladstone to Lord Granville. [Add. MS. 44543, fo. 20]

[*Copy*]. Strawberry Hill. Dec. 3. 73.

I do not know whether you think of taking any step on Sir H. Elliot's No. 404 about French designs on the Red Sea.[2] But as that is not a quesn of policy only a manifestly embraced fact, I shd suggest whether it wd be well to have any information the F.O. possesses on the territorial rights on the W. slope of the Red Sea & of the Gulf of Aden looked up, tho' it may possibly prove to be very indefinite.

935. Lord Granville to Mr. Gladstone. [G.D. 29/62]

Copy. Decr 3. 73.

This is an important note from Argyll [3]—the Turks are behaving very ill, but for us to authorize the troops to expel them seems to be a measure that should not be taken departmentally, and my impression is that the Govr cannot yet have received the late instructions sent by the Porte.

936. Mr. Gladstone to Lord Granville.[4] [G.D. 29/62]

10, Downing Street. Dec. 6. 73.

Neither of us are Russophobists but Elliot's Telegram of today [5] reports to us, for perhaps the fiftieth time, the scandalous conduct of Ignatieff.

[1] An undated exchange between Gladstone and Granville on Bright's health ending: 'I talked over some knotty things with him which I should like much to report to you after Cabinet if it breaks up early. W.E.G.', received by Hervey 15 Dec., but possibly belonging to the cabinet of 1 Dec., G.D. 29/62; and a further exchange during that cabinet, Add. MS. 44641, fos. 237–40, not printed.

[2] The Khedive sought British recognition of his claims to sovereignty, under Turkey, on the Red Sea coast. France also claimed parts of the coast. Elliot to Granville, No. 404, 13 Nov., received 24 Nov., answered Granville's request for an opinion on these two topics; see Vivian to Granville, No. 45, 22 Sept.; Granville to Elliot, No. 230, 23 Oct.; mem. by Hertslet, 21 Jan. 1874, F.O. 78/3187.

[3] Argyll to Granville, 2 Dec., enclosing tel. from the Resident at Aden wishing to restrain Turkish advances by force, G.D. 29/51; cf. second letter, 2 Dec., on his wish to instruct the Resident to use troops, G.D. 29/25A; Granville to Argyll, 2 Dec., that representations would be renewed at Constantinople, G.D. 29/22A; see also above, nos. 909, 910.

[4] No. 936 marked: 'Answd in the negative G[ranville]'; see below, no. 937.

[5] Untraced, but see 'extender', Elliot to Granville, No. 449, 8 Dec., recounting Ignatyev's attempt to convince the Austrian representative that Elliot was responsible for the Turkish mem. on the Bosnian question to which he objected, F.O. 78/2273.

That man seems to be both fox and firebrand & will yet I fear make a wa in Europe before he is done.

Query whether it would be right to let some newspaper probably the Time show up his doings, & to provide it with the material.

It would be a rare & exceptional proceeding but he is a rare & exceptiona vagabond.

937. Lord Granville to Mr. Gladstone. [Add. MS. 44169, fo. 289]

Private. Bowood. Dec 7/73.

The little visit to Windsor went off well. The Queen in high good humor bu did not allude to any political subject, excepting the appointment of the new Frenc Ambassador.[1]

She desired General Ponsonby to see me, but I had nothing to say to him and he could not conceive what she wished him to say to me unless about the futur management of the South Kensington Museum.

I told him that I had nothing to tell him—that I did not like the transfer,[2] bu that I believed the Trustees had already recd a communication on the subject that Aberdare agreed with me, so that the matter would receive full consideration but the difficulty of objecting was somewhat encreased by Cole's outrageous conduc —& that I did not think the Queen's objection to letting the Cartoons go unde the Trustees was valid, as they were a more independent body than the presen managers, who were Gov officials.

I will return you Clarendon's letter,[3] which surprised me.

Query Ilchester, Falmouth, Portsmouth, & Carysfort. But I cannot guarante any to accept.

Ignatieff is too bad. As soon as I got the telegram, I reflected what could b done with it. I am afraid publication in the Times would hardly be fair to Ellio & Reschid the latter having made the communication *confidentially* to Elliot. Beside a public complaint might make it difficult for the Emperor to carry out the intentio of removing him from Constantinople to be Governor of Bessarabia.

I have told Lyons, who is sensible & discreet to speak to Schouvaloff from me—[4] To say that I do not pretend to dictate what instructions are to be sent to Russia Diplomatists but that as I do not believe Ignatieff has been instructed to tell the Turks to refuse our claims on the Turks as to the neighbourhood of Aden, or to tel the Austrians that it is the English Ambassador who prompts Turkish State papers offensive to Austria or to tell the Turks that we side with the Persians and the Persians

[1] Cf. Granville to the Queen, tel. 3 Dec., reporting a French enquiry whether she would accept the duc de la Rochfoucaud de Bisaccia as French ambassador and supposing that she could not object, G.D. 29/36.

[2] Relates to the question of the union of the South Kensington and British Museums and the transference of the Raphael cartoons from Hampton Court to the former.

[3] 5 Dec., refusing the captaincy of the Corps of Gentlemen at Arms, Add. MS. 44441, fo. 175 ; offered, 1 Dec., Add. MS. 44543, fo. 20 ; see above, nos. 882, 884, below, 943, 945.

[4] There is no private letter from Granville to Lyons on this subject in G.D. 29/109.

that we side with the Turks, when the English & Russian Govts are pursuing the same object I am glad to have a private & safe opportunity of letting him know how the matter stands.

938. Mr. Gladstone to Lord Granville. [G.D. 29/62]

Hawarden Castle. Dec. 9. 73.

In my hint about Ignatieff I did not mean to suggest a full communication of confidential particulars so as to commit parties; but I am much better pleased to find that a superior mode of action is open to you.

I hope the Queen will not understand that there are differences of opinion among us about South Kensington further than as regards leanings anterior to examination.

Panizzi is very strongly of opinion that there should be a Commission on the Union, & on the state of the two Establishments.

My own 'leaning' is to the Union: I began with prejudice against the Trustee Government, and thus far I have been converted by experience—while open to be reconverted.

I am quite willing to recommend to the Queen any one of the four Peers you name, according to your comparative Estimate.

939. Mr. Gladstone to Lord Granville. [G.D. 29/62]

Hawarden Castle. Dec. 10. 73.

If you approve, I should like to go as far in the letter to Northbrook respecting young Lesseps and his companion as to authorise the civilities & attentions on the part of the agents of the Government which as travellers in remote parts of our Indian dominions they may greatly need, but subject to the reservations which you properly make. You will find in pencil words which would give effect to this view which is I think no more than may fairly be conceived to be implied in the very nature of a letter of introduction.

I have read the India Office letter of Nov. 29 with much regret. It seems to me most imprudent to show our teeth on the subject of this railroad. Even if it were a bad scheme we might perhaps trust to the physical & financial difficulties in its way to stop it. Undoubtedly it is needless & would be premature to commit ourselves in its favour; but to show our teeth on a request of this kind is a policy in my opinion worthy of Japan as it was 20 years ago, and one which would be utterly scouted in Japan of today.

I have not written to Argyll without hearing what you thought but pray send him this note if you think fit.[1]

[1] See India Office to Foreign Office, 29 Nov., refusing to support Victor de Lesseps's expedition to investigate the possibility of connecting the Indian and the Russian Asiatic railways, F.O. 65/879. See also Argyll to Granville, 26 Nov., on the inaccessibility of India as her best defence, G.D. 29/25A; Foreign Office to India Office, 13 Dec., enclosing Granville's proposed letter to Lesseps with a draft introduction to the Viceroy, F.O. 65/879. The latter has Gladstone's pencilled amendment offering 'normal offices of courtesy or goodwill'; see also Granville's note of explanation for Argyll on the draft; Argyll to Gladstone, 22 Dec., sent on to Granville, 24 Dec., G.D. 29/62.

How well Rothery writes. How strange to have the Legitimist Chief for French Ambassador.[1] How ominous is the removal of Fournier from Rome.

940. Mr. Gladstone to Lord Granville. [G.D. 29/62]

Immediate. Hawarden Castle. Dec. 14. 73.

1. I heartily enter into the spirit of your Draft Affghan–Turcoman Dispatch:[2] but it strikes me as worth your consideration whether a few words near the end, which I have placed within brackets, are not rather over-definite & might not, if they were to get out (as I suppose is possible) place us in an awkward position & diminish our freedom of action.

1. In the face of Russia—who would I think likely enough reply to us 'by all means give the Ameer as soon as you like as much assistance as you like & so we shall have the peace well kept'.

2. As regards the Ameer who might be able to quote this as a definite pledge.

As the best way of explaining my idea I inclose my substitute for consideration. I do not think it weakens the passage.

2. Cowper writes to know when he can resign.[3] It would be very desirable to avoid, if we can, more refusals of positive offers.

3. Townley asks time—in a letter more no than yes—I do not know how to get at him but it is very desirable that he should accept.[4]

941. Lord Granville to Mr. Gladstone.[5] [Add. MS. 44169, fo. 295]

[16 December 1873].

Cardwell was going off by the train, saying that Welby had seen him, and probably had already told you of his figures.

He could not believe it would [be] the wish of any one to reduce the Battalions below 520, or to disband any. He should be very glad if any one could suggest the reduction of the estimates, but he had been working at that end all the autumn, with the result he had mentioned to me.

I am to see him at 3 tomorrow.

[1] See above, no. 937.

[2] Enclosed in Foreign Office to India Office, 20 Dec., but is not with it in F.O. 65/879; printed draft, 20 Dec., and a printed copy of the final dispatch, to Loftus, No. 23, 7 Jan., F.O. 65/901. It drew Russia's attention to Afghanistan's fears that the coming expedition to Merv would violate her territory and the agreement of Dec. 1872/Jan. 1873; a copy of Gladstone's substituted passage, Add. MS. 44543, fo. 26.

[3] Cowper to Gladstone, 6 Dec., asking when his resignation of the captaincy of the Corps of Gentlemen at Arms might take effect, Add. MS. 44441, fo. 182; see above, nos. 882, 884, 937.

[4] Gladstone to C. W. Townley, 9 Dec., offering the lord-lieutenancy of Cambridgeshire, Add. MS. 44543, fo. 23, and above, p. 415, note 1.

[5] A note by Granville, 17 Dec., that he entirely agreed with Gladstone, on Kimberley's letter, that the recruitment of a native force in West Africa for the Ashantee War by payments per head should be stopped, G.D. 29/62, not printed.

942. Mr. Gladstone to Lord Granville. [G.D. 29/62]

Early. Hawarden Castle. Dec. 18. 73.

Please to read the inclosed letter from Sir T. Fremantle, and also an accompanying Memm of Gurdon's.[1]

The case is a little puzzling. Fremantle was Sec. at War and Sec. for Ireland before leaving Parlt: Peel one day said to him 'Why do you not lay yourself out for the Speakership?' And an admirable Speaker he would have made. His Parliamentary career began 47 years ago, his official career 39. Upon the whole I incline to think we should give him G.C.B.

I have tried to find (roundabout) what he looks to, but thus far without success.

943. Lord Granville to Mr. Gladstone. [Add. MS. 44169, fo. 297]

Foreign Office. Dec 20/73.

In consequence of what you said as to not wishing to meet with fresh refusals, I in a very guarded manner, sounded Ilchester as to whether he would like to have Cowper's place—saying nothing about his representation of any office—a question which might be treated separately.

He was very doubtful at first, but he would now accept if you make him the offer, which I hope you will do.[2]

Poltimore on account of health, and his not liking to attend the beginnings & ends of sessions, but with many expressions of personal & political devotion to you, has written to ask me to place his resignation in your hands of his office of Treasurer and *whip* in the H. of Lords.

Bessborough would like to have Monson in his place.[3]

I hardly know what to say as to Freemantle [*sic*]. The only objections to a Peerage are the number you are making, & the promise to Hammond, and the fact that although Freemantle was a Peelite, I believe his political opinions have for some years not been up to the Gladstonian mark—and as a rule I have not found that the atmosphere of the Lords liberalizes sons who have stood on Tory Principles. Peel is hardly an authority on this point.

I share Gurdon's opinion about the G.C.B—as to the extension of the claims it will create. I should have thought the K.C.B sufficient. It is a matter for him to consider whether he will take it—I have a further difficulty, in Odo Russell's claim as Ambassador to a G.C.B. & I believe you have only one vacant.

I doubt whether any Ambassador has been one so long without it.

[1] Fremantle's retirement from the chairmanship of the Board of Customs followed the amalgamation of the Boards of Customs and Inland Revenue. Fremantle's letter has not been traced but F. Goulburn wrote to Gladstone, 17 Dec., that Fremantle would prefer an honour to a special pension, Add. MS. 44441, fo. 222. The mem. by Gurdon indicated a peerage as suitable, G.D. 29/62. He became Baron Cottesloe in Jan. 1874; see below, nos. 972, 974–6.

[2] Ilchester accepted the captaincy of the Corps of Gentlemen at Arms; see above, nos. 882, 884, 937, 940.

[3] Monson accepted the office of treasurer of the household *vice* Poltimore but was not charged with any parliamentary responsibilities, 30 Dec., Add. MS. 44441, fo. 249.

I also send you a letter from Lowe.[1] From what you have said, I suppose you would not like to have Fitzmaurice in the Under Secretaryship. I believe Lowe's description of his qualities to be correct, but I do not know what his position is in the Commons.

I have no objections to Freemantle's Peerage, excepting those I have mentioned and those referring to his politics and those of his son might be obviated by proper assurances.

944. Mr. Gladstone to Lord Granville. [G.D. 29/62]

Hawarden Castle. Dec. 21. 73.

I am afraid I must trouble you to read the inclosed very strange letter from Playfair.[2] As I cannot suppose it to be wilful I can only describe it as one of the most deplorable official blunders I have ever known. It disappoints me extremely for, after the assurances he gave I was as sanguine as you in my anticipations.

Your happy methods of dealing with men cause your aid to be invoked on all occasions. I have often profited by it, and on this occasion I do not ask it, but knowing your kind interest in Playfair I did not like to write him the severe letter which as matters stand it requires without letting you know the situation of affairs.

It will be necessary not only that he shall express privately his regret but that (without public retraction) he shall seek opportunities of handling matters officially & publicly in a different and indeed an opposite sense.

945. Mr. Gladstone to Lord Granville. [G.D. 29/62]

H[awarde]n. D. 22. 73.

1. I have proposed Ilchester to the Queen.
2. Also Monson.
3. Fremantle's case is peculiar. I think I could not offer him the K.C.B. Station enters into these questions. He had been at the very door of the Cabinet as Sec. at War and Sec. for Ireland, before he became Chairman of Customs which was in some sense a descent: hence a little difficulty; but I think the K.C.B. plainly would not be suitable, though the G.C.B. would. (Are you perfectly sure of your *facts* as to the urgency of Ld O. Russell's claim? Manifestly he ought to have had K.C.B. first: for he does not come under our exception for old men.) On the other hand I certainly cannot guarantee Fremantle's politics. But I think he would do good in the House of Lords: if he had any sort of intercourse with the present Conservative Leaders, however slight, he would certainly help to keep them straight and if you think this the best way of dealing with him, we might let him run in couples with Hammond.
4. I have suggested to Lowe that we had better meet & talk over the case of

[1] Lowe to Granville, 19 Dec., suggesting Lord Edmond Fitzmaurice for the parliamentary under-secretaryship of the Home Office, G.D. 29/66.

[2] Postmaster-general to the Treasury, 20 Dec., on the salaries of post office employees, see below, no. 948 note.

he Home Secship, with that in the B. of Trade, when we come to town.[1] I think hat with Harcourt—James & Playfair—Fitzmaurice would be rather strong.[2] But nother serious question is whether we ought not to try to move Bonham Carter.

46. Lord Granville to Mr. Gladstone. [Add. MS. 44169, fo. 303]

rivate. Walmer Castle. Dec 23/73.

The Queen's Solicitor took an unconscionable time in preparing the alterations which were desired by the Duke of Edinburgh—& the other Lawyers have been ery long.

It was only after pressure that they got anything in shape for the Law officers.

They are of opinion that some of them were very good, and indeed indispensable, out others the 3 Law officers called upon me to explain were quite unreasonable. asked the Chancellor to communicate with one of them, and they are now perfectly agreed. In the meantime I got from Brunnow an opinion which appeared to be quite sincere that it was most undesirable for the Duke's present & future pecuniary nterests that anything *unreasonable* should be proposed. Reports of the Duke's parsimony had reached the Russian Court and anything which appeared grasping on his part would be resented.

I wrote this recently to the Queen in answer to a note I had received from her. In her answer, she told me that the Princess Royal had already informed her of the fact.

Time is most urgent, and the Queen does not require to see the draft. If you do not, & will trust to the Chancellor & Law Officers, please tell Tenterden so.[3]

947. Lord Granville to Mr. Gladstone. [Add. MS. 44169, fo. 307]

Walmer Castle. [24 December 1873].

I send you a letter from Halifax [4]—who is anything but a foolometer, and has great knowledge both of the facts, and of public opinion concerning them.

At the same time I do not appreciate the line of arguments he suggests.

We do not advance because we think the best way of preserving our enormous Indian Empire is to remain where we are.

The Russians rightly or wrongly yield to the apparent necessity of protecting each new acquisition which they make, in the same way as we did at an earlier period of our Indian History.

I have had an alarmist letter from the D of Cambridge [5] with which I have not

[1] Gladstone to Lowe, 21 Dec., Add. MS. 44543, fo. 34.

[2] I.e. as yet another 'new man' admitted to the government.

[3] See memoranda by Tenterden on the Marriage Treaty, Oct.–Dec., G.D. 29/106.

[4] Halifax to Gladstone, 22 Dec., proposing to strengthen the language that Loftus was instructed to use in St. Petersburg. He wished to expose the Russian assertions that they were 'only doing as we do' and would like to do it 'so that Europe might see it too', G.D. 29/64; and Granville's reply, 27 Dec., *ibid.*

[5] The duke of Cambridge to Granville, 19 Dec., on his concern about Central Asia and Russia, who probably thought 'that because of the approaching marriage and consequent alliance nothing will be said'; and reply, 20 Dec., G.D. 29/72.

troubled you, in which he states his opinion that the last Treaty with Khiva, is mos dangerous to our position in India.

948. Mr. Gladstone to Lord Granville.[1] [G.D. 29/62]

Hawarden. Xmas D. 73.

1. I am much relieved and pleased by your Telegram: but in what a stat of chaos poor Playfair must have received his office from the hands of Monsell.[2]

2. I send for perusal a curious letter from Ayrton.[3]

3. I send a message to London resp. the Marriage Treaty in the sense o confidence.[4]

4. As regards Halifax's letter, I am by no means sure that the task he suggest is as easy as it appears to him, or that *his* recital would be other than the beginnin of a series of bitter recriminations. He selects his own period of comparison; afte the Punjab, after Scinde, after Burmah. I have never heard of a Russian annexatio as bad as the annexation of Scinde. I had just entered the Cabinet when it wa done: done by Ellenborough in India, most reluctantly acquiesced in by Peel' Cabinet, every member of which, if I recollect right, decidedly disapproved of it.

There can be no doubt I think about your title to touch up Russia more sharpl about the Schouvaloff assurances; [5] if there is anything to be gained by it.

A happy Christmas.

949. Mr. Gladstone to Lord Granville. [G.D. 29/62]

Hawarden. Dec. 26. 73.

1. Playfair's letter,[6] returned herewith, is all that could be desired, so far a he himself is concerned.

2. I remember the case of Elliot and G.C.B. He got it, on account of hi having to represent the Queen at a great Suez Canal function, sooner than he woul otherwise have had it.

3. I am doubtful about the expediency of passing any one through the C.B and K.C.B. at full gallop in order to save the rule. But perhaps it will do if we tal this over in January.

[1] Granville to Gladstone, 25 Dec., on his disapproval of the plan of putting South Kensingto Museum under the Trustees of the British Museum, and his agreement to the new proposa Add MS. 44169, fo. 309, not printed.

[2] Playfair sent to Granville his letter to Gladstone, 24 Dec., explaining that the letter t the Treasury had been written in his name without his approval, which he would not have given Granville telegraphed its substance to Gladstone, G.D. 29/62; see also Playfair to Granville 26 Dec., G.D. 29/25A.

[3] Ayrton to Gladstone, 22 Dec., agreeing to transact all his business with the Queen i writing, describing the growth of conservative feeling in the country and his dissatisfaction wit his official career, Add. MS. 44441, fo. 226.

[4] Gladstone left a blank here which Granville noted on the back meant that 'he did no require the last Treaty draft to be sent to him before it was forwarded'.

[5] See above, no. 810. Relates to the drafts of Granville to Loftus, No. 23, 7 Jan. 1874, sti under discussion; see above, no. 940 note.

[6] See above, nos. 944, 948.

4. The offer of G.C.B. would of course amply pay the debt to Fremantle. But I do not doubt he would really like the Peerage [and] not care much about the other. I certainly would not think of *this* alternative without your free & full assent. And the question arises what I should say to him about politics if we take that course. Could I say more than that I hoped I might view him as an independent politician & one who would not enter the H. of Lords as an opponent? What is our standing ground with Hammond on this matter? And is it completely settled with him that we propose him for a Peerage?

Our marriage [1] comes off tomorrow. The kindness of one and all, great & small, has really been almost too much for us.

950. Mr. Gladstone to Lord Granville. [G.D. 29/62]

Hawarden. Dec. 27. 73.

I have written the inclosed note to Monson.[2] I do not know whether you would wish me to say any thing about attendance in the H. of Lords, but I am really afraid lest if it be put into the offer it should make him bolt, and I take it there is no doubt about your title to require it. I did not mention it in writing to Lord Ilchester.

Please to send on the note if you approve of it.

2. I likewise send for your perusal a letter this day received from the Queen with copy of my reply.[3]

I thought the proposal about the function of second whip would come better from you than from me.

P.S. I send a note from Biddulph about Marriage presents, with my reply: they seem to be a matter for your consideration.

951. Mr. Gladstone to Lord Granville. [G.D. 29/62]

Hawarden Castle. Dec. 29. 73.

The time approaches for settling new Cabinets.

What do you say to Monday 19th? [4] I should come to London on the Thursday preceding & have some preliminary communications about Estimates.

What do you say?

Ought I then to tell Bright what I have mentioned to you?

Our marriage was celebrated on Saturday—most happily, in all but the point of weather, which was but middling.

[1] Agnes Gladstone married E. C. Wickham, later dean of Lincoln, 27 Dec.

[2] Gladstone to Monson, 27, 29 Dec., offering a lordship in waiting, corrected to the treasurership of the household, Add. MS. 44543, fo. 37, G.D. 29/62; see above, nos. 943, 945.

[3] The Queen to Gladstone, 26 Dec., and reply, 27 Dec.

[4] Gladstone did not record a cabinet meeting on 19 Jan. He was ill and Granville again represented him, Fitzmaurice, ii. 118, and below, no. 969.

952. Lord Granville to Mr. Gladstone.[1] [Add. MS. 44169, fo. 313]

Walmer Castle. Dec 31/73.

I wish you joy with all my heart, and many happy new years.
Your dates will suit me perfectly.

953. Lord Granville to Mr. Gladstone. [Add. MS. 44170, fo. 1]

Walmer Castle. Jan 1/74.

Every possible good wish for this & many other happy new years. I will make a point of being in London during a part of your week—probably on the 9th.

954. Mr. Gladstone to Lord Granville. [G.D. 29/62]

Hawarden Castle. Ja. 3. 74.

1. I got your reply to my query about date for Cabinet : but not to that about Bright.

2. Did you read an Article in the Times, I think of Tuesday, about the vacant Irish Judgeship.[2] If not, pray do.

3. The Memorandum placed by Mr Thomson in the hands of the Shah appeared to me rather officious, especially considering how sharply it condemns certain parties.[3]

4. Goschen feels the great pressure of demands for ships at this & that place in all parts. I recommended him to submit to you informally a list, with any suggestions, of those which he has now scattered all about.[4] The French Navy Estimates are nearly 1 md below those of 1869.

955. Lord Granville to Mr. Gladstone. [Add. MS. 44170, fo. 2]

Walmer Castle. Jan 4/74.

I thought your question about Bright was whether you were certain of my obeying your summons for the 15th, and therefore might summon him. I do not know what else it can be unless it is whether you should confide to him your plans of the budget, which I should answer affirmatively or whether I was ready to speak to Cardwell about Estimates, which I should be ready to do, reserving to myself the amount of pressure I could *personally* bring.

[1] Granville to Gladstone, 30 Dec., on Wolverton's dislike of the proposal of a peerage for Fremantle, and 31 [?] Dec., on Monsell's peerage, Add. MS. 44169, fos. 312, 314, not printed.

[2] The chief barony of the Exchequer (Ireland). Chief Justice Pigot died, 22 Dec. See Spencer to Gladstone, 24 Dec., urging the appointment, before the new term, of Christopher Palles, the attorney-general, Add. MS. 44307, fo. 182. Gladstone's reply, 30 Dec., sent the leader of *The Times*, 30 Dec., p. 7, on reducing the number of Irish judges by appointing the senior puisne judge. Spencer, 2 Jan. 1874, again urged the immediate appointment of Palles, *ibid.*, fo. 189.

[3] See enclosure in Thomson to Granville, No. 137, 13 Oct., on the internal condition and the foreign policy of Persia, F.O. 60/351.

[4] There is no letter on this subject between 2 Nov. and 1 Jan. 1874 in Add. MS. 44161 ; but see Gladstone to Goschen, 1 Jan. 1874, on the problem's being perennial and suggesting the submission of a list to Granville, Add. MS. 44543, fo. 42.

I have often told Goschen that the only demands for ships which I really make are those accompanied with a recommendation. But there are many which I forward, because I think the request may be granted supposing the Ships in that part of the world have nothing better to do.

I did give a caution for the future to Thompson [*sic*].[1]

856. Lord Granville to Mr. Gladstone. [G.D. 29/62]

Walmer Castle. Jan 5/74.

The Chancellor sent me your letter about the scurrilous pamphlet. I have answered, & send you a copy of my letter.[2]

I desired Loftus' telegram to be immediately forwarded to you—the money arrangements seem liberal—& I do not think the Queen can object to the Chaplain clause—as the Emperor, probably at the desire of the Empress insists upon it.[3]

P.S. Lord Archibald Campbell sent me the enclosed scurrilous long and tiresome poem [4] by the authors of "the coming K" which was a still more personal attack upon the Prince of Wales. If you look at the end, you will see an attack, or rather a vulgar unfeeling quiz of the Queen.

Lord A. C. suggested that it ought to be suppressed.

I answer by the usual argument against giving encreased importance to things which had little.

857. Mr. Gladstone to Lord Granville. [G.D. 29/62]

Hawarden Castle. Ja 6. 74.

1. You have answered my question—many thanks.

2. I do not think I need trouble you to come up before Saturday the 17th; *unless* it is quite convenient, in that case the sooner the better.

3. My daily business between reading and writing—unfortunately aggravated at this moment by some local but important cares & calls—is so serious that I am not properly able to collect my thoughts for a review of the "situation" which however I feel very necessary. I am very desirous to know whether we regard it from one & the same point of view, & I will write in this sense the moment I can manage it. Pray read a little pamphlet on the "Probable position of the Constitutional Party in the present crisis". It is *smeared* with Disroute all over; and contains a new bid for the ultramontanes!

[1] See Granville to Thomson, No. 1, 2 Jan., advising abstention from further representations, F.O. 60/360.

[2] See Selborne to Granville, 4 Jan., enclosing a pamphlet by 'Mr Robertson of Doundouneline belonging to a sort of Republican Club which meets at The Hole in the Wall, Clerkenwall', with Gladstone's letter; Granville's reply, 6 Jan., on there being no need for immediate action, G.D. 29/67.

[3] Relates to the Russian Marriage Treaty; see above, no. 856 note.

[4] *The Siliad, or the Siege of the Seats*, by the authors of *The Coming K——* (1875); i.e. Aglen A. Dowty, British Museum catalogue; but cf. S. Halkett and J. Laing, *Dictionary of Anonymous and Pseudonymous English Literature*, which gives E. C. G. Murray as the author of *The Coming K——*. The poem poked fun at the recent difficulties of the government, at the Prince of Wales, and the Queen.

958. Mr. Gladstone to Lord Granville. [G.D. 29/62]

Hawarden Castle. Jan 7. 74.

1. I return your inclosures with thanks—and am glad you concur. Reflection rather confirms my bias. The *Kenealy* in the case might throw all manner of dirt on the Queen's long seclusions and command a good deal not of sympathy perhaps but of notice.

2. In a day or two I will send you some correspondence with H. M. about Prince Leopold.

3. Can I see the Siliad? or get it? which might be best.

4. The Chaplain Clause was really a matter of expression. No doubt was ever raised about the propriety of the *thing*: our way was the more prudent for this country at least.

959. Mr. Gladstone to Lord Granville. [G.D. 29/62]

Hawarden Castle. Jan 8. 74.

I am sorry to send so long a letter but the subject is very stiff.

If you think the view I have taken equitable and give it your concurrence in main points, you are quite free to show the letter to Cardwell.

960. Mr. Gladstone to Lord Granville.[1] [G.D. 29/29A]

Private & Confidential. Hawarden. Jan 8. 1874.

The signs of weakness multiply, and for some time have multiplied, upon the Government, in the loss of controul over the legislative action of the House of Lords the diminution of the majority in the House of Commons without its natural compensation, increase of unity and discipline, and the almost unbroken series of defeats at single elections in the country. In truth the Government is approaching, though I will not say it has yet reached, the condition, in which it will have ceased to possess that amount of power, which is necessary for the dignity of the Crown and the welfare of the country: and in which it might be a godsend, if some perfectly honourable difference of opinion among ourselves on a question requiring immediate action were to arise, and to take such a course as to release us collectively from the responsibilities of office.

The general situation being thus unfavourable, the ordinary remedies are not available. A Ministry with a majority, and with that majority not in rebellion, could not resign on account of the adverse manifestations even of very numerous single constituencies, without making a precedent, and constitutionally a bad precedent: and only a very definite and substantive difficulty could warrant resignation without Dissolution, after the proceedings of the Opposition in March last; when they, or at any rate their Leader and their Whips, brought the Queen into a ministerial crisis and deserted her when there. If then we turn to consider Dissolution, what would be its result? In my opinion, the very best that could happen would be that we should

[1] Printed without the starred sections, Morley, ii. 479–82.

come back with a small majority composed of Irish Home rulers and a decided minority without them: while to me it seems very doubtful whether even with Home Rulers counted in, we should command a full half of the House of Commons. In a word, Dissolution means either immediate death, or at the best Death a little postponed, and the party either way shattered for the time. For one I am anxious to continue where we are, because I am very loath to leave the party in its present menacing condition, without having first made every effort in our power to avert this public mischief. If I have made myself intelligible up to this point, the question that arises is, can we mark out such a course of policy for the Session, either in the general conduct of business, or in some departments and by certain measures, as will with reasonable likelihood reanimate some portion of that sentiment in our favour, which carried us in a manner so remarkable through the Election of 1868? I discuss the matter now in its aspect towards party: it is not necessary to make an argument to show that our option can only lie among things all of which are sound in principle. First then I do *not* believe that we can find this recovery of vital force in our general administration of public business. As men, notwithstanding the advantage drawn from Bright's return, the nation appears to think that it has had enough of us, that our lease is out. It is a question of measures, then: can we by any measures materially mend the position of the party for an impending Election?

* The conduct of the Ashantee campaign does much credit to the Ministers concerned: but all they can do, all that fortune can do in this direction, is to save us from a specific danger. The Ashantee war might have been our death, it cannot be our life, any more than the Abyssinian War could prolong the existence of the last Government.*

Looking to legislation, there are but three subjects which appear to me to be even capable of discussion, in the view I have presented. They are Local Taxation, the County Suffrage, and Finance. I am convinced it is not in our power to draw any great advantage, as a party, from the subject of Local taxation.

* I think it admits of a large and good measure, a measure which while granting pecuniary aid shall introduce needful improvements and obviate future inconveniences if not dangers. But the rate payers are a good deal demoralised, as such, partly by the working of our present law as to the incidence of new burdens, partly by the nature of the agitation which has been so astutely and ably prosecuted. They want money; and are at present rather indifferent about any thing except money. Now in the game of offering money, first the Tories are completely beforehand with us, secondly they will outbid us if we enter into a competition. I have no doubt that if we must deal with the chief difficulties of the case, I do not abandon the hope that we may do it solidly and with credit: but I am certain we cannot make it an effective means of taking the weights out of the other scale, and putting them into ours.* Equally strong is my opinion with respect to the party bearings of the question of the County Franchise. We have indeed already determined not to propose it as a Government. Had we done so a case would have been opened at once, comfortably furnished not with men opposing us on principle, like a part of those who opposed in 1866, but with the men of pretext and the men of disappointment, with intriguers and with egotists. And I believe that in the present state of opinion they would gain their end

by something like the old game of playing redistribution against the franchise. * But supposing an extreme supposition—that this were not so, and that the majority were well united on the question, there is nothing to prevent the Tories from supporting the measure. I am indeed arguing what we have already decided. Some good this measure may do in the hands of an independent member, but also, if it be proposed and not carried (as is probable) some harm: *we* cannot adopt it, to stand or fall by.* Can we then look to finance as supplying what we want? This is the only remaining question. It does not admit, as yet, of a positive answer. But it admits, conditionally, of negative answers. It is easy to show what will prevent our realising our design through the finance of the year. We cannot do it, unless the circumstances shall be such as to put it in our power, by the possession of a very wide margin, to propose something large, and strong, and telling upon both the popular mind, and the leading elements of the constituency. *We cannot do it, if the Ashantee war should continue, and should constitute a serious, perhaps even a sensible, burden on the account for 1874–5. We cannot do it, if any other source of great expenditure should be suddenly opened upon us.* We cannot do it, without running certain risks, of the kind that were run in the Budget of 1853: I mean without some impositions, as well as remissions, of taxes. We cannot do it, without a continuance of the favourable prospects of harvest, and of business. Lastly we cannot do it unless we can frame our Estimates in a manner to show our desire to adhere to the principles of economy which we proposed and applied with such considerable effect in 1868–70. But, subject to the fulfilment of these conditions, my opinion is that we *can* do it: can frame a Budget large enough and palpably beneficial enough, not only to do much good to the country, but sensibly to lift the party in the public view and estimation. And this although a serious sum will have to be set apart, even in the present year, for the claims of local taxation.

* A few words of explanation on the last of my conditions. I do not expect great things, but I do not think we can proceed without things great enough for the public eye to perceive, and to measure them. The state of markets, and course of prices, which were so terribly against us last year, will I hope afford some aid. The ironclad shipbuilding, which was a good deal forestalled on & after the outbreak of the German War, will surely now admit of great contraction. I will not, however, go into details *; but if we can get from ¾ of a million upwards towards a million off the Naval and Military Estimates jointly, then as far as I can judge we shall have left the country no reason to complain, and may proceed cheerily with our work; though we should not escape the fire of the Opposition for having failed to maintain the level of February 1870: which indeed we never announced as our *ultimatum* of reduction. I have had no communication with those of our colleagues, who would most keenly desire reductions, I might say, with any one. *When Bright agreed in August to take office, the subject of expenditure of course was opened between us: and I then expressed my hope that we should at any rate give some evidence of good will and good intention in the matter. I do not know whether he (for example) would be satisfied with what I have here sketched; but I am strongly of opinion that under the circumstances he ought, and from his general reasonableness I trust that he would.* I will only add, that I think a broad difference of opinion among us on such

a question as this, would be a difference of the kind which I described near the opening of this letter, as what might be in certain circumstances, however unwelcome in itself, an escape from a difficulty otherwise incapable of solution.

Let me now wind up this long story by saying that my desire in framing it has been simply to grasp the facts, and set aside illusions which appear to me to prevail among sections of the liberal party, nowhere so much as in that section which believes itself the most enlightened. If we can only get a correct appreciation of the position, I do not think we shall fail in readiness to suit our action to it; but I am bound to confess [myself] not very sanguine, if the *best* come to the best, as to immediate results, though full of confidence, if we act aright, as to the future and early reward.[1]

961. Mr. Gladstone to Lord Granville. [G.D. 29/62]

H[awarde]n. Jan 11. 74.

1. On Mr Jervoise's No 112 of 73,[2] I can I think explain Lord Russell's declaration that the autonomy of Ireland is asserted at Rome.

When I saw him shortly before leaving London, I mentioned to him the article in the Osservatore Romano which boasted of the leadership of the Irish R.C. clerical body in the movement for *autonomy*. He has probably taken my words. They are true—I have been rather surprised at seeing no explanation of this matter in the dispatches from Rome. I care not much whether the Pope interferes to keep his Irish in order; but this publication was a distinct impertinence.

2. I inclose a letter from Cardwell received today.[3] The Cabinet will meet before the Deputation comes. I do not agree in Cardwell's flattering view of my political position. It will not be needful to add to what I have already said, as to its substance: but I of course could not recede from it.

3. We have had a grievous blow here in the death of the Agent [4] who was a valued friend of 28 years' standing. The business of replacing him would have been a grave one at any time: it now comes at a most difficult period. I must wait for his funeral on Thursday and shall not come up until Friday morning. I ought to be in C.H.T. at 3 Pm.

[1] The cabinet decided, 23 Jan., on dissolution, Add. MS. 44641, fo. 245; announced 24 Jan., carried out, 26 Jan. Cardwell's and Goschen's refusal to reduce further the service estimates contributed to the decision; see Cardwell to Granville, copy, private and confidential, 15 Jan., Add. MS. 44120, fo. 210; Morley, ii. 483–7.

[2] Jervoise to Granville, No. 112 confidential, 31 Dec., reporting Antonelli's words minimizing the connection of the Irish Catholic bishops with the home rule movement and complaining of Russell's letter to Sir G. Bowyer, 4 Dec., F.O. 43/123; see above, nos. 926, 927; and for Russell's letter, *The Times*, 15 Dec., p. 18.

[3] Cardwell to Gladstone, private and confidential, 10 Jan., on Trevelyan's campaign for the county franchise and the anxiety of Harcourt, Palmer and himself that Gladstone should not reply favourably to a deputation of his supporters, Add. MS. 44120, fo. 206. He said Gladstone was 'the turning point of people's politics' who might give their votes but not their confidence to Disraeli.

[4] Burnett had managed the Hawarden estates since 1845.

962. Lord Granville to Mr. Gladstone. [Add. MS. 44170, fo. 9]

Private. Walmer Castle. Jan 12/74.

I have written to Cardwell enclosing your excellent letter, and leaving to him whether he should answer it, or talk over the matter with me in London.[1]

I send you two letters of the Duke of Cambridge. The last was in answer to mine saying that I had consulted the Treasury, who had informed me it was impossible to remit the duty on the Grand Duchess's plate, & asking him to specify the fund from which he thought the duty might be paid.[2]

963. Lord Granville to Mr. Gladstone.[3] [Add. MS. 44170, fo. 11]

Confidential. Burn.

I do not trouble you with [the] correspondence[4] I have had with those two men of iron, the P. of W[ales] and the D. of C[ambridge] exhorting me to be *firm* in Central Asia. The comments from the former are mingled with violent complaint as to his [*sic*] the new uniform (which I hear had already been ordered from Poole)—saying that things were changed since his father's time, and that I of all people should be aware of the course of progress . . .

964. Lord Granville to Mr. Gladstone. [Add. MS. 44170, fo. 12]

Private. Walmer Castle. Jan 12/74.

Tenterden has sent me his letter to you.[5] I am very sorry that the Treaty should have been sent without the explanations.

The Treaty [department] has been overwhelmed with work. I hear the Department was up all one night. Owing to the delay of Adlerberg in answering my letter of October, and to the unjustifiable subsequent delay of the Duke & his solicitor, and the usual procrastinations & differences of opinion among the Govt Legal advisers, time has become so short, that everything has been squeezed. You are quite justified in putting the responsibility upon me—& I now 'sleep with my two ears on my pillow' as the Chancellor Law officers and the Queen's conveyancer are agreed in the advice they have given me on a matter which I do not understand.

It would have been better if the mode of remittance had in the first instance been. . . .[6]

965. Lord Granville to Mr. Gladstone. [Add. MS. 44170, fo. 14]

Walmer Castle. Jan 12/74 9 Pm.

C[ardwell] has returned me your letter in a blank cover. It may be in consequence of my ending my letter " Let me know whether you will send me any

[1] See Cardwell to Granville, 15 Jan., assuming that they would talk over Granville's letter enclosing no. 960, G.D. 29/53.

[2] Not traced.

[3] This undated scrap may not be a separate letter but a postscript to no. 962.

[4] Not traced.

[5] Not traced.

[6] This letter is incomplete and no copy has been found.

nswer, or whether you will like to talk over matters in London, where I shall be efore the end of this week" or he may have written to you, or his note to me may ot have been put in the envelope.[1]

I am very sorry to hear of your loss. It must be a serious matter, and one of those hings which requiring personal attention must take up much of your time.

I will write on Jervoise tomorrow. The Post is going.

66. Mr. Gladstone to Lord Granville. [G.D. 29/62]

Hawarden Castle. Jan 13. 74.

After thanking you for your letters received today, I have several points to nention cursorily: but first let me express my earnest hope that you are in no way nxious about Lady Granville, whom you recently mentioned as not quite strong.

1. I have directed to be sent to you for perusal some letters about the position f Prince Leopold—of which it will be time enough to speak when we meet.

2. After a long delay, I have had a kind and satisfactory letter from General chen[c]k acquitting me so far as he is concerned of all evil intention about the J.S.[2] I do not trouble you with it, out of pure compassion.

3. You could not I think have adopted a better or more promising mode of roceeding with my (colossal) letter.

4. I have had a letter from Ponsonby, for the Queen, about the Duchess of E's *uggage*—perhaps this is the same question as that of the plate. Both are new to ne. I have telegraphed for information.

5. I quite understand the difficulty about the Treaty. It is in effect a marriage ettlement, & a very complex one. The drafting & the substance are two different ffairs & (I think) the layman can do little in the former. In my daughter's little ettlement the other day after settling the substance I never looked at the deed, or do I habitually read deeds in which I am interested when the purport has been ettled. This however is perhaps in a measure because it is hardly possible.

6. When the Queen started the subject of gross & nett payment from Russia, er notion was to act in favour of the married Couple as against spoilers, not as gainst the Emperor. But I understand our difficulty, particularly after what has een got, in *seeming*, even, to press him further.

67. Lord Granville to Mr. Gladstone. [Add. MS. 44170, fo. 16]

Walmer Castle. Jan 15/74.

Lady G. is still in bed, but her general health is very good.

Your letters about Prince Leopold seem to be excellent. I am not sure that should not prefer, although the Queen might object, that the full allowance should

[1] See above, no. 962.

[2] Schenck to Gladstone, dated 14 Feb. 1873, but marked 'received Jan. 20, 74, received first n draft in Jan. 1874', Add. MS. 44437, fo. 148. It answered Gladstone to Schenck, 28 Nov. 1872, on his personal position during the civil war and the references to him in the American case for the Geneva tribunal; see above, nos. 670, 760, 765, 794, 796.

be granted with an assurance on his part of returning it, as long as he lived with his Mother.

I cannot believe in the possibility of his staying on.

Habit and his health all induce the Queen to forget that he is grown up and Oxford which has immensely improved him, must have given him a notion of the sweets of liberty.

As to deeds, Lord Campbell told me that he had never read one, brought by his solicitor.

If Lady G. continues pretty well, I shall be in town tomorrow evening.

968. Mr. Gladstone to Lord Granville. [G.D. 29/29A]

Most Private. 10, Downing Street. Jan 17. 74.

Short Mem. on Cardwell's letter.[1]

1. The comparison to be drawn should I think be not with 1869–70—but with 1870–1 as it stood before the Franco-German War.

I should like to see the same comparison, on *this* basis. It is certainly the proper one. That of 69–70 was purely *intermediate*.

2. The Purchase Vote as I understand it is automatic—the sketch would really give an increase of 100 m. on the Estimates.

3. With reference to the closing words, I have had *no* communication direct as yet, except in terms quite general.

4. The *authorities* give me figures thus

Surplus 74–5	$4\frac{1}{2}$	m
I add to their 'low' estimate of Rev.	$\frac{1}{2}$	m
	5	m
New taxes I hope	2	m
	7	
Funds required		
Loss by Inc. Tax	4,775	m
by Sugar D.	1 960	m
by Local Tax^{n} (at least)	800	m
	7 535	m
For minor remissions, Surplus, & margin	465	m
	8	m

[1] See above, nos. 961, 962, 965.

969. Mr. Gladstone to Lord Granville. [G.D. 29/29A]

11 C.H.T. Jan 19./74.

I will make careful use of my enforced silence [1] to consider whether & how it is possible to frame an appeal to the constituencies, suitable & effectual in all respects, without any allusion to differences of opinion upon Estimates. It is certainly hard. I must speak of perseverance in economic efforts and the plan & purpose so far as my mind is concerned being perfectly clear & a kind of foregone conclusion.

970. Mr. Gladstone to Lord Granville. [G.D. 29/29A]

10, Downing Street. Jan 24. 74.

I see that the draft to Odo Russell [2] giving an account of the interview between Duc de Decazes and Lord Lyons is simply narrative and gives no instruction. It is very difficult I suppose to interfere in a question so immediately German as that of the Mandamus on the Bismarckian Laws. But if this be so might we not do the F[rench] G[overnment] a good turn by stating at Berlin, in view of the late declaration of Duc de Decazes about Italy, that we are impressed with the belief that they are endeavouring in good faith to extricate themselves from the trammels in which they were involved by the prior & continuous policy of France from 1849 onwards respecting Rome, & that we hoped Germany would do everything to help & encourage them so to extricate themselves, & to secure a firmer position in the face of the Pope & Clergy, in the manner least likely to arouse national susceptibilities.

971. Mr. Gladstone to Lord Granville.[3] [G.D. 29/62]

10, Downing Street. Feb. 4. 74.

Lord Lyons No 118 [4] which I have read since seeing you appears to show that the French Govt compelled to snub the Bishops in France is playing tricks in Turkey to court the Pope by urging the Porte, with some success, to put down the usages & trample on the feelings of the national party of Armenians and so give free scope in that country also to Papal Absolutism.

[1] See above, no. 951 note; Gladstone's mem. of topics to be discussed; mem. on the reduction of service estimates, modifying the conclusions of no. 960; mem. on the case for dissolution, 20 Jan.; mem. for Cardwell and Goschen suspending the argument about estimates since the decision to dissolve would be based on more general financial grounds, Add. MS. 44762, fos. 3–9.

[2] No. 24 confidential, 23 Jan., recounting his conversation with Münster arising from Decazes' appeal for British good offices with Germany, who had protested against the charges of French bishops on German anti-Catholic legislation, F.O. 64/798. The draft ended with a sentence, framed by Granville, reserving any instruction. A sentence was later added to draw Germany's attention to Decazes' declaration, and to Britain's confidence in French good faith in the words of no. 970.

[3] Gladstone to Granville, 29 Jan., on an application for an ecclesiastical benefice, Add. MS. 44543, fo. 57, not printed.

[4] Lyons to Granville, No. 118 confidential, 31 Jan., on the French ambassador's interference at the Porte in the Armenian Church question, F.O. 27/2044. See also Granville to Locock (*chargé d'affaires*, Constantinople), No. 22, 16 Feb., enclosing the dispatch and instructing him 'to advise the Porte not to give way to or encourage isolated representations' by any one signatory of the Treaty of Paris, F.O. 78/2326.

I hope that in sending this dispatch to Constantinople you will be disposed to suggest to Sir H. Elliot that he should however mildly warn the Porte against becoming a catspaw for any such purpose.

972. Mr. Gladstone to Lord Granville. [G.D. 29/29A]

Feb. 6. 74.

I was concerned to hear that your departure on Wedy afternoon was due or partly due to your having had a less good account of Lady Granville. I hope this was not so ; or at least *is* not so. Our matters have got much worse since you went : and thinking over the duties of the moment I am inclined to think it might be right at once to submit the non-political Peerages, viz. Hammond and Fremantle ; if it is to be done at all. Fremantle is good for 10 or 15 years more, and he will if in any contact with the present Opposition there tend to purify it. There is also the case of the Maharajah which I should be rather inclined to submit.[1] I have thought a good deal though not yet half enough over the probable situation. The points that most dwell upon my mind are 1. our moral & honourable obligation to give effect if we can to the financial pledges rather than hand over the 5 m[illions] to D[israeli]. 2. The question whether after the Ashantee [success ?] (you will have seen the happy news) & especially the Dissolution we can be justified in withdrawing ourselves from the judgment of Parlt on our acts.[2] This I think you will find a weighty consideration. In this age & country, nobody can censure an outgone government.

973. Lord Granville to Mr. Gladstone. [Add. MS. 44170, fo. 33]

Walmer Castle. Feb 6/74.

I send you a list of Dips who have claims for honors.

Odo's G.C.B. depends on your final decision as to Freemantle, because I believe there is only one Grand Cross vacant.

Please talk a word with Wolverton as to F.'s peerage.

What an Election. I do not however in the slightest degree regret the time of it.

You go out as you come in a great minister, and we shall soon have a frightful clamour for you.

Pray tell Mrs G. that Lady G. has got rid of all her troubles, and I hope will soon be able to enjoy a holyday with her spouse.

I shall have the pleasure of dining with you on Monday week.

[1] The honours conferred by the out-going government were : G.C.B., Odo Russell ; dukedom, the marquis of Westminster ; viscountcies, Lord Sydney and Cardwell ; baronies, Fortescue, who had lost his seat in the election, Fremantle, Hammond ; see below, nos. 973–6.

[2] The Ashantee capital had fallen, 3 Feb. By 6 Feb. the strength of the Conservative reaction was plain. By 12 Feb. the elections were over and Disraeli had a majority of fifty, Buckle, *op. cit.*, v. 283. Gladstone resigned, 17 Feb., without meeting Parliament, Guedalla, i. 445–7 ; Morley, ii. 492–4 ; Buckle, v. 285–8 ; mem. by Gladstone on conversation with the Queen, 7 p.m., 17 Feb., Add. MS. 44762, fo. 28.

974. Lord Granville to Mr. Gladstone. [Add. MS. 44170, fo. 28]

No 2. Walmer Castle. Feb 6/74.

I have only time to write a line.

I have anticipated some of your remarks in another letter.

I am against the Tory little game preserving Maharajah, swelling the number of your peerages, and in opposition to (what Halifax says) would be liked in India & by Anglo-Indians.

I should prefer Wols[el]ey if not premature.

I have asked you to speak to Wolverton about Freemantle's Peerage, if he is to have it instead of the G.C.B. I think at any rate, he might be sounded about his son, not by you, but by some 3d person—by me, if you like.

I do not attach much importance to your no 2 consideration about meeting Parlt. They are sure to say you have got into a great mess—from which you have been extricated by the skill of that army which you have tried to destroy—the thing is over, & we are not going to take any further notice of it.

No 1 is a very different pair of boots. I would give anything to abstract the 5 m from Dizzy's manipulator. But can it be done. How if they turn out Brand. How if they carry a vote of censure upon anything in both Houses upon the address.

How if you cannot obtain a modification of the estimates from either of the Departments.

You cannot turn out either C[ardwell] or G[oschen] at this moment. If they consent, is it usual to lay the estimates before the address.

I only start these points, for your consideration.

As to forming a new Govt hereafter, I do not know, but as an opposition, grace a vous, we go out unusually strong.

in haste as the housemaids write.

975. Mr. Gladstone to Lord Granville.[1] [G.D. 29/29A]

11, Carlton House Terrace. Feb. 7. 74.

I presume you will answer Bismarck's kind Telegram. Please to mention me in your reply or not as you think proper. 2. I will inquire about honours; but I think there are hardly any except the G.C.B. 3. I have got from Wolverton all I can about Fremantle. I should call his feeling a faint dislike. So the question is to do or not to do. But I have not the least objection to the sounding, if *you* can manage it. It should be soon! I agree about the Maharajah. 4. As to the impending crisis of our fate, one important element I admit will be the feeling of the party. I have asked Peel [2] (whose first feeling seems rather to be with you) to learn what he can. I tend to harden in my own view, principle & precedent seeming to me alike clear. There are four precedents of our time—1835, 1841, 1852, 1859, under three ministers. The only case the other way is that of 1868 of which the circumstances were altogether

[1] No. 975 printed Morley, ii. 492, without points 2 and 3 and the last sentence.

[2] To Peel, 6 Feb., asking for his views on the causes of the Liberal defeat and on the course to be followed in resigning before or after meeting Parliament, Add. MS. 44543, fo. 61. Cf. Morley, ii. 494–6.

peculiar. But I admit it to be very doubtful whether we should get beyond the Address. On the other hand I admit freely that I have no title to press my view beyond a certain point. I rejoice to hear your good account of Lady Granville.

976. Lord Granville to Mr. Gladstone. [Add. MS. 44170, fo. 35]

Walmer Castle. [8 February 1874].

I telegraphed thanks, and the pleasure it would give me to communicate the Prince's congrats to the Queen & to you. Today I have told Count Munster the same things from you.

I have written the enclosed letter to Freemantle. Please burn it, or send it to Wetherell to copy and forward.

I will run up on Tuesday.

Please forward the box to the Queen with the Marriage correspondence

Will you dine with me on Tuesday.

Has it ever crossed you to make your Cheshire neighbour [1] a Duke.

977. Mr. Gladstone to Lord Granville. [G.D. 29/29A]

11, Carlton House Terrace. Feb. 9. 74.

1. I think your letter to Fremantle as good a specimen of what a firm hand can do in a nice case as ever I saw. 2. Tomorrow unfortunately I dine with Panizzi. Could you dine here Wednesday? 3. Your suggestion about Westminster has often crossed my mind & I have every disposition to recommend it. 4. I told the Queen what I thought of the Elections—she acknowledges in a civil letter; & will be glad when I can tell her any thing *more.*[2] Evelyn Ashley writes in agony (for his election) at the rumour of *immediate* resignation.

978. Lord Granville to Mr. Gladstone.[3] [Add. MS. 44170, fo. 37]

18, Carlton House Terrace. Feb 17/74.

Bessborough says he believes that Spencer would like the offer of an extra K.P. to mark the approbation of his Ld Lieutenancy (not to interfere with the present vacancy being given to Carysfort).[4] An extra K.P. was given to Mayo.

If you think fit to mention it to the Queen, it might be as well to consult her whether there is any objection to a K.G. taking the Irish order, but I should think there was none.

[1] The marquis of Westminster.

[2] Gladstone to the Queen, 6 Feb., and reply, 8 Feb., Guedalla, i. 443–4.

[3] Granville to Gladstone, 17 Feb., on the Queen's irritation at the failure to repair parts of Kensington Palace, Add. MS. 44170, fo. 39, not printed.

[4] The fifth earl of Carysfort was invested with the order of St. Patrick, 31 Aug. 1874, in the place of Lord Howth, who died 4 Feb., but an extra K.P. was not created for Lord Spencer W. A. Shaw, *The Knights of England* (1906), i. 104. Spencer was offered a marquisate, see to Granville, 14 Feb., G.D. 29/25A.

979. Lord Granville to Mr. Gladstone. [Add. MS. 44170, fo. 41]

Private. Walmer Castle. March 3/74.

I go to town tomorrow afternoon. I dine with Clanwilliam, but I shall hope to see you (if not tomorrow evening,) on Thursday morning. I want much to consult you about myself in the Lords. Bessborough's letters rather perplex me.

Sydney tells me [1] that Disraeli told him that the speech must be on the 19th, whether he is elected or not.

980. Mr. Gladstone to Lord Granville. [G.D. 29/62]

11, Carlton House Terrace. Mch 4. 74.

I dine with Panizzi who does not like one's coming away early: but I expect to be at home tomorrow at any time before 4.45 when I go to the House.

A letter in D[aily] News yest[erda]y & Article today—letter in Times EPB. (evidently Bouverie) & article on it—may be read with some advantage.

981. Lord Granville to Mr. Gladstone. [Add. MS. 44170, fo. 43]

Private. Ealing. March 5/74.

Childers caught Lord Selborne and me as the train was leaving Waterloo yesterday evening to say that the House of Commons Members of the late Cabinet wished to meet at my house—I have since recd a telegram from Hartington stating that they would come at twelve on Saturday.

As in all probability it is to make some communication to you, perhaps you will be kind enough not to make any engagement for the morning.

I will tell you on Saturday morning the pith of what Selborne & Cardwell think.[2]

982. Mr. Gladstone to Lord Granville. [G.D. 29/29A]

11 Carlton H. Terrace. March 12. 1874.

I have issued a Circular [3] to Members of Parliament, of the Liberal party, on the occasion of the opening of Parliamentary business.

But I feel it to be necessary that, while discharging this duty, I should explain

[1] Sydney to Granville, 2 March, G.D. 29/25A.

[2] For Gladstone's first suggestion to Granville of the execution of his decision to resign the leadership, see Fitzmaurice, ii. 135–7. He announced his eventual resignation at the cabinet dinner, 16 Feb., Morley, ii. 497–9. For memoranda of his reasons, see Add. MS. 44762, fos. 39, 41. See Hartington to Granville, 5 March, on the efforts of the late cabinet to persuade him to stay, G.D. 29/54. He agreed to remain nominal leader for one session 'to be consulted and to appear on emergencies', Hartington to Granville, 12 March, *ibid.* See also Forster to Granville, 13 March, G.D. 29/56; but cf. Halifax to Granville, 27 Feb., on Hartington's assuming the lead in order to re-unite the party, G.D. 29/25A. The session began, 5 March.

[3] See draft and fair copy, announcing his intentions, Add. MS. 44762, fo. 29. For first draft of no. 982, 5 March, and amendments, 7 March, *ibid.*, fos. 37, 38. For a further draft and a draft in Granville's hand with some variations, see Add. MS. 44170, fos. 45, 48.

what a circular could not convey, with regard to my individual position at the present time.

I need not apologise for addressing these explanations to you. Independently of other reasons for so troubling you, it is enough to observe that you have very long represented the Liberal party, and have also acted on behalf of the late Government from its commencement to its close, in the House of Lords.

For a variety of reasons, personal to myself, I could not contemplate any unlimited extension of active political service. And I am anxious that it should be clearly understood by those friends with whom I have acted in the direction of affairs that, at my age, I must reserve my entire freedom to divest myself of all the responsibilities of leadership at no distant time.

The need of rest will prevent me from giving more than occasional attendance in the House of Commons during the present Session.

I should be desirous, shortly before the commencement of the Session of 1875 to consider whether there would be advantage in my placing my services for a time at the disposal of the Liberal Party, or whether I should then claim exemption from the duties I have hitherto discharged.

If, however, there should be reasonable ground for believing that, instead of the course which I have sketched, it would be preferable, in the view of the Party generally, for me to assume at once the place of an independent Member, I should willingly adopt the latter alternative. But I should retain all that desire which I have hitherto felt for the welfare of the Party. And if the gentlemen composing it should think fit either to choose a leader, or to make provision *ad interim* with a view to the convenience of the present year, the person designated would of course command from me any assistance, which he might find occasion to seek, and which it might be in my power to render.

983. Lord Granville to Mr. Gladstone. [Add. MS. 44170, fo. 55]

H of Lords. May 4/74.

F Cavendish showed me your letter on the debate of tonight on Ashantee—and I spoke to Cardwell, Kimberley Hartington and Goschen on the subject. They entirely agreed that our part was to defend the past, to say that the late Gov had purposely postponed any decision as to the future, and to abstain from opinions or advice, to vote if possible for a previous question.

They said they would give the same advice to Forster & Huguessen [*sic*], inculcating upon them that if they did not agree they must take care to mark that they were speaking for themselves alone.[1]

All those that I have mentioned with F Cavendish, Wolverton Peel and others

[1] R. W. Hanbury, Conservative M.P. for Tamworth, moved the withdrawal of British administration from the Gold Coast. Hugessen defended the Liberals' policy. The colonial under-secretary dissociated the government from a policy of 'unlimited expenditure' on 'a crusade against barbarism' and the House divided on a motion for adjournment, *Hans. Parl. Deb.*, 3rd ser., ccxviii. 1592–1664.

are anxious that as you come only occasionally to the Commons, that you should not attend on the County Franchise.[1]

I own their arguments appear to me to make a strong case, that it would place you & others in a difficulty.

What are your chief objections to the Archbishop's Bill.[2] Lord John was wretched—Derby cautious but not perfectly judicious to my mind.[3]

984. Lord Granville to Mr. Gladstone. [Add. MS. 44170, fo. 59]

[6? May 1874].

I have called in Portland Place, but both Mr & Mrs Hankey were out. I will telegraph to you tomorrow morning.[4]

They say that last night was good—the Speaker says that Dizzy does not attempt to lead the House.

985. Mr. Gladstone to Lord Granville. [G.D. 29/29A]

Hawarden Castle. May 7. 74.

Many thanks to you for solving my difficulty with Hankey. I shall now give up the idea of coming for Trevelyan's Bill, though I do it with regret. On the subject of the Agricultural labourers and their movement, I would recommend you to read a small book called 'The Revolt of the Field'.[5]

As to the Licensing Bill, it would seem to me imprudent to touch it on the second reading, so far as I understand the case.[6] But with this gratuitous enlargement of the hours it might well be called, in our jargon, the "additional Facilities for Drunkeness Bill".

With respect to the Archbishop's Bill, I do not know that I yet fully understand it. In writing to Wolverton I called it silly. This was a bad word: but I think it an ill-considered measure on a very difficult subject. *We* effected a good deal

[1] On 13 May G. O. Trevelyan moved the second reading of his Household Franchise (Counties) Bill, but failed to carry it, *Hans. Parl. Deb.*, 3rd ser., ccxix. 206–60. Gladstone was not in London. The Liberals were divided on the timing of the county franchise; see above, no. 961 note.

[2] The Public Worship Regulation Bill, introduced by the archbishop of Canterbury in the Lords, 20 April. The second reading was due on 11 May.

[3] Russell moved in the Lords for correspondence with Germany, Austria, Russia and France on the maintenance of the peace of Europe, 4 May. Derby answered and Russell withdrew the motion, *Hans. Parl. Deb.*, 3rd ser., ccxviii. 1564–9.

[4] Hankey sought to promote closer relations between the leaders and back benchers of the Liberal party by a series of dinner parties. Gladstone, having accepted an invitation to the first, excused himself through Wolverton who asked Granville to explain to Hankey; see Hankey to Granville, 6 May, G.D. 29/25A; Wolverton to Granville, 6 May, Add. MS. 44170, fo. 58; Granville to Gladstone, tel. *ibid.*, fo. 61.

[5] A. W. Clayden, *The Revolt of the Field* (1874), 234 pp. Relates to the strike of the agricultural labourers of East Anglia for higher wages; defeated by July after the Farmers' Association had refused to employ members of the National Agricultural Labourers' Union.

[6] Cross's Intoxicating Liquors Bill, introduced in the Commons, passed its second reading without a division, Harcourt and Lowe speaking briefly, *Hans. Parl. Deb.*, 3rd ser., ccxix. 75–150. It repealed sections 19–22 and 35 of the 1872 act (on adulteration and the right of entry) and modified the hours of closing.

in Church Legislation, by requiring much previous consideration among all parties & a large amount of consent. The Archbishop has, with consultation among the Bishops only, introduced a Bill which largely increases Episcopal power: no concurrence of the Government, no measures taken to secure the assent of the Clergy, but on the contrary the measure announced to them by the Times, a proceeding most imprudent, and, I think, scarcely decent.

All this seems to place the Bill under prejudice and diminish its chance of fair play.

I thoroughly approve of giving the people who attend, or desire to attend, the Church some better controul than they now have over the ill-judged or arbitrary changes made by the Clergyman. I would go a long way in allowing them to claim a continuance of the *status quo*: and it has always been my opinion that, if legislation be requisite (& I cannot wonder that many think it so, though I am not sure as to my own view), this is the safest time for it.

But this Bill has no regard to the *status quo* at all. It gives an immense facility of challenging any proceeding in divine service, however rooted in local practice, however approved by an entire congregation. But as to the judgment, the challengers seem to be dependent on each one individually of 27 or 28 Bishops, acting with the aid of Assessors, in the appointment of whom I understand he has a large share.

I seem to see here too much facility in *raising* questions; too little security of having them properly settled.

True there is an Appeal: but, when the Appeal reaches the final Court, it becomes subject again to all the delays, costs, and trammels of the old procedure.

There are two other points which I think most objectionable.

First the tendency to introduce in each Diocese different states of legal usage! according to the leanings and temper of each Bishop.

If variety in single Churches is not desirable (my opinion is that, when there is more than one Church accessible to the people, much variety ought to be allowed, but under this Bill what the Bishop rules for one Church he must rule, it is plain, for all) variety between one *Diocese* & another is very far worse and as I think a most serious evil.

The other is that the Bill proceeds upon this principle, that neither doctrine nor moral conduct require the legal securities which are necessary for the externals of Divine Worship. This is an entirely novel principle, and one which I must think long & much before adopting. There is much to be said for the direct contrary. Our rubrical laws are exceptions to the general character of our law: consisting, as they do, of an immense number of positive directions of things to be done, and incessantly done, by 22000 Clergymen all over the country. It seems to me to lie in the nature of things that such laws cannot, I would almost say ought not to be exactly obeyed. Their general spirit may be fairly followed, and yet particular breaches here and there may creep in, and may become so much the habit of the place that for the people they gradually become as it were the law. I am of opinion it ought not [to] be in the power of every individual Bishop with his Assessors to decide whether these practices shall be altered or not.

Another point of a serious nature is this. The Bishop has at present, with large but well understood executive powers, a great moral influence, and every really able & competent Bishop governs his Diocese *mainly* by this influence. I fear that if he is to be turned into what must be practically the character of a criminal judge over his Clergy, he will lose much more in moral influence than he gains in judicial power.

You will observe that I have not taken any objection to the Bill on the ground of unfairness to particular persons or parties. I see such objections are taken, but I do not feel sure that they lie justly against the measure.

I think the whole subject however of very great importance and I shall by no means shirk the consideration of it. I can see how in some things the Bill might be much improved. I am afraid you will think this letter, though a long one, very inadequate in its treatment of the measure: and so it is. I will however beg you kindly to keep it, for I might wish to look at it again.

If you see Wolverton please to thank him much on my part about the Hankey business.

Have you been asked to Windsor to meet the Emperor of Russia?

986. Lord Granville to Mr. Gladstone. [Add. MS. 44170, fo. 69]

18, Carlton House Terrace. May 9/74.

Many thanks for your letter.

The Handsome Donkey [Hankey?] was a good deal put out at first but ended in perfect good humour. He is it appears violently opposed to the extension of the County Franchise.

I told the Members of the House of Commons what you said about the licensing [bill]. They will act on your line, but as Lowe is to be spokesman, I cannot answer for the shades.

I am extremely obliged for your criticism on the Archbishop's Bill. We propose to criticize freely, but to vote for a second reading. Selborne has an entirely new bill for Committee which he will move as an amendment. I have not seen it.[1]

We have just been asked for the Banquet for the Czar on Thursday at Windsor.

Derby answered well a wonderfully foolish speech of Napier & Ettrick.[2]

987. Lord Granville to Mr. Gladstone. [Add. MS. 44170, fo. 71]

Niddry Lodge, Kensington. June 13/74.

I have recd. a note from Goschen asking me to urge Forster not to support Lyon Playfair on his motion next Monday for a Minister of Instruction. Lowe

[1] Relates to the second reading of the Public Worship Regulations Bill, 11 May, when Selborne and Grey were the Liberal spokesmen, *ibid.*, 2–65.

[2] Lord Napier and Ettrick asked whether the new government accepted Granville's dispatch to Loftus, 17 Oct. 1872, on the boundary of Afghanistan, and would defend the latter against unprovoked attack. Derby accepted the dispatch but refused to exceed its literal meaning and Granville spoke in support, 8 May, *ibid.*, ccxviii. 1906–17.

is going to oppose it strongly, and Goschen says that the repetition of the same difference of opinion between two of our colleagues as took place on the 25th clause will have the worst effect in the H. of Commons.[1]

I shall not move without hearing from you. Hartington summoned a meeting of the Commons ex ministers (with Cardwell) at my house to consider the course to be taken on the 25th clause, as there was a great difference of opinion.[2]

We met, Forster was determined to speak and vote in its support—the other M.P's to vote against it: & they thought it impossible to vote without speaking. Forster was rough & Bright rather offensive to him—but it was settled that Forster & Lowe were to speak, to avoid the appearance of answering one another, & to draw it as mild as possible in their respective directions.

Neither party were satisfied with the way this plan was respectively carried out—& there was much soreness.

It is a pity that we should be so much disunited, particularly as the Gov is certainly as little harmonious as possible.

Their popularity is on the decrease in the House of Lords, and it was a very strong measure Salisbury and Carnarvon staying away on the Appellate Jurisdiction Bill.[3]

3 fifths of the majority were liberals.

Dizzy is ill with gout in both feet, and very low.

I am afraid I shall miss you on the 15th, as we are to go to the Prince & Princess of Wales for Ascot.

Tell Mrs Gladstone that the Westminsters are delighted with Grosvenor's marriage, that it is almost certain that Waterford will marry Lady Blanche Somerset and it is said that Pembroke has been refused by Lady Gertrude Talbot.

988. Lord Granville to Mr. Gladstone. [Add. MS. 44170, fo. 76]

June 16/74.

Many thanks for your letter, & after communication with F Cavendish and Hartington I wrote to Forster & to Lowe—Urging the first not to support Playfair & asking the latter whether if Forster consented to remain silent on condition that Lowe would do so, he, Lowe would consent. Lowe answered in the affirmative but Forster was out, and I have recd no answer up to this date from him, but I see

[1] Goschen to Granville, Saturday [12 June], G.D. 29/25A. Granville sent to Forster a note from Gladstone, 14 June, agreeing that he should not support Playfair's motion on grounds both of policy and party, G.D. 29/29A, not printed. It did not reach him in time; see below, nos. 988, 989, and T. Wemyss Reid, *Life of . . . William Edward Forster* (1888), ii. 59–63. Goschen told Forster of Gladstone's note and prevented a division, but he and Lowe had already spoken in opposite senses, *Hans. Parl. Deb.*, 3rd ser., ccxix. 1589–1623.

[2] I.e. on the second reading of Richard's abortive bill to abolish clause 25 (safeguarding the parents' free choice of school) of Forster's Education Act. Forster and Lowe spoke against each other and twelve Liberals voted for the bill, *ibid.*, 1304–58.

[3] I.e. to amend the Supreme Court of Judicature Act (1872), committed, 11 June, when a motion to retain the Lords as the supreme court for Scotch and Irish appeals was defeated, *Hans. Parl. Deb., loc. cit.*, 1359; see also above, no. 852 note.

from the report that he spoke—& I presume Goschen to whom I told all that had passed was unsuccessful in stopping him. The result is damaging to the plan.

Many thanks for the rest of your letter. It was not reported, but I said a few words on the Scotch Patronage bill, throwing doubt on the expediency of the Measure.[1]

I hope you will come to town next week.

We are in a small pretty house of Villiers Lister.

989. Lord Granville to Mr. Gladstone. [Add. MS. 44170, fo. 78]

June 21/74.

I send you the enclosed note from Forster.[2]

I do not understand the delay in the receipt of the letter, as I sent a man in a cab with it.

990. Lord Granville to Mr. Gladstone. [Add. MS. 44170, fo. 79]

Private. 18, Carlton House Terrace. June 25/74.

I saw Freddy Cavendish this morning, who kindly gave me news of you all. He told me, saying it was to me alone, of some of your future arrangements. I should like to press upon you that with whatever largeness and delicacy you decide to act, you should take care either by yourself or by some one else, that all proper arrangements should be made for burdens of all kinds connected with a house & place falling upon the estate. I think even more than this ought to be done.[3]

Freddy tells me that you intend to come up soon, but that you do not mean to be in time to vote against home rule.[4]

You know how anxious I have been for your frequent presence in Parliament, but if you are not able to come for Home Rule, I am not sure with the present sad excuse, that I should come for some time.

In the opinion of several of our late colleagues, of Dodson and one or two private members who have spoken to me, although the Gov is blundering & losing ground, our party is more disunited than ever, & that for the present there is as much chance as ever of some of our disaffected taking the first opportunity of separating themselves in debate from you or any other leader.

I believe the autumn will make a great difference.

Pray say again all that is most kind to Mrs Gladstone. I need not say how deeply touched I was by the remarkable letter you sent partly in answer to mine.

[1] Hansard reports Granville ' who was very imperfectly heard ' as ' understood to say ' that he would support the measure but that a larger one was needed ; committee stage, 9 June, *ibid.*, 1252–3.

[2] See above, no. 987, note 1.

[3] Relates to arrangements on the Hawarden estate consequent on the death of Sir Stephen Glynne, Gladstone's brother-in-law, 17 June.

[4] For Butt's motion for Irish home rule and the debates, 30 June, 2 July, which Gladstone did not attend, see *ibid.*, ccxx. 700–92, 874–965. Gladstone to Granville, 26 June, on his return to London after his niece's funeral, and his position in the party. G.D. 29/29A. not printed.

991. Lord Granville to Mr. Gladstone. [Add. MS. 44170, fo. 83]

18 C. H. T. July 14/74.

I have just recd the enclosed.[1] The same thing has been said to me by quantities of our friends, but I have not troubled you with any suggestions as I do not wish to trouble you with my ideas on a matter, on which you have thought so much, & which is personal to you—but I do not think I ought to keep from you the opinion of such a man as Cardwell.

I need not say that I should be glad if you could put a spoke in the wheel which Dizzy is rolling with such complacency.

It does not seem to me that after your speech and the offer of your resolutions, you are bound to expose the latter to a greater defeat than will be the fate of the opposition to the 2d reading.

PS. Whether Cardwell's suggestion as to amendments is judicious or not, I will not say. I should prefer your saying that seeing the temper of the House, you see no practical use in proceeding to a division on your resolutions.

992. Lord Granville to Mr. Gladstone. [Add. MS. 44170, fo. 88]

18, Carlton House Terrace. [19 July 1874].

Luncheon?

How can one deal with the enclosed—a report of a speech which is sent for revision 35 days after delivery.

I did not say one sentence of it—in most cases the reverse.

I could compose a speech in the same sense as that which I made, but I have no recollection of what I actually said.

993. Mr. Gladstone to Lord Granville.[2] [G.D. 29/29A]

Penmaenmawr. Aug. 7. 74.

I think I ought to report to you about my affair with Harcourt.[3]

In such Speeches as I had heard from him on the Archbishop's Bill he had been studiously offensive but I was quite willing to take no notice, partly because of the scandal as respects the Liberal party, and partly I fear from the small value I set on his good opinion.

[1] Cardwell to Granville, 14 July, asking him to persuade Gladstone not to move his resolutions on the public worship bill, for party reasons, and suggesting amendment in committee, Add. MS. 44170, fo. 86. For Gladstone's speech (cf. no. 985), his resolutions, 9 July, the resumed debate, 15 July, in which he did not speak, and the formal withdrawal, 16 July, see *ibid.*, 1372–92, ccxxi. 13–89, 118–19.

[2] Granville to Gladstone, 25 July, asking for an address, Add. MS. 44170, fo. 89; Gladstone to Granville, 27 July, on the divisions in the party, G.D. 29/29A.

[3] On the conclusion of the Commons' proceedings on the public worship bill, Wednesday, 5 Aug., Harcourt attacked Salisbury's speech in the Lords, complimented Disraeli, and confronted Gladstone with legal and theological argument. Gladstone declined to argue but rebuked Harcourt for a lack of good taste and courtesy in launching his learning on the House, *ibid.*, 1341–66; cf. A. G. Gardiner, *The Life of Sir William Harcourt* (1923), i. 273–9; *Gladstone to his Wife*, edited A. Tilney Bassett (1936), pp. 204–5; Buckle, *op. cit.*, v. 323–8.

On Wednesday however instead of making any reparation to me, in defiance of all regularity, and without any practical issue before him, he spoke at me for above an hour (I believe): since even his slimy, fulsome, loathsome eulogies upon Dizzy were aimed at me, and I rather think the affair was got up between them, but in D. I have nothing to complain of. It was quite plain that he meant business, namely my political extinction, and thought that Ritualism afforded a fine opportunity. To this I do not much object, but the end being plain & grossly indicated, and as I did not like the manner or the tools employed, I bethought me that for the sake of the party from which I am not divorced in feeling, nor formally in fact, I must say something, and therefore I did so, though I felt obliged to observe limits of time, out of regard & respect to the House, which he had not observed. Those near me & some who came to me thought I had no choice, and I hope you will be of opinion I did not wantonly offend. What he thought, he best knows.

However I regret it *extremely*. It is a new scandal & a new difficulty for the party. I feel for those who are to come after me, in regard to their dealings with him. I am not angry with him, I do not respect him enough to be angry. But as to the future. He thinks himself a Disraeli, but he is not at present one; though he is a most able speaker in offence, I doubt his pluck & efficiency in defence. But [what] he perhaps does not perceive is that Dizzy himself, who is an extraordinary man and a genius, would not have been able to mount but for the most singular manner in which Derby & G. Bentinck played into his hands, the latter of the two first by his life, and then yet more by his death.

Forgive this piece of amicable confession and believe me. . . .

994. Lord Granville to Mr. Gladstone. [Add. MS. 44170, fo. 91]

Walmer Castle. Aug 8/74.

Many thanks for your note of the 7th, which odd to say I got here this evening.

I cannot conceive there being a doubt about your answer to Harcourt. It was a masterpiece and everybody is of the same opinion.

I *know* that it is the opinion of some of the present Cabinet, that Harcourt's & Dizzy's speeches were concerted,[1] but they are not sure whether it was to save the bill, or to drive in the wedge to oust Salisbury.

The conversation in the H. of Lords was arranged between Salisbury, Carnarvon, Hardy, and—Cairns. The whips knew nothing of it, nor Derby.

Although as you said in your speech, Harcourt has undoubted ability, nothing would give me greater pleasure, than to see him join Dizzy, which is anything but an unlikely occurrence. He would [be] a fatal gift to the Tories.

I presume that Dizzy has no other object, than to give a notion of his sagacity, in the mysterious allusions he makes to Foreign affairs . . .[2]

[1] See Meade to Granville, 18 Aug., telling him the speeches were concerted, G.D. 29/25A.

[2] In the Queen's speech at the close of the session, 7 Aug., *Hans. Parl. Deb.*, 3rd ser., ccxxi. 1416. Two further paragraphs of no. 994 on private legal business, not printed.

995. Mr. Gladstone to Lord Granville.[1] [G.D. 29/25A]

Copy. Hawarden Castle. 2 Nov. 74.

I sent to Murray my M.S.[2] by the post of yesterday. This has not been done without much deliberation. I have even consulted as far as I could under this roof, people whose views I thought might be useful to me, & brought two R.C. friends here that they among others might read it. I cannot explain fully on paper. Suffice it to say I have thought as well as I could about the *party*, to which I am sanguine enough to think it may be rather beneficial than otherwise. We have had since the Irish measures were completed, no *hold* whatever on the R.C.'s, except a handful. I have certainly felt the great religious interests of Christendom, which are deeply concerned in the Papal & Ultramontane proceedings. But my proper & main motive has been this: the conviction I have that they are waiting, in one vast conspiracy, for an opportunity to direct European war to the re-establishment by force of the temporal power; or even to bring about such war for that purpose—I desire in homely language to do the little in my power to put a spoke in their wheel. At the same time, the pamphlet may prove to be a trumpery affair; but I have thought it necessary alas to be prepared for the event of its making an impression. The title will be something like this "The Vatican Decrees in their bearing on civil allegiance—a political expostulation" (i.e. with British & Irish Roman Catholics).

The Priest party will be furious: the moderate men only embarrassed if they are too timid to do their duty. My wish is to help them in doing it. In this category Ripon may stand.

The whole circumstances have vividly recalled to me the trouble of mind I went through before publishing the letters to Ld Aberdeen about Naples—another difficult case in which I was obliged to act for myself because no one else could have the same point of view.

996. Lord Granville to Mr. Gladstone. [Add. MS. 44170, fo. 99]

Venice. Nov 10/74.

I was delighted to hear from you. I have waited a day or two, in hopes of getting your pamphlet before answering. Indeed it is very difficult to give an opinion until one has read it. I have no doubt it will create a great sensation, & it would certainly not be right of you to suppress opinions which you may think will be of use.

As a party question, it will of course set the whole of the Catholics against us, (including Ripon, of whose openness to reason on religious questions, I have given up all hope.) Acton's friends are a mere handful. He never would raise the number of subscribers to the Home & Foreign beyond a thousand. On the other hand I

[1] Granville to Gladstone, 22 Aug., inviting to Walmer and reporting his intention to go abroad, 7 Sept.; 31 Aug., describing Harcourt's autograph at Highclere; 25 Sept., on his crossing to Calais that evening, Add. MS. 44170, fos. 95–8; Gladstone to Granville, 25 Aug., declining the invitation; 1 Sept., thanking for his note; 2 Nov., covering no. 995 which was also sent to Wolverton, G.D. 29/29A, not printed.

[2] *The Vatican Decrees in their bearing on Civil Allegiance: a political expostulation* (John Murray, 1874); cf. *Gladstone to his Wife*, ed. Tilney Bassett, pp. 205–6; Morley, ii. 502–3, 509–12, 515–20.

ıave no doubt your pamphlet will give great pleasure to a large majority of the ountry, if it is written as I suppose it will have been.

The pros & cons as to the continent appear to me to be thus. It may do much ;ood in enlightening the world as to the monstrous assumptions of the present apacy.

On the other hand I doubt whether these encyclicals & etc have much practical olitical effect in Catholic Countries, & whether declarations from you may not upport what appears to me the injudiciously violent action of the G[erma]n Gt.

In the meantime I long to see your pamphlet.

I am at last convalescent & can do all one wishes to do in travel.

I was in bed during the 5 days Thiers was at Voltri, & did not see him once. rom the accounts I heard from my wife & Mme Galliera age is beginning to have ts effect. He is exceedingly bitter—the wrangles between him & Mme Galliera ıis hostess must have been sharp.

" Le Marechal McMahon est un homme parfaitement nul."

Mais, Monsieur, vous m'avez dit avant sa nomination à la Presidence " C'est ın très grand homme de guerre " Comment peut-il être un homme parfaitment nul ?

& again

Puisque M. Montalivet est devenu Republicain, vous le verrez à Nice.

Madame vous me dites des méchancetées.

Comment, Monsieur, est ce que vous me faites un procès de tendances ?

Non, Madame, je vous fais un procès de faiblesse. Vous êtes sous l'influence le vos amis, vous avez peur d'eux.

Mais, Monsieur, si j'avais peur d'eux, je n'aurais pas le plaisir de vous voir ici— t si j'étais peureuse, je n'oserai pas vous entendre. Eh bien je vous dirai, que le tout ce que, vous m'avez dit ces quatre jours, je ne crois pas un mot. Je ne rois pas que vous êtes républicain, je ne crois pas à votre amour pour l'Italie, ni votre enthousiasme pour le Roi Victor Emmanuel. Je crois que vous dites tout a pour la cause, dont vous vous êtes fait le champion. Est ce que je dis vrai.

He would not answer, and on going out she took his arm, & said nous nous lisputions, mais il n'y a que des amis qui peuvent disputer.

Madame, quand on discute avec moi, il faut être de mon avis.

Ah Monsieur, pourquoi ne me vous l'avez pas dit d'abord.

Our weather is divine, & Lady G. in ecstasies with Venice.

Can I buy you a Palace. They are the only things which seem cheap & really old.

97. Mr. Gladstone to Lord Granville. [G.D. 29/29A]

Hawarden Castle. Nov. 25.74.

Your letter of the 10th besides a fair report of you and your doings, and an nimitable report of Thiers's *duellista,* contained a most fair & acute appreciation f my pamphlet not as to the contents which you had not seen but as to the fact of ublication. I hope it has long before this reached you but I have not had your ddress & can only trust to forwarding from your house in London. I will now give ou as exactly as I can the various opinions and impressions which it or the report of it made before publication on the various persons with whom I had an opportunity of communicating.

Sir A. Gordon. Feared movement to repeal Act of 1829
Lord Acton. Feared magistrates & Boards of Guardians wd behave worse.
Mrs G. Malcolm. Delighted.
Mr de Lisle (R. C.). Anticipated much good.
Mr Knowles (Ed. Contemp. Review) much pleased.
Panizzi. Much pleased.
Lacaita. Thought he had objected but had not!
Wife and Son. Not displeased.
All these saw the MS or Sheets.
These upon description
1. Wolverton. did not seem dissatisfied.
2. Cardwell. Much pleased.
3. Huxley (reported by Knowles) mightily pleased.

Such was the state of opinion *ab intra*. But I felt and feel the case to have been one in which I could make no one but myself responsible.

I am very well pleased thus far with the result. The Times and Pall Mall Gazette made their efforts at first to write it down: but within a week had to come round. The impartial Spectator is about half-pleased. But what I regard as most important is the course of the discussion it has raised among the Roman Catholics themselves, who are writing in all manner of different senses. The result must be injurious to the pestilent opinions which have so grievously obtained the upper hand in that Church, and to the party which *means* to have a war in Europe for the restoration of the Temporal Power. To place impediments in their way, and in the way of that war, has been my principal purpose, & to effect this by an appeal while there is yet time to public opinion.

It is possible I may have to write again: but I do not as yet see a necessity for it. Nothing like a detailed answer has been yet tried.

Acton has written two letters in the Times which in their historical character are I apprehend quite impregnable, and which deal very heavy blows. On the other hand the Spectator remarked even of the first, 'this blow should have been struck from outside not from within'. And I own I do not see in what way his personal position can be defended in argument. Of this I have not said a word to him.

The effect on the Liberal party I think will be good. No R.C. vote is to be had, except for a price. Those who can pay the price will have the vote whether they be L. or C. But the price must lie in the future, not in the recollections of the past. And it is probable that for each R.C. vote gained we lose several Protestants. Even in the fervour of 1868 we could not carry Liverpool; perhaps because we had there a large and enthusiastic R.C. support.

And now you must be tolerably weary of the subject. In general politics, I see no daylight. The Wenlock Election [1] did not make a bad impression because

[1] The by-election was caused by the succession of G. C. Forester to the barony, 10 Oct. The borough, which had been represented by a Forester from 1678 with only short interruptions elected C. T. Forester, a nephew.

we lost no seat: but was very bad. We had an excellent Candidate, they a stick. Nothing will rally the party but a cause: or such portentous blundering as is almost beyond hope or fear.

There is a horrid Marriage case, Mr G. case, of which you at F.O. must have been cognisant, and which may make a great row on the score of Papal Aggression.

998. Mr. Gladstone to Lord Granville. [G.D. 29/29A]

Private. Hawarden Castle. Dec. 7.74.

When I wrote to you on the 25th from Scotland, I said nothing had then occurred to show it would be necessary for me to write again about the Vatican Decrees.[1] Since that time, however, matters have changed a good deal. The pamphlet, which then had only just come out in a popular edition, has circulated very widely indeed; and not only (besides all manner of others) have five of the Roman Bishops in England made answers, three of them in separately published Pastorals, but Manning has advertised a reply, from under the shadow of the Vatican, and this Reply will exhibit all that the united strength of the Curia can effect. I have little doubt that it will require an answer from me. The matter is a serious one; having gone into it, I must go through: happily, if I keep myself clear of theology proper, the goal is not very far off; and no one will be more delighted than I to get out of so thorny a business. My hope is that I may have somewhat increased the difficulties in the way of a violent restoration of the Temporal Power: and perhaps, though this is only a collateral result, may have done something to set people like Ripon a little on their guard for the future.

It would be too early, while you are still abroad, to discuss the matter in its party aspect, I mean as it affects my own pledge to consider, before the Session comes, the question of active leadership. I believe the publication has tended to strengthen, and *hearten*, the party generally: against which is of course to be set such estrangement of R.C.'s (not estranged already) as it may possibly have produced. But there would, at least such is my first thought, be [this] much to say against any act of formal leadership on this particular ground, that it would widen the breach with the Irishmen in the H of C. There is also much else to say. No progress whatever in my opinion has been made towards effective union. The calls for me as leader (which are not unanimous) really amount to this: men feel that the party is in the ditch, and they want to have somebody responsible for getting them out of it. Also the religious question generally—which we could manage while we were in power—has now passed out of our hands, and is a great difficulty in *my* way. What, in this province, the next Session may bring about, I cannot tell. But the Church of England has been brought to the brink of a most serious crisis, which may take the form of schism, disestablishment, or both. It is I believe still avoidable: but only by an amount of selfcommand, high-mindedness, & circumspection, on the part of the highest Church authorities, very different from that which they exhibited during the last Session. While this question remains unclosed, any *strapping* up

[1] See W. E. Gladstone, *Vaticanism* (1875), in reply to Manning's pamphlet; T. J. Capel, *A Reply to W. E. Gladstone's Political Expostulation* (1874), and others.

of the relations between the party and me can only I fear constitute a new danger. Then, we have no public object on the pursuit of which we are agreed. And, while this is so, I suspect that the best and only victories the party can obtain are such as we obtained last year, with some credit and satisfaction, on the Endowed Schools Bill.

I hope you have enjoyed all your Tour & been free from gout & cares.

In some early letter I shall hope to hear the probable time of your return.

999. Lord Granville to Mr. Gladstone. [Add. MS. 44170, fo. 106]

Savona. Dec 10/74.

Your letter has followed me with some circumlocomotivity. We do not with malice intent, imitate the late Duke of Devonshire, who when travelling in Italy, used to desire his letters to be sent to Frankfort, or Vienna but our change of plans lead to nearly the same result.

I got your copy of *the* pamphlet and some others almost immediately after I had written to you. I need not say with what interest I read & reread it.

At Florence Beaumont was doubtful, Lady Margaret, Tom Potter, & Lacaita much pleased. The Italians generally approving, but puzzled why you should have thought it necessary.

If I had written to you, my letter would not have been quite the same every day —and even now after receiving your full, & charming letter, I prefer talking it over with you, than troubling you with the long catalogue of pros and cons that occur to me.

I do not know the marriage case, or have forgotten it.

We have had a charming journey, since my gout departed. Travelling by the road short journeys along the Riviera perfectly delightful. We are going so slowly, that we shall not reach Walmer till the last day of this month.

The enormous profits you must be making by your pen will I trust make it unnecessary to let C.H.T.

At home the Gov seem most prosperous, with the exception of Dizzy, who does not appear to be in a condition to fight his cabinet, or to stand real Agitative work in the House of Commons.

Even without a " cause " I trust you will resume the place in earnest, in which *all* so much desire that you should be. Indeed it appears impossible that you should not do so.

Lady G. sends 1000 messages to you & your's.

1000. Lord Granville to Mr. Gladstone. [Add. MS. 44170, fo. 109]

San Remo. Dec 14/74.

I was charmed to find another letter from you here (of the 7th).

It is clearly desirable that you should not continue what in one sense may be called controversy longer than is necessary, and you should certainly not reply to small criticisms by small men—but if the Curia with the sanction of the Pope,

& through his legate Manning [replies], you have foemen worthy of your steel, & a just reason for one more pamphlet.

They will probably succeed in many small details, but I cannot conceive anything approved by the Pope, not confirming your principal argument.

I should cut my reply down, so as to make it as short as possible, & I would get some [one] like Acton to mark unmercifully anything that would touch the corns of the Catholics without being necessary for your argument.

I agree with most of what you say about home politics.

The question of disestablishment is an immense difficulty, but I think neither that nor any minor question need interfere with a real but passive leadership of the liberal party during the present session.

It is with something of a pang, only mitigated by the thoughts of the children at Walmer, that we are wending our way homewards along this lovely coast.

1001. Lord Granville to Mr. Gladstone.[1] [Add. MS. 44170, fo. 113]

Walmer Castle. Jan 5/75.

I came to town yesterday for 24 hours.

Wolverton gave me your draft, and commentary today.[2] I have hardly had time to read it, still less to answer it with any care.

But I should be sorry to receive such a letter.

I feel sure that your decision would be injurious to the party, & suspect it would be disadvantageous to yourself.

A great party should have a recognized leader in Parliament more especially the party favoring progress, but not unanimous as to the rate at which the progress should be made.

The absence of a recognized leader, must lead to disorganization and to such habits of indiscipline, as will not be overcome by any sudden enthusiasm for a cause, or for an individual.

With you (I should almost say in existence, but certainly) in the House of Commons, and occasionally taking part in the Debates, it is impossible that any individual, or any combination of two or three should have any authority. I doubt any one being foolish enough to attempt it.

As to yourself the question is more doubtful—there might be immediate ease and your reputation is so great, and your hold on a large portion of the Country so strong that secession will not affect your power of resuming your Parliamentary position when you choose to do so. But you would grievously disappoint the liberal party, with the exception perhaps of William Harcourt ; and a few others, and you would discontent your late colleagues in the Commons—& when duty compelled

[1] Granville to Gladstone, Mentone, 15 Dec., enclosing an untraced letter from Lady Russell, Add. MS. 44170, fo. 112, and reply, 21 Dec., G.D. 29/29A, not printed.

[2] No. 1003. Cf. Wolverton to Granville, 7 Jan., G.D. 29/25A ; see drafts and notes for no. 1003, Add. MS. 44762, fos. 147–70. It was read at a meeting of the late cabinet at Granville's house, 14 Jan., Granville to Argyll, who with Bright was absent, 14 Jan., G.D. 29/22A ; Fitzmaurice, ii. 141–4 ; Morley, ii. 503–5 ; *Gladstone to his Wife*, ed. Tilney Bassett, pp. 206–11 ; Mary Drew, *Catherine Gladstone* (1919), pp. 82–6.

you to take up some worthy cause, and attempt to lead it to a successful issue you would find a machine completely out of gear.

The question of overwork is serious, but with your extraordinary mental activity and fecundity, and with your temperament, will you ever find yourself in a position in which you will not strain your physical strength.

In the present state of affairs, your duty as leader of the opposition would not require hourly attendance or minute criticism of every act and every measure of the administration.

When once you had assumed the leadership, you could advantageously depute to others a considerable amount of the work.

I presume no one expects, or wishes to turn out the present Gov during the present session or for many more.

I reserve for our meeting the discussion of the Catholic Vote, the possible legislation on the Church of England, & other points strongly put forward in your commentary.

I will call on you at six on Saturday, & shall be at your orders all Sunday, & Monday morning. On Saturday, we shall dine at 7, to go to the play. Would either dinner or play be in your line.

I will try to arrange my thoughts more clearly before we meet.

I return your draft but keep the Commentary.[1]

1002. Lord Granville to Mr. Gladstone. [Add. MS. 44170, fo. 120]

Savernake. Jan 12/75.

I return you your draft. In any case I think I should omit the last sentence, as it will enable people to say 'what does he mean'—and does not appear necessary.

You have no idea how disagreeable it is to me, after the habits which I have acquired during the last years, to disagree with you on any point.

The Archbishop of Canterbury told Sydney last week that Russell Gurney had offered to introduce a bill this session, but that he had declined, thinking further legislation undesirable.

I shall be in town early on Thursday.[2]

1003. Mr. Gladstone to Lord Granville.[3] [G.D. 29/29A]

11, Carlton House Terrace. Jan 13. 1875.

The time has, I think arrived when I ought to revert to the subject of the letter which I addressed to you on the 12th of March.

Before determining whether I should offer to assume a charge, which might

[1] No. 1001 printed, Fitzmaurice, ii. 140, with verbal differences and a summary of the last four paragraphs.

[2] Cf. Forster to Granville, 12 Jan., arranging to come to London on 14 Jan., and asking Granville to express his conviction of the need of Gladstone's leadership if he was too late for the meeting, G.D. 29/25A; Hartington to Granville, 13 Jan., on the difficulty of his offering himself as a candidate for the leadership, G.D. 29/22A.

[3] Published in the newspapers, 15 Jan.

extend over a length of time, I have reviewed, with all the care in my power a number of considerations both public and private, of which a portion, and these not by any means insignificant, were not in existence at the date of that letter.

The result has been that I see no public advantage in my continuing to act as the leader of the Liberal Party; and that at the age of sixty-five, and after forty-two years of a laborious public life, I think myself entitled to retire on the present opportunity. This retirement is dictated to me by my personal views as to the best method of spending the closing years of my life.

I need hardly say that my conduct in Parliament will continue to be governed by the principles on which I have heretofore acted: and, whatever arrangements may be made for the treatment of general business, and for the advantage or convenience of the Liberal Party, they will have my cordial support. I should perhaps add that I am at present, and may for a short time be engaged on a special matter, which occupies me closely.[1]

1004. Lord Granville to Mr. Gladstone. [Add. MS. 44170, fo. 122]

Carlton H. Terrace. Jan 14/75.

I have recd your letter of the 13th.

I have communicated to you in detail the reasons which make me profoundly regret, and deprecate the conclusion at which you have arrived.

Your late colleagues share these feelings to the fullest extent, and have regretted the failure of their endeavour to persuade you to come to a different decision.

We have no doubt that the liberal party, in and out of Parliament, will feel as we do on the subject.

The observations we have addressed to you, are prompted by considerations of public advantage for the future, and not merely by our sense of your great service, and our sentiments of personal admiration and attachment.

1005. Mr. Gladstone to Lord Granville. [G.D. 29/29A]

Hawarden Castle. Jan 17. 75.

Many thanks for your letter; for what it contains (not forgetting the P.S.)[2] and because it *is* a letter.

And let me now thank you heartily and warmly for all your kindness, and say how sorry I am for the worry I bring on you. These thanks are due also to my other colleagues, in their several degrees of nearness.

I return your inclosures. The answer to Playfair is I think excellent. Only I would take care with Adam that he calls the meeting, if it is called, in deference to those who ask it, states this in his circular, and leaves it to them to manage it.

[1] The last sentence, though crossed through in a copy in the Granville papers, was published.

[2] See Granville to Gladstone, 16 Jan., enclosing Playfair to Granville, 15 Jan., and copy of the reply, 16 Jan., Add. MS. 44170, fo. 124, not printed; enclosures with Playfair's answer, 17 Jan., Fitzmaurice, ii. 145–7. Playfair with Fawcett and others favoured Forster's leadership, but wished for the election of a leader at a meeting of the parliamentary party. Granville wrote to Adam to ask whether he would summon the meeting and told Playfair.

Except as to the fact of calling, it should be like a meeting which was held automatically after the defeat in 1866—unless, & until, some arrangement is made which it may be thought wise to propose or support from your quarter, but I would not give this sort of character to the meeting as such & in the first instance.

In general, leadership has been I think spontaneously rather than formally determined. And in your good management I dare say Hartington will get quietly into the saddle, or rather upon the pillion.

Now for a variety of matters, partly collateral.

My wife thought I ought to write to the Queen or to Ponsonby.[1] I had considered this & come to the conclusion that I had no *locus standi*. I did not therefore see my way. It would have been a narrow ground, to give the assurance that I would look to any matter affecting the Queen or R. family, until definitive arrangements were made. Were my relations to the Queen more personal than they have been, I should write. On this matter I should have consulted you, had there been time.

You are unquestionably right about G. Bentinck. Dizzy was comparatively nobody till the death in 1848.

I should like to have had conversation with you on a subject which it is hard to avoid though it can hardly be a pleasant one to you: Greville, Reeve, Hayward. I have not read a great deal yet of the book.[2] To judge from the Review, C. Greville was not scrupulous enough in the getting of his materials. But *non constat* that he would have published any of the offensive parts. In this publication Reeve appears to me to have exceeded all bounds, and to be as entirely, as if he were exclusively (which he may be) responsible. But there is one portion of the subject on which I take the strongest view. I think the offence he has committed against the Crown, being a servant of the Crown, so gross, especially in reference to Queen Adelaide & the Duchess of Kent, but also in reference to William IV that it is a marvel to me how he can continue to hold his office and I think he ought not to hold it. But I have said, & probably shall say, this to no one, *solely* because I feel myself put out of court by Reeve's proceedings in the Edinburgh Rev.[3]

Would you kindly send me, at your convenience, the *scraps* of mine which you have: & I will send you, if you like, a copy of what I read on Thursday, as part of the res gestae.[4]

Kindly say all good things for us at Savernake.

1006. Lord Granville to Mr. Gladstone. [Add. MS. 44170, fo. 125]

Private. Bowood, Calne. Jan 19/75.

1000 thanks. I will say nothing to you about the thanks you so kindly convey; but I will give your messages to our colleagues.

[1] See Gladstone to the Queen, 21 Jan., on his resignation, Guedalla, i. 453.

[2] *Greville Memoirs. A Journal of the Reigns of King George IV and King William IV*, ed. Henry Reeve (1874), 3 vols., being the first part of the work completed in 1887. Cf. the Queen to Martin, 26 Oct., *Letters*, 2nd ser., ii. 354.

[3] Probably in publishing the article on Alsace-Lorraine, see above, nos. 307, 310, 314, 319.

[4] See above, no. 1001 note.

I have written to Adam in your sense. He does not seem to have recd the letter sent to him by Sydney.

I gathered from Playfair's first letter, that he was in favor of Hartington, but a note this morning announces that he finds that the general feeling amongst all classes of liberals is in favor of Forster, and that he himself although ready to serve cordially under Hartington, would prefer Forster.

Hartington entirely approved my language about himself, and has written in the same sense to W. Harcourt, who has pressed him.[1] The advocacy of the latter would be fatal to his being selected.

I remember when we were last in opposition a complaint against you, that you always sat next to Forster, and were always talking to him!!

I entirely agree with Mrs Gladstone about your writing to the Queen—& I do not think it at all too late to do so. To compare small things with great, I remember her speaking with emphasis on the contrast between Ch Greville & W. Bathurst, the latter only having written upon his retirement. She is frantic with Reeve.

I shall be at Longleat Warminster till Friday or Saturday—then in London till Monday or Tuesday when we go to Althorp.

Nothing can be more sensible than Lansdowne. I hear that the office is loud as to the contrast between him & Cardwell, as compared with Pembroke & Hardy.

I will send you the first draft of reasons.

1007. Lord Granville to Mr. Gladstone. [Add. MS. 44170, fo. 137]

18, Carlton House Terrace. Jan 23/75.[2]

I am just come to town, & have only seen Adam for five minutes.

He says he has had great difficulty in gathering the opinions. Of 50 M.P.s there is a slight majority for Hartington, but the Forsterites are much the most active & keen.

I also found a letter from Hartington, enclosing one for Adam, absolutely declining to be put up in opposition to Forster.[3]

I have written to say that I shall not show it, at all events not till after I have seen Hartington at Althorp on Tuesday evening.

What colleagues are in town, dine with me today, viz. Carlingford, Goschen, Adam & Freddy Leveson. Cardwell comes up tomorrow, or Monday.

Adam wished me to see Fawcett, Morley & Trevelyan, with K. Hodgson Whitbread & Dodson on Tuesday.[4]

I will write again.

[1] See Hartington to Granville, 17 Jan., 20 Jan., on his writing to Harcourt in the sense of Granville to Playfair, 17 Jan., on the election of a leader at a party meeting, G.D. 29/22A; cf. B. Holland, *The Life of Spencer Compton, Eighth Duke of Devonshire* (1911), i. 140–3.

[2] No. 1007 is bound in the volume as if dated 28 Jan.; but Granville was at Althorp, 28 Jan., in London, 23 Jan.; the dates of Hartington's letter and Gladstone's reply make 23 Jan. more likely as the correct date. It is also that in Gladstone's docket.

[3] Hartington to Granville, 22 Jan., G.D. 29/22A, printed Fitzmaurice, ii. 150–2; cf. earlier letters, 19, 21, 22 (first letter) Jan., all urging that Forster should lead in the Commons, *ibid*; Holland, *op. cit.*, i. 143–7.

[4] See also Adam to Granville, 1.47 p.m., 26 Jan., on Harcourt's dissatisfaction with the proceedings over the leadership and refusal to act under Forster and Forster's statement to Fawcett and Mundella that he did not wish for it, G.D. 29/25A.

1008. Mr. Gladstone to Lord Granville. [G.D. 29/29A]

Hawarden Castle. Jan 27.75.

I am sorry, rather than surprised, to hear of difficulties about the choice of a leader in the Commons ; not because there is any difficulty in the act, but because of the condition & habits of those who have to perform it. I received this morning from Kinnaird a note, in which he says that there is to be a fight for it and that it will not be very creditable. It will indeed be the very last degree of the ridiculous to which a party can be reduced, and for party purposes matter of ridicule weighs more than dishonour. I do hope measures will be taken to prevent men from making fools of themselves at the meeting next week. The dictate of common sense seems to me plain enough. If the party are not generally agreed, some friends of the respective candidates, or non-candidates, should agree to adjourn the meeting, without any thing approaching to debate, for further consideration of the subject. There are two dangers : one a public squabble, the other an unreal conclusion & appointment. There is but one good thing that such a meeting *can* do : namely to register with marked signs of unanimity and loyalty a foregone conclusion. To imagine it to be deliberative, while it is headless, is I think a fatal error. Supposing they are not prepared to agree, the party can do for a time without a leader in the Commons. The truth is, it has peccant humours to purge, and bad habits to get rid of, and it is a great question whether this can or cannot be best done without first choosing a leader. You see my talk is still of the shop. And the upshot is that if I can be of any use in writing to Kinnaird (or any one else, or otherwise [)], I hope you will let me know.

My impression is that though those you mention may be keen, they will encounter an opposition keener still. Indeed I think they would drive even John Bright to some act of violence.

Our present notion is to come up about the 12th, & probably go to Brighton for a few days at most immediately afterwards.

Pray remember us kindly at Althorp. It would have been delightful to go but I am drowned in historical books & boundless correspondence.

1009. Lord Granville to Mr. Gladstone. [Add. MS. 44170, fo. 129]

Althorp. Jan 28/75.

I cannot say how much obliged I am to you for your letter.

I think one from you to some independent member would be of the greatest use.

I go to town early tomorrow, and will let you know after seeing Adam, whether it would be better to write to Kinnaird, or to some other friend.

As far as Adam has been able to ascertain, *numbers* are as nearly equal as possible.[1] Quality appears to be much the other way.

I send you a note from Portman.[2] His advice does not appear to me to be prac-

[1] See Adam to Granville, 27 Jan., estimating Hartington's supporters at 43 and Forster's at 32, *ibid* ; cf. Playfair to Granville, 27, 28 Jan., analysing the opinions of Scottish members to whom he had written, *ibid*.

[2] 27 Jan., describing his part in persuading Althorp to lead the Commons when Earl Grey, the leader of the party, was in the Lords, Add. MS. 44170, fo. 133.

ticable at the present moment. The Speaker tells me confidentially that he is for Hartington, & that he believes the majority are so. He recommends that at the meeting, a vote should be taken, if it is numerous enough to include Hartington's friends. If not that it should be adjourned.

It appears to me with you, that two things must be avoided—a running down of Hartington by Fawcett, Mundella & Samuelson, and by Lowe & Harcourt of Forster—also an attempt by Fawcett or others to lay down a programme, on which the party is certain to split.

Hartington came back from his speechifying last night—rather dissatisfied with his speech which he was obliged to hurry over & disarrange, in consequence of Kimberley & others speaking at unconscionable length—Rather less reluctant than he was to go on with the candidature.

I will write again tomorrow from London, where I shall be early.

Why Brighton v. Walmer which is entirely at your disposal for any length of time.

1010. Lord Granville to Mr. Gladstone. [Add. MS. 44170, fo. 140]

Confidential. 18, Carlton House Terrace. Jan 30/75.

I have seen Adam, Playfair, and Forster.

The upshot is that the latter will absolutely decline being put forward, and hopes to convince his friends that he is right.

We wish to keep the fact a profound secret for the present.[1]

Adam, I think, would be the best person to whom you could write, as you kindly offered.

Kinnaird has been talking violently on Hartington's side, and it is better that you should not appear to favor either candidate, when there will be no necessity. But an exhortation to unanimity, dignity, & cordiality, might possibly be of great use.

Forster has behaved well. He was elated, as was not unnatural at first, with the prospect of succeeding you, but his sense of the difficulty of his situation has been daily strengthened.

P.S. The notes which I had in my hand have disappeared in the flibberty gibbetty way papers have, but I shall find them with better light tomorrow.[2]

Forster has just sent me word that he has seen Fawcett, who was at first indignant, but has consented to accept Hartington, with an understanding that his being leader does not prevent people expressing their advanced liberal opinions.

1011. Lord Granville to Mr. Gladstone. [Add. MS. 44170, fo. 144]

Private. 18, Carlton House Terrace. Feb 1/75.

Thanks for [your] note, and enclosure.[3] Forster will probably make use of the latter with some of his friends this evening.

[1] On Forster's withdrawal see Reid, *op. cit.*, ii. 96–7.
[2] The papers on the letter of 13 Jan., see above, no. 1005.
[3] Gladstone to Granville, 31 Jan., enclosing an open letter for Adam, G.D. 29/29A.

Adam's direction is 43 Parliament Street.

I have recd a violently kicking letter from Harty Tarty this morning.[1] I hope his genuine reluctance may be overcome.

If not too much trouble a line from you to him might turn the scale.

Bright takes the chair.[2]

I send you the notes of reasons for your —— resignation.[3] I should like to treat them, as old Lord Bessborough used to treat his playing cards, when luck was adverse, and tear them into small bits, & put them in the fire.

You do not mention Brighton again, so I hope poor Walmer has a chance.

Argyll has written me several letters, all breathing the spirit of a very free lance.[4]

1012. Lord Granville to Mr. Gladstone. [Add. MS. 44170, fo. 146]

18, Carlton House Terrace. Feb 2/75.

In re John Russell. I never intended to make any reply to Lord Russell—though I may make a civil allusion on Friday to his being the exception to those who have diminished the acerbity of the attacks on Foreign Policy, in consequence of Derby not having done any very foolish thing that we know of.

I am told I must issue a programme on Friday.

This I utterly decline to do. But I propose to say, that no one can accuse our party of not having a policy when it was in power.

That certainly the Tories had none in opposition, and the result as far as elections are concerned, has been favorable to them. That it remains to be seen whether they have any policy now.

That we have not only no expectancy of turning them out at present, but no wish. That our assurances as to avoidance of factions & embarrassing tactics may be therefore more confidently relied on than those which often have been given. But this will not prevent close observation and determined action which may not be altogether unavailing, if the Gov enter upon a retroactive course.

May I say this as being the policy I know you would have adopted if you had not retired—and if so, is there anything more, which you think it may be advisable to say.

Am I right in supposing that Northcote's estimate for the revenue was half a million more than yours, and if so, may that be said.[5]

Nothing more from Harty Tarty.

[1] Hartington to Granville, 31 Jan., against accepting the leadership, G.D. 29/22A.

[2] At the Reform Club meeting of the Liberal members of the House of Commons, fixed for Feb. 3. Hartington was there chosen as leader in the Commons; see below, no. 1013, and Halifax to Granville, 4 Feb., approving the decision, G.D. 29/25A; Holland, *op. cit.*, pp. 147-8.

[3] See above, no. 1005.

[4] Not traced.

[5] The session opened on 5 Feb. In the debate on the address Granville followed the conciliatory line he had laid down but did not mention Gladstone nor allude to Northcote's estimate of the revenue, *Hans. Parl. Deb.*, 3rd ser., ccxxii. 22–30.

1013. Lord Granville to Mr. Gladstone. [Add. MS. 44170, fo. 149]

Feb 3/75.

You will see in the papers, that the meeting went off without a hitch, and was altogether satisfactory although without anything of Enthusiasm—Freddy Cavendish is said to have done very well, and to have warmed the meeting more than others.

Of course this account is second hand, but all my informants agree.

1014. Lord Granville to Mr. Gladstone.[1] [Add. MS. 44170, fo. 152]

House of Lords. May 11/75.

Wolverton at my request has asked K Hodgson to move the resolutions. K H entirely agrees with you, and with the resolutions, but he will not move them. I have asked Wolverton whether he could suggest any other competent and fit M P —but he could not.

Hubbard certainly persevered with his motion on the 2d reading which is fixed for Thursday.[2]

1015. Lord Granville to Mr. Gladstone.[3] [Add. MS. 44170, fo. 162]

[6 August 1875].

I saw in the papers that you went away yesterday; and only learnt from your housekeeper that you were not gone. I wished particularly to tell you that Hartington is going after much doubt and consideration to attack Dizzy this evening for his Mansion House speech.[4]

We think that Dizzy can have no good rejoinder, but will fall back upon bad jokes against Hartington, & recrimination against the late Gov.

If you could be in your place your presence would somewhat restrain him, and he may say things which you ought to answer.

I shall try again to see you.

1016. Lord Granville to Mr. Gladstone. [Add. MS. 44170, fo. 164]

Walmer Castle. Nov 5/75.

How good of you to write to me. It is always a great pleasure.

[1] Gladstone to Granville, 27 April, urging decision on policy over Northcote's budget, G.D. 29/29A; Gladstone to Granville, 3 Feb., accepting the 'programme' of no. 1012 and lamenting the decline in quality of the Commons, G.D. 29/29A; and reply, 4 Feb., Add. MS. 44170, fo. 151; not printed.

[2] Relates to the second reading of the Local Authorities Loans Bill in the Commons, Thursday, 13 May. Hubbard was against increased facilities for borrowing and protested against the second reading but brought forward no motion. No resolutions were moved on the Liberal side, *Hans. Parl. Deb.*, 3rd ser., ccxxiv. 605–11.

[3] Granville to Gladstone, undated, 5, 11, 28 June, informing him of the death of a niece, asking him to deputise at Oxford and thanking, Add. MS. 44170, fos. 153, 155, 159, 161, not printed.

[4] Hartington, 6 Aug., sought to show the failure of Disraeli to redeem his pledge 'to elevate the condition of the people'. He hoped to expose Disraeli's appeal by social legislation for the popular vote and his claim that the Conservative was the people's party, *Hans. Parl. Deb.*, 3rd ser., ccxxvi. 652–67.

I shall try if possible to run up to London to see you, but I am afraid it will be difficult to get away from some people we expect.

We were asked to Chatsworth but unluckily we had engaged ourselves to Bowood.

This affair of Turkey is very serious—&. you can see by the Pall Mall the wild ideas that are springing up on the subject. I am always trustful in Derby's good sense, but I do not feel so confident as to his resistance to any sudden pressure, which appears to represent Public opinion—& there may be at any time a reaction in his cabinet against his cautious policy. The Standard always appears to be on the edge of criticizing him.[1]

It appears that the fugitive Slave instructions were based on a reference to the Law officers.[2] Their opinions [were] embodied as a matter of course in an instruction to the admiralty who put them forward as a matter of routine. The admiralty are not responsible, but Halifax Childers or Goschen would have sent a private query to the F.O.

I doubt whether James is quite right as to his law—but in a matter of such interest to this country as the slavery, it is absurd to allow a technical point to overrule us in dealing with Barbarous nations.

I am glad of your promised performance at Greenwich.

We are delighted to hear of Mr W. Gladstone's success at Hawarden.

1017. Lord Granville to Mr. Gladstone. [Add. MS. 44170, fo. 168]

Walmer Castle. Nov 9/75.

I am sorry to say I cannot run up to town as I had hoped. We have fresh people coming here every day this week.

Beyond the pleasure of seeing you, & taking stock of the present, I should have liked to consult you about a speech Hartington is to make at Bristol next Saturday. He intends to go on in the same strain about Education as he did the other day, but to make the necessity of improved local Gov, and of reforming it on right principles his great hobby horse. He thinks, & probably with justice that it is a subject on which there is less of difference of opinion among liberals than any other.[3]

I do not think he will say much about Foreign Affairs excepting the Fugitive Slave instructions.

[1] Granville replies to Gladstone's letter of 3 Nov., in which he wrote, ' the Turkish repudiation [of part of the interest on foreign loans contracted since 1856 (see below, no. 1036)] looms in my view as one of the greatest political events ', G.D. 29/29A.

[2] See Admiralty instructions, 31 July, to the commanders of naval stations and the naval officers abroad laying down rules for the surrender of fugitive slaves taken on board British ships, F.O. 84/1430, Parl. papers. [C. 1413] (1876). lxx, 257. The anti-slavery society agitated against the restriction of the naval officers' discretion as a reversal of policy. The instructions were suspended, 6 Oct., and after a cabinet meeting, 4 Nov., withdrawn, Parl. papers, *loc. cit.*, pp. 272–3 ; Buckle, *op. cit.*, v. 396–8 ; see below, nos. 1017, 1027–35.

[3] He spoke again at Derby on education, 20 Nov., *The Times*, p. 10. For the Bristol speech see *ibid.*, 14 Nov., p. 10, and Reeve to Granville, 26 Nov., G.D. 29/25A.

Our weather here is mild & changeable. Was not Forster's rather a wild speech,[1] and Stansfield's a good one.[2]

1018. Lord Granville to Mr. Gladstone. [Add. MS. 44170, fo. 170]

Walmer Castle. Nov 13/75.

1000 thanks for your letter,[3] which I recd in bed where I have been kept but for a short time from cold caught in my knee. I am up & well again which I hope shows that there is not much gout about me.

I sent off your hints to Harty Tarty. I have not yet seen his speech, my Observer having failed me today.

I return the statement. Nothing can be more shuffling & evasive than the answer of the French Gov, and the refusal to give permission to your writings to be colportés in France is unworthy of a Gov professing to be liberal in it's principles. At the same time in the balanced state of Parties in France, and the excitement of Public opinion the matter may not have been quite simple for them.

Does Mrs Gladstone know Mr Moor, and does she approve of his being here, drawing the children.

1019. Mr. Gladstone to Lord Granville. [G.D. 29/29A]

Hickelton. Nov. 28. 75.

I am glad to think you were not alone at Walmer when the startling news arrived about the purchase of the Khedive's interest in the Suez Canal.[4] We reckon that Cardwell was with you. But you may like to know how it strikes other friends, & even what are the sentiments of a disembodied spirit like myself.

Amid the conflicting statements that have appeared, I find the meeting point of them all in the version which seems as follows

a. The purchase is immediate

b. The payment is immediate

c. For a term of years the Khedive guarantees 5 per Cent upon the money: after which we get the Dividend yielded by the concern

d. In some manner it is subject to the consent of Parliament; and I *imagine* they are hardly in a condition to pay the four millions themselves outright, though some finance-agent may do it on the strength of the pledge to apply to Parliament.

[1] Forster at Edinburgh urged the transformation of 'our Colonial Empire into a Federation of . . . commonwealths', *The Times*, 6 Nov., p. 10. For his speech on education, *ibid.*, 8 Nov., p. 6.

[2] For Stansfield's speech at Bury, on education, but avoiding controversial points, and the Conservative blunder over the fugitive slave instructions, see *ibid.*, 8 Nov., p. 8.

[3] Gladstone to Granville, 11 Nov., suggesting that Hartington speak on the *Vanguard* minute, the slave instructions, and Froude's mission (see below, no. 1030 note) with enclosure about the French government, G.D. 29/29A. Cf. Hartington to Granville, 15 Nov., G.D. 29/22A.

[4] The contract with the Khedive for the purchase of nearly a third of the Suez Canal shares was ratified, 26 Nov., completing a negotiation begun, 15 Nov. The payment was made in three instalments by the Rothschilds, 1, 16 Dec., 5 Jan., at a commission of 2½% and in anticipation of a parliamentary grant; Buckle, *op. cit.*, v. 439–52; Parl. papers. [C. 1391] (1876). lxxxiii, 131.

e. There is no present sign of an intention to summon the two Houses for the purpose.

A storm of approbation seems to swell, almost to rage, on every side.

I write in mild language, out of respect, such respect as is due, to the sense of what seems an overwhelming majority. But my opinion on the imperfect information before me is this. If the thing has been done in concert with the other Powers, it is an act of folly, fraught with future embarrassment. If without such concert, it is an act of folly fraught also with present danger.

I am aware of no cause that could warrant or excuse it, except its being necessary to prevent the closing of the Canal. But that cause I apprehend could not possibly exist. The closing of the London & North Western would be about as probable.

You may remember that in our Cabinet we discussed the neutralisation of the Canal and the purchase was suggested or named.[1] As far as I recollect, we peremptorily set aside the purchase, and found no reason then to prosecute the neutralisation, partly because it was difficult, but principally because we found we stood so well as things are, that there was no motive to desire a change.

The substance of this has been sent to Hartington who was away on Friday morning. Freddy & I were of one mind at the first blush.

1020. Lord Granville to Mr. Gladstone. [Add. MS. 44170, fo. 172]

Walmer Castle. Nov 28/75.

What do you think of the purchase of less than one third of the Suez Canal shares. I presume the Times got the news from the Rothschilds, and the Telegraph from Derby.

As regards my first impressions, which I mistrust, it appears to be very foolish.

I presume it is without precedent—(is it not,) that the Gov should become part shareholders of a private undertaking over which by normal means they can have no control.

Is it not enough of a political measure, to induce and justify other countries in taking precautionary means.

Is it not possible that Lesseps, and the Rothschilds have duped the Govt into giving this great impetus to the value of Suez Canal shares, by threatening them with a purchase by French Capitalists.

Is it the intention of the Gov to buy in the open market another 100,000 shares at enhanced prices, in order to have an effective control. If they do so, cannot the remaining Shareholders still get them into endless difficulties.

Will it not give rise to all sorts of international difficulties, & questions.

Is the canal to remain subject to the discretionary powers, which we have always maintained, belonged to the Sultan.

[1] Childers in the Liberal cabinet had urged the purchase and neutralization of the canal. For discussion in the Liberal cabinet and the appointment of a cabinet committee, see Childers to Granville, 22 July 1870, and reply, 13 Aug., G.D. 29/54; for Lowe's objections to Childers's detailed plan of purchase, 16 Aug. see Lowe to Granville, 18 Aug., G.D. 29/66; see also Granville to Childers, 24 Aug., reporting Lowe's and Gladstone's views, G.D. 29/54; below, nos. 1024, 1025.

Ought so great a responsibility to be taken without immediately consulting Parliament.

We go to London tomorrow.

I suppose that the quieter we keep about the Suez Canal at present the better.

1021. Lord Granville to Mr. Gladstone. [Add. MS. 44170, fo. 176]

18, Carlton House Terrace. Nov 29/75.

I hear today[1] that you are at Hickelton, & will not therefore have got my letter. I am not shaken by the chorus of the Press, and of public opinion, which is undoubtedly one way—with two exceptions—the Economist, and the Saturday review, which are both good—you should read them.

I hear the Govt settled it in one day—& without of course any knowledge of facts. They mean to make play of our refusal to give moral support to Sutherland and Pender when they wished to buy the whole of the canal.

The fact of the Govt having only acquired *ten* votes in the whole concern (no shareholder being allowed to hold more, and every owner of 25 shares having one), would at any other time have thrown ridicule on the scheme.

I presume there is no doubt that we ought to keep quiet till Parliament meets, which it ought to have done in ten days, & to do which would have been in their interest.

I have written to ask Hartington & Forster,[2] to be merely oracular, till we have an opportunity of consultation.

We go to the Grange Alresford, today.

1022. Lord Granville to Mr. Gladstone. [Add. MS. 44170, fo. 179]

The Grange, Alresford. Dec 1/75.

Delighted to get your letter, which I only recd this morning.

Poor Childers took our view—Stansfield willingly agreed to be oracular tonight at some meeting.[3]

Forster takes our view.[4]

Lowe told Cardwell he thought it a great coup for the Govt—but I do not know whether he thinks [it] a wise act.

Cardwell is alarmed at the concurrence of public opinion.[5]

[1] See Halifax to Granville, 28 Nov., on Gladstone's excitement against the purchase, his own more moderate views but fear that it might entail the occupation of Egypt, G.D. 29/25A.

[2] Granville's letters not traced, but see Hartington's reply, 30 Nov., agreeing to be cautious but proposing to attack the failure to summon Parliament, G.D. 29/25A. Cf. Hartington to Granville, 28 Nov., on the purchase turning out ' a most successful coup ', G.D. 29/22A.

[3] Childers's and Stansfield's letters not traced.

[4] Cf. Forster to Granville, 3 Dec., supposing that had he ' been in a cabinet which had suddenly to decide whether or no to accept the offer ' he ' would have voted for acceptance ', G.D. 29/25A.

[5] Cardwell to Granville, 1 Dec., approving generally of the purchase, as Goschen did, and commenting on the failure to summon Parliament and the popularity of the government, *ibid.*; see also from Hartington, 5 Dec., *ibid.*; Goschen, 5 Dec., against any display of hostility but limiting his approval to the political aspect, G.D. 29/22A; Halifax, 6, 14, 21 Dec., approving the purchase, but minimizing the difference of opinion, Lowe, 7 Dec., and Lansdowne, 28, 29 Nov., G.D. 29/25A.

Fawcett seems to have taken a sensible line on the subject.

I cannot say how pleased I am at having taken exactly the same view as the disembodied spirit of this very foolish business.

1023. Mr. Gladstone to Lord Granville.[1] [G.D. 29/29A]

H[awarde]n. Dec. 10.75.

Many thanks for Mr Arnold's interesting letter. I hope foreign will and English eyes do not disagree as much in your case, as in mine.

I send for your perusal a letter from Lefevre,[2] not so wise as his speech at Reading. In reply I said of course it was not for me to advise, except that he should consult you: but if he wished to know my opinion as an individual it was much against his proposal.

As I understand the case of the B[oard of] T[rade] letter it was one which never should have been written without previous approval by F.O. *They* will probably produce it.

I rack my brains upon the great stroke of genius. I should fully accept Derby's minimising process,[3] but I am wholly at a loss to make out a case which will justify or excuse it. And the manner in which it was received really makes me blush for my Countrymen and for their press. But I have always felt that while for domestic purposes our press is admirable we have no security whatever from it against even the most outrageous follies in matters of foreign policy.

You see Northcote begins to think of his Nemesis. I hope all who egged him on will stand by him in his retreat: & he will do well enough.

I hope also you have no influenzas—we have all been on our backs.

Argyll suspends his opinion for further information.

1024. Lord Granville to Mr. Gladstone. [Add. MS. 44170, fo. 181]

Bowood, Calne. Dec 13/75.

I return you Lefevre's letter with many thanks. He has not written to me, but will of course be guided by your advice.

From his account, the Gov cannot make much capital out of this Bd of Trade letter.

What I am told they mean to do, is to hold you & me up to contumely for having refused Sutherland & Pender support in a project of buying the Canal from Lesseps—& they say that you refused on the ground that it might give rise to

[1] Gladstone to Granville, 4 Dec., commenting on d'Harcourt's report of Derby's aims in buying the Suez Canal shares and on Sir A. Gordon's standing for Aberdeenshire as a Conservative, G.D. 29/29A, not printed.

[2] Lefevre to Gladstone, not traced, but probably related to Board of Trade to Foreign Office, 26 Jan. 1871, recommending the neutralization of the Suez Canal and its management by an international commission. Lefevre had interviewed Lesseps officially over his proposals for purchase, July 1870. The letter and those of 29 March 1871 and 22 Jan. 1872 were published as an appendix to *Correspondence respecting the Suez Canal*. Parl. papers. [C. 1392] (1876). lxxxiii, 317 ff.

[3] For Derby's repudiation of the connection of the purchase with the Eastern question or a protectorate over Egypt see his speech, 27 Nov., Buckle, *op. cit.*, v. 453.

Foreign complications. I will look for what correspondence may have passed on the subject. I remember seeing S & P at the F.O. and they appeared to me to have no company, no plan, & no offer from the French Company.

Charles Howard, Freddy Leveson, & Portman disapprove of the Purchase. This financial Mission [1] seems to be a great aggravation of the error of the purchase, and of the mistake in not calling Parlt together.

But I shall keep myself quite uncommitted publicly till we meet and talk the matter over.

Wolverton was in great force, but requiring the support which a wife alone can give, under the responsibility of buying an estate, & building a house.

I gave a hint about Gordon's previous wish to represent Aberdeenshire, but it is not clear from your note whether the application was made at the last general election or at the previous one.

1025. Mr. Gladstone to Lord Granville. [G.D. 29/29A]

Hawarden Castle. Dec. 15. 75.

1. Gordon's application was at the *last* Election.

2. I have no recollection of having objected to any purchase of the Suez Canal by an English Company on the ground that it would lead to political complications. My rather vague remembrance is like what you report, of a *proposal* without a *scheme*.

3. Within a few days I must answer, & in the negative, the inclosed invitation from Southampton. I have sent a great many of these chilling replies—and I think of adding a word of sympathy. Shall I, may I, go so far as to say that in *my* opinion the two years we have had of Tory and Reactionary Government have done more to lay up trouble for the future than the immediately preceding twenty years of all administrations. Pray put an extinguisher on this if you think fit. Of course in any case I shall give it as a mere individual opinion.

1026. Lord Granville to Mr. Gladstone. [Add. MS. 44170, fo. 185]

Bowood, Calne. Dec 16/75.

I think you are quite right to decline resolutely to stump. In my small way, I have persistently done so.

As to the incisive phrase in your proposed reply, my first impulse was to write " by all means " but on 2d thoughts I am against it. I entirely agree, but in the present state of public opinion it would not be understood & would be thought to be overstated—and I think you should appear judicial in your utterances.

I liked Hartington's speech,[2] but I do not admit that Forster is more liberal

[1] The mission of enquiry into Egyptian finances under Stephen Cave, paymaster-general; see Parl. papers. [C. 1396] (1876). lxxxiii, 87, and his report, 23 March, [C. 1425], *loc. cit.*, 99.

[2] Hartington spoke at Sheffield, 15 Dec., *The Times*, 17 Dec., p. 6.

than I am. I agree with him in principle as to the county Franchise, though I may differ as to the appropriate time.

He is more identified with the great middle class, but I think him more Tory than I am as to Education, Colonies, & expenditure.

1027. Lord Granville to Mr. Gladstone.[1] [Add. MS. 44170, fo. 190]

Walmer Castle. Dec 22/75.

Thanks for your letter & observations.

I have recd the same extract from Sheffield.[2] But have sent no answer.

I have not the slightest recollection of such instructions, and am glad that your recollection is the same.

But I have been a little nervous. As, however much against the sentiment of the country, and non obstantibus Harcourt & James, in strict international law, a man of war ought not to receive slaves *within territorial limits*.

I have privately consulted a friend in the F.O.[3] He tells me that if such instructions had gone, they must have been sent to the Prime Minister—that there is no reference in the Index to such instructions, & that the man who *was* at the Head of the Slave Trade Department has no recollection of such a document. But he says that without examining the papers themselves he cannot be sure, & that he cannot do so without attracting the attention of the present people, who are certainly not aware of the existence of such a paper.

1028. Lord Granville to Mr. Gladstone. [Add. MS. 44170, fo. 193]

Walmer Castle. Dec 26/75.

From what I hear, I believe our recollections are correct, and that I issued no instructions about fugitive slaves when I was at the F.O. but that there were some older ones.

How sad poor de Vesci's death.

& though I was not intimate with him, I am sorry for Stanhope's loss. It is an individuality gone.

1029. Lord Granville to Mr. Gladstone. [Add. MS. 44170, fo. 195]

Walmer. Jan 18/76.

I send you 3 letters on the Fugitive slave question.[4]

All the private information I have been able to get confirms my recollection

[1] Gladstone to Granville, 21 Dec., partly printed Fitzmaurice, ii. 148, replying to no. 1027, has not been traced.

[2] An extract from a Sheffield newspaper, quoting an Admiralty Order of 1871 as a precedent for the withdrawn circular of 1875, was sent to Granville and Gladstone, Fitzmaurice, ii. 159. The extract from the East India Station Orders, 1871, was printed in Parl. papers. [C. 1413] (1876). lxx, 309.

[3] H. Hervey; see to Granville, 21 Dec., G.D. 29/25A. Cf. Vivian (head of the slave trade department, 1871) to Granville, 23 Dec., confirming Hervey's information but stating that there were some older instructions, *ibid*.

[4] Not traced but see Lefevre to Granville, 15 Jan., on there being no instructions on fugitive slaves while he was at the Admiralty, G.D. 29/26Ai.

that I issued no instructions. But I have written to Derby to be allowed to see the papers to which H. Lennox & A. Egerton alluded.

1030. Mr. Gladstone to Lord Granville. [G.D. 29/29A]

Hagley. Jan 19.76.

I ought to have returned the inclosure on an earlier day: but I am now & continually driven to put off writing the letters I ought & wish to write for the sake, or through the presence of others that I ought not & wish not but cannot help.

I think Lord Derby's view of the Suez Canal is only *relatively* the right one: right that is in comparison with others that are more and more dangerously wrong. What is the harm which has attended or is likely to attend private proprietorship in this case? Who can say that joint State proprietorship, which by the very force of the terms is all foreign is either theoretically free from objection, or likely to be free from difficulties in practice?

The Danube Commission is no precedent? There is no joint stock enterprise.

About the Slavery question again I do not think B. quite sees the point which is (true or not) that there is a certain principle of English law applicable & hitherto applied to the case, but on this occasion contravened.

However I suppose you will move to obtain 'papers' in the first instance in all these matters

Suez
Cape
Slavery
Vanguard etc.[1]

and will then have more daylight.

I am going to London tomorrow for Friday and Saturday—then to Harwarden—to return about the 2d. when I shall be at No 4 C. Gardens for Feb. & March.

What sad sad deaths there have been. I understand poor Ld Russell does not take in what has happened.

1031. Lord Granville to Mr. Gladstone. [Add. MS. 44170, fo. 196]

Walmer Castle. Jan 20/76.

Derby has given orders for me to see everything. But I also learn from Childers who has been to the Admiralty, that there were two letters from the F.O. to the Admiralty dated Jan & May 1870 giving precise instructions. They were to be

[1] The session began 8 Feb. These subjects, except the *Vanguard*, were covered by the Queen's speech and the debates on the address. Papers on them were laid by command: on fugitive slaves, [C. 1413] (1876). lxx, 257, circulated before Parliament met (below, no. 1034); on the purchase of the Suez Canal shares, [C. 1391], [C. 1392] (1876). lxxxiii, 131, 173, laid 8 Feb.; on the Cape, the mission of J. A. Froude and the proposed conference there of South African states and colonies, [C. 1399] (1876). lii, 97, laid 10 Feb.; on the loss of H.M.S. *Vanguard*, 1 Sept., the proceedings of the subsequent court martial and the Admiralty minute revising its decision, [C. 1384] (1876). xlviii, 665, laid 11 Feb.

sent to the Commodore on the East India Station, & the letter was embodied in the Station order of 1871.[1]

In one case two, and in another a large number of slaves came on board two ships at Anchor in Madagascar waters, the Captains refused to give them up, & the Commodore proposed to approve, but thought the owners should be compensated. Lord Clarendon disapproved, & laid down the doctrine that if they had escaped from the shore to a ship of war *beyond* the territorial limits, they should *not* be given up, but if within the territorial limit, that we had no right to take them away, unless they had been recently imported in defiance of our Treaties. In the latter case though coming on board within the Foreign jurisdiction they were to be detained, & the case reported to the proper authority for decision.[2]

You will observe that there is a considerable distinction between Clarendon's instructions, and the first circular of the present Govt— But I am glad I did not stump during the autumn or I should probably have put my foot in it. More by luck than by good guidance, Hartington & Forster said nothing fatal to our position as it turns out to be.

Will you look at your Cabinet notes. I have no recollection of the subject having been mentioned.

1032. Lord Granville to Mr. Gladstone. [Add. MS. 44170, fo. 200]

Walmer Castle. Jan 30/76.

I have recd the enclosed from Arnim.[3]

His quotation does not appear to mean that it was the English Gov who thought his appointment to the London Embassy inadmissible or who attributed to him the defects mentioned. I might in my reply state this, adding that I have no recollection of any queries having been addressed to me on the subject, or of my having given an opinion as to his fitness. (But that if such had been the case, I doubt whether I should think myself at liberty to give him any details on the subject).

I have on reflection written to Odo for Bismark's despatch, and for any light he can throw upon it.

I send you a letter of Hammonds.[4] Wylde assured me that it had been the

[1] Childers to Granville, 19 Jan., G.D. 29/26Ai; see above, no. 1027 note. Cf. Hartington to Granville, 19 Jan., on Harcourt's also having seen the paper 'which makes a party attack impossible', G.D. 29/22A. Gladstone's reply to no. 1031, 24 Jan., G.D. 29/29A, not printed.

[2] Clarendon to Consul Pakenham (Madagascar), 16 May 1870, F.O. 84/1433; Parl. papers. [C. 1413] (1876). lxx, 306.

[3] Arnim to Granville, 26 Jan., on Bismarck's publication of a mem. on Britain's refusal of him as Bernstorff's successor because of his 'esprit d'intrigue et manque de veracité'; see also Odo Russell to Granville, private, 4 Feb., stating in reply to Granville that Arnim had never been officially proposed; Granville to Arnim, 6 Feb., refusing to intervene between Arnim and Bismarck but denying that he had disparaged Arnim, G.D. 29/26Aii. For Granville's private deprecation of Arnim's appointment, Granville to Russell, 12 Feb., 8 April 1873, G.D. 29/110, Knaplund, *Letters from Berlin*, pp. 90, 98. Granville wrote 'query omit' against the words in brackets.

[4] Hammond to Granville, 24 Jan., that the Admiralty Orders of 1871 were not based on Foreign Office instructions, and recounting the *Dryad* case, G.D. 29/26Aii; see also further letters from Hartington, 22 Jan., Coleridge, 12 Feb., Hammond, 23 Feb., *ibid.*

universal practice for the F.O. to deal with each case as it arose, but he was not clear as to the principle on which they were decided. I send you Selborne's view.

1033. Mr. Gladstone to Lord Granville. [G.D. 29/29A]

Hawarden Castle. Feb. 1. 76.

In the matter of Arnim's letter (which I return, with Hammond's), I fear my recollection will do but little to help you. The matter was one in which probably I should only have observed, not interfered, because my knowledge of the personnel of European diplomacy is very narrow. However I have a sort of recollection: and it is to the effect that on the last vacancy various names were made known to us as having been reviewed at Berlin, and that Arnim's was among them: but of the reason alleged I have no remembrance and I should say pretty strongly the British *veto* was never exercised. I think the words *used* by Arnim do just signify that it was; but then I see no evidence that they are a quotation.

If you omit the passage you have marked for possible omission, you might guard yourself in the sentence which precedes it by a preamble ' without entering into any collateral matter ' or something of that sort.

The letter looks to me as evidently framed to help his case against Bismarck by showing how implicitly we accepted his statement, which he fully expects to find false. You see I am growing diplomatic in my old age.

Ought not Enfield's memory to be routed up on the subject of the Slave Circular?

I go to town tomorrow and hope to be with you on Friday.

You may I think safely summon me by postcard, putting simply day and hour, not signing, and not posting *with* a lot for others; as I am a clandestine person.

Hoping, and fearing, soon to meet you.

1034. Mr. Gladstone to Lord Granville. [G.D. 29/26Ai]

4 C[arlton] G[ardens]. Feb. 5. 76.

1. The Slave papers [1] exhibit a singular picture, and one far from creditable to the internal machinery of the F.O.

First Palmerston surrenders fugitives.

Next C[larendon] reverses this policy, with no reference to the contrarity.

Thirdly he revises his reversal—again with no reference to the change.

And lastly the cases on which the letter of Jan 6 was written seem all to have been cases of slave-trade slaves.

In all this I see no discredit to the Minister but a good deal to the Office, whose duty it is to keep alive tradition, a matter far beyond the power of an individual's memory.

As to myself, was it not a strange proceeding to send me the draft of Jan 6. 70 without the least intimation that it overset a previous policy?

But the communication to Parliament of the dispatch of May 16/70 is a most important fact.

2. I think you brought away the B[oard] of T[rade] MS? which I presume is included in the printed papers.[2]

[1] See above, no. 1030 note.

[2] See above, no. 1023.

3. I send Lord Russell's letter [1] —and I hope he will not publish it in its present form. Query would it be right, as regards the Danish paragraphs, to give a hint to Lady Russell?

(I am glad to hear she has got her grandchildren out of the hands of Mr Spalding.)

I return your inclosures.

1035. Mr. Gladstone to Lord Granville. [G.D. 29/26Ai]

4, Carlton Gardens. Feb. 8. 76.

In the new situation created by Disraeli's practised legerdemain, as far as I am able to see my way, I am for persevering, with the almost certainty of being beaten on the division. [2]

I ask myself whether in good faith there is work for a Commission, as distinguished from the work fit for Govt and Parlt? The answer is no. It is a fetch, and would have to be so called.

I think also that the Paragraph in the Speech points to communications with Foreign Powers more or less resembling those in the case of the Slave Trade: which would be very objectionable.

It seems to me also as if a *parallel* notice might with advantage be given by some fit person to this effect: in the event of the issue of the R. Commission, to pray for the suspension of the Circular & so forth.

Having said this I have to add that I shall implicitly accept your decision whatever it may be.

1036. Mr. Gladstone to Lord Granville. [G.D. 29/29A]

4, C[arlton] G[ardens]. F. 18. 76.

1. I suppose you & Hartington will talk together about the Suez Canal Debate & I only write to say I will do in it whatever you wish, except of course summing up & concluding it which would put me in a false position. [3]

2. Dizzy much mismanaged his statement last night and exposed the Queen to a snub. [4] But the vice of the proposal lies in the title Empress, and I fear that

[1] Russell to Gladstone, not traced.

[2] Disraeli disarmed the opposition by announcing the appointment of a royal commission to report upon the international obligations applicable to the reception of fugitive slaves. In the debate on the address Hartington merely argued that the commission was unnecessary. On 22 Feb. Whitbread failed to carry two resolutions against the surrender of fugitive slaves and for the withdrawal of the Admiralty's amended circular, 23 Dec., *Hans. Parl. Deb.*, 3rd ser., ccxxvii. 685–765, 820–97.

[3] The government asked for the grant for the purchase of the Suez Canal shares, 14 Feb. The opposition appealed for the postponement of the vote but the debate was only adjourned to 21 Feb. Lowe spoke for the Liberals, Gladstone spoke at length and Hartington concluded, *ibid.*, 266–88, 563–77, 584–607, 644–52.

[4] In introducing the Royal Titles Bill enabling the Queen to add a title to her style by proclamation, Disraeli avoided naming the title, but Liberal critics assumed that it would be Empress, *ibid.*, 408 ff. See Granville to the Queen, 24 Feb., Granville to Ponsonby, 26 Feb., on the Liberals' attitude and on Disraeli's neglect to agree with the opposition before introducing the bill, G.D. 29/22A; the first printed Fitzmaurice, ii. 161–2.

may also be thought its only virtue. I thought what you said on Feb. 7 particularly wise.

I think I must say something for the Bondholders of the *1854* Turkish Loan when their case comes on. I think it very strong.[1]

1037. Lord Granville to Mr. Gladstone. [Add. MS. 44170, fo. 202]

Private. Carlton Gardens. March 15/76.

Everybody refused to move—and at eleven we decided that he had better do it himself, as Anderson would not hear of yielding to Noel. Hartington I think wished to move.[2]

He says from the tone of many liberals, that he has even doubt of their votes. " Queen & Prince of Wales anxious—recd great kindness " etc.

The Queen rejects our proposal—I should guess with anger.

1038. Lord Granville to Mr. Gladstone. [Add. MS. 44170, fo. 205]

18, Carlton House Terrace. May 1/76.

James has given notice of a question for tomorrow.[3] It recites without naming him, the promise of Sir Stafford Northcote, asks whether that was the view of the Govt at the date, when the speech was made, and asks whether the words of the proclamation in the opinion of the Govt carry out that view. (I have not got the words but that is the substance).

Selborne has given notice that he will tomorrow call the attention of the Lords to the Proclamation, and ask the Gov̦, what in their opinion is its operation & effect. He will go fully into the subject, and make a long speech, a debate will probably follow, which will exhaust in the Lords the question of breach of faith on the part of the Govt.[4]

But what is to be done in the Commons, if as is certain the answer in both Houses is unsatisfactory.

[1] In Oct. 1875 Turkey had repudiated half the dividend on the state debt for the next five years. Recently published arrangements for the repayment of the 1855 loan made it a charge upon the Egyptian tribute appropriated to the repayment of the loan of 1854, and made no alternative provision for the 1854 bondholders. Derby had asserted that the British guarantee of the 1854 loan, 27 June 1855, gave her only the right to use her moral influence to gain its repayment. Gladstone to Granville, 22 Feb., on his speech in the Suez Canal debate, G.D. 29/29A, not printed.

[2] The Royal Titles Bill went into committee in the Commons, 16 March. Hartington moved a resolution that agreed to some appropriate addition but rejected the impairment of ' the ancient and Royal Dignity of the Crown by the assumption of the style and title of Emperor '. Anderson and Noel spoke as well as Harcourt but they failed to carry the right wing of the party, *Hans. Parl. Deb.*, 3rd ser., ccxxviii. 75–160. The bill passed the Commons, 23 March, and the Lords, 7 April, and received the royal assent, 27 April.

[3] Implying that the proclamation issued under the Royal Titles Act did not restrict the use of the title Empress to imperial occasions, to which Northcote had pledged the government on 20 March. For James's question, 2 May, *ibid.*, 1982.

[4] For Selborne's speech, the chancellor's reply and a short debate see *ibid.*, 1953–81.

Some of the party have begun a requisition to Adam to call together a meeting of the party. I presume an unusual proceeding.

What in your opinion should Hartington do. I do not like the notion of a vote of Censure. But is the Govt to go perfectly scot free, after an evasive answer to James' question.

3 or 4 dine here tomorrow to settle their course. If you could telegraph to me in time I should be grateful.

By (Rossa) I shall understand *Hartington*
(John)—*James*
(White)—*Selborne*
(action)—(Vote of Censure).

1039. Lord Granville to Mr. Gladstone. [Add. MS. 44170, fo. 210]

18, Carlton House Terrace. May 3/76.

Many thanks for your telegram.[1]

Selborne's speech was a gem—so simple & convincing— The impression of the M P's who heard it, and there were many, thought the debate quite one sided.

Harcourt however who says that the Proclamation is a blunder denies that Selborne made out a case of *bad faith*, but then his personal feeling for Dizzy puts such a supposition out of the question. He wished Hartington to move it.

After much discussion and the proposal of longer & more detailed resolutions it was settled that the best would be

" that in the opinion of this House, sufficient provision has not been made in the proclamation issued under the Royal Titles Act for restricting the use of the title of Empress ".

I was deputed to press Bright to move it. His only doubt, but a considerable one, is whether it is the sort of speech he can make. He was to give his answer in the House to Adam this afternoon.

If he refuses, which I think he will do, James who is in possession of the subject from having put the question is ready to move the resolution.

Bright asked me whether you would come up. I said that I did not know, but that I thought without consulting you or myself, that if Bright was the mover you would probably do so.

Please read Selborne's speech.

1040. Mr. Gladstone to Lord Granville. [G.D. 29/29A]

Hawarden Castle. May 4. 76.

I have not as yet read the debate in full but upon the case as it seems to stand I think you could hardly avoid taking issue. But does not the argument apply in the Lords as much as in the Commons?

[1] Gladstone to Granville, draft tel. 2 May: 'No vital objection to action if you are quite sure pledge remains unfulfilled . . .', Add. MS. 44170, fo. 209. James gave notice of the resolution and moved, 4 May, substantially as in no. 1039 but referring to the government's declarations during the passage of the bill. It was taken as a vote of censure and debated, 11 May, *Hans. Parl. Deb.*, 3rd ser., ccxxix. 51.

I cannot help supposing that in *our* House the division must improve though to what extent is uncertain.

I do not wish to speak but will not shirk it if you think it desirable when the time comes.[1]

It will not, I presume, be before next week. We go to Hagley today, and to London on Saturday or Monday. For a few days my wife and I are to be at No. 21.

She thanked you on my behalf for your most kind & feeling letter on the sad catastrophe of Lyttleton's death. It is the most mysterious dispensation I have ever known. Had a thousand men been before me, and had I been told that to one of them this would happen, and asked to which, I should have gone over the nine hundred & ninety nine before taking him. It is God's will, and doubtless is for good.

His son is a fine fellow: indeed all his sons are.

Have you seen a Paragraph in Pall Mall G. today about Canon Pope? This proceeding could not have more silly, if another Pope had been in question.

1041. Mr. Gladstone to Lord Granville. [G.D. 29/29A]

73 Harley Street. May 25. 76.

A word to say that Sir T. Dakin asked me to present the Prince Warden of the Fishmongers and I in declining on the ground of absence said I would *ask* you if he liked. This he took I find for your having agreed. I write in case you should see with surprise an unauthorised use of your name.

1042. Lord Granville to Mr. Gladstone. [Add. MS. 44170, fo. 214]

Holmbury. June 8/76.

What a good speech you seem to have made at the Political Economical Club.

But why do you quote page 17 in the Contemporary Review,[2] a sentence so inexplicable (at least to me) as that of Mr Martineau. . . .[3]

1043. Mr. Gladstone to Lord Granville. [G.D. 29/29A]

H of Commons. June 9. 76.

I am so glad that you have found matter of interest & provocation to thought in my paper printed in the last Contemporary.

If you will read the two articles of Martineau from which I quote I think you will find that the sentence I have cited is nearly the easiest in them . . .[4]

[1] Gladstone was present during the debate but did not speak. The motion was lost by 108 votes, *ibid.*, 370–470.

[2] 'The Courses of Religious Thought', *Contemporary Review*, 6 June 1876; reprinted W. E. Gladstone, *Gleanings of Past Years, 1844–78* (1879), iii. 95.

[3] A passage on the difference between an atheist and an agnostic has been omitted.

[4] A short passage continuing the discussion of agnosticism has been omitted.

Hartington has just put his question and been answered. The production of papers is again postponed.[1]

What I think unsatisfactory to the last degree is not the mere want of papers nor our ignorance in detail as to the steps taken by the Government but what seems, by negative evidence, to be a refusal on their part to recognise any obligation to procure from Turkey the fulfilment of the engagements so solemnly given to Europe in 1855–6 and so shamefully broken. From the Queen's Speech until now there has never been a word, at least in the House of Commons, which recognised these obligations. The only act which by implication acknowledged them was the Andrassy Note and that Disraeli defended by saying they did not like to remain isolated & the Turks themselves wished them to join in it. It is some recognition of this kind that we want. I do not feel sure that I shall myself be able to keep silence a great deal longer if it still be withheld.[2]

P.S. You may like to read the last page & a half of the inclosed letter. The writer is an unionist [?] scholar.

1044. Lord Granville to Mr. Gladstone. [Add. MS. 44170, fo. 216]

Holmbury. June 10/76.

On the whole I had rather not attack Martineau.

I reserve some remarks on agnostics till we meet.

With regard to Turkey my impression is that when the papers are produced, there will be materials to show that they have been without initiative in suggesting any solution of the pending question, and that they have been lukewarm in pressing the Turks to do what was right towards the Christians but I apprehend that in answer to the question whether they acknowledged the obligation of the Porte to fulfil the assurance given in the Treaty of 1856, and whether they had urged the Sultan to do so, they would simply answer in the affirmative.

1045. Lord Granville to Mr. Gladstone.[3] [Add. MS. 44170, fo. 218]

[20 June 1876].

Sorry to miss you—our meeting yesterday came to nothing.

W. Harcourt was very strong as to the case against the Gov in the Winslow affair, but equally strong against the law which Clarendon passed.[4]

[1] Hartington asked whether it was intended to lay papers on the negotiations connected with the Berlin Memorandum in the developing Eastern question and was answered by Disraeli with an appeal for forbearance, *Hans. Parl. Deb., loc. cit.*, 1605–9.

[2] Cf. a short speech on these lines by Gladstone in the debate on the address, 8 Feb., seeking to broaden the approach to the Turkish question from that of political expediency to those moral and historic considerations which obliged the powers to demand reforms, *Hans. Parl. Deb.*, 3rd ser., ccxxvii. 102–7.

[3] Gladstone to Granville, 12 June, on the Eastern question, G.D. 29/29A, not printed.

[4] The refusal of the American request for the surrender of the accused American Winslow raised a question of the interpretation of the extradition treaty with the United States, 1842, and the law which executed it, 1843, see Parl. papers. [C. 1482], [C. 1526] (1876). lxxxii, 1, 125. The opposition asked whether papers would be laid, 11 May. Harcourt asked again 16, 23 May, *Hans. Parl. Deb.*, 3rd ser., ccxxix. 777, 1113. Granville opened an important debate in the Lords, in which he and Selborne supported the American interpretation, 24 July, ccxxx. 1768 ff, and ccxxxi. 371–414.

Cardwell thought it was doubtful whether we had so strong a case against the Gov.

He & Forster doubted whether it was expedient to move in the matter, the Gov having plausible & popular ground to rest upon. Selborne was as strong as Harcourt as to the strength of the case, but doubted whether we should not do real harm as to the future settlement of the case by backing up the Americans at this moment.

James & I were of the same opinion. So nothing was decided.

It is possible that the Eastern question will be discussed on Friday, on a motion of Tom Bruce.[1] If so we ought to have a previous meeting.

The movement of the fleet which is popular now as a proof of vigour against Russia, was only decided upon after urgent appeals from Elliot for protection for the Greeks against the Turks.

1046. Mr. Gladstone to Lord Granville. [G.D. 29/29A]

73 Harley St. June 27. 76.

I saw Lord Stratford de Redcliffe today, went over the more prominent points of Derby's speech with him, and mentioned to him that in the Times Report two consecutive sentences of yours were utterly irreconcileable one with another.

We were agreed upon the following propositions.

1. (With Hammond) that the Government were quite wrong in allowing themselves, without any note or utterance, to be excluded from the initiative.

2. That Lord Derby was wrong in saying this was a civil war & we had no more business with it than any other civil war, referring apparently to Austria & Hungary as an example. *Because* this civil war arises out of the alleged nonfulfilment of engagements taken by the Sultan in 1855–6 to his own subjects, which we, apart from our interests, are under obligation, *in common* with the rest of Europe, to promote the fulfilment of.

3. That the dispatch of the fleet to the East, unexplained, has a distinct tendency to encourage the Turk in refusing to fulfil his own engagements. And lastly I pointed out that the present state of things is really just that in which the papers ought to be produced and the proceedings of the Government accounted for. For Lord Derby clearly intimated that the mediation of the Berlin note had dropped to the ground, had not been succeeded by any other, and that the Sultan was now corresponding with his own subjects. If any further mediation takes place it will be from a new starting point. What pretext is there for continued reserve?

Lord Stratford said he would rather have cut off his hand than subscribed the tripartite Treaty of Guarantee.

He is as sensible as ever of the mischief of Russia's having the Dardanelles—or rather the Bosporous.

And he decidedly inclines to the plan of settling the controversy by the grant of autonomy.

[1] Bruce on Thursday, 22 June, on an appeal for forbearance from Disraeli, did not press his motion asking for papers on the Eastern question and there was no debate, *ibid.*, ccxxx. 255, 265–8

1047. Lord Granville to Mr. Gladstone. [Add. MS. 44170, fo. 222]

18, Carlton House Terrace. July 2/76.

I propose telling Derby tomorrow that on Tuesday, [or] the day following, I shall ask him whether the time is not come for the production of the papers. I believe Hartington will do the same, or ask the question at once.[1]

Lord Russell has given up his question tomorrow.

I can hardly believe Lady Russell that he seriously intended to go up. He is utterly unfit for any such exertion. He says that he is for Mr Canning's policy. Making friends with Russia & Greece, & turning the Turk out of Europe.[2]

1048. Mr. Gladstone to Lord Granville. [G.D. 29/29A]

18, Carlton House Terrace. July 26.76.

I am sorry to find on calling that you are not expected till Friday night.

I lost no time in coming to say that Bruce in his motion, and Forsyth in an amendment, call upon us *inter alia* to vote approval of the proceedings of the Government. This I for one cannot do. I can hardly suppose you or H. will do it.[3]

But it raises very grave questions.

I must speak my mind. I am not obliged to divide.

But I could hardly refuse to join any others who might resolve on dividing. As to moving, the question seems to me to revive under the compulsion now offered to us.

My first impression is that an amendment might be moved

1. to have out the words of approval.

2. to lament the surrender by the Govt of more than of the initiative, & of the principle of European concert.

3. leaving alone the rest of Bruce or Forsyth as the case may be.

I inclose their notices though you will probably have seen them, to be certain that you may see the tuck we are invited to [join] in. My digestive organs are not strong enough.

1049. Mr. Gladstone to Lord Granville. [G.D. 29/29A]

H of C. July 27. 76.

Your Telegram reached me at the House. Adam has telegraphed his reply

[1] Granville in the Lords asked when there would be papers on the Eastern question, Monday 3 July, and Fawcett in the Commons, 4 July. Papers were promised as soon as possible, *ibid.*, 847, 946.

[2] See Russell to Granville, 3 July, excusing himself from the Lords and advocating association with Russia and France in the Eastern question, G.D. 29/22A. Granville sent the letter to Derby, Derby to Granville, 3 Aug., *ibid.*

[3] Cf. Granville to Gladstone, tel., 27 July: 'Hartington and I think impossible to agree with Bruce or Forsyth', Add. MS. 44170, fo. 224. The first important batch of Turkey papers had been laid on 21 July, [C. 1531] (1876). lxxxiv, 255. The debate followed, 31 July, on Bruce's motion favouring a policy of seeking equal treatment for the several races under Turkey's authority. Forsyth's amendment referred more precisely to the treaties of 1856. Neither was critical. Gladstone spoke but the debate did not proceed to a division, *Hans. Parl. Deb.*, 3rd ser., ccxxxi. 126–225.

begging Hartington to come up & hoping also for you. The state of the case as far as I know is this

1. E. Fitzmaurice has given notice of a motion involving blame; and I believe it is pretty certain that whatever the 'front bench' does there will be such a motion from some quarter.

2. As to myself I own I should be compelled (as at present minded) to vote with the Govt against the "previous question".

3. Kimberley Cardwell Lowe Forster (now) are against the previous question.

4. K. & C. wish to avoid moving a Censure. I presume they mean a negative to the vote of approval. I saw K. C. was fast on the bench.

4 [*sic*]. What seems absolutely necessary is, early conference of your principal friends.

5. It seems to me that the question between a negative simple and a negative in the shape of blame is one of policy only.

I am very sorry this inconvenience has fallen upon you in a manner so untimely. Adam will also telegraph briefly to you.

1050. Mr. Gladstone to Lord Granville. [G.D. 29/29A]

Hawarden. Aug. 7. 76.

In returning your letters from Lord Russell I may say that I also have one which was written in a more complacent mood.

There were two subjects on which I should have *dwelt* but for the belief that the debate must last and that others would handle them: the Bulgarian atrocities, and the pretended colonisation of European provinces with Circassians, one of the worst things the Turks have done.

I hope you will make sure before the prorogation that the results of the inquiry in Bulgaria will be published at once, not bottled up till February, with the prospect of a debate on July 31.

As a party question this affords no despicable material, but there are much higher interests involved. Lord Russell jumps over the difficulty that the charges against Turkey are not yet formally proven: but I hope it is recognised that if, and when, they are shown to be valid, we shall all come down upon Turkey pretty freely in respect of them. The subject *might* cause carnage in an amendment to the Address next February.

There is something horrid in reflecting that, while horrors were going on, our fleet was at Besika Bay within a few hours sail & not only was not there to arrest them but was believed by the perpetrators to be there for the purpose of securing their impunity.

Though I took my journey hither in the hope of finality I am of course available to run up in case of need on Turkish or other matter.

I was not sorry to be out of the Education *fracas* in which hardly any side is to my mind quite right.

1051. Lord Granville to Mr. Gladstone. [Add. MS. 44170, fo. 226]

18, Carlton House Terrace. Aug 19/76.

Il Conte d'Almaviva's son is—what do you think of the new Peerage? [1] & have you read Freemantle's address to the Electors of Bucks, and do you remember his father's assurances as to his son's politics, when you were considering the Peerage.

Can you make head or tail of the Eastern policy of the Gov.

I do not know whether it is true that they have been suggesting their good offices to Turks & Servians, & if so, whether it is done at the request of other powers. If not, and they are acting on their own hook, it is as foolish a bit of "spirited Foreign policy" as I ever heard of.

1052. Lord Granville to Mr. Gladstone. [Add. MS. 44170, fo. 228]

18, Carlton House Terrace. Aug 25/76.

I have been so occupied with domestic concerns, varied by a little attention to a mild gallop that Carrington is determined to give Freemantle in Bucks [2] that I forgot you did me the honor of asking my advice on the questions. I prefer the speech, which may be very useful, to the subscription.

I tried to throw cold water upon the election, as it will cost Carrington at least 5000£, I am told, without a chance. But I am delighted that he is determined to go on, & shows great energy and dash.

I have recommended a very clever little liberal lawyer to him, who will get up the Bulgarian atrocities well.

I do not wish it to be known that I wrote the address. I am glad you like it. I wrote it under orders to be extremely civil to Dizzy, and to kick up a dust.

It is wonderful how Dizzy's attention to young men answers. Carrington spoke to me of him with great regard. Said he had come to him on his father's death (whom you may remember a selfish old dandy, who believed his brother was made of glass) threw his arms round his neck, wept, and offered him two Lord Lieutenancies for the future.

The Rothschilds are behaving abominably.

Freemantle cannot speak, and broke down at Ailesbury. Carrington says his brother must and shall speak.

Lady G. is going on as well as possible. The change of weather is invaluable.

[1] Disraeli's promotion to the peerage as Lord Beaconsfield, 16 Aug.

[2] Thomas Fremantle, son of Thomas Fremantle, made first Baron Cottesloe by the out-going Liberals in 1874, won Disraeli's Buckinghamshire seat, 22 Sept., as a Conservative against Rupert Carrington, younger brother of the third Baron Carrington and William Carrington, Lib. M.P. for High Wycombe.

INDEX

The figures refer to the numbers of the letters, not to the pages